Petty Justice:
Low Law and the Sessions System in Charlotte County, New Brunswick, 1785-1867

PATRONS OF THE SOCIETY

Blake, Cassels & Graydon LLP

Chernos Flaherty Svonkin LLP

Gowlings

McCarthy Tétrault LLP

Osler, Hoskin & Harcourt LLP

Paliare Roland Rosenberg Rothstein LLP

Torys LLP

WeirFoulds LLP

The Osgoode Society is supported by a grant from The Law Foundation of Ontario.

The Law Foundation of Ontario
Building a better foundation for justice in Ontario

The Society also thanks The Law Society of Upper Canada for its continuing support.

Petty Justice:
Low Law and the Sessions System in Charlotte County, New Brunswick, 1785-1867

Paul Craven

Published for The Osgoode Society for Canadian Legal History by
University of Toronto Press
Toronto Buffalo London

www.utppublishing.com
www.osgoodesociety.ca
Printed in the U.S.A.

ISBN 978-1-4426-4991-0

Printed on acid-free, 100% post-consumer recycled paper with vegetable-based inks.

Publication cataloguing information is available from Library and Archives Canada.

University of Toronto Press acknowledges the financial assistance to its publishing program of the Canada Council for the Arts and the Ontario Arts Council, an agency of the Government of Ontario.

Canada Council for the Arts Conseil des Arts du Canada

ONTARIO ARTS COUNCIL
CONSEIL DES ARTS DE L'ONTARIO
an Ontario government agency
un organisme du gouvernement de l'Ontario

University of Toronto Press acknowledges the financial support of the Government of Canada through the Canada Book Fund for its publishing activities.

Contents

List of Figures

List of Tables

Foreword

THE OSGOODE SOCIETY FOR CANADIAN LEGAL HISTORY

Local administration and law enforcement in pre-Confederation Canada was largely done through a coterie of appointed officials, most notably the justices of the peace, but also including constables, parish officers, overseers of the poor, and the like. Justices and grand juries met at sessions courts to make local regulations, and justices and other officials enforced those regulations as well as the common law and provincial statutes. Justices exercised a minor civil jurisdiction and shared petty criminal jurisdiction with the sessions court. This system, inherited from Britain, has not previously been closely examined for Canada, and Paul Craven's masterful study of its operation and decline is thus a landmark in our legal history. In a remarkably deeply researched study of one county, Craven weaves together an intimate knowledge of the individuals involved and the law to comprehensively explain and illustrate how the system worked, who used it, and how private and public roles and interests overlapped and interacted.

The purpose of the Osgoode Society for Canadian Legal History is to encourage research and writing in the history of Canadian law. The Society, which was incorporated in 1979 and is registered as a charity, was founded at the initiative of the Honourable R. Roy McMurtry and officials of the Law Society of Upper Canada. The Society seeks to stimulate the study of legal history in Canada by supporting researchers, collecting oral histories, and publishing volumes that contribute to legal-historical scholarship in Canada. It has published ninety-six books on the courts, the judiciary, and the legal profession, as well as on the history of crime and punishment, women and law, law and economy, the legal treatment of ethnic minorities, and famous cases and significant trials in all areas of the law.

Current directors of the Osgoode Society for Canadian Legal History are Robert Armstrong, Kenneth Binks, Susan Binnie, David Chernos, J. Douglas Ewart, Violet French, Martin Friedland, Philip Girard, William Kaplan, C. Ian Kyer, Virginia MacLean, Patricia McMahon, Roy McMurtry, Madeleine Meilleur, Janet Minor, Dana Peebles, Paul Perell, Jim Phillips, Paul Reinhardt, William Ross, Paul Schabas, Robert Sharpe, Alex Smith, Lorne Sossin, Mary Stokes, and Michael Tulloch.

The annual report and information about membership may be obtained by writing to the Osgoode Society for Canadian Legal History, Osgoode Hall, 130 Queen Street West, Toronto, Ontario, M5H 2N6. Telephone: 416-947-3321. E-mail: mmacfarl@lsuc.on.ca. Website: www.osgoodesociety.ca.

R. Roy McMurtry
President

Jim Phillips
Editor-in-Chief

Preface

This is a book about local justice and administration in the colonial period. That it happens to be set in Charlotte County, New Brunswick, is due to the unusual depth and extent of the surviving sources for that place. I came to this project knowing little about the province and its history and so owe a great deal to Janice Cook, whom I was fortunate to employ as a research assistant (on David Frank's recommendation) before she joined the Provincial Archives of New Brunswick (PANB), and to others on its staff who educated me graciously and made my intermittent research visits pleasant and productive.

I am indebted to numerous colleagues for advice and assistance of various kinds. Harry Arthurs and Douglas Hay first stimulated my interest in low law; the late Peter Oliver encouraged me to write about it; Jim Phillips, his successor as Osgoode Society editor-in-chief, has been a constant source of enthusiasm. Joshua Smith generously shared research material. David Bell and Gail Campbell, among other New Brunswick specialists, helped set me straight at various points along the way, as did St Andrews local historian David Sullivan. Members of the Toronto Legal History Group (now the Osgoode Society Legal History Workshop) patiently put up with draft versions of many of the chapters in annual instalments and this book is the better for their comments and suggestions. I am indebted to Douglas Hay, Craig Heron, and Mary Stokes for critical readings of particular chapters, to Balfour Halevy and Marianne Rogers for guidance to and through the legal literature, and to students in several iterations of my York University graduate course on low law for their insights.

Jim Phillips, Philip Girard, and two anonymous reviewers made helpful comments on the whole text, and I hope now to have answered most of their questions and addressed most of their concerns. I also have to thank Len Husband of the University of Toronto Press, where Wayne Herrington provided a painstaking copy-edit and Ani Deyirmenjian supplied essential advice and assistance with design and production. Credit is due to Byron Moldofsky of the University of Toronto Department of Geography who made the maps in figures 1.1 and 1.2, and to PANB for permission to reproduce the images in figures 2.1, 2.2, 4.1, and 12.1. William Kearns and Becky Schaefer assisted with record linkage and index preparation respectively.

Financial assistance was provided by the Social Sciences and Humanities Research Council of Canada, by York University, and by the Osgoode Society for Canadian Legal History.

Finally but most importantly, thanks to ML who found room for this project over many years.

A note about the footnotes

The footnotes use short form citations for archival materials, newspapers, and other published works. Full references will be found in the source list and bibliography. Statutes are cited by regnal year, calendar year, and chapter number; unless otherwise specified they are acts of the New Brunswick legislature. The footnotes use these additional abbreviations:

JHA New Brunswick. Journal of the House of Assembly.

JLC New Brunswick. Journal of the Legislative Council.

CCGS Charlotte County. General Sessions. Minutes.

CCSS Charlotte County. Special Sessions. Minutes.

WPO Winslow Papers Online.

CCGS and CCSS minutes are interspersed in the general sessions minutebooks, PANB RS148/a/2/a. The CCSS entries include special sessions to which all the justices in the county were invited as well as meetings of the magistrates of St Andrews. The volumes in this series cover these date ranges:

1. CCGS Sep 1785 – CCGS Apr 1815
2. CCGS Sep 1815 – CCSS Nov 1834
3. CCGS Apr 1835 – CCSS Sep 1841
4. CCGS Sep 1841 – CCSS Oct 1863
5. CCGS Apr 1864 – CCGS Apr 1877

Chapter 1

Introduction: High law, low law, not law

> '. . . the description of a high law and a low law is hardly to be found in any book I have yet met with.'
>
> Clarke et al., *Bank*, 412

On October 24, 1805, George Leonard, superintendent of trade and fisheries for North America, preventive officer of His Majesty's Customs in New Brunswick and a member of the province's executive council, seized the American sloop *Falmouth* off Campobello Island in Passamaquoddy Bay for a breach of the navigation acts.[1] In the litigation that followed, described by one historian as 'comic opera,' local customs officers on both sides of the border testified in New Brunswick's court of vice-admiralty against Leonard's seizure.[2] The act provided that no goods should be loaded aboard ship in a British possession unless the ship had been built in Britain or its colonies and its master and three-quarters of the crew were British subjects.[3]

1. The sloop was detained by Charles Edward Leonard, George's son and deputy, who conducted it to Saint John where it was formally seized in his father's name.

2. Condon, 'Leonard, George.' For the organization and jurisdiction of the colonial admiralty courts see Stone, 'Admiralty.'

3. [GB] 7&8 Wm.III (1695) c.22, s.2.

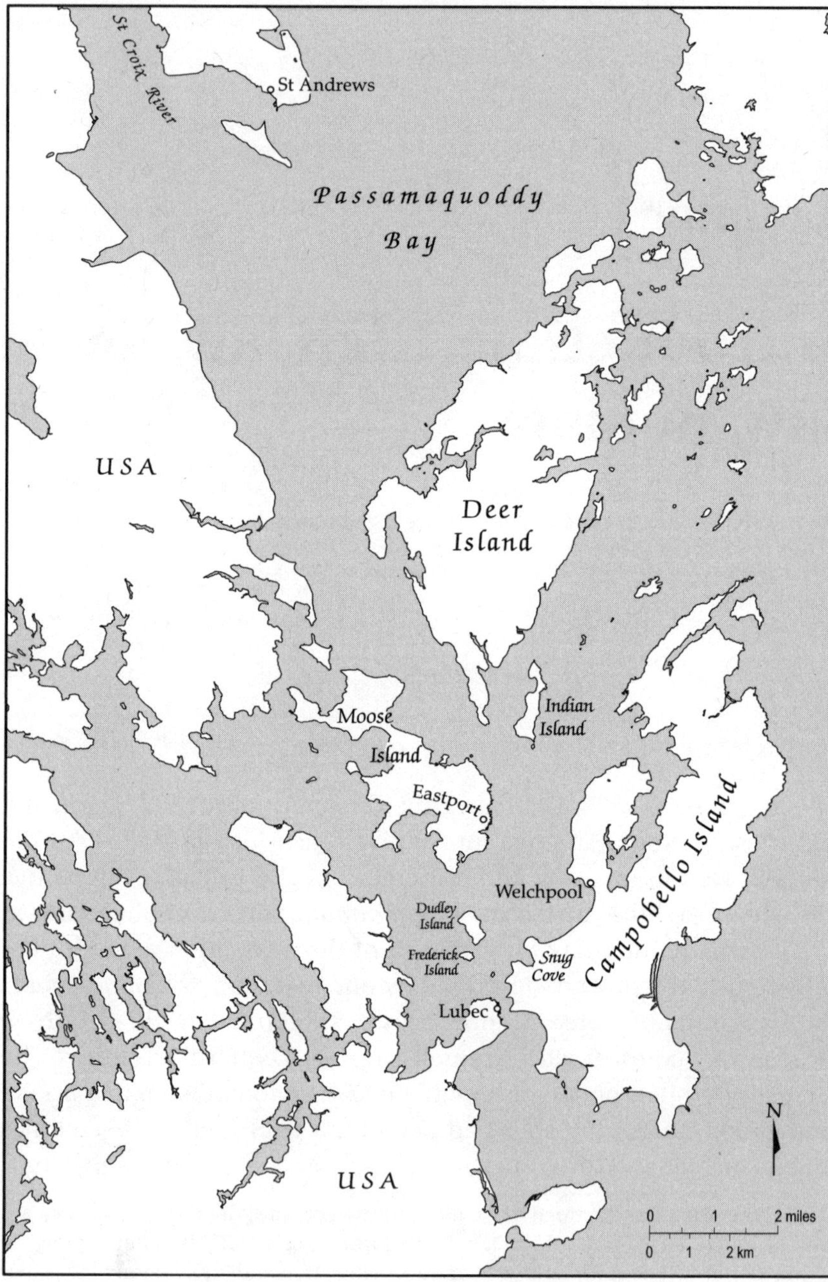

Figure 1.1 – Passamaquoddy Bay, 1805

The prosecution maintained that the *Falmouth* had been loaded in British waters. There were two main branches to the defence. The first was that the waters in which the *Falmouth* had been taken belonged to the United States under the 1783 treaty that ended the revolutionary war. The second was that the same waters were deemed 'neutral' according to a long-established practice and mutual understanding of the rules of trade in the region. The first argument rested on formal substantive and interpretative legal principles of universal application, on the high law of nations. The second rested on informal practices and understandings entirely local in their application, on the low law of the Passamaquoddy plaster trade.[4]

The *Falmouth* had received a document from the American customhouse at Frederick Island clearing it for St Andrews, New Brunswick. The sloop anchored in the channel between Dudley and Campobello islands where it received 120 tons of plaster from two Nova Scotia schooners which had first made entries at the British customhouse at Campobello. The purpose of these arrangements was to evade both the navigation acts' restriction on foreign lading and the U.S. tonnage duty on foreign vessels in American waters. By long-standing agreement between the local customs officials the midstream waters of the channel ('the lines') were considered neutral as a convenience to trade. The U.S. clearance to the *Falmouth* was not intended to send it to St Andrews (where it would not have been allowed to enter in any event) but rather to permit it to bring its cargo of foreign plaster into American waters without having to pay the tonnage duty. The Nova Scotia schooners' entries at Campobello were to

4. Plaster of paris (gypsum) was mined in Nova Scotia for use as a fertilizer in the southeastern United States. The case is reported in an anonymous pamphlet, *The Question respecting the right of the United States of America, to the Islands in Passamaquoddy-Bay, By virtue of the Treaty of 1783, considered in the Case of the Sloop Falmouth* ... (cited below as *Falmouth Pamphlet*): copy in CO 188/13 encl. in Leonard to Castlereagh, 16 Feb 1806. Leonard, who was pressing for an investigation of the Saint John customs officials, claimed that 'much of the evidence and observations on the Trial have been withheld from publication in the pamphlet from delicacy to those Officers ...' Solicitor general Ward Chipman, who argued the case for the prosecution, is the likely author of the pamphlet: see Leonard's letters to Winslow, 14 Dec 1805 and 20 Dec 1805, and to Merry, 20 Aug 1806, published in part in W.O. Raymond, ed., *Winslow Papers, A.D. 1777-1826*, Saint John, 1901, and now accessible as digital images of the original letters: *WPO.*

permit them to transship their plaster on the lines. A few years before this, it had been common practice for small vessels from the British provinces to unload their plaster on the wharves of Campobello to be purchased and loaded by larger American ships bound for American ports. Leonard's activities had put an end to that illicit practice. The customs officers had arranged to revive and legitimize the trade by permitting plaster to be transferred at anchor on the lines.

The prosecution argued that the channel was a British waterway. American shipping had a treaty right to navigate it but not to discharge or take on cargoes. To establish British ownership of the channel Chipman and Leonard argued for a reading of the peace treaty that would make all the islands of Passamaquoddy Bay—including Frederick Island where the U.S. customshouse was located and Moose Island, the site of the town of Eastport—part of New Brunswick. This was the real purpose of the prosecution as Leonard explained in private correspondence.[5] If the waters were British then the local officers' agreement to treat them as neutral was at best unenforceable and at worst fraudulent, a 'bare-faced attempt to violate the existing laws of both nations.' Here the prosecution relied on the rule of law, giving English admiralty authority for the proposition that the navigation laws 'are to be construed and applied with great exactness' and that, 'If there is a rule of law on the subject binding the Court, I must follow where that rule leads me, though it leads to consequences that I may privately regret, when I look to the particular intention of the parties.'[6]

Judge William Botsford found for the prosecution on the secondary issue, holding that the *Falmouth* was seized in British waters.

---

5. 'The condemnation of the Vessel is a second consideration—the first is to obtain a Right by the Treaty to all the Islands in the Bay of Passamaquoddy and the waters which surround them . . . ,' *WPO*, Leonard to Winslow, 20 Dec 1805.

6. *Falmouth Pamphlet*, 18, citing the judgment of Sir William Scott in the case of *The Hoop, Cornelis Master*, (1799) 1 Robinson's Admiralty Reports, 196. This was not an ordinary navigation acts case but involved trading with the enemy. Compare Scott's judgment in *The Betty Cathcart, Gillespie Master*, ibid., 220, at 221, from which Chipman seems to have extracted the first passage quoted above: 'The revenue and navigation laws are certainly to be construed and applied with great exactness . . . At the same time it is not to be said that they are not subject to all considerations of rational equity . . . '

Although some authors have claimed otherwise he did not accept the Chipman-Leonard thesis that all the islands belonged to Britain, but rather accepted that 'the citizens of the United States are in possession' of Moose, Dudley, and Frederick islands, 'over which the United States claim and exercise undisturbed jurisdiction.'[7] The islands to the west of the channel belonged to the United States, those to the east to Britain. By the law of nations, each of them had dominion to the midpoint of the waters dividing them. Since the evidence showed that the *Falmouth* sat at anchor closer to Campobello than to Dudley island it must have been in British waters when it received its cargo. Botsford also found authority in Lord Mansfield for the proposition that it made no difference whether cargo was transferred between vessels in territorial waters or was landed by one and laden by the other.[8] He rejected the low law defence: 'The British Custom-House officers in assenting to the line of the neutral or common waters on the Campo-Bello side, exceeded their authority as Officers of the Customs, by determining a matter of general law.' The vessel and its cargo were lawfully seized but in the circumstances—presumably the customshouse practice—costs were not awarded.

There are at least two ways of thinking about the customs officers' arrangements although they are not mutually exclusive.[9] The first, and the one advocated by Leonard and adopted in greater or lesser degree by subsequent commentators, is that the customshouse

7. MacNutt, *New Brunswick*, states at p.140, 'The judgment was a legal assertion of Britain's right to Moose Island.' Condon, 'Leonard, George,' claims that the judgment 'effectively asserted Britain's right to Moose Island.' This was the prosecution's position but not what Botsford decided. See his decree as reported in *Falmouth Pamphlet*, 28: 'I know of no public act of our Government from which I can infer its denial of the jurisdiction exercised by the United States over the Islands on the Western side of the channel, or a disavowal of the right claimed by them to the same; I am therefore to consider this passage or channel as conterminous, and dividing this Province from the United States.' The *Falmouth* case is not mentioned in Carroll, *Good and Wise Measure*.

8. Citing *Berns v. Rucker*, (1760) 1 Black Rep. 313. Botsford also found authority in Adam Smith for the proposition that the navigation acts were the palladium of British commerce: *Falmouth Pamphlet*, 27.

9. The idea of 'creole' officials in a 'borderlands' context as discussed in J.M. Smith, *Borderland Smuggling*, may be a third way of thinking about it, distinguishable by the primacy it gives to high law in assessing legitimacy.

officers were corrupt, incompetent, or both. Colin Campbell, subcollector of customs at St Andrews and heir to the arrangement that had been worked out by his predecessor in office, former Charlotte county sheriff John Dunn, was also agent for the *Falmouth*. His son—future Charlotte county sheriff Colin Campbell Jr—owned the seized cargo. In the case of this particular sloop the British customs officer most closely concerned had a personal pecuniary interest. But it was never suggested that the *Falmouth* was treated differently than other American vessels trading on the lines. To conclude that Campbell was corrupt (by the standards and expectations of his time) it would be necessary to show that it was wrong for him to engage in the trade, either because the trade itself was improper or because it was improper for an officer to participate in the trade he was employed to regulate. There are difficulties with both of these propositions, as will be seen more fully later on.

The second way of thinking about the customs officers' arrangements is to take them at face value as a method of ordering and regulating social relations—in this case, international trade—in circumstances where the maintenance of trade was understood to benefit both communities notwithstanding that the boundary between them had not yet been determined definitively. Leonard's and Chipman's attempt to use the *Falmouth* seizure to support British territorial claims shows that they were in question. The community benefit of the Passamaquoddy plaster trade was simply described by lieutenant governor Smyth in 1812: 'as the Americans are the only purchasers of this article, which we exchange with them for flour, the advantages of the Trade are reciprocal.'[10] And in fact despite Botsford's high law court having given primacy to a high law account of the dispute, it was the low law version that won out in the medium term. Fearful of further antagonizing the Americans while embroiled in a European war, the imperial government directed Leonard to make no more seizures in Passamaquoddy Bay.[11]

10. CO 188/18, Smyth to Bathurst, 31 Oct 1812.

11. CO 188/13, Ludlow to Leonard, 26 Jun 1806, communicating instructions of Anthony Merry, British ambassador at Washington, ibid., 29 Apr 1806.

Understanding low law

This is a book about local justice and administration in a British colonial setting. My approach is institutional and prosopographical. I am interested in *how* things worked—systems, methods, and practices—and also in *who* made and used them—the actors, their motivations and interactions. The institutional framework is important but so is individual and collective agency. In this approach the most telling moments often involve fractures of various kinds when systems fail to work, actors are unable to manage, or institutional friction overcomes function. These fractures occur on many levels: material and ideological competition within the local setting; conflicts among local, central, and imperial authorities; clashes between what Norma Landau has called patriarchal and patrician tendencies within the structures of paternalist authority;[12] ultimately, given the time and place of this study, the increasing strain of centrifugal local exceptionalism against centripetal liberal universalism.

From a legal-historical point of view, the focus of this study is the 'low law' of justices of the peace, customs and forestry officials, constables and other parish officers, and 'commissioners' of various kinds. Douglas Hay has argued, 'In a market, there must be expensive justice and cheap justice, and, historically, this has, in large measure, translated into high justice and low justice.'[13] One aspect of 'low law' is that it is law for the lower orders, law as a commodity rather than a specialty. Another is that as statute law it ousts the common law thereby making 'high' law irrelevant within its domain:[14]

> The substance of 'low law' was delegated parliamentary authority over the activities of the labouring population: magistrates acted under statutory powers which gave them very wide discretion to prosecute acts which could be construed as criminal in cases of vagrancy, offences against the poor laws, petty theft, poaching, or breach of contract.

This is the sense in which Hay and I used the term in our study of the

12. Landau, *Justices*, 3f, 359f, and see further below.

13. Hay, 'Time, Inequality,' 171. I take 'low justice' to be a subset of 'low law' for reasons discussed later in this section. See as well Hay, 'Legislation, Magistrates,' 59.

14. David Lemmings, 'Introduction,' in Lemmings, *British and Their Laws.*

master and servant acts.[15] Here, though, I want to go beyond 'low justice' to consider 'low law' as an administrative, legislative, regulatory, and judicial whole. Simply put, I want to think about the various roles of the New Brunswick justices of the peace and other low law officials as together constituting a single method or institution notwithstanding that some of these roles were spelled out in particular enactments, others inferred from the general statutory scheme, still others derived from the broad discretion to 'keep the peace' granted by the justice's commission, and some simply made up on the spot.

A working definition of low law in this larger sense might begin with a general notion of 'law' as rules and methods of social ordering enforced or required by the state,[16] and then proceed to distinguish rules and methods pertaining to the formal legal system which constitutes 'high law' from those belonging to other institutions and actors.[17] Any definition of low law requires it to be set off not only from high law but also from other institutionalized rules and methods of social ordering that are not directly enforced or required by the state.[18] There are no bright lines separating these three species

15. 'Introduction,' in Hay and Craven, *Masters, Servants.*

16. This does not require a unitary state or any particular configuration of more or less autonomous state institutions, but only the general idea of state power *sui generis.* Here, however, we are dealing with public officials invested with state authority by appointment and jurisdiction.

17. The distinction made here between high law and low law is therefore quite different from the distinction between high (typically appellate) courts and low courts (typically of first instance) implied by Karsten, *Between Law and Custom.*

18. A broader pluralist account of 'low law' than is advanced here might do away with the requirement of state engagement. For example, Ramsay, 'Consumer Law' names private complaint handling as a source of low law:

> Legal centralism is still influential in consumer law and 'high law' as represented by decisions of appeal courts or the European Court of Justice continue to be the focus of attention. The vast amount of 'low law' that is generated in small claims courts, administrative tribunals, ombudsmen, and the private complaint handling practices of firms remains relatively unstudied.

Similarly, Bell, 'Legal Pluralism' at 88 and see Arthurs, 'Labour Law.' Customary and other conventional normative systems are important methods of ordering to be considered alongside law, but that does not mean that they *are* law. As it seems to me, the danger in conceptually divorcing 'law' from 'rule' is the implied neglect of state power and its social foundations.

of social ordering (high law, low law, not law) and the boundaries between them will often resemble tidal estuaries where fresh and salt water combine. Low law becomes interesting in its own right when it is distinguishable not only in volume but in kind from high law, when the discontinuity is charged with tension about the meaning of 'law.'[19] The particular defining institutions of low and high law are historically contingent. In liberal democratic societies today, high law is marked out constitutionally by the judiciary, institutionally by the hierarchy of courts, and ideologically by 'the rule of law.' Low law is found in a plethora of regulatory, administrative, and quasi-judicial agencies, boards, and commissions. In colonial New Brunswick, as in many other places in the British empire in the eighteenth and nineteenth centuries, high law belonged to the common law courts and to such specialist high courts as vice-admiralty, some of whose judges also had a role in executive government,[20] while the key institution of low law was the sessions system of county governance by justices of the peace.

A mixture of adjudication, legislation, and administration typified the work of both high law and low law at least until relatively recent times. Low law then and now includes policing. Formerly, however, the term 'police' encompassed not only crime detection and prevention but also minor criminal trials, the adjudication and collection of small debts and similar claims, social welfare, assessment and taxation, public works, municipal legislation and enforcement, business regulation and licensing, as well as the preservation of public order and civic peace. Most studies of low law emphasize the criminal law aspects but this was a small part of the justices' work and one that was often avoided by otherwise active justices.[21] While crime and

19. Arthurs, *Without the Law.*

20. In New Brunswick judges sat on His Majesty's Council until 1832 when it was replaced by separate legislative and executive councils. With the exception of the chief justice, who chaired the new legislative council, judges no longer sat on either body. The proceedings of H.M. Council sitting in its legislative capacity from 1786 to 1830 were published subsequently as the *Journal of the Legislative Council of the Province of New Brunswick* (2 vols., 1831) and are cited here in sequence with its successor JLC.

21. Thus the equation of low law with 'everyday criminal justice' in Fyson, *Magistrates,* 95 is overly restrictive.

punishment receive their due in this book, attention is paid as well to the justices' roles in debt collection, municipal finance, social welfare, and provincial politics and to the non-adjudicative roles of other low law officials.[22]

The 'sessions system' of county governance by appointed justices was the central institution of 'police' in this larger sense. It was staffed almost entirely by part-time volunteers and appointees without special training or professional qualifications.[23] The fact that crime prevention and prosecution, municipal legislation and its enforcement, poor relief, public works, assessment and taxation were all entrusted to local elites with business, professional and family interests of their own raises questions about the extent to which they used public office for private purposes. The magistrate sitting as judge in his own cause is a familiar trope.[24] More generally, however, the uses of office in promoting or defending the holder's private (as distinct from mere class) interests have been largely neglected in the low law literature. The relationship of private interest and public office is one of the core themes of this book.

This book is also interested in the interplay of high and low law. As already noted, the boundary between the two is brackish at best. In part this is due to the ebb and flow of judicial attitudes and practices which may range from enthusiastic reception and endorsement of low law decision-making through varying degrees of deference all the way to close, critical, even hostile, supervision and review.[25] Low law officials react and respond to high law supervision not only by compliance but by adaptation and evasion as well. Insulated from effective review they may adopt and evolve methods and practices quite unlike those of the courts in analogous circumstances. Low law is not

22. However I have not tried to provide an exhaustive catalogue of low law activity. In particular I have ignored sessions' limited role in schooling and skirted the details of making and maintaining by-roads, bridges, and highways.

23. A legally-trained clerk of the peace was the usual exception.

24. Examples include Hay, 'Patronage, Paternalism,' Frank, 'Let But One,' and the David Owen cases in chapter 2 below.

25. A recent example of the first in the low law realm of Canadian labour-management relations is *Communications, Energy and Paperworkers Union of Canada, Local 30 v. Irving Pulp & Paper, Ltd.* 2013 SCC 34; a standard account of the last in the same realm is Weiler, 'Slippery Slope.'

high law writ small. The differences may be celebrated and protected (for example by privative provisions in the empowering statutes) or may come under attack as incompatible with the rule of law or the monopoly of legal professionals. The discretion and autonomy of low law officials and institutions on the one hand, and the problem of supervising and controlling them on the other, are the second and third core themes of this book.

A final core theme is the tension between local and external forces in shaping the community and its institutions, especially low law institutions. As Norma Landau showed, paternalist rule by resident gentry can involve the spirited defence of local institutions, individuals, and interests from external pressures ('patriarchal' rule) or efforts to undermine these in favour of the perceived benefits of more global institutions and values ('patrician' rule). Laura Edwards has described the reshaping of early American legal institutions along somewhat analogous lines.[26] In mid-nineteenth-century New Brunswick, as power and resources were transferred from Whitehall to Fredericton, from council to assembly, and then again from assembly to provincial cabinet, tensions between patriarchs and patricians threatened the viability of the sessions system and contributed to its eventual demise. In order to explore this theme fully, I have tried to understand the course of New Brunswick political, economic, and legal history from a local standpoint.[27] My account, based largely in local records and journalism, therefore differs in some respects from the standard version in W.S. MacNutt's magisterial history which is written largely out of central and imperial sources.[28] All history may not be local history, but this one is.

As these reflections suggest, low law means more than 'law on an

---

26. Edwards, *People and their Peace.*

27. Mostly perforce from a St Andrews standpoint since records and newspapers from other parts of the county are sparse.

28. MacNutt, *New Brunswick.* Compare, for example, my discussion of the deputy land surveyors as low law officials based largely on their correspondence inwards (chapter 5) with MacNutt's account of the Commissioner of Crown Land's domination of his office which is based largely on his correspondence outwards. Similarly, while MacNutt (275) relies on a derisive comment by a defensive lieutenant governor for his characterization of C.R. Hatheway as a corrupt trading magistrate the view from St Andrews was quite otherwise (chapter 6).

everyday level, as it was administered in myriad small contexts and affected the lives of ordinary people,'[29] although it means that too. Low law and high law emerged concurrently out of centralizing efforts to stem social conflict and impose the King's peace in late medieval England.[30] High law used the royal courts to determine disputes among the propertied; low law relied on members of the local gentry to keep the peace among the lower orders, manage county and parish affairs, and mediate relations with the central authorities. Low law was overwhelmingly statute law administered by part-time justices of the peace (JPs), borough justices, and other lay officials. As judges and as county governors the JPs exercised a good deal of autonomous discretion attributable both to the central government's reluctance to alienate the volunteer peacekeepers upon whom it relied to maintain local order and to the high courts' reluctance to engage with the enormous volume of petty disputes they decided or actively to supervise their work.[31] This characteristic autonomy and discretion enabled JPs to preserve and promote local institutions and interests—including their own proprietary interests—even in the face of central government policy. Not until the mid-nineteenth century, when increasingly large slices of their former authority were parcelled out to agencies, boards, and commissions, did English justices of the peace lose their capacity to manage local affairs in what they took to be the interests of the local community.[32]

Similar institutions were recreated in the British North American colonies (and elsewhere in the empire) and with similar results.[33]

29. Phillips et al., *Essays X*, 15.

30. Palmer, *Black Death.*

31. Hay, 'Dread.' For an extended discussion of the low law autonomy of employment relations in this context see the editors' introduction to Hay and Craven, *Masters, Servants.*

32. See generally the Webbs' 11-volume *English Local Government* and more recently Eastwood, *Governing Rural England* and *Government and Community.*

33. For an international overview see Skryme, *Justices of the Peace*, vol. 3. Studies of the justices of the peace and related institutions in pre-Confederation British North America include Fyson, *Magistrates* (Quebec and Lower Canada), Lewthwaite, 'Law and Authority' (Newcastle District, Upper Canada), Murray, *Colonial Justice* (Niagara District, Upper Canada/Canada West), and Weaver, *Crimes, Constables*, chapter 1 (Hamilton, Upper Canada/Canada West). Mostly these emphasize criminal justice. For early urban institutions see Girard, 'Rise and Fall' (Halifax) and

High court judges sat on the colonial governors' executive councils until well into the nineteenth century, while the great bulk of petty judicial and administrative business was managed by lay magistrates (JPs) and other local officials. Two features in particular distinguished low law in these colonies. First, in the absence of a substantial educated landlord class embued with a tradition of governance, the colonial commission of the peace was drawn from a relatively shallow pool of more-or-less respectable, more-or-less propertied inhabitants, often with little social distance from the neighbours over whom they were placed. Second, while in England the justices were the Janus-faced guardians of the boundary between local and central versions of law and order, in the colonies they managed local relations with both provincial and imperial governments, sometimes playing one off against the other in furtherance of local interests.

This book explores the world of colonial low law from a vantage point near the intersection of King and Water streets in St Andrews, the shire town of Charlotte county, New Brunswick. Located in the southwest corner of the province and sharing a long-disputed border with the state of Maine, the county was populated initially by a number of Loyalist group settlements. Charlotte's original magistracy was made up largely of worthies who had served in similar public capacities in the American colonies. Despite their Loyalist origins and their continuing competition with Americans over territory and resources they retained close business and social ties across the international boundary. This included organizing a flourishing cross-border trade which the imperial customs administration stigmatized as smuggling and which was alternately weakly defended and half-heartedly suppressed by the provincial government at Fredericton.

Although Charlotte was geographically quite large and by New Brunswick standards populous its low law administration was domi-

Acheson, *Saint John*, especially chapter 2. See also J.K. Wilson, 'Quarter Sessions' and Baker, 'Small Claims.' For a brief discussion of the justice of the peace in early America see Conley, 'Doing It by the Book,' 257. With a few exceptions (for example, Snell, 'County Magistracy') historians of colonial America and the early Republic have paid little attention to the justices of the peace. They are scarcely mentioned in Tomlins and Mann, *Many Legalities* except for one contribution, Bushman, 'Farmers in Court.' Edwards, *People and their Peace* is inattentive to the literature about the English JP and so fails to notice significant continuities and parallels.

nated by the magistrates of St Andrews who in lay life were the leading merchants, bankers, and shipowners of the town. Their hegemony was contested by competing groups of businessmen within the county—the traders and proprietors of the island parishes (Campobello, Grand Manan, and West Isles); the shipbuilders and lumbermen of St Stephen and Milltown, border communities further up the St Croix river; and would-be rivals in St George parish and elsewhere. The St Andrews businessmen-magistrates were also locked in regional competition with their counterparts in the much larger port city of Saint John. These various business associations and conflicts helped shape the magistrates' conduct as local administrators and judges.

Unlike justices of the peace in England and in many of its colonies, the New Brunswick magistrates had exclusive civil jurisdiction in actions under five pounds. A few of them were also appointed to the inferior court of common pleas which shared concurrent jurisdiction with the supreme court in larger civil actions.[34] In the credit-based economy of a nineteenth-century trading community there was an enormous volume of petty civil litigation arising out of disputes about dishonoured notes, overdue accounts, trespasses (for example, cutting trees on someone else's land), unpaid wages, and other everyday incidents. Because of the overwhelming number of cases and a reluctance to sit in judgment over (and thereby risk alienating) their own customers and suppliers, the leading businessmen-justices tried to avoid the exercise of this part of their jurisdiction. At St Andrews they solved this dilemma by encouraging Charles Reid Hatheway, a half-pay officer without commercial involvements, to take on the bulk of the justicing business. For their part they continued to dominate county administration and filled most of the county's seats in the provincial assembly and legislative council.

---

34. For ICCP jurisdiction see note 62 below. New Brunswick JPs' civil jurisdiction resembled that of early colonial New York where the Duke of York's laws gave single JPs summary civil jurisdiction to £5 and constituted courts of judicature of three JPs to hold jury trials in civil disputes up to £20. Later in the seventeenth century New York courts of sessions were given unlimited civil jurisdiction subject to review in cases over £5, and later still inferior courts of common pleas were introduced on the New England model: Goebel et al., *Law Enforcement*, 18-24.

In examining the day-to-day business of justicing this book examines Hatheway's role as de facto town magistrate of St Andrews. Despite his disengagement from ordinary commerce and the ineffectiveness of his attempted forays into provincial politics,[35] Hatheway's career was indelibly marked by the county, regional, provincial, and imperial competition that shaped magisterial conduct in New Brunswick. He began in the service of the county's leading landlord, Campobello proprietor David Owen, but they had a profound falling-out when Hatheway took the side of the St Andrews businessmen-magistrates in opposition to Owen's highly idiosyncratic management of his island parish and the cross-border plaster trade which he briefly dominated and they coveted. Owen pursued a vendetta against Hatheway at Fredericton and in a voluminous correspondence with the imperial authorities in London, resulting eventually in a mass of litigation and a rare, although ultimately ineffective, attempt by the provincial government to prosecute Owen for misconduct as a magistrate.

Already tainted in some quarters by his involvement in the Owen affair, Hatheway's reputation came under attack in Fredericton a few years later when tensions between the St Andrews magistrates active in the cross-border trade and the imperial customs officers at that port spilled over into public recriminations. Thomas Wyer, the county's most prominent businessman-cum-justice of the peace-cum-provincial politician, charged that James Morton Spearman, HM Collector of Customs, had challenged him to a duel. Spearman was prosecuted at the bar of the assembly, where Hatheway was called as a witness and denounced as a perjurer. At about the same time a provincial commission on judicial reform produced a statistical report identifying Hatheway as the most active magistrate in the colony. His detractors stirred up rumours that he promoted unnecessary litigation in order to line his own pockets. The newly-arrived lieutenant governor, who apparently did not understand the extensive civil jurisdiction of New Brunswick magistrates but was well-versed in the English demonization of 'trading justices,' promptly re-

35. Hatheway ran for the assembly in 1827 and 1830 but on both occasions withdrew before the polls closed: Anon., *Elections*, 159. The 1827 Charlotte election, its candidates, and its consequences are versified in Scott, *Early Reminiscences*, 45ff.

moved Hatheway from the commission of the peace. It took seven years and a change of lieutenant governors before his St Andrews colleagues managed to have him restored. He remained an active justice until shortly before his death in 1869.

The sessions system came under increasing attack from the mid-1840s. Although the Charlotte magistrates and their supporters successfully resisted the pressure for municipal incorporation until it became mandatory throughout the province in the 1870s, provincial enactments for the election of parish officers and for grand jury oversight of county finances limited their administrative autonomy to a degree. More importantly, the county's heavy indebtedness for public works, including the new jail and courthouse at St Andrews, along with the tax burden imposed on local ratepayers by the province's determination to download the cost of pauper immigration, made for a shift in the justices' relations with the provincial assembly. Where they had once dominated the county's seats in the legislature and insisted on appropriating Charlotte's share of provincial revenues to their own projects, they now faced electoral competition from ratepayer advocates as well as from newly-minted officials appointed by Fredericton to oversee areas of administration, for example emigrant arrivals, that had formerly been their exclusive concern.

The end of the sessions system was hastened by the emergence of party politics at the provincial level in the 1850s. Not only did the enlarged provincial stage offer new opportunities for prominence, but party patronage generated new justices of the peace by the dozen while the increasing centralization of provincial administration undermined the scope and authority of the county bench. The justices' role in local governance was steadily lessened. Two of their lay courts were abolished and replaced by a professional County Court, although individual justices of the peace retained their small claims jurisdiction. Within a few years of Confederation both local governance and the administration of petty justice in New Brunswick were transformed.[36]

36. Bell, 'Legal Pluralism,' 86: 'New Brunswick is a jurisdiction which has gone to perhaps unique extremes to eradicate the local, the non-standardized and the non-professional from the administration of justice.'

Charlotte county

Charlotte county sits on the north and east sides of Passamaquoddy Bay in the Bay of Fundy, bordering Maine to the west by river and sea. By the early eighteenth century the Passamaquoddy nation of Algonkians who inhabited the region when the first Europeans arrived had largely withdrawn across the St Croix river in retreat from punitive raids by New Englanders although some seasonal encampments and mission sites remained when the Loyalists arrived.[37] The area had briefly been a focus of French colonization—De Monts and Champlain built a habitation on an island near the mouth of the St Croix in 1604 only to abandon it after a brutal first winter—but by the late seventeenth century, despite the granting of a few seigneuries, there was just a handful of Acadian families in the region, none of whom seem to have remained or returned after the expulsion of 1755. The government of Nova Scotia, of which the region then formed a part, promoted settlement from New England in the early 1760s, and in 1765 a large district extending over much of what was to become New Brunswick was erected as the county of Sunbury.[38] While most of the New Englanders settled at Saint John or up its river valley a few moved further west to take advantage of the fishery, lumbering, and trading opportunities in the Passamaquoddy region. The Nova Scotia government made several large land grants in the area, including the grant of Campobello island to the Owen family of Glansevern, Wales, in 1767.[39] Captain William Owen established a company to recruit British artisan and agricultural settlers for Campobello. Thirty-eight indentured servants 'of almost all trades and callings' arrived with Owen and fifteen members of his ship's crew in 1770 to find part of the

37. First nations people protested the destruction of a cross at the site of St Andrews in 1784 (Raymond in Vroom, *Glimpses*, XXI, 16 Jun 1892, quoting John Curry's evidence to the boundary commission) and the magistrates of St Andrews negotiated a neutrality agreement with Passamaquoddy chiefs at the outbreak of war in 1812 (CO 188/18, Minute of Council, 10 Jul 1812). Local placenames—Indian Point, Indian Landing, Indian Island—reflected the continuing presence of aboriginal people in the area.

38. Sunbury county NB is a small fragment of the original Sunbury county NS.

39. Davies, 'William Owen,' 189.

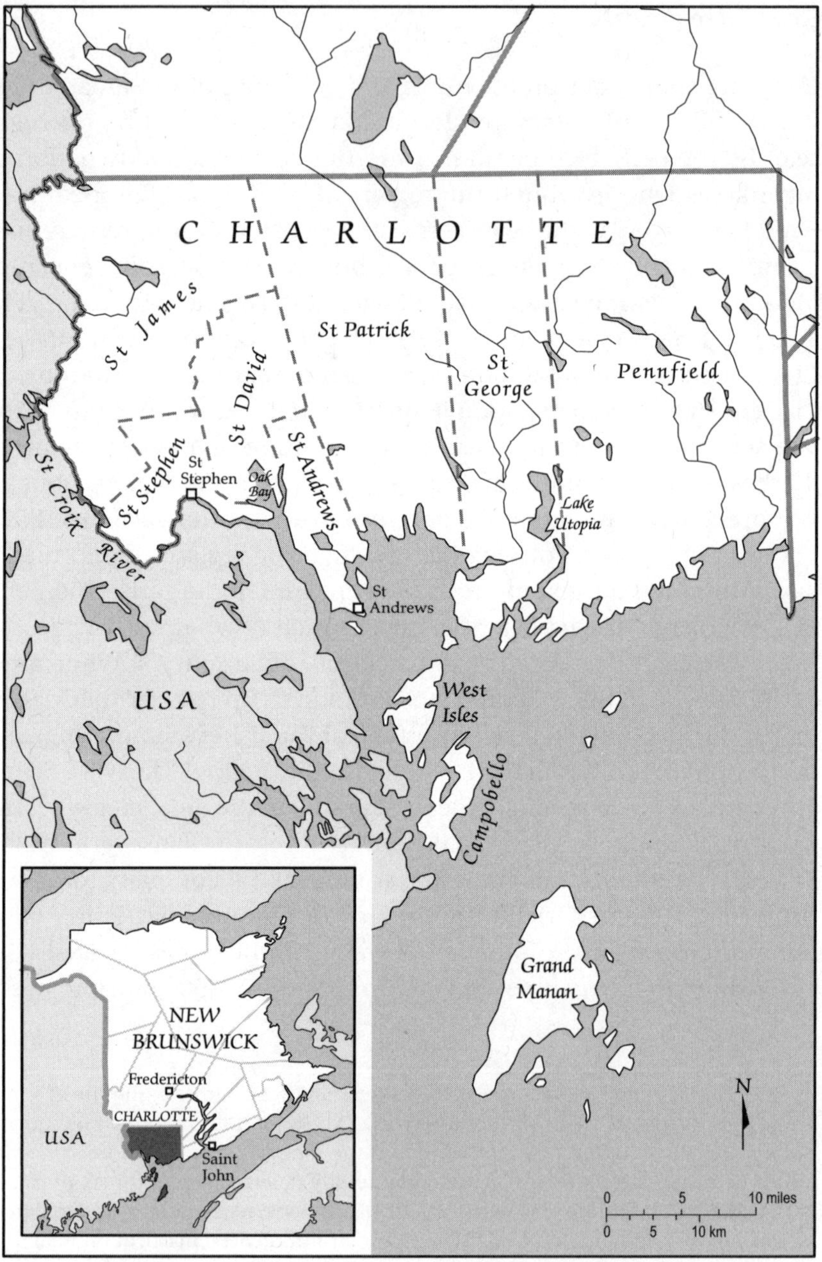

Figure 1.2 – Charlotte county and parishes, 1805

island occupied by three New England families.[40] By 1780 or thereabouts there were permanent settlements on several other islands as well and the beginnings of a lumbering community of as many as twenty families, most of them from Machias, on both sides of the St Croix river at what were to become St Stephen, NB, and Calais, Maine. There were isolated trading posts and fishing camps elsewhere in the region.

The Revolutionary War and its aftermath transformed the region politically and demographically.[41] About thirty-five thousand refugees made their way to Nova Scotia from the beginning of the conflict of whom about twelve thousand came to Sunbury. In addition, some three thousand Loyalist troops were landed at Saint John in 1783 when their regiments were disbanded. Nearly two thousand Loyalists arrived on the shores of Passamaquoddy Bay in 1783-4. Most came as members of settlement associations. St Andrews was founded by an association of merchants and officials from Massachusetts, many of them Scots in origin, some born in Britain and others first-generation colonials. They had fled to Penobscot early in the war expecting a new British colony to be established there.[42] The St Andrews population was strengthened by disbanded soldiers. Refugee British officials from New York who had spent a disastrous winter at Port Matoun in Nova Scotia, travelled upriver to St Stephen under the leadership of Nehemiah Marks. Pennfield parish had its origins in an association of Quaker Loyalists.[43] Members of the Cape Ann Association, 'economic Loyalists' from New Hampshire, took lands near Oak Bay in what was to become St David parish.[44]

---

40. According to Owen, they 'chearfully acquiesced in coming under my jurisdiction': W. Owen, *Narrative*, 120. See also W. Owen, *Journal*. The leading New Englander, Robert Wilson, assumed control of the island after Capt. Owen's departure and remained a thorn in the side of the captain's nephew: see D. Owen, *Statement* (copy with Owen's handwritten emendations in CO 188/28) and chapter 2 below.

41. See generally Acheson, 'Denominationalism'; E.C. Wright, *Loyalists*; R. Fellows, 'Loyalists and Land Settlement'; Condon, 'Loyalist Arrival'; MacNutt, *New Brunswick*, chapter 3; Wynn, 'Population Patterns.'

42. Nason, 'Meritorious.' For the history of the Penobscot colony project, Sloan, 'New Ireland.'

43. When its original settlement at Oak Bay failed the association removed to Pennfield Ridge: Holmes, *Loyalists to Canada*.

44. Acheson, 'Anonymous Loyalists' suggests the complexity of their motives.

John Curry and forty other pre-Loyalists had been granted some fifteen thousand acres in what was to become St Patrick parish in 1784 but few settled there until the arrival in 1790 of former 74th Highlanders who had come to St Andrews in 1783 when the regiment was disbanded.[45] A group settlement of disbanded Royal Fencible Americans led by Peter Clinch became St George parish; another of disbanded Gaelic-speaking troops at Scotch Ridge formed the nucleus of what was to become St James parish.[46]

Group settlement, often reflecting common origins or shared experience, along with the relative isolation of the various communities, made for pronounced differences among the parishes. Acheson contrasts commercial Anglican/Presbyterian St Andrews, focused on the West Indies 'triangle' trade, with industrial Methodist St Stephen, where American logs were transformed into British sawn timber, although both centres were also active in lumbering, shipbuilding, and (often at least notionally illicit) cross-border trade.[47] Campobello with its mix of pre-Loyalist New Englanders and the remnants of the Owen settlement attracted a few ex-military British and Loyalist officers interested in the profitable plaster export trade, often considered a cover for smuggling. The ordinary settlers there and on the other islands depended mainly on the fishery for their livelihoods. In the back country most households worked at lumbering in season supplemented by small-scale subsistence farming of what was generally poor soil.

Each of the group settlements had a few prominent well-to-do

45. LaVorgna, 'St. Patrick's,' 22f.

46. St James was severed from St Stephen in 1803.

47. Although historians of early New Brunswick have made much of religious movements and denominational conflicts, these rarely figured significantly in Charlotte county low law. (The Temperance movement is another story, as will be seen.) Sabbatarian complaints appear infrequently in the local court records. Despite early rivalry between Anglican and Methodist ministers for the souls of St Andrews, religious coexistence was the norm as different congregations shared resources and often contributed to one another's building funds. Crypto-Catholic John Dunn served as county sheriff and customs officer despite the officially Protestant establishment: J.M. Smith, *Borderland Smuggling*, 31. While instances of religious intolerance are known—for example, W.F.W. Owen was particular about the adherences of his Campobello tenants—there was no local counterpart to the sectarian rioting experienced in other parts of the province, for which see See, *Riots in New Brunswick*.

local leaders, the so-called 'professional Loyalists' who dominated commerce, the professions, and officialdom, and a larger contingent with few resources who found it hard to carve out an existence. Of the two thousand or so Loyalists who arrived by 1785 it has been estimated that as many as a thousand had returned to the States by 1803, victims of a prolonged commercial depression. The population stagnated and declined until the end of the Napoleonic wars when the revival of the British timber market sparked economic growth and renewed British immigration, especially of Irish Protestants. This more than doubled Charlotte's population by 1824 and doubled it again to about eighteen thousand by 1840. But the end of the colonial tariff preference in the 1840s produced a second long depression and emigration of the native-born. St Andrews and St Stephen were especially vulnerable because of their reliance on international trade. This second out-migration was accompanied by an intake of largely Catholic and impoverished Irish famine refugees, some of whom quickly moved on to the United States while others remained at St Andrews to labour on the docks and in railroad construction.[48] Although St Stephen's population revived in the 1850s as lumbering expanded under Reciprocity, much of its growth was accounted for by internal migration from other parishes in the county, both driven by and reinforcing the decline of St Andrews.[49]

Institutional development and the sessions system

Loyalist dissatisfaction with their reception and treatment by the government of Nova Scotia quickly led to the partition of the old province and the creation of New Brunswick in September 1784. Governor Thomas Carleton arrived in November.[50] In June of the following year he issued a proclamation establishing Charlotte county and its parishes, naming its officers, fixing its shiretown or seat at St Andrews, and establishing its courts.[51] These were not the first local courts for

48. Chapter 10.

49. For the most part this paragraph summarizes Acheson, 'Demography.'

50. Carleton's commission was demoted to that of lieutenant governor in 1786 when his older brother Guy became governor general of British North America.

51. The county and parish boundaries were confirmed by the first act of the province's legislative assembly, 26 Geo.III (1786) c.1. The original parishes were St

the region. In 1767 Nova Scotia governor Lord William Campbell gave a commission to James Boyd, a Scottish trader who had arrived at Indian Island four years earlier, to serve as the first justice of the peace in the Passamaquoddy region.[52] In 1770 Captain Owen, his ship's master, and his clerk were also appointed.[53] Two years later the Nova Scotia legislature provided for a court of general sessions of the peace for 'the district of Passamaquoddy' at Campobello because of the difficulty of travel to the Sunbury county seat.[54] John Curry, who first became a justice of the peace in 1774, later deposed that courts of general sessions of the peace had been held at Campobello from 1770 until the beginning of the American war:[55]

> during that time (as might fully appear by the Docketts of said courts, had they not been taken from the deponent with several other books and papers by an American Privateer in the year 1778) Moose Island, Deer Island, Indian Island, and all other islands in said Bay of Passamaquoddy were within the jurisdiction of the Province of Nova Scotia, and that the inhabitants of all the islands in the said Bay were regularly summoned and attended the different Courts held at Campobello.

In February 1783 the governor of Nova Scotia issued a new commission of the peace for the Passamaquoddy district, naming Curry, Philip Bailey, Robert Pagan, and William Gallop as justices. Curry was

---

Stephen, St David, St Andrews, St Patrick, St George, Pennfield, and West Isles, the latter comprising Grand Manan and Campobello as well as Indian, Deer, and several lesser islands.

52. Kilby, *Eastport*, 109. The commission is reproduced in Vroom, *Glimpses*, 'Additions and Corrections,' 13 Oct 1892. NYPL Chalmers, NS volume, includes documents relating to Boyd's Passamaquoddy sojourn. Boyd seems to have removed to Halifax not long afterwards but his son, also named James Boyd, settled at St Andrews in 1819 and will figure prominently in what follows.

53. W. Owen, *Narrative*, 116. While in residence Owen dealt with minor crimes (ibid., 123) and performed marriages as a single justice (ibid., 123, 138). On June 4, 1771, just before he left the island for good, he and his fellow Campobello justices (but no other Sunbury magistrates) held a special sessions to celebrate the King's birthday, summoning a jury to view and report on the state of settlement; for its presentment, ibid., 153ff.

54. [N.S.] 12 Geo.III (1772) c.2.

55. Reproduced in Kilby, *Eastport*, 110. As Owen did not record a court of general sessions in his journal for 1770-1 it is unlikely that any was held before 1772.

a long-time resident of the area, having established a trading post at Indian Island in 1770 and pursued various other opportunities on the islands and up the St Croix since then.[56] Captain Bailey of the Royal Fencible Americans was a newly-arrived Loyalist: like Curry, he was to receive a substantial grant of land for group settlement in St Patrick parish the following year. Pagan was one of the leaders of the Penobscot Association, while Gallop, a master mariner, had been a loyal privateer during the revolution. Both settled at St Andrews. In his 1798 testimony to the boundary commission[57] Pagan said he had attended a court of general sessions for the Passamaquoddy district at Campobello under his Nova Scotia commission, but if so no court documents appear to have survived.

Governor Parr's 1783 commission had named one pre-Loyalist and three Loyalist justices. It was overtaken by governor Carleton's 1785 proclamation,[58] naming one pre-Loyalist (Curry) and fourteen Loyalists including Pagan and Gallop. The Charlotte bench included two of the three leading figures in the Penobscot Association, Pagan and his father-in-law Jeremiah Pote; the third, Thomas Wyer (Pote's other son-in-law), was named high sheriff. Six other St Andrews grantees were named to the bench along with two Pennfield Quakers (both of whom had served in arms during the revolution); Peter Clinch and another St George grantee; Nehemiah Marks, leader of the Port Matoun Association; and Moses Gerrish, a Harvard-educated Loyalist who had been granted the island of Grand Manan subject to settlement conditions that he was subsequently unable to meet. That eight of the fifteen justices were St Andrews grantees showed

---

56. In 1770 Lord William Campbell visited Campobello and asked Owen and Curry to obtain information about the boundary between Nova Scotia and Massachusetts: *WPO* 9-18, Interrogatories administered to John Curry Esq by Phineas Bruce Esq acting on behalf of the United States of America, St Andrews, 23 Oct 1797.

57. The peace treaty of 1783 had established the St Croix as the boundary with the United States but which river was the 'true' St Croix remained unsettled and was referred to international arbitration. Pagan was not a disinterested witness, of course, but his discovery of the ruins of the 1604 habitation in accordance with Champlain's sketch helped to settle the question. Pagan's testimony about his archaeological investigations is reproduced in Kilby, *Eastport,* 124f.

58. The clerk of the peace wrote out a copy of the proclamation at the beginning of the county's general sessions minutebooks, PANB RS148/a/2/a/1.

the prominence Carleton intended for the shiretown.[59] Curry, Pagan, and William Anstruther were named justices of the inferior court of common pleas. Joseph Garnett, a St Andrews military Loyalist who had not been granted land, received appointments as clerk of the peace, keeper of the county records, and puisne judge of the monthly clerk's court.

The proclamation established and staffed three local courts.[60] The county's justices were to assemble for up to five days twice a year in April and September in general sessions of the peace with the broad powers of its English counterpart to do anything that justices of the peace in sessions ought to do.[61] Unlike general sessions, the inferior court of common pleas was designated a court of record. It was to be held concurrently with sessions to try civil actions between forty shillings and fifty pounds except those involving title to land, subject to review for error by the supreme court.[62] That it was to be con-

---

59. The proclamation also named two coroners: Jacob Buffington, one of the two Pennfield justices, and Samuel Spencer, a St Andrews grantee.

60. See also Donovan, 'Origin.'

61. It had 'full Power and Authority to enquire of, hear and determine within the County aforesaid all and all Manner of Felonies, Imprisonments, Riots, Routs, Oppressions, Extortions, Forestallings, Regratings, Trespasses, Offences, and all and singular other evil Deeds and Offences whatsoever within the County aforesaid from time to time perpetrated, done, arising, or happening, which to the Office of Justice of the Peace are incumbent or do in any manner belong or which hereafter shall happen to belong or be incumbent or which in any manner before the Justices of the Peace at the Sessions of the Peace ought or may be enquired into, heard and determined, together with the corrections and punishment thereof, and to do and execute all other things within the County aforesaid and the Liberties and Precincts thereof as fully, freely and entirely, and in as ample a manner and form as Justices of the Peace of us our Heirs and Successors anywhere within that part of our Kingdom of Great Britain called England by the Laws, Statutes or Customs of England, or by any other Legal Method whatsoever heretofore had or exercised or hereafter to be had or exercised, could, might or can do, and in as ample Manner and Form as if the same had been in these our Letters particularly and by Special Words expressed, contained and mentioned; And that you or either of you the Said Justices of the Peace of Us, our Heirs and Successors in the County aforesaid, may have and exercise Jurisdiction in all Causes, Matters and Things whatsoever, which to Justices of the Peace of our Said County in any Manner do or ought to belong.'

62. Actions under ten pounds and those for slander or assault and battery were to be exempt from review. ICCP jurisdiction was amended by 26 Geo.III (1786) c.9 and again by 35 Geo.III (1795) c.2 which made it concurrent with the supreme court's

ducted in the same manner and using the same procedures as other courts of record and made subject to writs of error in the province's supreme court shows that it was to be the bottom rung of the hierarchy of common law courts, belonging more to high law than to low. Both sessions and common pleas were to be held at St Andrews.

The third court, called the clerk's court, was to be held monthly or more often at locations throughout the county[63] to determine small claims up to forty shillings. It was to be staffed by the clerk of the peace in association with any one justice and to have an expeditious and inexpensive procedure modelled on the English sheriff's courts where a single twelve-man jury heard all the trials on court day. The proclamation set out a detailed sketch of procedures but it is uncertain whether they were ever put in practice. In 1786 the first provincial assembly changed the rules. Although it was still called the clerk's court, a single justice was to officiate and decide cases alone or, at the defendant's election, with a jury of three.[64] An act of 1791, described by Carleton as 'experimental' and limited to two years duration, transferred all the powers of the clerk's court to justices of the peace.[65] It was continued for a further two years then replaced in 1795 by an act giving any justice of the peace *ad hoc* civil jurisdiction up to three pounds and effectively abolishing the clerk's court.[66]

---

subject to the ICCP defendant's right to remove actions or appeal judgments greater than £10 into the supreme court. By 42 Geo.III (1802) c.7 ICCP was given exclusive summary jurisdiction over claims worth from £5 to £20 not involving title to land.

63. The proclamation says 'in some convenient place in each and every township or district,' but this was before the parishes were formally established.

64. 26 Geo.III (1786) c.10. An amending bill passed the assembly in 1789 but did not receive council assent. It came before the legislature as a bill 'for the abolition of the Clerk's Court' (PANB RS24 S4-B7) in response to petitions from Sunbury county and was amended and renamed in committee (JHA 1789). It would have abolished the clerk's court, transferred its jurisdiction to each and every JP, and set fees for his services: PANB RS24 S4-B14.

65. 31 Geo.III (1791) c.4; CO 188/04, Carleton to Grenville, 10 Jun 1791.

66. 33 Geo.III (1793) c.1; (1795) 35 Geo.III c.1. I say 'effectively abolishing' because although s.18 of the 1795 act expressly removed the jurisdiction of the clerk, repealed the 1786 statute, and provided that small debts were not to be sued for in any other court than before a single JP, the 1786 act was notionally revived when the 1795 act expired in 1802 and was not repealed by its replacement: see note 68 below. 50 Geo.III (1810) c.17 s.18 provided that, 'the Justices of the Peace, in the several Counties, shall respectively have concurrent jurisdiction with the Clerk's Courts,

When it expired in 1802 the assembly expanded the justices' exclusive civil jurisdiction to five pounds.[67] Carleton urged disallowance because the sum was 'much too large to be thus decided on in a Country where from necessity persons of small property and slender information, and liable to local and other prejudices, are often in the Commission of the peace.'[68] Despite a lengthy legal opinion worrying that the powers given to justices by the act infringed on the original jurisdiction of the supreme court and limited its powers of review, the imperial government eventually confirmed the new act.[69]

As in England and elsewhere in the British empire, the court of general sessions of the peace was the hub of local governance.[70] Justices of the peace from across the county assembled in the shire town to pass local by-laws, hold jury trials of regulatory, morals, and minor criminal offences, assess taxes, approve county expenditures, license taverns and appoint a variety of officials. Local bills to be introduced in the assembly were given a first public reading there.[71] The sessions grand jury inspected the courthouse and jail, conducted pretrial investigations of indictable offences, and made presentments on such topics as disorderly houses, bootlegging, bad roads, decay-

---

in the respective Counties,' in matters under forty shillings. This may have been intended to ensure that no part of the English county court jurisdiction remained unprovided for in New Brunswick: JLC 5 Mar 1810. But there is no evidence that a clerk's court was ever held in Charlotte. Curiously, 'An act to appoint a clerks court in the Town of St Andrews' was read at September sessions 1828 but there is no act with that title on the statute books nor is such a bill mentioned in JHA or JLC.

67. 42 Geo.III (1802) c.5. The 1795 act had a two-year limit but was continued for a further five years by 37 Geo.III (1797) c.1.

68. CO 188/11, Carleton to Hobart, 26 Apr 1802, explaining that the bill had been 'passed by Council and assented to by me without sufficient deliberation.' He also pointed out that the act tacitly repealed former enactments without identifying them expressly as required by the royal instructions to avoid uncertainty as to what laws were in effect. This may explain the notional revival of the 1786 act noted above.

69. CO 188/11 for the unattributed legal opinion, dated March 1802; CO 188/12 for the Order-in-Council of 18 May 1803 approving the act.

70. In England and other colonies the court met quarterly, hence the term quarter sessions. In New Brunswick the court met just twice a year in general sessions.

71. An exception was made for a bill establishing new fire regulations for St Andrews which had been 'read and approved of at a public meeting at the Court House in Saint Andrews, the Inhabitants of which place only are interested in the provisions thereof': JHA 1828, 14.

ing bridges, and public nuisances. Sometimes it could serve as a check on the bench. For example in April 1787 the grand jury presented 'that thro' the multiplicity of Business or some other causes the Magistrates have not paid that attention to the Laws in general of the Province that they are required to,' in particular a recent act empowering sessions to regulate the use of weirs and nets in rivers and streams.[72] By the middle of the nineteenth century the sessions grand jury had acquired a more formal supervisory role as auditor of county accounts.[73] Appointment to the sessions grand jury was a first mark of local prominence and often a precursor to office.

While the bulk of the local legislative and financial business of the county was conducted in general sessions, the justices sometimes assembled out of sessions for particular purposes, whether to appoint a replacement for an official who had left the county, to provide for a local emergency such as a fire or smallpox outbreak, to examine a prisoner, or to respond to an enquiry from the provincial executive. There was no jury at these meetings, which were usually held in private. All the county justices might be called to such gatherings (although only a handful might attend) in which case they were minuted as 'special sessions.'[74] Sometimes however the call went only to justices residing in town, and these were typically minuted as 'meetings of the magistrates of St Andrews.' (Neighbouring justices in other parishes are known to have met occasionally to deal with collective matters of purely local concern, but as the county clerk of the peace was not involved their meetings were not noted on the sessions minutebook.)

In addition there was a great deal of judicial and related business to be conducted out of sessions by the minority of justices who chose to make themselves available to hear lesser criminal and regulatory cases (either alone or with one or two other justices as the particular statute required) or the still smaller number who were willing to

---

72. 26 Geo.III (1786) c.31. The bench thereupon adopted regulations for the St Croix fishery proposed by the St Stephen parish officers.

73. Chapter 9.

74. Unlike Fyson's Quebec justices the St Andrews magistrates did not hold regular petty sessions for summary trials but something of the sort developed at St Stephen later in the nineteenth century.

decide small civil claims. The sessions system encompassed not only general and special sessions but also the activities of justices out of sessions; some of the latter were in principle to be reported to general sessions although this did not always happen in practice. Appendix A.1 lists some of the powers assigned by statute to justices in and out of sessions. Typically where regulatory authority was assigned to general sessions enforcement of the regulations fell to justices out of sessions.

The sessions system also encompassed the duties and conduct of parish officers, notionally appointed or approved by the justices in general sessions but often nominated (and after 1850 elected) by parish or town meetings. The parishes were administrative subdivisions of the county without ecclesiastical significance but equivalent to townships elsewhere. Each had its own clerk, tax assessors and collectors, overseers of the poor, school trustees, constables, roads commissioners and surveyors, as well as inspectors of various kinds, fence viewers, and other petty officials all drawn from among the local ratepayers to serve for a year at a time. In St David, the only Charlotte parish with a long continuous series of surviving appointment records (Table 1.1), about a fifth of the ratepayers held parish office each year.[75] Many of them held multiple offices and some filled the same offices year after year. Over a period of sixty years the parish had just five clerks. Weighers of hay served an average of nine years each, inspectors of bricks eight years, school trustees five. Farmer, reformer, and sometime provincial cabinet minister James Brown served continuously as St David school trustee from 1826 to 1852, returning to that office again in 1854 and 1865. Mill-owner Tristram Moore JP held parish office for forty-three years, thirty-three of them as inspector of timber. He also served as assessor of rates, school trustee, commissioner of highways, and overseer of the poor. Other justices of the peace also held concurrent parish offices although this could be controversial.[76]

75. PANB RS148/A/3; PANB RS148/C/3/m/1.

76. See chapter 3.

Table 1.1 – St David parish officer appointments

Officer	1805	1825	1845	1865*
Commissioner of Highways	3	3	3	3
Surveyor of Highways	7	18	38	43
Overseer of Poor	3	3	3	3
School Trustee	-	3	3	3
Town Clerk	1	1	1	1
Constable	2	3	3	6
Fence Viewer	3	2	9	5
Pound Keeper	1	3	6	5
Surveyor of Lumber	3	8	-	-
Surveyor of Timber	-	-	6	3
Hogreeve	1	8	13	17†
Assessor of Rates	3	3	3	3
Collector of Rates	-	1	1	1
Inspector of Hay	1	2	3	-
Inspector of Bricks	-	2	2	-
Inspector of Staples	1	-	-	-
Revisors of Election	-	-	-	3
Totals:	29	60	94	102

* Elected; see chapter 12.
† 'Hogreeve and field driver'

Other offices intersected with the sessions system. The high sheriff of the county, though appointed by the provincial executive, was responsible to sessions which determined his salary.[77] The county

77. Sheriffs took fees for their civil functions, legislative appropriations for their electoral functions, and were paid by the county for the 'criminal part' described by Charlotte high sheriff Thomas Jones in justifying his £50 annual salary: 'Some of these duties are, pursuing, apprehending, and safe keeping all Her Majesty's enemies, and all offenders against the Law and after their condemnation, I am to execute their punishments, whipping or hanging or whatever else it may be. I am chief conservator of the Peace; I have to interfere and stay all quarrels, broils and riots. I have to obey the Magistrates, and see their warrants properly executed. I have charge of the Jail, and am answerable for the safety and health of all confined. I have to execute the Queen's writs of Scire facias and Extent gratuitously, where the parties prosecuted have no property—this is often attended with great expence, the parties being often at a great distance, the Records have to be searched, Jurors summoned, and an Inquisition held. I have to collect, and am answerable for all fines to be paid the Queen for which I receive no fees. I have also by the first day of May in each year, to file

clerk of the peace, another provincial appointee paid by sessions, was the county's chief executive officer. The county treasurer was named by and responsible to sessions for the county accounts.

Equally important were the less formal intersections between sessions and other institutions of colonial governance. Sessions had limited taxing authority; if it required funds for major capital projects or to pay down the county debt it needed special statutory authority from the provincial legislature. So long as the provincial assembly functioned as a committee of county representatives to parcel out available resources and some of the county's four assemblymen were also justices of the peace, the integration of sessions and assembly business was normally quite easily achieved.[78] There were points of contact between the sessions system and the judiciary: a handful of county justices of the peace also held commissions on the inferior court of common pleas[79] and justices of the peace in their ministerial capacity conducted pretrial investigations and committed accused for trial at the circuit court.[80] The supreme court on circuit visited Charlotte county once or twice a year in most years. Its grand jury was selected, as one judge put it, 'from those persons possessing influence and standing in different parts of the county,'[81] but justices of the peace were not overrepresented. Although many, perhaps most, of those appointed JP had previously served on circuit grand juries, the circuit grand juries only occasionally included a JP. One or two senior justices sometimes sat on the circuit bench to share the benefit of their local knowledge with the presiding judge.[82] The lieutenant

into court a list of Jurors throughout the County, for which the Justices are to pay me, what they think proper—this is included in the 50 pounds': PANB RS148/a/1, 7 Apr 1841.

78. Appendix A.3 and chapter 9.

79. Every JCP was a JP but only a few JPs were JCPs.

80. But see chapter 8.

81. G.F. Street's address to the Grand Jury, Charlotte Circuit 1846, as reported by *Standard*, 29 Apr 1846. On this occasion of Street's first circuit since his appointment to the supreme court bench, the county magistrates proceeded 'by arrangement' to his lodgings and presented him with an address of welcome.

82. Few circuit minutes survive for Charlotte county and local newspapers only occasionally listed the circuit grand jury so it is difficult to quantify participation by justices of the peace. There were two JPs on the grand jury at the August 1825 circuit; the same grand jury included several who were to be appointed to the county bench

governor often consulted the supreme court judges before appointing justices of the peace, so participation on circuit grand juries was a way of becoming known to the judiciary. Some justices of the peace held other public offices that occasionally touched on their role as local governors in unexpected ways, as for example when one magistrate drew on provincial funds entrusted to him as commissioner of buoys and beacons to relieve the county when it was on the verge of bankruptcy.[83] The county militia reflected the hierarchy of governance: many of its commissioned officers also held commissions of the peace or other county offices (sheriff, clerk of the peace) and were at the same time leading businessmen.[84]

St Andrews and the 'junto'

In 1769 nineteen-year-old Robert Pagan, son of a Glasgow sugar refiner, came to Falmouth, Massachusetts (now Portland, Maine) to participate in the West Indies trade. With his brother Thomas he established the firm of Robert Pagan & Co. as a subsidiary of a Greenock merchant house, invested in lumbering and shipbuilding, and built up a prosperous trading business. He married the daughter of Jeremiah Pote, a Falmouth merchant and selectman, and thereby gained a connection to another Pote son-in-law, the customs official Thomas Wyer. By 1776 the Pagans, Potes, and Wyers were forced to flee Falmouth as Tory sympathizers. They regrouped four years later at Castine on Penobscot Bay, which was being promoted as a Loyalist haven, the site of a proposed British colony to be called New Ireland. Pagan became the most prominent entrepreneur in the region, a magistrate, and the highest-ranking civil official once Dr John Caleff, chief promoter of the New Ireland project, left for England to lobby for it there. The British government abandoned the project dur-

in later years. At the August 1826 and 1827 Charlotte circuits, supreme court justices Chipman and Botsford respectively were joined on the bench by the county's senior JP, Hugh Mackay, 'and others their fellows,' although just one at a time. There were no justices on the grand juries at these circuits: PANB RS32/A/2. Two of the 1853 grand jurors had the same last name and first initial as two justices: *Standard*, 16 Nov 1853.

83. Chapter 9.

84. Chapter 3.

ing the peace negotiations, ceding the Penobscot region to the United States. Pagan and his associates cast about for a new commercial territory under the British flag. They selected the peninsula in Passamaquoddy Bay just east of the new boundary line. It offered an adequate harbour, a short route to West Indies ports, an 'inexhaustible' supply of timber, a good fishery, little or no competition from existing businesses and ready access to American markets. In 1783 the Pagan brothers, Pote, Wyer, Caleff, William Gallop, and Colin Campbell established themselves as the official agents of the Penobscot Associated Loyalists and began negotiating for land grants, surveys, and other necessities. In September of that year six hundred and thirty-nine members of one hundred and forty-five households took transport from Penobscot to St Andrews where they were allocated lots in accordance with the town plan, zoning decisions, and building code that the agents had prearranged with a view to its 'systematic and expeditious settlement.'[85]

Penobscot Association agents dominated the list of official appointments in the new Charlotte county. They used their positions as magistrates, sheriff, customs officer, land surveyor, and assemblymen to control development in their commercial interest, to resist American challenges to the international boundary,[86] and to offset competition from other groups in the county.[87] They also ensured their preeminence as landholders and businessmen by acquiring key waterfront property in St Andrews and millsites in its hinterland. The Pagan, Wyer, Gallop, and Campbell families controlled forty per cent of the St Andrews water lots and the best mill privileges in the region.[88] Pagan, Wyer, and Pote continued to assemble property by purchase

85. Nason, 'Meritorious,' 45; Macmillan et al., 'Pagan, Robert.'

86. Along with his archaeological researches to prove the 'true' St Croix, Pagan joined with Campbell and Curry to resist U.S. claims to Moose Island (now Eastport, Maine) and Dudley Island: CCGS 9 Sep 1790; CO 188/2, Carleton to Grenville, 13 Aug 1791 encl. Campbell and Pagan to Odell, 20 Jan 1791.

87. In 1803, for example, Pagan and his associates at St Andrews successfully opposed a St Stephen group's petition for land to extend its mill holdings there. Pagan argued in the assembly that the lands were required for county purposes and had the request referred to general sessions, where he used his influence to substitute a 21-year lease for the grant: Nason, 'Meritorious,' 122f.

88. Ibid., 68, 71.

from the original grantees, acquiring thirty-nine town lots and 'numerous' rural properties in the vicinity of their millsites between 1784 and 1802.[89] They lent money on mortgages and financed settlement by advancing funds against labour, lumber, and fish.

The vision of the St Andrews merchants was to make their port the sole entrepôt for the produce of the Passamaquoddy region. But by the end of the eighteenth century some serious obstacles had emerged. The imperial government established a naval timber reserve on the boundaries of St Andrews thereby cutting off supplies to the group's mills and limiting the expansion of the settlement. This favoured the sawmills and shipyards of St Stephen, located at the head of navigation on the St Croix with an unimpeded forest hinterland. Merchants and lumbermen in other parishes resented the concentration of wealth and authority at St Andrews and the efforts of the Pagan group to extend operations throughout the county as a way of offsetting the limitations of St Andrews. From Campobello David Owen bewailed the St Andrews 'hive . . . which sting me at every vent.'[90] St George patriarch Colonel Hugh Mackay denounced the St Andrews 'Junto,' saying that 'peace and tranquility will never be effectually established in this County' while Pagan and his associates among the Charlotte assemblymen remained on the commission of the peace.[91]

Robert Pagan died in 1821, his brother-in-law Thomas Wyer three years later.[92] A second generation inherited their vision for St Andrews. Led by Wyer's son (also named Thomas) this new junto included clerk of the peace Harris Hatch, the wealthiest man in the county, and 'squire' John Wilson, promoter of British North America's first railroad project, the St Andrews & Quebec, which was designed to extend the shire town's hinterland to the Saint Lawrence and make St Andrews the leading British port on the continent. Robert Pagan had been among the founders of the Bank of New Brunswick in 1820; Hatch, Wyer, Wilson, and others, several of them surviving Penobscot

89. Ibid., 102f. Between 1786 and 1810 ten St Andrews merchants were involved in ninety per cent of land transactions: ibid., 105.

90. NLW Glansevern #8400, Owen to chief justice Ludlow, 1 Jul 1790.

91. Mackay to Edward Winslow, 1 Jun 1803, in Raymond, *Winslow Papers*, 490f.

92. Their father-in-law, Jeremiah Pote, died in 1796.

Loyalists or their sons, founded the Charlotte County Bank in 1825.[93] Like their predecessors members of the second junto combined private business with public office as justices of the peace, of the common pleas, assemblymen, and legislative councillors. And like their predecessors, they attracted resentment and resistance from other parts of the county. By the 1840s, and especially following the second Thomas Wyer's death in 1848, the St Andrews merchant-justices were struggling to preserve their hegemony in the face of deepening economic distress, heightened regional competition, transformative demographic shifts, and a new politics and morality trumpeting temperance and accountability.

This book combines biographical narrative with thematic analysis to explore various facets of the operation of low law in pre-Confederation Charlotte county. The narrative focuses on the fortunes and reverses of the St Andrews 'junto' and on the careers and interactions of three justices in particular: David Owen, a younger son in a prominent Welsh family, whose patrician disdain for colonial institutions and actors sat uneasily with his attempt to maintain a caricature of English rural squirearchy on his Campobello Island estate; Charles Reid Hatheway, a younger son of Loyalists who became the de facto town magistrate of St Andrews and relied on justicing to supplement his meagre income as a junior half-pay officer; and James Boyd, son of the pre-Loyalist trader JP, a St Andrews grocer and populist patrician politician permanently at odds with his fellow St Andrews magistrates.

The thematic analysis falls into three parts. Part I, 'Petty justices,' examines relations between the St Andrews junto and its rivals in the island parishes up to the early 1830s focusing on local and metropolitan efforts to control the magistracy and other low law officials. Chap-

93. 6 Geo.IV (1825) c.12. The bank's shareholders profited by financing the county debt for which many of them were accountable as magistrates and other public officials with fiscal responsibilities: chapter 9.

ter 2 considers attempts by the St Andrews junto to deal with David Owen by mobilizing both popular support and the machinery of high law. Chapter 3 begins with the junto's first experiment with collective self-regulation in the case of two West Isles justices and continues with the provincial executive's failed attempt to bring the heavy guns of the *ex officio* criminal information to bear on Owen. Chapter 4 examines the conflict between the imperial customs establishment and the local magistracy at St Andrews, leading to lieutenant governor Campbell's decision to remove Hatheway from the Charlotte bench in 1832.

Part II, 'Doing substantial justice,' focuses on dispute resolution aspects of low law, beginning in chapter 5 with the front line officials of the province's land and timber bureaucracy. Chapter 6 considers the business case for justicing through a detailed examination of Hatheway's activities in 1840-1, the first year of his reinstatement to the Charlotte bench. Chapters 7 and 8 analyse Hatheway's civil and crown dockets respectively in the twenty years after 1847 to examine the uses and meaning of 'substantial justice' as dispensed in magistrates' parlours.

Part III, 'The sessions system and its enemies,' explores administrative low law in Charlotte county. Chapter 9 examines the roles of sessions and the county's assemblymen in public works and public finance, particularly in building Charlotte's gaols and courthouses. Chapter 10 considers the local administration of poor law with a focus on the consequences of the Irish famine immigration, 1847-50. Chapter 11 addresses liquor licensing and prohibition, exploring how the temperance movement helped to transform the Charlotte bench in the late 1850s. Chapter 12 examines the sessions system in decline in the decade leading up to Confederation when municipal incorporation was an available but not yet universal alternative. It concludes with a brief overview of the main themes of this book.

Part I

Petty justices

> 'They have declared, Master William, that I am the first Character this day in North America. Excuse my Vanity.'
>
> David Owen JP, 1791

Part I: Introduction

The Charlotte county bench was far from united or even harmonious at any time in its history. The local interests of particular towns and parishes, competition among business and political rivals, territorial jealousies, even conflicting ideals of honour and respectability exemplified in attitudes towards duelling all ensured a constant hum of bickering that at times broke out into violent antagonisms. The bench was not a unit but neither was it a fragmented collocation of individuals. Instead there were recognizable patterns of stable and shifting alliances. The St Andrews junto, the most remarkable and long-lived example of the former, persisted for two generations. In contrast the much looser cluster of arch-Tories and island traders around Campobello patrician David Owen was constantly in flux as his outrageous machinations alternately attracted and repelled his hangers-on.

This Part examines one theatre of conflict, the struggle between St Andrews and the island parishes for control of the plaster trade and other opportunities as it played out in low and high law settings during Charlotte's first half-century. The larger context of this local struggle, the questionable legality of the trade itself, involved provincial revenue policies and the imperial customs establishment. Nevertheless some of the conflicts examined here ostensibly had nothing to do with business rivalries but involved local taxation, militia organization, the propriety of justices occupying parish offices, electioneering, mutual insults, and physical assaults.

As these tensions played out they revealed a range of improprieties as magistrates used their official powers to overawe dependants, fend off local and extraregional competitors, manipulate legal outcomes to serve their own interests, repay their allies, and undermine their enemies. Efforts to counter these improprieties in turn revealed the limits of self-regulation, judicial supervision, and executive oversight. Competing blocs of justices experimented with a variety of control strategies: getting up petitions; calling on rivals to resign; making calculated use of the machinery of high law; appealing to the provincial executive and to Whitehall; promoting the territorial division of parishes and even the county to enhance immediate local autonomy. Provincial strategies that relied on the high law courts, most notably the attempt to prosecute David Owen for misconduct by means of an *ex officio* information, were unavailing, as too was one lieutenant governor's attempt at personal diplomacy. His successor's heavy-handed use of the executive power to remove justices from the commission had immediate practical effect but it undermined local authority and helped set the stage for a new theatre of conflict over the proper balance of local and provincial power.

Chapter 2

The trials of David Owen, 1787-1803

The Reverend David Owen M.A., senior wrangler (1777), and Fellow (1779) of Trinity College, Cambridge, came to New Brunswick in October 1787, in his thirty-third year, to wage law.[1] He expected to stay six months, a year at most. When he died at Campobello in December 1829 he had lived forty-two years on the island, straying no further afield than occasional visits to Saint John, Fredericton, Boston, and Philadelphia.

Owen's mission was to supervise litigation to recover the family property at Campobello. His swashbuckling uncle Captain William Owen RN had been promised the whole island in 1767 for services rendered as secretary to Nova Scotia governor Sir William Campbell. When it was objected that the grant was too large for a single individual, Captain Owen named his three young nephews—Arthur Davies, David, and William Jr, sons of his older

1. Some of the biographical writing about David Owen consists of unverifiable folklore and demonstrable misinformation. Much of both originates in the writings of Kate Gannett Wells, who was relied upon in varying degrees by Ganong and others. See, for example, Wells, *Campobello* and 'David Owen,' and Vaughan, 'At Campobello.' Many of the sources quoted without citation in Nowlan, *Outer Island* are nowhere to be found. Ingersoll, 'Owen, David' is factually more reliable (except that Owen was never a judge of common pleas: CO 188/35, Odell to Owen, 5 Feb 1827). Davies, 'Welsh landlord,' is generally reliable as well as creative in its speculations but here I give my own view of Owen's character and motivation.

brother Owen Owen—as co-grantees. Having spent 1770-1 establishing a foothold at Campobello, apparently without serious contention from the New England families already squatting there, Captain Owen departed on His Majesty's service to India, where he went missing in 1778, eventually to be declared dead.

By the mid-1780s the three nephews' joint claim to the island was vulnerable on several fronts. Although Captain William never married, he had left two acknowledged sons by Sarah Haslem, his housekeeper, one of them born on Campobello. They might have pressed a claim under their father's will which left all his possessions to his 'adopted' children.[2] There was the risk of claims by members of the joint stock company organized to settle the island who had lost considerable investments there during the American war when the company's agent abandoned the island and returned to England. In his absence, Robert Wilson, one of the New England squatters whom Captain Owen had suffered to remain, managed to attach some 2500 acres—including the entire cleared and improved part of the island—on a purported debt by the company, and shortly thereafter drowned.[3] When the three-year equity of redemption expired in 1783, the lands and buildings he had held under mortgage were sold at auction to settle his estate. They came into the hands of Charles Morris, the remarkably acquisitive surveyor general of Nova Scotia, who sold them in 1785 to Gillam Butler; and he in turn sold or leased parts of the property to his nephew by marriage, Thomas Storrow, to his business partner, and to other Loyalists who settled on the island. Moreover, Mary Wilson, Robert's widow, continued to live on part of the disputed property whether as Butler's notional tenant or otherwise.[4]

---

2. Davies, 'Welsh landlord,' 404. In fact, Campobello passed to uncle William's younger son, William Fitz William Owen, after David's death: chapter 9.

3. John Curry JCP, administrator of the Wilson estate, reported to the proprietors in January 1785, 'I ever thought Mr Wilson was indebted to the Company: what his views was, in proceeding in the manner he did, *God only knows*... I think if he had lived his intentions was not to defraud the Company, but to have settled honestly with them.' Curry caused this letter to be published after the second trial in the Wilson ejectment (below), 'to counteract certain insinuations which are industriously circulated to [the proprietors'] prejudice': *Gazette* 29 Jun 1792.

4. NBM Hazen S38-1 F4-24, Morris to Ward Chipman, Jul 1787; D. Owen, *State-*

Into this legal quagmire stepped Jonathan Bliss, a Massachusetts lawyer-politician who had been living in England since the outbreak of the American war. In 1784 he was angling for an appointment to the newly-created province of New Brunswick where his close friend Benedict Arnold, then also living in England, proposed to enter the West Indies trade. Arnold had connections with the promoters of the proposed New Brunswick Academy—one of whom, Jonathan Odell, had negotiated the general's defection to the British side during the American war—and also with Campobello, where Nathan Frink, his former aide-de-camp, had established a trading business.[5] Bliss and Arnold proposed that David should come out to New Brunswick, take a position at the new college, and represent the brothers' interest on the spot while Bliss secured their title to Campobello in the colony's courts.[6]

David eventually declined Arnold's project: 'The College is a Burlesque. The Tuition he offered a sham.'[7] Nevertheless, Bliss had succeeded in setting the hook. Arthur and William agreed to share the costs of litigation and to pay David's living expenses for a year. (This at any rate was their position; David always maintained that they were to cover his expenses until he had recovered the whole island or disposed of it, neither of which was achieved in his lifetime. In a statement of account filed in 1817, Owen charged his brothers with £100 sterling per annum in 'salary,' as well as their share of his legal and living expenses, all at compound interest.) Bliss left for New Brunswick

---

ment; Glansevern #1162, David Owen to William Owen, 23 Oct 1787 (encl.).

5. While living in Saint John, Arnold had a wharf and warehouse on Campobello, where he retreated after the riot which followed the trial of his slander suit against Munson Hayt. Barry K. Wilson's claim that there is no contemporary evidence for the riot (*Arnold*, 208) is sufficiently answered by David Owen's letter to brother William, Glansevern #1200, 15 Sep 1791: 'General Arnold was burnt in Effigy at St John's; and would have been killed by the Mob, unless some Officers of the 54th Reg't had exerted themselves to save his Life ... Mrs Arnold was in Fits the whole day. He was down in Campo Bello a few days, and in considerable danger when here for the people remember his exploits at New London, where many lost a Brother or some relation.'

6. This sentence is a reconstruction based on comments in David Owen's correspondence from New Brunswick.

7. Glansevern #1162, David Owen to William Owen, 23 Oct 1787. Also #1162a (encl.): 'Arnold's proposals seem visionary. He is not liked here. There is no College founded, only a small School. It was well I did not come out with him ...'

in February 1785 as its newly-appointed attorney general. He gave the Owens detailed advice about how to prepare for the lawsuit, even going so far as to recommend that they employ St Andrews resident David Mowatt, captain of the brig *Providence* on which David was to take passage to New Brunswick, to accompany him to the Navy Office to examine Captain Owen's death certificate so that he could prove it in court. David complained bitterly for years thereafter that brother William, a barrister at Lincoln's Inn, had negatived this and other advice in order to skimp on expenses.[8]

Alden Nowlan's suggestion that Owen left England 'because of his resentment at not having received a lucrative appointment in the church'[9] is untenable. There is no evidence that Owen had any interest in becoming a parson. Indeed, he resented his parents' decision to confide his schooling to his uncle Edward, rector of Warrington, whom he described as 'peevish, silly and superstitious' and 'proud to a degree inconsistent with true Xtianity.'[10] David had had enough of life at the vicarage. Moreover, he already had a good living, his Trinity fellowship and seniority, with its annual dividend of about £200.[11] The fellowship imposed no duties,[12] and its only condition was that he not marry. Despite the folklore that he had been Pitt's tutor, or even the King's, there is no evidence that David ever tutored anybody. (Pitt did not attend Trinity; he was a Pembroke man.) The quality of dons at this time has been described by a subsequent Master of the college as 'very poor.' The majority of fellows, having nothing to do, 'devel-

8. For example, Glansevern #1166, David Owen to William Owen, 8 Jul 1788; #1729, David Owen to A.D. Owen, 10 Dec 1790; #1735, David Owen to A.D. Owen, n.d. [likely Jun 1792].

9. *Outer Island*, 49.

10. Glansevern #4034, David Owen to Mary Jones, 18 Jul 1808.

11. David estimated his 1807 dividend at £216: Glansevern #1220, David Owen to William Owen, 16 Mar 1808. It would have fluctuated with agricultural prices in England.

12. '...unless they were the minority who were tutors or other college officers, fellows had few tasks to perform: they were left to their own devices for a lifetime': Searby, *History of Cambridge*, 101, where Searby also points out that in the eighteenth century residence rules were not enforced; at p. 112 he reiterates that 'until the reforms of the 1870s Cambridge fellows did not have an obligation to perform tasks in return for their guaranteed stipend,' which took the form of 'dividends or shares in the profits from the college's estates, rather than salaries' (p. 95).

oped uninviting personal eccentricities,' while the ban on marriage accounted for the 'queerness of their manners.'[13] While David was absent in New Brunswick his interests at Cambridge were looked after by the leading figure in the small group of fellows who took an active part in college affairs,[14] Trinity's senior tutor, Thomas Jones, who like David had graduated as senior wrangler (1779). Jones was probably David's half-brother, Owen Owen's son by his housekeeper.[15] When Jones died in 1807 Owen commenced a contretemps with his successor over his books and furniture: he also complained that Jones had dishonoured his bills and misplaced a valuable bond[16] and that Jones's executor was in league with Pagan and Wyer, to whom Owen owed money.[17]

The *Providence* reached Saint John on October 3, 1787, after eight weeks at sea.[18] On October 8 David Owen first set foot on Campobello, where he immediately sent his servant John Lloyd to serve eviction notices on Gillam Butler and Mary Wilson.[19] Ten days later he was at the capital, hoping to avoid litigation by persuading the lieutenant governor and council to settle the brothers' claim by executive fiat.[20] This was unavailing: 'The contest between the Grantees of

---

13. Trevelyan, *Trinity*, 74.

14. Although he was a member of the Seniority, the eight senior fellows responsible for governance, I have found no evidence that David took any part in College affairs while in New Brunswick. The only acknowledgment of any responsibility to the College comes in a 1791 letter to brother William: 'I hope yet to see you soon; especially as my Seniority requires my attendance. You shall not, however, see me without Cash enough to do away both your and Arthur's black looks for the Expenditures made unavoidably here on our Acct': Glansevern #1200, above.

15. Venn, *Alumni Cantabrigienses* II:3, 608; Marsh, *Thomas Jones*, 1, says only that Jones 'lost his father at an early age.' D.W. Smith, 'Berriew and Trinity' gives an extended account of Jones's relations with the Owen family.

16. Glansevern #4032, David Owen to Mary Jones, 15 Jul 1807; #4033, David Owen to Mary Jones, 3 Sep 1807; #1746, David Owen to A.D. Owen, 17 Oct 1807; #1219, David Owen to William Owen, n.d. [likely Dec 1807]; #4034, David Owen to Mary Jones, 18 Jul 1808.

17. Glansevern #1220, David Owen to William Owen, 16 Mar 1808.

18. *Gazette* 10 Oct 1787. Owen's shipmates included James Glenie who was to become as irritating a gadfly to New Brunswick officialdom as Owen himself: Godfrey, 'Glenie, James.'

19. Glansevern #1160, David Owen to William Owen, 10 Oct 1787.

20. Glansevern #1161, David Owen to William Owen, 23 Oct 1787: 'I have been

Campobello and Gillam Butler being a question of Law—they are referred to the Courts of Justice.'[21] In renewed consultations with Bliss, Owen learned that Butler had mortgaged his deed to one McGill. 'Pray consider this Business,' he urged brother William:[22]

> I find that an Ejectment cannot be obtained till next July, & Mr Bliss says I must Prove my Title, contrary to your suggestions—A Non Suit here would be a terrible business—I fear a Jury—McGill is an Officer in the Army & pitied for having a Mortgage, but the Council are all Americans—Every thing is American.

As Bliss filed suit in the supreme court against Butler,[23] David peppered William with instructions: the Navy Office certificate of Captain Owen's death is insufficient; it must be certified by a notary or under the seal of the City of London; William must ascertain whether Captain Owen's natural son Edward has copies of any papers respecting the original sale; William must have his servant copy all the proceedings into a book; Arthur must acquire notarized copies from the parish register to prove the brothers' births and send out the probate of Captain Owen's will with the letters of administration and powers of attorney; if Edward is coming out[24] he could bring all these with him, as well as sworn affidavits by his mother and guardian of his own identity; and so on and so on—'You have no Idea of the Nature of our Courts.'[25]

Some of the documents arrived but in July 1788 as the trial date approached Bliss again warned David that affidavit evidence of Captain Owen's death was not admissible in an action for trespass or ejectment. A live witness was required to prove the death certificate.

---

up the Country at St Annes, about 90 miles from here with the Governor—No Communication but by Water—It took me 6 Days.'

21. PANB RS6/B, 12 Oct 1787.

22. Glansevern #1161, above.

23. PANB RS42, 1787, Arthur Davies Owen v. ___ [*sic*]. For ejectment at common law in England, see Woodfall, *Landlord and Tenant*, chapter 14.

24. Edward might have had a claim to some small islands, not included in the original grant of Campobello, by his father's will.

25. Glansevern #1161, above; similarly #1163, David Owen to William Owen, 28 Oct 1787, in which David asks for a certificate from the Campobello Company acknowledging the brothers as grantees and sole proprietors, and #1164, David Owen to William Owen, 28 Dec 1787, enclosing a copy of Bliss's requirements.

'The difficulty,' explained Bliss, 'is in the form.' The trial would have to be postponed.[26]

The Butler ejectment came on for trial at the Charlotte County circuit in August 1789.[27] Joshua Upham presided, accompanied on the bench by the three senior magistrates of the county, John Curry, Robert Pagan, and Colin Campbell. Curry was also sworn as a witness for the plaintiff, and Pagan for the defence. Solicitor general Ward Chipman,[28] attorney for the defendants, sought to introduce evidence of the Nova Scotia sheriff's sale to Morris and his subsequent sale to Butler but after hearing lengthy technical arguments Judge Upham upheld Bliss's objections to their admission. The trial seems to have taken most of the day. The jury retired for two hours and returned in the evening with a verdict for the Owens against all the defendants but Mary Wilson.[29] Reporting the judgment, Bliss explained that 'Evidence was adduced, which it seems was satisfactory to the Jury, that Mrs Wilson has been in possession upwards of twenty years; by which they were of opinion that an Action was barred, notwithstanding one being out of the Province & beyond the Sea.' He recommended against moving to set the whole verdict aside because of the Wilson 'irregularity,' advising instead that a new ejectment suit be filed against her. (Owen immediately instructed him to commence an action.) Finally, Bliss observed, the defence had filed a bill of exceptions to Judge Upham's opinion, to be argued next term: 'I have no doubt in my mind that their exceptions will be overruled, and that we shall obtain Judgment according to the Verdict.'[30]

---

26. Glansevern #4359, Jonathan Bliss to David Owen, 9 Jul 1788; also #1166, David Owen to William Owen, 8 Jul 1788 and #1721, David Owen to A.D. Owen, 8 Jul 1788.

27. PANB RS36/A/1. The record identifies the plaintiffs as the three Owen nephews and their late uncle, and the defendants as Gillam Butler, Jonathan Stover, Albert Rightman, Neil McCurdy, Thomas Storrow, Andrew Lloyd, and Mary Wilson. According to Vroom, *Glimpses*, CXXIII, 5 Jul 1894, Stover, McCurdy, and Storrow had all purchased lots on Campobello from Butler, while Storrow and Lloyd had leased large acreages from him. Mary Wilson was Robert Wilson's widow.

28. Chipman was also crown clerk on circuit and advocate general in the court of vice-admiralty.

29. The Wilson farm amounted to some 200 acres. The jury also excepted Head Harbor Island (40 acres) on the ground that it was not part of the original Owen grant.

30. Glansevern #1170, David Owen to William Owen, 2 Sep 1789.

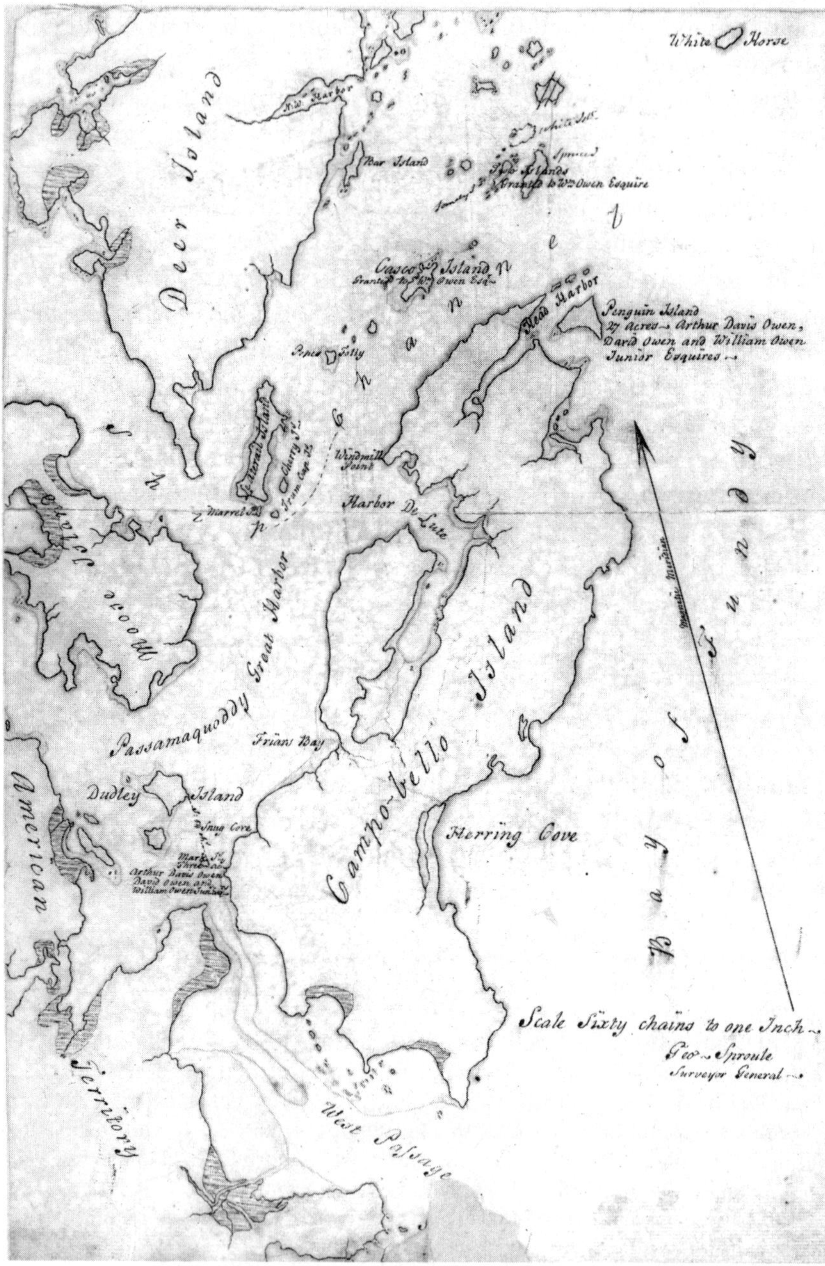

Figure 2.1 – George Sproule's plan of Campobello, 1800
(PANB H3-203-38-1800)

At the same circuit court, David Owen defended a suit by prominent Saint John merchant John Black, Robert Pagan's business partner in the naval mast trade and an associate of Pagan's brothers in that city.[31] In August 1788, William Owen had refused payment of a bill for £50 drawn by David in Black's favour. David's brothers had previously complained about his expenditures, and he in turn had rebuked them for doubting his thrift: 'The necessaries of life here (for comforts there are few) are extravagantly dear ...'[32] David first learned that William had protested his bill when sheriff Thomas Wyer arrived at Campobello with a capias for his arrest: 'I know not what cause, on your part, could operate to bring me into such disgrace, anxiety & Trouble ...'[33] Then in November John Black himself arrived at Campobello. What took place between them can only be imagined, but the upshot was that Black sued Owen for trespass and assault and battery. His claim for £500 damages was reduced by a jury of inquiry to £11/14 and sixpence costs after Owen had the venue changed from Saint John to Charlotte county. Nevertheless, Owen had to pay an additional £19 to his lawyers, on top of their charges for the Butler ejectment: 'The Devil is in their fees.'[34]

Notwithstanding the Black affair and the legal fees David Owen was greatly uplifted by the ejectment verdict. 'You may be surprised,' he wrote home, 'but I have now no wish to return. This Climate agrees

31. Nason, 'Meritorious,' 146f.

32. Glansevern #1166, David Owen to William Owen, 8 Jul 1788, containing advice of the bill to Black (endorsed by Mowatt) and two others.

33. Glansevern #1167, David Owen to William Owen, 25 Aug 1788. Black and his partners sued in the supreme court for the balance of the account: PANB RS32 1788, s.n. James Hunter v. David Owen.

34. Glansevern #1160, above: 'Have paid Bliss £36, Hardy £6 and Blowers of Halifax 7/10 amounting to near £50 ... Black's Attorney [Chipman] wanted a Set of Bills for the Damages & Costs in £30 Sterling if I have no remedy by appeal I must pay it so; or suffer a Capias ad Satisfac'm. [Elias] Hardy the Counsel with Bliss seems no way satisfied with his payment on Account in £6 ... The argument upon the Appeal will cost as much as the Original Action. They being allowed travelling expenses ...' For the litigation see PANB RS32 1788, John Black v. David Owen, and PANB RS36/A/1 Aug 1789. Owen instructed Bliss to appeal the Black damages. Elias Hardy issued a precipe for a capias returnable in May 1790, but nothing further appears to have been done: PANB RS32 1790, David Owen v. John Black. David estimated his expenses in the assault and capias to be £60 at least: Glansevern #1725, David Owen to A.D. Owen, 28 Dec 1789.

with me. I have conquered all difficulties, & am looked up to.'[35] By now he was well settled in at Campobello. Rather than take lodgings at Saint John—the original plan—he had moved into quarters on the island where he was amusing himself with his house and garden. In December 1788 he sent brother Arthur a lengthy panegyric on the splendours of Campobello (not least the fecundity of its women),[36] and a year later, when Butler's application for a new trial had been denied, David proclaimed that he could now 'live happily and like a Prince among my settlers.' He laid out a comprehensive plan for managing the island, including everything from investments in lumbering and shipbuilding to supplying a monthly 'frolic' for the tenants—'This will keep them in good humour and not cost much'—and even gifts of cheese and flannel stockings to keep Bliss content.[37]

There were two clouds on David's horizon. One was his brothers' unwillingness to sink yet more money in Campobello futures; the other was the widow Wilson. The former was to draw him into ruinous speculations and estrangement from his family; the latter was to become an obsession that would involve him in unending litigation for the rest of his days.

Owen's second attempt to defeat the Wilson claim came on for trial at St Andrews in August 1791. It was a disaster. The jury disregarded Judge Upham's direction to find for the plaintiff. In an account written thirty years later, Owen asserted that liquor had been supplied them 'through a back window' and that the foreman later boasted of having 'worn out' the other eleven.[38] At the time, though, it was Owen who was worn out: 'I shall leave this place in a few Minutes half dead with Fatigue of the Circuit Court – Shall advertise Campo Bello forthwith ...'[39] Owen's application for a new trial was granted but when it came on in February 1792, 'The Chief Justice came the Circuit and instead of giving us the Cause, as every one expected, gave it against us and in the most indecent manner. An ig-

35. Glansevern #1170, above.

36. Glansevern #1722, David Owen to A.D. Owen, 15 Dec 1788, apparently intended as an advertising brochure for prospective tenants or purchasers.

37. Glansevern #1725, above.

38. D. Owen, *Statement.*

39. Glansevern #1199, David Owen to William Owen, 26 Aug 1791.

norant Jury, altho' Special, did as he directed and a verdict was again given in favor of Widow Wilson.'[40] Bliss, reported Owen, was deeply chagrined.[41] David drew up a bill of exceptions to Ludlow's judgment and paid to have it filed in the supreme court,[42] but nothing ensued. In his 1822 pamphlet, Owen gives his version of how the case was 'hung up' interminably:[43]

> In 1803 the File of the Supreme Court was searched for the Bill of Exceptions; but no such Bill could be found. Judge Upham ... being informed of this, observed, that 'perhaps they will find another'—and about ten years afterwards, a Bill, different from the one signed by the Judge at Saint Andrews, was found on the File.

'How or when this Bill was made and filed and the original Bill embezzled,' he wrote in another late account, 'are facts yet unknown to the Plff.'[44]

David Owen gives offence

All the while that David Owen was entangling himself with the high law of supreme court judges and juries and the leaders of the provincial bar, he was also making his mark on petty justice in Charlotte. Within a few months of his arrival he was already at odds with the St Andrews junto. Robert Pagan returned home one Saturday evening in April 1788 to find that 'a poor woman named Boyle with two young children' had been brought from Campobello and left there by Owen's servant without claim to settlement in the parish under the province's

40. Glansevern #1738, David Owen to A.D. Owen, 6 Sep 1792; PANB RS36/A/1, Aug 1792.

41. Glansevern #1738, above.

42. He imagined it was to be 'sent home to the King in Council': Glansevern #1739, David Owen to A.D. or William Owen, 6 Sep 1792; for delivery of the bill to Elias Hardy to be filed, CO 188/28, David Owen's ms. 'Reports' of supreme court cases in which he was concerned. In his accounts for 1792, Owen includes £1.0.9 for 'Bill of exceptions sealed by the Judge as it was drawn by D. Owen and a Packet sent,' as well as £104.8.9$\frac{1}{2}$ to Bliss 'in Eject causes' and £63 to Hardy. Garnett also received £5.

43. D. Owen, *Statement.*

44. CO 188/28, Owen's 'Reports.'

version of Elizabethan poor law. He convened a special sessions, ordering the paupers to be sent back to the island along with a copy of the proceedings so that Owen 'may be informed of the conduct of his Servant therein, which the Court cannot suppose [him] to [have] been heretofore acquainted with.'[45] Although Owen maintained good relations with justice of the peace Daniel McMaster, who lived on Campobello from time to time,[46] he resented Pagan and the other 'Scotch wretches' and 'Americans' who dominated St Andrews including some, like half-pay Loyalist officers Christopher Hatch and Nathan Frink, who did business on Campobello.[47]

Inevitably the ejectment verdict brought David into direct conflict with Butler's associates and tenants, some of whom were prominent and well-connected in county society and local business. His attempts to extract back rent drove Mrs Butler and her children to flee the island in an open boat. When Mrs Storrow sought refuge with L.F. Deslesdernier, the U.S. Customs collector on nearby Frederick Island, Owen brought sheriff Dunn from St Andrews to seize her belongings. Dunn declined Owen's orders to break down Deslesdernier's door because he doubted his jurisdiction: Frederick Island was disputed territory.[48] On his way back to Campobello Owen seized

45. CCGS 28 Apr 1788. For New Brunswick poor law see chapter 10.

46. McMaster had a brother in London, whom David recommended to William as a useful contact. While the Butler suit was ongoing David arranged for Daniel to take charge of the island under power of attorney during his absences at Saint John and Fredericton, 'to prevent accidents': Glansevern #1165, David Owen to William Owen, 2 Jul 1788. Owen also found a temporary ally in attorney and clerk of the peace Joseph Garnett, whom he recommended to William Owen (Glansevern #1173, 1 Dec 1789) and employed in some of his early litigation. In January 1790 David boasted, 'The report Garnett has made here of my connexions at home has made me of more consequence that I could have supposed': #1175, David Owen to William Owen, 8 Jan 1790.

47. Glansevern #1738, above, suggesting that Campobello and the other islands should be separated from Charlotte county: 'while we have anything to do with Saint Andrews, with some Scotch wretches there, we can have no good of the Island.' Frink (Benedict Arnold's former aide-de-camp) and brothers Christopher and Hawes Hatch were New Englanders who had served in the British forces during the revolutionary war and retired on half-pay to Charlotte county: Sabine, *Biographical Sketches* I:522. Christopher Hatch lived and traded on Campobello while Frink had business interests there.

48. Chapter 1.

Storrow's cow.[49] Ann Appleton ('Nancy') Storrow was a strong woman with some powerful allies. Her husband Thomas, a British army officer, was away in Jamaica at the time; her brother-in-law Henry Barlow Brown was a St Andrews attorney and deputy clerk of the peace. Ann immediately made formal complaints about Owen's seizure to two New Brunswick magistrates and one in Massachussetts,[50] and sent this detailed account to Brown:[51]

> [O]n Monday last Captain Hatch, and some other gentlemen, knowing my distress at the loss I had sustained, went to [Owen] and offer'd to purchase the cow at the market price with the intent that she should be restored to me again, Sir he absolutely refused them at any rate, and openly exulted that he had it in his power to deprive me for ever of the use of her, he said he would bid her up as high as 30 dollars rather than they should have her.

As the news circulated Owen's reputation, already sullied, took a turn for the worse: he 'is held in universal detestation by every one.' The leaders of St Andrews society organized to rescue Ann: Robert Pagan offered her the use of a house; other families contributed money; Colin Campbell and Thomas Wyer arranged to collect her from Frederick Island; Brown offered to keep her in firewood.[52]

Ann had calculated on Owen's jealously for his reputation—'I suppose Owen will be raving mad, when he finds that I have made the

49. A recent interpretation sees in the incident not merely an attempt by Owen to exercise his landlord's right to recover back rent but also an assertion of both personal proprietorial and provincial claims to the disputed island: J.M. Smith, 'Rogues,' 82f. Owen asserted several claims to Frederick Island, originally on behalf of his cousins through Uncle William's estate, and later on his own account, arguing that the Campobello grant encompassed Frederick, Dudley, and even the much larger and extensively populated Moose Island (the site of Eastport, Maine), to all of which Massachusetts was asserting a claim. For one statement of Owen's claim, CO 188/12, Owen to Lord Hobart, 29 Dec 1803; for the Charlotte magistrates' concerns about jurisdiction, CCGS 9 Sep 1790; for Chipman's account of the territorial dispute, CO 188/10, Chipman to Carleton, 26 Dec 1798.

50. MHS Storrow, Storrow to her unnamed aunt, 17 Feb 1790. Higginson, *Cheerful Yesterdays* includes a brief memoir of Nancy Storrow at 7–9.

51. MHS Storrow, Storrow to Brown, 5 Feb 1790.

52. MHS Storrow, Storrow to her aunt, 17 Feb 1790.

matter so publick.'[53] She knew her man. On February 22 Owen stormed down to Hatch's Campobello wharf and forbade the master of the ship that was lying there from taking off any more boards: when asked why, 'he told him he would Stove every water Cask of the Ships on the Shore for that there was people about him that would do or say anything of him.' Owen then pointed to Hatch's house and exclaimed, 'There were two Damb'd Whores in that House ... that were at the bottom of it.'[54] The shipmaster told Hatch, who went with brother Hawes and a visiting officer named Thomas Walker to confront Owen. Christopher Hatch recounted what followed:[55]

> [A]t first he denied it, but on being pressed hard he said he meant the women in my House, I Caned him Handsomely, & went out of his House; in about a minute he run out with a Pistol, ... yet when he found I was armed, & ready to receive him, Dunghill like the Coward wheeled, and run into his House.

The story became the talk of the county and was freely embroidered. 'Owen gave out his skull was fractured, which idea occasioned a great deal of wit among the bucks of St Andrews for that his head was hurt say they every one but himself knew long ago.'[56]

Announcing his intention to prosecute the Hatch brothers and Walker, Owen beat a strategic retreat to Saint John in search (he said) of medical attention. The legal outcome seemed a foregone conclusion even to so sympathetic a witness as Ann Storrow:[57]

> I suppose it will be an expensive piece of business to Hatch. His committing the outrage in Owen's house will make against him tho every one thinks he served Owen perfectly right, and that the provocation he received was sufficient to excuse him. However the law you know must be satisfy'd.

---

53. Ibid.

54. NBM Hazen F9-3, Hatch to Lindsay, 26 Feb 1790.

55. Ibid. 'Dunghill': cockfighting slang for a game cock that wasn't, per Grose, *Dictionary*, 58.

56. MHS Storrow, Storrow to Mrs Butler, 5 Apr 1790. Owen's contemporaneous version was that he was attacked 'by three half pay Refugee Officers who are interested in the [Butler-Wilson] Suit on the pretext of having said something unhandsome of the Wife of one of them': Glansevern #1178, David Owen to William Owen, 5 Mar 1790.

57. MHS Storrow, Storrow to Mrs Butler, 5 Apr 1790.

Hatch asked Ward Chipman to defend the assault and to prosecute Owen for defamation:[58] 'This mans Character is established thro this province, but as he is fixed as a great pest to Society in this County, I should think it best to have the Action for the Assault tryed here ...' Chipman's advice was not encouraging:[59] 'There is no doubt that behavior so slanderous & provoking, will fully justify you in the eyes of the *world*, for taking satisfaction in the manner you did ... and it is only to be regretted, that by having recourse to law, he has so great an advantage over you.' Owen's words were not defamatory at common law, nor did they amount to lawful provocation. 'The principal thing to be determined upon is whether you will let judgment go against you by default ...,' which might result in lower costs should a local jury of inquiry award small damages.

Both Storrow and Chipman underestimated the capacity of Charlotte's low law establishment to protect one of its own. To begin with, when Owen sent a posse from Saint John with a supreme court warrant to arrest Hatch ('I have engaged to give them 10 Guineas if they succeed') sheriff Dunn refused to deputize them on the ground that bail had already been granted.[60] Then the grand jury at April general sessions refused to find bills against the three accused. Next day the jurors asked to be discharged from further attendance as they had completed their business. Robert Pagan, presiding, referred the question to deputy clerk Henry Barlow Brown, who said that he expected Owen 'to embrace the first opportunity which the weather would allow him' to come from Campobello to prosecute the assault. The grand jurors objected that Owen was not bound to appear and it would be inconvenient for them to remain so Pagan discharged them. Christopher Hatch immediately asked to be released from his recognizance over Brown's objection that bail should be continued. 'The Court having inquired whether any Complaint upon Oath relating to the Assault & Battery was officially lodged in the Court, and being answered in the negative, unanimously agreed that Mr Hatch be forthwith discharged from the Recognizance above mentioned.'[61]

58. NBM Hazen, F9-4, Hatch to Chipman, 27 Feb 1790.
59. NBM Hazen, F9-5, Chipman to Hatch, 1 Mar 1790.
60. Glansevern #1180, David Owen to William Owen, 12 Mar 1790.
61. CCGS 8 Apr 1790.

The very next morning, David Owen appeared before the bench to complain that despite all his precautions, 'he had been surprised as he feared.' He objected to Brown's conduct and that of the magistrate who took Hatch's recognizance. He challenged the jurisdiction of general sessions, saying that Hatch should have been bound over to the next circuit because the supreme court had issued its warrant against him. The justices unanimously rejected his complaints, and after a brief conversation about the previous day's proceedings Pagan cautioned Owen not to take the courtesy the court had shown him as either an apology or an explanation, but only 'as information of their proceedings the day before, to a brother Magistrate who had not then attended but was now present.'[62] Owen had to return to Campobello with nothing more than an order for his assailants to make a peace bond. He contented himself by writing a long account of the whole affair to chief justice Ludlow, complaining that, 'in the County of Charlotte, a Magistrate may be dangerously wounded, in his own Castle, & the assassins escape, with the Sanction of suppositious Justice,' and demanding, 'that the present matter be prosecuted to punishment and the "Hive" broke into, which sting me at every Vent, at the same time offering honey to my hands.'[63]

Owen continued to press for the 'assassins'' arrest, even sending writs to England in hope of catching Walker.[64] His civil suit in trespass and assault and battery against Christopher Hatch came on for trial in August 1791 at the same Charlotte circuit court that defeated Owen's action against Mary Wilson, and where Hatch himself was a grand juror. The trial came at the very end of the sitting and was enlivened only by the fact that one witness—David Owen's servant John Lloyd—was sworn twice, first for the prosecution and then for the defence. The petit jury found Christopher Hatch 'not guilty' and a few months later Chipman's motion for judgment nisi causa was granted in the supreme court.[65] Hatch remained in business as

---

62. Owen had been appointed to the commission of the peace in June 1788: PANB RS538/B/5 and see further below.

63. Glansevern #8400, above.

64. Glansevern #1183, David Owen to William Owen, 18 Jun 1790; #1185, David Owen to William Owen, 20 Jul 1790.

65. PANB RS36/A/1, 23 Aug 1791; ibid., 27 Aug 1791; PANB RS32/B, 7 Oct 1791.

a Campobello merchant heavily involved in the cross-border plaster trade[66] and retained his standing in the local community: he was to serve as foreman of the sessions grand jury at least five times between September 1792 and April 1818 and served on the circuit grand jury in 1811. An ally of David Owen's sometime ally Hugh Mackay, Hatch became assistant deputy surveyor general of the King's woods in 1809.[67] His son Harris and grandson Wellington were to become clerks of the peace and fill other county offices.

David Owen judges in his own cause

The St Andrews hive had not finished with David Owen. The next episode began just a few months after Hatch's acquittal and it also involved Owen's servant John Lloyd, whose indentures were to have expired in November 1791 and who had expressed a wish to return to England. Perhaps in an effort to keep him available to testify in a renewed assault on the Wilson encroachment Owen decided to permit Lloyd to manage a store at Harbor de Lute 'upon trial.'[68] David wrote home in September 1791 boasting about the success of this venture: 'He has all the Custom, is well liked; and, I believe, will do very handsomely for himself and us. He is honest & very attentive.'[69] But in March of the following year the store was broken open and its con-

---

Owen employed Elias Hardy in this action: PANB RS32 1791, David Owen v. Christopher Hatch. In April 1792 when Hatch made an appearance at the Charlotte sessions to answer to his recognizance in the assault prosecution the court informed him that the indictment had been removed by certiorari into the supreme court, returnable in May 1792, but there is nothing in the surviving court records to suggest that there were any further proceedings.

66. Hatch's Campobello store account book contains entries at least as late as 1808: PANB MC207/3/1. Also *WPO* 12-24, Hugh Mackay to Edward Winslow, 1 Jun 1803: Hatch 'occasionally resides upon CampoBello' and is 'a principal dealer' in plaster.

67. Ibid., Mackay to Winslow, 20 Aug 1807; ibid., Hatch to Winslow, 23 Apr 1809, complaining that Pagan, McMaster, Wyer, and other St Andrews notables were cutting crown timber without license. When Hatch died in 1819 the Halifax-based surveyor general of the woods lamented the loss of a valuable deputy: PANB RS7 vol. 98, 1420, Wentworth to Smyth, 21 Apr 1819.

68. Glansevern #1196, David Owen to William Owen, 16 Jun 1791.

69. Glansevern #1200, above.

tents (variously described by Owen as worth 'twenty shillings and upwards' or £100) stolen.

Relying on his own authority as a justice of the peace Owen arrested two Campobello fishermen, Peter White and Hezekiah Marks, and had them conveyed to jail in St Andrews on suspicion of felony. With the memory of Hatch's release by the court of sessions still fresh in his mind, Owen drafted the warrant of committal to keep them 'until the next general gaol delivery for the County of Charlotte,' thereby denying them bail. In England, where assizes were held on a fixed schedule, this form of commitment was a usual method of proceeding outside of London. But in New Brunswick at this time the four supreme court judges were on strike for improved travel allowances, refusing to go on the prescribed regular circuits to hold trials away from the capital.[70] The county would have to request, and the government to order, a special commission before Marks and White could be tried.

A week after sheriff Dunn took the two accused into his keeping[71] Owen issued a warrant for the arrest of John Lloyd, 'lately indendted [*sic*] Servant to David Owen of Campo Bello, [who] hath absconded himself from his Master's Service without a discharge: and while in such service hath made away with Goods and Articles which were under his Charge, without giving an Account of the same.'[72] A few days later Owen decided to send Lloyd back to England notwithstanding that he was a 'necessary evidence' against the widow Wilson as well as Marks and White.[73] In the event he waited until after the second Wilson trial and then followed Lloyd's departure with a letter to brother William urging him not to pay his wages as 'he has been very sly here.'[74] When David made up his accounts for the year 1792 he set off against the wages owing to Lloyd since 1789 an entry for 'sugar & sundries squandered by you and not entered in your books' to the

70. MacNutt, *New Brunswick*, 99.

71. NBM Hazen F54-23(1).

72. NBM Hazen F44-19.

73. Glansevern #1205, David Owen to William Owen, 24 Mar 1792; #1730, David Owen to A.D. Owen, 29 Mar 1792; #1732, David Owen to A.D. Owen, 6 Apr 1792.

74. Glansevern #1210, David Owen to William Owen, 18 Oct 1792; #1213, David Owen to William Owen, 5 Dec 1792.

value of £55.13.0, leaving a large balance in David's favour.[75]

Marks and White lay in gaol at St Andrews. They applied to April general sessions for bail or an early trial. The justices regretted that Owen's mittimus deprived them of power to grant bail. Sessions resolved to apply to Ward Chipman as clerk of the crown for a commission to have them tried and to recommend in the mean time that the supreme court grant a writ of habeas corpus at the county's expense. In mid-May, sheriff Dunn appointed a deputy to take Marks and White to Judge Upham's chambers at Fredericton where habeas corpus was granted. A court was ordered to be held in August.

The entire calendar of the court that opened at St Andrews on August 21 was Owen business. Chief Justice Ludlow presided with county justices John Curry, Robert Pagan, and Colin Campbell on the bench. There were three trials scheduled: The King v. Marks; The King v. White; and Owen v. Wilson. The retrial of the Wilson ejectment came on first. While the petit jury was out considering its verdict the grand jury, among whom were justices Ninian Lindsay and Nathan Frink, came into court to say 'that they had examined the witnesses for the Crown against Hezekiah Marks and Peter White but found no Ground for an Indictment.'[76] No sooner were the prisoners discharged than they retained Chipman to prosecute Owen for false imprisonment.[77] County clerk Joseph Garnett, once Owen's friend and confidante, encouraged the prosecution, sending Chipman a copy of the warrant for Lloyd's arrest—'the business, to me, has a strange complexion indeed'—and setting out the case against Owen:[78]

> That Mr Owen has acted both as Party and *Judge* in this Matter, I have no Doubt ... and I think that, altho' no proof could be

75. Glansevern #1214, David Owen to William Owen, 6 Dec 1792.

76. PANB RS36/A/1, Aug 1791.

77. Sheriff Dunn served Chipman's notice of prosecution dated 25 Aug 1792 on Owen at Campobello on August 31: NBM Hazen S38-F11-37. This predates the letter of 12 Sep 1792 by which Marks and White seek Chipman's opinion and retain him to prosecute: ibid., S38-F11-43. Owen retained Hardy for the defence. White returned to Campobello where he drowned in 1806. Owen thereupon applied for letters of administration of White's estate 'as his Landlord and chief Creditor': *WPO*, Owen to Winslow, 20 Nov 1806.

78. NBM Hazen S38-F11-45.

> produced against them to induce any Suspicion, whatever, yet he first took their Recognizances, which he afterwards burned, and then retook & committed them ... the Cruelty of which committment and its consequences you are no stranger to, & the people in this County feel for.

Just as in the affair of Storrow's cow, the attack on his character and reputation stung Owen smartly. He wrote Chipman, whining of the hardships he was suffering by the 'hive's' litigation: 'It may be sport to you, but it is little short of death to me, to see the efforts of five years labour ... done away with by party violence.' Requesting that writs be served upon him as inexpensively as possible and that no advantage be taken of his ignorance of the rules of court, Owen showed his adversary one concluding flourish: 'The Triumphs of a Court, when founded in Injustice, are but the trophies of a Victim, which one day must be sprinkled with the Water of its own Transgressing.'[79]

David Owen floats a boat

Assisted by geography, weather, American and imperial policy, and colonial necessity, the chief business of Charlotte county's shoreline communities was illicit trade.[80] At the creation of the province, its first governor was instructed to put a stop to the business. Just a month after his arrival Carleton issued his proclamation against the 'mutual intercourse' between New Brunswickers and Americans, 'under color of which many persons have carried on an irregular trade contrary to the Act of Navigation.'[81] Imperial, provincial and local officials were duly appointed, but their efforts were doomed to futility from the start. There were too many fog-shrouded inlets, too many inducements, and too great a dependency on American flour and other goods for anything more than token or symbolic enforcement of the laws of trade. And it is telling that the first major show trial—for illegally importing American whale oil under pretence of its being a New Brunwick product—resulted in 1786 in the conviction of

79. NBM Hazen S38-F11-40.

80. For a comprehensive overview of the issue in this period, see J.M. Smith, *Borderland Smuggling.*

81. CO 188/3, 17.

Gillam Butler of Campobello. Sentenced to three months' imprisonment and a £500 fine, Butler broke gaol but was recaptured and had to pay up. Carleton proposed to use the enormous fine to pay Ward Chipman's arrears of salary as acting attorney general for a year and build gaols in the several counties.[82]

There was a great deal of money to be made in the carrying trade, in expediting American transactions with the British West Indies by vessels built and registered in the province, in nocturnal transfers between New Brunswick and American boats, in evading custom house rules, in burying British goods under loads of Nova Scotia plaster consigned to U.S. destinations and American manufactures in imported flour barrels, in excise avoidance of every imaginable description. The official working assumption (not unwarranted) about enterprise of any sort was that it must be a ruse. Thus when Benedict Arnold proposed to establish a rum distillery at Saint John, Carleton responded to London's concerns on behalf of West Indies planters, 'I know not at present how to estimate the quantity he might be able to distill, nor how much more, under colour of such distillation, might be introduced by illicit importation from the United States.'[83]

The Butler-Storrow enterprises, like those of Frink, McKenzie, Hatch, and others, were all premised on the favourable location of Campobello close by American harbours for unregulated international trade.[84] Frink was so intent on pursuing his opportunities there that in 1793 he offered to lease the island from the Owens, writing to William in London when David declined his offer, so that David had to justify his refusal by saying that the tender was 'intended to deceive,' and that Frink was 'by no means a fit Tenant, supposing no Fraud intended.'[85] David ran the Butlers and Storrows off the island, and waged a war of attrition against Hatch, McKenzie, and Frink, but it would be a mistake to imagine that he did so to purge Campobello

82. CO 188/3, 193; PANB RS330, Carleton to Sydney, 6 Apr and 13 Oct 1786; Carleton to Steele, 4 Jul and 5 Dec 1787. Chipman had acted as attorney general until Bliss arrived in the province.

83. CO 188/3, Carleton to Sydney, Oct 1787.

84. The full absurdity of the situation was laid bare in the *Falmouth* trial of 1805, where imperial customs officers defended a breach of the navigation acts against the province's chief enforcement officer: chapter 1.

85. Glansevern #1746, above.

of illegal traders. On the contrary, David imagined that the terms of the grant gave him 'most probably certain royal privileges' including freedom from custom house duties 'upon his Vessels clearing coastwise and within the Bay of Fundy for parts of that Province, where by his Grant he considered the Trade to be free, and not encumbered by subsequent conditions.'[86] Those 'parts' included Moose Island, claimed and occupied by U.S. citizens but still in Owen's view part of his personal free trade zone. By anyone else's reckoning, David Owen was as much a scofflaw and illicit trader as any of the merchants and magistrates in the county.

One early incident shows us something of Owen as a man of business during the years of the Butler ejectment, the 'assassins,' and the Marks and White prosecutions. It strongly suggests that David, like his brother magistrates, was more than willing to put his role as justice at the service of his commercial interests.

Not long after his arrival at Campobello, Owen began to realize that his success as a landlord was bound up with the prospects for trade. As early as 1788 he capped a lengthy account of how he was settling his lessees by proposing to 'build a stout Vessel annually, load it with Ton Timber and sell both it and Cargo in England. This addition would encourage the tenants to clear their Lands, bring others and Trade to the place.'[87] A year later, reporting the verdict in the first Butler ejectment, David advised his brothers that he had drawn a bill on them for £40 sterling, 'to pay for Iron of a vessel building one-third at my Expense.' This was to encourage his tenant Bowen Smith, a ship's carpenter, to carry on his trade.[88] But his brothers rebuked his expenses and refused his bills, and soon the vessel came to represent all David's hopes, 'by which I must sink or swim.'[89] His efforts to find a buyer at Saint John failed as rumours of impending war spread in early 1790; Smith reneged on his promise to pay two-thirds the cost of construction; and by the end of the year Owen had run out of cash and was in desperate straits. He had advanced more than £180 to

86. CO 188/12, Owen to Hobart, 29 Dec 1803.

87. Glansevern #1721, David Owen to A.D. Owen, 8 Jul 1788.

88. PANB MC996, Owen to Howell, 5 May 1818. I am grateful to Joshua Smith for this reference.

89. Glansevern #1175, above.

build the vessel, despite his intention to do no more than 'furnish Iron and Naval Stores' from his own funds. In December 1790 David pleaded for another £150 to fit her for sea: 'which, if I do and you answer the same, you will make me happy—if not, miserable ... I have no other hope but from Navigation.'[90]

A few days later Richard Batchelor, a Saint John customs officer, visited the Campobello shipyard armed with a warrant to break open locks in search of contraband. He interrogated a local blacksmith about cordage and iron imported illegally from Boston and tore boards from Smith's dwelling house to make his search.[91] Batchelor returned to Campobello in February. Owen encountered him at Snug Cove where (Owen deposed) he was assaulting and terrifying two seamen. Batchelor evaded Owen's attempts to arrest him and escaped, assaulting Owen as he did so.[92]

At September sessions 1791 Owen, the Campobello blacksmith, and one of the terrified seamen were named as crown witnesses against Batchelor for breaking open Smith's house and other buildings, for taking property away 'under color of office,' and for assaulting the two sailors. Nathan Frink was named as crown witness in an indictment against David Owen for assault and battery on Batchelor. The business was put off until the following April sessions, when Batchelor had the indictment against him removed by certiorari to the supreme court. His complaint against Owen seems to have hung in the air until 1795 when it was finally dismissed. For years after this, Owen fulminated against the abuse of authority by the Saint John customs officers, complaining about the misuse of writs of assistance, the impropriety of Batchelor's warrant, the irregularity of his proceedings, and so on.[93] But this was all bluster to cover up the real issue: that Batchelor had come to Campobello to seize iron and ships' stores illegally imported by Owen for the completion of his vessel.

Batchelor's visits occurred in December 1790 and February 1791. In December 1790, Owen reported that the *Owen* had been launched

90. Glansevern #1729, above.

91. CO 188/18, McEachern deposition.

92. CO 188/18, Owen deposition.

93. For example, CO 188/18, Owen's petition to the Prince Regent in Council, 4 Jun 1812.

two months previously, 'and I have only to provide for the remainder of the expense to complete her Hull for sea.'[94] In January 1791 he advised brother William (then on the Oxford circuit) that he had drawn another £60 for the vessel: 'it will be profitable.'[95] Then on February 16, just days before Batchelor's return, he explained that 'the Severity of the Weather has detained her loading near five Weeks longer than expected ... She is now loaded, and will sail in a few Days for Antigua ...'[96] It seems very likely that Batchelor's visits to the shipyard in December and Snug Cove in February were intended to intercept contraband destined for the good ship *Owen*, and that in arresting Batchelor for assaulting and terrifying two sailors, David was rescuing his own crew.

David Owen calls a meeting

By the autumn of 1801 hostilities between David Owen and the St Andrews establishment had reached such a pitch that the junto was tempted to move against him directly. Two sets of complaints by Owen tenants about his conduct as landlord and justice sparked bitter contests in the county sessions and provincial politics, helping to set the stage for Ward Chipman's unprecedented attempt to prosecute him for misconduct as a magistrate twenty years later.[97] Owen's proclivity for using his office to harass his tenants undoubtedly offended the junto's sense of propriety and of the dignity of the county bench but as we shall see the St Andrews magistrates had other more material interests in bringing him to heel as well.

In October 1801, Francis Mathews[98] Jr complained to Nathan Frink that Owen had issued a warrant charging him with having 'harboured in his dwelling house Women of Bad fame and used threats at different times to prevent divers Merchants and other persons from

94. Glansevern #1729, David Owen to A.D. Owen, 10 Dec 1790.

95. Glansevern #1190, David Owen to William Owen, 8 Jan 1791.

96. Glansevern #1192, David Owen to William Owen, 16 Feb 1791: Owen drew another £40 'to send her away paying the Wages of Seamen & Port Charges &c.'

97. Chapter 4.

98. Spelled Matthews or Mathis in some documents. Francis senior and his sons were frequently caught up in Owen litigation as they lived on the boundary of the Wilson 'encroachment.'

prosecuting their Lawful occupations and aided and assisted in the Commission of divers Acts to the Great disturbance of the Neighbourhood and evil example of others.' Mathews had been arrested on the authority of this warrant and taken before Owen who had required him to find sureties for his good behaviour.[99]

Mathews did not seem particularly concerned about Owen's vague allegations except for the one about bad women. He told Frink that he and his wife had taken a poor transient woman into their home while she was awaiting passage to Nova Scotia on the schooner *Maggott*, letting her spin yarn to pay for her board. As Frink recalled the episode, Mathews was 'irritated at Mr Owens making an act of hospitality and even humanity criminal by his construction of Law and from which he had been liberated on Bail but a few moments before.' He wanted Frink to issue a warrant for the arrest of David Owen. 'And now Sir,' said Mathews, 'if this was criminal in me it must be more so in Mr Owen to keep a Whore in his house, and I demand a warrant against him for keeping Hannah Smith who is another mans wife.'

Despite Alden Nowlan's description of Hannah Smith as Owen's 'mistress' for forty years[100] there is no more evidence for a sexual relationship between David and his long-suffering housekeeper than between Francis Mathews Jr and his spinning boarder. Against the precedents of David's father and uncle, both of whom fathered children on their housekeepers, we might set Ann Storrow's characterization of Smith as 'the Vestal virgin of Friar's Bay.'[101] Smith seems to have been lacking in lasciviousness. Although she had once married a sea captain, she took to neither his name nor his bed. In her old age she sustained a lengthy interrogation about David Owen's last days by relatives seeking to contest his will but admitted nothing.[102] Whether or not David Owen was bedding his housekeeper is beside the point.

---

99. The papers in Owen's suit against Frink for libel and altering a document (dated 1802-4) including Frink's deposition and a copy of Owen's warrant for Mathews, were found in the much earlier PANB RS32 1789, The King v. Nathan Frink (embezzling the King's stores).

100. Nowlan, *Outer Island*, 54.

101. MHS Storrow, Storrow to Mrs Butler, 5 Apr 1790.

102. Glansevern #14357, 'Interrogatories exhibited to Hannah Smith late Housekeeper to D. Owen Esq. ...,' 5 Nov. 1830.

What was important was the appearance of the thing. Mathews's complaint brought Owen's private respectability and public character both into question.

Frink found himself in an 'awkward situation.' He told Mathews that it was not the sort of matter that required immediate action. Instead he would make a note of the complaint, recording his refusal to act, so that if Mathews wanted to make an issue of it at the court of sessions he could complain to the grand jury about both magistrates at once. Dissatisfied by this, Mathews exclaimed: 'Then Sir, there is Law enough for Mr Owen to punish his poor Tenants, but there is no Law for them to call him to account.' Nevertheless Frink made a note of the complaint on the bottom of the recognizance that Owen had forced Mathews to execute. The next day Owen's clerk came to where Frink was working and demanded that he return the Mathews documents to Owen as they were his property. Frink refused, saying they must be lodged with the clerk of the peace. True to his word when Frink attended at the opening of the April 1802 general sessions he delivered the warrant and recognizance into court. This was to have significant repercussions in what followed.

In the mean time another Owen tenant complained to the St Andrews justices. In November 1801 Benaiah Dow, a Campobello fisherman and deputy sheriff, arrived at St Andrews in the custody of a constable. They were accompanied by Owen's clerk who carried a letter from his master to the magistrates of the town:[103]

> Benaiah Dow stands committed, convict of an assault upon me—Also of breaking open my House with intent declared, and begun to be put in Execution with a Musket, to commit Murder on my Body; from Which Murder he was restrained with difficulty by two Young Men then in the house . . . I am in danger from the Villain. You will take care how he is managed.

As senior magistrate, Robert Pagan convened a meeting of all the jus-

103. PANB RS32 1803, The King v. Robert Pagan, depositions on rule to show cause why an information should not be granted against him for a libel. Some of the documents in PANB RS32 1802, David Owen v. Benaiah Dow, are referred to and belong in the Pagan casefile.

tices then at St Andrews. Six of them[104] assembled to examine Dow and the constable, schooner captain, and clerk who had escorted him from Campobello. When they learned that the affray had begun when Owen forcibly attempted to prevent him from entering the part of the house he occupied as Owen's lodger, the magistrates (mindful perhaps of the Marks and White affair) unanimously agreed to admit Dow to bail instead of imprisoning him.

Dow used the opportunity of this meeting to complain of Owen's 'arbitrary proceedings and conduct' as a magistrate, saying that as deputy sheriff he had within a short time served thirty-five persons with processes issued by Owen, all of which had later been settled or compromised and not reported to general sessions. The captain and the constable, both Campobello residents, supported Dow's complaint. The justices regretted that there was nothing they could do about these grievances in special sessions. They conceived that the proper mode of redress was by application to general sessions where the grand jury or county justices, once convinced that Owen's conduct was oppressive, might petition the lieutenant governor to deal with him.

Not long after this, however, Nathan Frink and John McKenzie, two of the magistrates who had attended the November special sessions, returned to St Andrews from business on the island and requested another meeting to consider Campobello residents' complaints, 'of their suffering unjustly from summonses, warrants and ex parte Affidavits, issued, made and taken' by Owen.[105] At this meeting there was a heated debate about whether Owen's fellow justices had the power to redress such grievances. Pagan's view—that the 'most constitutional' way of proceeding was for the aggrieved individuals to bring their complaints to general sessions for transmission to the executive government—again prevailed.

But early in January 1802, David Owen himself arrived at St Andrews and sent a note around to the various magistrates calling them to a special sessions at the clerk's office. As senior magistrate,

104. Pagan, McMaster, Frink, Daniel McLachlan, John McKenzie, and county clerk Donald McDonald JP.

105. The meeting was attended by justices Frink, McKenzie, Pagan, McMaster, and clerk McDonald.

Robert Pagan took umbrage at Owen's presumption 'in coming up and in his own name summoning a meeting of the Magistrates by a Common Constable.' He was prevailed upon by his fellow justice, brother-in-law, and business partner Thomas Wyer to waive his objection if Owen would solicit his attendance personally. This was eventually arranged, although it required clerk McDonald's intervention as well, and on the evening of January 8 six of his brother magistrates gathered at the clerk's office, Pagan insisting on his right to preside.[106] After an unpleasant exchange between Owen and justice McKenzie, whom Pagan with some difficulty restrained, it was time for the main business of the evening.

Owen denounced his fellow magistrates for having released Benaiah Dow from custody. Dow had returned to Campobello where he was circulating a libellous petition to have Owen removed from the commission of the peace, encouraged, Owen charged, by some of the magistrates present. He had called this special sessions to have warrants issued against Dow on four new charges. Two of these were ancient history, and the third—that Dow had entered Owen's parlour 'and did by force leave a Letter there, not belonging to his Office'—was a farce. They were quickly dismissed by the justices.

Owen's fourth charge was that Dow had rescued a prisoner from a constable. McKenzie told the meeting that while he and Frink were loading a schooner at anchor off Campobello the day before, Owen refused to allow anyone on board to set foot on the island. When a seaman took a boat to shore to collect something from Dow, Owen ordered his servant to arrest the man and take him to his house. Dow told the sailor the servant was no constable and offered to let him spend the night in his room at Owen's house. Next morning Owen discharged the seaman from custody. The magistrates divided on whether a warrant should issue against Dow for this 'rescue.'[107] The motion failed and Owen was thereupon advised to seek redress from

106. Pagan, McMaster, Wyer, McKenzie, McLachlan, and Lindsay attended, along with Owen and McDonald.

107. McLachlan, McMaster, and clerk McDonald voted to issue a warrant; Lindsay, McKenzie, Pagan, and Wyer voted against; Owen abstained. The following year, Owen recommended McLachlan, McMaster, and McDonald as friends of the executive government in St Andrews: *WPO*, 12-8, Owen to Winslow, 19 Feb 1803.

a magistrate of his parish.[108] Owen's four complaints, the vote on the motion, and the parting advice were dutifully recorded by clerk McDonald.[109]

But the minutes did not record the discussion that followed, in which Owen accused Pagan of having encouraged Dow to circulate a petition against him. Pagan denied having ever 'seen a line' of it and told Owen that if he had indeed issued thirty-five processes and compromised them without the knowledge of sessions,[110] he was 'unfit to hold the office of a Justice of the Peace.' Should the governor learn that Owen was guilty of 'such flagrant abuses of his commission' he would break him as a magistrate. Owen challenged Pagan to name one such warrant, to which he replied with two, one of which Owen said was a distress for damages in which the sessions had no power and the other a warrant for militia fines.[111]

So incensed was Owen by these events that he asked the Supreme Court to issue a criminal information against Pagan for libel. He also began civil and criminal suits against Nathan Frink, one of the justices who had pressed for action against him;[112] registered official complaints against Frink and two other justices who had attended the meeting; complained to Lord Hobart, secretary of state for the colonies, that Pagan had tampered with a jury and engaged in other mischief; and manoeuvred to depose sheriff Dunn, who had assisted in circulating the petition on Campobello.[113]

Neither Dow nor his sureties appeared at the April 1802 sessions

108. Campobello was part of the parish of West Isles until March 1803 when Owen succeeded in his campaign to separate it: (1803) 43 Geo.III c.4, s.2.

109. These minutes are in the supreme court casefile but not in the sessions minutebook.

110. Daniel McMaster's deposition dated 23 Aug 1802 adds that it was understood they were compromised 'for value.'

111. Owen had McDonald copy into the record his own version of the minutes which included these comments and Pagan acknowledged them in his deposition dated 8 Feb 1803.

112. Owen was himself presented by the grand jury at the Apr 1803 general sessions for alleged misconduct in the Frink prosecution: see further below.

113. Another head of complaint for Owen was that Pagan had warned Dunn that as high sheriff he could be held liable if any warrant served by deputy sheriff Dow at Owen's behest was successfully challenged and damages awarded.

nor did he answer when called again in September.[114] He may have been avoiding arrest for debt, for in January of that year Owen had filed suit against him in the supreme court for £43.1.10 on account.[115] Owen seems to have dropped this suit, probably in exchange for Dow's deposition in the libel action alleging that Pagan had authored the impugned petition.[116] But it was at April sessions that the Mathews papers with Frink's emendations came into Owen's hands. That he was there at all and how he came to receive the documents are consequences of another event that pointed up a deep political division on the county bench, the unexpected demise of his former ally and subsequent antagonist, county clerk Joseph Garnett.

David Owen adds insult to injury

Owen had not attended the April 1800 sessions where deputy clerk Henry Barlow Brown read an extraordinary sickbed letter from a dying Garnett[117] in which he assured the public that its papers were to be 'readily found in my office, among their proper books, or on their files, probably, from my various indispositions and infirmities, not in so methodical a manner as might be wished and expected.' In fact, there were no files or papers to be found for hundreds of sessions and common pleas cases dating back to the creation of the county.[118] Garnett also referred to some 'claims uncompensated on the County for actual services of a public nature during the space of fourteen years

114. This is the last time this proceeding is mentioned in the CCGS records.

115. PANB RS32 1802, David Owen v. Benaiah Dow.

116. See further below. Dow was still living on the island some years later. In May 1805 Benaiah Dow and Stephen Mitchell, described as 'fishermen of Campobello,' purchased a schooner from John Kent of Grand Manan: PANB RS431 (bonds).

117. His hope, 'during a painful a tedious and an awful process, in the view of obtaining relief from those excruciating agonies I am labouring under without intermission,' to be preserved, 'from an otherwise impending, a rapid, an alarming, and a most loathsome *Dissolution*,' went unfulfilled.

118. Owen reported to Hobart that there were no records for a thousand cases tried before 1802: CO 188/12, 29 Dec 1803. This would make ICCP a court of record without records. The court's surviving minutes (PANB RS431) include several suits involving Owen in 1800-2:

last past.' In fact, the county accounts were in complete disarray.[119] In his closing benediction, Garnett wished for a restoration of the 'social unanimity' of the county: 'May all Mankind discard the pernicious doctrines of modern Liberty & Equality and place a just value upon civil subordination which protects property, and upon Regular Governments which Secures the Natural Rights of Man.'[120]

Garnett was no more, and in September 1800 the justices appointed Brown to replace him as county clerk 'pro tem' until the wishes of the lieutenant governor were revealed. The office of county treasurer, by contrast, was within the gift of sessions. The bench divided along fairly predictable lines, Pagan, Wyer, Frink, Porter, and McLachlan voting for Brown, and Hugh Mackay, the two McMasters, Elisha Andrews (who was to replace Dunn as sheriff in 1803), and McKenzie for Donald McDonald. Except perhaps for McKenzie and McLachlan, it was the insubordinate hive versus the friends of regular governments. The vote was tied so sheriff Dunn was appointed treasurer pro tem, the succession being put off until the next sessions.[121] This gave the provincial executive time to act. In October 1800 it appointed McDonald to succeed Garnett as register of deeds and wills; in February 1801 he became county clerk.[122] Social unanimity was

Plaintiff	Action	Defendant
David Owen	capias in case £200	Benaiah Dow
David Owen	capias in case promises £600	Benaiah Dow
David Owen	capias in debt £200	Benaiah Dow
David Owen	capias	Benaiah Dow *et al.*
David Owen	capias in case £200	Craig & Tinning
David Owen	capias in case sur trover £20	Rebecca Garnett
David Owen	capias in debt £10	George Peck
David Owen	capias	George Peck
David Owen	capias in trespass £10	Hibbert Hunt Jr
Benaiah Dow	capias in case trespass £300	David Owen
John McKenzie	capias in case promises £80	David Owen
Duncan McEachern	(for blacksmith work)	David Owen

119. As early as 1788, James Campbell recorded that the county was three years in arrears to him for money laid out to build the gaol: 'Mr Garnett is to give me an order for it how soon the business of the Sessions is over, for he is so methodical that he cannot be broke in upon with different business at once': NBM Hazen, Campbell to Ward Chipman, 9 Sep 1788, and see chapter 9.

120. CCGS Apr 1800.

121. CCGS Sep 1800.

122. PANB RS538/B/5.

restored and a second division averted at April sessions 1801 when clerk McDonald declined nomination as county treasurer, permitting Brown to be acclaimed.[123] Once the executive had signalled its approval of the settlement by appointing Brown a notary public,[124] the county justices turned to the business of sorting out Garnett's affairs, first at special sessions called for the purpose in the summer of 1801, and then at general sessions in April 1802.

Just weeks after the angry meeting with his brother magistrates over the Benaiah Dow affair David Owen returned to St Andrews to enjoy a personal triumph, the public reading at April general sessions of the bill then before the legislature to erect Campobello as a separate parish. And there were more triumphs in store. After taking Owen's evidence the grand jury returned true bills against Benaiah Dow, Francis Mathews Sr, and John McKenzie. Mathews was bound over to September sessions; McKenzie was granted a continuance at Frink's request. Owen remained to make a magnanimous gesture towards clearing up the Garnett confusion: moving a resolution that county officers be paid annually, he promised to donate £10 each year for that purpose. He was appointed, along with Daniel McMaster and Nathan Frink, to examine and compare the sessions records with the original documents in the clerk's office and report to September sessions. It must have been this duty that put the Mathews papers, with Frink's annotations, into Owen's hands.

A few days before the September 1802 general sessions the Saint John *Royal Gazette* published what purported to be David Owen's address to the independent freeholders of Charlotte county, offering his services in the next general assembly. It concluded with an interesting campaign promise: 'I look forward to a just Counterpoint for the accumulated Insults of fifteen years Maturation; for injurious Offences, which can only be expiated by just punishment; OR, atoned for, WITH ——' A similar text appeared on a handbill with the printed salutation, 'In behalf of the Junto. I am with respect, Your obedient Servant, THE GOOSE HIMSELF.' The surviving copy has a handwritten amendment to the signature: 'or Hannah the Gander' (Figure 2.2).

David Owen was present when general sessions opened at St

123. CCGS Apr 1801.

124. PANB RS538/B/5, 14 Aug 1801.

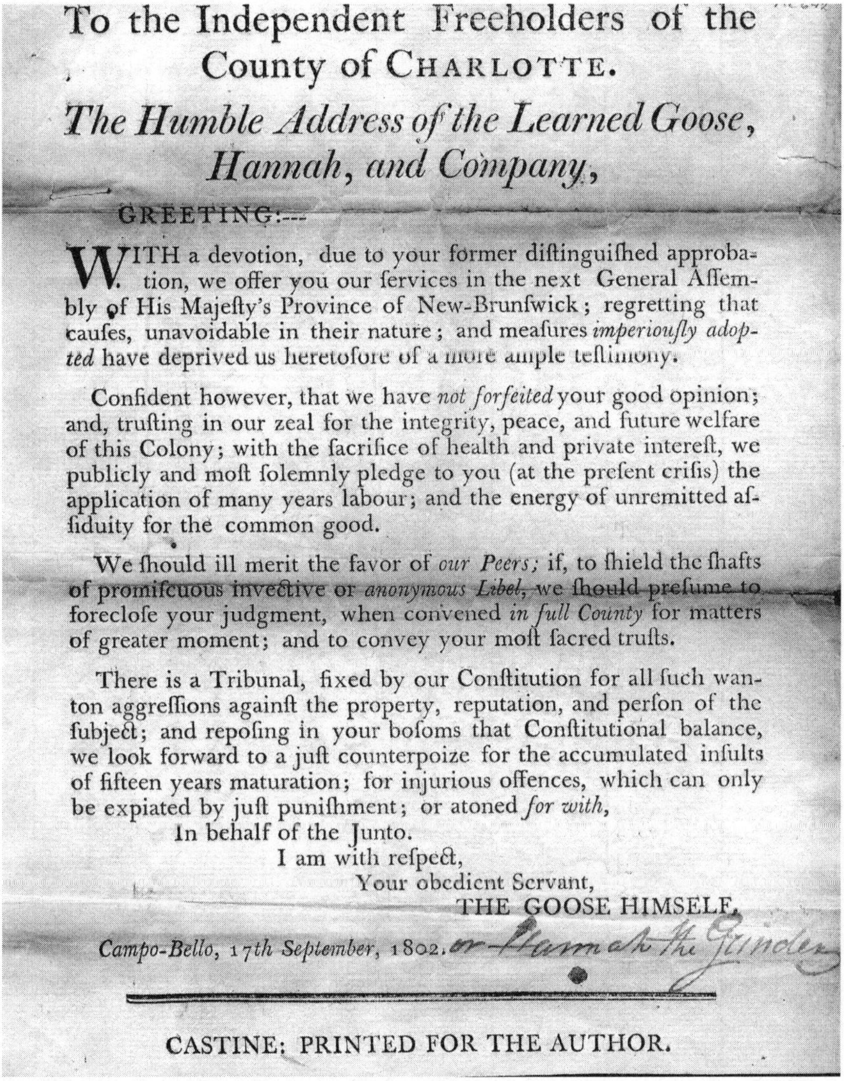

To the Independent Freeholders of the County of CHARLOTTE.

The Humble Address of the Learned Goose, Hannah, and Company,

GREETING:---

WITH a devotion, due to your former diſtinguiſhed approbation, we offer you our ſervices in the next General Aſſembly of His Majeſty's Province of New-Brunſwick; regretting that cauſes, unavoidable in their nature; and meaſures *imperiouſly adopted* have deprived us heretofore of a more ample teſtimony.

Confident however, that we have *not forfeited* your good opinion; and, truſting in our zeal for the integrity, peace, and future welfare of this Colony; with the ſacrifice of health and private intereſt, we publicly and moſt ſolemnly pledge to you (at the preſent criſis) the application of many years labour; and the energy of unremitted aſſiduity for the common good.

We ſhould ill merit the favor of *our Peers;* if, to ſhield the ſhafts of promiſcuous invective or *anonymous Libel,* we ſhould preſume to foreclose your judgment, when convened *in full County* for matters of greater moment; and to convey your moſt ſacred truſts.

There is a Tribunal, fixed by our Conſtitution for all ſuch wanton aggreſſions againſt the property, reputation, and perſon of the ſubject; and repoſing in your boſoms that Conſtitutional balance, we look forward to a juſt counterpoize for the accumulated inſults of fifteen years maturation; for injurious offences, which can only be expiated by juſt puniſhment; or atoned *for with,*

In behalf of the Junto.

I am with reſpect,

Your obedient Servant,

THE GOOSE HIMSELF.

Campo-Bello, 17th September, 1802. or Hannah the Grinder

CASTINE: PRINTED FOR THE AUTHOR.

Figure 2.2 – Nathan Frink's 'election squib' (PANB MC642-MS1)

Andrews on September 21. His committee on sessions records reported the following day. On September 23 the seventeen grand jurors presented a true bill against John McKenzie, Ninian Lindsay, and Nathan Frink for 'wickedly and maliciously devising and intending unjustly to vex and aggrieve David Owen ... and to deprive him of his reputation, and to bring him into contempt and scandal ...'[125] The court adjourned until the afternoon when McKenzie, Lindsay, and Frink, having first called for the bill against them to be read, asked the clerk to record, 'that they lament that the Court was not competent to hear and determine the charge.'

Next morning the court granted one grand juryman's application for dismissal. On the margin of an extract from the sessions minutes he sent to Lord Hobart, Owen wrote: 'Robert Pagan, Justice, tampered with the Jury at this period.'[126] The grand jury retired, now sixteen in number, then sent in a note requesting that it might 'amend an error' in the bill against McKenzie *et al.* When court resumed at six o'clock that afternoon, David Owen was on the bench along with Pagan, Frink, McKenzie and three other justices. The grand jurors were called in and declared Owen's bill against the justices 'ignoramus,' i.e., that there was no case to meet. The court thanked and dismissed them and then promptly adjourned. The county turned its collective mind to the general election.

Stars and daggers

These squabbles have to be seen not only as ripples in village puddles but also as local eddies of provincial tides. Three larger contests form the background in this period: the first constitutional, over

125. The grand jury dismissed other complaints against McKenzie, Dow, and another of Owen's tenants, George Peck: CCGS Sep 1802. The substance of the bill is not in the minutes; it is copied (with the substance of the charge suppressed by ellipsis) in CO 188/12, Owen to Lord Hobart, 29 Nov 1803.

126. His complaint, headed 'Case of an Indictment, erased by a Judge,' set out that Pagan 'did instruct the Jury, deliver the Foreman a Volume of Burn's Justice and authorise one Juror to be dismissed — And that he was the sole cause, from Malice and prosecution in the Supreme Court ag't him (Robert) for similar practices, of the embezzlement and destroying of the aforesaid Record, in manner and form, *under Color of Office ...*': CO 188/12, 4 Apr 1804.

the relative prerogatives of executive and assembly; the second territorial, over the western boundary with the United States; the third imperial, over the effective reach of the navigation acts to curb the province's illicit trade with its near neighbour. In each of these, Charlotte county and its magistrates played important roles. The county's four assemblymen—three of them justices—formed half the bloc of 'runaways' whose desertion of the 1801 assembly precipitated the 1802 general election. The boundary question involved substantial parts of Charlotte. It turned in the first instance upon a determination of the 'true' river St Croix from among three alternatives, and here Robert Pagan had played the crucial part by uncovering archaeological evidence to sustain the British position. Then the contest turned to the islands of Passamaquoddy Bay, most immediately to Moose, Frederick, and Dudley islands just off the western shore of Campobello. The trade question implicated many of the leading merchants and justices of Charlotte and in its intersection with the boundary question it pointed out Campobello as a nest and haven of smugglers and illicit traders.

The political struggle between adherents of the provincial executive and discounters of the executive privilege, never far beneath the surface of assembly proceedings, came to a head in 1801. The ostensible issue was whether the power of appointing the clerk of the assembly rested with that body or was the lieutenant governor's prerogative. Twice the assembly sent up a revenue bill with a clause for the payment of its clerk; twice council sent it back down for removal of the offending clause. At this point eight of the twenty-four members quit town claiming that the work of the session was done. This left a plurality on the side of privilege although not a quorum of the House. Nevertheless they made the requested amendment and voted supply whereupon the lieutenant governor prorogued the session and called a new election.

It is difficult to come up with appropriate labels for the two voting blocs that emerged in the 1801 session and reappeared in 1802. Despite contemporary cries of 'partyism' they were not political parties so to use such terms as 'liberal' and 'conservative' to distinguish them is more likely to obscure than to illuminate. Nor should we follow Joseph Garnett to distinguish between the friends of subordination and its enemies, or David Owen to distinguish between those who were 'attached to all loyal exertions of the Executive' and those who were not,[127] for these descriptions, while contemporaneous, are nonetheless partisan. 'Job Creon' described the two groups as 'steadfasts' and 'runaways': this was perhaps clearer but hardly more neutral.[128] Perhaps the safest contemporary characterization was made by another anonymous pamphleteer who simply identified the former affiliation as '†' and the latter as '⋆' while sagaciously noting that, 'the leaders of the (⋆) party are the principal importers,' who stood to gain a premium by putting off the taxation measures in the revenue bill.[129] Among these mercantile adherents of the 'runaway' bloc were Charlotte county members Robert Pagan, David Mowatt, James Campbell, and Ninian Lindsay.[130]

Despite his ongoing battles with the supreme court judges and other members of the executive council there can be no doubt that David Owen would have been 'steadfast' had he remained a member of the assembly in 1801. He had indeed been elected in the 1795 general election but, as a petition of twenty-four freeholders complained in 1798, 'from the situation of his Health and other Avocations,' he had never attended the House nor did he appear likely to do so.[131] His seat was declared vacant for non-attendance[132] and Ninian Lindsay succeeded to it in the resulting by-election.[133] Our pamphleteer listed him as '⋆Ninian Lindsay⋆' and noted, 'The one marked on both ears with his master's sign, is a late puppy that barks only by rote.'

On October 1, 1802, a week after September sessions, sheriff John Dunn announced that the election of four members to represent Charlotte county would take place at polls to be held in the parishes of

127. *WPO*, Owen to Winslow, 18 Jul 1803.

128. [Anon.], *Steadfasts and Runaways*, attributed to executive councillor Edward Winslow by MacNutt, *New Brunswick*, 115n42.

129. [Anon.], *Elector's Mirror*.

130. Robert's brother William, member for Saint John, was also in this group. The only Charlotte member who was not also a justice of the peace was Wyer's brother-in-law David Mowatt, the shipowner whose brig *Providence* had brought David Owen to New Brunswick in 1787.

131. PANB RS24, S13/P9.

132. JHA, 31 Jan 1799.

133. JHA, 24 Jan 1801.

St George, St Stephen, and St Andrews. Owen immediately protested, presumably because there was to be no poll on Campobello or anywhere in West Isles.[134] There were seven candidates, three of the '⋆' persuasion and four of the '†'. Although he had convinced himself that he had done what was necessary 'to secure Col Mackay's Election & my own,' for David Owen the outcome was a pointed one:[135]

Robert Pagan	252	Ninian Lindsay	243
Hugh Mackay	204	Joseph Porter	182
James Campbell	161	Daniel McMaster	142
		David Owen	3

Porter, a Charlotte JP and another of Pagan's puppies, had signed the 1798 petition to unseat Owen, who now launched a campaign to keep him out of the assembly on the ground that he was an alien. Owen claimed that Porter had lived in the United States as a citizen for ten years after the revolution and so was not qualified for election as a 'faithful subject' of the Crown.[136] Owen and Mackay also schemed to replace the sheriff, Owen claiming to have been 'deprived of a fair issue of the contest' by Dunn's conduct of the election.[137]

David Owen stirs the hive

As 1803 began, David Owen was at daggers drawn with assemblymen-justices Pagan, Lindsay, and Porter, justices McKenzie and Frink and sheriff Dunn. These skirmishes played out in the Supreme Court, Charlotte general sessions, and *sub rosa* intrigue carried on in cor respondence with the provincial executive and the imperial government.

134. *Royal Gazette* 26 Jan 1803.

135. *Gazette*, 30 Oct 1802. I have not found the pollbook, but it is a fair speculation that the only votes for Owen were those of Mackay, McMaster, and himself.

136. PANB RS24 S16/P15. Porter had been appointed to the commission of the peace in October 1799: PANB RS538/B/5. Owen petitioned to unseat him: JHA 1803, pp.16, 18, 20, 29. The House split evenly on a motion to postpone the question until the next session, the Speaker casting the deciding vote in favour. Witnesses were to be examined at St Andrews before Henry Barlow Brown and Donald McDonald.

137. *WPO*, Owen to Winslow, 18 Jul 1803. For the machinations against Dunn, ibid., Owen to Winslow, 19 Feb 1803, Mackay to Winslow, 1 Jun 1803, and the discussion below.

Owen's application for a criminal information against Pagan in the Benaiah Dow affair came before the supreme court in February 1803.[138] Bliss had advised him to drop the matter but, Owen wrote, 'I cannot accede to [his] motive for relinquishing my cause agt R. Pagan, after having perused the Affidt and taken a very large Fee.'[139] Owen's best evidence was Benaiah Dow's affidavit that Pagan had given him verbal directions to have attorney Daniel Tillotson prepare a petition charging Owen 'with Cruelty, Oppressions, Extortion, and especially with compromising Recognizances for Money.' Dow afterwards delivered up to Owen both the petition and Tillotson's note to Pagan seeking clarification of what was required.[140] He closed his affidavit by declaring, 'And I know not of one Instance wherein the said David Owen received Fees, as a Justice of Peace.'[141] Having so deposed, Benaiah Dow returned to Campobello, his debt to Owen apparently forgiven.

Chief Justice George Duncan Ludlow and his associates accepted Pagan's claim—Owen variously called it an 'expurgatory oath' and a 'Compurgation Oath'—that he had never seen the paper circulated by Dow.[142] The court discharged Pagan with costs against Owen[143] who thereupon complained to Lord Hobart that Ludlow was guilty of

---

138. Ibid., Owen to Winslow, 18 Jul 1803. At least one leaf of this letter is missing. The letter is not in Raymond, *Winslow Papers.*

139. Ibid. In his accounts for 1802 (Glansevern #14351-5) Owen charged £25.9.0 for 'the expences of prosecuting for a Libel bro^{t}. to C. Bello to disturb the Settlers,' including £3.13.8 'Attorney's Bill for prosecuting,' and in those for 1803 he charged over £100 for 'prosecuting the Libellers and attending at Frederickton to get C Bello and its appurtenances erected into a a separate Town and Parish,' including lawyers' fees of about £25 to Bliss, £5 to Charles Peters, £7 to Ward Chipman, and £20 to J. Whitman.

140. The petition is not in the extant case file. Owen later claimed that just one person, 'an American,' had signed it, which if accurate is not surprising given the dependence of his tenants and his reputation for vindictiveness in litigation and otherwise.

141. PANB RS32 1803, The King v. Robert Pagan. The casefile also includes letters from Tillotson to Pagan in which he gives meandering and evasive accounts of his role in the affair.

142. This, at any rate, is how Owen recalled the reason years later: CO 188/28, Owen's 'Reports'; *WPO*, Owen to Winslow, 18 Jul 1803, referring to Pagan's 'expurgatory oath'; Owen's complaint to Hobart (below) that Ludlow had allowed Pagan's 'Compurgation Oaths.'

143. *Royal Gazette*, 2 Mar 1803.

'illegal perversion of the law, delay and refusal of justice.'[144] The complaint fell on deaf ears, perhaps because the chief justice's brother was presiding over the province in Carleton's absence. Revisiting the case twenty years later, Owen at least had the satisfaction of observing, 'The Sheriff, whose Deputy B Dow had been, was dismissed from Office and soon afterwards one of the Justices was put out [of the] Commission; the other died.'[145]

At the same sitting Owen also tried to launch criminal proceedings against Nathan Frink and John Dunn. Owen's complaint against Frink included 'his acquiring by indirect means the possession of *my* Warrants & his exposing them to public contempt to answer private revenge ... returning my Warrants with Bonds attached & indorsed with Scandal to the Bench of Sessions ... '[146] Owen also complained that Frink had libelled him in the 'learned goose' hand-bill. The court dismissed it as 'an election squib' and declined to award criminal informations against either Frink or Dunn.[147] Owen's responsibility for these efforts to prosecute 'at the suit of the King, whose name and authority is often used as a covering to the vilest purposes' was outed by Nathan Frink in a letter to a Saint John newspaper: 'The fact is, that the Learned, Reverend, and Worshipful DAVID OWEN, Esquire, (insti-

144. CO 188/12, Owen to Hobart, 4 Apr 1804.

145. CO 188/28, Owen's 'Reports.' McKenzie may have been removed from the commission of the peace. He did not appear on the bench at sessions after April 1803. In 1803 Owen was non-pross'd in a suit he had brought against McKenzie two years earlier (PANB RS42 1801; PANB RS32/b Oct 1803). Owen had complained to the surveyor general about 'gross impositions' in the 1790 grant of a mill seat to McKenzie: CO 188/12, Owen to Sproule, 19 Oct 1802 and see *WPO*, Uniacke to Owen, 30 Aug 1802. The 'other' magistrate was James Campbell, one of the Charlotte MHAs of the '⋆' persuasion in 1802. Owen considered him to have been implicated in the mill seat grant: PANB RS13/27/a/2, Owen to Carleton, 'Caveat,' 28 Jul 1802 (and see the Uniacke letter cited above). Campbell died in December 1802 when he fell from the roof of his Beaver Harbour mill: *Royal Gazette* 15 Dec 1802.

146. This of course referred to Frink's notation on the Mathews papers. The court dismissed as 'surplusage' Owen's complaint that Frink had interlineated Owen's recognizances by requiring those bound to attend sessions to be 'of good behaviour' in the interim: *WPO*, Owen to Winslow, op. cit.

147. For the Frink dismissal, *Royal Gazette*, 16 Feb 1803. The article about the Dunn dismissal appeared in the same issue of the *Royal Gazette* but has been clipped out of the microfilmed copy. It is referred to in Frink's letter to the editor, below.

gated by the devil, or some other evil spirit), instituted the suits . . .'[148]

Even before the election, Owen and Hugh Mackay had schemed to oust Dunn from the shrievalty. In July 1802 they recommended Captain Robert Vardon as 'a faithful, loyal Subject and warmly attached to the Government,' suitable and willing to be appointed high sheriff.[149] Council issued a commission to Vardon but had to cancel it when he declined the appointment.[150] Mackay told the executive that Vardon was prevented from accepting it 'by the intimidation and threatenings of a certain party in the County,' and Owen reported that Vardon was 'threatened with Suits' if he accepted.[151] Council next decided to give the appointment to Elisha Andrews. While Vardon's commission had been openly directed to county clerk Donald McDonald the new commission was sent in secret to Hugh Mackay and Daniel McMaster. Dated March 17, 1803, it was still under wraps on April 12 when general sessions opened.

Alerted by the Vardon affair to his impending removal from office, but unaware of the Andrews commission, Dunn's supporters had organized a two-pronged action at the sessions. The grand jury brought in a presentment against David Owen for having removed the Mathews warrant and recognizance from the county records so that he could file them in the crown office to support his aborted prosecution of Nathan Frink. It also unanimously adopted a resolution 'sincerely lamenting' Dunn's decision to 'retire' from office and hoping that he would continue in public service. Dunn replied thanking them for their 'unexpected' tribute and the whole was sent off to Saint John to be published in the newspaper.[152] According to Owen, Dunn only learned of Andrews's appointment after the close of sessions:[153]

> The Commiss. to the present Sheriff was not known, at this

148. *Gazette* 26 Feb 1803. Frink undertook to publish the proceedings in full, but does not appear to have done so.

149. PANB RS13/27/a/2, Owen and Mackay to Odell, 16 Jul 1802.

150. PANB RS538/B/5, 10 Jan 1803. Vardon had been a British naval officer during the American war, and subsequently settled in Charlotte county. He does not appear to have involved himself in county affairs.

151. *WPO*, Mackay to Winslow, 1 Jun 1803; ibid., Owen to Winslow, 18 Jul 1803.

152. *Royal Gazette*, 4 May 1803. The resolution is dated Apr 15 and the letter from grand jury foreman Peter McCallum to the publisher Apr 18.

153. *WPO*, Owen to Winslow, 18 Jul 1803.

> time, to this Tool of party. He clearly expected, that no one in the county would accept the Office. For, when Mr E Andrews, on the next Monday after the Sessions, did by my directions notify his being duly sworn into that office ... Mr J Dunn forgot himself & made use of the following Language –viz.– 'That the Sheriffs commission had been offered to every vagabond in the county,' and being asked by Mr Andrews, 'whether he meant to insinuate that he (Mr Andrews) was one,' he answered, 'Not, but that it was as likely to be offered to a vagabond as a Gentleman.'

Owen was delighted that the Andrews appointment had been made 'without the special knowledge and first motion of Mr President Pagan,' and insisted that the publication of the grand jury encomium was proof positive of Dunn's unfitness for office.[154]

But with Dunn disposed of Owen had still to counter the charge of misconduct in removing the Mathews papers with Frink's annotations from the county records. He recognized that his best escape was to deal directly with 'Mr President.' We have only his own self-serving account of what took place. He invited Pagan to 'fix another place & time & bring his friend, with this caution, not to take it as a challenge, where all such matters could be soon settled.' Pagan was evasive and seemed to want Owen to challenge him outright. There was a brief meeting between Pagan, seconded by Porter, and Owen, supported by Mackay, but to no avail.[155] Owen beat a strategic retreat. For the time being, he would abandon his quest for justice in the county sessions, the supreme court, and the provincial executive. Instead, he would seek his remedy at the seat of empire.[156]

154. Dunn retained his office of deputy collector of customs at St Andrews.

155. *WPO*, Owen to Winslow, 18 Jul 1803.

156. CO 188/12, Owen to Hobart, 29 Dec 1803.

Figure 2.3 – Chestnut Hall, St Andrews, built in 1824 for clerk of the peace Harris Hatch (Kerri Chrus, Ross Memorial Museum, 2008)

Chapter 3

High noon at Campobello: St Andrews and the islands in the 1820s

On April 9, 1822, the eight justices of the peace then attending Charlotte general sessions, all of them residents of St Andrews, resolved to complain to the lieutenant governor about three absent colleagues for conduct 'derogatory to the character of Magistrates.'[1] One chose to resign rather than stand an investigation and immediately gave up his commission.[2] West Isles magistrates Gilbert Ruggles and Warren Hatheway stood their ground.[3] Ruggles wrote in his own defence and provided character references including three of the St Andrews justices who had joined in the resolution.[4] Hatheway produced a petition signed by one hundred and seven residents declaring him to have given 'universal satisfaction' as a magistrate and to be 'the most

1. The eight St Andrews magistrates were Thomas Wyer Sr, Thomas Wyer Jr, James Campbell, Colin Campbell, Daniel McMaster, John Wilson, Peter Stubs, and (in a rare appearance) Rev. Jerome Alley.

2. This was Daniel McLachlan; the resolution provided the option to resign.

3. CCGS Apr 1822; PANB RS76, Charlotte magistrates' petition, 13 Apr 1822.

4. Thomas Wyer, Peter Stubs, and John Wilson (together with Charlotte's senior magistrate, Hugh Mackay) stated that they had 'never heard, or known, any thing of him, derogatory to the character of a Magistrate, except the altercation between him and Warren Hatheway . . .'

suitable person in the parish' for that position. The county's clerk of the peace submitted affidavit and documentary evidence in support of the sessions resolution. A few weeks later the provincial executive issued a new commission of the peace for Charlotte county in which their names did not appear.[5]

This incident is noteworthy for several reasons. It was the first time the Charlotte magistrates used their principal collective institution, the general sessions of the peace, to discipline their own members on their own initiative.[6] Certainly complaints against justices had been heard and determined at sessions before, but always as individuals subject to due process of law for such offences as assault or selling liquor without a license, not for abuse of office or conduct unbecoming a magistrate. Individual justices had complained to one another or to the government about a fellow magistrate's conduct before this and had even sought criminal informations in the supreme court, but there had been no official collective action by the county bench per se. The last time the question of a general complaint had arisen was in 1801 when Robert Pagan advised Benaiah Dow that the most constitutional method of breaking David Owen as a magistrate was to get up a petition that sessions could recommend to the provincial executive. Now however the magistrates decided to act on their own motion.

The 1822 resolution points up the increased tension between the St Andrews justices and those of other parishes in the county. It had been moved and adopted on the first day of sessions, even before the grand jury was sworn. It was most unusual to have more than three or four justices present at the opening of sessions; to have had eight was unheard of. As was often the case, none of the magistrates from other parishes was present, not even the county's senior justice Hugh Mackay (St George parish), who appeared the following day, charged the grand jury, and presided over the remainder of the session. In all, eight Charlotte county justices who did not attend the

5. PANB RS538/B/5, 9 Aug 1822. The usual executive procedure for adding or dropping magistrates was to issue a new commission of the peace for the county superseding former commissions.

6. Compare Landau's account of self-regulation in eighteenth-century Middlesex in 'Trading.'

first day of sessions took their places on the bench on subsequent days, including justices residing in West Isles,[7] Campobello, Grand Manan, St George, St David, and St Patrick parishes. It is hard to escape the conclusion that the St Andrews magistrates packed the court on opening day to ensure passage of the resolution, although it is also possible that some magistrates who would otherwise have attended chose to stay away because they had wind of the motion.

Warren Hatheway and Gilbert Ruggles

The parish of West Isles comprised Deer and Indian islands and a host of little islets in Passamaquoddy Bay between St Andrews and Campobello.[8] The largest by far was Deer Island, which, like Campobello, had been granted to a single proprietor with a view to colonization. The original grantee sold the island in 1770 to Thomas Farrell, a British officer.[9] It is not clear when Farrell arrived at Deer Island, how long he remained, or what steps he took to develop the place. Loyalist families who had settled there complained in 1805 and again in 1812 that they had been unable to secure title to their lands and improvements. Their complaints were not remedied until after Farrell's death in September 1822.[10]

Gilbert Ruggles and Warren Hatheway were Massachusetts Loyalists and first cousins, descendants of Ebenezer Hatheway and Welthea Gilbert who married in 1744. Their daughter Welthea Hatheway and her husband Richard Ruggles, son of General Timothy Ruggles, were Gilbert's parents, while their son Ebenezer Hatheway and his wife Mary Hatheway (another cousin) were parents to Warren.

Richard Ruggles and his family settled at Annapolis Royal, Nova Scotia, after the revolution. By 1805 Gilbert Ruggles was living in

7. Hatheway sat on the fifth day. Ruggles did not occupy the bench, but he was a witness for the prosecution in one case and put up bail for a defendant in another.

8. Campobello and Grand Manan had been parts of West Isles until they became parishes of their own by 42 Geo.III (1803) c.4, s.2 and 56 Geo.III (1816) c.10 respectively.

9. Farrell was said by Hugh Mackay to have fought on the American side during the revolutionary war: Mackay to Odell, 31 Aug 1805, pressing the claims of Deer Island Loyalists, in Barto, *Passamaquoddy*, 72.

10. For the early history of Deer Island see ibid., chapter 5.

Charlotte county and was of sufficient age and respectability to be appointed to take special bail in the inferior court of common pleas.[11] He was in business at Deer Island by 1817 and became a justice of the peace the following year. He described himself as a 'trader' in court documents in the 1820s.[12] Ruggles remained at Deer Island for a time after losing his place in the commission, then removed first to St George and then to St Andrews, where he served as a poor house commissioner in the early 1830s.[13]

Warren Hatheway was born in Massachussetts in 1773. The family came to New Brunswick as Loyalists, settling on a grant at Burton in Sunbury county.[14] Warren was living in Charlotte county by 1802 when he was presented at general sessions for selling liquor without a license. He was an early ally of David Owen's against the regional dominance of St Andrews, assuring him 'in confidence' (as Owen nevertheless disclosed) 'that he never was on a grand Jury, which acted with so much hasty virulence' as the one that presented Owen for misconduct in April 1803.[15] By 1805 Warren was operating a store on Bar Island just off the shore of Deer Island.[16] He is identified as a merchant of Deer Island in legal papers in 1811, 1815, and 1816 when he was named to the commission of the peace.[17] He served

---

11. *Sentinel*, 20 May 1805.

12. Capias for Ghradus Johnston at suit of Gilbert Ruggles, reciting the contracting of a debt at Deer Island on 13 May 1817 (the promissory note in the same file is dated 30 May 1817): PANB RS431/A, Ruggles v. Johnston (1821); PANB RS538/B/5, 5 Oct 1818.

13. Ruggles was licensed as an auctioneer for St George parish in 1828 (PANB RS538/B/5, 13 Feb 1828) and served as roads commissioner in 1829 (CCGS 25 Sep 1830). PANB RS148/C/3/j/1 St Andrews assessment list, 1831; *Courier*, 2 Aug 1833. He served on the grand jury at September sessions 1833. Ruggles subsequently left St Andrews and, apparently, the province: the obituary for his son Charles, dead in Demerara of the 'black vomit,' identifies Gilbert as 'formerly of St Andrews' (ibid., 19 Mar 1842).

14. Sabine, *Biographical Sketches*, I:525. Warren was living at Burton in 1798 and at nearby Sheffield in 1801: NBM, Jarvis family papers, Warren Hatheway to Munson Jarvis, 14 Aug 1798; PANB, RS157/A2/5 RMV/CSU/2/1, Sunbury County General Sessions, 1801.

15. *WPO*, Owen to Winslow, 18 Jul 1803.

16. CCGS, 23 Sep 1802; Barto, *Passamaquoddy*, 69ff.

17. PANB RS431/A, Warren Hatheway v. Israel Andrews (1811), Warren Hatheway v. Murdock McLean (1811), Warren Hatheway v. Thomas Adams (1815), Warren

as a captain in the county militia until December 1819 when he was replaced by Charles Reid Hatheway—his younger brother, of whom more below—upon leaving the province.[18] Warren kept a store at Eastport on Moose Island, a short distance from Campobello, and probably removed there for a time. Eastport was occupied by British forces during the War of 1812 and not returned to American control until 1818. In 1821 when Warren married an Eastport woman the notice identified him as 'merchant, of Deer Island,' so he had returned to New Brunswick.[19] His name appears in the November 1821 commission of the peace for Charlotte.[20] He left the county again shortly after losing his commission and settled permanently at Eastport.[21]

The third main player in the Ruggles–Hatheway saga was one of the original Deer Island loyalists, Ghradus Johnston, a farmer and fisherman who served as a parish constable for West Isles. Johnston was a client of Ruggles, and Ruggles in turn was a client of Hatheway.

As Gilbert Ruggles later told it, he and Warren Hatheway had been 'on the most friendly footing' until June 22, 1820, when Ruggles issued a writ for the arrest of Fenwick Bell, the captain of Hatheway's schooner *Ruth.* Constable Johnston took Bell off the *Ruth* and was about to take him to gaol in St Andrews when Hatheway arrived on the scene, beat and abused Johnston, and rescued Bell.[22] Hatheway had a different version, in which Johnston had boarded the *Ruth* when she was already at sea and so abused the crew that after bring-

---

Hatheway v. Samuel Dean (1815), Warren Hatheway v. Samuel Lovejoy (1816); PANB RS538/B/5, 22 May 1816.

18. Militia general orders, 1 Dec 1819, newspaper clipping attached to page in PANB RS538/B/5.

19. Warren's 'consort,' Nancy Hatheway, died in November 1820 at Deer Island, aged 44; he married Hannah Peavey at Eastport in August 1821: *Sentinel,* 18 Nov 1820, 11 Aug 1821. Warren submitted a customs drawback petition from Deer Island in March 1821: PANB RS24 S29-P71.

20. PANB RS538/B/5, 23 Nov 1821.

21. Warren's co-partnership 'in trade in the West India & European business' with his son, Charles Henry Hatheway, was dissolved in 1823, leaving the accounts with the son at Deer Island for collection: *Sentinel,* 6 Jun 1823; an infant child of Warren and Hannah Hatheway died at Eastport in 1826: ibid., 18 Nov 1826; Warren was elected to the Eastport school committee in 1828: ibid., 12 Apr 1828.

22. PANB RS76, Ruggles to Smyth, 6 May 1822. The mittimus was signed by Ruggles and David Owen.

ing the schooner to anchorage they abandoned ship, 'all sails flying, and in imminent danger.' Learning that Johnston had taken Bell to Ruggles's store, Hatheway went there and expostulated with his cousin, who replied, 'You have reigned long enough; it is my turn now. I will take Captain Bell where I please, and that will be before Mr. Owen.' Hatheway eventually persuaded Johnston to accompany him and Bell to St Andrews. Upon their arrival Johnston asked to see Thomas Wyer, by then the senior magistrate of the town. Wyer refused to get involved but sent them to an attorney who declared the warrant defective. Johnston thereupon agreed to release his prisoner in exchange for Hatheway's and Bell's undertaking not to prosecute him for false arrest.[23]

The immediate upshot of these events was a flurry of litigation. Johnston sued Hatheway in trespass for assault and rescue but did not show up for the trial.[24] Then Ruggles sued Hatheway in defamation for accusing him of partiality as a magistrate and for saying his warrants were 'no better than brown paper.'[25] This earned him a judgment for forty shillings. In return Hatheway had Ruggles arrested for debt and required him to find nearly £200 bail.[26] Ruggles thereupon sued Hatheway for false imprisonment.[27] In the mean time, Johnston signed a declaration that he had never had any grounds of complaint against Hatheway. This led to Ruggles suing Johnston for libel. When Johnston retracted his statement, blaming Hatheway for tricking him into making it, Ruggles had him arrested for several old debts.[28] Offers of arbitration between the cousins—'to leave all their difficulty to three men each paying their own costs'—came to naught.[29] Finally, more than two years after the event, Hatheway had to face a criminal

23. This summary of Hatheway's account is based on his deposition sworn in open court at the St Andrews circuit on 20 Sep 1822 and recorded in the back pages of the ICCP minutebook for 1822-3 (PANB RS431/B/1/1).

24. PANB RS42 1820, Johnston v. Hatheway.

25. PANB RS42 1820, Ruggles v. Hatheway.

26. PANB RS42 1820, Hatheway v. Ruggles.

27. PANB RS42 1820, Ruggles v. Hatheway.

28. PANB RS431/A 1821, Ruggles v. Johnston; PANB RS76, Johnston affidavit, 27 Apr 1822.

29. C.R. Hatheway deposed that he had acted as go-between and made offers of arbitration on his brother's behalf but that Ruggles was unwilling.

prosecution at the circuit court.

Taken altogether, Hatheway and Ruggles had accused each other of interfering with a constable in the exercise of his duty, rescuing a prisoner, issuing an improper warrant, interfering with a witness, suborning perjury, malicious prosecution, false imprisonment, and partiality. None of this was enough to cause their brother justices to interfere, much less to seek their resignations for conduct derogatory to the character of the magistracy. The St Andrews justices decided to act only when Ruggles and Hatheway took their dispute out of the wharves and storehouses and courtrooms and into the public press.

It began in October 1820 when *The King v. Warren Hatheway* was adjourned because Johnston did not appear to prosecute. Gilbert Ruggles was disappointed at first but became incensed when he was shown correspondence with the attorney general accusing him of having persuaded Johnston to make a groundless complaint.[30] When Hatheway made his comments about partiality and brown paper warrants, Ruggles could restrain himself no longer. In September 1821 he inserted an advertisement in the St Andrews and Eastport newspapers over the by-line, 'A friend to Justice,' stating that Hatheway had avoided the trial by bailing Johnston out of gaol and sending him on a fishing voyage to Labrador.[31] Hatheway responded immediately, announcing in the St Andrews *Herald* that Johnston had apologized to him and identified Ruggles as 'the person who seduced him' to complain.[32] Two weeks later, after the close of the Charlotte circuit, Hatheway inserted a similar response in the Eastport *Sentinel*, this time adding a charge that Ruggles had arranged for 'three rancorous vagabonds' to give false testimony at the defamation trial.[33] Ruggles fought back, filling 'nearly three columns' of the *Herald* with his counterclaims.[34] Hatheway purchased nearly two columns of the same newspaper to recite his version of the recent lawsuits along with the certificate of one of Ruggles's witnesses in the slander trial that he had

30. PANB RS76, Ruggles to Smyth, 6 May 1822.

31. The issues of original publication in both newspapers have not survived, but the advertisement is reproduced in Warren Hatheway's responses, noted below.

32. *Herald*, 25 Sep 1821.

33. *Sentinel*, 9 Oct 1821.

34. *Sentinel*, 3 Nov 1821. The Oct 1821 issues of the *Herald* have not survived.

had to coach two others to remember the words, 'which we were told by Mr. Ruggles to swear to,' and offering fifty pounds reward for the production of the 'vagabonds' at the next court.[35] But when the next court opened in April, the justices moved quickly to have Ruggles and Hatheway broken as magistrates.

Warren Hatheway's tribulations did not end with his removal from the commission of the peace. He had still to endure the adjourned criminal trial, which finally came on at the Charlotte circuit in September 1822. He seems to have felt vindicated there, judging by the letter he wrote to the presiding judge, Ward Chipman, shortly afterwards:[36]

> I cannot help expressing my grateful acknowledgements for your indulgence at the September Circuit and was happy your Honor discovered something of the conspiracy that has so long been in operation against me. I have been persecuted this two years past with such calumny and corrupt perjury as your Honor doubtless saw a sample of at court . . .

Hatheway must have hoped that Chipman would intervene with the executive to have him restored to the commission of the peace because he recited his innocence, objected to the lack of a hearing before the Charlotte magistrates, pointed out that his parishioners had petitioned in his favour, and claimed that there was now, 'not a Magistrate in the Parish capable of administering an oath . . . those who were appointed that were respectable have refused to serve in consequence of the disrespect shown me.' His own theory of why he had been broken had nothing to do with newspaper advertisements:[37]

> My situation in the West Isles has become envious to some of the St Andrews Gents . . . I have owned more navigation, done more business, and paid more into the revenue than every Magistrate in the County together, and this not being done in the Town of St Andrews has excited in them an envious disposition . . . and from this source have all these conspiracies arisen

35. *Herald*, 1 Jan 1822, 8 Jan 1822; also in *Sentinel*, 12 Jan 1822.

36. NBM Hazen, W. Hatheway to Chipman, 20 Nov 1822. The outcome of the trial is unknown.

37. Ibid.

> and representations been made to the Government, ... and from this was I supplanted from the Magistracy ...

Was there more to the St Andrews magistrates' decision to rid themselves of their troublesome West Isles colleagues than irritation with their attacks on each other in the public press? Or was Hatheway's grandiloquent notion of a conspiracy against him just one more indication among many of his unsuitability for the magistracy?

There was a history of commercial rivalry between the St Andrews junto and the West Isles merchants and traders. In 1805, when Thomas Farrell applied for a re-grant of Deer Island despite having sold the entire island on one occasion and parts of it on others, St George patriarch Hugh Mackay supported the Loyalist squatters and opposed Farrell's petition. Were it to succeed, he predicted, Robert Pagan of St Andrews would be 'the principal gainer.' In particular, Mackay urged the provincial executive to endorse Warren Hatheway's claim to Bar Island, just off the Deer Island shore, 'as he will be awkwardly situated in regard of his improvements, should it be granted to any other person—but more particularly to Farrell.' Hatheway personally delivered Mackay's letter to the provincial secretary.[38] In 1810 Farrell received his re-grant including Bar Island. Seven years later, perhaps as a consolation prize, Warren Hatheway was granted six small islets in Passamaquoddy Bay.[39]

Pagan, Wyer, and their associates at St Andrews had long been seeking to squeeze out commercial rivals in the islands. Beginning in the 1790s they had established strategically-located outposts at Indian Island and elsewhere in the bay to draw the trade in fish, timber, and contraband away from Saint John. Pagan acquired 300 acres and a mill seat on Deer Island from Thomas Farrell and installed his associate John Campbell on Marvel Island to supervise his fishery interests. The Pagan businesses forged an alliance with Daniel McMaster and his three brothers, well connected in Halifax and with substantial interests on Grand Manan in the southernmost reaches of Charlotte county.[40] The McMasters also owned property in West Isles and op-

38. Mackay to Odell, 31 Aug 1805, in Barto, *Passamaquoddy*, 72.
39. PANB RS686, W Hathaway [*sic*], 26 May 1817.
40. Hugh Mackay supported the McMasters' effort to acquire all the ungranted

erated out of Campobello.[41]

The Pagan businesses were facing a crisis in 1821-2. When Robert Pagan, the founding patriarch of St Andrews, died in November 1821 his associates' commercial and political control of the county was under attack on several fronts. St Andrews, hemmed in by crown timber reserves, had already reached its development limits and was being outpaced by the rapid growth and prosperity of St Stephen parish.[42] Saint John interests sought to destroy Charlotte's dominance of the lucrative gypsum trade with the United States, launching a 'plaster war' that saw provincial gunboats and British naval cruisers seizing coasting vessels in Passamaquoddy Bay.[43] In the wake of the April 1822 resolution to oust Ruggles and Hatheway from the magistracy, merchants and proprietors in West Isles, Campobello, and Grand Manan rallied around David Owen's secessionist project of uniting the three island parishes in a new county free from the control of St Andrews.[44]

Robert Pagan presided over his last general sessions of the peace in September 1821. Of the eight St Andrews magistrates who convened for the opening of April sessions 1822 five had been his long-term business partners or close associates and the fortunes of the remaining three were wholly bound up in the preservation of St Andrews' regional hegemony. However sincerely they might have wished to protect the 'character of Magistrates' from being smeared in the newspapers, their desire to protect their own business interests, social prominence, and political power by getting rid of troublesome rivals must have been overwhelming. But Hatheway and Ruggles were small fry compared to the self-styled 'principal proprietor'

---

land in Grand Manan, in which they were allied with Christopher Hatch and Donald McDonald: Mackay to Winslow, 20 Aug 1807, in Raymond, *Winslow Papers*, 588, and chapter 5 below.

41. Nason, 'Meritorious,' 29, 114f, 140, 145f.

42. Ibid., chapter 5.

43. J.M. Smith, *Borderland Smuggling*, chapter 7.

44. CO 188/27, Owen to Smyth, 3 Jul 1821; CO 188/28, petition of Warren Hatheway and others (West Isles), 18 Jul 1822; PANB RS7, Owen petition to the King, 20 Jul 1822; CO 188/30, Owen to Bathurst, 2 Aug 1822; PANB RG1 RS339 A/2a/1823/a5, Owen to Chipman, 10 Apr 1823; CO 188/28, petition of Moses Gerrish and others (Grand Manan), 24 Jun 1822.

of Campobello, whose separatist intrigues, studied disregard of others' interests, and reckless proclivity for setting cats among pigeons made him a formidable irritant.

David Owen's plaster war

When last we encountered David Owen in December 1803 he had determined to have nothing more to do with the 'iniquitous proceedings' and 'fraudulent warfare' of his fellow Charlotte county justices, the judges of New Brunswick's supreme court, the members of the legislative assembly, and the province's lieutenant governor and council, preferring to address his numerous complaints directly to the imperial cabinet and royal family. Though many pens were broken and seas of ink consumed in this transatlantic correspondence over the next quarter century, Owen could not insulate himself and his island fiefdom entirely from local institutions. He might refuse to attend the courts of general sessions at St Andrews but he still had to apply there for renewals of his liquor license, to complain about a parish constable who refused to do his duty, or to secure a replacement when he was unwilling to fill a parish office himself.[45] He might prefer not to sue in the provincial courts but could not avoid being sued in them.[46] Pressed by his creditors and victimized (as he saw it) by the repeated refusals of his agents in England to honour his bills, Owen was even forced into financial arrangements with the despised St Andrews 'hive', most notably Thomas Wyer who was angling for possession of Campobello and its thriving illicit trade.[47] Nor would

45. Owen applied for a liquor license by correspondence to the April 1804 court, sent a letter of complaint about a constable to the September 1806 court, and wrote to the September 1804 court refusing to serve as assessor of rates and to the September 1807 court to have an April grand jury presentment against him for selling liquor without a license quashed. The Harris Hatch correspondence (PANB MC207) includes several letters from Owen excusing himself from attending sessions and listing various items of business he wants dealt with there.

46. Supreme Court casefiles (PANB RS42) in this period include McKenzie v. Owen (libel, 1805), Brown v. Owen (debt, 1805), Barlow v. Owen (debt as security for defaulter, 1806), Cook v. Owen (promises, 1810).

47. Glansevern #1219, David Owen to William Owen, with enclosures, Dec 1807; Glansevern #1220, David Owen to William Owen, 16 Mar 1808; PANB RS431/F1, Hatch to McDonald, 5 Dec 1807.

he forgo the endless round of petty litigation against his own tenants.[48] Moreover, the London recipients of his petitions, memorials, and complaints continued to insist on referring them to Fredericton for investigation.

Owen had long been suspected of involvement in the contraband trade. During the 1812-14 war provincial commander Thomas Saumarez had kept him under surveillance, 'owing to reports having been made to me of his opposition to the laws upon many occasions.'[49] British naval officers patrolling in Passamaquoddy kept a weather eye on Owen whom, as proprietor of the most 'notorious place for illicit trade' in the whole Bay of Fundy and the only magistrate on the island, they believed to be 'in favor of the smugglers' because he profited personally from their activities.[50] Owen himself acknowledged the local importance of what he referred to as 'the business at the lines termed by His Excellency Smuggling,' although he distanced himself from the lieutenant governor's characterization of it.[51]

The plaster trade in Passamaquoddy Bay had been largely left to its operation after the *Falmouth* trial.[52] It attracted renewed attention following the 1812-14 war particularly after Moose Island, occupied by the British during the hostilities, was returned to U.S. control.[53] The burning question was no longer the disputed ownership of the islands in the bay, but whether the trade was to be monop-

---

48. For example, PANB RS431/A 1805, Owen v. Davidson & Martin; PANB RS42 1807, Owen v. Peck; PANB RS42 1807, Owen v. Hunt, Hunt & Hunt; PANB RS42 1808, Owen v. Mathis; PANB RS42 1808, Owen v. Beckwith; PANB RS42 1808, Owen v. Parker; PANB RS431/A 1810, Owen v. Mathis.

49. CO 188/20, Saumarez to Bathurst, 15 May 1814.

50. PANB MC996/6448, George Pechelle to unknown, 28 May 1822. I am indebted to Joshua Smith for this reference.

51. CO 188/30, Owen to Wilmot, 4 Aug 1822.

52. Chapter 1.

53. While Moose was under British military governance several Charlotte county merchants, including John Wilson and Cadwallader Curry, set up establishments there. Wilson described himself as 'Merchant of Moose Island' in several ICCP affidavits and depositions: for example PANB RS431/A, Wilson v. Hill, 22 Aug 1816, Wilson v. Flagg, 24 Feb 1819. He later petitioned for relief from bonds he had given there: PANB RS24 S33-P33, 1 Feb 1825. CO 188/30, Deposition of C. Curry, 11 Oct 1822. Wilson was commissioned JP in 1822 and Curry in 1830.

olized by the 'fair traders' of Saint John, owners of large ships who wanted the benefit of the carrying trade to markets in New York, Baltimore, and Philadephia, or left to the 'free traders' of Passamaquoddy, owners of the small coasting schooners that brought plaster to the lines for transshipment to American vessels. Within Charlotte county the issue resolved itself into a battle between the merchants of St Andrews—who hoped to compete with their Saint John counterparts for the American carrying trade if the free traders could be made to desert the lines in favour of their port—and the traders of Campobello and West Isles who hoped to profit from the use of their wharves and stores if the schooners were prevented from exchanging their cargoes at sea. As always the rhetoric against the free traders was larded with unproven allegations that the exchange of plaster for flour was a mere cover for smuggling tea, British and American manufactured goods, and Indian cotton, although local customs officials maintained that there was more opportunity for clandestine exchanges of contraband along the province's long and still-disputed land boundary with Maine than in the coasting trade.

In 1816 the assembly banned transshipments of plaster on the lines or its landing anywhere in New Brunswick but Saint John or St Andrews and prohibited exports of plaster to any U.S. port east of Boston.[54] If successful these measures would have evicted small coasting vessels from the international trade, but the immediate passage of countervailing American legislation prohibiting the importation of plaster in any but American vessels meant that their only consequence was to drive free traders from the island wharves back to the lines.[55] Then in 1818 the imperial government investigated com-

---

54. 'An act for the encouragement of the Trade of this Province in Plaster of Paris, otherwise called Gypsum,' 56 Geo.III (1816), published without chapter number in the annual volume for 57 Geo.III (1817) and as 1816 c.32 in the 1817 compilation. It had been suspended pending a similar Nova Scotia enactment and imperial assent. The act required shippers to post bond and pay a ten shilling fee: the bond (but not the fee) was to be cancelled upon production of a certificate that the plaster had been landed at Saint John or St Andrews.

55. CO 188/23, Dawson to Hailes, 10 Mar 1817. Dawson, British consul at Baltimore, predicted that American importers would get around the trade restrictions, as they had the wartime embargo, by smuggling plaster at Passamaquoddy and transporting it overland. According to another contemporary account, 'the Americans

plaints by general John Coffin, a New Brunswick executive councillor who had moved to England the previous year, of extravagant fees exacted by the Saint John customs officers from the coasting trade. The enquiry confirmed that the Collector at Saint John was taking fees to which he was not entitled, but more importantly it exposed serious flaws in the organization of the department. All of New Brunswick was a single port (the Port of Saint John) whose two chief officers, the Collector and Comptroller, shared between themselves all the fees they collected at the harbour in Saint John and half the fees collected by their subordinate officers at the various outports. A council committee recommended that the department be reorganized on a salaried basis, that customs fees in excess of salaries be remitted to the treasury, and that the outports of Charlotte county (which together brought in as much in fees as the harbour of Saint John) be made a separate port with its headquarters at St Andrews.[56] This last reform was implemented in May 1820 and the following year St Andrews became a free port where American vessels could trade directly for British goods destined for American markets.[57] No sooner had the town become a free port with an autonomous customs house of its own than the junto ordered all ships entering Passamaquoddy Bay to clear at St Andrews instead of the island offices as formerly.[58]

---

now obtain this article clandestinely as neither the Navy nor the Custom House Officers will take cognizance of the transactions' on the lines: ibid., General Coffin to provincial agent Bonner, 26 Sep 1817.

56. CO 188/24, Report of Council Committee, 24 Aug 1818.

57. Proclamation, 21 Mar 1821, reprinted in *Sentinel*, 9 Jun 1821. At first the customs officers at Saint John attempted to undermine St Andrews's new status by insisting that it applied only to the town and not to the outports in Charlotte county: see CO 188/27, 'Humble Address of Merchants and Other Inhabitants at St Andrews,' 25 Jun 1821 and correspondence relating thereto. This was resolved by the establishment of an autonomous customs house at St Andrews; some of the repercussions are examined in chapter 4.

58. *Herald*, 2 Apr 1822. The notice is signed by Wyer as deputy provincial treasurer. Junto intimates Colin Campbell and John Dunn were appointed collector and comptroller of customs respectively at St Andrews: *Royal Gazette*, 22 Oct 1822 (notice dated 14 Oct).

New legislation in 1820, designed to overcome the American retaliatory law by imposing a duty on plaster *arriving* in Charlotte county, produced a new flush of illicit trade.[59] The so-called 'plaster war' might better be described as the eighteenth brumaire of Stephen Humbert, for that Saint John merchant and assemblyman stepped into the shoes formerly worn by George Leonard as the provincial preventive officer charged with enforcing the new duty. Like Leonard before him he armed a vessel, had his son appointed deputy, and set off for Passamaquoddy to make seizures. He met concerted and sometimes violent resistance from the plastermen and received little or no assistance from the local customs officers and the commanders of naval vessels cruising in the region. Most of the few craft he managed to seize were released to their owners by the government. By now the trade had shifted to the west side of Passamaquoddy Bay in the waters off Lubec and Eastport 'without reporting at any Office whatsoever.'[60] While recognizing U.S. ownership of Moose, Dudley, and Frederick islands, the New Brunswick legislature resolved that all the waters of the bay 'to the western shore' were in Charlotte county. The attorney general directed Humbert to seize plaster vessels owned by British subjects in what for all other purposes were acknowledged to be American waters.[61] As its critics had foreseen, attempts to enforce the law pushed up the price of plaster and so the incentive to engage in the illicit trade.

By 1820, David Owen, then in his late sixties, was fighting a plaster war of his own. He wrote to county clerk Harris Hatch at St Andrews, demanding to know 'the nature of the Monopoly plaister Bill, wh[ich] is said to have passed the House and to be seen in operation to destroy the western lands from St Johns' Harbour—and drive away

59. Charlotte traders imported plaster from Nova Scotia for resale to American shippers. 60 Geo.III c.19 (1820) imposed a duty of 7/6 per ton on plaster entering the county, to be enforced by a special 'preventive officer' with powers of search and seizure; its companion act 60 Geo.III c.20 (1820) provided for plaster imports at Saint John and prohibited its landing anywhere else in the western parts of the province. 3 Geo.IV (1822) c.32 and 4 Geo.IV (1823) c.16, which applied one per cent of the duty towards the maintenance of an armed revenue cutter, were disallowed by London in 1824: CO 188/30, Council minute, Whitehall, 19 Oct 1824.

60. PANB RS24 S29-Z6, Wright to Wetmore, 13 Jun 1820.

61. Ibid., Wetmore to Humbert, 24 Jun and 3 Aug 1820.

the population.'[62] Owen's first plan of attack was to agitate for disallowance of the act. He complained to Lord Bathurst, secretary of state for the colonies, that although the bill was 'of unusual and the most extraordinary nature' it lacked the suspending clause required by the royal instructions and was no more than an effort by Saint John to 'impound' the plaster traffic and deprive Campobello of 'all the sources of foreign trade.'[63] A month later he raised the stakes. Endorsing the protest of a Nova Scotia plasterman whose schooner had been forcibly boarded and searched under the new provisions Owen insisted that the seizure was illegal: 'I beg therefore, as I have long ago prayed, that I may be allowed to surrender all my Grants from the Crown of lands situate in the Bay of Passamaquoddy' in exchange for one hundred and fifty thousand pounds compensation.[64] He painted a bleak picture of the impact of the 'plaister bill' on his island:[65]

> The whole may fairly be called the deserted Village.[66] The Plaister landing ... [which] by a moderate compensation paid for Beachage brought me in a very handsome income are now wholly unoccupied and the wharves erected by me at great expense for the chief purpose of lading and unlading that article with greater facility and with less wastage, are also untenanted ... In Welch Pool, a few months ago, many labourers and Mechanics had full employ. But now most of them have quitted the place for want of employment, and some Merchants, who intended to settle in that town, relinquished their intentions.

In Owen's opinion, the provincial legislature's only purpose was 'to destroy the trade of this place.'[67] He demanded that Campobello be made a free port.

62. PANB MC207, Owen to Hatch, 11 Apr 1820.

63. CO 188/26, Owen to Golbourn, 15 Apr 1820.

64. CO 188/26, Owen to Bathurst, 25 May 1820, enclosing protest of Peter McArthur and James Reed, 23 May 1820. Ghradus Johnston, the constable in the Hatheway–Ruggles affair, was among the armed enforcers and refused to show his authority for arresting the captain when challenged. For the compensation claim, CO 188/18, Owen's petition to the Prince Regent, 4 Jun 1812.

65. CO 188/30, Owen to Wilmot, 4 Aug 1822.

66. Owen's allusion was no accident: the Irish poet's nephew, Henry Goldsmith JP, a business associate of Wyer, had been collector of customs at St Andrews. His son Oliver would later publish *The Rising Village, with Other Poems* (Saint John, 1834).

67. CO 188/28, Owen to Bathurst, 23 Apr 1824.

A serpent in the garden

In June 1821 one of Owen's wharves was temporarily sequestered by the crew of a British warship on an anti-smuggling cruise. Replying to his protest against this 'outrage,' lieutenant governor Smyth advised that if the naval officers had exceeded their authority Owen must look for his remedy in the civil courts.[68] This became the provincial executive's principal motif in an oratorio for five voices that was to sound without intermission until Owen's death in December 1829, its echoes still reverberating in the St Andrews customs house imbroglio of the 1830s.[69] Owen's tediously-reiterated part was a chorus of longing for a separate county with its seat at Campobello.[70] The other voices belonged to the colonial office in Whitehall, whence the Owen–Smyth correspondence and much more made its way; to the St Andrews 'hive' from whose oppressive rule Owen's panacea was designed to rescue the island parishes; and to Charles Reid Hatheway, one of Warren's younger brothers, whom Owen recruited to deliver his protest to Fredericton.

Hatheway was born at Burton in January 1789, a younger son in a large but relatively undistinguished Loyalist family.[71] At age twenty he became a lieutenant in the Charlotte county militia—brother Warren was a captain—but seems still to have been living in Sunbury county where he served as grand juror and surveyor of roads in 1812.

68. CO 188/27, Owen to Smyth, 3 Jul 1821; ibid., Smyth to Owen, 13 Jul 1821.

69. Chapter 4.

70. For example CO 188/30, Owen to Bathurst, 2 Aug 1822: By erecting the new county, the King will earn 'the gratitude of his numerous Subjects resident in the whole Bay of Fundy where trade in Plaister Paris, Grindstones & other articles the produce of their lands naturally centers at those islands and in which they have been materially and without cause disturbed.' Owen reported that he was willing to pay for the new county's gaol and courthouse; in other correspondence he promised the Society for the Propagation of the Gospel to build a church to be staffed by their missionary on condition that the Bishop of Nova Scotia and his New Brunswick archdeacon would lobby on behalf of his separatist project.

71. His father, Ebenezer Hatheway, had resigned his commission in a loyal regiment after quarrelling with a superior officer. He turned privateer, was captured by American forces, and made a daring escape from confinement in Simsbury Mines. After the Revolution he was granted 112 acres at Burton but no half-pay. His mother, Mary Hatheway, was rumoured to sympathize with the whigs: Sabine, *Biographical Sketches*, 525f ('Hathaway'); Hill, *Loyalists*, 104; NBM Hatheway papers.

Later that year he was promoted captain in the Charlotte militia and in the spring of 1813 became an ensign on the British establishment in the New Brunswick Regiment. He was promoted lieutenant in August 1814. The only record of his wartime service that he preserved was his account for £130 7s 7d expenses in carrying public dispatches from Frederiction to Quebec, Quebec to Fredericton, Fredericton to Halifax, and Halifax back to Fredericton. When the New Brunswick Regiment was reduced in the summer of 1816 he married Julia Clements and moved to Deer Island. When brother Warren left the province in 1819 Charles succeeded him as captain commanding the Deer Island company in the second battalion, Charlotte county militia, with rank from July 1812.[72] He fleshed out his income as a half-pay officer with minor provincial appointments as seizing officer and auctioneer.[73]

In December 1819 Hatheway called at Campobello to display his new commission: 'I observed, en passant, that all Com[missions] of *new Invention* were illegal,' Owen characteristically replied, 'unless sanctioned by an Act of the whole Legislature.'[74] But in the summer of 1821 he recruited Hatheway to carry his protest against the naval 'outrage' to the lieutenant governor.[75] Hatheway must have carried out this mission to the satisfaction of both men for on Owen's recommendation Smyth included him in a new commission of the peace later that year[76] and Owen hired him as his agent or manager on Campo-

72. The wartime account and Hatheway's record of his military appointments are in the slim collection of his papers at NBM. Although the account is dated 1815, Hatheway signed it as an ensign. See also Facey-Crowther, *Militia List* and PANB RS538/B/5. For the Sunbury appointments see PANB RS157 A2/14/RMV/CSu/2/1; for the marriage, *Courier*, 11 May 1816.

73. PANB RS538/B/5, 3 Jun 1819 (seizing officer), 14 Jun 1820 (auctioneer); he was appointed notary public, 10 Apr 1823. Charles made several appearances as witness and juror at Charlotte general sessions in April and September 1821. Owen later claimed that Hatheway had been trying unsuccessfully to earn a living in this period by smuggling: see further below.

74. CCA MC349, Owen to Hatch, 22 Dec 1819. Owen was presumably referring to the seizing officer position but his main purpose was preening self-display.

75. CO 188/27, Owen to Smyth, 3 Jul 1821. Owen also sent a petition to make Campobello a free port.

76. PANB RS538/B/5, 23 Nov 1821.

bello in May 1822.[77] Five years later, when their relationship had dissolved into a morass of mutual recrimination and civil and criminal litigation, Owen recorded that it had begun when Hatheway moved from Deer Island to occupy the disused custom house at Snug Cove as Owen's tenant.[78] When Owen's then-overseer died in February 1823 he appointed Hatheway as his agent and attorney and arranged to have him included in the commission of the peace.[79] Hatheway was soon hard at work taking depositions from Owen's clients in the campaign to make Campobello a free port, surveying and advertising building lots, witnessing leases, compiling assessment lists, and serving as the landlord's bully boy.[80] Owen prosecuted two of his ten-

---

77. In a contemporaneous Supreme Court deposition, Owen described Hatheway as having been his 'servant' on 16 May 1822: PANB RS42 1822, David Owen v. James Wilson et al.

78. During the 1812-14 war the customs office was relocated to Moose Island. Once Eastport was again ceded to the United States, Owen refused to permit the customs department to use the house, ostensibly because it would not pay him back rent for the time it had been unoccupied during the war. He also refused to lease a lot on Campobello to the local customs officer on the basis of aesthetic objections to the architectural drawings of the house he proposed to build. In the result a customs office was established on tiny Rowan (or Rouen) Island just off the southern tip of Indian Island, a great inconvenience to shipping that ensured Owen a minimum of interference. More than ten years later St Andrews officials were still complaining that the deputy-treasurer for West Isles 'lives on a little island, a mere small rock; and if a smart breeze should blow ... a vessel might come in to any other part of the West Isles, and discharge her whole illicit cargo, before the officer could arrive to interfere': *Courier*, 11 Mar 1831, reporting the legislative debate on the provincial treasurer's accounts. The correspondence between Owen and the customs officials is in CO 188/30, David Owen complaint, 4 Aug 1822, encl. A through F.

79. CO 188/35, Owen protest against further proceedings in the criminal information against him, 19 Jul 1926 [Owen, Protest]. For the criminal information see chapter 4.

80. CO 188/30, depositions of John Paterson (24 Sep 1822) and Cadwallader Curry (11 Oct 1822); *Sentinel*, 9 Mar 1823 advertising lots and assuring prospective purchasers that Campobello was soon to become a free port; PANB RS42 1824, Hatheway v. Owen; CCA (uncatalogued) plans of four Deer Island lots, 3 Dec 1825 signed by Hatheway as surveyor; PANB RS431/A, lease, David Owen to Robert Kelley, 10 May 1823; PANB RS148/c/3/b/1, Campobello assessment lists, 11 Apr 1823. Nowlan, *Outer Island*, 55f gives an account of Charles's role in an eviction: 'But when Hatheway, accompanied by the sheriff, went to claim the property he was attacked by a crowd led by Sarah Wilson, Mary's daughter-in-law, who brandished a sword that had been carried by Robert Wilson during the French and Indian War. Parker

ants for assault and sued them for damages occasioned by the loss of Hatheway's services while recovering from a beating they had given him during an attempted eviction.[81]

Charles Reid Hatheway in his early thirties, captain of a militia battalion, a newly-minted justice of the peace clothed as well in the petty authority of a landlord's bailiff, was surely something of a martinet. This may have been the quality that attracted Owen to him in the first place, but before long Charles's sense of duty was to set the two men at odds. The difficulty was that where Owen saw conspiracy and contempt Charles saw legitimate authority. Their increasingly rancorous differences set private property against public authority, drew Hatheway into alliance with the hated St Andrews 'hive,' and drove Owen to make a fetish of the separatist project. An increasingly frustrated provincial executive finally decided to prosecute Owen for sedition and misconduct in office, producing such a transatlantic storm that the new lieutenant governor felt obliged to come to Campobello in a futile attempt to pacify him.

Through most of the 1820s five discordant voices sounded their simple motifs in rough counterpoint. The ostensible issues were many and varied, ranging from precedence in the county commission of the peace to command of the Campobello militia; from taxing aliens to building roads; from clearances for plaster vessels to the seizure of leather from a tanyard; from armed resistance and riot to the destruction of an apple orchard. They all had at bottom Owen's dogged and unyielding persistence in lobbying for separation from Charlotte county. No matter what the specific dispute, each of the five voices sounded its own distinctive motif. Owen sang of conspiracy and oppression, Hatheway of duty and necessity. The 'hive' hymned St Andrews's hegemony. Three lieutenant governors and two presidents of council joined in the provincial executive's chorus, 'Let the courts decide,' while four successive secretaries of state for the

---

kept the house.' Nowlan did not cite his sources and the year he gives for this incident (1816) cannot be correct; see note 81 below.

81. PANB RS42 1822, David Owen v. James Wilson et al.; CCGS 17 Sep 1822, The King v. Daniel Cashman and James Wilson Jr. This was part of the continuing saga of the Wilson 'encroachment' which had preoccupied Owen since he first set foot on the island in October 1787.

colonies sang the imperial anthem: 'Will no-one rid us of this turbulent priest?'

The incidents of this lengthy struggle cast light on several low law themes. These include recruitment to the magistracy, the compatibility of magisterial with other county and parish offices, and such abuses of office as excess of jurisdiction, acting as judge in one's own cause, and barratry. This decade of demands and recriminations is especially rich in illustrations of the techniques available for supervising and controlling the justices, although for the most part fumbled or ineffective. They include private litigation, both civil and criminal; collegial intervention by the county bench at general sessions (as seen in the Warren Hatheway–Gilbert Ruggles affair); and various steps available to the provincial executive, including the exercise of its appointment power, investigations by the law officers, and the use of the *ex officio* criminal information. It also shows how patronage, petitioning, and appeals over the heads of those responsible could delay and indeed stultify centralizing efforts to impose imperial or provincial control on even the most idiosyncratic and troublesome local administration, especially when the administrator was an important proprietor.

Militia troubles

New Brunswick's first militia act, passed in 1787, required 'every person' between the ages of sixteen and fifty to enlist in a regimented or independent militia company.[82] By 1794 'every person' had become every white male inhabitant or resident, sixteen to sixty years of age, and companies and regiments were to muster for training, discipline, and exercises four times each year.[83] Regiments were organized by

82. For general background see Facey-Crowther, *Militia.* Failure to enlist, to appear at muster, or to behave appropriately there was punishable by fines imposed by the company commander and enforced by one of its noncommissioned officers acting in the role of a constable to serve process, seize property, and convey delinquents to the county gaol. In 1802 militiamen were protected from arrest for debt on muster day or during actual service: 42 Geo.III (1802) c.1. This provision was omitted from the 1805 legislation but reinstated by 47 Geo.III (1807) c.12.

83. 34 Geo.III (1794) c.1. Later legislation required free blacks to form 'pioneer' companies subordinate and subservient to regimental battalions in case of actual

county:[84] in practice their staffing generally mirrored the local administrative hierarchy. The 1808 militia act did away with independent companies, provided relief from attendance for those who lived far from the mustering site, and required some exempts to pay a fee in lieu of participation.[85] This was refined in 1810 by requiring company captains to make annual lists of exempts in their district. The enforcement system was modified, so that fines for nonattendance were to be recovered before a justice of the peace while fines for misconduct were to be enforced as previously by the captain's warrant served by a sergeant or corporal.[86] In 1814 there was an innovation: 'all persons other than British Subjects, and who shall have resided for the space of two months in this province' had to pay forty shillings annually to support the militia.[87] The 1816 act reduced this 'alien tax' to thirty shillings and made it enforceable before a justice of the peace at the suit of the company's quartermaster.[88] Further refinements in 1822 required company captains to make annual lists of aliens and provided relief for those who had taken the oath of allegiance *before* the 1812-14 war.[89] The militia act was amended the following year to provide that no fine was to be enforced by a company captain without first summoning the delinquent to show cause why it should not be imposed. The summons was to be served by a civil constable rather than a militia noncom as formerly.[90]

At Campobello David Owen had commanded a militia company from its formation in 1797 until July 1812 when he resigned in a fury because neither the lieutenant governor nor the colonial secretary nor the Prince Regent would support his refusal to have the company

service: 45 Geo.III (1805) c.1. Black pioneer companies were required to muster with their battalions by 53 Geo.III (1813) c.1.

84. 32 Geo.III (1792) c.1.

85. 48 Geo.III (1808) c.1. Certain professions and occupations were exempt from muster although not from actual service, as also were Quakers: 27 Geo.III (1787) c.1.

86. 50 Geo.III (1810) c.9. Some exemptions and exempt fees were modified by 52 Geo.III (1812) c.8.

87. 54 Geo.III (1814) c.21.

88. 56 Geo.III (1816) c.6.

89. 3 Geo.IV (1822) c.23.

90. 4 Geo.IV (1823) c.27. This act 'to explain and amend' the militia laws managed to confuse matters further by the reference in its preamble to a non-existent 'Act for the organization and regulation of the Militia of this Province,' 49 Geo.III (1809).

participate in a muster and inspection at Indian Island as ordered by the battalion commander, Thomas Wyer.[91] In Owen's view 'his' company was not required to leave the island except when called out under martial law to defend against actual invasion or insurrection. He carried on a vituperative campaign against his successor as company commander, whom he described as having 'not a foot of land in the District, born in the north of Ireland of mean parents, a serjeant lately in His Majesty's 8th Regiment and who secured a spot on Campo Bello Island for the purpose of curing fish,' and whose appointment he thought was 'to serve the ends of all those who had been the cause of all his complaints to the parent state.'[92] He complained that by making fines for delinquency recoverable before the captain rather than a magistrate, the militia act put his tenants 'at the mercy of this creature.'[93] He refused to attend a court of inquiry into these complaints at St Andrews because to do so would be 'inconsistent' with and 'contradictory' to his position that Campobello militia concerns were to be dealt with at Campobello.[94] His insistence that the Campobello company was independent of the Charlotte regiment was one of the planks in Owen's platform for separation from the county.[95]

When Hatheway became Owen's agent and moved to Campobello he was captain of the Deer Island militia company. He considered resigning his commission there but Owen encouraged him to apply

---

91. PANB RS559/a/1/a, Wyer to Owen, 12 Jun 1812. For the date of Owen's resignation, *Royal Gazette*, 10 Aug 1812 (giving his name as 'Owens') and see Facey-Crowther, *Militia List*, 74. Owen later insisted that the July 1812 date was a scandalous libel, he having in fact resigned in 1811 before the declaration of war, but he continued to style himself 'commanding officer' in 1812: C0188/19, Encl. G-3, certificate of David Owen, Commanding Officer, 4 Jun 1812. Elsewhere Owen insisted that he had not resigned at all but merely 'deposited' his commission 'as a matter expedient, in the hands of the Colonel,' while assuring the provincial secretary that 'I ought to have command of my own Militia:' Owen, Protest.

92. CO 188/19, R.O. Jones (on behalf of Owen) to Bathurst, 1 Mar 1813.

93. CO 188/20, Owen to Goulbourn, 15 Apr 1814.

94. CO 188/19, Owen to Lord Liverpool, 27 Apr 1813 (encl.), complaining that 'a certain party residing [at St Andrews] always injured' his interests.

95. The executive rejected this claim, stating 'that under the present Militia Law no independent Companies are authorised or recognized': CO 188/35, Odell to Owen, 5 Feb 1827.

for a transfer to the Campobello company instead.[96] The claims of the existing commander posed a difficulty but Major Harris Hatch, clerk of the peace at St Andrews, resolved it solomonically, dividing the company in two and making Hatheway captain of the new one.[97] Hatheway began proceedings to collect the alien tax and sent Owen a list of twelve 'delinquents' because as captain 'it would be illegal for me to act as a Magistrate and would thank you to proceed against them.'[98] Owen at first refused to have anything to do with the alien tax, telling him that 'the Militia Law was a damned rascally arbitrary Law that it was made by a set of ignorant rascals & that it would cause a rebellion in the Province.' He threatened to prosecute Hatheway or anyone else who would try to enforce it against his tenants.[99] A few days later, however, Owen consented to preside over what he termed a 'special sessions' to examine the alien tax informations. Richard Ferris, the battalion quartermaster, attended to prosecute and Hatheway was there as an observer.

Owen gave several versions of how he managed this 'special sessions.' On his own showing he went out of his way to obfuscate the proceeding, using every technical and formal device he could come up with to defeat the tax.[100] He began with a lengthy reading of the commission of the peace, something that was not required even at general sessions. He refused to accept Ferris's list of delinquents, insisting instead that he must make a separate complaint against each of them using a form Owen found in Burn's *Justice*.[101] When Ferris

96. CO 188/35, Hatheway affidavit, 21 Jun 1824.

97. CO 188/35, Petition of Abijah Gregory, 1 Mar 1825; Owen, Protest. Owen claimed that the division was unlawful because the existing company was not up to strength. Clerk of the peace Harris Hatch took command of the new third battalion of the Charlotte militia comprising West Isles, Campobello, and Grand Manan when it was created in 1822: *Royal Gazette*, 26 Nov 1822.

98. PANB RS76, Hatheway to Owen, 26 Jul 1823.

99. PANB RS559/A/1/a, Hatch to Shore, 1 Jan [1824] encl. Hatheway to Hatch, 12 Nov 1823. Owen never denied using these words but claimed that the conversation was privileged as between him and his 'attorney.' See, for instance, PANB RS76, Owen deposition, dated 27 Jul 1823 but reporting events as late as September of that year.

100. Owen, Protest. See also CO 188/35, Owen memorandum, 4 Aug 1823.

101. Burn, *Justice* was the leading English magistrates' manual. Shortly after arriving in New Brunswick, Owen asked to be sent a copy of 'the last Edition but one,'

pointed out the Militia Act provision, Owen informed him:

> The words 'other than' were in lieu of the words in the former Militia Act 'not being' and that the Act by him quoted was *in pari materia* and the negative disqualifications by which he claimed title to receive the penalty, ought to be by him, the Informer, negatively set forth in his charge ... the point had been fully argued and settled by unanimous opinion of all the Judges of HM Court of KB in England; and was adjudged to be a point settled by the constant tenor of all the authorities and that this Court could not proceed otherwise.

According to Hatheway, Owen then told the aliens, 'I have summoned you here to answer to the Qr Master for an Alien Tax, but he having refused to file in such a complaint as will justify my Acting the Court is therefore at an end & I have nothing more to do with you.'[102]

These proceedings did little to endear Hatheway to the privates in his new company or to increase their respect for him. A few weeks later, when as senior captain he mustered both companies for regimental training and inspection, the junior captain treated him contemptuously and some of the men on parade refused to recognize his command.[103] An attempt was made to patch the quarrel over dinner with Owen, Hatheway, Majors Harris Hatch and Thomas Wyer, and Adjutant William Hatch all present.[104] Nevertheless the next day Hatheway issued orders against sixteen or seventeen militiamen for absence or disorderly conduct on parade and gave them to his sergeant to execute. Owen reprimanded the sergeant (his tenant), saying that the act required service by a constable. He threatened to

---

i.e., that of 1785, which was current at the creation of the province: Glansevern #1181, David Owen to William Owen, 13 May 1790.

102. CO 188/35, Hatheway affidavit, 21 Jun 1824. Quarter master Ferris also gave an affidavit (ibid., n.d.): 'Several Aliens appeared to stand trial and Mr Hatheway was also there. Mr Owen said he could not proceed against those Aliens unless I made out a complaint against each Alien according to a form which he then showed me in a Book. I referred him to the Alien List then before him told him the persons present had refused paying the Tax & I was ready to prove it if he wished. A few minutes after Mr Owen said the court was at an end, that he could not proceed in consequence of my refusing to file in proper complaints (or words to that effect).'

103. Owen, Protest; PANB RS76, Owen deposition, 27 Jul 1823.

104. William Hatch seems to have been Harris's cousin, the son of father Christopher's brother Hawes Hatch.

drive the Campobello constable off the island if he had anything to do with Hatheway's writs. When Hatheway told Owen that he was under orders to enforce the militia law, Owen replied, 'Well, by the Almightly God, before I will allow you, Hatch, or anyone to harass and dragoon my men on this Island with such a damned rascally, arbitrary Militia Law, made by a set of pimping rascals about Fredericton I will sacrifice every drop of blood in my body.'[105]

Hatheway persisted and acting now as magistrate sent constables to seize property under writs of execution for the unpaid fines. The constables reported that the delinquents were 'clubbed together & so violent that they could not arrest them.' Hatheway enlisted the support of West Isles magistrate G.D. Berton and went with a constable to seize a boat belonging to two of the delinquents. A crowd assembled. The boat was rescued and the constable assaulted. No-one present would respond to the magistrates' calls for assistance. Even Cadwallader Curry, a merchant and 'the most influential person in the settlement,' refused to assist, saying he feared his property would be destroyed if he did so. Berton reported that 'there appeared to be a general disposition to treat authority with contempt in a more open way than I have ever before witnessed in this province.'[106] The constable having gone to St Andrews to swear an information against his assailants, Owen had him arrested and harangued him after which he refused to attend general sessions to prosecute.[107] Another constable, also an Owen tenant, initially swore affidavits supporting Hatheway's version but subsequently deposed in Owen's favour.[108]

Parish business

Just as Owen believed his island's militiamen should not have to pay the alien tax, so was he convinced that the parish was exempt from

105. CO 188/35, Hatheway affidavit, 21 Jun 1824.

106. CO 188/35, Berton affidavit, 21 Jun 1824; ibid., Memorandum of Hatheway and Berton, 13 Nov 1823, appended to Morgan affidavit, 12 Nov 1823.

107. CO 188/35, J.M. Parker deposition, 21 Jun 1824; ibid., Wetmore to Douglas, 8 May 1827.

108. CO 188/34, Morgan petition for relief from bonds, 25 Feb 1825, accusing Hatheway of asking him to perjure himself before the sessions grand jury. Owen paid the fee for this petition.

Charlotte taxes[109] and other obligations imposed by the junto at St Andrews, whom he accused of conducting county business in secret sessions.[110] He did all he could to frustrate Hatheway's attempts to conduct Campobello parish business as tax collector and surveyor of highways, advancing as a legal principle the incompatibility of parish and customs offices with those of a justice of the peace, obstructing Hatheway's attempts to bring taxation cases to trial, and encouraging his tenants to sue Hatheway personally for official conduct. He also appealed to the law officers of the crown to have Hatheway removed from the commission of the peace for holding incompatible public offices.

Hatheway had been careful to avoid adjudicating the alien tax cases even though they were nominally at the suit of the quartermaster. But in the summer of 1824, when Hatheway met resistance in his attempt to seize leather from John Milliken's tan yard in his capacity as a customs official, he called for the assistance due him as a magistrate.[111] Owen encouraged Milliken to contest the seizure on the ground that Hatheway could not act as both seizing officer and magistrate. The issue was joined again when general sessions adopted a resolution, 'that no magistrate be appointed to any parish office in the county of Charlotte, excepting the offices of school trustees and Surveyors of Lumber.'[112] Hatheway held parish office as gauger of casks and surveyor of lumber for Campobello, which Owen insisted fell within the ban. Owen petitioned the lieutenant governor to pre-

109. Hatheway claimed that when he was appointed assessor of rates he discovered that no county taxes had been collected on Campobello, and that when he later asked for the 'parish book' to document this claim Owen refused to let him see it, saying there was no law to enforce the tax and the people 'did right in standing out': CO 188/35, Hatheway affidavit, 21 Jun 1824, and see chapter 9.

110. CO 188/35, Owen to Odell, 5 Feb 1825.

111. Milliken was one of the aliens on Ferris's list. In or about 1818 customs officers had seized leather which he claimed to have manufactured at his tannery on Moose Island but which fell under suspicion for several reasons, not least that it was 'of too good a quality to have been manufactured by John Milliken who was thought a very indifferent workman.' The claimants in vice-admiralty were two Fredericton saddlers, recent immigrants from the United States: PANB MC996/6447, 'Case on the Part of the Prosecution, 49 Sides of Leather,' n.d. I am grateful to Joshua Smith for this reference.

112. CCGS, 13 Apr 1824; rescinded 13 Apr 1825.

vent Hatheway acting as a justice of the peace while he occupied these offices, 'and thereby the inhabitants of Campobello and all others may be relieved from the Extortions and oppressions which they suffer under colour of his office; and without the expense and trouble of numberless lawsuits, which they are not able to prosecute.'[113]

The executive did not do as Owen requested and the county bench rescinded its resolution. Milliken had to content himself by suing Hatheway for damages while Owen made do by promoting a private prosecution for barratry alleging that Hatheway was 'a continual disturber of the peace' and 'a common and turbulent sower of discord between his neighbours.'[114] The grand jury at April sessions 1825 accepted the bill after clerk Hatch (who was Hatheway's defence attorney in Milliken's pending lawsuit as well as his commanding officer in the militia business) refused to allow the tanner to testify before them—but it also found a true bill against Milliken for assaulting Hatheway in his tan-yard. At the next sessions, held after the civil trial in which Milliken collected thirteen pounds damages and sixpence costs for the improper seizure,[115] both were discharged upon payment of costs and Hatheway was appointed surveyor of roads for the parish of Campobello.[116]

Hatheway's appointment was the junto's answer to Owen's open declaration of war on the Charlotte magistrates, his 1824 protest that as Campobello was his private property its roads could not be public highways and the county bench could not interfere.[117] His object was 'to have the Parish of Campobello considered as Exempt from the Power of the Court of Sessions of Charlotte County.' This was too much for the law officers, who nevertheless sought to protect lieutenant governor Douglas from the same charge of prejudice that

---

113. CO 188/34, Owen to Douglas, 25 Feb 1825. Owen signed the petition on behalf of himself and his tenants and added the names of Cadwallader Curry, John Paterson, John Milliken, and Abijah Gregory. The last two were alien tax defendants.

114. CO 188/34, copy of true bill attested by Owen.

115. PANB RS36/A2, 11 Aug 1825. Hatch moved unsuccessfully to have the verdict set aside: PANB RS36/B, 1 Mar 1826.

116. CCGS 20 Sep 1825.

117. CO 188/35, Owen's printed protest, 21 Sep 1824. At April sessions 1825 the bench refused to receive a return by Curry and Paterson, 'styling themselves commissioners of the parish of Campobello': CCGS 12 Apr 1825.

Owen had brought against Bliss and Hatheway:[118]

> The Law must take its course and it belongs to the King's Court of Justice to determine whether the Parish of Campobello is or is not part of the County of Charlotte, as also who are or are not the Parish officers duly appointed, and what acts of theirs were or are legal and valid, and particularly whether any Highways have been laid out and established or can be legally laid out or established on the Island of Campobello. We forbear submitting any opinion on that point because it may so happen that Your Excellency may be called upon in your Judicial Capacity in the Provincial Court of Error to decide thereupon, and the case ought not as we conceive to be prejudged or in any way prejudiced.

Nevertheless Hatheway's appointment as surveyor of highways led to the one ground of complaint against him that was taken seriously by the law officers. Acting as surveyor, Hatheway laid out roads on Campobello and assessed statute labour obligations on the residents; acting as justice of the peace, he issued process to enforce those obligations. While for Owen the issue had everything to do with Campobello's independence from control by St Andrews (and perhaps from the laws of New Brunswick more generally), for the law officers it raised a question about the proper limits of magisterial authority. When Hatheway petitioned for relief from Owen's obstruction of his efforts as 'a Magistrate and a Parish Officer' to enforce the statute labour act,[119] Owen countered by accusing him of misconduct in accepting an appointment incompatible with his office as justice of the peace.[120] Attorney general Wetmore, smarting no doubt under the lash of Owen's repeated reminders of patronage and moral indebtedness,[121] seized the opportunity to chastise Hatheway and call him to

118. CO 188/35, Wetmore and Peters to Douglas, 27 Dec 1826.

119. CO 188/35, Hatheway to Douglas (petition), 30 Nov 1825.

120. CO 188/35, Owen to Wetmore, 2 Dec 1825.

121. Owen had successfully lobbied the colonial secretary to have Wetmore appointed attorney general in 1811; he had also supported Wetmore's failed bid to become British agent in the boundary negotiation of 1815, when Chipman got the appointment: CO 188/21, Owen testimonial, 18 Feb 1811; ibid., 2 Apr 1815. Owen believed judges Chipman and Bliss, both of whom had been rival candidates, to be prejudiced against him for supporting Wetmore: CO 188/28, David Owen's ms. 'Re-

account, accusing him of having 'united in your one person the Office of Party and Judge, contrary to the first principles of Justice,' and opining that the office of surveyor of highways was not only incompatible with that of justice of the peace, 'but degrading to the magistrate' who accepts it.[122]

Hatheway replied that Owen had been made a commissioner of highways in 1821, 'at his own request,' and that several other county justices had accepted parish offices in recent years. As for himself, he had accepted the appointment only because the former incumbent had been driven off the island by Owen's threats and harassment and no-one else was willing to serve. He denied any illegality: once he had delivered the statute labour list to the commissioners of highways his duty as surveyor was done; when the commissioners applied to him as justice to issue process against the delinquents he was no longer an interested party. As for the incompatibility, 'I did suppose there was a degree of inconsistency in a Magistrate holding any Parish office, but its having been practised for a number of years in other Counties in the Province as well as in this without any interference of His Majesty's Attorney General (to my knowledge) was induced to think there was no impropriety in it . . .'[123]

The following year Hatheway complained that Owen had persuaded several residents to sue him for fines he had assessed against them and then deprived him of his defence by repeatedly adjourning the proceedings. In this and other ways Owen had made it 'utterly impossible for him to perform the duties of his office so effectually as he wishes and Justice requires . . .'[124] By then the place was in an uproar. Owen was encouraging his tenants to resist constables and deputy sheriffs sent from St Andrews; their attempts to serve warrants and enforce executions for unpaid fines and taxes resulted in riotous res-

---

ports.' Wetmore represented Owen in dozens of lawsuits between 1801 and 1821. Never one to trust his lawyers, Owen confided to his agent John Wilkinson that he believed Wetmore had 'privately & without any authority signed a retraxit' in his endless legal battle against the Wilson encroachment, 'and that this was the secret cause of his delay in proceeding with the suit': Glansevern #14378, 'Copy of a paper put into the hands of John Wilkinson in the year 1826 by the late David Owen Esq . . .'

122. CO 188/35, Wetmore to Hatheway, 24 Dec 1825.

123. CO 188/35, Hatheway to Wetmore, 25 Jan 1826.

124. CO 188/35, Hatheway to Douglas, 14 Feb 1827.

cues. Wetmore advised the new lieutenant governor, Howard Douglas, that while Owen's was 'an extraordinary mode of proceeding,' Hatheway had indeed acted illegally and improperly by combining the offices of surveyor and magistrate. Solicitor general Peters concurred in his colleague's opinion at least to the extent that Hatheway was 'giving unjustifiable and unnecessary trouble to Your Excellency and that his proper course is an appeal to the Courts of Justice for redress, if he has been injured.'[125] Nevertheless, the law officers had ultimately to acknowledge the truth of Hatheway's defence, 'in regard to the general practice which prevailed in the Sessions of the Peace and which had taken its origin in the great difficulty which existed in the infancy of the Province, of finding suitable persons to fill the various Parochial appointments.' They pointed out that Hatheway had not acted corruptly and recommended acceptance of his tacit apology. Under the 'peculiar circumstances' of 'extreme hostility' between Owen and Hatheway it would be inappropriate to prosecute him.[126]

---

125. CO 188/35, Wetmore to Douglas, 21 Mar 1827, endorsed by Peters, 28 Mar 1827. Owen sued in trespass for cutting down trees and fences; Hatheway's defence was that he acted in his official capacity to clear trees and illegal fences from the public highway. The papers in this suit are mixed in with others involving the same parties, but it does not appear to have gone to trial: PANB RS42 1825, Owen v. Hatheway.

126. CO 188/35, Wetmore and Peters to Douglas, 30 May 1827.

Chapter 4

The empire strikes back: Executive action, 1824-32

The naive young officer whom Owen had taken into his confidence and employ had become a 'pimping spy and snake in the grass,' a willing tool of the enemy at St Andrews.[1] Hatheway's complaint about Owen's obstruction of the militia law prosecutions was referred by Major Hatch to the adjutant general 'for the information of the President and Commander in Chief.'[2] It arrived at Fredericton during the brief presidency of Ward Chipman, who had long experience of Owen as counsel to several of his antagonists and victims over the years.[3] It was now time for Owen to be sprinkled with the water of his own transgressions. Without much in the way of investigation or advice Chipman directed the law officers to prosecute him.[4] Chipman's death a few days later did not so much delay matters—his son

1. CO 188/35, Owen to Odell, 5 Mar 1827.

2. PANB RS559 Militia A/1/a, Hatch to Shore, 1 Jan 1823 [but must be 1824].

3. Chapter 2. Owen later argued that Chipman held a grudge against him because Owen had lobbied the Prince Regent to remove him from the international boundary commission in favour of Wetmore: CO 188/35, Owen to Odell, 5 Mar 1827.

4. CO 188/35, copy of Council minute, 27 Jan 1824. In explaining the affair to Howard Douglas, the next lieutenant governor, the law officers stated that the prosecution was instituted under the 'express order' of President Chipman in Council: ibid., Wetmore and Peters to Douglas, 27 Dec 1826.

Ward Jr, the solicitor general, gave his opinion almost immediately[5]—as did attorney general Thomas Wetmore's reluctance to act against a regular client and sometime patron. Wetmore dithered and delayed until the province's new administrator put his foot down, expressing 'the greatest surprise that so long a period should have been allowed to elapse without any legal steps having been taken.'[6] Even so, the information was not prepared and exhibited until July and another year passed before the case came on for trial in August 1825.

In July 1824 Wetmore informed the Supreme Court that David Owen JP of Campobello was a disaffected subject, 'contriving and endeavouring unlawfully, maliciously, factiously and seditiously' to disturb the peace and bring the government into hatred and contempt, 'creating false opinions and suspicions,' and 'obstructing and preventing as much as in him lay the due course and administration of Law and Justice.'[7] There were three specific counts. The first alleged that Owen, acting as a magistrate, unlawfully and corruptly acquitted several Campobello residents from liability to pay the alien tax. The second accused him of seditious speech in his two private conversations with Hatheway about the 'rascally arbitrary' militia law. The third charge, the one viewed most seriously by the solicitor general in his correspondence with Wetmore, turned on an incident remarkably similar to that which had precipitated the Warren Hatheway–Gilbert Ruggles imbroglio three years earlier. It alleged that Owen had interfered to release a Campobello resident from arrest by a constable sent from St Andrews on Hatheway's complaint that he had threatened and verbally abused him.

Proceeding by *ex officio* information allowed the government to prosecute directly, without indictment by a grand jury or leave of the

5. PANB RS8, Chipman to Wetmore 13 Feb 1824, stating that it was impossible 'under present circumstances' for him to consider the matter fully but that there could be 'no doubt as to the propriety of at once filing an information for the rescue of the man arrested under the warrant from the Justice at St Andrews and before Easter Term.' Chipman Sr died on February 9.

6. PANB RS8, Wetmore to Bliss, 13 May 1824; the quote is from Bliss's endorsement on this memorandum, dated 15 May 1824. For Wetmore's dithering, see his correspondence with Chipman, 13 Feb, 11 Mar, 26 Apr, 1 and 5 May, 1824, and with Bliss on May 13 and 14.

7. Copy of information in CO 188/35, Douglas to Bathurst, 5 Jun 1827 (encl. #7).

court.[8] It put the accused to the significant expense of mounting his defence regardless of the outcome.[9] In England, as Joseph Chitty explained in 1816, informations could be filed by the attorney general at his discretion for any misdemeanour tending, 'in his opinion, to disturb the government or immediately to interfere with the interests of the public or the safety of the crown.'[10]

In proceeding by *ex officio* information the attorney general, unlike private prosecutors, was not bound by recognizance to appear and prosecute so it was entirely at his discretion when and how to commence, suspend, or drop the prosecution. He could not be called as a witness nor was he liable to an action for malicious prosecution. He was entitled to amend the information at any time and to have the matter tried by special jury at his election.[11] In short, this was an extraordinary form of proceeding by which the Crown could effectively suspend many of the protections to which accused persons were normally entitled.

New Brunswick's attorney general followed English King's Bench procedure carefully. The formulaic opening and closing passages of Wetmore's information recite nearly verbatim the same form supplied

---

8. Leave was required in ordinary criminal informations, thereby allowing the accused to require the prosecutor to show cause, as for example in Owen's information against Pagan discussed in chapter 2.

9. '[A]s it is beneath the dignity of the crown either to receive costs or to pay them': Chitty, *Practical Treatise*, I:848.

10. Ibid., I:845. In his review of Staffordshire cases in King's Bench, Douglas Hay has found that *ex officio* informations were used infrequently and (except for two cases involving attacks on excisemen) exclusively to prosecute Jacobite rioters and their sympathizers: the crown, he argues, used the extraordinary route of informations because it could not get indictments from the county's Tory grand juries in these cases. The Staffordshire cases include several criminal informations brought against magistrates for official misconduct, but none of them were filed *ex officio*: Hay, *King's Bench*. For the use of ordinary (not *ex officio*) criminal informations to control the English magistracy, Hay, 'Dread.' For the various disabilities that applied to a private prosecutor seeking to proceed by information rather than indictment, Chitty, *Practical Treatise*, I:855f, and for the special case of (ordinary) informations against magistrates, ibid., I:873f.

11. '[A] practice which has been objected to as too unfavourable to the subject, when the influence of the crown is opposed to a single individual, and state policy is in question': ibid., I:848.

in Chitty's 1816 treatise.[12] A little more than a year after the information was filed, the case came on for trial at circuit in St Andrews before John Murray Bliss and a special jury. The presiding judge apparently was unconcerned about his impartiality despite being the prosecutor's father-in-law, having participated in the council at which the prosecution was ordered, and having subsequently, as administrator of the province after Chipman Sr's death, nagged the reluctant attorney general to get on with it.

Wetmore prosecuted for the Crown. David Owen (having exhausted the legal resources of the Wetmore–Bliss clan) was represented by Alfred Locke Street.[13] The minutes of the 1825 Charlotte circuit give only an outline of the proceedings, although they do list the jurors and witnesses.[14] The judge's notes have not survived and there are no extant newspaper reports of the trial. There remain sev-

12. Chitty cites 11 Harg. St. Tr. 266 for the form. An extraneous '*for our said Lord the King*' in Wetmore's conclusion may have been a transcription error in the original or in the later (1827) copy from which I have taken the text.

13. Street was a St Andrews lawyer, Rev. Jerome Alley JP's future son-in-law. He was Owen's counsel of record in almost all the litigation I have found from 1824 on. Alfred's nephew George Dixon Street studied law in his office; he became Wyer's son-in-law in 1835: *Bay Pilot*, 17 Aug 1882. Alfred's father was Samuel Denny Street, whose appointment as Clerk of the Assembly in opposition to Carleton's wishes had helped to precipitate the 'stars and daggers' crisis described in chapter 2. There was no love lost between the Streets and the Wetmore–Bliss clan. Street *pere* fought an inconclusive duel with J.M. Bliss in 1800; in 1821 Alfred's brother, Fredericton lawyer George Frederick Street, killed Wetmore's eldest son in another duel. Street was acquitted on his trial for murder after an address by Chief Justice John Saunders stressing the importance of character. George Frederick occasionally represented Owen at the Supreme Court in term, for example in the ejectment mentioned in note 17 below. Owen wrote to London supporting S.D. Street's abortive 1822 attempt to have the colonial secretary overturn Lt.-Gov. Smyth's choice of E.J. Jarvis for a Supreme Court vacancy in favour of his own application. Owen dismissed Jarvis as young, inexperienced, and the son of a blacksmith turned Saint John alderman (hence not to be trusted on either class or regional grounds): CO 188/28, Street to Owen, 14 Oct 1822; Owen to Wilmot, 17 Oct 1822. London did overrule Smyth but appointed William Botsford instead. This was Street's third failed attempt to become a Supreme Court judge. (Jarvis received as a consolation prize appointment as a crown law officer in Malta; he returned to the Maritimes as chief justice of P.E.I. in 1828.)

14. PANB RS36/A/1, 9 Aug 1825. The Crown called C.R. Hatheway, Harris Hatch, Peter Stubs JP, Richard Ferris, James M. Parker, James Price, John Lank, and Daniel Todd; the defence called Abijah Gregory, Colin Campbell, Joseph Russell, Josiah Coffin, David Owen Morgan, Cadwallader Curry, and John Milliken. A number of Char-

eral partial versions of what transpired: reports by the law officers and Judge Bliss in December 1826, and David Owen's multiple (and sometimes inconsistent) retellings intended to pressure the government to discontinue proceedings against him and to prosecute Hatheway instead. The 1826 reports were ordered by the new lieutenant governor, Howard Douglas, to help him navigate the treacherous waters stirred up by a hurricane of Owen grievances sent his way both directly from Campobello and via London.

The official reports said little more than that the charges were 'fully investigated' in a trial that lasted twelve hours; that it appeared to Judge Bliss that 'the whole rested upon the credit to be given' to Hatheway's testimony; that he charged the jury that they must convict Owen of using seditious words if they believed Hatheway; that the jury deliberated overnight and declared upon coming into court the next morning that 'there was not the least probability of their ever being able to agree'; and that they were discharged by consent and a new trial ordered.

As might be expected, David Owen's account was more highly coloured. He emphasized four points: pretrial intimidation, judicial bias, corrupt testimony, and jury misconduct. He claimed that a few days before the trial he had received an anonymous letter urging him to compromise with Hatheway to avoid 'ruin,'[15] and that an *agent provocateur* had infiltrated his dining room in an attempt

lotte worthies were on the special jury, at least eight of them St Andrews residents. Several had signed the petition to make St Andrews a free port. Several had already served on sessions grand juries; almost all of them would do so at some point. They included a fireward and a port warden as well as the future cashier of the Charlotte County Bank, the future contractor for the St Andrews' waterworks, a future customs officer and lighthouse commissioner, a future deputy treasurer, the future lessee of the fish house on the St Andrews market wharf, and several who would serve in such offices as assessor of rates, surveyor of masts, and commissioner of timber drives or booms.

15. Owen considered the letter to be an extortion attempt by Hatheway: PANB RS8, Owen deposition, 12 Sep 1826; CO 188/35, Douglas to Bathurst, 5 Jun 1827, enclosing *inter alia* a copy of the anonymous letter and Owen's commentary about it; ibid., Owen to Odell, 5 Mar 1827. In solicitor general Peters's opinion, the anonymous letter was 'a ridiculous thing' and a waste of the government's time: CO 188/35, Peters to Wetmore, 23 Dec 1826. Peters had succeeded Ward Chipman Jr as solicitor general on the latter's elevation to the Supreme Court bench.

to have him incriminate himself. Owen argued that Bliss was personally prejudiced against him because he had favoured Wetmore for attorney general. Moreover, wrote Owen, when Street objected to the manner of proceeding by *ex officio* information Bliss declared in open court that the attorney general had been 'ordered to do it.' Owen charged that this gave rise to 'a violent presumption, amounting to full proof, that the Judge had taken cognizance of the matter in Council,' and ought therefore to have disqualified himself. On the other hand, Owen maintained that Bliss directed the jury to acquit on the rescue and alien tax counts, leaving only the charge of seditious language to be determined on the jury's assessment of Hatheway's credibility.[16] Owen argued that Hatheway's motives were corrupt, saying that he had acknowledged in open court that he would not have complained had Owen not refused his extravagant demand for compensation 'for extra services in his office of Agent.'[17] Finally,

16. Owen develops these arguments most extensively in CO 188/35, Owen to Odell, 5 Mar 1827: 'if Judge Bliss used any stronger expressions in his charge than ordinary the Attorney General might be aware, that if personal excitement existed, it arose in the first instance from the active part which I took in having him appointed into the office he now holds by sending at his request his first application to Lord Castlereagh for the appointment in preference to Mr Bliss and several other applicants, and further by procuring from Mr Percival, as a token of Friendship and his long standing intimacy with me, the Patent which he apprehended that otherwise he should not have obtained.' Owen had impugned Bliss's judicial competence in his 1822 letter (note 13 above) supporting S.D. Street's aspiration for a Supreme Court appointment.

17. Owen also maintained that whatever he might have said to Hatheway in private conversation was privileged as between principal and agent. Hatheway's suit in debt and assumpsit for unpaid wages due him for carrying out Owen's commissions was referred to arbitration by Peter Stubs (of St Andrews), Cadwallader Curry, and John Chaffey (both of Campobello): PANB RS36/A/1, 9 Aug 1825. They awarded damages to Hatheway and for several years thereafter Owen held a grudge against Curry, whom he had recently recommended for the magistracy: CO 188/34, Owen to Odell, 9 Nov 1824. As Hannah Smith recalled (Glansevern #14357, above), Owen was 'exceedingly hurt by Mr C Curry's giving countenance to the proceedings of Hatheway,' but they were reconciled during Owen's last illness, and he named Curry as an executor. The damages in this suit were eventually compromised to settle proceedings in other litigation between Owen and Hatheway involving a contested mortgage and ejectment: see exchange of correspondence between counsel and other materials in two casefiles (which seem to contain papers from several different suits between Owen and Hatheway) in PANB RS42 1825, David Owen v. Charles Hathe-

Owen maintained that eleven of the jurors were in his favour and that the hold-out, James Campbell Jr, communicated improperly with the judge while the foreman 'was dozing from fatigue,' thereby ensuring the jury's dismissal and the order for a new trial.[18]

A second trial before Bliss was scheduled for August 1826 but he was unable to go the circuit and was replaced by Judge Chipman, who recused himself as the author of the principal count in the information.[19] In the interim, Owen had embarked on a campaign aptly described by the new solicitor general: '[T]he sole object of Mr Owen appears to me to change the relative situation of himself and Mr Hatheway, that is to say, to have the present prosecution suspended against himself and a prosecution instituted against Mr Hatheway in place thereof ...'[20] Shortly before the second trial was to commence Owen submitted a lengthy protest to Chief Justice Saunders challenging the legality and propriety of the *ex officio* information and rebutting the charges against him.[21] At about the same time he swore out (before himself) his deposition in the affair of the anonymous letter, suggesting for the first time that before Hatheway came to Campobello he had been trying to make his living as a smuggler.[22] He also sent a long letter to Bathurst with sixteen enclosures setting out a matted web of complaints against Hatheway and Douglas and concluding, characteristically:[23]

> I therefore beseech Your Lordship to separate the three Parishes, of Campobello, West Isles and Grand Manan, from

---

way, and PANB RS42 1824, Charles Hatheway v. David Owen, as well as PANB RS32 B (Supreme Court minutes in term), various entries, Jul 1825 to Mar 1827, in particular 26 Feb 1827.

18. Owen's most detailed account is in CO 188/35, Owen to Odell, 5 Mar 1827, written in response to the government's *nolle prosequi* on the information. Campbell became customs collector at Campobello in 1834.

19. PANB RS36/A/1, 9 Aug 1826, ordering that the case be made a *remanet*; CO 188/35, Wetmore and Peters to Douglas, 27 Dec 1826.

20. CO 188/35, Peters to Wetmore, 23 Dec 1826.

21. PANB RS339/A/2a/1823/a19, Owen to Saunders, 19 Jul 1826 (miscalendared as 8/9/1823).

22. Owen sent copies of the protest and deposition to Fredericton via his new agent, John Wilkinson: PANB RS8, Owen to Douglas, 12 Sep 1826.

23. CO 188/34, Owen to Bathurst, 24 Sep 1826.

> Charlotte County, and thereby to relieve the Inhabitants without delay. I leave the name of the new County to your Lordship's choice.

Owen's campaigns against Hatheway and Douglas

Owen's revenge encountered several pitfalls. His attempt to incriminate Hatheway as a failed smuggler was not taken seriously by the law officers.[24] His efforts to have Hatheway removed from the commission of the peace and replaced with two Owen nominees—'a thing never before denied me by any other person'[25]—came to grief when one candidate, John Paterson, was convicted of a fraud on the revenue at the same circuit that tried the *ex officio* information and the other, Cadwallader Curry, declined the appointment, 'assigning as a reason, that he would not act with Mr Owen.'[26] Nor did self-help—setting his dogs on Hatheway; denying him access to the parish records; forbidding constables from serving his writs on pain of losing their leases; ejecting a mortgagee who rented to him—accomplish his purpose.[27] Not only did Hatheway remain on the island and in the magistracy, but he was promoted Major in the county militia and commissioned (by judges Saunders and Bliss no less) to take affidavits in the supreme court, two marks of executive and judicial ap-

---

24. Jacob Mabee's deposition alleging that Hatheway had recruited him for a smuggling adventure in 1817 was taken by Owen in August 1825 (on the very day of the trial in *R v. Owen*, although he was not called as a witness for the defence). Mabee was master of the brig *David Owen*; Hatheway had listed him for the alien tax. The law officers recommended against proceeding (other than by private prosecution) on this charge: 'It will not we apprehend be deemed necessary for us to enter at large into the considerations which have led to the recommendation, but we beg to observe that the transaction stated by Mabee is now nearly of Ten Years standing.' *Royal Gazette*, 18 Feb 1823; PANB, RS13/27/a/2, 24 Dec 1825; CO 188/35, Wetmore and Peters to Douglas, 27 Dec 1826.

25. CO 188/34, Owen to Odell, 9 Nov 1824.

26. CO 188/35, Douglas memorandum, n.d. (stamped 'received' 6 Jul 1827). Paterson was convicted of smuggling rum. Curry became a JP in 1830, the year after Owen's death, and see note 17 above.

27. Hatheway itemized these and other Owenisms in the deposition read by the executive council when it ordered Owen prosecuted, although none of them were particularized in the information: copy in CO 188/35. The mortgage and ejectment are mentioned in note 17 above.

probation extended to him in the face of Owen's attacks.[28] Owen's project of forcing the crown to file an *ex officio* information against Hatheway was thereby foiled. This was not the end of Owen's campaign; indeed, his very last public communications were three renewed attacks on Hatheway, penned in August 1829.[29] Rather than commence the private prosecution recommended by the law officers as his only remedy, he recycled his tales of Hatheway's perfidy to press his case against the lieutenant governor himself.

When news of Howard Douglas's appointment first reached New Brunswick, David Owen had high hopes that his grand project might be realized at last. Months before the new lieutenant governor departed England, Owen was writing to him and Bathurst urging separation from Charlotte.[30] Douglas had hardly set foot in the province before receiving yet another petition from Campobello complaining about St Andrews' regional imperialism.[31] He replied that the matter was under consideration and that he planned to visit the island the following summer to judge for himself.[32]

That the question should have been reopened at all was a testament to Owen's power of making a nuisance of himself. Lieutenant governor Smyth had attempted to end the matter three years earlier by offering to put the separation petitions before the Assembly. Owen had declined, explaining his reluctance by saying at one point that 'the course of petitioning the Crown having been begun, no other could with propriety be taken,' and at another that Smyth's offer entrenched on the Royal prerogative, for just as the old King had separated New Brunswick from Nova Scotia, so should the new one sep-

28. NBM Hatheway Papers, 6 Mar 1826 (promoted Major); ibid., commission to take affidavits, 29 Jan 1827.

29. CO 188/39, Owen to Murray, 12 Aug 1829 (accusing Hatheway of smuggling); ibid. (a second letter of the same date, denouncing Hatheway's abuses of authority as surveyor of highways); PANB RS13/27/a/2, Owen to Odell, same date (highways complaint again). Owen signed his will on September 8, added a codicil naming Curry as executor on November 12, and died on December 10, 1829.

30. Bathurst asked Douglas to take the subject under consideration: CO 188/30, Douglas to Horton, 27 Mar 1824.

31. CO 188/34, Owen to Douglas, 3 Sep 1824. Douglas was sworn in at Fredericton on 28 August.

32. CO 188/34, Charles Douglas to Owen, 1 Oct 1824. Charles Douglas, the lieutenant governor's son, acted as his private secretary.

arate Campobello from Charlotte.[33] It seems unlikely that Bathurst's willingness to have the new lieutenant governor reexamine the question proceeded from sympathy for Owen's views and rather more likely that the prospect of Owen turning up at Whitehall, as he threatened to do on more than one occasion, motivated the advice.[34]

Douglas, unlike his predecessors, made it a point to see the province with his own eyes. The occasion for his visit to Campobello a few weeks after the inconclusive trial of the *ex officio* information (and only two days after Hatheway was appointed surveyor of highways) was the mustering of the third battalion of the Charlotte militia at Indian Island. Douglas travelled to Eastport where he was met by the province's revenue cutter and taken to Campobello. In the afternoon he crossed to Indian Island where he was met by Major Hatch under a seventeen-gun salute echoed by another from deputy-treasurer Jouett on Rowan Island. Douglas, who was unwell, returned to Fredericton immediately after inspecting the troops, regretfully declining the officers' invitation to dinner upon hearing that Government House was on fire. 'His Excellency's hasty departure and under such circumstances, cast a damp over the spirits of all present; and the men were shortly after dismissed.' The officers' appetites were undampened, though, and under the presidency of Major Hatch and vice-presidency of Captain Hatheway they regaled one another and some of the local gentry with numerous toasts, including one proposed by Hatch to the King, the army, the navy, and the lieutenant

33. CO 188/35, Owen to Odell, 5 Mar 1827; CO 188/30, Owen to Wilmot, 15 Oct 1822.

34. CO 188/34, Owen to Bathurst, 15 Sep 1826: 'At the advanced age of Seventy four Years, it can hardly be expected, that I may with safety undertake a voyage to England to remove in person (if possible) the numerous Evils of which I have so frequently complained.' PANB MC416, Owen to Bathurst, 2 Jan 1827, enclosed in Bathurst to Douglas, 31 Mar 1827: 'This place being yet under the oppressions stated in my communications of the 24th last September, I have again to remind your Lordship thereof ... and to declare that if my great age and infirmities will not prevent me, I must endeavour in the ensuing Spring unless relief is had before that time, to return to England for redress ...,' and Bathurst's covering letter to Douglas: 'If Mr Owen should arrive in this country he will probably appeal to the King in Council and I therefore trust that his case has been carefully investigated by you with the assistance of His Majesty's Council and you will not fail to transmit any document or report in his case for my information.'

governor and another by Hatheway to the civil and military officers of New Brunswick: 'May they always set up to the old adage—"England expects every man to do his *duty*."'[35]

There is no contemporary account of Douglas's meeting with Owen in September 1825. A year later Owen gave his version in complaining to Bathurst that Douglas 'has injured me in many points and is prejudiced beyond measure.' Douglas replied with an account of his own.[36] Owen's story of their meeting is a catalogue of carefully documented grievances, many of them already described. Some of the others included Owen's allusion to his correspondence with the Bishop of Nova Scotia (whose see included New Brunswick) which concealed another grudge against the lieutenant governor. Shortly after arriving in the province Douglas had commissioned a survey of religious institutions to be transmitted to the Society for the Propagation of the Gospel. The report included the observation that Campobello 'has a place of worship in a state of decay, originally intended for a Church ... This Island is principally the property of one Individual.' The Reverend David Owen's response was to promise to build and endow a proper church and apply to the SPG for a missionary to serve in it—but only after the seat of a new county had been established at Campobello, an object for which he entreated the Bishop's intervention.[37] Owen also complained that Douglas had accepted an honorary appointment as major of the Saint John militia which was 'incompatible' with his office as commander-in-chief of the province. Worst of all, Douglas had 'expressly declined a separation of the County on the general ground whereon it was prayed for; saying, that we had not force sufficient to coerce the tumults of the Islands. To that I replied that the St Andrews faction caused the existing tumults, and by removing the cause the effect would be removed.'

Each head of complaint was answered patiently and at length by

35. *Sentinel*, 25 Sep, 1 Oct 1825, emphasis in original. For Douglas's indisposition, CO 188/35, Douglas to Bathurst, 5 Jun 1827.

36. CO 188/34, Owen to Bathurst, 15 and 24 Sep 1826; CO 188/35, Douglas to Bathurst, 5 Jun 1827.

37. CO 188/34, Owen to archdeacon Best, the author of the report, 26 Dec 1825. Owen had this letter printed and sent copies to Douglas, Bathurst, and the SPG among others.

Douglas in his exculpatory account of their conversation:[38]

> All these alleged grievances took their origin from circumstances which occurred long before my time. When I did see myself at liberty to pronounce any decision upon these cases that decision was the reverse of oppressive and prejudicial to Mr Owen, as will appear by my having put a stop to proceedings which my Predecessor, with the advice of the Council, had directed the Law Officers to institute, and in this conciliatory disposition towards Mr Owen, did that visit to him originate, which he now makes ground for complaint against me personally.

The most striking thing about Owen's bitter complaint of prejudice is that it was made on the heels of Douglas's decision to abandon the prosecution of the *ex officio* information. In December 1826 the law officers had recommended, and Douglas had agreed, 'that the ends of public justice have been sufficiently attained,' and that, 'however indiscreet Mr Owen may have been in making use of improper expressions, we do not think he can justly be suspected of being either a seditious or disaffected subject.' They had, however, rejected all of Owen's complaints against Hatheway as having originated 'in high resentment excited by Disputes and Altercations upon matters altogether of a private nature . . . The law has provided remedies for all injuries and the Courts of Justice are wide open for the parties to enter who conceive themselves to have been injured.'[39] The provincial secretary was directed to write to Owen rejecting several recent grievances—that he had not been given due precedence in the commission of the peace; that he was entitled to exclusive command of the Campobello militia—but communicating as well that the proceedings against him were to be stayed.[40]

It is not difficult to see why Douglas's decision to stop the prosecution should have unleashed a new torrent of abuse and invective from Campobello. A few weeks after his conversation with Owen, Douglas had reported against the separation project, saying that Owen's

38. CO 188/35, Douglas to Bathurst, 5 Jun 1827.
39. CO 188/35, Wetmore and Peters to Douglas, 27 Dec 1826.
40. CO 188/35, Odell to Owen, 5 Feb 1827.

views were 'very erroneous.'[41] In January 1826, Bathurst agreed that separation was 'inexpedient.'[42] The real cause of Owen's renewal of his grievances was his insistence on reopening the separation file by persuading London that it had been misled by a biased local administration. So vociferous were his complaints that on two occasions Bathurst felt obliged to require Douglas to justify his conduct. Having compiled the fat dossier of correspondence and reports on the topic that makes up the bulk of the New Brunswick despatches for 1827, Douglas sent his aides to Campobello on two separate occasions to invite Owen's attendance at a Council called to investigate his complaints. Owen refused to meet the emissaries or even to accept the letters they tried to deliver. Council responded with a resolution condemning Owen's 'contemptuous and factious' conduct.[43]

Still Owen kept up the campaign, gaining new hope from every change in the imperial administration and renewing his lobbying as Goderich succeeded Bathurst, Huskisson succeeded Goderich, and Murray succeeded Huskisson.[44] Bathurst's successors did not bother calling on Douglas for answers. The New Brunswick executive had communicated its final word on the subject in a Council minute transmitted to Whitehall in May 1827:[45]

> The general charge of injury and prejudice made against His Excellency is most extraordinary. Courtesy, Condescension, and kindness are distorted into conduct of deep and sinister design ... This exhibits a lamentable picture of the perversion of Mr Owens mind.

This was the official version. Personally Douglas tried, 'not at least [to] forget that he is an old Gentleman, and have only to lament, that

41. CO 188/31, Douglas to Bathurst, 10 Nov 1825.

42. PANB MC416, Bathurst to Douglas, 4 Jan 1826.

43. CO 188/35, Council minute, 18 Jul 1827.

44. For example, CO 188/36, Owen to Huskisson, 30 Oct 1827: 'After such a mass of letters and petitions with all other apparent requisites to cause us to have relief, it seems to be superfluous to add anything to this reference, except my most earnest desire that the evils complained of may be speedily removed ...' See also CO 188/39, Owen to Murray, 12 Aug 1829 (two letters reiterating the old complaints against Hatheway).

45. CO 188/35, Report from His Majesty's Council, 31 May 1827.

he should have so misapplied his talents and misdirected his course of life, as to have become a disappointed querulous old man.'[46]

Nevertheless, it would be hard to conclude that Owen got everything wrong in this contest. His reluctance to enforce the province's militia act was partly vindicated by the wholesale revision of the alien tax provision shortly afterwards.[47] The plaster act and the province's enforcement machinery, to which he had objected so vociferously, were soon repealed or disallowed.[48] The rule requiring vessels to clear at St Andrews before proceeding to Campobello was overturned although customs seems to have delayed implementing the new instructions until after his death.[49] On the issue of 'incompatible' offices, which he had so forcibly and insistently raised, Owen's position had been recognized in principle if not in practice.

It would be harder still to conclude that the provincial executive got everything right. Above all, the Owen affair demonstrated the utter failure of its reliance on the courts to control the magistracy, whether by private or public prosecution. All that remained was the executive power of removal from office, a remedy Douglas's successor was to wield quite ruthlessly before long. Nor had its interventions accomplished the restoration of public order on Campobello even after Hatheway finally gave up the good fight and left the island. In January 1829 Charlotte's high sheriff had to call out the St Andrews Rifles as a *posse commitatus* after meeting violent resistance there.[50] There could be no resolution in Owen's lifetime. On his deathbed he demanded that his body to be sent to Wales for interment. He would not be buried in New Brunswick where, 'he said with great emphasis, "I have been most cruelly used."'[51]

---

46. CO 188/35, Douglas to Bathurst, 5 Jun 1827.

47. Compare sections 6 and 7 of the 1822 militia act with sections 16 and 17 of its 1825 counterpart.

48. The plaster act was repealed in 1821; the act for a revenue cutter was disallowed in 1824.

49. *Sentinel*, 1 Dec 1828 (Owen letter), 3 Mar 1829 (Dawson letter), 18 Aug 1830.

50. *New Brunswick Courier*, 31 Jan 1829, copying *Herald*. The Rifles was a militia company commanded by captain James Boyd, of whom more below.

51. Glansevern #14357, above. His body was accordingly sealed up in a lead coffin and shipped home. The story that sailors broke open the casket to drink the preservative spirits, throwing what remained of Owen into the sea, is as exemplary

The Spearman affair

Owen's death silenced one of the most extreme champions of aristocratic privilege in the colony but the melody lingered on among some members of the legal and military establishment. Its St Andrews choristers included Alfred Locke Street, Owen's last lawyer, and the recently-appointed collector of customs James Morton Spearman, a British army officer on half pay. They enlisted the sympathetic support of the new lieutenant governor Archibald Campbell to bring the St Andrews junto to heel. Among the collateral victims of these latest brawls were Charles Reid Hatheway, dropped from the commission of the peace in 1832, and Colin Campbell, former collector of customs but now high sheriff of Charlotte, dismissed in 1840.[52] This was not merely a local vendetta: the larger picture was composed of such great questions of contemporary public policy as judicial reform and imperial devolution. This being Charlotte county allegations of illicit trade and tensions among local, provincial, and imperial authorities about its regulation meant that the larger picture contained a miniature of local rivalries, enmities, and alliances that must figure in any explanation.

Customs duties were a principal source of New Brunswick's public revenue. By a settlement worked out in 1826 imperial duties were turned over to the provincial treasury net the expenses of collecting them.[53] Widespread resentment of the cost of the imperial apparatus and of its control from London remained, particularly as changes in imperial trade policy cut into local revenues. Just before the 1831 legislative session the newspapers observed that while only four per cent of the provincial revenue was spent collecting it, officers' salaries

---

as it is apocryphal.

52. Some of the same characters who worked to have Hatheway dismissed played similar roles in sheriff Campbell's downfall in the wake of charges that he had played favourites in an election. Campbell's enemies included Alfred Locke Street and his nephew George Dixon Street in particular. Thomas Wyer (G.D. Street's father-in-law) wanted the sheriff's job for his brother-in-law David Mowatt so Campbell could expect no aid from that quarter, nor from county clerk Harris Hatch who wanted the job for one of his sons. Like Hatheway, Campbell collected hundreds of signatures to petitions for his reinstatement; like Hatheway, this availed him not at all. See for example PANB RS8/1/15, Campbell to Odell, 26 Mar 1839.

53. See in general MacNutt, *New Brunswick*, chapter 9.

accounted for more than three-fourths of the money collected by the St Andrews customhouse. Vacancies in the customs establishment were 'immediately filled by persons sent out from England to the exclusion of the natives of the Province.'[54] When the assembly met in February–March 1831, Stephen Humbert drew attention to the difference between the provincial treasurer, 'an industrious, respectable and worthy man,' who attended every day at his office to manage the accounts of the whole province at a salary of £600 a year, and 'the Custom House gentlemen of Saint John [who] are driving about the streets with their tandem sleighs, and horses, and bells, and furs, and receiving £1500 a year a-piece, while the Collector's name is signed to the custom house papers by a clerk.'[55]

St Andrews custom revenues fell from £3330 in 1829 to £2860 in 1830, due in part to the opening of British West Indies ports to American vessels in November 1830.[56] Declining revenues brought stricter enforcement of the letter of the law and both factors put pressure on local shipowners and merchants in the carrying trade. During the 1831 session Thomas Wyer presented a petition complaining of the 'arbitrary and oppressive' conduct of the St Andrews customs officials.[57] The petition was referred for comment to collector Spearman,

---

54. Letter of 'An Old Settler' at Pleasant Ridge, possibly Thomas Wyer, reprinted in *Courier*, 12 Feb 1831.

55. *Courier*, 19 Feb 1831. The provincial treasurer, Richard Simonds, was brother to Charles Simonds, another stern critic of the Custom House: see, for example, ibid., 19 Mar 1831. The assembly resolved to address the King proposing a reduced custom house establishment with substantially lower salaries: JHA 31 Mar 1831; this proposal was accepted: *Courier*, 25 Feb 1832.

56. Reporting on the further decline in 1831, the St Andrews customs officials blamed as well the repeal of imperial duties on grain and lumber effective June 1831 and, most importantly in their opinion, the New Brunswick legislature's decision in 1831 to decommission its revenue cutter, which 'has acted as a Premium on Smuggling, and that to an enormous extent.' These cannot explain the 1830 decline. PANB RS13/17/b/10, Spearman and Saunders to Odell, 10 Jan 1832.

57. JHA 14 Mar 1831; *Courier*, 19 Mar 1831. This 'Petition of William Kerr and other merchants of St. Andrews complaining of oppressive measures on the part of the Customs officers at that port and praying that the House take their grievances into consideration,' 14 Mar 1831, and that of 'James Douglas and ten others pointing out to the House that they did not sign the petition against the Customs officers at St. Andrews, and praying that the House make note that not all merchants in St. Andrews sanction that petition,' 30 Mar 1831, are missing from the assembly records.

who replied with a vindictive report 'on the character of the memorialists.'[58] One of the petitioners was 'almost constantly in a state of intoxication'; another was 'a small farmer ... formerly a shipbuilder and smuggler'; a third was 'a fraudulent bankrupt ... and a notorious smuggler.' Of Charles Reid Hatheway, now residing at St Andrews, who had signed along with Wyer, Wilson, Ker, and other junto stalwarts, Spearman said he knew nothing, 'except that he occasionally imports a barrel of flour for his own use.'[59]

Spearman identified John Wilson JP, one of St Andrews' leading merchants, as the instigator of the petition and called him 'a notorious smuggler.' Wilson had opposed what he considered to be Spearman's 'arbitrary and harsh' treatment of the plastermen.[60] There was bad blood between them personally stemming from a lawsuit for back rent.[61] Nor did Wilson get along with Spearman's customs house colleague, comptroller Frederick Saunders. In August 1830 Wilson and Saunders argued over some routine customs business. When Wilson told Saunders he was no gentleman, Saunders allegedly kicked him and beat him about the head and body. Wilson sued Saunders for the assault and was awarded £280 in damages.[62] Saunders took a leave of absence and returned to England.

When the assembly reconvened in January 1832 Thomas Wyer rose on a point of privilege, complaining that Spearman had chal-

---

58. His list is reproduced in Mowat, *St Andrews*, 99-100.

59. Testifying at Spearman's trial before the bar of the House, Hatheway gave the identical account of his personal dealings with the St Andrews customs house: *Courier*, 11 Feb 1832.

60. *Courier*, 7 Apr 1832. Wilson paid for the reprinting of this letter which the *Herald* had published in February.

61. Wilson had sued Spearman for rent due in 1830: PANB RS42 1830, Wilson v. Spearman, resolved in Wilson's favour at arbitration. Spearman approved a warehouse owned by Wilson for bonded goods (PANB RS23/17/b/10, 3 Dec 1828), then revoked the approval (after the lawsuit but before the petition) in favour of one owned by James Rait (ibid., 22 Nov 1830; *Royal Gazette*, 8 Dec 1830). In his newspaper correspondence (note 60 above) Wilson attributed Spearman's hostility to the lawsuit. Spearman gave his own account of their relationship in closing submissions on his trial at the bar of the House of Assembly (*Courier*, 18 Feb 1832) and sued Wilson for libelling him in the press.

62. PANB RS42 1830, Wilson v. Saunders; *Courier*, 25 Feb 1832 copying *Herald*, reporting that the Supreme Court had affirmed the verdict in term.

lenged him to a duel over words spoken in the House during the previous session. A Speaker's warrant issued for the arrest of Spearman and his second, Captain Thomas Jones,[63] for trial before the bar of the House. Wyer's witnesses—Wilson, Hatheway, and St Andrews *Herald* editor Peter Stubs—were commanded to attend to give evidence.[64] At the trial, Wyer claimed that Spearman had sent Jones to him with a letter demanding an apology or 'such satisfaction as is due from one gentleman to another,' for statements Wyer had made when introducing the petition.[65] Wilson was called to prove that when Wyer sought his advice about the letter he took it to be a challenge. Stubs was called to prove that Spearman and Jones had asked him to publish an attack on Wyer as 'a liar, a scoundrel and a coward' in the columns of the *Herald*.[66] Hatheway testified to a conversation he had with Jones in the street: he said Jones told him he was carrying a challenge from Spearman to Wyer and that Spearman wanted to make an example of Wyer in order to convince the assembly to stay out of custom house affairs.[67] In his closing submissions, Jones acknowledged

63. Jones was a Charlotte county JP residing at St George. Like Hatheway, he was a half-pay officer: *Courier*, 28 May 1831. He served as acting comptroller of customs at St Andrews during Saunders's leave of absence: PANB RS8, Appointments & Commissions under Governor's Private Seal. In 1834 he was offered but declined the position of sub-collector at West Isles: *Standard*, 26 Jun 1834. He became High Sheriff of Charlotte in 1840, remaining in that office for a quarter century until his death on the slopes of Vesuvius while vacationing in Europe: ibid., 15 Mar 1865 copying *Globe*.

64. JHA 26 Jan 1832. Stubs had not signed the 1831 petition.

65. The letter itself was not in evidence as Wyer had returned it to Jones and the defence did not produce it at trial.

66. Perhaps this was the same document as the 'address to the officers of Colonel W's battalion' that the Saint John *Courier* declined to publish: *Courier*, 28 May 1831.

67. The closest thing to a verbatim account of the trial is the *Courier* report by George Blatch who was himself called as a witness in his unofficial role of legislative reporter. Reporting the trial from the gallery, he complained in the published account about the heat and noise and a raging headache that prevented him from taking in all that was said. He seems to have been at his worse during Hatheway's testimony in chief, writing that he could give no 'connected account' as 'the noisy bustle in the gallery was so great, that we could scarcely hear five words together of this witness's statement of facts.' It is hard to judge whether Blatch's difficulties were real or diplomatic. My assessment of the testimony is based on his account of Hatheway's cross-examination, *Courier*, 11 Feb 1832.

having had a conversation with Hatheway on the street but denied having told him that he was delivering Spearman's 'challenge.'[68]

Spearman's defence had four branches. The first was that he had not objected to Wyer's speech as delivered in debate in the House but rather to the edited version that Wyer had prepared for publication: 'Such a speech might be innocent and proper, while it was kept within the walls of that hon. House, but it might become a foul and calumnious libel when promulgated abroad.'[69] The second line of defence was that as an army officer who might return to active service he had to defend his honour. A brother officer in the East Indies might treat him with contempt unless he could show that he had not left Wyer's aspersions unanswered. All he had wanted, he assured the House, was Wyer's assurance in writing that he had not intended to stigmatize Spearman's private character. Third, he argued that if Wyer's witnesses, all of them magistrates, had really believed that he was issuing an unlawful challenge they would have acted to keep the peace. That none of them did so proved that it was not a challenge. The final branch of the defence was that Hatheway was a liar whose testimony should be given no weight.

The defence made a concerted effort to undermine Hatheway's credibility. When Spearman attempted to cross-examine him on this point the Speaker ruled that the defendants could only question him about the material facts but that they could call other witnesses to attack his credibility. They called Owen's former lawyers George Frederick Street (himself a famous duellist) and his brother Alfred along with prominent banker-politician John Robertson for this purpose.[70] Their testimony does not appear in the published account of the trial: 'The evidence ... tending solely to impeach the veracity of an individ-

---

68. *Courier*, 18 Feb 1832. In cross-examining Hatheway, Spearman suggested that Wyer had sent him to accost Jones. Hatheway denied having spoken to Wyer about the matter before meeting Jones.

69. Compare Todd, *Parliament*, pp.42f: '... although members are protected in the House in freedom of speech, yet both Houses have held that that protection does not extend to the *publication* of their speeches, as it would then be in the power of any member to pronounce, in his place, notorious libels upon individuals, under pretence of its being necessary for the information of the House.'

70. For the Streets see note 13 above.

ual, the Reporter does not consider it his duty to publish it.'[71] The Streets were of course well aware of the significant part Hatheway's credibility had played in Owen's trial on the *ex officio* information seven years before. Owen had touched on this in his subsequent campaign against Hatheway: 'A man stamped in a Court of Justice with the names he heard at St Andrews is surely unfit for any office, civil or military which conveys the Ideas of honor or reputation.'[72] Hatheway's failure to respond to challenges to his credibility showed him to be dishonourable, on the same principle that required Spearman to defend his honour against Wyer's allegations. William Boyd Kinnear moved for evidence 'to prove Mr. Hatheway's character for veracity to be bad' but the motion failed along with an amendment to permit Spearman and Jones to call three additional witnesses to challenge Hatheway's credibility.[73] In summing up, Spearman 'animadverted on the inconsistency' of Hatheway's evidence.[74] Jones closed his defence insisting that Hatheway's account of their conversation was 'most untrue.' This statement was met by 'an expression of popular feeling' from the gallery. Spearman and Jones were acquitted.

Wyer arranged to have the official record amended to show that he had not initiated the charge against Spearman but had merely reported it when called upon in the House to do so.[75] He agreed to drop his criminal prosecution of Spearman in exchange for Spearman's undertaking not to sue him for libel.[76] Instead Spearman sued John Wilson and John Stubs, who had replaced his father Peter as publisher of the *Herald*, for publishing Wilson's letter against Spearman. The trial

71. *Courier*, 11 Feb 1832.

72. CO 188/35, Owen to Wetmore, 2 Dec 1825.

73. JHA, 9 Feb 1832.

74. Blatch chose not to publish the details.

75. JHA 9 Mar 1832. The amendment was moved by Edward Barron Chandler who had also testified at the trial. Chandler represented Westmoreland in the assembly and supported Simonds and Wyer on the customs question.

76. Hatheway took the depositions of Wyer, Wilson, and Stubs when they swore out criminal informations against Spearman but did not provide evidence of his own: PANB RS42 1831, R v. Spearman. The attorney general commenced prosecutions of Spearman and Jones in May 1831 but they had not yet come to trial: *Courier*, 28 May 1831. PANB RS76, Spearman to Peters, 24 Mar 1832: 'I shall of course drop all thought of proceeding against Col Wyer for libel. Had I not received your letter I should undoubtedly have prosecuted him.'

in *Spearman v. Wilson* lasted four days in October 1832. His illuminations of the draft minutes (Figure 4.1) exhibit the Supreme Court clerk's tedium with these lengthy proceedings. Judge Chipman took an hour and a half to charge the jury, which deliberated for four and a half hours before returning, at ten in the evening, with a verdict for Spearman and damages of one shilling.

Hatheway, Wilson, and Stubs filed expense claims for their appearances before the assembly.[77] A few days later lieutenant governor Campbell delivered written rebukes to the three St Andrews justices, expressing his 'surprise and displeasure' that although they believed a challenge had passed they did nothing to preserve the peace and so 'neglected the most important duty of magistrates.'[78] Stubs replied with a long self-exculpatory letter.[79] In the interim, having given up his newspaper and remarried, he became cashier of the Charlotte County Bank and its associated St Andrews Savings Bank in which both Wyer and Wilson were directors.[80] Stubs remained on the commissions of the peace and of common pleas until 1835 when he absconded from the colony with nearly £700 of depositors' money.[81] Wilson does not appear to have replied to the lieutenant governor's letter but he also retained his commission as justice of the peace.

Spearman took no legal action against Hatheway, who neverthe-

77. JHA 2 Mar 1832; *Courier*, 10 Mar 1832

78. PANB RS13, 12 Mar 1832.

79. PANB RS343/B/2, 27 Mar 1832; PANB RS13, 25 Apr 1832.

80. The remarriage is noticed in *Courier*, 17 Dec 1831.

81. *Courier* copying *Standard*, 23 Apr 1835. A new commission without Stubs's name issued on 25 Nov 1835. Wyer and his fellow directors were voted £702/12/5 by the assembly in 1839 'to remunerate them for losses sustained by the failure and defalcation of the Cashier,' and a further £279/3/10 the following year, 'to relieve them from the reponsibility occasioned by the defalcation of the Cashier': JHA 1839, 415; 3 Vict. (1840) c.59. The bank's depositors had petitioned the legislature for reimbursement and for an act to compel 'the recovery of sums due from the Justices of the Peace ... and the President and Directors of the Charlotte County Bank' (JHA 1837-8, 17) but the savings bank directors 'at last determined to pay the Depositors in full ... without further trouble or litigation': PANB RS623/A/1/a, Andrews to Wetmore (clerk to the legislature), 8 May 1838. Stubs had been a Charlotte magistrate since 1821. He died in Scotland in Oct 1840: *Standard*, 27 Nov 1840. A son by his first marriage, also named Peter, was a lawyer and compiler of Stubs, *N.B. Manual*. Another son, John, took over the proprietorship and editorship of the *Herald* in August 1831: *Courier*, 20 Aug 1831.

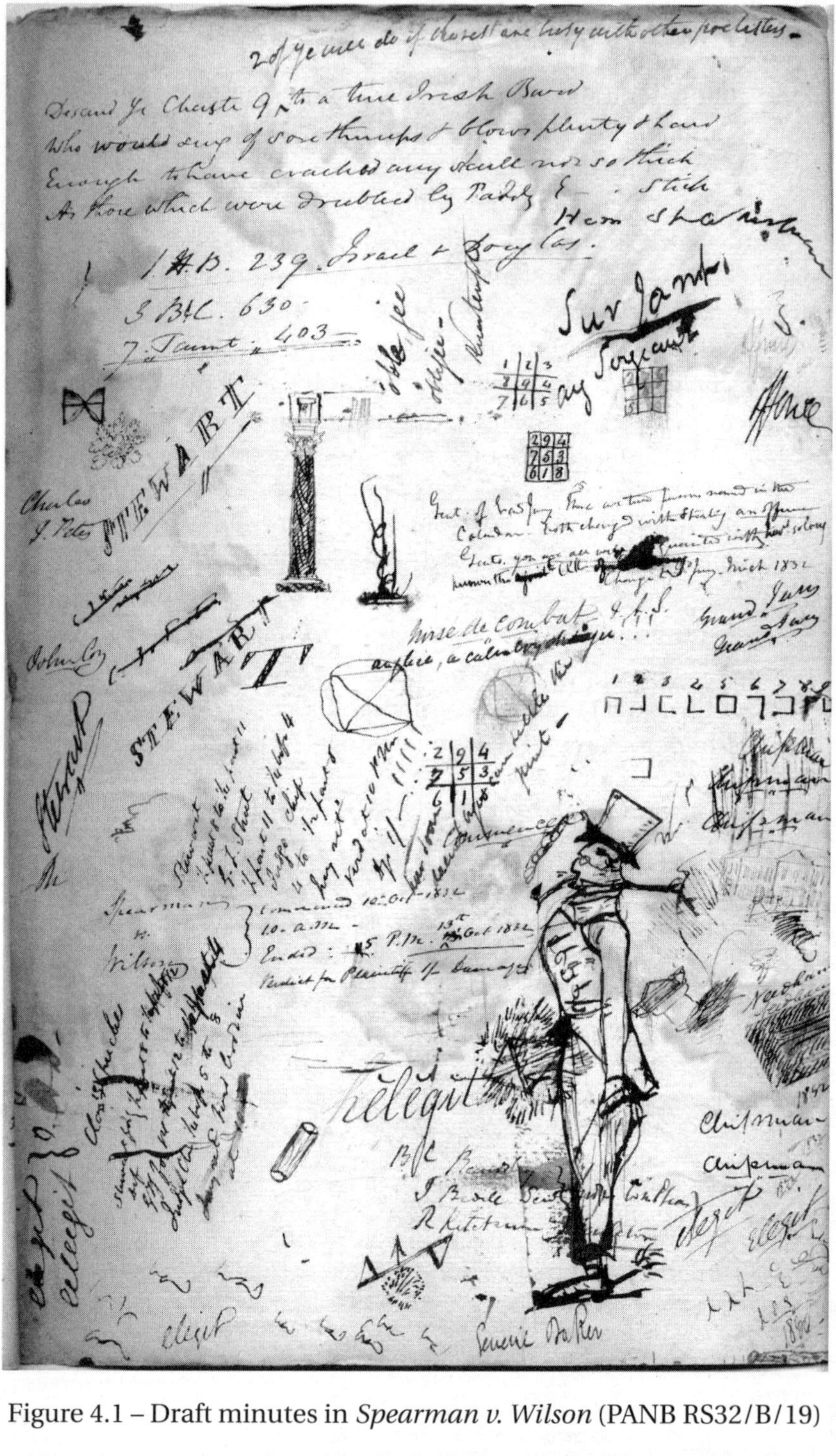

Figure 4.1 – Draft minutes in *Spearman v. Wilson* (PANB RS32/B/19)

less suffered the severest consequences. In October the executive council reviewed a file of papers about his conduct and advised to omit his name from the next commission of the peace for Charlotte.[82] No-one informed him of this decision. In November he attended two special sessions, one to consider new quarantine regulations and the other to deal with jail breaks and statute labour.[83] In December, when the new commission was issued, he immediately petitioned the lieutenant governor to be told why he had been removed, complaining that he and his wife and nine children 'stand degraded in the community.' Hatheway asked for a 'strict and impartial inquiry' into his conduct and an opportunity to save himself and his family 'from falling victims to ex parte representations and blasting their prospects for ever.'[84] Three months later, having received no reply from Campbell, Hatheway submitted petitions from Charlotte county residents asking for his reinstatement. These were laid before council but no action was taken.[85]

Having still received no reply from the provincial government, Hatheway next wrote Lord Goderich, secretary of state for the colonies, complaining of 'the insult & indignity to which his feelings are thus subjected by removal from office without any reasonable or probable cause assigned,' and enclosing copies of the petitions he had sent to Campbell.[86] The first, from St Andrews, had two hundred and sixty-five signatures including those of the sheriff and under-sheriff, justices Stubs, Wyer, Wilson, and Ker, the county treasurer, two barristers, two attorneys, three clergymen, three surgeons, a notary public, two schoolteachers, an auctioneer, and several militia officers. The second, from other parts of the county, had three hundred and forty-eight signatures including those of several justices, assemblymen, and militia officers. A third, from Grand Manan, had another fifty-one names. Hatheway also supplied a notarized certificate that the letters and petitions were true copies of the originals sent

82. Encl. in CO 188/46 v.2, Campbell to Hay, 3 Nov 1833.

83. CCSS 2 Nov, 19 Nov 1832.

84. PANB RS7, Hatheway to Campbell, 3 Dec 1832.

85. PANB RS7, Ex. Co. Minutes, 4 Mar 1833.

86. CO 188/47 v.3, Hatheway to Goderich, 28 Mar 1833; he sent a second request a year later: CO 188/51, Hatheway to Goderich, 20 Feb 1834.

to Campbell.

By the time Hatheway's letter reached the colonial office Lord Goderich had been succeeded by Lord Stanley. He must have requested information from the provincial executive because in June 1833 he was sent a copy of the council resolution.[87] His permanent undersecretary sent Hatheway's correspondence to Campbell requesting that he return it with his comments and that he point out to Hatheway that he should have addressed his concerns to the lieutenant governor before writing to Stanley (as of course he had done)—the resulting 'delay and inconvenience cannot be attributed to this office.'[88] Campbell sent a brief reply in November enclosing council's file of documents and making vague allusions to 'numerous complaints of improper conduct' against Hatheway, to his 'well known disreputable character,' and to his reputation 'as an encourager of litigation for his own private emolument.'[89] This was far from satisfactory. Stanley wrote a scathing reply, beginning with Campbell's neglect to give Hatheway notice of the 'loosely thrown together' accusations, let alone an opportunity of refuting them, and continuing with the failure even to acknowledge his correspondence. Then the colonial secretary reviewed the evidence against Hatheway, which amounted in his estimation to 'a few jejeune paragraphs,' some 'vague allusions,' letters from an unsuccessful defendant and his friend making a 'trifling' accusation supported by 'futile' evidence, and one 'distinct and intelligible charge' unsupported by information or evidence. If Hatheway was indeed well known as a disreputable character, then perhaps council's decision was amply justified:[90]

> But I am compelled to add that I have looked through your dispatch in vain for any explanation of the grounds upon which above 600 persons, many of them in situations of high trust and respectability have been induced to volunteer, in regard to a person notoriously disreputable their high testimony to

87. CO 188/49, Baillie to Stanley, 24 Jun 1833.

88. PANB MC378, v.13, Hay to Campbell 28 Jul 1833. A further evidence of the care with which Hatheway's letter had been read at Downing Street was Hay's reference to him as 'late magistrate in the County of Northumberland.'

89. CO 188/46, v.2, Campbell to Hay, 3 Nov 1833.

90. CO 188/49, Stanley to Campbell, 8 Feb 1834.

> the integrity, uprightness and judgment with which he has discharged his magisterial duties, under their immediate observation.

Campbell replied at length, despairing of the 'many very improper characters and inefficient persons' in the New Brunswick commissions of the peace.[91] Among them, Hatheway had been 'particularly pointed out' to him 'as one whose character and integrity had been publicly impeached and as one who had caused such miseries amongst the poor by promoting litigation for his own advantage and encouraging petty and vexatious suits.' Hatheway's own report of the volume of his business to a recent commission was evidence enough of this. The petitions should be discounted because it was well known in New Brunswick that 'partizans go round with a sheet of paper, headed by a few names of their own party, and persuade the ignorant and unwary to sign' by misrepresenting its purpose. 'I do not say that this system was pursued in the case of these petitions, but it certainly does appear that 219 names affixed to one of them and 23 to another are all in one handwriting.' (Campbell seems not to have noticed that the petitions sent him via Stanley were notarized copies of the originals, hence very likely all in the same hand.) He proceeded to make an assertion that has survived as the sole reference to Hatheway's career in the historical literature: 'I am moreover well informed that these petitions were hawked about the public houses in St Andrews and other parts of the county, for the purpose of obtaining the names of persons who neither knew nor cared for their contents.'[92] Hatheway had not been apprised of the case against him because there was no specific charge. To have told him that he was dismissed because of his bad character would have wounded his feelings needlessly. Campbell concluded his defence by citing the attack on his credibility at the Spearman trial: 'I cannot conceive anything more disreputable to a person in the situation of a gentleman, and holding His Majesty's Commission in the Army than his lying under a stigma of this kind publicly cast upon his character.'

91. Campbell was a scourge of the provincial magistracy: for examples see notes 105 and 108 below.

92. MacNutt, *New Brunswick*, 275.

Campbell's despatch reached London after yet another changing of the imperial guard. Lord Glenelg, the new colonial secretary, was not inclined to inquire too closely into his predecessor's affray with the lieutenant governor. That Hatheway, a half-pay officer and captain of militia, was a man without honour sufficed to close the file:[93]

> There can be no doubt from the circumstances stated, which prove that he is a person whose testimony is not to be believed, that the address got up in his favor is a fraudulent document, that the statement of his emoluments is not correct, and that a man who could allow his veracity to be impeached before the Bar of the Assembly without any attempt at retrieving his character must be most unfit to be a magistrate.

Glenelg told Campbell that his government's only mistake had been to neglect acknowledging receipt of Hatheway's letters. Should Hatheway inquire again he was to be told that the selection of justices of the peace was 'a high and solemn trust of which the discharge must be to a great degree discretionary,' so no reasons could be given.[94]

A trading magistrate

After quitting Campobello in 1829[95] Hatheway had settled at St Andrews where he quickly established a debt-collection practice second to none in the province. While his extensive caseload was not before council when it recommended his removal, Campbell relied on the statistics to press his case on London after the fact. That statistics even existed is the consequence of another substantial public policy issue in the 1830s, the high price of civil justice.

Concerns about costs and delays in the supreme court found legislative expression in bills to extend the jurisdiction of the magistrates at the expense of the high court judges. In 1830 the legislature had to be prorogued without voting supply when the judge-dominated

93. CO 188/49, Minute, 21 Jul 1834.

94. CO 188/49, Glenelg to Campbell, 10 Jul 1834. The provincial secretary advised Hatheway that H.M. Government concurred in his removal from office: PANB RS13/A/2, Odell to Hatheway, 24 Oct 1834.

95. CO 188/42, vol. 2, Hatheway to Odell, 30 Jul 1832, states that he had lived for more than three years 'within a few rods of Colonel Wyer,' i.e. in St Andrews.

council refused its consent to an assembly bill to give JPs jurisdiction in smuggling cases. The legislature was immediately recalled, council's assent was extorted, and within a month Hatheway and Stubs were holding the first of many special sessions at St Andrews to deal with seizures of illegally imported goods.[96] The Saint John Chamber of Commerce complained that 'much injury and distress result to the inhabitants of this Province generally in consequence of the numerous Law Suits at all times existing in it, but more particularly from the circumstance of the greater part of such suits being carried on in the Supreme Court, where the costs are so heavy and oppressive.'[97] Debt collection in the justice's court was an expeditious and inexpensive proceeding, especially when compared to proceedings in the higher courts. Justices of the peace were always available; the other civil courts sat only a few weeks each year and their tariff was much steeper. During its 1831 session, the assembly debated bills providing for judges' expenses, expanding the JPs' criminal jurisdiction, giving them a limited jurisdiction in tort, trover, contract, and other civil cases, and increasing the limits of their debt jurisdiction. Expanding the scope of low law was as popular a topic as trimming the customs house salaries.[98] As Edward Chandler put it in debate, 'There certainly was, throughout the country, a strong prejudice against judges, lawyers, and legal proceedings, in consequence of the many fees payable to them and the enormous expenses of providing witnesses in civil causes.'[99]

In the spring of 1832 Ward Chipman, Robert Parker, and William Boyd Kinnear were appointed to report on the judicial institutions of the province, which were felt to be 'deficient in simplicity and perspicuity.'[100] They prepared a recommended schedule of fees in the Supreme Court: '[A]s we are well aware that the public attention will

96. NBM Hatheway Papers, 'Record of Surveys.' Hatheway took notes of these sessions in his surveying notebook.

97. *Courier*, 30 Apr 1831.

98. The two were sometimes explicitly linked, as by Stephen Humbert in the legislative debate quoted earlier: 'The law is good in itself, no doubt, but the administration of it is grievous and oppressive ... The Custom House system, Sir, is another grievous burden ...' *Courier*, 19 Feb 1831.

99. *Courier*, 26 Feb 1831.

100. Letters patent of the Commission, reciting the assembly's address.

be very much directed to this branch of the subject, we have bestowed upon it a careful consideration.'[101] By this schedule, the minimum taxable costs on a default judgment[102] in a summary action over £10 involving a single defendant and no execution amounted to £1.4.2 in attorney fees, five shillings and threepence for the clerk, two shillings and sixpence for the judge, and six shillings for the sheriff, for a grand total of £1.17.11 (a penny short of thirty-eight shillings). By contrast, the whole cost of a default judgment without execution on a £5 debt in the justice's court was two shillings.

In March 1832, shortly after Spearman's acquittal in the House, the Chipman commission circulated a questionnaire to the province's magistrates asking how many trials they had conducted and writs issued in the previous three years and for other details of their practices.[103] The commissioners tabulated the returns and summarized them in their report.[104] They listed twenty-two Charlotte county justices, seventeen of whom had replied to the circular (Table 4.1). Four of the five who reported no civil business lived at St Andrews. The most active magistrate in the county, indeed in the entire province, was Charles Reid Hatheway.[105] He held more trials than the City Court of Saint John.[106] While the great bulk of his business originated

101. *Report . . . by the Commissioners appointed to inquire into the Judicial Institutions of the Province,* 2 Jan 1833, 19.

102. Default judgments were granted to plaintiffs when the defendant did not appear at trial to contest the debt.

103. Except for one in the Nathaniel Hubbard (Sunbury county) papers (NBM Hubbard, F21 #126) the original returns have not survived.

104. There are numerous difficulties with the statistical tabulations, not the least of which is that the 'addenda et corrigenda' published by the Commission are inconsistent with the tables they are intended to correct.

105. Among justices Hatheway's only competition was William Wilmot of Fredericton, with 1946 summonses and 404 writs of capias. Wilmot reported 1394 trials but these included statute labour suits, which may not have been included in other justices' returns. Wilmot was also removed from the commission of the peace as a trading justice; his case was exacerbated by the report that he plied his trade while confined as a debtor within the York county jail limits. William Wilmot is not to be confused with Malcolm Wilmot of Westmorland county who lost his commission in 1835 after arresting lieutenant governor Campbell for travelling on a Sunday.

106. The City Court reported 677 trials in the three years; Hatheway 747. In 1840, St Andrews had a population of 3682 and the whole of Charlotte county just over 18,000. The City of Saint John's population was about 19,000: Holbrook, *Census.*

Table 4.1 – Returns of Charlotte county magistrates for 1829-31

Name	Summons	Capias	Judgments	Trials
Abbott, Samuel	326	60	287	66
Allanshaw, James	0	0	0	0
Armstrong, Thomas	459	81	331	115
Campbell, Colin	0	0	0	0
Clinch, Patrick	805	24	449	160
Curry, Cadwallader	n/a	n/a	n/a	n/a
Frankland, William	66	23	47	0
Hatheway, C.R.	3584	121	2698	747
Jones, Thomas	382	113	205	10
Ker, William	0	0	0	0
McCallum, Peter	n/a	n/a	n/a	n/a
McKay, Hugh	113	7	152	96
Moore, Tristram	412	51	463	457
Mowatt, David	0	0	0	0
Paterson, John	n/a	n/a	n/a	n/a
Porter, George M.	n/a	n/a	n/a	n/a
Stubs, Peter	0	0	0	0
Upton, Aaron	n/a	n/a	n/a	n/a
Vernon, Moses	62	0	33	50
White, James	55	6	55	55
Wilson, John	3	0	0	0
Wyer, Thomas	23	0	10	7

in St Andrews he had issued processes into every parish of the county.

Although the Chipman commission's statistics did not form part of the evidence against Hatheway in council, Campbell relied upon them in justifying the decision to London.[107] In November 1833 he submitted a copy of the Chipman commission's tabulation as proof of Hatheway's 'unworthy traffic' as a 'trading justice.'[108] He added

107. Council met in October; Chipman's report is dated the following January.

108. CO 188/46, vol. 2, Campbell to Hay, 3 Nov 1833. In this letter Campbell named William Wilmot (note 105 above), 'second only to Mr Hatheway' in this 'shameful traffic,' and Hugh Munro as other 'faulty individuals' he had dismissed from the commission of the peace. Munro had refused to act as a justice in Gloucester county because of his quarrels with the clerk of the peace; he was also in trouble with the Crown Lands department for cutting timber with a license: CO 188/50, file of documents transmitted 29 Oct 1834.

that 'on a trial before the Supreme Court of Fredericton a short time ago, two gentlemen of unblemished reputation in the province made affidavit that from their personal knowledge of Mr. Hatheway, they considered him a person unworthy of being believed upon his oath.' This appears to conflate the Owen and Spearman trials, the former in the supreme court on circuit at St Andrews, the latter before the bar of the assembly in Fredericton. The two unblemished gentlemen must have been the brothers Street.

Three of the complaints forwarded by Campbell to London claimed that Hatheway encouraged litigation. In protesting Hatheway's adjudication of a suit against him Henry Beamish asserted that 'litigation is encouraged to the fullest extent in this town by Mr. Hatheway in order to put fees in his pocket.' But the substance of his complaint (supported by one of the jurors in the case) was that Hatheway showed partiality to his creditor in overturning Beamish's objections to his jurisdiction and in charging the jury. James Douglas JCP, a merchant and Charlotte County Bank director whose name had headed the petition opposing Wyer's anti-Spearman initiative,[109] deplored Hatheway's 'reprehensible conduct' in 'encouraging and promoting vexatious suits.' He complained specifically that when the master of one of his ships applied for the arrest of six deserting seamen Hatheway insisted on 'the tedious process' of issuing six separate warrants: 'The consequence was that the men had ample time to make their escape and did so.' No doubt Hatheway's conduct and its consequence vexed justice Douglas but this was clearly not a case of 'encouraging vexatious suits.' James Boyd, grocer, captain of the St Andrews Rifles, and treasurer of the poor house, was a rival election candidate and long-standing antagonist of Hatheway's. He volunteered 'that I believe he is in the habit of creating business in his court, thereby causing litigation which otherwise would not take place, and know of his extorting from the ignorant and unwary 5 per cent in addition to the fees charged by him for what he terms receiving and paying over.'[110] Boyd's complaint had been copied to Hatheway, who

109. Note 57 above.

110. Boyd made a second complaint, but it did not involve encouraging litigation. Boyd and Hatheway had been unsuccessful candidates in the October 1830 general election: *Courier*, 16 Oct 1830.

replied that the charge of extortion was untrue and that he did not create but rather suppressed litigation. He explained the five per cent surcharge to cover his trouble in keeping money paid into court, issuing receipts, and making change as a convenience to litigants.[111] Not satisfied to leave well alone, Hatheway went on to complain that Boyd was 'resorting to all means in his power to annoy and injure me, and that his motives in complaining of me were not so pure as might appear by the complaint.' Hatheway had proceeded against some fifty St Andrews residents who refused to pay the assessment for a municipal fire engine. Boyd, 'although a militia officer,' had organized the tax revolt and used 'many intemperate expressions which breathed the spirit of insubordination.' His 'enmity has originated from being defeated in attempting to resist the law in cases where I have been called upon to enforce it, and for which causes my feelings have been wounded.'

In responding to the solicitor general's investigation[112] Hatheway answered each of Boyd's specific complaints but again proved unable to resist the temptation to say more than was called for:[113]

> It has also been said for the purpose of giving a colouring of truth to the assertion that I promote litigation, that I receive from 3 to £400 a year for Justice fees, whereas in fact I have never received £350 during a period of nearly eleven years I have been a magistrate which I can make appear to the satisfaction of any impartial person.

Lieutenant governor Campbell seized upon this statement when Lord Stanley demanded particulars of the grounds for Hatheway's removal from the magistracy. Campbell argued from the Chipman commission statistics that Hatheway's claim not to have received £350 in eleven years could not possibly be true. Campbell assured Stanley that the lowest fee allowed to the magistrate in cases that proceeded by summons was 3/1 although more was often charged depending on the number of witnesses and other circumstances. By

111. Hatheway said that he had taken legal advice from J.W. Chandler 'that I had an undoubted right to do so.' Hatheway to Odell, 30 Jul 1832, no. 2 of the 'sundry papers.'

112. No. 3 of the 'sundry papers.'

113. Hatheway to Peters, 28 Aug 1832, no. 4 of the 'sundry papers.'

his own report, Hatheway had issued more than 3500 summonses in three years. By Campbell's arithmetic, his fees must have exceeded £550 just for three years of summonses, let alone the greater fees allowable for capias actions and the additional five per cent he charged 'without any legal authority.'

Campbell's calculation was exaggerated and self-serving. Claiming that costs of 3/1 were obtainable 'provided the suit go on to judgment and execution which they almost invariably do,' he ignored Hatheway's return of nearly a thousand summonses which had not resulted in judgment, let alone execution.[114] If every case in which he gave judgment had gone to trial and execution, Hatheway's fees would have been more like £425 than £550. But the majority of his judgments did not involve trials. The Chipman commission calculated typical bills of costs in justices' courts. Hatheway held 747 trials, which would have earned him about £170 at the Chipman commission rate if all had involved a jury.[115] Chipman's statistics show that in the whole province, about one in five trials before justices involved a jury. If this proportion held for Hatheway he would have had about 158 jury trials. In fact he reported only 60 jury trials, for which his total fee at the Chipman commission rate would have been about £14. He held 687 trials without a jury (and probably with fewer witnesses). The justice's fee for all his trials would have totalled about £125.[116] Hatheway issued 1951 judgments without trial. If every judgment had gone to execution he would have earned about £220.[117] By this mea-

114. The Chipman commission observed that justices commonly took no fee for a summons unless and until it was returned. Hatheway's practice at this time is not known but the later evidence suggests that he only made a docket entry once a summons had been returned: chapter 7.

115. Typical bills of costs are set out in statement no. 12 of the Appendix to the report. Where there was a trial by jury, the justice was entitled to 6d for the summons, 6d for the venire, 1s for the trial and judgment, 9d for the execution, and 4d for each subpoena to a witness, for a total of 4/9 in a jury trial involving six witnesses and going to execution. *Pace* Campbell, fees to the justice in suits commenced by capias were typically lower (4/3) because they were estimated to involve only three witnesses.

116. At the Chipman commission rates, assuming three witnesses instead of six, Hatheway's fee in the average trial without jury with judgment for the plaintiff and execution would have been 3/3.

117. He was entitled to 6d for the summons, 1s for the judgment, and 9d for the

sure Hatheway would have earned at most about £330 over the three years. Since some proportion of the judgments would not have resulted in an execution a lower total is likely. It is much less far-fetched to estimate Hatheway's income from justice's fees at about £300 over the three years than at Campbell's figure of £577.4.9.[118] When it is considered that Hatheway had probably done little private debt collection before he arrived at St Andrews in 1829, his claim to have received no more than £350 in his eleven years as a justice is conceivable, all the more so if his return included administrative as well as civil cases.[119] Nevertheless, Glenelg accepted Campbell's calculations as showing that Hatheway's 'statement of his emoluments is not correct.' There was nothing more to be said.

The conflicts of the early 1820s reviewed in chapter 3 were largely confined to warring factions within Charlotte county. By the middle of the decade, however, they had spilled over into provincial and even imperial affairs. In part this was because the particular irritants were local manifestations of broader issues and disputes: imperial commercial policy; provincial control of Crown revenues; relations between the executive and the assembly. In part it was due to the personal agency, predilections, and experience not only of local combatants like Owen and Hatheway or Spearman and Wyer but of their counterparts on the larger stage as well. Chipman's snap decision to prosecute Owen was largely attributable to their mutual history. The

execution.

118. If half the judgments resulted in execution his fees would have amounted to £13 for jury trials, £99 for trials without jury, and £183 for judgments without trial.

119. The Chipman commission observed that many of the justices included in their returns prosecutions for statute labour, commutation, or fines. If Hatheway had counted these cases, his aggregate fees would have been lower (for example the fifty fire engine assessment cases at 3s each). Unfortunately the commissioners made no attempt to sort out which justices were reporting which sorts of proceedings, except for William Wilmot who was said to have included statute labour cases.

distinctive interventions by lieutenant governors Douglas and Campbell had at least as much to do with their respective personalities as with historical necessity. The almost inexplicable readiness of a succession of colonial secretaries to at least seem to pay attention to Owen's endless petitioning stemmed from the courtesies due to one of their own background, education, and class as well as anxiety that he might otherwise return to make a nuisance of himself in person at Whitehall and at the foot of the throne.

The broader significance of these events is in what they show about the relationship between the local operation of the sessions system and the institutions of provincial and imperial governance. Part III returns to this theme in examining local administration in the context of provincial finances and politics. First though, Part II turns to a different set of questions raised in part by the Chipman commission's investigation and lieutenant governor Campbell's offensive against the 'trading magistrates'—questions about the role and conduct of low law officials in dispute resolution both within and without the formal justice system.

Part II

Doing substantial justice

'I ought not to notice such vermin . . . I defy them to injure me.'

James Boyd JP, 1849

Part II: Introduction

Justices of the peace were protected from vexatious prosecutions for technical irregularities in their proceedings so long as they did 'substantial justice.' This Part provides a close examination of what justices and some other low law officials actually did and how they did it in their dispute resolution roles both in and out of court.

It begins in the woods of Charlotte county, as critical a contested resource as the wharves of St Andrews and the islands, but where the main low law functionaries were the deputy surveyors of the Crown Lands agency. Unlike justices of the peace, deputy surveyors had no civil or criminal jurisdiction. They were public servants on the front lines of the province's single most powerful bureaucracy, a close analogue to the imperial customs establishment. Their technical role of imposing linear order on the landscape by chain and compass was echoed in their low law role of maintaining social order by mediating disputes, peace-keeping and surveillance. In this their purpose was not unlike the justices', and like the county's magistrates its surveyors were not immune from using their public role in the service of private interest.

Surveying was a business, but so could be justicing. Charles Reid Hatheway eventually won reinstatement in the magistracy at the request of many of the county's justices because unlike them he was not engaged in commercial business and so could act impartially in the business of justicing without impairing a private commercial interest. Chapter 6 examines the business of justicing, its activities, market, and remunerative potential, through an analysis of Hatheway's first year back on the bench. Chapters 7 and 8 look at civil and criminal justicing respectively through a detailed analysis of Hatheway's court ledgers and papers, supplemented where possible by the less extensive records of some other Charlotte JPs, to show in practical terms how substantial justice was done. Like the surveyors in the woods, the active justices of St Andrews and elsewhere emphasized local dispute resolution, trial avoidance, and the maintenance of social order through peace-keeping and surveillance.

Chapter 5

In the woods: Low law and the Crown Land Office

The new commission of the peace that issued in December 1833 deprived Hatheway of more than the dignity of his magistracy; it meant the loss of about half his income as well. He owned no property but his house lot in St Andrews. So far nothing had come of his application for a grant of wilderness land made two years earlier. He could hardly support himself, his wife Julia, and their nine children ranging in age from eighteen months to sixteen years, on his lieutenant's half-pay alone. And Julia was five months' pregnant with their tenth child.[1] To shore up his sagging finances Hatheway began hustling for clients for his surveying practice. This and the 500 acre grant he finally received in 1834 brought him into contact with another branch of low law—the local administration of crown lands and forests.[2]

1. NBM Hatheway Papers, item 18, list of children's birthdates.

2. Hatheway's grant was for his military service during the War of 1812. His request to the colonial office in May 1831 was transmitted to the lieutenant governor with directions to comply with it in August of that year: PANB MC416, Hay to Campbell, 11 Aug 1831. However the land was not actually granted until January 1834. Hatheway accepted 500 acres of wilderness land surveyed by DLS Mahood on the second range, Flume Ridge, St Patrick (later Dumbarton) parish, near the St Andrews & Quebec Railroad reserve: PANB RS686, 31 Jan 1834; JHA 1840, Crown Land Returns

When the province was established, the crown domain was put under direct imperial control: the surveyor general was appointed for life by London, land grants were administered by the executive (the surveyor general was not at first on council), deputy land surveyors were appointed by the lieutenant governor, and forest reserves were administered from Halifax by the surveyor general of the King's woods.[3] Beginning in 1817 the revenues were dedicated to provincial uses but land policy remained under imperial control. In 1824 the colonial secretary appointed Thomas Baillie commissioner of crown lands and surveyor general of New Brunswick. As with the imperial appointees to the customs department, Baillie's large salary, authoritarian ostentation, and personal extravagances earned him the envy and dislike of many in official Fredericton. Unlike his counterparts in customs, however, Baillie built a generally effective (although not incorruptible) system of policing the disposition of lands and forests, which were as enticing to squatters and timber poachers as the fog-bound islands and inlets of Passamaquoddy were to illicit traders. His plans for alienating the public domain produced substantial revenues which greatly reduced the executive's dependence on legislative appropriations. For this reason his administration came under the same concerted attack in the assembly as that of his less productive counterparts in the customs, most notably in the 1833 session. The legis-

appendix, lxxxii. It does not seem to have yielded an economic return in the short term. Nearly twenty years after accepting the grant Hatheway permitted Michael Noonan to occupy lot 9, 'until sold, and to build a log house and remain there rent free, but to prevent trespassing and cutting of logs and timber, as also on adjoining lots': NBM Hatheway Papers, 4 October 1851. When Hatheway sold the lot to his son, C.E.O. Hatheway, in 1853, Noonan agreed to rent it from him; by a subsequent agreement he was permitted to cut hay: ibid., 2 Apr 1853, 5 Apr 1854. Later correspondence in the CLO papers indicates that C.R. Hatheway sold lot 8 to John Sullivan in 1865: PANB RS637, Hatheway to John Sullivan, 19 Aug 1865; NBM Hatheway papers, J.A. McCallum (DLS) to Hatheway, n.d.; see also PANB RS637, McCallum to Connell, 30 Jul 1867. Hatheway's sketch in this letter shows four 100-acre rectangular lots (numbered 6 through 9) on one side of the road reserve, and an irregular 100-acre parcel between the road and the river. There was a dispute about the width of Sullivan's lot: Hatheway advised Sullivan to 'get an *authorised* Surveyor to find out and prove' the correct bounds, which probably explains McCallum's involvement.

3. R. Fellows, 'Loyalists and Land Settlement,' Thomson, *Men and Meridians,* I:138.

lature was finally to gain control of the crown lands in 1837 although Baillie kept his office of surveyor general (but not his commissionership) along with his full salary until he retired in 1851.[4]

The Crown Lands Office (CLO)[5] consisted of a central office with salaried officers in Fredericton and a number of local deputy land surveyors (DLS) who worked on a per diem and commission basis.[6] The deputies were personal appointments of the commissioner of crown lands until 1837 and of the executive council on recommendation of the surveyor general thereafter. Their role in protecting crown timber overlapped with that of the seizing officers commissioned by the lieutenant governor in council. (Hatheway's seizing officer commission dated from 1823, a year after his older brother Calvin Luther was appointed a DLS for Charlotte.)[7] It took a very long time for Charles Reid to win a CLO deputation, not least because his St Andrews enemy James Boyd had a friend at head office. In 1840, when Baillie's personal bankruptcy forced him to vacate the office temporarily—he had sunk his considerable all in peat bogs—Hatheway was deputized by his locum,[8] but he does not seem to have been assigned any work and was struck off the list when Baillie was reinstated two years later.[9]

---

4. MacNutt, 'Baillie, Thomas,' MacNutt, *New Brunswick, infra.*

5. Once the assembly gained control of crown lands and abolished the commissionership, the office became the Crown Lands Department. I have used the CLO acronym throughout for simplicity's sake.

6. The purchaser of crown land was liable for the payment of DLS fees and expenses at a fixed rate per diem; the surveyor was assigned by warrant from the surveyor general. Deputies carried out surveys for the CLO itself at a lesser rate and could accept private surveying jobs for which they generally charged more. (However, printed instructions issued in 1852 provided for a charge of fifteen shillings per day, 'whether the same be paid by Government or by private applicants.' An undated edition of the instructions specified a rate of twenty shillings a day for surveys at crown expense.) Deputies were entitled to a commission on the land sales they conducted. After 1830 they also received £50 annually in commutation of their former fees for laying out and inspecting timber berths: Baillie to Harvey, 23 Feb 1838, printed in JHA 1837-8, app. 3 (n.p.).

7. Calvin Luther Hatheway (1786-1866) lived at Saint John, where he served as a justice of the peace 1838-44, and then moved to Sunbury county. He was active in the temperance movement and wrote a history of the province. His son George Luther Hatheway became premier of New Brunswick in 1871.

8. NBM Hatheway papers, commission dated 12 Feb 1840.

9. Hatheway's name does not appear on the list of deputies prepared by Baillie

Hatheway persisted, as did Boyd. The day Charlotte DLS and former sheriff Colin Campbell died Boyd informed Baillie of the circumstances, adding, 'C.H., I suppose, will be looking out for an appointment to the vacancy which he by no means deserves from you.'[10] Not long afterwards Boyd's prediction was borne out and in applying for the deputation Hatheway told Baillie, 'I have reason to believe, and it is thought so by many others, that I have been falsely represented to you by persons interested in preventing my having an appointment in your Department.'[11] Baillie turned him down but Hatheway persisted, sending in a bundle of survey reports and field books to support a renewed application.[12] Eighteen months later he finally received his deputation, Harris Hatch and Thomas Wyer giving bond for his faithful and diligent performance.[13] By then his seven years in the wilderness were well over, and he had been back in the magistracy five years.

But long before becoming an official deputy with access to CLO assignments, Hatheway had been conducting surveys for private, civic, and corporate clients. His duties as David Owen's factotum at Campobello in the early 1820s included laying out boundaries between lots. He surveyed and mapped lots for Deer Island clients.[14] His parish office of surveyor of highways did not require its holder to run his own lines, but Hatheway did so.[15] His surveying notebook,

---

in May 1843: PANB RS7, vol. 98, p.1319.

10. PANB RS637, Boyd to Baillie, 31 Aug 1843.

11. PANB RS637, C.R. Hatheway to Baillie, 20 Sep 1843.

12. Ibid. (Baillie endorsement on reverse of letter); PANB RS637, C.R. Hatheway to Baillie, 14 Mar 1844.

13. NBM Hatheway Papers, 'Record of Surveys,' copy of bond, 26 Jul 1845. Hatheway took the oath of office on 29 Aug 1845.

14. CCA (uncatalogued), 'Map of McNeill and other lands in Deer Island,' signed by Hatheway, Campobello, 3 Dec 1825.

15. NBM Hatheway Papers, 'Record of Surveys'. Similarly, in 1843-4, Hatheway and Hugh Morrison were jointly appointed commissioners under a legislative grant for making a sewer in St Andrews. They took a five per cent commission on the appropriation. In addition, Hatheway charged £5 for 'exploring, surveying, levelling, preparing plans, including pay for an Assistant,' and Morrison charged £15 for '40 days services superintending and overseeing the work.' The auditor found Morrison's charges objectionable, but passed Hatheway's without comment: JHA 1844, app., cxciv, Report on Special Grants.

begun in 1827, shows him quite busy in various parishes in 1827 and 1828, less so in 1829, then with no work at all from December 1829 until April 1833, when he and William Babcock were chosen as arbitrators to adjust a disputed line between two properties in St Andrews. Once out of the commission of the peace, however, Hatheway actively promoted his services in competition with the surveyor general's deputies. One of them complained to head office:[16]

> No doubt you may have heard of a Mr Hathaway in St Andrews, who is so fond of making himself noticed in public that he sends his Circulars printed throughout the County offering to survey three days for the sum of 20/ and can run a Line to a hair which you may suppose answers his intended purpose.

Hatheway's introductory cut rate offer did not last; before long his standard fee was comparable to the guinea a day commonly charged by Charlotte deputies in their private practice.[17]

Hatheway was most active as a land surveyor between 1833 and 1842 with work in every parish but Campobello and Grand Manan. Among his private clients were some of Charlotte's leading businessmen, including county clerk Harris Hatch and justices Thomas Wyer, James Allanshaw, and Nehemiah Marks.[18] He received public commissions to explore and survey lines for roads and was employed on occasion by deputy land surveyors to run baselines.[19] His most substantial piece of business in the period was the preliminary survey 'to explore a route and ascertain the practicability of making a Rail Road from [St Andrews] to the Highlands (so called) on the borders of Canada,' as DLS (and *Standard* editor) George N. Smith's associate over several weeks in November–December 1834.[20] Once restored to the magistracy, Hatheway's surveying activity declined, despite his

16. PANB RS637, Allan to Beckwith, June 1834.

17. Hatheway charged James Allanshaw & Company 22/6 per diem for sixteen days' services; his account also included per diem charges for chainmen, axemen, and luggagemen: PANB RS637, copy of account dated 29 Sep 1835, sworn before Thomas Wyer, 28 Jul 1836.

18. NBM Hatheway Papers, 'Record of Surveys.'

19. He supplied examples of these in his 1844 application for a deputation: PANB RS637, Hatheway to Baillie, 14 March 1844.

20. Their report is reproduced at the end of the (unpaginated) CLO return, JHA 1837-8 app. 3. They were hired by the acting committee of the St Andrews &

1845 deputation, and consisted in the main of such public commissions as the St Andrews common (1842), highways (1843), the St Andrews sewers (1844), and the new gaol limits (1850). Hatheway moved with relative ease between justicing and land surveying because there was a traditional area of overlap between the two spheres and because of their fundamental similarity as state-sponsored modes of dispute resolution.

Low law and the CLO

The fortunes of Charlotte's businessmen-magistrates were intimately tied up with the crown lands administration. Early on, the fiat of the Halifax-based surveyor of the King's woods had curtailed St Andrews' expansionist ambitions by establishing a naval timber reserve just outside the town, cutting it off from its prime hinterland and thereby contributing to the growing importance of its rival, St Stephen.[21] The lumbering, sawmilling, and timber export businesses that were the foundation of New Brunswick's economy had their earliest flowering in Charlotte county.[22] Early St Andrews magistrates Thomas Wyer, Robert Pagan, John Campbell, and Henry Goldsmith all held valuable millsites individually or in partnership with one another. When Christopher Hatch became deputy surveyor of the King's woods in 1809, he complained that the Charlotte magistrates had done nothing to restrain the 'great depredations' on crown timber: 'none opposed it because it suits every person':[23]

> Mr Pagan owner of saw mills and purchases large quantities of timber, Messrs McMasters, Porter, Wyer, Campbell, Lindsay, Cristy, all engaged in this business; Col. Mackay concerned in logging & timber teams ...

By the 1830s Charlotte's new generation of lumber barons was well represented on the county bench, John Wilson, George M. Porter, Nehemiah Marks, James Allanshaw, and James Rait prominent among

Quebec Rail Road Association: Harris Hatch, lumbermen-justices John Wilson and James Rait, and bank director-physician Samuel Frye, all of St Andrews.

21. Nason, 'Meritorious,' 85-8.
22. Wynn, *Timber Colony*, 20.
23. *WPO*, C. Hatch to Winslow, 23 Apr 1809.

them. Their fortunes depended on ready access to trees, rivers, and millsites within the control of the crown land office.[24]

The personnel of local crown lands administration had long overlapped with that of the Charlotte magistracy. For example, Donald McDonald had been at various times deputy land surveyor, justice of the peace, and county clerk of the peace, while Colin Campbell Jr served as justice of the peace, deputy surveyor, and high sheriff of the county as well as collector of customs at St Andrews.[25] Jacob Allan was both DLS and JP.[26] This overlap cannot be explained by a mere shortage of qualified men in the early days of settlement: as late as 1867, Patrick Curran of Milltown took a deposition as a JP and endorsed it 'correct' as a DLS.[27] Other Charlotte county deputy surveyors had close family connections to the local bench: Christopher Hatch was the father of long-time clerk of the peace Harris Hatch; Edward Jack was a son of county treasurer and sometime tide-surveyor David W. Jack, Thomas Wyer Jr's brother-in-law.

24. See, for example, the contest between the Porter brothers and Marks over 19,000 acres licensed to the Porters but sold to Marks, in which Ninian Lindsay was also implicated as agent for an American consortium. A select committee of the legislature charged with reporting on their petitions and counter-petitions noticed, among other things, that, 'If the sale were cancelled, and the Logs were cut under Licence, a large proportion of the Lumber would inevitably escape the payment of Export Duty by being shipped on the American side, a practice which has prevailed in that quarter for many years past.' JHA 1845, 170-4, 217-8. In the same session, another legislative committee dealt with claims arising out of the James Rait estate. Rait, who died a bankrupt, had been the original purchaser of part of the land in question between the Porters and Marks: ibid., 269-70; JHA 1846, 280-1; JHA 1847, 144-5. For another disputed claim by the Porters, dating back to 1841, see JHA 1846, 136-9, and the Attorney General's opinion, ibid., 141-2. For collusion between the Porters and Marks, see PANB RS637, deposition of David Upton, 22 Jan 1845.

25. For an example of McDonald acting as both DLS and JP, see below at note 56. On one occasion Campbell declined to survey the St Andrews commons boundary line, not because he was interested as a bordering landowner but because he was a magistrate (and so shared responsibility for the administration of the commons); the Charlotte bench requested the surveyor general to appoint a 'disinterested deputy' to conduct this survey: CCSS 13 Jun 1827.

26. James Albee JP is identified as a 'surveyor' in the 1851 census, although he does not seem to have been a DLS. Conversely, Hatheway's census entry shows him as Justice of the Peace but not as a surveyor.

27. PANB RS637, Curran deposition, 3 Aug 1867.

In addition, the magistrates had a direct hand in policing some aspects of the forest industry under provincial legislation sponsored by Charlotte MHAs who were also county justices. By an act of 1805 the justices in general sessions were to make regulations and appoint officials to ensure that timber collected in the various booms was safely delivered to its owners.[28] They were given regulatory control over the timber drives by acts of 1827 and 1835.[29] An 1830 act empowered them to fine sawmill-owners on the New Brunswick side of the St Croix for throwing waste into the river to the detriment of navigation.[30] The justices were also peripherally involved with crown lands administration as certifiers of deputies' accounts.

Despite these convergences of personnel and responsibility, however, the main justification for viewing deputy land surveyors as low law officials is what they did and what it meant. While 'land-surveying' was a fairly recent coinage,[31] the term 'surveyor' had been in use since medieval times, and had acquired a complex of related meanings. Like the similarly-formed 'overseer,' 'overlooker,' 'supervisor,' and 'superintendent,' 'surveyor' denoted someone in charge of people or things, especially in an official capacity.[32] According

28. 45 Geo.III c.14 was introduced by Robert Pagan; it was amended in 1823 by 4 Geo.IV c.7 (confirmed by 5 Geo.IV (1824) c.6) to provide penalties, recoverable before a single justice, for breaches of the regulations. The April 1832 general sessions enacted a detailed set of boom regulations and appointed commissioners to carry them into effect. The regulations were reviewed and revised intermittently, for example CCGS Apr 1839 and CCGS Apr 1842. Regulations for the upper boom in St George parish, passed in 1849, 1853, 1855, and 1863, are collected at the back of CCGS vol. 4.

29. 8 Geo.IV (1827) c.15, introduced by Hugh Mackay, continued by 9&10 Geo.IV c.16 (1829) and 7 Wm.IV c.20 (1837); 5 Wm.IV (1835) c.31, introduced by James Brown (not a JP until 1846) in compliance with a petition from John Wilson JP, 'and others, Merchants, Mill Owners and Lumberers in the County of Charlotte': JHA 1835, 335.

30. 10&11 Geo.IV (1830) c.12, introduced by Joseph N. Clarke, continued by 7 Wm.IV c.20 (1837): s.2 suspended its operation until similar provisions were adopted by the Maine legislature. The act was repealed and replaced with similar provisions (except the suspending clause) by 8 Vict. (1845) c.58.

31. According to the *Oxford English Dictionary* [*OED*] it first appeared in print in 1771.

32. *OED*, 'surveyor,' 1a and 1b, dating from the 1440s and so used as late as 1872. Within this range of meanings, the term had been applied to an estate manager [1e (1485, 1782)]; the principal magistrate of a district [1f (1548, 1679)]; and a censor [1g

to one Charlotte DLS, supervisory abilities figured prominently in the qualities desirable in a land surveyor. Reporting on an assistant whose mathematical knowledge and technical skill surpassed his own, he supplied this caveat: '*But* a thorough knowledge of the woods and ways and a *full determination* to drive business through thick and thin is most desirable in the Surveyor as having charge of many men.'[33] The surveyor as petty official occurred in several New Brunswick low law contexts. Surveyors of highways mustered and supervised statute labour on the roads.[34] Surveyors of fish and of lumber were responsible for the quality and quantity of exports.[35] Surveyors of rivers, who kept navigable streams clear of obstacles, had the power to impress labour.[36] There were surveyors of hay,[37] of grindstones (in Westmorland county),[38] and of dams.[39] These were all parish officers, but the term 'surveyor' was used in other official contexts as well. For example, the provincial treasurer's deputy in excise matters at major ports was called the tide surveyor.[40]

(1663)]. A second group of meanings relates to architecture and building, a third to land surveying, and a fourth to the valuation of real estate.

33. PANB RS637, Allan to Beckwith, 28 Dec 1831 (emphases in original).

34. C.R. Hatheway's tribulations as surveyor of highways on Campobello are discussed in chapter 3. The powers and duties of commissioners and surveyors of highways were first set out in 26 Geo.III (1786) c.32 and then elaborated, revised, suspended, revived, and continued in a long list of pre-Confederation statutes: 27 Geo.III (1787) c.5; 29 Geo.III (1789) c.8; 31 Geo.III (1791) c.3; 36 Geo.III (1796) c.7; 37 Geo.III (1797) c.6; 41 Geo.III (1801) c.7; 45 Geo.III (1805) c.16; 50 Geo.III (1810) c.6; 52 Geo.III (1812) c.3; 54 Geo.III (1814) c.7; 56 Geo.III (1816) c.24; 58 Geo.III (1818) c.3; 5 Geo.IV (1824) c.14; 7 Geo.IV (1826) c.23; 9 Geo.IV (1828) c.13; 10&11 Geo.IV (1830) c.31; 1 Wm.IV (1831) c.33; 2 Wm.IV (1832) c.29; 3 Wm.IV (1833) c.20; 6 Wm.IV (1836) c.2; 3 Vict. (1840) c.45; 6 Vict. (1843) c.24; 13 Vict. (1850) c.4; 25 Vict. (1862) c.16.

35. 26 Geo.III (1786) c.50; 27 Geo.III (1787) c.11; 28 Geo.III (1788) c.9; 37 Geo.III (1797) c.4; 43 Geo.III (1803) c.7; 50 Geo.III (1810) c.23; 54 Geo.III (1814) c.2; 56 Geo.III (1816) c.13; 59 Geo.III (1819) c.11; 9&10 Geo.IV (1829) c.23; 1 Wm.IV (1831) c.45; 7 Wm.IV (1836-7) c.10; 8 Vict. (1845) c.81; Vict. (1861) c.18.

36. 26 Geo.III (1786) c.33, providing that surveyors of roads shall also be surveyors of rivers.

37. 26 Geo.III (1786) c.33.

38. 7 Geo.IV (1826) c.16.

39. 11 Vict. (1848) c.20.

40. At St Andrews, Wyer's brother-in-law David W. Jack served as tide surveyor from 1825 until his appointment as deputy treasurer in 1839.

Unlike the parish officers, whose appointments and authority derived from statute, deputy land surveyors derived their authority from the crown prerogative by way of the surveyor general. An act of 1791 mentioned 'persons not properly deputised, nor acting under oath,' as a cause of 'great confusion, uneasiness and disquiet' about property rights in land.[41] It provided that deputies were to take an oath of office and act under the surveyor general's specific warrant; the grantee requesting the survey was to pay them ten shillings a day.[42] It was repealed as 'ineffectual' in 1812, however, and not replaced.[43] In 1835, probably at Baillie's urging, a bill was introduced 'to regulate the Office of Deputy Surveyors in this Province.'[44] It would have required deputies to swear an oath of office, to give bonds for their faithful performance, and to act only on the surveyor general's warrant. It proposed to make it an offence for anyone not so qualified to run lines between grants or lots, except only commissioners and surveyors of highways laying out public roads and landowners surveying on their own land. The bill was given the three-months' hoist and died on the order paper.[45] The experiment was not repeated. Shortly after the crown lands passed into provincial control council resolved, 'It being essential to the public interest that all Officers, Clerks, &c., &c. should be persons of good character, and in all respects properly qualified for [their] duties ... that in future no Deputy Surveyors, Clerk, or other Officer attached to the Department of Surveyor General, be appointed without the authority of his Excellency the Lieutenant-Governor, in whom the whole patronage of the Department should be vested.'[46]

41. 31 Geo.III (1791) c.8. The other causes mentioned were running lines by compass without adjusting for magnetic deviation and marking only the fronts of the grants, leaving their rear boundaries uncertain. Recipients of grants could have their boundary lines marked by the surveyor general or his deputy with stone pillars or wooden posts, to be registered in the CLO. Tampering with surveyors' landmarks was punishable by a £5 fine on summary conviction before two justices of the peace.

42. Where the surveyor general acted personally (as for example in Figure 2.1 above), he was entitled to fifteen shillings a day.

43. 52 Geo.III (1812) c.4, which also corrected certain grants of land in Charlotte made under the seal of Nova Scotia before the creation of the province by substituting true north for magnetic north in the descriptions of the boundary lines.

44. PANB RS24 1835, bill 86.

45. JHA 1835, 395.

46. JHA 1839, 387, printing a council committee report of 11 Nov 1837.

This transferred the patronage from the surveyor general to council (and rescued it preemptively from the assembly) but otherwise made no provision to regulate the deputies whose direction and supervision remained at the surveyor general's discretion.[47] Only after a major administrative and political scandal in 1861 were CLO procedures reformed and the surveyor general obliged to make regular reports to the assembly on the workings of his office.[48]

Like the justices, the DLS had a prime role in the imposition and maintenance of order. Their work not only marked out physical boundaries, but also drew lines between settlement and lumbering, and between deserving and undeserving claimants. They policed and prosecuted offences and compounded with offenders. Like the justices, the DLS were profoundly engaged in the resolution of civil disputes. They were involved in state surveillance, and they actively mediated between local interests and provincial policy. In all these activities the deputies, like the justices, operated informally within the sphere of state authority but just outside the boundaries of the law courts to deliver what they represented as substantial justice to deserving subjects.

Deputy land surveyors were not the same as justices of the peace, of course: they had no power to dispense summary justice; they had less autonomy and less scope to exercise discretion. Unlike the justices, they reported directly to a central office, took their orders from it, and sought direction in difficult cases (although they often suggested what those directions should be). They were not judges or quasi-judicial officers; their authority was administrative and regulatory; they did not so much make decisions themselves as advise the surveyor general. Nevertheless they had and used the power of effective recommendation as the knowledgeable officials on the ground and familiar with the circumstances. Even such a hands-on manager as Baillie generally deferred to his deputies' advice while some of his

47. Sometimes the deputies deputized in turn; for example, DLS Jack employed an assistant 'to protect the Magaduvic and Digdeguash waters from trespassers ... I have agreed to give him one half of my quarter of the Stumpage for helping me': PANB RS637, Jack to Inches, 4 Jun 1856.

48. Although the assembly had regularly received crown land returns the first 'Report of the Surveyor General of New Brunswick' was made in 1862.

successors were not much more than rubber stamps.[49]

Finally, like those of the justices, the deputies' private economic and social interests intersected with their public role and official duties as the transformation of attitudes towards governance, patronage, and political morality over the first half of the nineteenth century turned perquisite into peculation and opportunity into impropriety.

Surveillance and classification

'Surveyor' implied not only superintendence but also surveillance. Surveyors of highways were empowered to collect the names of everyone in their district for statute labour purposes.[50] Deputy land surveyors exercised a more far-reaching power of surveillance although they lacked specific statutory authority for it. In conducting large-scale explorations and surveys they reported on the character of the local population in general and on particular individuals, while in recommending land grants and sales they often commented on the merits or demerits of the applicants whose petitions they typically drafted.[51] They filed their reports with the CLO at Fredericton where the surveyor general (except for a few years following the province's creation) was an executive councillor. The colonial administration's knowledge of individuals and communities in the hinterland was derived as much from deputy surveyors' reports as from the occasional correspondence of justices of the peace or observations passed on by circuit judges.[52]

49. See, for example, the Select Committee on Crown Land Department's summation of James Brown's regime as surveyor general, JHA 1861, 164. Evidence taken before the committee is discussed below.

50. 9 Geo.IV (1828) c.13, s.2.

51. An 1843 order in council set the DLS's maximum fee for preparing land petitions at two shillings and sixpence: *Courier*, 21 Oct 1843. They did not always charge a fee: for example, in returning a survey and receipt one DLS noted, 'these people being very poor I act gratuitously as their Agent in this Business': PANB RS637, Mahood to Baillie, 8 Aug 1832.

52. One Supreme Court judge prefaced his observations by noting 'that a Judge on the Circuit has not much opportunity of making himself acquainted with the state of such parts of the County as it is not in his power to visit ...' and restrained himself from making any inquiries beyond those specifically requested on behalf of the executive: PANB RS8 (Magistrates), Parker to Chief Justice, 10 May 1838.

An early example is DLS Donald McDonald's lengthy report on outstanding Charlotte county land grant applications, focusing largely on the personal merits of the claimants.[53] A Pennfield applicant was praised for his 'former industry and application' but had to be rejected as he was 'now in a state of absolute insanity and confined by a chain to the space of a few feet in one corner of his house.' Another applicant's 'character for honesty industry and loyalty will be found to merit all he asks.' At St George, two lots might be granted to an applicant's sons who, if not yet of age, 'at least they are of full size and strength, and well calculated for the purposes of cutting and clearing woodland.' A St David applicant 'is of age and well acquainted with the nature of clearing and improving woodland. His ability to erect mills, otherwise than his labour and industry is only in common with other farmers sons in the country.' A tenant of David Owen's, applying for land at St David, 'from his former services, and long residence in the country seems to merit attention – in his family of eight children, are 4 or 5 fine Boys, and being brought up in the Country, may soon become useful Settlers.' At St Stephen, 'a very industrious, Loyal, and useful Settler' deserved relief for having expended his industry for ten years on the wrong lot due to a mistaken survey. Another applicant's 'steadiness and perseverance in the improvement and cultivation of land' entitled him to additional lots.

McDonald gave an extended account of Grand Manan, pointing out, 'From its frontier situation, ..., it may become a very dangerous, or a very important acquisition to the future welfare and safety of the Province; much will depend in this Respect on the Loyalty and integrity of its Inhabitants.' There was a great deal of contention about property rights on the island, with various absentee and resident claimants relying on licenses of occupation issued by Nova Scotia in 1783, subsequent sales, conveyances and bequests, and actual occupation and improvement. No-one had clear title to any of the land.[54] McDonald lamented that the original licensees had not been 'more guarded in the description and characters of some of the set-

53. PANB RS637, McDonald to Sproule, 1 Jan 1806.

54. Similarly Cape Breton was originally settled under licenses of occupation by the governor of Nova Scotia so that title to land was uncertain until finally confirmed by legislation in 1850. I am grateful to Philip Girard for this information.

tlers' they introduced, many of whom abandoned their situations, passing their improvements on to friends and relations who claimed the lots in opposition to the licensees. The situation on Grand Manan was further complicated by the colonization efforts of Dr John Faxon, an American emigré, who had purchased a substantial tract of land from one of the licensees.[55] On the one hand, 'it must be acknowleged from the exertions of the present occupants ... it promises soon to be a very regular and extensive Settlement'; on the other, McDonald wondered about the loyalty of the American settlers at this strategic location. Acting as magistrate, he had administered the oath of allegiance to several of them, although he doubted its efficacy:[56]

> Several of the said deponents are men of some property, friends to order and Government, and will probably make useful and Loyal Subjects, tho it is very doubtful notwithstanding their oaths that they all will, the report, current in circulation at the time of the Survey, that the Island would soon be ceded to, and taken possession of by the State of Massachusetts, however vague, seemed to gain almost universal Credit, and tho alarming to a great many was far from being universally so.

McDonald declined to make a recommendation for or against a grant confirming the Faxon lands in his 1806 report, stating only that 'the measure merits enquiry and deliberation.' Three years later, however, having returned to Grand Manan on a warrant of survey intended to clear up the competing applications, he dealt at length with Faxon's claims, describing some of them as gross misrepresentations and in general charging the doctor with fraudulent speculations in vacant crown land.[57] In reporting to the surveyor general, McDonald observed that he had 'very fully complied with your appeal to my candor, in stating any fraud or collusion I may discover on the part of any of the applicants.'[58] Along with his denunciation of Faxon's

55. Another complication was McDonald's anxiety to assist his McMaster relations with their competing claim to the Faxon tract: see further below.

56. In 1807, however, Dr Faxon nearly precipitated a brawl at an Eastport tavern when he defended the British stance in the *Chesapeake* affair: J.M. Smith, 'Rogues,' 167.

57. PANB RS637, McDonald to Sproule, 18 Apr 1809.

58. Ibid. For Sproule's instruction, UNB MG/H46a, Sproule to McDonald, 20 Feb 1807.

land agency he pulled no punches in characterizing one unsuccessful claimant as 'said to be a Deserter from the British Navy' and another as 'more deserving of the Whipping-post than of any Lands from the Government.'

A quarter century later, DLS Smith reported on ungranted lands in Pennfield and St George. He returned the usual commentary about poor but deserving squatters and singled out Daniel M. Wilson as the neighbourhood tyrant. One squatter, an American citizen married to Wilson's daughter, 'defied all authority to dispossess him, but about a year ago his wife's sister laid a child to his charge, and he was obliged to fly to avoid old Wilsons rage, who threatened to shoot him.' Another had to keep his cow tethered because Wilson had fenced off the nearby pasture without any authority to do so. Wilson had managed to take possession of the old St George townsite and commons, accumulating allotments from disappointed would-be settlers 'for a bottle of rum or a pound of tobacco':[59]

> He settled here some years ago, on being obliged to fly from the States, and by a trick of gross deceit partook of the Sacrament and went thro' the forms of naturalization.
>
> His language and example are very pernicious—he declares openly against Monarchy and regularly celebrates the 4th of July. His acts of cruelty and treachery to the settlers round the shores are heard in all quarters. He is universally dreaded and detested. But the fear of his desparate acts will operate strongly against the sale of the lands in his neighbourhood, unless some measure can be adopted to restrain his disorderly conduct.

In distinguishing between deserving and undeserving applicants for land, the deputies also pressed for local exceptions to department rules. In 1827 the old policy of free grants on condition of settlement duties was replaced by a new imperial policy of auctioning off crown lands to the highest bidder. This opened up a field for speculation and threatened to squeeze out the small settler. A few years later the system was modified to permit instalment purchases of tracts up to

---

59. PANB RS637, Smith to Baillie, 12 Sep 1832. Wilson was a frequent customer at the bar of Charlotte general sessions. He was indicted for assaults on at least three separate occasions in 1817, 1820, and 1829.

200 acres at prices fixed by the CLO; larger tracts were to be sold at auction. Charlotte deputies pressed against Baillie's preference for lumbering over settlement and championed the poor but deserving squatter. For example, Smith pleaded the cause of one who despite 'a good character for industry and sobriety ... is unable, tho' willing, to purchase, and if driven off the land, he should go on the Parish.' In the same report he approved of recent efforts to enforce the terms of former grants but feared they would weigh most heavily on the poorest settlers: 'The fear of offending the rich, and the uncertainty of success, have prevented applications for escheat.'[60] Another Charlotte DLS pleaded the case of some settlers who had cut logs on land that they were buying on the instalment plan. CLO rules forbade removing timber before full payment was received: 'I am sure it is not the intention of the Cr[own] to make an example of these poor Devils and let pass with impunity other persons whose property is worth thousands of pounds.'[61]

Once the legislature acquired control of the crown lands in 1837 the policy preference shifted still more decisively to lumbering by making cheap annual leases available. Under the new policy crown land could only be sold in hundred-acre lots 'not valuable for lumbering purposes,' to landless purchasers who intended to settle on them. The applicant had to prove that he was deserving and pay the full price set by the CLO before taking possession, although current squatters had the option of buying by instalments at a higher rate.[62] Twelve years later the balance shifted somewhat when the assembly empowered the provincial executive to survey, divide, and sell vacant crown land 'to persons who are willing and able to improve the same.' This was accompanied by an innovation in allowing for payment in kind by labour on the roads,[63] and by a substantial giveaway of the

60. PANB RS637, Smith to Baillie, 12 Sep 1832.

61. NBM Mahood, Mahood to Beckwith, 7 Apr 1834.

62. 8 Wm.IV (1837) c.2, s.5; the base price was fixed at 2/6 per acre. Squatters could buy the lots they occupied at that price or by four annual payments based on 3/0 per acre (s.1).

63. 12 Vict. (1849) c.4, known as the Labour Act; 12 Vict. (1849) c.19, known as the Commutation Act. The latter was little used: JHA 1862, 'First Report of the Surveyor General of New Brunswick,' 11. One Charlotte DLS claimed never to have heard of the commutation act until a dispute arose: PANB RS637, Curran to McMil-

crown domain to railway promoters, for example the grant of twenty thousand acres between St Andrews and Woodstock to John Wilson's St Andrews & Quebec railroad company in the same session as the Labour Act.[64]

The Labour Act came under heavy criticism from its inception, when the colonial office predicted 'much difficulty in getting the work on the road economically and effectually performed.' In 1855 the assembly's roads committee recommended its reconsideration, saying that despite the legislature's good intentions great frauds had been practised.[65] As late as 1862, and in the wake of an unprecedented scandal, the new surveyor general reported a history of 'such gross abuses in [the Labour Act's] administration, and, such a perversion of its spirit by applicants,' that increasingly stringent regulations had been required. Nevertheless,[66]

> There is still an impression in the minds of many that either by misrepresentation or collusion, a considerable amount of Labour has been returned which either has never been performed, or paid at rates much higher than ought to have been allowed; and it yet remains for the Executive to prepare some measure by which it may be clearly ascertained what work has been and is being done under the Labour and Commutation Act, and also for securing trustworthy certificates of residence and improvements.

Part of the difficulty arose from the interposition of parish com-

---

lan, 2 Dec 1861.

64. 12 Vict. (1849) c.60. The home government worried 'that such extensive grants would seem to occasion of diverting the intention of a Company established for a particular purpose, to other objects unconnected with their proper functions ...' Grey to Head, 5 Apr 1849, printed in JHA 1850, 109. The railway grants created a lot of work for surveyors: in 1862, James Boyd recommended a client for a deputation, complaining that DLS Jack was in railway company employment and neglecting his CLO surveys: PANB RS637, Boyd to McMillan, 6 Mar 1862.

65. Grey to Head, 5 Jul 1849, in JHA 1850, 111; JHA 1855, 230.

66. JHA 1862, 'First Report of the Surveyor General of New Brunswick,' 11. A more sanguine account of the benefits of the Labour Act is set out in JHA 1867, 'Sixth Report of the Surveyor General of New Brunswick,' ix. In that year, an order-in-council cancelled all sales under the Labour Act commenced before 1861 but not yet completed, giving partial relief to purchasers who had performed labour or made improvements but failed to fulfil all the conditions of sale.

missioners of highways (later, Labour Act commissioners) between the DLS and the CLO. Nevertheless the Labour Act and regulations revived and formalized the DLS surveillance role by requiring purchasers to prove compliance with their settlement duties and to pay for previous occupiers' improvements at valuations set by the deputies, who were also empowered to receive applications for land.[67]

Dispute resolution and avoidance

May 1834 found Hatheway on a private surveying job in St David:[68]

> Set my Compass on a corner between John Pagan & Robert Tower ... found that Pagan had enclosed and improved a large piece of Tower's land which Pagan admitted but said he would not give it up without being paid for the improvements and also said that Towers told him the line run where his (Pagan's) fence then stood.

One way of thinking about land surveyors is to view them as independent experts who used their technical skills to establish a factual basis for decision-making. Allowing for their independence, there are still two problems with this approach. The first is that it ignores their efforts to mediate between disputants and to persuade them to accept a resolution short of litigation.[69] The second is that it overstates their expertise and the reliability of their fact-finding. Acting as state agents, Charlotte's deputy land surveyors attempted to resolve disputes on the ground or, when this did not succeed, to intervene by advising the CLO (and through it the executive government) about the

67. JHA 1864, App. II, 'Regulations for the Management of the Crown Lands Department ...' (adopted in 1861), 124. Labour Act applicants had to verify their petitions by oath before a JP.

68. NBM Hatheway Papers, 'Record of Surveys.'

69. Even some aspects of formal CLO policy were predicated on dispute avoidance. For example, the practice of auctioning off the right to cut hay on 'wild meadows' was justified, despite its infinitesimal contribution to revenues, by the necessity 'to invest some individual with a legal right to cut the grass ... in order to prevent the collisions which would otherwise occur': JHA 1862, 'First Report of the Surveyor General of New Brunswick,' 10.

outcomes they preferred. Their understanding of land law and departmental regulations was sometimes at odds with that of the civil courts. The deputies sought to help parties and the CLO avoid litigation, not only because it was troublesome and expensive but because they favoured different outcomes than those expected from the courts. In most cases we only know about these efforts when they were unsuccessful and the dispute was carried into the CLO, the legislature, or the courts. Reports of unsuccessful mediation make it clear that informal dispute resolution was an everyday aspect of the deputies' role and that they thought it to be effective in the majority of cases. Unsuccessful mediations were reported as exceptions to the general rule.

'[I]t is such a fighting time among the farmers,' one DLS complained, 'that is they have got their harvests in & they have not else to look to but their lines so that I have no time to do anything.'[70] Some farmers would stop at nothing to accumulate land at the expense of their neighbours. In the new Clarendon settlement at Lepreau where many purchasers were buying their land under the Labour Act, ox-team owner Robert Ogden was accused of refusing to haul for anyone who did not sign a petition to declare him sole roads commissioner.[71] In March 1861 Ogden called a parish meeting:[72]

> We did not go as we knew that no man having respect for himself would be seen in Ogdens Rum Shanty to attend a meeting called by him, however his Brothers and friends met and voted him in commissioner, and his Brother Ben, Magistrate, a man that has told me he was never but 6 nights in School in his life.

Having first laid out a road that cut several acres off a neighbour's property, Ogden prevailed on one of his brothers to bury a dead child there so he could have the lot set aside as a graveyard, cutting merchantable timber on the property all the while.[73] DLS Kerr's attempt

70. PANB RS637, Jack to Inches, 14 Aug 1857.

71. PANB RS637, Boyd and others to Brown, 3 Mar 1860; ibid., Fisher to Brown, 13 Jun 1861.

72. PANB RS637, Floyd to Gowan, 3 Jun 1861. Magistrates were not elected officials in New Brunswick; presumably this makeshift was adopted by the Clarendon settlers because there was no JP in the neighbourhood.

73. PANB RS637, John Iddiols to James Brown, 15 Jan 1861.

to resolve the situation was ineffectual and Ogden's neighbour finally addressed his grievance to the CLO.[74]

Deputies sometimes anticipated difficulties when they received their warrants of survey. In one instance DLS Allan asked for 'such instructions as I shall be warranted in when I make the Survey as certain lives have already been threatened with Guns and Axes.'[75] DLS Jack warned head office about competing claims to a lot, saying that he supposed one of the disputants 'will be favoring the Surveyor General with lots of letters on the subject he is rather a celebrated character here.'[76]

In 1859, DLS Curran went to St James to survey a Labour Act lot for John Gleason. The land described in the warrant infringed on some improvements made by a neighbour, John Ross, which Curran appraised and reported. He was then directed to amend the Gleason survey and lay out new lines for Ross. Gleason objected that this would cut him off from the main road and threatened to petition the House of Assembly.[77] Curran attempted to work out an accommodation but Ross refused to allow him to survey new boundaries except as directed by the CLO. 'I got well abused by Mr Ross because I would not do what he wanted,' Curran reported, ' and I left them without getting them reconciled ... he is the most contrary & unreasonable man that I have met with yet.'[78] He proposed to return in the spring 'and get them to rights.' Before he could do so, Ross complained to the surveyor general that Curran was unfairly favouring Gleason and demanded that a different DLS be appointed to run the lines accord-

74. PANB RS637, McCutchin to Inches, 25 Oct 1860; ibid., McCutchin to Gowan, 17 Oct 1862. When the community rejected the graveyard and Ogden's brother removed the coffin to his own land, Ogden petitioned to have the property set aside for a school. For another dispute at Clarendon see ibid., Oldrieve to McMillan, 13 and 20 Jan 1862.

75. PANB RS637, Allan to Power, 2 Oct 1838.

76. PANB RS637, Jack to Inches, 29 Dec 1860.

77. If the Martin Gleason who successfully petitioned in 1849 to 'be secured in the possession of a lot of Land' in St James (because he had been crippled by the bursting of a gun) was John's father, John would have been eighteen or nineteen when he applied for land under the Labour Act: JHA 1849, 225; R.F. Fellows, *Census, 1851.* These were the only Gleasons in the St James parish census.

78. PANB RS637, Curran to Inches, 12 Mar 1860.

ing to the CLO's original directions.[79] When Curran's views were solicited he explained that he had tried to 'divide the land fairly and put an end to their disputes.'[80] A second DLS, appointed by the surveyor general to examine the conflicting claims, found that Ross was entitled to all he asked.[81] This was not the end of the matter, however, for three years later Gleason informed the surveyor general that he and Ross had agreed to exchange lots with one another 'to end the dispute' between them, and asked for deeds to issue accordingly.[82]

The case is interesting because it shows DLS Curran attempting to negotiate a fair and equitable outcome even in the face of clear directions from headquarters. He did not view his primary role as a technical expert adept in the use of compass and chain but rather as an agent of social peace among the neighbours (whose opinions he solicited and reported) and of reasonable accommodation between the disputants: 'There is bad feeling between them and both are contrary, and I shall be glad when it is settled.'[83] When he spoke of 'getting them to rights' the right he had in mind was not Ross's property right but rather the right ordering of social relations in the settlement. If in this case Curran exceeded the limits of his discretion, it was not so much on account of the personalities involved as because the CLO had revised its directive in response to his original report. Had Curran not reported that Gleason's warrant of survey infringed on Ross's improvements but silently gone about seeking a mutual accommodation instead, the result might have been not only different but also more typical. At the end of the day, the dispute was ended not by CLO fiat but by the former adversaries' agreement to swap lots.

Deputies intervened to protect the interests of settlers from the otherwise overwhelming pressure of lumbering. When Freeman H. Todd applied for a timber license in St James several petitioners for land in the neighbourhood appealed to DLS Curran, saying that Todd had threatened to 'strip their lots this winter.' Curran advised the surveyor general that 'they are all industrious working men' and argued

79. PANB RS637, Ross to Brown, 27 Feb 1860.
80. PANB RS637, Curran to McMillan, 24 Nov 1862.
81. PANB RS637, Campbell report, 12 Jun 1862.
82. PANB RS637, Gleason to McMillan, 8 Feb 1865.
83. PANB RS637, Curran to McMillan, 24 Nov 1862.

that 'the paltry sum obtained for the Licence would be no compensation for the discouraging of the settlers.' His recommendation was accepted.[84] Other deputies intervened in similar disputes between Labour Act petitioners and the railway company whose land grants encompassed their lots.[85]

The deputies also attempted to mediate disputes between competing lumbermen. DLS Allan stepped delicately around ambiguous arrangements made by the CLO that appeared to award overlapping cutting rights to two companies, assuring Baillie that the mistake 'is *highly satisfactorily* explained in your esteemed favour of the 15th inst,' but going on to say that since he had visited the area in dispute, 'I hope Your Honor will consider me regular in reporting the case.' He proceeded to set out the facts, identify the relevant factors, and make a recommendation that departed from Baillie's earlier disposition:

> Mr Douglas has been at considerable expence in cutting roads clearing out the Brook & in preparation for the winter work, and if there has been any remissness in Mr Douglas in sending forward either applications or the Timber Duties at the proper time which may have happened in such a season as the last unfortunate one I should be sorry that he should suffer so much as he must inevitably do if the present collision is permitted to exist.
>
> I am probably saying more than is consisting with my duty, but when I see matters as I have seen this I think it but right I should state it. Should there be any Licence to Hasty or others on the ground there I am aware of the difficulty of withdrawing but I should hope that the parties would only be permitted at *farthest* to take what Timber is actually licensed if a more favourable compromise between the parties by your Orders cannot be effected.[86]

As with Curran's efforts to accommodate Gleason, Allan sought discretionary substantial justice in the face of legal rights asserted on the strength of the surveyor general's authority.

84. PANB RS637, Curran to McMillan, 2 Dec 1861 (endorsed).
85. For example PANB RS637, Stevens to McMillan, 2 Feb 1865.
86. PANB RS637, Allan to Baillie, 20 Oct 1834, emphases in original.

Nevertheless prominent disputants could use their influence to get their way in the CLO and even to overcome unfavourable court decisions. Consider, for example, Moses Vernon and his son James. Vernon *père*, the son of a Quaker loyalist who helped found the Pennfield settlement, was a mill-owner and moderately active justice of the peace.[87] In the 1820s he was one of several St George grantees whose bounds were surveyed in the winter: discovering in the spring that some of the land was under Lake Utopia, they applied to the government for compensation. Vernon had lost eighteen acres, for which he received a new grant of more than four hundred. This was apparently not enough, for when DLS Smith visited the area in 1831 Vernon pointed out a hemlock stump which he claimed marked one of his bounds. Smith was convinced this could not be the case, indicating instead another hemlock marked by DLS McDonald years before. Smith refused to run a new line as Vernon wished, 'being unwilling to conduce to his acquisition of 150 acres of Crown land surreptitiously.' Nevertheless Vernon arranged for DLS Mahood to run the line, 'but he was totally uninformed on the matter and simply obeyed Mr. Vernon's directions, who never mentioned a word of our debate until the line was finished.' Smith wanted the CLO to 'come to a decision' on Vernon's new line and divide the surreptitiously appropriated land among a group of poor and deserving squatters: 'These four actual settlers are married to 4 sisters – are perfectly sober – very industrious & live in the greatest harmony together.'[88]

Not long after this, DLS Mahood found himself the brunt of Vernon's sharp practices. In the spring of 1834 he surveyed a block of land for James Vernon, Moses's son and business partner. When James

87. He reported fifty civil trials to the Chipman commission. His wife was the daughter of Charlotte mill-owner James Campbell JP. Like his father-in-law Vernon was interested as both mill-owner and JP in regulating timber drives and booms. In 1818 he participated in a meeting of magistrates to petition for a passage through the Magaguadavic boom; in 1835 he served on a committee of magistrates to appoint timber drive commissioners: CCGS, 20 Apr 1818; *Standard*, 19 Mar 1835. He was commissioner for the great road from St Andrews to Saint John—the disputed lots discussed below were along this route—and in the mid-1830s moved to the latter city, setting up as a timber exporter. His widowed daughter became W.F.W. Owen's second wife.

88. PANB RS686; PANB RS637, Smith's report, 16 Nov 1831.

pronounced himself satisfied and said he had 'no wish whatever' to purchase more land on that stream, Mahood proceeded to lay out an adjacent lot for Henry McPherson. In the mean time, unbeknownst to Mahood and McPherson, James Vernon went to Fredericton to apply for the same land. He returned with a warrant of survey directed to Mahood which he kept from the DLS despite encountering him several times. A week after Mahood had completed the McPherson survey, Moses Vernon handed him the order in favour of his son, urging him to go and survey it immediately. ('He spoke rather passionately concerning it,' Mahood recorded in his journal.) Mahood declined, saying he would have to write to the CLO first. James Vernon took Mahood's letter to Fredericton and returned with a letter directing Mahood to survey a lot for him and to refrain from doing anything which would 'occasion any difficulties to the department.' An embarrassed Mahood wrote a lengthy explanation to the acting surveyor general, 'not knowing what representations Mr Vernon might have made respecting me, to you when he was last in Fredericton.'[89]

Mahood surveyed another fifty acre grant for James, this one adjacent to a Vernon millsite in Lancaster parish, Saint John county. Shortly after James began developing the site, neighbouring landowners complained that his grant infringed on their properties. The government encouraged them to test their title by an action of ejectment, undertaking to cover the expenses if their claim was upheld.[90] At the same time, the CLO sent its most senior official, Andrew Inches, to verify Mahood's survey at Vernon's expense, and when he proclaimed the bounds to be good Vernon felt himself safe in defending the ejectment.[91] The suit against him succeeded, not for any flaw in the survey but because the legal descriptions of the plaintiffs' properties were sufficiently imprecise to comprehend the land subsequently granted to Vernon.[92] Vernon petitioned the assembly for relief and within five years of the adverse judgment he was voted more than a hundred and fifty pounds credit against future crown land pur-

89. PANB RS637, Mahood to Beckwith, 10 Jun 1834; NBM Mahood, 16, 20, and 29 May 1834.

90. PANB RS637/156, Law officers' opinion, 17 Mar 1851.

91. JHA 1847, 168.

92. 4 NBR (2 Kerr) 351.

chases. The plaintiffs had to wait nearly ten years before their £44 expense claim against the government was upheld by the crown law officers.[93]

The deputies preferred to avoid litigation, which put their work into question and cost them court days for which they were grudgingly compensated if at all.[94] One DLS advised Baillie to withdraw a particular lot from sale, 'as I am sure there will be interminable Lawsuits respecting it.'[95] Another simply observed that none of the licensees in his district complied with regulations without suggesting that anything should be done about it.[96] At least some deputies recognized a disjuncture between their determinations and those of the courts. For example, in the first Vernon dispute noticed above DLS Smith complained that the courts ignored the 'obvious' and 'common sense' meaning of the word *or* in formal descriptions of land grants, making a 'real stumbling block both to Proprietors and Surveyors':[97]

> [I]f a line be described as running South 11° West 40 Chains *or* to the north line of a grant to C.D., the Surveyor, one should think, would be warranted to lay off the 40 chains, if he found them, and proceed onward until he met C.D.'s north line; but the Lawyers and Judges say, 'No. You must lay off the 40 chains, if you find them, and then stop—but if you meet C.D.'s north line *before* the 40 chains are completed, you must *stop at that line*.'
>
> This appears like Government saying, 'Head I win, Harp you lose'—but I understand it has always been ruled so by the Bench of this Province ...

93. For examples of other legislative grants to compensate landowners and unsuccessful litigants for past CLO mistakes, JHA 1850, 147f (report on two petitions involving land granted to Rev. James Alley, JP).

94. For example, PANB RS637, McDonald to Sproule, 10 Aug 1811, requesting that he be sent his report and plan of survey for 'the trial I am so unfortunate to have depending.' When DLS Mahood was subpoenaed by the Crown to appear as a witness in a supreme court trial relating to a land grant, the auditors objected to his account for twelve days attendance at Fredericton, saying, 'whatever may be the merits of the case, it is a matter for consideration whether it can properly come under the head of disbursements' in the CLO: JHA 1837-8, Appendix, n.p.

95. PANB RS637, Mahood to Baillie, 15 Jul 1847. Baillie complied.

96. PANB RS637, Jacob Allan report on lumber inspection, 25 May 1837.

97. PANB RS637, Smith's report, 16 Nov 1831, original emphases.

Smith suggested referring the question to the crown law officers, 'so that we should act according to some fixed and legal principle, instead of the tampering hesitancy under which we are often compelled to shift, without giving satisfaction to contending parties, our employers, *or ourselves.*'

These discrepancies between substantial and procedural justice and between low and high readings of what the law required were compounded by the shortcomings of survey technique. Early surveys relied on compass bearings without understanding or accounting for magnetic variation. In many cases only the fronts or the lateral lines of grants were actually measured, the remaining bounds being left to extrapolation. The 'permanent' monuments marking bounds were more often than not wooden stakes hammered into the ground or blazes cut in the bark of (sometimes dead) trees.[98] Surveyors' equipment was neither standardized nor centrally calibrated. In 1785, deputies were warned to be 'particularly careful that the Instrument you use in all surveys is correct and true.'[99] Despite sending his instrument to 'the most eminent Artist I could hear of in Boston,' DLS McDonald confessed in 1803, 'I have not that implied confidence in it yet that I could wish.'[100] Half a century later, when Baillie asked the lieutenant governor for permission to send the CLO's in-house instruments to London for repair and adjustment,[101] deputies were still supplying their own idiosyncratic equipment.[102] An 1848 inspection

98. On all three points see 31 Geo.III c.8 (1791), which was itself soon repealed as ineffectual. Printed instructions for deputies in 1824 required them to 'attend minutely' to 'local variation and other peculiarities in the Magnetic Needle,' and to 'be very particular to run out one side and part of the rear line,' drawing solid lines on their plans for the measured portions and dotted lines for the extrapolations. New instructions issued in May 1852 attempted to improve the accuracy of surveys not only by further technical specifications but also by requiring the DLS to administer an oath to chainmen, to measure their chains, and to avoid contradicting previous surveys without prior authorization. For a late example of lost landmarks, PANB RS637, Bunten to McMillan, 5 Apr 1862.

99. Sproule circular, quoted in Thomson, *Men and Meridians*, I:139.

100. PANB RS637, McDonald to Sproule, 9 Apr 1803.

101. PANB RS637, 16 Dec 1845.

102. For example, in applying for a DLS appointment Hatheway noted, 'The Instrument I use is a brass Compass card four inches diameter wedge needle with Ball and socket has been compared with the instruments used by Deputies Smith, Ma-

found that 'almost all the chains are of imperfect lengths.'[103] There was no formal training, although after 1824 'gentlemen applying for deputations' were notionally required to 'give their gratuitous attendance at the Surveyor General's Office for at least three months' and to pass an examination.[104] Andrew Inches reported in 1846 that several deputies were 'not competent':[105]

> They are, generally speaking, unwilling and unable to bear the expence of procuring new or better instruments, and throughout all the Deputies belonging to the Department, there are probably not more than two or three who at all attempt improvement, or any better acquaintance with the theory of their business.

Technical accuracy was also compromised by policy. Instead of a systematic centralized approach to laying out provincial land, Baillie protested, the government allowed 'every individual who may wish to purchase 100 acres of Land to have a separate Survey made, and to become the paymaster of the Surveyor. It is virtually taking the Surveying of the Province out of the hands of the Government and placing it in the hands of ten thousand irresponsible persons.' Returning to the subject the following year, he argued 'that the man does not live on the face of the earth who can correctly compile those surveys.'[106] Considering these obstacles the deputies' task of resolving disputes was often, as DLS Allan's remark suggested, less a matter of applying mathematics than of managing men.[107]

---

hood, Allan & Campbell and by an approved instrument of Col Marks and found correct.' PANB RS637, Hatheway to Baillie, 20 Sep 1843.

103. PANB RS637, Surveyor General circular.

104. PANB RS637, printed instructions for deputies, n.d. (1824). Applying for a permanent deputation in 1852, Edward Jack listed plane geometry, algebra, and trigonometry among the subjects on which he was prepared to be examined, claiming familiarity with 'such parts of Surveying and Engineering as are advertised to be taught in Kings College, Fr[edericto]n by Mr McMahon Cregan': PANB RS637, Jack to Wilmot, 9 Oct 1852. Five years later he wanted his brother to spend a month or two copying plans in the office so that he too could apply for a deputation: ibid., Jack to Inches, 7 Sep 1857.

105. PANB RS637, Inches report on land surveyors and seizing officers, Sep 1846.

106. JHA 1848, 43; ibid. 1849, 105.

107. Above, at note 33.

Order and disorder

In early March 1843 DLS Mahood set off by sleigh and snowshoes to inspect the timber cut on crown licenses in the backwoods of Charlotte county. He slept in settlers' cabins, in timber shanties, and under canvas in the snow. On three consecutive nights he was troubled by dreams, which he recorded in his journal:[108]

> On Saturday night last I dreamed of travelling with my horse & sleigh along a road in the woods and seeing a wolf coming towards me, I got out of the sleigh and was taking off the cover of my gun to fire. Just so I awoke.
>
> On Sunday night I dreamed that there had been a child of mine killed and that I had had some concern in it . . . I was there and was alarmed lest I should be found out.
>
> Last night I dreamed . . . [that] I was in the water and was teaching my son James to swim . . . his mother wading out from a Point to meet him . . . and told her that as he could now swim he would perhaps after be attempting it alone and told her to watch him and not allow it lest he would be drowned.

Days spent imposing order on the landscape and its human exploiters contended with nights of imagined ferocity and panic. For this long-serving paragon of the crown land service, disorder would win at the last.

William Mahood was born in County Cavan, Ireland, about 1811 and emigrated to New Brunswick with his parents and two brothers in 1818.[109] He studied surveying under DLS Smith at St Andrews in 1830 and was deputized by Baillie the following year.[110] Based at Magaguadavic in St George parish he soon distinguished himself by the accuracy of his surveys and the elegance of his draftsmanship. He received a provincial commission as seizing officer in 1835 and moved to St Andrews to become Local Deputy for Charlotte in 1843, thereby succeeding Colin Campbell and forestalling Hatheway's application.[111]

108. NBM Mahood, 7 Mar 1843.

109. They were protestants. In adulthood, William belonged to the Church of England; his brother Samuel, who became a DLS for Queen's county, joined the Methodists.

110. PANB RS637, Mahood to Wilmot, 30 Aug 1852.

111. PANB RS637, Executive Council, Mahood to Steves, 10 Nov 1854.

In addition to the usual duties of a DLS, Mahood was commissioned to survey the county boundaries[112] and to prepare a plan of all the public roads. He made the first detailed map of Charlotte county. Mahood's voluminous surviving correspondence, journals, and field books illuminate the work of a busy DLS between 1830 and 1855.[113] They also reveal an inquisitive, observant, albeit sometimes impatient mind. Mahood's notebooks record the details of his daily work and expenditures but include as well neighbourhood sketches, family, church, militia, and election incidents, weddings and funerals, folk remedies and recipes, music, lyrics and poetry, graveyard inscriptions, and dreams.

Mahood spent many days each year measuring out and marking the boundaries of grants, timber licenses, lots, and road allowances—sometimes in the face of determined opposition[114]—but this was far from all that his DLS duties entailed. There was the logistical work of organizing men and supplies for surveying expeditions, seemingly endless paperwork in preparing field notes and reports of surveys, days in the CLO at Fredericton copying plans, long winter treks through the lumbering districts to count stumps and audit licenses, writing correspondence and petitions for land-seekers both great and small, conducting sales of land, leases, and seized timber, making up accounts, testifying in court, patching up quarrels between neighbouring landowners, valuing real estate, woods, and improvements, detecting timber poaching and pursuing the offenders, exploring uncharted country for the railroad company, advising head office, and negotiating relations with a succession of surveyors general.

July 1838 found Mahood in the role of detective as he tried to track down some lumber he had seized for nonpayment that spring. Finding that much of it had been cut into boards by a Lepreau sawmill operator who had bought the logs from the delinquent lumberman,

112. NBM Mahood, book #16, 21 Oct 1845-19 Dec 1845. For his difficulties in getting paid for this work, JHA 1846, Appendix, Report on Public Accounts, ccvi-ccvii; JHA 1847, 329.

113. NBM Mahood; PANB RS637/7/d/0/7 and infra.

114. He abandoned one survey when the neighbouring settler threatened him with an axe, but disregarded another's threat of a lawsuit: PANB RS637, Mahood to Baillie, 12 Jun 1837; ibid., Mahood to Wilmot, 23 Feb 1853.

he spent the better part of a day trying to convince both parties to enter into bonds for the duty owed. When they could not find the necessary security Mahood travelled to Saint John in search of the lumber which had been shipped there. Arriving in the evening, he made some inquiries then went to the theatre. The next morning he learned that three cargoes from the Lepreau mill were lying on a wharf in Portland ('called St Helena from its being isolated') mixed in with other boards. Having first marked the piles of deals with the crown's broad arrow, Mahood made inquiries among the timber merchants, only to discover that part of the Lepreau shipments had been sold and some already sent to Europe. He hunted up another DLS and set him to watch over 'St Helena' while Mahood searched the other wharves where purchasers of the Lepreau timber were known to keep their stocks. Unable to find any more of the missing boards, he arranged for the court of vice-admiralty to serve a monition on one of the purchasers. On his way home to St George, Mahood stopped again at the Lepreau mill where he marked a pile of boards and cautioned the operator not to cut or remove any more of the marked lumber. This investigation took five days in all. A month later, Mahood returned to Lepreau where he found a Saint John schooner loading the seized lumber. After halting the transfer Mahood seized all the sawn lumber and logs at the mill, leaving a man in charge 'with orders to prevent any person taking them away.'[115]

This was not an isolated incident: Mahood seized about three hundred thousand superficial feet of lumber cut on James Rait's license at Port Lepreau in April 1839. Despite a promise from Rait's agent to leave the logs until they were paid for, when Mahood visited one of the mills in August he found them being sawed into boards.[116] Again in 1846 a Lepreau sawmill cut logs seized by Mahood despite his warning against 'touching any of them until they were settled for.'[117]

115. NBM Mahood, 9-13 Jul 1838, 9 Aug 1838. Sawmilling appears to have been a cutthroat business in the Lepreau area: see, for example, the case of a mill operator charged with the capital crime of arson by four of his woodsmen, allegedly to extort money from him: *Courier*, 26 Nov 1842, copying *Chronicle* and *New Brunswicker*.

116. Ibid., 11 Apr 1839, 16 Apr 1839, 7 May 1839, 14 Jun 1839, 25 Aug 1839.

117. Ibid., 12-14 Oct 1846, 12 Nov 1846.

The provincial timber statutes permitted licensees who cut more trees than they had bargained for to pay stumpage or duty on the excess.[118] A legislative investigation of the casual revenue accounts submitted numerous 'interrogatories' to the CLO querying discrepancies between DLS reports of excesses and receipts of duties. Many of the answers revealed settlements, deductions, and other adjustments.[119] Mahood's responsibilities included negotiating with the lumbermen for the excess cut, often taking bonds or promissory notes for future payment.[120] It could be difficult to collect what was owed. While at St Stephen for an auction in February 1843 Mahood called twice on one licensee for unpaid dues but he was not at home. This was repeated the following morning; in the afternoon, when Mahood finally tracked him down, the delinquent said he could not pay just then as his money was in the bank. Two days later Mahood returned by arrangement, collected the money, then 'travelled homewards eighteen miles in the storm.'[121] When payment was not forthcoming, Mahood was responsible for advertising and selling the seized lumber.[122] The amounts involved could be substantial. In 1842 James Allanshaw JP petitioned the assembly for an adjustment of his accounts with the CLO, which claimed he owed almost £18,000 for timber cut on his various leases, including the excesses. He supplied certificates from Mahood showing that his cull had been deficient over several years to the value of about seven hundred pounds. A legislative committee recommended 'that under all the circumstances of the case, [Allanshaw] should be relieved on surrendering all the Leases, and paying immediately the sum of £1,100.'[123] When

118. For an overview, Wynn, *Timber Colony*, chapter 6.

119. In making his return, Baillie observed that it 'was prepared by the Accountant of the Crown Land Office, but whether correct or not it is impossible for me to say.' JHA 1840, App., Crown Land Returns &c., clv.

120. For example NBM Mahood, 26 Apr 1843.

121. Ibid., 8-11 Feb 1843.

122. For example, the twenty-four thousand feet cut in excess by John Campbell on the Rait block 'which he had neglected to pay for and which had been condemned and was now offered for sale at 10/ per thousand': ibid., 28 Jan 1843, 8 Feb 1843.

123. JHA 1842, 286: 'The case is involved in some complexity and difficulty, and the Committee feel satisfied that by adopting this course, the true interests of the Government will be served.'

James Rait JP died a bankrupt in self-imposed exile, his creditors and executors wrangled with the government for years over his timber dues and licenses.[124]

Making collections was aggravating and time-consuming, but it was essential if the DLS was to receive any pay for much of this work.[125] Mahood and his colleagues worked on commission. When it was payable, at what rate, and on what amounts were continuing topics of contention.[126] Not long after his appointment as local deputy for Charlotte, Mahood received a stinging rebuke from Baillie who accused him of employing an 'insolent and dictatorial tone' in correspondence about his five per cent commission on land sales, which Mahood had copied to the Receiver General. Mahood thought he should receive five per cent of the purchase price under the new regulations; Baillie's position was that he was only entitled to five per cent of the initial instalment made on the day of the sale. (To make matters worse, MHA James Boyd was encouraging his constituents to pay nothing down at the sale.)[127] At the height of the assembly's struggle with the executive over control of crown lands, the Board of Audit disallowed numerous CLO accounts including many of Mahood's. Among these was his claim for expenses incurred in seizing

124. Rait had fled to Jamaica to escape his debts. PANB RS637, Thompson to Baillie, 16 Aug 1842; ibid., Andrews to Baillie, 20 Dec 1850; and see references in note 24 above.

125. See, for example, the complaint of Mahood's successor, enclosing his account of lumber cut in his district: 'I have had a great deal of trouble to collect it. I have been dunning for one week. I think the fact of taking a note for Stumpage which I did has not a good effect and I do not know but that it discharges the logs at any rate. When a country man gives a note for a debt he considers it paid.' One lumber company dishonoured its note, '& I have been dunning ever since.' PANB RS637, Jack to Inches, 16 May 1856. On another occasion Jack complained that he had 'not made a living this winter out of the Surveyorship as the county is so poor that I do not get half paid for what I do': ibid., Jack to Brown, 3 Mar 1856.

126. As was whether the deputy could protect his commission on the original amount when the offender settled for a lesser penalty. For example PANB RS637, McCallum to Connell, 28 June 1867: 'I cannot see by what right Mr R claims exemption from paying $\frac{3}{4}$ of my lawful dues, because the Government seen fit to take his Bond for four hundred dollars, in payment for the Stumpage, exclusive of my dues.'

127. PANB RS637, Mahood to Baillie, 16 Aug 1843; Mahood to Receiver General, 16 Aug 1843; Mahood to Baillie, 22 Aug 1843 (two letters, one enclosing Boyd correspondence); Mahood to Baillie, 3 Oct 1843.

lumber, which the Board thought could not be paid before the lumber was actually sold. This time Baillie came to his defence, pointing out that seizures were handled differently in the CLO than in customs or the treasury because its officers were unsalaried. The auditors would have none of it: 'The practice of the Custom House and Treasury is precisely similar, the charges are never paid till the article is sold, the salary has nothing to do with it.' The Board also objected to (among other things) Mahood's charges for surveying timber leases submitted before the lessee was bonded, and for inspecting the timber cut on a lease: 'This appears an extraordinary charge. [The lessee] has given bonds under his five year lease, and the regulations require him to exhibit an attested account of all Lumber cut by him. Why was this inspection considered necessary?' Baillie's explanation: 'Notwithstanding the Bond supervision is necessary as a check upon the party, and the Crown has upon all occasions been benefitted by it.'[128]

Deputies were entitled to a fixed per diem rate for actual land surveying duties, payable in most circumstances by the recipient of the grant or license. Like many of his colleagues, Mahood experienced difficulties in collecting these payments. The church was notoriously reluctant to pay surveying fees for its grants.[129] So, sometimes, was the local bench. On one occasion Mahood was laying out a public street between Thomas Hitchings's mill privilege and a common: 'The Magistrates went off and one of the Commissioners sneaked off and T.H. Hitchings also leaving me alone, all afraid to have to pay me.'[130] The Board of Ordnance refused to pay Mahood's account for surveying the military lands at St Andrews except by a note subject to

128. JHA 1837-8, Appendix, 'Report upon sundry accounts of disbursements ... dated 9th December 1837,' n.p.

129. For example PANB RS637, Mahood to Beckwith, 24 Nov 1832; Beckwith to Greenwich church wardens, 24 Nov 1832. When DLS Smith surveyed a grant for Rev. Jerome Alley JP, however, 'no doubt was entertained' of Alley's liability for the fee, which Smith applied to his son's tuition at Alley's school: PANB RS637, Smith to Baillie, 22 Feb 1845.

130. NBM Mahood, 23 Jun 1846. When the Charlotte bench decided to expand the public landing at St Stephen it passed an order for the county DLS to make the necessary survey, 'and that the expence be paid by the Rents arising from the Public Landing': CCGS 19 Apr 1836.

discount, 'which I cannot afford to pay.'[131] The most difficult client of all was the provincial government itself. Mahood's account for surveying the Charlotte county boundaries was ruthlessly trimmed by the auditor general.[132] Mahood made a detailed rejoinder and petitioned the legislature several times, but the account was never fully paid despite the surveyor general's certification that the work 'appears to have been most satisfactorily performed' and the charges reasonable.[133] When Mahood sought compensation for time he had spent preparing a plan of county roads for the use of the assembly, the government's initial response was simply that it had no funds for the purpose.[134]

Like other deputies, Mahood also held a provincial appointment as seizing officer. He applied for additional appointments although without success. Requesting copies of the crown land regulations to distribute among railroad construction workers he complained, 'Had I been appointed Emigrant agent for this place, I could have given more information to the emigrants than any other person in this place could have done.'[135] When Thomas Wyer's death vacated the office of receiver of crown debts for Charlotte, Mahood put in his bid for the job: 'It is in some measure connected with my situation and the duties could be performed much better by me than any other person.'[136]

Mahood's surveying and drafting skills were highly respected. Patrick Clinch JP, commissioned to lay out a road through unexplored wilderness, retained him to make a baseline: Mahood's 'skill as a surveyor, together with his knowledge of the country, ... enabled him at the first attempt, to run a line, without any perceptible deviation from a straight one.'[137] When the brothers Porter challenged the sale of crown lands in the former Rait block to Nehemiah Marks JP the assembly put the issue on hold pending a re-survey, naming Mahood

131. PANB RS637, Mahood to Baillie, 22 Jul 1848.

132. JHA 1846, 304, 307; ibid., Appendix, Report on Public Accounts, ccvi.

133. PANB RS687, Mahood to Baillie, 20 Feb 1844.

134. After a round of petitions, however, he was voted £10 in 1849 (JHA, 297) and £5 in 1851 (JHA, 342).

135. PANB RS637, Mahood to Baillie, 26 Jun 1848.

136. PANB RS637, Mahood to Baillie, 8 Jan 1849.

137. JHA 1839, Appendix, lvi.

for the sensitive task.[138] When James Vernon petitioned the legislature over his defective title to a grant of crown lands, Andrew Inches, the senior official in the CLO, was sent to determine the accuracy of Mahood's work: 'after elaborate survey ... [he] ascertained the correctness of Mr. Mahood's survey, and also found that it was in strict accordance with ancient blazings, which he states to have been upwards of fifty years old.'[139] Mahood had no hesitation in praising his own precision, nor did he show much deference to his professional colleagues. On several occasions he noted errors in C.R. Hatheway's surveys, observing in one case that 'I crossed his line twice—in one place he was more than two rods to the N.E. of my line. The line he run is not straight.'[140]

So it must have come as a surprise to the surveyor general when Patrick Shea of Pennfield complained in May 1854 about Mahood's conduct in surveying the fifty acres he claimed under the Labour Act:[141]

> Mr Mahood has caused a great deal of trouble between the neighbours here for the last fortnight he has been among them for it seems he cannot run a straight line and particularly every afternoon for Petitioner says he has been part of three days on other surveys hunting Mr Deputy Mahood up in the woods for the Parties sometimes thought he might have been lost for any person can tell by the Gentleman's Manoeuvres he is altogether wrong in the head and is not on that account capable of doing duty correctly as a Surveyor.

Mahood requested a leave of absence to go to Boston for his health, his doctor reporting that 'his intellect has been evidently impaired, and I consider him quite unfit to attend to any business whatever.'[142] Within days, his wife Lucretia reported that William had been sent

138. JHA 1845, 171f.

139. JHA 1847, 168. According to its website, the Association of New Brunswick Land Surveyors holds two plaques with sections of trees blazed by Mahood in 1835 and 1844 respectively. The latter came from a white pine still standing in 1946.

140. NBM Mahood journals, 9 Dec 1846; for additional examples ibid., 28 Apr 1843 and 24 May 1846.

141. PANB RS637, Shea to Brown, 28 May 1854.

142. PANB RS637, Mahood to Wilmot, 31 Jul 1854; Gove to Wilmot, 3 Aug 1854.

to the provincial lunatic asylum.[143] Sending along several testimonials and endorsements from local notables, she begged surveyor general Wilmot to keep his job open for him and to ask the lieutenant governor to retain him in his commission as seizing officer. Wilmot appointed Edward Jack as a temporary replacement, promising to reinstate Mahood when he recovered from 'his unfortunate state of mind,' while regretfully declining her proposal that the CLO purchase the rights to Mahood's county map to help support the family in the mean time.[144] Before long Mahood announced that he was fully recovered and sought to return to work. A letter from his doctor urged that he be reinstated. But Wilmot was now out of office and acting DLS Jack would not give up the situation without formal instructions from the government which were not forthcoming until Mahood wrote at length to the new surveyor general. Mahood was back at work by January 1855.[145] He immediately contested Jack's claims to fees for seizures he had commenced but not completed and for work in the period between his medical clearance and formal reinstatement.[146]

Not long after Mahood's return, however, Peter Cassidy, a Lepreau Harbour settler, complained that in surveying for a neighbour he had cut off fifteen of the fifty acres he had marked out for Cassidy a few years before. '[E]very other survey he has made last week he has the neighbours at variance for he has run lines to interfere with one another.'[147] An intending purchaser reported that he had attended

143. Mahood was not the first crown lands official whose career was interrupted by mental illness. Surveyor general Anthony Lockwood was confined as a lunatic in 1823 after declaring himself the head of government and attempting to auction off the legislature's furniture.

144. PANB RS637, Lucretia Mahood to Wilmot, 9 Aug 1854, 14 Aug 1854; Wilmot to Lucretia Mahood, 19 Aug 1854; Lucretia Mahood to Wilmot, 21 Sep 1854; for William Mahood's unsuccessful petitions for aid towards publishing the map see JHA 1850, 91; JHA 1851, 71, 307; JHA 1854, 59; JHA 1855, 162, 257.

145. PANB RS637, Mahood to Wilmot, 15 Oct 1854; Gillmer to Steeves, 10 Nov 1854; Mahood to Steeves, 14 Nov 1854.

146. PANB RS637, Mahood to Inches, 19 Jan 1855, Jack to Brown, 3 Mar 1856; JHA 1855, 313, 357 (return of correspondence moved by Boyd); PANB RS24/1855/zz2, file 2, 'Schedule of correspondence between Mr Edw. W. Jack and the Crown Land Department . . .'

147. Ibid., Cassidy to Brown, 19 May 1855.

a sale at St Andrews to buy the lot he had applied for, but 'Mr Mahood was not in attendance (being sent to the Asylum) ...'[148] A Pennfield settler wrote to inquire whether his survey had been filed at the CLO: 'Mr Mahood was insane at the time he came to make the survey and ran several lines the last one I think is correct.'[149] Lucretia confirmed that he was back in the lunatic asylum, quite deranged in mind.[150] She applied, unsuccessfully, for CLO employment for their son James.[151] William Mahood died at Carleton (and so in all likelihood at the asylum, which was located there) in August 1855 leaving Lucretia and three children.[152] He owed the CLO ninety pounds but had an outstanding claim for stumpage which the surveyor general personally collected and kept in his own hands, 'as I wanted directions from the Government what to do with it; they directed me to pay it to the Receiver General's office, on account of the claim against Mahood. I had intended it for the Widow until this decision; this reduced his debt to about £60, which we lost.'[153]

Public, local, and private interest

Changes in New Brunswick's crown land policy were interrelated with changing, sometimes contested, ideas about public service, responsibility, and accountability. Before the mid-1820s, the privatization of the crown domain occurred by gracious dispensation—grants of land, licenses of occupation—in recognition of service, loyalty, or other merit. These were discretionary gifts bestowed by the provincial executive whose members were entitled to fees for every grant. Some of the surveyor general's duties were farmed out to deputies whose compensation also depended on fees and commissions. This period of executive patronage was interrupted when the colonial office appointed Thomas Baillie as commissioner of crown lands and shortly thereafter abolished the fee system in favour of direct sales of crown land. Over the next decade Baillie supervised an admin-

148. Ibid., Buchanan to Brown, 7 June 1855.
149. Ibid., Woodberry to Brown, 24 Sep 1855.
150. Ibid., Lucretia Mahood to Brown, 2 June 1855.
151. Ibid., Lucretia Mahood to Inches, 19 Sept 1855.
152. *Chronicle*, 17 Aug 1855.
153. JHA 1861, Appendix, Crown Land Evidence, 32.

istration divided between the salaried civil servants of the CLO and the commissioned field staff of deputies. So long as crown land revenues insulated the executive from accountability to the assembly, the CLO staff and deputy surveyors were responsible to no-one but Baillie. Despite his tendency to micromanage and despite efforts by senior staff, particularly chief draftsman Andrew Inches, to exercise authority over the field officers, the deputies retained a good deal of autonomy. After 1837, the assembly used its newly-won power of the purse to make the crown lands department accountable to the legislature. One consequence of this somewhat ungainly sidling towards responsible government was a contest over the departmental patronage. Because provincial politics were dominated by local and regional interests this meant the appointment and discipline of local deputies: James Boyd's meddling in the choice of Colin Campbell's successor as Charlotte DLS is an early example. Baillie managed to retain effective control of the department's central staff as long as he remained surveyor general. Ten years after he left, however, and in an emergent climate of party politics,[154] scandal punctuated the career of the office's most senior civil servant. In its wake the surveyor general became formally responsible to the assembly for the conduct of his staff. The politicization of crown land policy and procedure and the struggle over departmental patronage transformed both the public's expectations of the deputies and their self-image.

The first generation of surveyors considered their deputations to be entitlements and their participation in public life to be corollary to the pursuit of conscientious self-interest. DLS McDonald's spirited attacks on Dr Faxon's Grand Manan speculations were not motivated solely by suspicion about the American purchasers' loyalty or his disgust at land fraud. McDonald's sister had married into the ; McMaster clan, Faxon's rivals for ungranted island property. McDonald applied for land on the island and reported in his own favour. Surveyor general Sproule rejected McDonald's specific application because the land in question had already been allotted to Faxon but he authorized the DLS to find and survey other unoccupied land for the McMasters. McDonald appealed, giving Sproule a reasonably frank (albeit confi-

154. Chapter 11.

dential) account of his interest:[155]

> Besides the very central and convenient allotments already made, there is hardly a Spot on which a Hill of potatoes could be planted, within miles of the shore, but what is now, under some pretence, laid claim to, and that chiefly by encroachments from American Citizens ... and that the Objection to Our Application as it may respect the Settlement and Improvements of the Island, will apply with greater force against numerous and various Proprietors, whose politics in many instances may be at this time hostile to the welfare of us, Our Country, and Government.

McDonald recruited support for his application from Charlotte patriarch Hugh Mackay,[156] lobbied the chief justice for support in council, and delayed executing the warrants of survey for which he had been sent to Grand Manan pending the executive's decision on the McMaster claims.[157]

McDonald understood that his job entailed the assessment of applicants for grants as much as it did the measurement and valuation of land and improvements. His deputation was sufficient evidence of his own loyalty and desert and so of his entitlement to executive largesse. While he might be open to 'selfish imputations' if he used his position to shut out a worthy applicant, the public interest coincided with his own when his application ousted useless, disloyal, or undeserving ones. McDonald's apparently acceptable elision of private and public interest is evident as well in his complaints about dif-

155. UNB MG/H46a, Sproule to McDonald, 20 Feb 1807; PANB RS637, McDonald to Sproule, 20 Aug 1807, disclaiming 'any selfish imputations' on the ground that he had applied only out of 'duty' to his 'widowed sister and orphan family.'

156. Mackay sent Edward Winslow an account of the McMasters' claim, adding that 'twenty odd years uninterrupted intimacy and friendship with their uncle Mr. McDonald and other relatives & connections in this Country, makes me feel peculiarly interested in the success of their intended application.' He also pointed out that the grant would benefit Christopher Hatch, 'whose interest and prosperity I have much at heart,' to whom Moses Gerrish, McDonald's partner in the application, had promised a portion: Raymond, *Winslow Papers*, 588-90. Ten years earlier, Gerrish had been implicated along with James McMaster (Indian Island), Nathan Frink (Campobello), and others in a smuggling ring: PANB RS42 1796, King v. Thomas Ross et al., affidavit of Colin Campbell, 30 Sep 1796.

157. PANB RS637, McDonald to Sproule, 22 Sep 1807.

ficulties in collecting his fees: 'I could with some degree of patience bear all this, was it for the accommodation of useful, Loyal, or deserving Settlers. But it is too indignant to see the Government and its Officers trifled with, for the Speculative convenience of, generally speaking, a very different description of applicants.'[158]

With the shift from grants to land sales and timber licensing during the Baillie regime, however, the DLS office was increasingly commercialized. Deputies had long been required to post performance bonds and take an oath of office.[159] Unlike parish and county surveyors of lumber and fish, who from 1829 on were restrained from trading in the articles they regulated,[160] neither the oath nor the regulations forbade the DLS from engaging in land speculation. Even the failed draft enactment to give deputy land surveyors a monopoly of the work would not have required them to abstain from land dealing in their private capacity.[161] Nor did the various circular letters and printed instructions for deputies issued by the CLO from time to time expressly forbid land dealing.

The mounting attacks on Baillie's administration in the 1830s did not focus in the main on charges of speculation in the CLO but rather on agency capture by the lumbering interests. Even under the former regime there had been complaints of deputies colluding with trespassers and taking unauthorized license fees. In the Miramichi region, armed conflict erupted between rival lumberers and a deputy surveyor was formally investigated for partiality.[162] In Charlotte, former DLS Colin Campbell came under the eye of Robert Gowan, who as 'John Gape' led the journalistic assault on Baillie's unreformed

158. PANB RS637, McDonald to Sproule, 28 Nov 1808.

159. R. Fellows, 'Loyalists and Land Settlement,' 9.

160. Before 1829 surveyors of lumber were sworn to the faithful and diligent discharge of their duty; by 9&10 Geo.IV c.23 (1829) s.3 they had to swear as well, 'that I will not directly or indirectly be a dealer in, or interested in the buying and selling of any article of Lumber, either on my own account or on account of any person or persons whatsoever ...'

161. PANB RS24 1835, bill 86 provided for this oath: 'I do swear that I will faithfully ~~justly and~~ truly and impartially execute the office of a Deputy Surveyor of Lands in this Province, according to the best of my skill and ability.' 'Justly and' are struck through in the handwritten draft, and 'and impartially' inserted after 'truly,' indicating that some consideration was given to the form of the proposed oath.

162. Wynn, *Timber Colony*, 139-41; ibid., 134.

CLO:[163]

> Heard that a Deputy Commissioner of Crown Lands in the County of Charlotte had been accused of injustice, and oppression, and fraud in his official capacity ... Would wish to know whether honesty is considered necessary in a Deputy Surveyor; is it a point of official etiquette to select the vilest ruffians that can be found to fill respectable and useful stations.

Campbell's repudiation of Gape's allegations contained an unhappy turn of phrase—'With his accustomed malevolence and total disregard for truth, he asserts that I was "thrust out of the Crown Land Office, sans ceremonie, because then uncontaminated by avarice," &c. This is an infamous falsehood.'— affording Gowan the obvious mocking riposte.[164] In fact, however, Campbell had given up his deputation in order to become high sheriff of the county. Ousted from the shrievalty without ceremony a decade later he considered his reinstatement as DLS to be 'a right and not a favor.'[165] That he should have felt the need to say so suggests that change was in the air. In the same year the lieutenant governor justified the abolition of stumpage because it had required 'a subordinate class of Officers [i.e., DLS] throughout the Country, in the exercise of extensive powers, and subject to undue influences.'[166] This was a far cry from McDonald's version of the DLS role.

While agency capture was to remain a persistent and perniciously recurrent demon of crown lands regulation, the great scandal that shook the CLO to its foundations originated not in its relations with the lumbering industry generally, but in land sales and speculation. Although the issue only surfaced in 1861, the investigation showed that land sales under false names (in part to circumvent the statutory limits on Labour Act and other instalment sales to individuals)

163. *Courier*, 13 Apr 1833. After the assembly won control of the crown lands Gowan was rewarded with a job in the CLO.

164. Ibid., 13 Jul, 27 Jul, 10 Aug 1833.

165. PANB RS637, Campbell to Baillie, 18 Apr 1843. Campbell also sought reinstatement as a justice, 'being at present liable to be called upon to serve as a Juror in the Court where I so long presided': PANB RS7, (Public Officials), Commission of Peace 1840-47, 195.

166. JHA 1844, 25, printing Colebrooke to Stanley, 28 Apr 1843: stumpage fees were replaced by an export tax on lumber.

along with speculation in crown lands by department officials and members of government had been going on for thirty years and more, flourishing during the railway boom. The chief culprit in the CLO was its senior officer and long-standing figurehead for probity and professionalism in the surveying business, Andrew Inches, who insisted to the end that he had done nothing morally wrong. He took the fall for the CLO and the attorney general was made to do the same for the government. The department was reconstituted and made fully accountable to the assembly. The investigating committee formulated a new ethos of public service: 'The practice which has long prevailed, of Officers in Public Departments acting as agents in connection with the business of the department, is looked upon with distrust, and is unsound in principle.'[167] New instructions were issued forbidding deputy surveyors and crown lands officials from dealing in public lands and timber berths or taking agency fees from individuals dealing with the department.[168] Two years later a legislative committee recommended Inches's reinstatement, 'as being a person well versed in the duties of the Department, cognizant of its details, and possessing a thorough knowledge of all matters on which information is constantly sought.'[169] In October 1895 Inches marked his sixtieth anniversary in the CLO: 'He entered when he was 18 years old. He is now 78.'[170] His brief fall from grace had been long forgotten.

The deputies' role had begun in the 1780s on the model of paternalist public service by autonomous gentlemen taking professional fees. Successive jolts of accountability—to a charismatic Baillie, to provincial auditors, to a succession of legislative committees—had limited the scope of private entrepreneurship and confined the DLS within an increasingly straitened framework of bureaucratic regulation and procedure. The Crown Lands Department of 1865 was a very different organization than its predecessor of eighty years before. Nevertheless, its deputies continued to dispense low law, improvise departmental policy, and pursue substantive justice within the emerging institutional and administrative environment.

167. JHA 1861, 130-5, 161-6 and minutes of testimony in JHA appendix.
168. JHA 1864, Crown Land appendix, 129 (approved 22 Apr 1861).
169. JHA 1863, 175.
170. *Daily Sun*, 15 Nov 1895.

Chapter 6

'Unconnected with mercantile pursuits': The justice business, 1840-1

Sir John Harvey replaced Archibald Campbell as lieutenant governor in 1837. He had hardly settled in at Government House before Charles Reid Hatheway renewed his campaign for reinstatement, asking why he had been removed from the commission of the peace and pressing for the opportunity to answer any charges against him.[1] The first intimation of a return to official favour came in December 1838 when Hatheway was reappointed as a notary public.[2] It is probably no coincidence that this happened just as Harris Hatch and Thomas Wyer were made legislative councillors.[3] Hatheway caused a stir at April sessions 1839 when he tried to have the grand jury adopt a resolution for restoring him to the magistracy.[4] Nevertheless a new petition signed by Harris Hatch, twenty-one justices (but not James Douglas),

1. PANB RS13/54/c/1838, Hatheway to Harvey, 28 Mar 1838.
2. PANB RS538/B/5, 20 Dec 1838.
3. *Courier*, 19 Jan 1839.
4. *Standard*, letter of 'Brittanicus' (likely James Boyd), 20 Apr 1839. In reply to this call for Hatheway to first rebut the charges against him, a 'Looker On' asked, 'What charges was he to rebut?' and answered his own question: 'Those which were instigated by malice, concocted and preferred in secret, and which he could not rebut for want of opportunity.' *Standard*, 4 May 1839.

and eleven lawyers (but not the Streets) recommended Hatheway's appointment to the Charlotte bench:[5]

> ...from being entirely unconnected with all Mercantile pursuits, [he] would be a very essential acquisition in performing the various and arduous duties of office greatly increased from being a Border County, and in which his Usefulness would be felt immediately in the community in which he resides and generally throughout the County.

Hatheway had the support of justices in every parish of the county including some of the most senior. Two-thirds of the magistrates attending April sessions signed the petition, as well as two-thirds of the county bench as a whole.[6] On March 14, 1840, the province's executive council approved a new commission of the peace for Charlotte including 'C.R. Hatheway in his former place.'[7]

Hatheway was sworn in on April 7 along with the new county sheriff, Captain Thomas Jones.[8] A week later Hatheway took his seat on the bench at April sessions.[9] He soon resumed his former role as one of New Brunswick's busiest JPs, writing on the inside cover of his memorandum book:

> In 4 years C.R. Hatheway paid over to County Treasurer and Commissioners of Poor £257.15.0. Gross amount paid over by all other justices from 1840 to 1844 inclusive £47.0.0.[10]

---

5. NBM Hatheway Papers, item #7, 25 Apr 1839. Harris Hatch styled himself 'MLC,' having been appointed to the legislative council along with Wyer. The magistrates were Mackay, Wyer, W.F.W. Owen, McCallum, Vernon, Wilson, J. and T. Moore, Clinch, Mowatt, Fisher, Knight, Garnett, Marks, Frink, Snell, Chaffey, Albee, Wetmore, McNeil, and Moses. The lawyers were G.S. Hill, J.W. Chandler, R.M. Andrews, T.B. Wilson, Wellington Hatch, S.G. Andrews, Peter Stubs, J.H. Whitlock, T.B. Abbot, G. Thomson, and W.B. Chandler.

6. Three justices in the November 1838 commission had since left the county.

7. This meant not only reinstatement but restoration of seniority as though he had never been struck from the commission. PANB RS538/B/5, 14 Mar 1840.

8. Jones had been Spearman's second in the Wyer challenge affair described in chapter 4: his testimony at the assembly trial had undermined Hatheway's credibility and contributed to his removal from the commission.

9. *Standard*, 17 Apr 1840; CCGS minutes, 14 Apr 1840.

10. NBM Hatheway Papers, item #18, n.d.

He continued his practice as JP (later JCP) until at least 1866.[11] When he died, aged 80, in 1869 his newspaper obituary remembered somewhat grudgingly that as a justice of the peace 'he was acknowledged to be at one time the most competent in this County.'[12] One of his sons inherited the family practice.[13]

Commission of the peace

Justices were made and unmade by having their names included in or removed from the commission of the peace for the county. These commissions were issued from time to time by the lieutenant governor exercising the royal prerogative. It was the convention in New Brunswick (as elsewhere) that each county's entire roster of justices appeared in each commission. This meant that every new commission replaced its predecessor and that a new commission for the whole county was necessary to add or remove even a single justice. While this convention had not always been observed in early New Brunswick—David Owen was appointed in 1788 without a new county commission[14]—it had become the accepted practice by the turn of the nineteenth century. The form of commission in use in mid-nineteenth-century New Brunswick (Appendix B) was very similar to that used in England when the colony was created.[15] At five places where the English commission referred to 'ordinances and statutes,' the New Brunswick version has 'ordinances, laws and

11. The last entry in C.R. Hatheway's justicing ledger is dated 12 Nov 1866. He attended sessions in April 1867 but not thereafter.

12. *Standard*, 21 Jul 1869.

13. Hatheway requested his son's appointment in 1861: PANB RS9, Meeting of 1 Jul 1861, Hatheway to Tilley, 16 May 1861. C.E.O. Hatheway became a JP in 1867 and attended September sessions: *Standard*, 19 Jun 1867; CCGS. Unlike his father he was well immersed in mercantile pursuits having operated a series of shops and agencies. He was involved with the St Andrews marine hospital and the local railroad. Shortly after becoming a JP he advertised himself as an auctioneer and commission merchant selling groceries at retail: *Standard*, 25 Mar 1868. His name appears as a magistrate inspecting the gaol as late as 1888: PANB RS375/B4. CCA holds one of C.E.O. Hatheway's justicing notebooks, 'Book no. 3,' 1879-82.

14. PANB RS538/B/5, 28 Jun 1788.

15. The comparison that follows is between the commission printed in Burn, *Justice*, III:5-7 and the 1845 commission of the peace for Charlotte county in PANB RS148/P/2/b, reproduced in Appendix B.

Table 6.1 – JCPs in commissions by precedence, Charlotte, 1830-40

Name	Mar 1830	May 1832	Dec 1832	Nov 1835	May 1836	Nov 1837	Mar 1838	Nov 1838	Dec 1839	Mar 1840
H Mackay	•	•	•	•	•	•	•	•	•	•
J Campbell	•	☠								
C Campbell	•	•	•	⧉						
T Wyer	•	↓								
P Stubs	•	•	•	👎						
T Wyer	↑	•	•	•	•	•	•	•	•	•
D McMaster	•	☠								
J Allanshaw		•	•	•	•	•	•	•	•	•
J Rait					•	•	•	•	•	•
J Douglas					•	•	•	•	•	◁
WB Kinnear									•	•
WFW Owen									•	•
J Wilson										•

Removed	👎	Dead	☠	Sheriff	⧉
Left county	◁	Precedence increased	↑	Precedence reduced	↓

statutes.' The New Brunswick version omits the English commission's references to outlawry, poisonings, enchantments, sorceries, and 'arts magick.' It also omits the English commission's provisions about referring difficult cases and about the keeper of the rolls. The consequence of the latter omission seems to have been that in England but not in New Brunswick the justice of the peace was a court of record for at least some purposes.[16] Some early-nineteenth-century commissions listed 'The judges of the Supreme Court, the members of His Majesty's council, the attorney and solicitor generals' before the names of the county justices but this practice ended in the mid-1820s.[17]

Justices of the peace were listed in the commission by precedence, based on the date of their first appointment. The senior magistrate in the county had a customary claim to preside at sessions, address the grand jury, and speak for the bench although in later years Charlotte general sessions elected its own chairman. The senior magistrate in each parish probably claimed a similar customary entitlement at local sessions and meetings of magistrates. The general ex-

16. Burn opens his discussion (III:1) with the claim that 'Justices of the peace are judges of record,' but this was not the universal view in England.

17. The whole formula appears in the 1816 Charlotte commission. It appears again but without the judges in 1818, 1821, and 1822 but is absent from the 1826 and later commissions: PANB RS538/B/5.

ception to the seniority precedence rule was that justices of common pleas were moved to the head of the list. Separate commissions were issued for the common pleas but every JCP was also a JP and appeared as such in the commission of the peace. When a justice of the peace was first named to the common pleas he leapfrogged more senior JPs in the commission and took precedence over them. Tables 6.1 and 6.2 show JCPs and JPs in every commission of the peace from March 1830 to Hatheway's reinstatement in March 1840. James Rait was first appointed in December 1832 when he ranked twentieth in precedence. He was named to the common pleas in March 1836[18] so when the next commission of the peace issued in May of that year he jumped to fourth place in the precedence list. When Hatheway was restored to the commission 'in his former place' in 1840 he was put in the seniority list between Patrick Clinch and David Mowatt just as he had been in 1830. Charlotte justices took their place in the seniority list seriously. David Owen fretted for years about losing his place as the oldest JP in the commission to more recently appointed JCPs, arguing that justices of the peace were entitled to precedence over those of the common pleas.[19] Peter Stubs, who had been JCP since May 1824, threatened to resign his commission when newly promoted Thomas Wyer was placed ahead of him in the March 1830 list. The slight was righted in the May 1832 list.[20]

Commissions of the peace distinguished between justices 'of the quorum' and others who were not. Two or more justices were necessary to constitute sessions, at least one of whom had to be a justice of the quorum.[21] Only justices of the quorum could perform marriages. In 1816 Moses Gerrish, the patriarch of Grand Manan, urged the appointment of another magistrate for the island: 'he should be appointed Quorum unus, to enable him to solemnize Matrimony; for if ever I should renew my oath, my stay here will be short, and where

18. PANB RS538/B/5, 24 Mar 1836.

19. CO 188/35 encl. copy of Owen to Douglas, 13 Sep 1826. He was advised that JCPs were placed at the head of the list in every county but Saint John 'by particular directions of the Governor and Council': ibid., Odell to Owen 5 Feb 1827.

20. PANB RS342/B/4, Petition of magistrates and residents of St Andrews to President Black, (n.d.).

21. Cf. Burn, *Justice*, III:14.

Table 6.2 – JPs in commissions by precedence, Charlotte, 1830-40

Name	Mar 1830	May 1832	Dec 1832	Nov 1835	May 1836	Nov 1837	Mar 1838	Nov 1838	Dec 1839	Mar 1840
P McCallum	⊕	⊕	⊕	⊕	⊕	⊕	⊕	⊕	⊕	⊕
T Armstrong	⊕	⊕	⊕	⊕	⊕	⊕	⊕	⊕	⊕	⊕
M Vernon	⊕	⊕	⊕	⊕	⊕	⊕	⊕	⊕	⊕	◁
W Frankland	⊕	⊕	⊕	⊕	⊕	⊕	⊕	⊕	⊕	⊕
W Ross	⊕	☠								
J Alley	⊕	⊕	⊕	⊕	⊕	⊕	⊕	⊕	⊕	▷
J Wilson	⊕	⊕	⊕	⊕	⊕	⊕	⊕	⊕	⊕	△
T Moore	⊕	⊕	⊕	⊕	⊕	⊕	⊕	⊕	⊕	⊕
P Clinch	⊕	⊕	⊕	⊕	⊕	⊕	⊕	⊕	⊕	⊕
WB Cripps	⊕	☠								
CR Hatheway	⊕	⊕	👎							⊕
J Allanshaw	⊕	△								
B Robinson	†									
A Upton	†									
D Mowatt	⊕	⊕	⊕	⊕	⊕	⊕	⊕	⊕	⊕	⊕
T Jones	⊕	⊕	⊕	◁						⧉
S Abbott	⊕	⊕	⊕	⊕	⊕	⊕	⊕	⊕	⊕	⊕
W Ker	⊕	⊕	⊕	⊕	⊕	⊕	⊕	⊕	⊕	⊕
G Porter	†	†	†	†	†	†	†	†	†	†
J Paterson	⊕	⊕	⊕	⊕	⊕	⊕	⊕	⊕	⊕	⊕
C Curry	†									
J White	⊘	⊕	⊕	⊕	⊕	⊕	⊕	⊕	⊕	☠
J Rait			⊕	⊕	△					
J Wilkinson			⊕							
W Fisher			⊕	⊕	⊕	⊕	⊕	⊕	⊕	⊕
J Knight			⊕	⊕	⊕	⊕	⊕	⊕	⊕	⊕
CH Jouett			⊕	⊕	⊕	⊕	⊕	⊕	⊕	◁
J Douglas			⊕	⊕	△					
W Garnett			⊕	⊕	⊕	⊕	⊕	⊕	⊕	⊕
N Marks			⊕	⊕	⊕	⊕	⊕	⊕	⊕	⊕
J McLachlan			⊕	⊕	⊕	⊕	⊕	⊕	⊕	⊕
J Frink			⊘	⊘	⊕	⊕	⊕	⊕	⊕	⊕
WFW Owen				⊘	⊕	⊕	⊕	⊕	⊕	△
J Allen					⊕	⊕	⊕	⊕	⊕	◁
IR Mather					⊘	⊘	⊘	⊕	⊕	◁
J Snell					⊘	⊘	⊘	⊕	⊕	⊕
R Thomson						⊘				
Jn Chaffey			†				⊘	⊕	⊕	☠
Js Chaffey								⊕	†	
R Lindsay							⊘	⊕	⊕	⊕
J Porter							⊘	⊕	⊕	⊕
J Albee							⊘	⊕	⊕	⊕
J Moore							⊘	⊕	⊕	⊕
AJ Wetmore								⊕	⊕	⊕
J McNeil								⊕	⊕	⊕
T Moses								⊘	⊘	⊘
C Craig								⊘	⊘	⊘
W Babcock										⊘
G Mackay										⊘
DA Rose										⊘
J Robinson										⊘

JP-Quorum	⊕	JP non-Quorum	⊘	Promoted JCP	△
Resigned	▷	Declined	†	Dead	☠
Removed	👎	Sheriff	⧉	Left county	◁

I am going there is neither marriage nor giving in marriage.'[22] The quorum distinction was preserved in mid-nineteenth-century New Brunswick but it was not a particularly salient one because all but a few of the most recently-appointed justices were included, as can be seen in Table 6.2. Magistrates were appointed to the quorum without regard to their service, knowledge, or experience. Lumberman George M. Porter was named to the quorum in every commission from 1830 to 1866 although he declined to take the oath of office and never attended sessions with the exception of a single day.[23] He took no part in any other duties of a justice.

Names were carried over from one commission to the next unless the county clerk of the peace advised that the justice had died, left the county, or had not taken the qualifying oath ('declines' in Table 6.2). William Boyd Kinnear, the Saint John lawyer-politician who had moved the assembly resolution about Hatheway's credibility and was to become solicitor general in the mid-1840s, was named to the Charlotte commission in 1839 so that he could examine witnesses under oath in his investigation of the Grand Manan church-burning in which Wilford Fisher JP was suspected of arson.[24] His was the only nonresident appointment in the decade. Kinnear remained on the list until 1842 when clerk Hatch pointed out that he lived in Saint John and did not attend sessions.[25]

While (as we have seen) there were differing opinions about whether a magistrate could serve in other public offices, it was well understood that the sheriff could not be in the commission of the peace. Colin Campbell JCP's name was removed from the next commission when he became county sheriff. When he lost the shrievalty he asked to be restored to the magistracy, giving vague English au-

22. PANB MC207, Gerrish to Harris Hatch, 12 Aug 1816.

23. On 21 Apr 1835 he attended to move a resolution that no tavern licenses be awarded for St Stephen. In 1851 he told the government that he did not consider himself to be in the commission of the peace having never taken the qualifying oath (chapter 7).

24. PANB RS13/A/3, Odell to Kinnear, 5 Dec 1839, instructing Kinnear to call on Harris Hatch 'before whom a partial examination has been instituted' to accompany him to the island. For more on Fisher see Ingersoll, 'Fisher, Wilford' and chapter 8 below.

25. PANB RS8, Magistrates, 1/3, Charlotte, return of magistrates, 1 Jan 1842.

thority for the practice and pointing out the need for an additional JCP because James Rait was leaving the province and Hugh Mackay was too old to attend court. Council considered his application but declined to comply with it.[26] Charles Reid Hatheway was the only Charlotte justice in the decade to be removed from the commission for misconduct (and the only one to be restored).

Appointment to the commission of the peace was a mark of prominence in the community.[27] The office carried with it a number of responsibilities but for the most part they were not obligations. Lieutenant governor Campbell had reprimanded John Wilson and Peter Stubs for doing nothing to keep the peace in the face of an apprehended duel but he did not remove them from the commission for it.[28] Like unsalaried volunteer justices elsewhere Charlotte magistrates varied immensely in the extent to which they participated in the responsibilities of office. Some justices were essentially inactive. The ancient St George magistrate and former MHA Hugh Mackay, first appointed in 1789, remained in the commission without any expectation of activity.[29] Among St Andrews magistrates the Anglican minister Jerome Alley rarely attended general sessions unless there was church business to transact and seems never to have acted in criminal or civil litigation although he sometimes lent his name and title to community petitions and pleas for clemency. Oddly enough he was the only Charlotte JP to join in a petition by Saint John justices for a provincial magistrates' manual.[30] He finally stepped down in 1839 after nearly twenty years of inactivity because he found the duties of a magistrate to be 'incompatible' with those of rector of the parish:

---

26. PANB RS7, vol. 96, Campbell to Odell, 4 Feb 1841 and endorsement.

27. This was true wherever there was a lay magistracy: see for instance Johnson, *Becoming Prominent*, chapter 3.

28. Chapter 4.

29. Clerk Hatch travelled to Mackay's home to swear him in, a privilege accorded to no-one else in the commission. Petitions by justices and others for 'a more efficient Magistracy' for St George resulted in the appointment of Patrick Clinch in 1838: PANB RS7, vol. 96, W.F.W. Owen to Odell [n.d.]; ibid., Wyer et al. petition, n.d. When Clinch decided to move to St Andrews to start a newspaper Mackay's inactivity was again urged as necessitating an additional new appointment: ibid., Wyer to Odell, 18 Feb 1842; ibid., James Brown to Odell, 9 Mar 1842.

30. PANB RS24 S30:P22 (1822).

'having declined the active duties of a Magistrate, I have hitherto neglected tendering my resignation, which it might have been better to have done long since.'[31] He was the only Charlotte magistrate to resign his commission (as distinct from declining to take the oath in the first place) in this period. The new commission of the peace that issued in March 1840 making four new appointments and reinstating Hatheway followed closely on a report by the county's clerk of the peace that nine of the justices named in the December 1839 commission were defunct: two had died, one (Rev Alley) had resigned, another had declined to qualify, and five had left the county.[32]

Among the more active justices some specialized in particular areas of responsibility. St Andrews auctioneer and consignment dealer William Ker handled much of the crown or criminal business out of sessions during Hatheway's exile.[33] Thomas Wyer, who had been a member of the provincial assembly continuously from 1828 until his appointment to the legislative council in September 1839, took a small part in local justice out of sessions but was more deeply engaged in county governance, public works, and taxation as well as in representing St Andrews and Charlotte interests at Fredericton. Wyer and his fellow legislative councillor, James Allanshaw, took turns presiding over the county's inferior court of common pleas.[34]

---

31. PANB RS7, vol. 96, Alley to Odell, 12 Jan 1839. Alley was first appointed to the commission of the peace in 1821.

32. Ibid., Harris Hatch certificate, 25 Feb 1840. Hatch retired in favour of his son in March 1840.

33. Sheriff Thomas Jones observed that Ker had been 'chief Police Magistrate for a length of time' (i.e., while Hatheway was out of the commission): PANB RG8 (Magistrates), Jones to Ker, 22 Aug 1840. Ker told the 1832 Chipman commission that he had held no civil trials in the past three years. Nevertheless, when former newspaper publisher John Stubs left town in 1834 he advertised that Ker would be collecting all debts under £5 due him in St Andrews, St George, and St Patrick. (Samuel Abbot JP was Stubs's collector in St David.) *Standard*, 20 Mar 1834.

34. PANB RS431/B/1/4, ICCP minute book, 1838-1858. Hugh Mackay, James Rait, W.F.W. Owen, and John Wilson were also commissioned justices of common pleas in 1840. Owen attended once, with Wyer. Wilson sat occasionally in 1840 and 1841, always along with Wyer or Allanshaw. Wilson had several suits in ICCP at these sessions. On April 14, 1840 Hatheway, reinstated as JP a month previously but not himself a JCP, joined Allanshaw on the common pleas bench. Perhaps this was a public display of acceptance by Allanshaw, who had not signed the petition for Hatheway's reinstatement.

Among the St Andrews magistrates in the 1840 commission, David Mowatt was a farmer. It is not clear whether the John McLachlan who held a tavern license in 1840-1 was John McLachlan JP.[35] Thomas Wyer was local agent for Lloyd's of London and a bank director. He and James Rait had substantial landholdings and other investments as did John Wilson, the town's leading merchant and mill-owner, a director of the Marine Insurance Association and the chief promoter of the St Andrews & Quebec railway scheme. Consignment dealer William Ker and shopkeeper William Garnett had served together in the local chamber of commerce.[36] Garnett had been made a JP in 1832 by the commission that excluded Hatheway. An attempt to set fire to his store in 1834 resulted in the establishment of a volunteer night watch in St Andrews.[37] William Babcock, first appointed JP in 1840, kept a store and a hotel. While the 1840 and 1841 general sessions were in progress, the local newspaper carried advertisements by Babcock offering salt and flour (to be 'sold on reasonable terms, for Shingles, or Lumber payments'), canvas and paints; by Wilson offering ship's rigging, fishermen's supplies, and a farm property; and by Ker offering wines by the cask and advances on cargoes consigned to Barbados or Jamaica.[38] Outside St Andrews, many of the magistrates in the 1840 commission were also businessmen. James Allanshaw was one of the county's leading mill-owners.[39] Among St Stephen justices, Nehemiah Marks and brothers George and John Porter were prominent lumbermen.[40] Wilford Fisher was the leading merchant on Grand Manan. The Moores of St David and Mackays of St George and St Patrick were lumbermen. Admiral William Fitz William Owen, on the other hand, had retired from the Royal Navy to succeed his late uncle David as principal proprietor of Campobello. Half the Charlotte county agents for the St Andrews *Standard* were magistrates.[41]

The St Andrews justices held a number of local and provincial

35. His subsequent career is described in chapter 10.

36. CO 188/33, Report of St Andrews Chamber of Commerce on price of flour, 11 Jul 1826.

37. *Standard*, 11 Sep 1834, 16 Sep 1834, and see chapter 8.

38. Ker's brother was a West Indies merchant in Grenada and Tobago.

39. Wynn, *Timber Colony*, 105.

40. PANB MC1081; ibid., 106f.

41. *Standard*, 11 Sep 1840.

public appointments beside their membership in the commission of the peace. Babcock was an alms house commissioner in 1840. Garnett, Ker, Mowatt, and Rait were licensed auctioneers; Garnett, Rait, and Babcock firewards; Mowatt and Clinch coroners; Hatheway a notary public; Rait and Wilson members of the board of health; while legislative councillor Wyer held any number of appointments at various times including those of supervisor of the great roads and commissioner to solemnize marriages, of light houses, of packets and of buoys and beacons. In 1845 he applied to be made collector of crown debts for Charlotte as 'I have no appointment under Government that brings in anything,' except his five per cent commission on the contingent expenses of the lighthouse commission, worth twenty pounds a year. As we have already seen, several St Andrews justices, including Lt. Col. Wyer, Major Garnett, and Captain Hatheway, commanded militia units, as did legislative councillor and former clerk of the peace Harris Hatch.

The St Andrews magistrates of 1840-1 made up a fairly intimate circle. James Rait and William Babcock were associated with John Wilson in the Chamcook Mill & Factory Company; all three along with Thomas Wyer were directors of the St Andrews & Quebec railroad company; Wyer and Wilson were directors of the St Andrews and Saint John Stage Coach Company.[42] A *Standard* correspondent pointed out the cliquish nature of the Charlotte County Bank directory: Harris Hatch was president, Thomas Wyer and James Street were father-in-law and son-in-law, John and Edward Wilson were brothers, and the remaining four directors (who included Grand Manan JP Wilford Fisher) lived so far away from St Andrews that they were rarely present at meetings.[43] There were other family connections as well. Thomas Wyer lobbied for years to have his brother-in-law David Mowatt made high sheriff of the county. William Garnett was son-in-law of Peter Stubs. Wyer and Mowatt were sons of two of the town's founding Loyalists and nephews of its original patriarch, while Garnett was probably the son of the county's first clerk of the peace. James Rait was a relative newcomer to St Andrews. By making large investments in tim-

42. 3 Vict. (1840) c.66; 6 Wm.IV (1836) c.31; 1 Vict. (1838)c.40. Magistrates from other Charlotte parishes were involved in these enterprises, as was Harris Hatch.

43. *Standard*, 10 May 1838. See 6 Geo.IV (1825) c.12 and *Courier*, 12 May 1832.

ber lands and other speculations he quickly achieved prominence, gaining appointment as justice of the peace in 1832 and as justice of common pleas in 1836. But by the time the 1840 commission issued, his affairs were in utter disarray. He fled to Jamaica to escape his creditors and soon died.

Business and family connections overlapped with each other and with other connections of mutual interest. The county's most prominent magistrates were often also its members of the provincial assembly. The powerful Pagan–Campbell–Wyer interest in St Andrews had been represented continuously in the House since the founding of the province although this was about to change with Wyer's elevation to the legislative council.[44] County members not only represented local interests at Fredericton but controlled significant resources, especially after the assembly gained control of crown land revenues in 1837. T.W. Acheson describes the emerging New Brunswick version of 'responsible government':[45]

> [M]ost important financial decisions were not made in the Executive Council but in the Appropriations Committee of the Assembly, where one representative from each county gathered to distribute most of the provincial revenue. The major concerns of the county representatives were for roads and other local public works ... Since these vital decisions were not taken by the government but by the county representatives in the Assembly, the divisions between the Executive and the Assembly were muted ...

What was good for the Wyer interest was good for St Andrews. In the 1839 session he served as Charlotte's representative on the all-important roads committee and sponsored a legislative grant of one hundred pounds to support the stage coach company.[46] One of his last achievements in the assembly before his translation to the upper house was securing an appropriation of nearly a thousand

44. Charlotte elected four members. The Pagan–Wyer–Campbell interest that dominated St Andrews was represented in the assembly by Robert Pagan (1786-1820), John Campbell (1820-27), and Thomas Wyer Jr (1828-39).

45. Acheson, '1840s,' 326.

46. JHA 1 Mar 1839. An additional grant to the same company was approved in blank on 15 Mar 1839, 'to enable them to keep up the establishment.'

pounds for the four former trustees of the St Andrews savings bank, 'to remunerate them for losses sustained by the failure and defalcation of the Cashier,' Peter Stubs.[47] The trustees who benefited from this largesse were John McLachlan JP, Harris Hatch, Samuel Frye M.D., and Thomas Wyer. The board of directors of the county bank, presided over by Hatch, included St Andrews justices Wyer, Wilson, Douglas, McMaster, and Rait.

C.R. Hatheway lived on the margins of this close-knit group. Although of Loyalist parentage like Wyer and Mowatt, he had grown up at Burton in Sunbury county. His wife had been raised in York county and he had no relatives at St Andrews. He was loosely associated with Wyer and Hatch interests through his opposition to David Owen and his involvement in the Spearman affair but as his fellow magistrates recognized and as he himself later put it in applying for appointment to the common pleas, Hatheway 'had no connection with any trade or mercantile business.'[48]

Unlike the idealized English eighteenth-century Whig gentleman justice, who might employ a man of business but was definitely not of that class himself, the St Andrews justices were overwhelmingly drawn from the ranks of commerce rather than landed property. They and their fellow Charlotte magistrates had petitioned for Hatheway's reappointment because his lack of business involvements made him especially suited to 'the various and arduous duties of office.' There were several reasons why those duties must have seemed 'incompatible', as Rev Alley had put it, with their various business interests. Receiving complaints, issuing writs, examining witnesses, and deciding disputes consumed a busy man's valuable time. The appearance of impartiality could be hard to maintain when judging one's own clients, suppliers, and competitors. Commercial success could be undermined by presiding over suits that pitted customer against

47. JHA 5 Mar 1839, and see chapter 4, note 81.

48. PANB RS7, vol. 96, Hatheway to lieutenant governor, 28 Feb 1848. He also pointed out that he had 'performed a great deal of duty' as a JP and 'have never had a judgment removed or set aside.' The executive seems to have agreed with his assessment that another JCP was needed at St Andrews but appointed James W. Chandler instead: ibid., 23 Feb 1849. Hatheway was finally promoted to JCP in 1855 at Harris Hatch's urging when Chandler resigned: PANB RS7, vol. 97, Hatch to Tilley, 30 Mar 1855; PANB RS538/B/5, 30 Oct 1855.

customer. The wise trader minded his own business.[49] Elsewhere lay justices organized regular 'petty sessions' to manage the press of low law business,[50] or called for the appointment of full-time stipendiaries.[51] At St Andrews, Hatheway's reappointment to the commission of the peace was a third kind of solution to the problem: a sort of Squire Dogsbody who could be counted on to keep the wheels of local justice in motion while neither overreaching his modest standing among the county elite nor gumming up the works by egregious conduct.[52]

Sites of magisterial activity

Justices acted collectively at the general sessions of the peace, at special sessions convened for the conduct of particular business,[53] at meetings of magistrates for a single parish,[54] and sometimes at public meetings called for various purposes. They might attend the quarterly sittings of the inferior court of common pleas or the twice-yearly visits of the supreme court on circuit.[55] They met in groups of two or three (and sometimes more) for tasks delegated by statute to a 'double' or 'triple' justice. They sat alone, typically in their own shops

49. In the 1832 Chipman commission returns only Wyer and Hatheway among the St Andrews justices reported holding civil trials. Wyer reported seven trials in three years, as against Hatheway's seven hundred and forty-seven. Other Charlotte parishes showed more widely diffused civil trial activity. See further chapter 7.

50. For example Fyson, *Magistrates*.

51. For stipendiaries in New Brunswick see chapter 12, at note 64.

52. In 1730s London one alderman dominated the criminal business due to the reluctance of other businessmen-justices to undertake this work. When he died, the other magistrates organized themselves to sit in rotation: Beattie, *Policing and Punishment*.

53. Hatheway attended special sessions on the county debt (26 Aug 1840), on payments for the new courthouse (5 Jan 1841), and to appoint commissioners of the poor (26 Apr 1841).

54. For example, a meeting of St Andrews magistrates to arrange for a new wharf, 15 May 1841.

55. ICCP sat concurrently with the general sessions in April and September, and in additional terms in July and December: 35 Geo.III (1795) c.2; 42 Geo.III (1802) c.7. The supreme court circuit had only recently been regularized by 8 Wm.IV (1837) c.4, fixing the Charlotte court for the fourth Tuesday in April and the Tuesday following the fourth Tuesday in October. Circuit minutes for this period have not survived.

or parlours, to receive complaints, issue paper, and adjudge small crimes and petty civil disputes. Most informally of all, they were expected to deal with circumstances and situations they might encounter on the streets and wharves as they carried on their daily business.

General Sessions of the Peace

The New Brunswick equivalent of quarter sessions elsewhere, the county general sessions of the peace convened at St Andrews on the second Tuesday in April and the third Tuesday in September each year. There were thirty-six names in the commission of the peace for Charlotte issued on March 21, 1840. Table 6.3 shows the number of days each magistrate was recorded as attending general sessions in April and September, 1840, and April 1841.[56] It is clear that proceedings were dominated by St Andrews justices and that some parishes, including the populous St Stephen, were badly underrepresented.[57] Hatheway and Wyer shared top honours for attendance, totalling seventeen days each.

Little judicial business was conducted at these three sessions. In April 1840, the grand jury found five true bills against four defendants, two of whom were tried and acquitted by the petit jury. Another gave bail to appear at the next sessions but there is no mention of the case

56. The minute book records justices 'present' each day. This tally underestimates the attendance of some justices who were in sessions committee meetings rather than on the bench. Large committees were struck to audit county accounts and allocate the tax burden among the parishes: they seem to have met for one and sometimes two days in each session while a few justices (sometimes just one or two) remained on the bench. The minutes record committee membership but not committee attendance. On the other hand, the tally probably overstates the participation of some justices who may have left the sessions room after putting in a token appearance at the beginning of the day.

57. According to the (notoriously unreliable) 1840 census, St Andrews and St Stephen were roughly equal in population at approximately three thousand five hundred each; St George and St Patrick each had about two thousand; the remaining parishes ranged between about seven hundred (Campobello) and one thousand six hundred (St David), most of them about one thousand. For West Isles the census report notes: 'Nearly 200 of the Male Population of this Parish were at Sea, at the time of taking the Census, and are consequently not included in the above return.' Holbrook, *Census*.

Table 6.3 – JPs in commission by parish: CCGS attendance (days)

Name	Parish	Apr 1840	Sep 1840	Apr 1841	Total
Thomas Wyer	St Andrews	3	7	7	17
James Rait	St Andrews	0	0	0	0
John Wilson	St Andrews	4	2	0	6
Charles R. Hatheway	St Andrews	6	4	7	17
David Mowatt	St Andrews	1	1	0	2
William Ker	St Andrews	4	0	8	12
William Garnett	St Andrews	0	0	3	3
John McLachlan	St Andrews	2	3	2	7
William Babcock	St Andrews	5	0	4	9
William F.W. Owen	Campobello	0	1	3	4
John Snell	Campobello	1	0	2	3
John Robinson	Campobello	5	0	0	5
William Frankland	Grand Manan	0	0	0	0
Wilford Fisher	Grand Manan	0	1	1	2
Cochran Craig	Grand Manan	0	0	0	0
Joshua Knight	Pennfield	0	0	0	0
Tristram Moore	St David	0	1	1	2
Josephus Moore	St David	1	0	0	1
Hugh Mackay	St George	0	0	0	0
Patrick Clinch	St George	2	0	1	3
Abraham J. Wetmore	St George	1	0	1	2
James Allanshaw	St Patrick	4	2	4	10
Peter McCallum	St Patrick	0	0	0	0
George Mackay	St Patrick	2	0	2	4
Thomas Armstrong	St Stephen	0	0	0	0
Samuel Abbott	St Stephen	2	0	6	8
George Porter	St Stephen	0	0	0	0
Nehemiah Marks	St Stephen	0	0	1	1
James Frink	St Stephen	0	0	0	0
Robert Lindsey	St Stephen	0	0	0	0
John Porter	St Stephen	0	0	0	0
James Albee	St Stephen	1	0	2	3
David A. Rose	St Stephen	1	0	2	3
Thomas Moses	West Isles	0	0	4	4
John McNeil	West Isles	1	0	0	1
William B. Kinnear		0	0	0	0

in the September 1840 minutes. A bench warrant issued against the fourth defendant but when he appeared for trial in September he was released on a peace bond at his prosecutor's request. In September 1840 sessions received a grand jury presentment for selling liquor without a license and determined a complaint by the overseers of the poor against John Irwin, a St Andrews trader, for fathering a bastard child. In April 1841 the bench disposed of presentments for liquor license offences by ordering proceedings out of sessions by the magistrates of the parishes concerned. There were just four other items of judicial business. The defendant in a case of common assault failed to appear thereby forfeiting his bail. In another assault case involving a father and son as co-defendants one was acquitted and the other convicted and fined five pounds.[58] The prosecutor in another case did not appear. The final item of business was another bastardy complaint: neither the putative father nor his security, St Stephen JP Nehemiah Marks, made an appearance.[59] Perhaps in deference to their colleague in the commission the magistrates did not order the recognizances escheated immediately but issued a writ of scire facias returnable at September sessions to show cause why execution should not issue.

While the judicial calendar was light—'chief justice' Wyer announced that there was only one prisoner confined in the county gaol on a criminal charge in September 1840—there was a lot of county business to transact.[60] The magistrates were paying particular attention to this aspect of their duties because the sessions grand jury had recently acquired enhanced powers to audit the county accounts and supervise tavern licensing.[61] In the wake of the assembly's acquisition of new fiscal powers, there was a surge of enthusiasm for closer scrutiny of public spending. Public meetings were held in several Charlotte parishes in 1841 to deplore excessive spending by the legis-

58. Hatheway had conducted the preliminary examination in this case.

59. It was not at all unusual for Charlotte justices to give security for recognizances. Whether they charged for their role as bondsmen is unknown.

60. *Standard*, 18 Sep 1840.

61. 3 Vict. (1840) c.23; 3 Vict. (1840) c.47. Addressing the grand jury in April 1840 justice Allanshaw praised the new legislation as 'most comprehensive' and deserving 'its best attention': *Standard*, 17 Apr 1840. For grand jury oversight see also chapter 9.

lature.[62] At the county level James Boyd, who successfully contested the by-election for Wyer's former seat, campaigned on a platform of enhanced powers for the grand jury 'as Supervisors of the County property and accounts.'[63] He complained that grand jury recommendations had been ignored by the magistrates in the past and called for both grand and petit jurors to be paid for their services.[64] Boyd's successful campaign against Patrick Clinch JP signalled not only a growing dissatisfaction with the magistrates' domination of county affairs but also the loosening of the Wyer interest's hold on Charlotte patronage.[65]

Hatheway sat on the sessions committee to pass the public accounts in April and September 1840 and chaired it in April 1841. The grand jury audited the work of the justices' committee at April sessions both years. In 1840 it made a number of general criticisms: there was an alarming increase in county expenditures; the justices had routinely ignored grand jury recommendations in the past; the Charlotte County Bank charged excessive interest on the county debt; constables' charges were exorbitant; the liquor laws were inadequately enforced. It also pointed out that several magistrates had not accounted for fines they had levied in assault cases.[66] The accounts for 1841 credited four justices with paying over fines to county treasurer D.W. Jack: A.J. Wetmore (St George, £2), J. Moore (St David, £4), G. Mackay (St Patrick, £1), and Hatheway (St Andrews, eight payments totalling £13/4/3.) The grand jury directly criticized individual accounts passed by the magistrates. It made no comment on the £10 paid Hatheway in October 1840 as commissioner for re-

62. *Standard*, 28 May, 4 June, 11 June, 18 June 1841.

63. *Standard*, 5 Oct 1839.

64. There had been an unsuccessful attempt to introduce legislation for the payment of county grand juries province-wide in 1839. Boyd's complaint was echoed by the April 1840 grand jury: see below.

65. Boyd was an ally of Charlotte's new high sheriff, Thomas Jones, who had supported Spearman against Wyer, Wilson, Stubs, and Hatheway in 1832. Boyd became a JP in 1845. He and Hatheway remained one another's *bêtes noires* for years to come.

66. *Standard*, 24 Apr 1840. The accounts themselves were not published. The following year, an anonymous correspondent (probably the newspaper publisher) took the justices to task for this: ibid., 9 Apr 1841. Sessions then ordered the accounts to be published no later than May 20 each year; the 1841 accounts appeared in the *Standard*, on 28 May 1841.

pairing the gaol, but it rejected claims by three other justices for fees in criminal cases:[67] 'No other Magistrates make such charges against the County, and the Grand Jury believe them to be contrary to law.' The clerk of the peace claimed fees for advice in criminal cases and for drawing up petitions and charged for disbursements, all of which the grand jury thought should be covered by his salary. It rejected several other accounts as extravagant, made a number of recommendations for future economy (among them that no grocer be appointed an overseer of the poor), and concluded by recording its 'indignation and surprise' at the provincial legislature's decision to grant £1500 to help cover recalled lieutenant governor Harvey's debts.

As committee chair Hatheway published the justices' reply, dealing first with the grand jury's strictures on fees: '[A]s your Worships have provided for limiting the fees to the express sums prescribed by law, in all future cases, they deem it inexpedient to recommend any measures for causing the said charges to be refunded ...'[68] The justices had anticipated the audit. Two days before the grand jury made its report the magistrates had resolved that 'no accounts for Judicial Services shall be paid or allowed by this Bench except when specifically provided for by statute.' Hatheway's reply dealt with the grand jury's other specific criticisms in a similar fashion: the justices had 'seriously deliberated on the salary to the Clerk of the Peace' before finding his claims to be 'in order.'[69] A constable's account condemned by the grand jury had been passed by the bench at a previous session so 'it would be inexpedient to recover it.' Accounts paid by the magistrates but not shown to the grand jury were either 'an accident' or 'not considered necessary to put before them.' Hatheway acknowledged the merits of some of the grand jury's more general recommendations while passing no comment on its criticism of the assembly.

---

67. Wetmore claimed £3/10/0, Knight 19s, and Ker £11/18/1. On 12 Apr 1841, Ker paid the county £15/8/7 in respect of his 'account audited April 1840.'

68. *Standard*, 7 May 1841. The reply, dated 20 Apr 1841, went on to say that the impugned charges were consistent with the table of fees and that their illegality was 'even now questionable.'

69. By 4 Wm.IV (1834) c.29 clerks of the peace were directed to advise and assist the justices on request in examinations of persons arrested for felony, and were entitled to 'reasonable compensation' out of the county funds by order of general sessions.

Having thus successfully defused the threat of transparency and accountability, Hatheway had established himself as an impartial defender of county governance. One telling incident occurred during the wave of public meetings that were called in several parishes to denounce the assembly's spending. Lawyer R.M. Andrews published an account of the St Andrews meeting, naming Hatheway among those present and implying that he had endorsed the protest.[70] Hatheway hastened to distance himself: 'That I was at the Court House a few minutes at its commencement is true, but as a spectator only. Mr. Andrews *knew* that I was averse to the getting up of such a meeting and that I refused to sign a requisition to the Sheriff for its publicity.'[71]

Crown business out of Sessions

Out of sessions, justices of the peace investigated alleged crimes and other public offences. Their fees for these services were established by ordinance in 1785 and reissued in 1834.[72] Numerous provincial statutes gave them summary jurisdiction to try a variety of petty criminal and regulatory offences either alone or with one or more fellow magistrates.[73]

There are two sources of evidence for Hatheway's crown business in 1840-1. One is his justicing ledger in which he kept records in his own hand of his crown and civil business;[74] the other is two files of

70. 'Now I know that five magistrates actually did sign the requisitions, and I saw, besides Capt. Owen, Chas. R. Hatheway and Wm. Babcock, Esqrs, both present': (*Standard*, 4 Jun 1841).

71. Ibid., 11 Jun 1841.

72. *An Ordinance establishing fees to be taken in the Province of New-Brunswick* (Fredericton, 1834).

73. In particular 9&10 Geo.IV (1829) c.21, giving two justices summary jurisdiction in cases of common assault which they were to punish by fine or up to one month's imprisonment in default of payment. Fines were to be paid to the overseers of the poor. Section 15 also gave the magistrates power to award costs (although fine and costs together were not to exceed £5). The liquor act, 3 Vict. (1840) c.47, provided in s.23 that costs in prosecutions before a single or double justice were to be regulated by the table of fees in civil suits (discussed in the next section) and costs in prosecutions at general sessions by the fees ordinance. See also Appendix A.1.

74. PANB RS463. There are three of these containing dockets and notes for 1841-49 (referred to as 'Ledger 1' below), 1849-67 ('Ledger 2'), and 1867-8 ('Ledger 3'). Starting later in the decade, Hatheway included notes of evidence in these ledgers,

loose documents in the county papers catalogued as 'pretrial complaints' and 'pretrial examinations,' the majority involving Hatheway but dating for the most part from the mid-1850s.[75] Hatheway recorded twenty-one crown cases involving twenty-four defendants in his docket between April 1840 and January 1841.[76] Table 6.4 summarizes these proceedings, showing the number of justices involved in the case, whether it was a preliminary examination or a trial (or both), the costs charged, and its disposition.

Some of the offences deserve special mention as arising out of the revision of the criminal law in the 1830s.[77] Justices sitting alone were given exclusive jurisdiction to deal with complaints of cruelty to animals, which were punishable by a fine of ten shillings to five pounds along with costs.[78] Cases 11a and 11b in Table 6.4 involved two co-defendants accused by its owner of mistreating a red mare. The felonious stealing (case 18), tried summarily before three justices, involved the theft of 'sundry articles of the value of twenty shillings.' The distinction between grand and petty larceny had been abolished in 1831 making all larceny felonious but the same enactment empowered general sessions to try thefts up to five pounds. Where the value of the stolen property was two pounds or less the accused could be admitted to bail. Accused who could not make bail and who would therefore remain in gaol for more than forty-eight hours before the next general sessions could be tried summarily by any three justices of the peace and punished by imprisonment for up to six months or by whipping.[79] In 1840 the province repealed and replaced its 1826 act for regulating seamen. Where the old act had given two justices

but not in 1840-1. The entry for one of the 1840 cases is marked '(see trial)' which suggests that Hatheway was keeping such notes separately in these years.

75. PANB RS148/d/3/a; RS148 d/3/c.

76. Hatheway did not record any crown cases in February, March, or April 1841. I have considered the date of the case to be the date on which it is first mentioned in the ledger.

77. See generally 1 Wm.IV (1831) c.14 which followed the English criminal law reform acts by declaring all the criminal statutes repealed in England to be of no force and effect in New Brunswick. The assembly then enacted new criminal legislation which, among other things, expanded the magistrates' summary jurisdiction. See further chapter 8.

78. 4 Wm.IV (1834) c.13.

79. 1 Wm.IV (1831) c.15.

Table 6.4 – Hatheway's crown proceedings from ledger, 1840-1

Case	Offence	JPs	Exam	Trial	Costs	Disposition
1	drunk	1	✓		6s 6d	24 hours gaol then discharged
2a	felony	3	✓		9s 6d	discharged
2b	felony	3	✓		(incl)	discharged
3	disorderly	1	✓		6s 6d	discharged
4	assault	2		✓	13s 9d	fined 15s plus costs
5	drunk	1	✓		6s 6d	discharged
6	aid desert	2		✓	15s 1d	fined £3 incl costs
7	drunk	1	✓	✓	7s 9d	committed to gaol
8	assault constable	2		✓	n/a	fined £2 10s plus costs
9	obstruct justice	1		✓	2s 6d	fined 10s
10	assault	2		✓	11s 6d	fined 15s incl costs
11a	illtreat horse	1		✓	£2 12s 3d	fined £1 plus costs
11b	illtreat horse	1		✓		[discharged?]
12	[unspecified]	1	✓		12s 6d	mittimus
13	larceny	1	✓		15s	mittimus
14	larceny	1	✓		10s	mittimus
15	assault	2		✓	£1 5s 7d	fined £1 5s 6d incl costs[!]
16	liquor license	2		✓	£1 5s 3d	fined £2 plus costs or 40 days gaol
17	drunk	1	✓	✓	6s 6d	discharged
18	felonious stealing	3		✓	6s 6d	one month imprisonment
19	assault	1	✓		8s 0d	[discharged?]
20a	assault	2	✓		13s 9d	recognizance
20b	assault	2	✓		13s 3d	recognizance
21	liquor license	1		✓	£2 2s 0d	fined

authority to impose a penalty of five to ten pounds for engaging or concealing a deserter the new one reduced the minimum penalty for this offence to two pounds and expanded its scope to include aiding, enticing, or assisting a seaman to desert (case 6).[80]

Slightly more than half these crown cases were tried summarily either by Hatheway alone (6 cases) or in association with another justice (7 cases). The rest were preliminary examinations. Six accused were discharged, two released on bail, and three sent to gaol to await their trials. What became of the last three is a mystery.[81] The two who were released on bail, were the Henry Simpsons, father and son, charged with assault and battery on a St Stephen grocer and provision dealer and tried at April sessions 1841.

Hatheway's ledgers for this period are not very revealing about the circumstances of the offences or the social location of the offenders.[82] About twelve per cent of the accused and a similar proportion of the complainants or victims were women. Hatheway imposed the fine in case 9 for 'obstructing me in proceeding in a cause when in the course of trial before me this day.' On the day in question the offender James Garrett, a frequent client of Hatheway's debt collection service, attended Hatheway's office to secure a default judgment in a civil suit. The fine Hatheway recorded on the crown side of his ledger must have been for a criminal contempt ('insolent behaviour …tending to interrupt the proceedings') as provided for in the legislation governing the justices' civil jurisdiction.[83] Some of the complaints were institutional: clerk of the peace Wellington Hatch brought the liquor licensing charges against accused who had been presented by the grand jury at sessions, while the drunk and disorderly complaints were made by Thomas Sime or Thomas Turner, two of the St Andrews poor house commissioners. Thomas Wyer was the complainant in case 6 (aiding a deserter) but whether he was acting in

80. 7 Geo.IV (1826) c.12; 3 Vict. (1840) c.62.

81. Their names do not appear in the minutes of the next succeeding general sessions. Circuit court minutes for this period have not survived nor are there crown-side case files for these three accused.

82. The more detailed minutes of crown and civil actions in Hatheway's later ledger entries are used in chapters 7 and 8 to explore these questions in depth.

83. 4 Wm.IV (1834) c.45, discussed below.

a public or private capacity is unknown. He did not judge the case. In proceedings where he acted with one or two other justices Hatheway was associated with Babcock five times, Wyer three times, Garnett and Fisher twice each, and Knight and Allanshaw once each. Three of these associates were not St Andrews residents.

The only extended account of crown side proceedings in which Hatheway was involved in this period is Wellington Hatch's record of an investigation in the late summer of 1840.[84] There is no reference to it in Hatheway's ledger. On August 19, Lydia Greenlaw and her daughter Elizabeth came to Hatheway to complain that a 'gang' of drunken sailors, accompanied by some women, had pulled down their house ('situated in the lowest part of St Andrews') and taken away their belongings the night before. On August 20 justices Wyer, Allanshaw, Hatheway, and Babcock met along with the clerk of the peace to examine the complainants and a witness in the presence of six of the accused. The Greenlaws and their witness each gave a statement under oath. The accused were given the opportunity to ask them questions. After their statements and answers were read over to them and explained the Greenlaws affixed their marks. The accused were not examined but the justices took evidence from a defence witness: Charles S. Howatson, a St Andrews boarding-house keeper, testified that he had shown one of the accused to bed on the evening in question and then locked up the house.[85] The accused were committed and the Greenlaws bound over 'to appear next court.' There is no mention of this affair in the September 1840 sessions minutes nor are there extant circuit court casefiles for any of the accused. Reading between the lines of the depositions the incident appears to have begun with a first attack on the Greenlaws' house the night before although they did not complain to the authorities until the second night when the sailors, their faces masked by handkerchiefs, 'commenced pulling the house immediately down and hunted all through the woods to find the goods and swore that if they did not find the goods they

84. PANB RS148/D/3/c, 'The Queen vs Sundry persons for pulling down a house,' 20 Aug 1840.

85. Howatson was the principal complainant in charges of judicial misconduct against Ker, who described him as a notorious crimp: PANB RG8 (Magistrates), Ker to Odell, 20 Aug 1840.

would knock their [Lydia's and Elizabeth's] brains out.' This suggests a dispute about the ownership of the new shirts and bedclothes the sailors' women took away. Whether this was a charivari, an ethnic brawl, an outburst of vigilantism, or all of these things, it hints at a practice of violent communal norm enforcement in competition with the magistrates' official police authority.[86]

A main purpose of Hatheway's ledger-keeping was to keep track of his fees. He wrote out tables of justices' fees in civil suits and in proceedings against seamen (but not of fees in crown cases) on one endpaper. However the 'costs' column in Table 6.4, which transcribes the amounts listed in the record of each case, is not a consistent guide to his income from crown cases. In some instances—for example, cases 2a, 2b and 18, in which he acted with two other justices—he indicates the whole amount as 'due to C.R.H.' At other places the distribution of costs is less clear. There is no explanation given for the very high costs in the animal cruelty case (11a and 11b), but as it arose in St Patrick and was tried in St Andrews some considerable part was likely constable fees and travel expenses. The ledger in this case merely notes, 'Costs paid by Deft & delivered to the parties' without indicating the justice's fee. The accounting in case 15, where the costs exceed the total fine including costs, is obviously in error. However, in several cases Hatheway noted the specific services for which he was charging fees. For example, case 12 has 'oath compt enquiry & mittimus, 2nd examination, 4 Evidences & recognizance' for a total of 12s. 6d. Case 19 is even more particular: 'compt oath & warrant 3/9, 3 Subs 1/, Examination 2/6, 3 Evidc sworn /9 — 8/ due.' This was an assault case, so it attracted the 2s. 6d. charge for an examination set out in the 1790 fees table. None of the other items are referable to that table, but they do correspond to fees allowed in civil cases as described below. This speaks to the contretemps between the justices and the grand jury in 1841 about what fees were permitted by law in crown cases. The civil

86. For ethnic violence in New Brunswick in the 1840s, see See, *Riots in New Brunswick* and, more generally, his 'Unprecedented Influx.' As he notes at page 13 of the book, though, See's research 'focuses on several communities scattered along the reaches of the Saint John River. It does not explore ... the southwestern counties rich in Loyalist traditions ... [which] lacked riots and socio-economic confrontations that achieved the drama and magnitude of those addressed' in his work.

fees for issuing writs, administering oaths, and so forth were certainly 'provided for by statute,' as the bench put it in their April sessions resolution although there was no statute providing for their application in crown cases other than liquor licensing offences. Nevertheless it seems to have been Hatheway's uncontested practice to apply the civil fee schedule to services unprovided for in other statutes. While it is difficult to estimate Hatheway's income from crown proceedings with any precision, it does appear that his fees amounted to between six and fourteen shillings in most cases, say ten shillings on average. By this estimate, which may be overgenerous, his income from crown cases in 1840-1 would have been approximately twelve pounds.[87]

Civil jurisdiction

New Brunswick magistrates had exclusive jurisdiction to decide most minor civil actions alone or with a three-man jury. The governing statute had recently been amended to define and clarify this jurisdiction: it included actions to recover debts up to five pounds and certain other civil actions for damages up to two pounds.[88] The amendments included a set of forms and revised tables of fees allowed to justices, constables, witnesses, and jurors, and to supreme court judges and attorneys in proceedings to remove a cause from the justice's court. The justice's fees are summarized in Table 6.5.

Hatheway's ledger includes three hundred and sixteen civil proceedings initiated between April 1840 and April 1841. The great majority (284, 90%) commenced with a writ of summons, although in thirty cases the defendant was arrested by capias and in two by a warrant. Slightly more than half (172, 54%) resulted in default judgments. Of the cases that went to trial, only eleven (7.5%) involved a jury. Al-

87. This assumes that Hatheway did not take fees in undocketed cases like the Greenlaw examinations where he sat in association with other justices.

88. 4 Wm.IV (1834) c.45, conferring jurisdiction in debt, in trespass (and trespass on the case) for injuries to personal property, and in trespass to real property. The main exceptions to jurisdiction were actions where land title was in issue, actions in which the crown was party, actions in debts over £5 which had not been reduced by payment to £5 or less, actions in debts by specialty that were not for a sum certain, and actions against executors, administrators, trustees of absconding debtors, and corporations.

Table 6.5 – Fees allowed Justices of the Peace in civil actions (1834)

Summons or capias	0s 9d
Copy of summons or capias	0s 3d
Affidavits for capias, and swearing	1s 0d
Subpoena	0s 4d
Copy or ticket of subpoena	0s 2d
Swearing witness or constable	0s 3d
Appointment of next friend or guardian	0s 6d
Venire	0s 6d
Swearing Jury	0s 6d
Adjournment	0s 6d
Trial and judgment	1s 3d
Judgment by default & assessing damages	1s 0d
Taking bail & justifying	1s 0d
Taking deposit	1s 0d
On money paid into Court by defendant pending suit, $2\frac{1}{2}$ per cent	
Execution	0s 9d
Execution against joint debtors requiring special endorsement	1s 0d
Certificate to suspend execution	0s 3d
Affidavit of service of summons & swearing	0s 0d
Affidavit to be taken by attorney or agent, & swearing	1s 0d
Copies of particulars &c, per 100 words	0s 6d
Return to Judge's order for removal	5s 0d

most two-thirds of the judgments (193, 61%) went to execution of which about twenty per cent were renewed or stayed. The process was expeditious from initial writ to trial and judgment but payment following judgment was frequently delayed—sometimes for months, occasionally for years—and in some cases was never collected.[89]

These civil proceedings were mostly actions to collect commercial debts (accounts and promissory notes) although they included a few actions for fines in liquor license offences following grand jury presentments (seven cases prosecuted in the name of the 'Clerk of the Court') and for taxes (nine cases prosecuted in the name of the 'Justices of Charlotte'). There was at least one action for each of trespassing on the plaintiff's property; impounding the plaintiff's oxen; wages owed the plaintiff's son; 'damage'; by a party for constable's fees—but as with the crown side of his ledger for this period, Hatheway recorded few details. The great majority of cases resulted in judgments for the plaintiff. In the few cases where the plaintiff failed to appear judgment was entered for the defendant to recover costs. Occasionally a plaintiff was nonsuited with the same result. A handful of cases are marked as 'settled' or 'compromised' and one was resolved by arbitration out of court: 'left by consent of plaintiff to 2 men and decided that defendant keep the table and pay JP costs.'

Leaving aside those involving institutional plaintiffs, there were 300 civil actions with 156 distinct plaintiffs and 247 different defendants. Table 6.6 shows the distribution of this community of litigants among the 300 actions. The vast majority of litigants, whether plaintiffs (90%) or defendants (93%), played that role just once or twice in the year under consideration. Ten individuals appeared as plaintiffs in a total of one hundred actions, a third of the total (Table 6.7): people in this group of ten defended only nine actions, just three per cent of the total. The ten major plaintiffs fall into three groups, all of them having extensive dealings with the less genteel elements of the St Andrews population. Sime and Chandler (a lawyer) were poor house commissioners and it seems likely that the majority of their suits were in that public capacity. David Polleys and James B. Brown held tav-

89. Against his record of one case decided in January 1841 and in which execution issued a month later Hatheway noted, 'examined by plaintiff 10 May 1852.'

Table 6.6 – Distribution of litigants in civil actions

Individuals appearing:	As defendants	%*	As plaintiffs	%†
Once	195	79	106	68
Twice	35	14	27	17
Three times	10	4	6	4
Four to five times	7	3	7	4
Six to ten times	0	0	7	4
More than ten times	0	0	3	2

* Per cent of all defendants. † Per cent of all plaintiffs.

ern licenses and so were well-situated to accumulate small debts.[90] The third group comprised proprietors of discount stores and boarding houses. We have already met C.S. Howatson, James Garrett, and John Irwin, who advertised 'Great Bargains!' at his New Brunswick Cloth & Fancy Store.[91] George Watson may have been, like Howatson, a sailor's boarding-house keeper and sometime crimp: in 1835 he had been bound over for trial as an accessory before the fact to mutiny and desertion.[92] Dry, goods retailer Dennis Bradley advised credit customers at his 'Cheap Store' that 'All those indebted to him, either by note or book account are requested to settle their respective accounts, which will be found to be the most satisfactory conclusion.'[93]

Despite the volume of petty civil business, this was not a particularly litigious community. Only twenty-two individuals appeared as both plaintiff and defendant, and of these three were among the ten most active plaintiffs, two were constables, and three tavern licensees. Few plaintiffs or defendants appeared in court more than once.

90. *Standard*, 2 Oct 1840. Polleys may also have held public office; he became provincial flour inspector at St Andrews in 1847.

91. *Standard*, 18 Sep 1840.

92. The prosecution arising from the desertion of seven sailors from the brig *Agenora* involved some of the usual suspects: Watson was committed for trial by justices Wyer and Allanshaw, while the arrest of three of the sailors (one of whom turned crown witness) was due to 'the exertions of Messrs [William] Babcock & Son and the prompt assistance of the civil authorities' at Eastport, Maine, whence they had taken the ship's longboat: *Standard*, 24 Dec 1835.

93. Ibid., 11 Sep 1840.

Table 6.7 – Ten plaintiffs accounting for one-third of civil actions

Individuals appearing:	As defendant	As plaintiff
Charles S. Howatson	2	6
David Polleys	0	7
George Watson	0	7
James B. Brown	4	8
Patrick O'Neal	3	8
Thomas Sime	0	8
Dennis Bradley	0	9
James Garrett	0	11
James W. Chandler	0	13
John Irwin	0	17

It is not difficult to construct an estimate of Hatheway's income from civil litigation from the schedule of fees and the accounting entries in his ledger. Each of his 316 cases was initiated by a summons, capias or warrant, for which he was entitled to ninepence.[94] Plaintiffs who wanted to have their debtor arrested by capias had to swear an affidavit that they believed the defendant was about to leave the jurisdiction or otherwise evade the obligation; there were 30 of these at a shilling each. Hatheway gave 172 default judgments at a shilling each and 144 trial judgments at one shilling and threepence apiece. There were 193 executions (ninepence each), 37 renewals (ninepence), and 6 stays (threepence). His 11 jury trials each involved a venire (threepence), administering an oath to the jury (sixpence), and another to the constable to attend them (threepence). The ledger entries make it difficult to assess how many witnesses had to be sworn (at threepence each) but this item is only specifically noted about 20 times. Hatheway took bail on 15 occasions at a shilling a time. He does not appear to have granted adjournments or taken money from defendants before trial,[95] and none of his cases was removed to the supreme court.

94. The ledger only records processes that were returned. The Chipman Commission reported in 1832 that justices commonly took no fee for a summons unless and until it was returned. Given the absence of any system for recording summonses that were not returned, it seems likely that Hatheway followed this practice.

95. The fee schedule in the 1834 statute was unusually verbose about justices' entitlement to income from funds passing through their hands: 'On money paid

Table 6.8 – Calculation of Hatheway's fees in civil suits, 1840-1

Item	Number	Rate	Shillings
Initial writ	316	0.75	237.00
Affidavit in capias	30	1.00	30.00
Default judgments	172	1.00	172.00
Trial judgments	144	1.25	180.00
Executions	193	0.75	144.75
Renewals	37	0.75	27.75
Stays	6	0.25	1.50
Venire	11	0.50	5.50
Jury oath	11	0.50	5.50
Constable oath	11	0.25	2.75
Witness oath	20	0.25	5.00
Bail	15	1.00	15.00
		Total:	826.75

Table 6.8 shows the calculation of these fees, which amount in total to a little more than forty-one pounds for the year. He earned an average of two shillings and sevenpence per cause, although his fee most commonly amounted to two shillings threepence.

Hatheway's limited involvement with other business activities and his loose alignment with the Wyer interest made him a valuable acquisition to the local bench. Like other mid-nineteenth-century communities lacking an independent gentry, Charlotte was governed by a local elite of merchants, industrialists, and bankers. Elsewhere such benches of businessmen often attempted to organize and delegate their day to day administrative and judicial responsibilities to paid officials (clerks, stipendiaries) or to more structured institutions (petty sessions, municipal corporations). These efforts were consistent with and contributed to the increasing professionalization and bureaucratization of local government and petty justice in the period. In Hatheway, however, the St Andrews elite discovered a third

into Court by a defendant pending a suit, before trial or judgment, two and a half per cent. or sixpence in the pound, but no per centage to be charged for receiving money on deposit in lieu of bail or upon execution.' The exception seems to have been directed at one of the practices for which Hatheway had been criticized in 1832, charging interest on moneys collected.

solution, one by which they could reduce the burden of governance without sacrificing paternalist control.

The availability of a single justice prepared to take on a substantial volume of business benefited not only his fellow magistrates but the larger community of traders and customers as well. While there is no indication that a significant backlog of cases had developed during the years Hatheway was out of the commission, limited access to petty justice may well have reduced the volume of such litigation. Without competent, expeditious, inexpensive, and accessible debt collection St Andrews businessmen might have been more reluctant to extend credit to marginal customers and more inclined to allow the indebtedness of creditworthy customers to cross the five pound threshold into the more costly jurisdiction of the common pleas. Easy access to an active justice uninvolved in ordinary commerce may therefore have improved the terms of trade for both businesses and customers in St Andrews.

Hatheway was an unusually active non-stipendiary justice. Figure 6.1 identifies (X) each day on which he participated in one or more of the justices' administrative or judicial functions. He was able to maintain his large family in circumstances of modest gentility suitable to his rank by combining his military pension, his justicing fees, and an occasional commission as a land surveyor. Hatheway received about £80 sterling, equivalent to £100 New Brunswick currency, as a lieutenant on half-pay.[96] In 1840-1 he earned about £40 in civil fees, £12 in crown-side fees, and £10 for administrative services[97] so that his total income as magistrate was between £60 and £65. If surveying brought in another £15 or £20 annually, Hatheway would have nearly doubled his half-pay. As a justice unconnected with business, Hatheway was thereby able to make a remunerative business of justicing.

96. NBM Hatheway Papers include his London agent's statements of account.
97. His account as jail commissioner may have included expenses.

Figure 6.1 – Hatheway's justicing calendar, April 1840 to March 1841

April 1840

Su	Mo	Tu	We	Th	Fr	Sa
	X		1	2	3	4
5	6	X	8	9	10	11
12	X	X	X	X	17	X
19	X	X	X	X	X	X
X	X	28	29	30		

May 1840

Su	Mo	Tu	We	Th	Fr	Sa
					1	2
3	4	5	X	7	X	X
X	11	12	X	14	15	16
17	18	19	20	21	22	X
X	X	26	X	X	29	X

June 1840

Su	Mo	Tu	We	Th	Fr	Sa
31	1	2	X	4	5	X
7	X	X	10	X	12	X
14	X	X	17	18	19	X
21	X	X	X	X	26	X
28	X	30				

July 1840

Su	Mo	Tu	We	Th	Fr	Sa
			1	2	X	4
5	X	7	X	9	10	X
12	X	X	X	X	X	X
19	20	21	X	X	24	X
26	X	X	X	30	X	X

August 1840

Su	Mo	Tu	We	Th	Fr	Sa
2	X	4	X	X	X	X
X	X	X	12	X	14	X
16	17	X	X	X	21	X
23	X	X	X	27	X	X
30	31					

September 1840

Su	Mo	Tu	We	Th	Fr	Sa
		1	2	3	4	5
6	7	8	9	X		X
13	X	X	X	X	18	X
20	X	X	X	24	25	X
X	28	29	30			

October 1840

Su	Mo	Tu	We	Th	Fr	Sa
				X	X	X
4	X	X	X	8	9	X
11	12	13	14	X	16	17
18	19	20	X	X	X	X
25	26	27	28	29	30	X

November 1840

Su	Mo	Tu	We	Th	Fr	Sa
1	2	3	4	5	6	X
8	9	X	X	X	13	X
15	16	17	18	19	20	21
22	23	24	25	26	27	28
29	X					

December 1840

Su	Mo	Tu	We	Th	Fr	Sa
		1	2	3	X	X
6	7	X	9	10	11	X
13	14	15	X	17	18	X
20	21	22	23	X	25	X
27	X	29	X	31		

January 1841

Su	Mo	Tu	We	Th	Fr	Sa
					1	X
3	X	X	X	7	X	X
10	X	X	X	14	X	X
17	18	19	20	21	22	X
24	X	26	27	X	29	X

February 1841

Su	Mo	Tu	We	Th	Fr	Sa
31	1	2	X	4	5	X
7	X	X	10	11	12	X
14	15	16	17	18	X	X
21	X	23	24	X	X	27
28						

March 1841

Su	Mo	Tu	We	Th	Fr	Sa
	X	2	X	4	X	X
7	8	X	X	X	12	X
14	X	X	17	X	19	X
21	X	X	24	X	X	X
28	X	30	X			

Chapter 7

Hatheway's civil docket, 1847-67

New Brunswick magistrates were not required to report regularly to the government but on a few occasions (like the 1832 Chipman commission) they were asked for statistics of their work. In March 1851 the assembly called for returns from all the magistrates in the province showing 'the number of Suits brought for the recovery of Debts or Damages under the Justices' Act ... [and] the number of Prosecutions for the recovery of Penalties and Demands arising from County and Parochial Rates or Assessments.'[1] The returns were

1. JHA 1851, 184. The very detailed requisition (moved by R.B. Cutler of Kent county) sought, 'Returns from all the different Magistrates and Justices in the Province, shewing the number of Suits brought for the recovery of Debts or Damages under the Justices' Act, The amount sued for,–Whether the Writ was Bailable or Common Process,–Whether tried by a Jury or decided by the Justice,–The amount recovered, and when nothing was recovered,–Also, the number of Prosecutions for the recovery of Penalties and Demands arising from County and Parochial Rates or Assessments,–The Return to shew the same separately, with the name or names of the Constable or Constables serving the Writ or Writs, and Execution in case of Execution being issued,–The amount of Justices' Fees, Constables' Fees, Witness Fees, Jury Fees, separately in each case,–Also, the Suits on which Execution was finally issued,–The cost of the Constable for travel and levy,–Whether property was sold, and if so, the nature and kind of property,–The Return to comprise a period of one year, and be ready to lay before this House at the next Session.' Provincial secretary Partelow thereupon sent a circular letter to all the justices, calling on them to supply the required information before the end of December: PANB RS13/A/7, Partelow to

tabled in the assembly in April 1852 and referred to a select committee, but no report was forthcoming.[2]

Table 7.1 – Charlotte justices reporting civil suits, 1851

Justice	Parish	Number	Parish %	County %
Hatheway	St Andrews	203	72	39
Ker	St Andrews	78	28	15
Moore	St David	15	100	3
Knight	St George	56	60	11
Clinch	St George	38	40	7
McCallum	St Patrick	10	59	2
McFarlan	St Patrick	7	41	1
*Albee**	*St Stephen*	*150*		
Rose	St Stephen	103	98	20
Grimmer	St Stephen	2	2	0
Craig	Grand Manan	12	100	2
McNeil	West Isles	2	100	0

* Record for 1849-50, not included in totals (see note 5).

Barely half of Charlotte's thirty-nine justices filed returns.[3] There were none from Campobello, Pennfield, or St James parishes. Of the twenty who did respond, eight had nothing to report. St Stephen's George M. Porter replied that he did not even consider himself to be in the commission of the peace, never having taken the qualifying oath. As for his brother John, then out of the country, George felt he could 'safely say, that he has never acted in the capacity of a Magistrate in the collection of debts in any case.' Nehemiah Marks reported having 'never issued a summons or had any cases before me as a magistrate.' Among the St Andrews justices, James Allanshaw 'never since I have been in the Commission tried a civil suit, my duties having been confined solely to criminal matters,'[4] while Dr McStay did nothing as a magistrate but attend the General Sessions. John Snell

magistrates, 5 Apr 1851.

2. JHA 1852, 57, 137, 265.
3. PANB RS539/C.
4. Nevetheless Allanshaw had tried many civil suits at common pleas.

laid out an elaborate tabulation with columns for the headings in the assembly resolution—then filled it with the single word, 'none.' James Street conveyed the same message more economically, while legislative councillor and former clerk of the peace Harris Hatch JCP, now signing himself 'Senior Magistrate for Charlotte,' disapproved of the whole enterprise:

> [S]ince I have held the situation of a Magistrate for the County of Charlotte, I have not issued a civil process, and I have not much inclination to do so, as I conceive the civil power given to the Magistrate, as is now the case, has a tendency to lessen his authority in his original criminal jurisdiction, and, therefore, compromises, more or less, the efficiency of the law, in that respect.

Twelve Charlotte justices reported among them 526 civil suits (Table 7.1), ranging from John Grimmer's two causes heard on the same day and involving the same plaintiff and John McNeil's two, both abandoned by the plaintiff, to substantial numbers heard by David Rose and James Albee at St Stephen and Hatheway at St Andrews.[5]

This chapter explores civil justicing through the lens of Hatheway's well-documented practice. The materials include his docket from June 1849 to February 1856, listing 890 civil suits, as well as a great number of loose papers from the 1850s and 1860s.[6] While the analysis in chapter 6 emphasized justicing as a remunerative business, the intention here is to look in some detail at the legal process, Hatheway's possibly somewhat idiosyncratic practice, and the economic and social relations that underlay both.

5. Albee submitted his unsummarized record for 1849-50 as he had been too ill to hear cases since then; Rose seems to have taken up the St Stephen civil work in his place.

6. Ledger 2. The 1849-1856 period was selected to facilitate linkage with the 1851 census and with assessment, parish officer, and other nominal information in PANB RS148. Unless otherwise specified references to 'the docket' in this chapter mean the 890 civil cases initiated in this 80-month period. The same ledger also contains Hatheway's notes of 'complaints and proceedings on Trials long since settled and disposed of' at pages 201-381. Examples for which specific source citations are not given are from those pages. The loose papers are for the most part in PANB RS148/C and D. The subgroupings in these record series do not consistently reflect the contents of the files.

Overview

As the 1851 assembly resolution suggested, civil suits could arise from private transactions ('debts and damages') or public obligations ('penalties and demands arising from ... rates and assessments'). Hatheway's return included 182 private suits and 21 tax collection cases. While his docket entries identify the subject matter of the dispute in only about a third of the cases, it is clear that the overwhelming majority of the suits he heard arose out of private disputes, most of them about goods and services received but not paid for. More than half of these (about 180 of 299 cases in which the cause can be identified from the docket entry) involved promissory notes; others included claims for specific items (flour, wood, meat, rent) or services (wages, wagon hire, medical services), while a small proportion sought compensation for damages, recovery of old unsatisfied judgments, or settlement of disputed accounts. In addition a relatively small number of cases were brought by county or parish officers to recover fines (for example, for hogs running at large), the dog tax, or other levies including statute labour on the highways.

Whether private debt or public obligation, the civil process had three phases. First a plaintiff came to the justice to initiate the suit and call on the defendant to answer it. Next came trial and judgment. Finally, if judgment was awarded it had to be collected and paid over and the costs of the process had to be recovered. The plaintiff and defendant were principal parties but they were by no means the entire cast. The JP was involved in all three phases; constables might be involved in any or all of them; witnesses and jurors might be involved at trial; one or both of the parties were sometimes represented by lawyers or other agents; sureties gave bail for defendants who had been arrested; others (referred to here as third parties) might be involved in various roles, most prominently as payors or payees.[7] In a minority of cases the sheriff and gaoler also had roles to play.

Numerous decisions had to be made in the process. The central formal determinations were the verdict and judgment at trial. These were preceded by many more informal decisions. The plaintiff had to decide whether and when to proceed against the defendant, for how

7. See the discussion of the court's clearinghouse role at page 261 below.

much, and in what forum. He (sometimes she) had to choose a JP and decide whether to proceed by arrest or summons. The defendant had to decide whether to contest the plaintiff's claim or accede to it by confession or simple nonappearance. Either party might offer to settle the claim, in which case the other would have to decide whether to accept or reject the terms. If there was to be a trial each side had to decide what evidence to adduce. Either could request a three-man jury failing which the magistrate would proceed summarily. After judgment was rendered the defendant had to decide whether or not to satisfy it (here there might be room for another round of settlement decisions); if it was not satisfied the plaintiff had to decide whether to press for an immediate levy on the defendant's property or to wait on events; if the defendant's property was insufficient the plaintiff had to decide whether to insist on sending him to the debtors' room at the county gaol and, if the defendant was utterly insolvent, how long to pay for his keep there.

These relatively simple proceedings, therefore, were founded on a complex series of economic and social calculations. While a quantitative analysis of the docket can reveal a good deal about how (and how well) the legal process worked and who was caught up in it, understanding the economic and social calculus of petty civil litigation requires a more intimate encounter with the specific circumstances of particular cases.

People

Nearly three thousand names are recorded for the 890 civil cases in Hatheway's docket. The majority of these cases (521; fifty-nine per cent) involved only three named players apart from Hatheway himself: typically one plaintiff, one defendant, and one constable. Slightly more than ten per cent involved just one or two individuals, twenty per cent involved four, and the remaining ten per cent of cases involved between five and nine. This counting of named individuals somewhat underestimates the number of people involved, however, because Hatheway did not consistently record jurors' names. Although only 48 jurors are named in the docket it records 66 jury trials, accounting for an additional 150 participants. Similarly, although

Hatheway recorded the names of witnesses in only 104 cases witness fees were charged in many others. More people were involved in the processing of these 890 cases than were named on the docket. Nevertheless the analysis that follows is necessarily restricted to those whose names are known.[8]

Hatheway's civil court was a largely male preserve. Except as witnesses in other people's suits women made only forty-seven appearances in their own names,[9] thirty of them as plaintiff, nine as defendant, and the rest representing their plaintiff husbands (or, in one case, mother), usually by receipting payments. Among the woman defendants only one—St Andrews boarding-house keeper Mary Coldwell—appeared more than once. Ellen Healey, the butcher's wife, was the most frequent woman plaintiff. Mary Lonergan, who kept house for tavernkeeper James Driscoll, sued three times, twice on promissory notes in her favour. Four other women—one a tavern-keeper, another a widow—sued twice. Women played more prominent parts in Hatheway's crown cases than in his civil proceedings.[10]

Many individuals appeared in the same role in Hatheway's court on more than one occasion in the eighty months analysed here (Table 7.2). The majority of plaintiffs appeared in that role more than

---

8. To identify repeated appearances by the same individual it was necessary to reconcile variant spellings (even within a single docket entry, as for example when a plaintiff's signature to a receipt is spelled differently from Hatheway's note of his name in the style of cause) and to distinguish as far as possible between different individuals with the same name. Hatheway recorded the parish of residence for defendants but not for plaintiffs or others named. Docket entries were linked manually to the 1851 census for Charlotte county and, where additional confirmation was needed, to assessment rolls, lists of parish officers, and other nominal sources. Repeated occurrences were taken to be the same individual where the normalized spelling of the name, the parish of residence, and any special qualifications (e.g., office or occupation) matched and the census contained only one adult individual with the corresponding characteristics. The 2998 names collected from the docket resolved to 904 distinct individuals; of these, 549 (61%) were positively linked to the alphabetized census compilation in R.F. Fellows, *Census, 1851*. William Kearns provided valuable research assistance in the first pass of the docket database and census linkage.

9. Examples of women suing in their own names and of husbands suing for wages earned by their wives or defending against obligations incurred by them are given below at pages 267 and following.

10. Chapter 8.

Table 7.2 – Principal roles in 890 civil suits

Role	All names	Distinct names	Approx. rate
Plaintiffs	895	310	3
Defendants	932	502	2
Constables	797	52	16
Witnesses*	104	89	1
Attorneys, agents	94	51	2
Third parties	92	75	1
Jurors*	48	29	2
Sureties	25	22	1

* Under-represented—see text.

Table 7.3 – Repeated appearances in role in 890 civil suits

Number of appearances:	1	2	3-5	6-10	11+	(Max)
Plaintiffs	175	56	43	20	16	(48)
Defendants	340	67	69	22	4	(20)
Constables	29	4	10	3	6	(471)
Witnesses	78	9	2	0	0	(5)
Attorneys, agents	38	5	4	3	1	(13)
Third parties	65	5	5	0	0	(5)
Jurors	20	6	2	1	0	(8)
Sureties	19	3	0	0	0	(2)

once (Table 7.3). Three plaintiffs appeared more than thirty times: the merchant firm Odell & Turner (32), butcher Thomas Healey (38, and his wife Ellen an additional 9), and blacksmith Michael Fauls (48). Four defendants, including a hotel-keeper, a farmer, and a mason, each appeared more than ten times. William Henan served as Hatheway's constable in more than half the cases (471). Moreover, many individuals appeared in more than one role at different times (Table 7.4): for example 86 people appeared as both plaintiff and defendant. Of the 904 distinct individuals named in the docket, 732 appeared in just one role, 122 in two, 34 in three, 10 in four, and 6 in five or more different roles. Among those with the greatest breadth of experience, St Andrews lawyer A.T. Paul appeared as attorney for both plaintiffs and defendants, as a plaintiff himself, as a witness, and as a third party. Tavern-keeper Charles McGee appeared as plaintiff, defendant, juror, witness, and third party. John Dougherty, another tavern-keeper, appeared as plaintiff, plaintiff's attorney, surety, and third party. Butcher and frequent plaintiff Thomas Healey also appeared as defendant, juror, and surety. When William Henan was not acting as a constable, he also appeared in the roles of plaintiff, defendant, plaintiff's attorney, defendant's attorney, and witness. A few years later Henan's experience of the legal system would broaden still further to include the roles of criminally accused and penitentiary inmate.

Table 7.4 – Multiple roles in 890 civil suits*

Role	Dft	Cbl	Wit	Att	3dP	Jur	Sur
Plaintiff	86	8	21	26	21	11	11
Defendant	–	11	21	13	20	11	11
Constable	–	–	6	7	6	2	1
Witness	–	–	–	7	8	2	2
Attorney	–	–	–	–	7	3	3
3rd Party	–	–	–	–	–	5	3
Juror	–	–	–	–	–	–	2

* Count of individuals in each pair of roles.

Not every plaintiff or defendant who made several appearances at Hatheway's justice shop can be considered a regular customer. While many of the plaintiffs who appeared more than five times brought just one or two claims at a time over many months, others brought a handful of claims all at once. Michael Fauls was in the former category, seeking one or two writs a week most summers, far fewer in the off season. Harris Hatch, for all his strictures against the civil jurisdiction, regularly sued his tenants for arrears of rent every June. William Craig, on the other hand, suing as commissioner of roads, filed all eleven of his suits on the same day. Hugh Morrison brought his nine dog tax suits within a few weeks of April sessions when the county and parish accounts were approved. *Charlotte Gazette* publisher John McLachlan brought a total of thirty-four suits between

October 1849 and May 1852, eight of them on one day in November 1850. He wound up the newspaper in December 1853 on account of unpaid subscriptions, and died the following year.[11] Thomas Wilson and the firm of Wilson & Bolton sent a list of more than fifty debts to Hatheway for collection in March 1854,[12] resulting in the launch of six lawsuits in July of that year. The merchant firm of Odell & Turner brought eleven of its thirty-two suits on the same day in December 1851, likely in the wake of a reorganization following Thomas Turner's death the previous year.[13] The other side of the coin was clusters of suits against a single defendant, like the nine filed against St Andrews mason Levi Handy in June and July 1853, representing a feeding frenzy by creditors anxious to collect what they could before the debtor lost everything. Handy owed the butcher, the doctor, the tailor, the tavern-keeper, the tavern-keeper's housemaid, and the dog tax collector as well as several of his workmen. Two years later Handy, now on the gaol limits, applied for weekly relief from his creditors. This set off a bidding war for his services. Michael Fauls offered a month's work at five shillings a day; constable Henan wanted a cellar wall built at seven shillings and sixpence; master mason George Thomson offered ten shillings (to be offset by a debt Handy still owed him). Even James Boyd, representing one of the original creditors, joined in, saying 'he will give the D employment at 5/ per day but refuses to give the offer in writing.'[14]

Most of the plaintiffs in Hatheway's court lived in the town or parish of St Andrews, but it was not uncommon for residents of other parishes to sue there: one St George fisherman filed eleven suits. There were plaintiffs from elsewhere in the province and beyond, most commonly Saint John merchants but including as well Halifax brewer Alexander Keith and Eastport (Maine) justice, legislator, and *Sentinel* editor Lorenzo Sabine. While the majority were St An-

11. *Patriot*, 16 Dec 1853; *Standard*, 28 Dec 1853, 11 Oct 1854. Patrick Clinch JP bought the press and type to start his own short-lived newspaper, the *Provincialist*.

12. PANB RS148/D/5.

13. *Standard*, 16 Oct 1850. His widow carried on the firm in partnership with his nephew Thomas Turner Odell. Hatheway docketed four other Odell & Turner suits as being brought by Turner's executors.

14. PANB, RS148/D/3, 24 and 31 May, 1855. For imprisonment for debt, the gaol limits, and weekly relief see further below.

Table 7.5 – Residences of defendants in 890 civil suits

Place	Suits*	Persons	Place	Suits*	Persons
St Andrews	629	297	Campobello	12	10
St David	26	22	West Isles	7	6
St George	76	50	Grand Manan	9	4
St James	1	1	Pennfield	4	4
St Patrick	133	80	Eastport	1	1
St Stephen	36	25	Unknown	2	2

* Total exceeds 890 as some had more than one defendant.

drews residents, more than forty per cent of the people named as defendants (accounting for a third of the total cases) lived outside the parish (Table 7.5). In twenty-four of the suits where the residences of both plaintiff and defendant are known neither lived at St Andrews. While some of these involved Charlotte residents suing others in their own or another parish several were filed by Maine residents against Charlotte defendants, mostly from the island parishes. In 1865 and again in 1867 the assembly adopted bills requiring causes to be tried before a magistrate residing in the same parish as one of the parties but both were rejected by council.[15]

Most plaintiffs and defendants represented themselves, but some appeared by agents or attorneys or brought counsel to the trial. Plaintiffs had representation in seventy-eight cases and defendants in fifteen. Hatheway used two methods of indicating that plaintiffs were represented. In twelve cases he styled the cause as 'Smith alias Jones v Brown,' indicating that Smith was the plaintiff and Jones appeared on his behalf. In these suits the 'alias' had an interest in the outcome.[16] In a case styled 'Doran alias Getty v. Sheffield' (24 May 1851), innkeeper Samuel Getty appeared to collect on a note to constable Peter Doran by St Stephen blacksmith Gideon Sheffield; judgment was given for Doran and an execution issued in Getty's favour. This appears to have been the culmination of a complex series of trans-

15. *Standard*, 24 May 1865; ibid., 12 Jun 1867; PANB RS24 1867, bill #91.

16. The interest of the 'alias' differed from the interest of the purchaser of a note. See page 244 below.

actions for the recovery of constable fees arising out of Getty's suits against Sheffield (1 March, constable McKewin), John Stinson, and Joseph Stinson (5 April, constable Doran). After John Wilson's death in April 1855, Hatheway styled suits by his widow to collect his debts as 'John Wilson alias Alice Wilson.'[17] Other 'aliases' included a shipwright, a baker, a blacksmith, and a lawyer. In other suits, Hatheway styled the person appearing for the plaintiff as his agent or attorney or, in one case of a minor child represented by her father, as her guardian. Similarly defendants' representatives were identified as agents or attorneys. The distinction between the two terms did not rest on profession as lawyers and laypersons appeared in both roles and in two cases the representative was styled 'agent and atty.' Three St Andrews lawyers appeared a total of twelve times as the plaintiff's or defendant's agent or attorney. It seems likely that attorneys appeared under a formal power of attorney while agents had more limited authority.[18] Thus William Trundle, an 18-year-old clerk, appeared as agent for the firm of Odell & Turner in six 1851 suits. Constable Henan appeared as agent for the plaintiff or defendant in several suits.[19] Agents' occupations included labourers, farmers, hotel and tavern keepers, skilled tradesmen, and fishermen as well as lawyers, clerks, and constables. Some appeared for family members, as did Sarah Smith for her 83-year-old deaf father, and others for neighbours in distant parishes. When George Christie sued Israel Hanson in Hatheway's court neither the plaintiff nor the defendant, both of whom lived out of parish, appeared personally.[20] When noone appeared for the defendant judgment was given for Christie on

---

17. There are examples of these notes with Hatheway's markings on them in PANB RS148/B/2/r.

18. RSNB (1854) c.137 s.19 provided that 'no attorney shall take any part in a cause if objected to by the opposite party, unless he make oath that his services are entirely gratuitous.' St Andrews lawyer A.T. Paul swore such an oath in Bradley v. O'Neal (24 Aug 1855) in which he was attorney for the defendant.

19. PANB RS24 1865 bill #70, providing that 'No constable shall act as the agent of Plaintiff or Defendant in the Trial of any Cause before a Justice of the peace,' passed the assembly but was rejected by council, probably because it also extended the JP's civil jurisdiction to £10.

20. There were two lumbermen named George Christie, one residing in St Stephen and the other in St James. Hanson was from St Stephen.

the strength of his agent's oath that the plaintiff's claim was just. Hanson's St Andrews agent subsequently paid Hatheway the amount owing to be forwarded to a second agent of Christie's.

Bringing suit

Charlotte county's economy depended on medium and long-term indebtedness.[21] Farmers, fishermen, and lumberers borrowed against future sales. Merchants financed their customers and were credited by their suppliers. Purchases were made on account or by promissory notes 'for value received' which often entered into circulation in place of money. This was not a cash economy. Hard New Brunswick currency was difficult to come by. At St Stephen 'American currency circulates to the almost total exclusion of any other,' a visiting Saint John journalist wrote in 1864: 'It is here called by the store keepers "bad" money, to distinguish it from the Province money which is, of course, good.'[22] Sessions resolved to collect St Stephen taxes 'in current American money with the exception of the amount assessed for county rates, which sum be collected and paid in legal currency.'[23] In the back country even dubious greenbacks were scarce. The proposed cancellation of the wolf and bear bounty was opposed on the ground that bounty certificates were the only media of circulation in some parts of the county.[24] Hard currency was in such short supply that from time to time even the St Andrews customs house had to tender for a small supply of sterling.[25] Payment in goods or services was common. Edward Stentiford's wagon works, offering sleighs and toboggans 'for sale on liberal terms,' advertised for 'Boards, Scantling, Shingles, Laths, Cordwood and Country Produce, or any other satis-

21. For the changing moral economy of debt in late-eighteenth-century America see Mann, *Republic of Debtors.*

22. *Morning Telegraph*, 14 Sep 1864.

23. CCGS Apr 1864.

24. PANB RS13/A/7, Partelow to Norwood (St Stephen), 8 Jan 1853. Allegations of fraud were common: for example PANB RS13/A/6, Partelow to Albee, 10 Apr 1849, asserting that many of the animals for which bounty was claimed in Charlotte had been killed in the United States.

25. *Standard*, 3 Jan 1855.

factory payment taken in exchange.'[26] Even promissory notes negotiated months in advance of their due dates were sometimes made payable in kind. Thus Thomas Carson gave Michael Fauls a note of hand payable in hemlock bark and Francis Mathews signed a note for $6.83, 'to be paid in fish at the market price in St Andrews.'[27] The great majority of notes were stated in monetary terms although they were not necessarily paid in cash. Where debt was the basis of exchange and times often hard, arrears were common. Every fall the *Standard* pleaded with subscribers to pay their accounts so that it could lay in a stock of paper for the winter. Storekeepers offered discounts for cash or for prompt payment. Bradley's 'British House' offered cut goods at Saint John wholesale prices for cash only.[28] The firm of Dimock & Wilson offered a twenty-five per cent discount just for paying a three-month note when due.[29]

In these circumstances a creditor had to consider carefully whether and when to sue for his debt. There was little point in pressing a debtor beyond the limit of his resources as he might just wind up in gaol at the creditor's expense. It was better to wait, if possible, until he had money in hand—a steady job, a crop, a ship in the harbour. For example, the firm of Odell & Turner sent Hatheway its account against a customer, pointing out, 'He gets his pension *today* about $25 and I shall feel obliged if you would proceed at once to collect the debt.'[30] If the debtor was being pressed by other creditors or if he seemed inclined to pack up and leave town, then one had to stake one's claim before it was too late. And if one's own creditors were pressing their claims, then it was time to call in one's debts to satisfy them. We can see a sophisticated understanding of these various calculations in DLS Mahood's advice to head office about proceeding on

26. *Standard*, 3 Jan 1855.

27. PANB RS148/D/4/a, 14 Feb 1857. The original notes are in PANB RS148/B/2/r, July 1852 (Carson) and 26 Mar 1861 (Mathews). This file, catalogued as Secretary-Treasurer records, contains a large number of promissory notes with Hatheway's jottings about proceedings on them on the reverse.

28. *Standard*, 3 Jan 1855.

29. RS148/B/2/r, 4 July 1853.

30. PANB RS148/B/2/e, T.T. Odell to Hatheway, 15 Oct 1867, emphasis in original. The claim was for $20, reduced from a larger amount to come within the magistrate's jurisdiction.

a note given for stumpage:[31]

> If the note taken from S Munson endorsed by G P Lancton ... has not been paid I would beg leave to suggest that it be put in train for collection immediately as Munson has taken away all the Lumber, but which was never released to him ... I am sure Munson is trifling about paying it, and never will if he can avoid it, but I think that Lancton would not allow himself to be sued if he was urged to pay. I have understood lately that both Munson and Lanctons Circumstances are rather precarious, and it will not be safe to let the note stand over any longer.

The justice's court was an important source of information for creditors making these decisions and also served as the local clearinghouse for intertwined debtor-creditor relations, as will be seen below.

Once a creditor had decided it was time to collect outstanding debts or accounts, his first cautious step was to advise the debtor to settle in order to avoid law costs. When Warren Hatheway was about to leave the province he advertised that he had left his books and accounts with his partner for collection: 'all those who do not improve the earliest opportunity to make payment of their respective debts, will be put to cost without any discrimination.'[32] One St Patrick farmer and lumberer wrote to another, 'I hold three Note of Hand against you which is all due by the 12 day of the Month this is to let you see how they stand at this time ... and I wish you to Pay it over to Me by the 12 Day of this Month without fail ...'[33] Creditors sometimes retained Hatheway to write their warning letters. The firm of Wilson & Bolton prepared four lists of 'persons ... to be written to by Justice Hatheway' at various points in 1854-5.[34] One of those named was William Mahood to whom Hatheway wrote two letters, the first answered, 'will pay soon,' the other, 'dead.' Among Hatheway's other notations against the names on these lists are 'written to,' 'disputes the demand,' 'will pay P soon,' 'says P promises to wait, P denies saying so,' 'has pd P,' 'sued,' 'summons issued,' and 'received

31. PANB RS7, Mahood to Baillie, 9 Jan 1844.
32. *Sentinel*, 1 Nov 1823.
33. PANB RS148/B/2/r, John Stewart to John Carmichael, 4 Jan 1856.
34. PANB RS148/D/5.

in full,' all indicating that the letters preceded legal action. The recipients of these letters often replied directly to Hatheway asking for more time: 'I beg you will not put cost on it as I am willing but not able to meet the demand at present times is very hard and money scarce with me but I will call and settle it as soon as I possibly can by forbearing with me awhile you will confer a great favor.'[35]

Some experienced Charlotte magistrates were unwilling to write dunning letters. Patrick Clinch explained his contrary view during an 1831 assembly debate on expanding the justices' civil jurisdiction:[36]

> If a Magistrate should investigate the nature of a case before granting a summons, he would cause himself very great trouble, he would be going out of his proper track, and would perhaps obtain an improper view of the case. He (Mr. C.) used sometimes to give himself much trouble in that way. He used to hear the statements of complainants, and would sometimes even write letters to parties, informing them of the complaints against them, and urging them if possible to settle the matter between themselves. But he found the inconvenience of such a course. Parties on both sides would come and tell him long stories, and how was it possible for him to form an opinion? He had therefore at last found it better to proceed exactly according to the law, and to grant summons, &c. whenever they were demanded. If a summons were improperly taken out, the aggrieved party would have his action against the aggressor, who would be punished by having to pay the costs.

In this light, Hatheway's letter-writing supports his claim to have suppressed rather than encouraged litigation.

If a dunning letter failed to persuade the debtor to pay up, the next step was to initiate a suit. There were two processes available to the creditor, summons and capias, and several other decisions to be made. When Benjamin Pettigrew of Bayside sent an indignant reply to one of his duns—'If I pay $20 it will be after it goes before the Judges at Fredericton. I will not be imposed on by such fellows.'—Hatheway noted at the bottom, 'P pressing his demand and Deft having concluded to resist P claim I have at the request of Plaintiff issued

35. PANB RS148/B/1/a, William Clarke (Flume Ridge) to Hatheway, 6 Dec 1861.
36. *Courier*, 12 Apr 1831.

a summons.'[37] More than ninety per cent of the civil suits recorded in Hatheway's docket were initiated by summons. This was the less expensive option and did not require an oath. Until the early 1860s when he began using preprinted forms, Hatheway prepared the writ in longhand on a scrap of paper.[38] A typical summons, issued at the request of a St Andrews shopkeeper against a customer in St Patrick parish, directed 'any Constable of the County' to

> Summon Patrick McGrath to appear before me at my Office in Saint Andrews on Saturday 9th August next at the hour of eleven in the forenoon to answer the demand of John Lochray for six dollars and sixty cents according to the bill of particulars hereto annexed, and make return forthwith, as by law directed. Dated the 28 July 1862

Hatheway signed the summons and handed it to a constable, who delivered it to the defendant and returned a written receipt:

> I acknowledge the debt herein claimed and a service thereon of the Summons. Patrick McGrath. Rec'd 2d August.

In this particular case McGrath also wrote a letter, likely giving it to the constable to return to the creditor:[39]

> Mr Loachrey Sir / Spare as much Cost as possible as there is no Cause of trial / I am promised Some money shortly may be the middle of the week and I shall send it to you / No more at present from yours / Patrick McGrath

Hatheway's docket for 1862 shows that John Lochary issued summonses for several of his debtors in late July and early August, four of them returnable on August 9, and that in McGrath's case judgment was issued 'by D ackndgt of Sums & debt $6.60.'

---

37. PANB RS148/B/2/e, Pettigrew to Hatheway, 7 July 1864. I have not found this suit in Hatheway's 1864 docket, so perhaps the plaintiff relented and withdrew his claim for unpaid wages.

38. Hatheway copied out blank forms for information and complaint on the first leaf of Ledger 2. Later he struck these out and made a note to 'Adhere to the forms laid down in the revised Laws of 1854.' Hatheway's writs did not follow the schedule of forms in RSNB 1854, c.137 verbatim but did not depart from them materially. In what follows I give examples of writs actually issued by Hatheway.

39. PANB RS148/B/2/r.

It was not unusual for defendants to attempt to negotiate upon receipt of a summons. Two brothers in St George wrote Hatheway acknowledging receipt of a summons and regretting that he had not written to warn them first: 'Please send no execution til the last of this month as we will send you the money the first of next month. We would have paid it sooner only that Mr Ludgate can't get any money in to pay me what he owes me.'[40] Defendants' letters were particularly likely when they were out of parish as travel by the constable and any witnesses would quickly elevate costs.[41] Alexander McMaster of St George, served with Samuel Getty's demand for ten dollars, returned it to Hatheway along with twenty-five shillings (five dollars)[42] and one shilling threepence costs:[43]

> You can tender him with the 25/ and if he does not see fit [to] take it and give me a clear receipt return me the money you can also say to him if this does not suit I will go to gaol and pay the debt as there is nothing doing here at present I would go sooner than pay more than I owe ...

Another St George defendant wrote to Hatheway:[44]

> Sir I recd a summons from you in favour of Mr Falls I did not think Falls would trouble me this year. From the talk I had with him in summer I fully intended to pay him what I owed him and does now. Dear Sir if you will use your Influence to stop any further proceedings I pledge myself to have the thing settled to your satisfaction on the 10th of June as I will have means on that day. The summons I send over to you. I think there is a mistake in it that you will not proceed on it.

40. PANB RS148/B/1/a, Bradley v. W and S Boyd, 18 Jun 1860.

41. PANB RS148/D/5 includes several examples, some of them acknowledging and paying the debt, others contesting the amount or disputing the form of the summons. For example, in January 1863 T.K. Parker of Deer Island acknowledged owing Odell & Turner 'a small balance of an account but denies ever giving Mr. Odell a note of hand' and disputed the summons because it was addressed to T.R. Parker. Of course St Andrews residents might just stop by Hatheway's office to haggle personally rather than send a letter.

42. New Brunswick officially converted to decimal currency in 1860. I have used the conversion table in *Standard*, 31 Oct 1860.

43. PANB RS148/D/5, McMaster to Hatheway, 28 Sep 1863.

44. PANB RS148/D/3/b, Stephen Murray to Hatheway, 29 Dec [no year].

A final example, also from St George:[45]

> I did not receive your Summons until the 21 I think I do not owe Mr Bradley quite that amount but I wish you to see him about it and let me know if it is so I do not want you to put costs on it times is hard here at present But I will try and Pay it as soon as possible if I can not pay it all at once I will send part I will have a look at the Books and see how we stand I think there is a mistake somehow.

The more expensive option available to creditors was to proceed by capias, a writ directing the constable to arrest the debtor and hold him until the trial. Creditors wishing to proceed by capias had to swear (and pay for) an oath that the defendant was justly indebted in the sum claimed, that the defendant was at least twenty-one years of age, 'and that there is danger of losing the debt' unless the defendant was arrested or held to bail.[46] Then the magistrate prepared a warrant directing the constable 'to take the body of' the defendant:[47]

> and him safely keep till he shall give good bail to answer the demand of John J Bartlett upon a Note for One pound Ten shillings, and to notify the said Defendant that the cause will be heard before me, at my Office, in St Andrews, the 31st day of this Instant at eleven o'clock in the forenoon. In default of Bail being given, you are required to bring the Defendant before me, that he may be dealt with as the Law directs.

The defendant's bail endorsed the back of the writ affirming that 'I do hereby consent to become bail for the within named defendant in this suit.'[48] John Rodgers, a St Andrews painter and glazier, was already in

45. PANB RS148/D/3/e, Hugh Brown to Hatheway, 22 Jun 1860.

46. PANB RS148/D/3/b and RS148/D/3/d include several examples of printed forms for the oath dating from 1859 and later. Hatheway's handwritten affidavits of capias oaths contain the same elements but in slightly different words: for example, PANB RS148/B/2/r, oath in Kearney v. McDonald, 8 Sep 1857. Women and members of the assembly could not be arrested on capias, nor was the writ available for claims under ten shillings: RSNB 1854, c.137, s.10.

47. PANB RS148/D/3/f, Bartlett v. McDole, printed form of capias, 22 Dec 1859. Hatheway indicated on its face, 'This writ to be served as a summons.'

48. PANB RS148/D/3/f, Kearney v. Slason & Rainsford, 18 November 1861. Compare RSNB 1854, c.137, s.12. Bail in this case was Hatheway's shopkeeper son, C.E.O. Hatheway, who would later take over his father's justicing business.

gaol when he was served with a capias at the suit of ship carpenter John Billings; tavern-keeper Charles McGee and grocer William Ballantine put up bail but Rodgers failed to appear for trial and judgment was entered against him.[49]

Only eighty-six of the eight hundred and ninety suits in Hatheway's 1849-56 docket were initiated by capias. Nearly a third of these were by plaintiffs who sued just once in the period and more than half by plaintiffs who sued no more than three times. Among Hatheway's more frequent customers there was no statistical correlation between the number of suits they filed and the proportion that was by capias. No plaintiff used the process more than four times. Just eight defendants were arrested by capias more than once in the period, and only one more than three times. Levi Handy, the gaoled St Andrews mason whose job prospects were so brightened by his application for weekly relief, was named defendant in seven capias suits, all of them filed within a two week period that began the day after he was served with a summons in another suit. All this suggests that the oath was taken seriously and the process reserved for exigent circumstances.

In thirty-four of the eighty-six capias suits, the defendant did not appear for trial, either because the constable had not found him or because he skipped bail.[50] On two occasions constable Henan, rather than producing the defendant for trial, appeared for him as agent and attorney and denied the debt; in neither case did the plaintiff appear. Of the fifty remaining capias suits, fourteen were tried the same day the capias issued, fifteen within a week, eight within the second week, and the rest within thirty-two days of the writ.[51] It is impossible to tell in what proportion of these the defendant secured bail for his appear-

49. PANB RS148/D/3/g, 5 May 1857. Capias issued on 4 May and the hearing took place on 16 May.

50. Hugh Copley, arrested by capias in November 1855 at the suit of James McLaughlan, had gone bail for McLaughlan's debtor William Watters the previous August. Watters had confessed judgment at trial after arrest on capias but could not be found when the constable went to levy execution against him. Copley paid the outstanding debt.

51. RSNB 1854, c.137, s.13 provided that 'After the defendant is arrested the constable shall take bail for his appearance ... but if no bail be offered he shall carry the defendant before the Justice ... and the defendant when brought there shall either deposit the sum sworn to and costs, or give bail ... or be committed to gaol by warrant of the Justice,' while s.14 provided that, 'The defendant shall be detained in cus-

ance at trial.[52] Most delays between the initiation of a capias suit and the trial were likely attributable to difficulties in finding the defendant and to travel time.

The choice between summons and capias was not the only one a plaintiff had to make. He had also to decide whom to sue and for how much. There were conventional variations in the form of promissory notes that had consequences for their enforcement at law. Where there was more than one debtor the phrasing of the obligation determined whether the plaintiff could choose to sue just one of them or had to proceed against all at once. Most notes were transferable, usually by 'order' of the original creditor but sometimes simply to the bearer, which had consequences for who could sue, what defences could be raised, and what evidence had to be led. For example in November 1855 William Cunningham of St Patrick signed a note promising to pay 'Robert Curry or order' in two months. In January 1856, Robert Curry endorsed the reverse, 'Pay the within note to William Boyd value received by me.' When Boyd was unable to collect from Cunningham he sued Curry who sued Cunningham in turn.[53] Where the balance on the note or account exceeded the £5 statutory jurisdiction, the creditor might decide to abandon the excess claim in order to use the relatively cheap and truly expeditious process before a magistrate.[54] Thus when the St David firm of Osgood & Co. sued Joseph Smith of Oak Bay on his note for £5/15/0 the firm's agent marked on the reverse, 'I abandon all over five pounds of the within note.'[55] In another such case the creditor attested, 'I abandon £1-4-6 of the within note & claim five pounds.'[56]

---

tody one day only for every two shillings of the sum stated in the warrant, whether he remain in custody thereon or be charged in execution ...'

52. There are some inconsistencies in Hatheway's recordkeeping and in many cases it is cannot be distinguished whether the securities given were for appearance at trial or bail following judgment.

53. PANB RS148/B/2/r, note and endorsements. Both suits appear in Hatheway's 1856 docket, with trial dates 15 Sep and 2 Dec respectively.

54. RSNB 1854, c.137, s.20 provided that 'If the plaintiff's demand exceeds five pounds, judgment shall be rendered against him with costs, unless he reduces it to that amount and abandons the overplus.'

55. PANB RS148/B/2/r, 14 Sep 1857.

56. PANB RS148/B/2/r, Thompson v. Huggins, Feb 1857.

Debt collection on notes and accounts was the mainstay of Hatheway's civil court but not its only business. Neighbours sued one another for damage to gardens[57] or crops caused by animals[58] or children[59] and to recover lost property.[60] County and parish officials sued for unpaid taxes[61] and other assessments.[62] Churches sued for pew rent[63] and the county agricultural society for membership dues.[64] Examples of particular kinds of disputes are given later in this chapter.

Trial and judgment

Whether the plaintiff proceeded by summons or capias, the writ indicated a date and time for hearing the cause. In nearly eighty per cent of the suits the hearing came within two weeks of the initial writ and more than ninety per cent were heard within three weeks (Table 7.6). Adjournments were very rare and in almost every case judgment was rendered on the day of hearing. What happened at the hearing depended on decisions the parties made, beginning with the decision whether to attend at all. Plaintiffs nearly always appeared, either personally or by an agent; in the fourteen cases where they did not costs were awarded to the defendant whether or not he appeared.

The majority of defendants did not appear at trial (Table 7.7). In some cases this was because the constable could not find them to serve the summons or take them under capias[65] and in others the defendant had already acknowledged the debt and returned a payment

57. Irwin v. Stentiford, 1 May 1860.

58. McCarty v. Dougherty, 27 Aug 1859.

59. Murphy v. Hanson, 16 Sep 1859.

60. McReynolds v. McGee, 20 Aug 1855.

61. Morrison v. Stentiford, 22 Apr 1856.

62. McCurdy v. Miller (statute labour), 23 Jul 1859.

63. Episcopal Church Corporation, St Andrews v. Billings, 13 Mar 1854.

64. Stevenson v. Smart, 12 Jan 1861.

65. A St George constable acknowledged receipt of a summons he was to serve: 'I do not know such a man residing in the parish at all events I will make all the enquiry I possibly can to find him.' PANB RS148/B/1/a, John Lynott to Hatheway, 7 Aug 1854. Upon learning that a defendant was away in Boston, another St George constable returned the summons to Hatheway to be renewed on his return: ibid., James Lynott to Hatheway, 9 Oct 1855.

Table 7.6 – Days between initial writ and hearing of 890 civil suits

Days	Per Cent	Cumulative
Same day	2	2
1–7 days	26	28
8–14 days	51	79
15–21 days	15	94
> 21 days	6	100

(or a promise to pay) in Hatheway's pretrial process. In many cases defendants who did not challenge the plaintiff's claim but were unable or unwilling to pay it immediately were content to let judgment go against them by default, thereby incurring law costs but avoiding the additional costs of travel or giving up working time to contest a lost cause. Hatheway recorded default judgments in nearly sixty per cent of the suits. In another thirteen per cent the defendants attended the hearing and confessed their indebtedness. For example, when George Rigley took out a capias against Thomas Rack for $24 arrears of house rent, reducing his claim to $20 to bring it within Hatheway's jurisdiction, Rack and his bail appeared in court the day before the adjourned trial date to 'acknowledge debt and costs in this case and request Judgt may be entered against me for same and will pay as fast as I can.'[66] In the result Hatheway held trials in just over a quarter of the 890 cases in the docket for this period.

Little can be said about the physical arrangements of Hatheway's court or its social ambience. It was held at his 'office,' which was almost certainly a large room at his house on King Street in St Andrews, a short block from the county courthouse and gaol.[67] He did

66. PANB RS148/B/2/e, 12 Jul 1864. The following day Hatheway issued judgment for the plaintiff with costs.

67. Hatheway's home, built in the early 1830s, replicates in its more modest frame construction the style and lines of Harris Hatch's elegant brick residence, Chestnut Hall (Figure 2.3), thereby asserting their alliance and relative status in the community. Images of the Hatheway house may be seen at http://www.historicplaces.ca/en/rep-reg/place-lieu.aspx?id=9851.

Table 7.7 – Disposition of 890 civil suits

Disposition	Number	Per Cent
Default judgment	521	59
Confession	117	13
Abandoned	7	1
Trial by JP	175	20
Trial by Jury	66	7
Other, unknown	4	<1

not employ a clerk—all the documents for his long career are in the same easily-recognizable hand as his personal correspondence and private notes—but there would have been a constable or two almost constantly in attendance although not necessarily to maintain order. Hatheway had to punish one of them for contempt when he 'put a question to an Evidence, kept speaking in contempt of the going on with the suit against the Dft and continued repeating his opinion and opposition to the proceeding although repeatedly required by me to be silent.'[68] On another occasion Hatheway attributed a mistake in his arithmetic to 'the excitement of the parties and interruptions.'[69] Reading Hatheway's trial notes and docket entries, one senses an ebb and flow of litigants, witnesses, lawyers, and spectators through the room, of people waiting their turn being recruited for juries, of the occasional impatient interruption, of men and women coming and going to sign papers and take or leave money, and of the intermingling of civil and criminal business.

The plaintiff or the defendant opted to have a jury in about a quarter of the civil trials. This decision was not taken lightly as it involved additional costs. The request had to be made the day before the trial. Hatheway issued a writ of venire in terms like these:[70]

> To any Constable of Saint Andrews. You are hereby required to summon and warn three persons duly qualified to act as Jurors

68. R v. Gallagar, 4 Oct 1852.
69. Healey v. Pye, 25 Nov 1864.
70. PANB RS148/D/3/e, 17 May 1856.

> and who are in nowise of kin to either of the parties to appear at my Office this day at 11 o'clock to make a Jury in a case in which James McMaster [is] Plaintiff and Isaac Kennedy Defendant.

In this case the jury consisted of hotel-keeper John Bradford, house carpenter Thomas Wren, and shipwright Samuel Billings. Bradford and Billings were habitueś of Hatheway's court; Billings had a suit coming on for trial that very day. The jurors were required to swear an oath to 'well and truly try this cause ... and a true verdict give according to the evidence.'[71] The jury heard the parties and their evidence in open court and delivered their unanimous verdict publicly. If they could not agree within three hours' deliberation they could be discharged and another jury impanelled unless the parties agreed to have the justice decide the cause himself.[72] This does not seem to have happened in any of the 890 cases, but in an 1864 suit that began with an evidentiary dispute about whether the defendant had paid his first week's board to the plaintiff's wife and then degenerated into an argument that culminated in the defendant's resentful offer to pay it again and the plaintiff's refusal to take his money, the jurors could not agree. After they were discharged by consent of the parties, the plaintiff withdrew his suit.[73] In 1866, in a suit for arrears of rent in which the defence was that the evicting landlord had failed to make repairs—'If you had fixed the house as agreed I should have paid you but you did not do so'—the jury took a view of the premises but could not agree and asked to be dismissed before their three hours were up. At this point the plaintiff withdrew his suit and was allowed to bring it on again after paying costs. At the second trial a month later a new jury heard the evidence, took a view, and found for the plaintiff landlord. By this time the leaking roof had been repaired.[74]

Perhaps the strangest, and in some ways the most revealing, of the jury tales from Hatheway's civil court occurred in the summer of 1863. James Burns had agreed to dig and stone James McCarroll's well for $26, the client to furnish the stone. When McCarroll queried the sufficiency of the well Burns drilled two test holes without reaching

71. RSNB (1854) c.137 sched.(I).
72. RSNB (1854) c.137 s.34.
73. PANB RS148/D/3/d, Wade v. Trites, 15 Feb 1864.
74. PANB RS148/D/3/b, Fauls v. Lane, 3 May 1866; 4 June 1866.

more water but refused to drill a third, telling him to wait and see whether the water rose or fell. The well remained unfinished because McCarroll did not supply any stone. After McCarroll refused part payment Burns filed suit, maintaining 'there was a good supply of water in the well for any family and more.' McCarroll's defence was that he did not want the well stoned until it had been deepened. To this point it was a simple and sadly familiar contractor dispute. The jurors retired, contemplated, and delivered their conclusion in writing:

> We the under signed find for the plaintiff six pound ten shillings [$26] and sixpence cost him the said plaintiff to stone up the well by the Defendant furnishing the stone Immediately. P.S. We have being to the well and fill satisfied in regard to the sufficiencty of water.

In Hatheway's view they had 'mistaken the law and their duty,' presumably because although they found for the plaintiff and awarded his demand in full (despite the incomplete contract) they also ordered specific performance against both parties. (A proper verdict would simply have compensated Burns on a valuation of the work he had actually done inasmuch as he was prevented from completing the contract by McCarroll's failure to supply him with stone.)[75] An hour after the jury was dismissed, McCarroll returned to Hatheway's office with a paper from St Andrews lawyer B.R. Stevenson. He demanded a copy of the judgment in the case, 'and threw down a dollar which I refused to receive and told him I could not record such a statement as a verdict.' Hatheway explained that he considered the proceedings to be 'null and void' and recommended that McCarroll leave his dispute with Burns 'to a couple of your neighbours to settle.' Saying he was willing to do so, McCarroll picked up his dollar and began to leave, but then stopped to ask who was to pay the costs of the aborted trial. When Hatheway said he expected each party to pay its own McCarroll threw down the dollar again and demanded a receipt in full for his costs, which Hatheway refused. Later that day Hatheway

---

75. In Kirkland v. Doak, 26 Mar 1859, a jury accepted the evidence of several carpenters about the value of extra work sued for, and in Main v. Chalmers, 15 Aug 1854, a jury found that the plaintiff had no cause of action as he had not completed the work contracted for.

told Burns that McCarroll wished to arbitrate their difference. Burns agreed. 'The P & Dft having both declared their willingness to leave the matter to men I considered myself discharged from any further action in the matter.' Four days after the trial, though, McCarroll returned to Hatheway's office, asked for his dollar back, and employed him to draft an arbitration agreement. Although Burns 'made no objection to the terms of the agreement or the arbitrators, [he] said he would not sign it but would go to Deft and with an Evidence tender his services and readiness to stone up the well.'[76] This was the end of the matter so far as Hatheway was concerned. He did not enter the suit in his 1863 docket but retained the draft arbitration agreement, for which McCarroll had paid him fifty cents, among his papers:

> Whereas a difference has arisen between the undersigned ...about the digging and stoneing up a well, we do hereby jointly and severally agree and bind ourselves each of us to choose a man to settle and determine all matters of difference between us as to the digging of the same and stoning and we authorise the said persons so chosen, to choose a third man to act with them. The said persons to give an award and decision of their doings in writing during this present week to us.

There are several inferences suggested by this story. Jurors sometimes attempted to do substantial justice, that is, to deliver what they considered to be just or fair outcomes unobtainable from formal or procedural justice. In his role as magistrate, though, Hatheway felt more constrained. He attempted to mediate this case only after concluding that the proceedings were a nullity, and when he did so his object was not to bring the parties to a settlement of their dispute but rather to suggest an informal procedure (non-binding arbitration) in which he would play no further part.

Although these disputes involved small sums of money the evidence before the jury could be quite complex, especially at the intersection of economic and familial relations. For example, when a son-in-law sued his father-in-law for the balance of an account the

76. PANB RS148/D/5, Burns v. McCarroll, 24 July 1863. This is based on Hatheway's draft memorandum of events, made (one assumes) in anticipation of further trouble.

jury heard evidence from both men, their wives, and six other witnesses about a multitude of transactions in the plaintiff's account and defendant's set-off including making and repairing boots and shoes, cash loaned, charges for moving house, boarding and nursing the defendant's daughter (the plaintiff's wife) when she was ill, and supplying feathers. There were disputes about who was to pay the servant girl's wages and who was responsible for shingling the roof. The jury sifted through the often vague and sometimes conflicting testimony and awarded the plaintiff about four-fifths of his original claim.[77]

With few exceptions (some of them discussed below), whether they were heard by a jury or by Hatheway alone, the contested suits turned on their facts. When lawyers were present their principal contribution was to raise technical objections which Hatheway generally overruled. The most common objections were that the justice lacked jurisdiction because the plaintiff's claim exceeded the statutory limit of five pounds (twenty dollars) or because title to land was at issue in the proceedings. James Cox sued Michael Hays for $19.93, the difference between the value of goods he had received and the hours he had worked helping to build a ship for Cox. Hays's lawyer B.R. Stevenson objected first to Cox's clerk giving evidence as he was the plaintiff's agent at trial, then to the court's jurisdiction because the original account before allowing for Hays's work on the ship exceeded twenty dollars. Hatheway overruled both objections and sent the case to the jury.[78] A contractor sued for £5 for painting railroad cars, having abandoned the rest of his account to bring it within the court's jurisdiction. Both parties were represented by counsel. When Stevenson, for the defence, moved for dismissal because the plaintiff had led evidence that he was owed more than he claimed, A.T. Paul for the plaintiff insisted on putting the case to the jury. Probably because there were lawyers involved Hatheway made a detailed record of his ruling:

> The Court considers that the 1st and 20th sections of the Act defining the jurisdiction of Justices in Civil Suits extends to the present case, and by the powers conferred by the 20th section

77. McLaren v. McCurdy, 16 Jan 1858.
78. Cox v. Hays, 25 Jul 1857.

> it *necessarily* follows that accounts exceeding five pounds must be adjudicated on where a part has been abandoned, to establish a balance and will therefore charge the Jury accordingly, when the parties dispute each others accounts the court considers that no decision can be given without going into evidence of the gross amounts of both accounts.

Having lost its motion, the defence called evidence about the plaintiff's shoddy work and his responsibility for the loss or theft of a quantity of lead from the painting shed. The jury gave a verdict for half the plaintiff's demand.[79]

The same counsel were present in a suit by the New Brunswick & Canada Railway & Land Company (successor to the old St A&Q) alias Julius Thompson, its manager, for trespass by cutting timber on its land. Stevenson, representing the defendant, first objected to the form of the summons because it did not fully identify the plaintiff. When this was overruled he objected to Hatheway's jurisdiction because title to land was at issue. He argued that the plaintiff had not proved title, and that 'being a corporate body [it] cannot sustain an action of trespass without showing a grant.' Hatheway dismissed the objection: 'Court considers an action can be sustained by showing occupation.'[80] Stevenson represented the plaintiff in an 1861 trespass case when R.M. Andrews, for the defence, raised the land title objection. Hatheway ruled that since the defence 'declines offering evidence to show title of land does in *reality* come in question, and the Plaintiff proving the line between her and Defendant being admitted by Defendant to be about right when run a few days ago … it appears to me I am justified in letting the case go to the Jury.'[81]

---

79. McLauchlin v. Hamilton, 20 Jan 1858, emphasis in original. Hatheway overruled a similar objection in Healey v. Pye, 25 Nov 1864. RSNB 1854, c.137, s.1 provided for the £5 limit, 'unless the same be reduced by payment or abandonment to that sum,' and s.20 allowed for set-offs and provided that 'If the plaintiff's demand exceeds five pounds, judgment shall be rendered against him with costs, unless he reduces it to that amount, and abandons the overplus.'

80. 3 Sep 1859.

81. Taggart v. Berry, 24 Oct 1861: emphasis in original. R.M. Andrews's subsequent conduct in this case figured in Hatheway's wariness of him, discussed in the next chapter.

Along with objections by lawyers there were objections to them.[82] When a defendant failed to attend a hearing that had been adjourned at his request Hatheway sustained an objection to Stevenson's attempt to act as his attorney without showing the defendant's written authority. The lay plaintiff—the very experienced Michael Fauls—raised the issue when Stevenson challenged the jurisdiction of the court.[83] While practically every case involving a lawyer also involved a procedural objection, lawyers had no monopoly over technicalities. In a suit by shipmaster W.J. Lord against farmer Marshall J.C. Andrews for freight in carrying his turnips to Saint John, Andrews claimed a set-off but acknowledged that he had not given Lord advance notice as the law required. When Lord magnanimously offered to allow the set-off anyway, Andrews abruptly left the court and judgment was given against him for the original claim less the set-off. Upon returning some hours later for the trial of a second suit for damages by detaining Lord's vessel at Saint John in a futile attempt to sell the badly frozen cargo Andrews challenged the court's jurisdiction, saying 'the law only allows action of trespass on real and personal property which he contends does not apply here and says he intends to prefer a claim for damages against P before a higher tribunal.' Lord wanted the case to go to the jury and said he was quite willing 'to have their verdict revised.' Hatheway overruled the objection—'The Court consider the word Suit means a wrong; injury; injustice; consequently and synonymous as damage and there being no higher tribunal of such a demand as low as forty shillings think this a fit question for the jury and within the meaning of the law.'—whereupon Andrews stated, 'I leave the court and will not attend the Trial or call any evidence.' Lord called several witnesses and the jury awarded him the £2 damages he claimed and £2/6/10 costs.[84]

Experienced litigants could produce and respond to the full repertoire of objections without benefit of counsel. In a case between Michael Fauls and Thomas Carson the defendant acknowledged signing a note of hand but objected to paying it because of 'the statute of limitations,' the want of consideration, and a concurrent action be-

---

82. For popular attitudes at the time, see Marquis, 'Anti-Lawyer Sentiment.'

83. Fauls v. Lynott, 22 Nov 1856.

84. Lord v. Andrews (two suits), 14 Feb 1856.

fore justice Ker on the same note. On the first point, Carson maintained that the date of the note had been changed to keep it current. On the second he said he gave the note for a barrel of flour which he never received. Unfortunately for him his own witnesses contradicted both points. Fauls produced Ker's certificate that the suit before him had been adjourned at Carson's request for want of a material witness and showed that at law Ker lost his jurisdiction when the adjournment was for more than a month. The jury gave a verdict for Fauls's entire claim and awarded him the costs in Ker's court as well as in Hatheway's.[85]

Hatheway rarely allowed requests for adjournment to secure the presence of a material witness. A defendant sought to have the trial put off two weeks to secure the evidence of his former clerk. In a former action on the same claim (twenty days' labour making hay) the plaintiff had been nonsuited. Hatheway ruled that 'D not having pled in any set off or taken out any subpoenas for Evidence and the want of a more satisfactory assurance of his ability and *desire* to have Constantine as an Evidence in a fortnight hence, and having admitted that he was sued by P in this Court in March last for same demand when Constantine was then a Clerk in his employ, that he, D, did not acknowledge the debt and the P having no proof it was not allowed, and that he D got a verdict for 10/ with costs against P under those circumstances the Court cannot sustain the application for putting off the case.'[86] Hatheway did allow an adjournment in the suit between Michael Fauls and Edward Lynott discussed above but not before Lynott produced an affidavit sworn before justice Chandler stating that justice Ker was a material witness but too ill to attend, and possibly even then only out of respect for a fellow magistrate. When Lynott did not attend the adjourned trial (and Stevenson's attempt to appear on his behalf was rejected) Hatheway ruled, 'The D not having appeared or using any effort within the knowledge of the court to procure Justice Ker testimony, do adjudge D to pay the P £5/0/0 with costs of suit.'[87] But Hatheway's very limited tolerance for technical

85. Fauls v. Carson, 14 Feb 1857. Additional documentation in PANB RS148/D/4/a, PANB RS148/B/2/r (note), PANB RS148/B/1/a (Ker's certificate).

86. Harris v. Watters, 28 Jul 1855, emphasis in original.

87. Fauls v. Lynott, 22 Nov 1856.

objections and dedication to expeditious proceedings have to be set off against the constraints which he apparently felt he had to observe in dispensing substantial justice.

Plaintiffs won judgments in about eighty per cent of the contested suits. This was true whether or not a jury was involved although suits were dismissed slightly more often when they came before Hatheway alone. The real benefit of a trial for many defendants was the discounting of their debt, whether because the plaintiff abandoned part of his claim in order to bring it within the jurisdiction of the court or because the court found against the plaintiff in some particulars or for the defendant in set-off. These monetary benefits to defendants were reduced or eliminated by the costs which were almost inevitably awarded against them when judgment was given for the plaintiff. The high rate of default and confessed judgments suggests that the calculus operated against contesting a suit unless there was strong evidence to undermine the plaintiff's claim or he had unreasonably refused to account for a demonstrable set-off. This is not to suggest that every decision to contest a suit was made rationally. Some defendants—like Marshall Andrews—were too emotionally entangled to forgo their day in court and one suspects that some others—Thomas Carson for example—delighted in the battle, win or lose.

Collections and recoveries

Whether the suit was decided by default, confession, abandonment, nonsuit, or trial, judgment meant someone had to pay money. That someone could pay up immediately, try to negotiate for a settlement or more time to pay,[88] or go home and wait for the opposing party to make the next move. Fewer than a quarter of the suits were finally

---

88. For example, in Sept 1863 James Boyd told Hatheway, who had issued a default judgment in his favour a few days earlier, that he was willing to wait until Christmas for payment, and followed this up with a note: 'On Mr Robt Townshend paying you the costs I consent to wait for a while longer.' Hatheway added a notation indicating that a constable told him in Feb 1864 that Townshend had paid Boyd in full: PANB RS148/D/1, Boyd to Hatheway, 8 Sep 1863. Hatheway's docket lists several suits brought by Boyd in the fall of 1863, some for fines in by-law offences and others for debts.

Table 7.8 – Last recorded step in 877 civil suits where judgment given

Step	Number	Per Cent
Payment	560	64
Execution	113	13
Settled	87	10
Trial	74	8
Gaol	12	1
Costs unpaid	11	1
Not found	8	1
Other	12	1

concluded on judgment day. In more than sixty per cent of them the victorious party (or occasionally the constable, if it was his fees that remained unpaid) applied to Hatheway for a writ of execution against the judgment debtor's property. More than a quarter of the executions had to be renewed one or more times before they were finally satisfied, the debtor was lodged in gaol or no longer to be found, or the judgment creditor simply gave up (Table 7.8).

One consequence was that while launching a suit and bringing it to judgment was remarkably expeditious the process of recovering the judgment and collecting costs could take a very long time if it succeeded at all. About a third of the suits were concluded within three weeks (in the sense that no further action was taken after that time). Two thirds were concluded within three or four months but the remaining third could drag on for years (Table 7.9). On average suits in which judgments were awarded involved two additional steps (executions, part payments, settlements, etc.) following the trial, but a quarter of them required between three and five additional steps and a few as many as eleven or twelve before the judgment was satisfied or the creditor exhausted.

Under the 1854 civil justice act a creditor could request an execution at any time within three years of the judgment.[89] Upon receipt of the requisite fee Hatheway would issue his writ in terms like these:[90]

89. RSNB 1854, c.137, s.38. Women and members of the assembly were exempt (s.39). The three-year limit was introduced by 6 Vict. (1843) c.13.

90. PANB RS148/D/4/b, Healey v. Summers, execution (printed form), 25 Oct

Table 7.9 – Time from first to last steps in 877 civil suits where judgment given

Time Elapsed	Cumulative Per Cent
1 week or less	9
2 weeks	24
3 weeks	31
30 days	39
60 days	56
90 days	64
120 days	71
180 days	77
1 year	89
2 years	96
3 years	98
15 years	100

> To any Constable of the County. You are hereby required to levy of the Goods and Chattels of Michael Summers of the Parish of St Andrews $20.00 which Thomas Healey recovered against him in the Court before me, and also $1.60 costs, amounting in the whole to $21.60 besides the costs of levying this Execution, and to have the money before me at my Office in St Andrews within thirty days from the date hereof, to be rendered to the said Thomas Healey. For want of Goods and Chattels whereon to levy, (after deducting wearing apparel and bedding, kitchen utensils and tools of his trade and calling to the value of fifteen pounds,) you will take the body of the said Summers and deliver him to the Keeper of the Gaol of the said County; and the said Keeper will take the said Summers into his custody and him safely keep for fifty days, unless the said sum with the costs thereon, be sooner paid: and how you shall have executed this Precept make return to me at the day and place aforesaid.

Default judgment in this case had been given in August 1860 and a first execution issued in October the same year. Hatheway's docket shows that it was renewed in November 1860 and May 1861: it is

---

1861.

not known whether this was because Summers could not be found, had made a partial payment (unrecorded by Hatheway), or persuaded Healey to give him more time. The writ given here was issued in October 1861, a year after the original execution and fifteen months after judgment.

If the constable could find the judgment debtor he would show him the writ and give him the opportunity to settle the debt. Failing payment he was to seize property and advertise it for five days before putting it up for public sale, returning to the debtor any proceeds above what was needed to satisfy the judgment and costs. If the debtor's property was insufficient the constable would take him to the county gaol where he could be kept one day for every two shillings of the judgment to a maximum of fifty days (including any days already spent there, for example on capias awaiting trial).[91] The execution against Summers yielded enough to pay all but $9.93 of the judgment and costs so Hatheway endorsed the reverse of the writ to limit his confinement to twenty-four days. Healey told Hatheway in January 1862, seventeen months after judgment, that he had been paid in full.

Imprisonment for debt was well established in Charlotte county.[92] The stone gaol (completed 1836) was designed to accommodate debtors in a large room on its upper floor while criminals were confined in cells below. By mid-century the practice was falling out of favour. Although attempts were made from time to time to abolish it altogether[93] the fundamentals of the system were little changed since 1791 when the assembly first provided for 'the support and relief of confined debtors.'[94] An imprisoned debtor could apply for a small weekly allowance to be paid by his creditor upon per-

---

91. RSNB 1854 c.137 s.40.

92. In 1831 the press reported that in the year past fifty debtors had been committed to the Charlotte county gaol on magistrates' warrants for debts under £5, one of them for 'the trifling sum of 6s. 8d.' *Courier*, 12 Feb 1831, copying *Herald*.

93. In 1850, when the maximum term of confinement for debt was reduced from twelve to three months, the attorney general said he favoured abolition: *Standard*, 17 Apr 1850. Attempts were made from time to time—'A Bill is now under discussion to do away with imprisonment for debt it is as long as the Moral Law and more like a Bankrupt Law than anything else.' PANB RS148/B/1/a, James Boyd (Fredericton) to Wellington Hatch, 20 Mar 1863—but debtors could still be sent to gaol in New Brunswick at Confederation.

94. 31 Geo.III (1791) c.14, am. 39 Geo.III (1799) c.6, am. 41 Geo.III (1801) c.5,

suading a magistrate that he could not support himself in gaol. If the creditor failed to pay the allowance the debtor was to be released and could not be imprisoned again on the same judgment but the creditor was still able to collect by seizure and sale of the debtor's property. The 1850 consolidation incorporated earlier provisions allowing the debtor to be released from 'close confinement' in the gaol to live and work within the county's gaol limits.[95] This required him to post a bond with two sureties to the sheriff for twice the value of the debt for which he had been imprisoned. Much of the de facto reform in confinement for debt from the 1830s on consisted in the intermittent reduction of the maximum period of imprisonment and enlargement of the gaol limits, which by 1867 had become coextensive with the county boundaries.[96]

Hatheway held several hearings on applications for weekly support. Unlike the Levi Handy cases described earlier, in most of them the creditor declined to appear, an order for support was granted, and the debtor was released the next day on receipt of the gaoler's affidavit that he had not been paid.[97] Evidently many creditors considered paying a weekly allowance to keep their debtor in gaol to be throw-

cont. 45 Geo.III (1805) c.19, am. 47 Geo.III (1807) c.2, rev. 50 Geo.III (1810) c.30, am. 59 Geo.III (1819) c.12, am. 3 Geo.IV (1822) c.15, am. 4 Geo.IV (1823) c.10, am 7 Geo.IV (1828) c.13, rep. 10&11 Geo.IV (1830) c.30, am. 1 Wm.IV (1831) c.43, am. 2 Wm.IV (1832) c.13, am. 3 Wm.IV (1833) c.18, rep. 6 Wm.IV (1836) c.41, cont. 3 Vict. (1840) c.31, cont. 8 Vict. (1845) c.42, am. 12 Vict. (1849) c.44, rep., consol., & am. 13 Vict. (1850) c.31, rev. RSNB 1854 c.124, am. 22 Vict. (1859) c.17, am. 23 Vict. (1860) c.28, am. 26 Vict. (1863) c.10.

95. CCGS Apr 1837 had ordered that 'all persons confined upon the said limits be at liberty to attend divine service on the sabbath days in the town plat of St Andrews.'

96. CCGS Apr 1831 ordered the sheriff to 'advertise in the public papers for persons to make an offer for maintaining the criminals and insolvent debtors who are unable to support themselves and that in the mean time the jailer maintain them as before,' and increased the gaol limits to the full extent permitted by the 1830 legislation. Hatheway was contracted by the county to survey and mark the gaol limits in 1850 and 1851. 30 Vict. (1867) c.28 applied to the whole province, extending the limits of every county gaol to 'any part' of the county, but did away with the weekly support entitlement for debtors who took advantage of the expanded limits.

97. For example, PANB RS148/D/3/b, Andrews v. Logan, 15 Sep 1859. A similar process obtained at ICCP: for example ibid., Boyd v. Atkinson (before Hatheway and Wilson), 7 Oct 1864.

ing good money after bad. The hearing before the magistrate served a double purpose though: in establishing the debtor's insolvency it also provided an opportunity to test whether he had any means remaining with which to satisfy the judgment. Stephen Greenlaw had been confined on the gaol limits for seven or eight weeks before applying for an allowance in December 1863. Cross-examined by his creditor's lawyer A.T. Paul, he testified that he had been unable to work for several weeks earlier in the year due to an injury. His wife had inherited a property from her father which they had mortgaged for more than the place was worth. He had other debts besides the mortgages and the judgment on which he was confined. He had discharged one of his minor sons from all obligations and had exercised no authority over him since August so he considered he had no right in the crop the boy had raised. While on the limits he had worked for several weeks at the shipyard but all his wages went to supporting his wife and four children. Dr Gove testified that Greenlaw had arranged for him to have some straw from his son's barn in part payment of a debt but it was not worth more than a dollar. At this point the hearing was adjourned until the following day when Greenlaw handed his creditor a quitclaim deed to the mortgaged property. Thereupon Hatheway ordered a weekly allowance of one dollar, the first instalment to be paid that day. After sundown, when the gaoler reported that he had received nothing for Greenlaw's support, Hatheway ordered him released from confinement.[98] Another confined debtor gave up some harness and hogsheads to the plaintiff before the allowance was ordered, the creditor refused to pay, and the debtor was released.[99] These examples suggest that creditors used the weekly allowance hearing to wring the last drop from their confined debtors and that debtors applied for the hearing not so much for the one dollar weekly pittance as in the expectation of being released.

98. PANB RS148/D/3/b, McCurdy v. Greenlaw, 11 Dec 1863.

99. PANB RS148/D/4/a, Johnson v. Sherar, 25 Sep 1862. Johnson was imprisoned as a judgment debtor in the Supreme Court where the same insolvent debtor legislation applied except that two justices, in this case Hatheway and Boyd, heard the application for weekly relief. PANB RS148/D/3/b, Connell v. Falconer, 13 Jul 1863 is a similar application before justices Hatheway and Bradley by a Supreme Court judgment debtor imprisoned on an execution apparently issued by Boyd.

It would be misleading to leave this topic without observing that many creditors were unwilling to pursue every debtor to the utmost extent of the law. W.C. McStay, a St Andrews physician who was made a JP in 1848, brought fourteen suits in Hatheway's court during the eighty-month period to collect on unpaid bills for medical attendance. All resulted in judgments, some of them paid immediately and others only after executions issued. In three of his suits, though, McStay asked Hatheway to stay the executions and paid the costs himself. In one of them he did so only after the constable returned the execution unsatisfied because the debtor had no effects on which to levy. In the remaining two, both filed in September 1850, McStay halted proceedings and paid the costs before the execution was returned. One of these defendants was described in the 1851 census as ninety-nine years old and 'very infirm,' and the other as eighty and 'deaf.' Other frequent plaintiffs including Michael Fauls and Thomas Healey asked for executions to be stayed on some of their judgments. Post-judgment settlements were quite common. In the suit between Lochary and McGrath which supplied the example summons and related correspondence (page 240) the plaintiff accepted $4 in settlement of the $6.60 judgment and paid the costs himself.[100] A few days after Hatheway awarded him judgment in full in his suit against Lynott (page 254) Michael Fauls attended at Hatheway's office and stated for the record, 'I hereby give up and abandon all further proceedings on the foregoing judgment at present.'

Hatheway's office as clearinghouse

> Dear Sir: John Carmichael is settle with me and I will take the £2 5s 0d he left with you and stop all proceeding against him on the note I left with you. Pleas to give me credit for the £2 5 0 on the Buckman suit against me and I will try to Pay the Balance as soon as Possible. Your obedient friend John Stewart.[101]

Hatheway's court was not only a place for reconciling small claims between distinct pairs of litigants but also a clearinghouse both for information about the current standing of one's debtors and creditors

100. Judgment was rendered on 9 Aug 1862 and the settlement entered on 14 Nov.
101. PANB RS148/B/2/e, Stewart (St Patrick) to Hatheway, 6 Aug 1857.

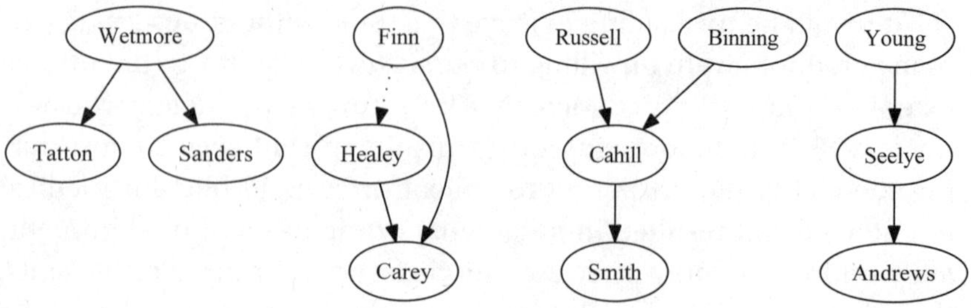

Figure 7.1 – Debtor → Creditor relations in four clearinghouse cases

and for the ongoing balancing of accounts in the complex web of obligations that constituted the debt economy. This was accomplished by the agency of the constable in levying executions and of the justice in setting off suits in which someone was a judgment creditor against others in which he was a judgment debtor (Figure 7.1). Hatheway's enterprise in turning his office into an unofficial local clearinghouse was sustained by the province's supreme court in the only known instance of judicial review of his justicing practice.

Hatheway issued an execution against Charles Wetmore on a judgment in favour of William Tatton, handing it to constable Henan. Tatton told Henan to do as he thought best in levying it. Henan had previously seized a quantity of ship timber belonging, as he thought, to Wetmore to satisfy an execution Hatheway had issued in a suit by Robert Sanders. There was more than enough timber to satisfy both judgments, so Henan advertised it for sale. However, on the day of the sale Benjamin Pettigrove claimed ownership of the timber, 'and not having been indemnified I abandoned the sale since which I could not find any goods or the Body of the said Charles J Whetmore whereon to levy.'[102] In this example, Henan's (ultimately unsuccessful) attempt to collect for Tatton depended on knowledge acquired while attempting to collect for Sanders, and Pettigrove's ability to intervene and stop the sale (and thereby deprive Tatton and Sanders of realizing their judgments against Wetmore) depended on information published by Henan in the normal course of his duties. In other

102. PANB RS148/D/4/b, return of execution, 9 Oct 1861.

cases the constable and the justice played a still more active part.

Patrick Carey sued Thomas Healey on a promissory note. At trial before Hatheway Healey admitted signing the note but objected to paying it because it was given without consideration. Constable Cain testified about the history of the affair. Three months previously justice Ker had issued judgment in favour of Carey against Dennis Finn, Healey's brother-in-law. When Cain went to levy execution against Finn, Carey agreed to take Healey's note for the amount of the judgment. Cain returned the execution to Ker as satisfied, 'and by request of the parties came with them to this Office when Justice Hatheway, by request of the parties, drew the note now in my hands and read it to them.' Healey signed the note and handed it to Carey. In giving judgment against Healey Hatheway ruled, 'Am of opinion that the D's giving the note was an open bonafide Transaction and that the P's giving up the goods levied upon was a valuable consideration and satisfactory to the D at the time.'[103] Where the Wetmore cases involved two plaintiffs and one defendant, the Carey cases involved two defendants and one plaintiff. Constable Cain was the vector carrying not only information but also the litigants themselves between Ker's court and Hatheway's, and Hatheway played active roles in both suits. His ruling against Healey recognized the common practice whereby judgment debtors settled with their creditors by providing a third party's promise of future payment thereby substituting for a bad debt a presumptively better one.

In the late 1840s Hatheway's clearinghouse activities twice resulted in litigation against him. Despite a favourable verdict, Hatheway complained to the provincial executive about the proceedings in the first suit because he was offended by James Boyd's charge to the jury. Judgment went against him in the second suit before A.J. Wetmore JP but Hatheway successfully challenged it on review. Both cases offer revealing glimpses of his practice. The fact that he was challenged suggests again that it was somewhat idiosyncratic. Hatheway certainly could not have conducted a successful clearinghouse without taking on a disproportionate share of civil justicing. By the same token, if plaintiffs had not appreciated his clearinghouse activ-

103. Carey v. Healey, 22 Sep 1855.

ities they need not have brought their suits in his court.

In October 1847 James Smith sued Hatheway before justice Boyd for nine shillings which he claimed as the balance of a judgment Hatheway had given in his favour against John Cahill.[104] Cahill owed money to Smith; George Russell and John Binning owed money to Cahill. Cahill got judgments against Russell and Binning and executions were issued against them. After levying on Binning constable Henan called on Smith and told him 'it would be a good time to get his money.' Smith and Henan went together to Hatheway's office where Henan gave Hatheway the money he had collected from Binning.[105] Hatheway paid Henan's constable fee out of this amount and gave the rest to Smith in part payment of his judgment against Cahill, saying that it was all he had in his hands at present. Smith then went to Boyd to sue Hatheway for the balance of the judgment.[106]

At the outset of the trial Hatheway challenged Boyd's jurisdiction, pointing out a section of the act regulating proceedings before justices in civil suits which provided that a justice who neglected or refused to pay over money lodged with him could be criminally prosecuted or sued for damages in the supreme court but not both.[107] Boyd overruled the objection and, having taken the evidence of the constables who collected from Russell and Binning, charged the jury in the following terms:[108]

---

104. Cahill had sued Smith but the jury gave judgment in the defendant's favour for 16/3 with costs amounting to £1/4/6: Ledger 1, 124. The trial was held on 27 Mar 1847.

105. Hatheway's docket entry in Ledger 1 shows that he tried Cahill's suit against Binning on 7 Nov 1846 and received payment in full on 15 May 1847. Henan had charge of the executions against Cahill (in Cahill v. Smith) and Binning. I have not found a record of Cahill's suit against Russell in Hatheway's book which together with the evidence that the money was not paid over to him suggests that it was tried by another justice, possibly Boyd.

106. PANB, RS13/54/c/1847, Boyd's minute of trial, Smith v. Hatheway, 22 Oct 1847. Henan and Smith may have been aware that Russell had also settled his debt with Cahill but the evidence at trial established that Hatheway had not received that money. Hatheway's trial record shows him paying Smith 'out of Binning debt' received from Cahill on 15 May 1847.

107. 4 Wm.IV (1834) c.45, in Berton, *Acts*, (referred to by Hatheway as 'Province Laws'), 694, marginal note 96.

108. Hatheway set out the charge in his petition 'in substance and nearly in the

> I don't consider the defendants objections valid. The law he quotes does not say he shall not be sued before another Justice for money he may refuse to pay over as a Magistrate. [A] poor man could not get his debt out of the Justice's hands if he had to bring his suit for it in the Supreme Court—but as it is proved that the defendant paid over to the plaintiff all he had collected from Cahil you will have very little to do. [H]ad it been otherwise I should have felt it my duty to charge you differently.

Hatheway complained to the lieutenant governor stressing the 'extraordinary situation' in which he was placed. Boyd had no jurisdiction. The plaintiff Smith was a 'notorious drunkard and a man of the lowest stamp in the community, a mere puppet' without any legal or equitable claim. Worst of all Boyd's charge to the jury put him in the position of having either to meet the case 'or be impeached with the charge of trying (in his Magisterial capacity) to deprive a poor man of his rights.' Boyd's conduct was bound 'to destroy public confidence and bring the Magistrates into collision and contempt.' The attorney general reported that there was no error or irregularity in Boyd's proceedings and that Hatheway had no cause for complaint.[109]

Details of what led up to the second suit against Hatheway are lacking but it is clear from Supreme Court justice Robert Parker's judgment that Hatheway had deducted from what he paid over to a plaintiff in one suit the amount he owed as defendant in another:[110]

> inasmuch as ... there was no ground of action by the Pff against the Dft [Hatheway] to recover back the money sent to the Dft

following words,' and supplied a statement signed by four witnesses in support of his account of the trial.

109. PANB RS7, Peters to Saunders, 3 Nov 1847. When Boyd was informed of the outcome he asked to see a copy of Hatheway's representations: 'knowing the man as I do, I have every reason to believe that he has made a false statement of the affair': ibid., Boyd to Saunders, 26 Nov 1847. The government complied with his request, but nothing further came of it: PANB, RS13/54/c/1847, Peters to Saunders, 15 Dec 1847; ibid., Saunders to Boyd, 18 Dec 1847.

110. PANB RS148/D/4/a, judicial review of A.J. Wetmore JP's judgment in P.D. Seelye v. Hatheway, 9 June 1849 (copy dated 2 Nov 1855). Hatheway's endorsement on the reverse refers to a subsequent trial before Patrick Clinch JP and seems to indicate that Seelye had been judgment creditor in a suit against Young and judgment debtor in a suit by Andrews, to whom Hatheway paid the proceeds collected from Young.

> while acting in the capacity of a Justice of the Peace in the recovery of demands against the Pff [for] which suits had been instituted – which said money appears to have been applied in part discharge of the said demands for which the said Pff was liable and not retained by the Dft to his own use, I do reverse the Judgment rendered in this case against the Dft with Costs to be paid by the said Pff to the said Dft, which costs I have taxed at the Sum of L5.19.0.

It is telling that the costs awarded in a Supreme Court matter heard in chambers exceeded the principal amount of the magistrate's civil jurisdiction.

These were not isolated instances. Money was paid to or by parties other than the litigants (excluding others directly engaged in the proceedings and entitled to fees or expenses, like constables and witnesses) in nearly ten per cent of the suits in which Hatheway rendered judgment in the eighty-month period. In some of these the third parties were members of the litigant's immediate family and in others they may have been acting as go-between for the litigant but it is a reasonable supposition that in many, perhaps most, of these cases the payment represented a clearinghouse transaction. Since in many other cases the docket simply notes that someone, often a constable, reported the matter settled or paid the clearinghouse function may have been still more pervasive than the naming of a particular third party indicates.

Common causes

In closing this discussion of Hatheway's civil practice in the 1850s and 1860s, it will be useful to describe some particular kinds of cases and specific issues that arose in several of them, with a view to illustrating the quality of civil justice dispensed in Hatheway's court. In some cases these anecdotes illustrate a legal point, in others they illuminate social relations, and the last of them is just too good a story not to repeat. Hatheway's papers in the municipal records are so extensive that it would be possible to multiply instances many fold. Here are just a few examples in each of just three of the areas in which disputes arose: wage claims, pilotage, and taxation.

Wages

Numerous claims for unpaid wages came before Hatheway, many of them simply because the employer could not or would not pay what he owed. Testifying in support of his application for a weekly allowance, Levi Handy explained that six of the plaintiffs whose suits had forced him onto the jail limits were men he had hired in 1853 to work for him in building Charles Thompson's steam brewery but could not pay. It seems likely that a significant proportion of the default and confessed judgments (about which few details are recorded) was for unpaid wages.[111]

The more interesting cases among those that went to trial were ones in which the wage rate had not been agreed in advance or the employer claimed a set-off for board, truck, or misconduct.[112] In several suits where wages figured either in the demand or a set-off there had been no prior agreement about or specification of the rate at which they were to be paid.[113] Lydia Johnson went to live with James Bickerton the day after he buried his wife. Seven months later she left him and sued for housekeeping wages. He resisted her claim but she brought two women to testify that they had heard him say he expected to have to pay for her services and another to prove that there

111. Supporting documentation exists in the occasional case. For example, PANB RS148/B/1/a, John McCarty v. William Tatton, 9 Feb 1856, in which McCarty won a default judgment against Tatton for wages due his (presumably minor) son. He led evidence to prove that Tatton had 'agreed to give P son James $12 per month to go in his vessel.' James testified to the correctness of his father's account which showed £6/3/9 offset by intermittent cash payments, tobacco, and coal for a balance due of £2/1/3. Some months later McCarty sued Tatton again on a note of hand. After Tatton was arrested on an execution the suit was compromised: ibid., 3 Dec 1856.

112. In a related case, a seaman's suit to recover the value of his carpenter's tools left on the vessel and retained by its master was dismissed for want of jurisdiction because the plaintiff deserted contrary to 'sec 243 the Shipping Act,' even though he subsequently returned to the ship and offered to work out his time. The master testified that 'The whole crew deserted when we came into this port [in distress]. The articles were signed by the men when on board of the vessel when she lay off in front of Eastport on the lines (so called), we were then on our way out to sea from this Port.' PANB RS148/D/4/a, Joseph Wilson v. James Hays (master of British brig *Prospect*), n.d. [1860].

113. Levi Handy had worked a few days for another mason when he applied for relief: his employer testified that they had not settled on a rate of wages.

was 'nothing wanting or amiss' in her conduct. The jury gave a verdict in her favour.[114] In Cox v. Hays[115] when the plaintiff presented his account for 'sundry goods' the defendant 'would not give P a note for the balance but said he would pay for it in work at some future time.' Hays later worked on a brig being built for Cox under master workman George Walker, who testified that he assessed his wages at 7/6 or $1.25 a day. At trial Hays said that he had been paid 7/7 or $1.40 a day at his previous employment, 'payable weekly in cash,' and that while he 'did not make a particular agreement with [Cox] about wages' he had expected 8/ or $1.60 a day. The jury gave a verdict for three-quarters of Cox's original claim, presumably adjusting the account by allowing Hays's set-off at a higher wage rate.

When Samuel P. Chase sued William Marshall for £4/11/6 for boarding him and his wife, Marshall requested a jury and put in his own claim for £4/18/9, including £3/7/6 for eighteen weeks' wages for his wife in 1853 and three days' wages for himself in 1855 along with a claim for boarding Chase's wife and '1 day of self horse & waggon moving your wife to my place.' Each party's story completely contradicted the other's. Samuel Chase insisted that Ann Marshall came to his house, asked to stay there, and 'did not do anything for me or my wife to my knowledge.' Eleanor Chase said she had advised Ann to board elsewhere 'where she could get some wages to pay [her] board' and that she 'did not work or assist me.' Ann Marshall testified that she had been working elsewhere when Samuel Chase 'came and got me to go and live with him and help his wife work.' The jury somehow arrived at a verdict for Chase for £2/14/0 so they must have allowed something for Ann Marshall's wages even if they accepted the balance of her husband's set-off.[116]

Hosa S. Greenlaw worked for Isaac Hanson, '3 weeks in swamping out roads and hauling back 8 days, 4 nights loading a woodboat, 15 days lathing P's house, 15 days tending a mason, 6 days digging potatoes, 10 days haying, 6 days hauling out bark, 1 day hauling bark, 1 day digging at a hill, 6 days hauling sand,' for which Hanson promised to

114. Johnson v. Bickerton, 17 Sep 1855.

115. Above at page 251.

116. Chase v. Marshall, 28 Nov 1857. Marshall's account for his set-off is dated at St James, 21 Nov 1857: PANB RS148/B/2/e.

pay him 'well.' He sued for the statutory maximum, claiming to have reduced his demand to that amount by allowing Hanson for 'cloth, a cap, and a pair of shoes which I call 20/.' Hatheway accepted Hanson's evidence that Greenlaw had paid for the cap, 'which from P own shewing makes his demand exceed £5' and adjudged him nonsuited and liable for the costs.[117]

While Greenlaw's case might be seen as an egregious example of formal trumping sustantial justice, William Pearn's successful suit against Thomas Anderson for £5 wages showed that it was nevertheless possible for an unsophisticated young labourer to turn the tables on his employer in Hatheway's court. Pearn testified,[118]

> I lived with D upwards of 18 months, I am nearly 16 years old, cannot read, made no particular agreement with D. He said he would clothe me and do what was right. He never gave me an outside coat or jacket, I have no drawers or any other articles of clothing but what I have on except the shirt now before the court, and to the best of my knowledge and belief the following is a true and just account of all I rec'd from D: Cash 3/, 2 straw hats and 1 wool hat, 3 blue cotton shirts, 1 calico vest, 2 pr socks and 1 pr new footed, 1 pr blue cotton trousers and 1 pr flannel, 1 pr boots, 3 pr shoes shop work, 1 pr of D old ragged trousers and 1 pr of his old ragged drawers cut short and patched up for me. I did all kinds of work D reqd and worked faithfully. I went in his woodboat bringing wood here, picking it up on the beaches, sometimes to load his boat, cut wood at the house, took care of the cattle, cleared out the stables, and last winter worked in the woods with him getting out lumber. I had some tobacco and pipes.

His widowed mother told the court that when she asked for some of William's wages, Anderson 'said he would give me what was fair then went quickly away,' while his wife promised to send her a barrel of flour which never arrived. In his defence, Anderson said, 'I can't make out an acct very well but swear that all the charges in my set off are correct, upwards of £11/16 - never agreed to give P wages - don't pretend that all the clothing charged was new.' To which Pearns replied,

117. Greenlaw v. Hanson, 7 Oct 1857.

118. Pearn v. Anderson, 23 Jul 1859. This was a jury trial by request of the defendant.

'You have charged me 7/6 for a saw lost, we used it on the beach, you passed it several times and saw it on the wood. I do not think I ought to pay for it.' The jury agreed and gave a verdict for £5 and costs.

Pilotage

Before 1863, piloting ships to and from the various harbours in Charlotte was regulated by the county. Common pleas appointed port wardens who controlled access to the occupation by the system of branch licensing while sessions prescribed when ships were required to employ pilots and the rates and fees to be charged.[119] The pilots made up a tight-knit group with close family connections and shared investments in their boats.[120] The duties and privileges of pilots had always been contentious at St Andrews. As early as 1798 sessions had banned a pilot for 'careless and improper conduct' and published the decision at Saint John and Halifax to make it 'as public as possible.'[121] Pilots sent collective petitions to sessions for revised regulations in several years and in 1835 they purchased a newspaper advertisement to publicize their struggle with shipowner and St Stephen magnate Nehemiah Marks JP over his continuing refusal to pay pilotage.[122] As

119. Pilotage regulation was taken out of the hands of the Charlotte justices and left to commissioners appointed by the provincial government by 26 Vict. (1863) c.36, sponsored by James Boyd.

120. Evidence given by J.H. Whitlock in a suit for pilotage heard by Hatheway showed that the pilot boat *Watchman* had five owners, the *John Conley* three, and the *Tormentor* about nine: Hugh Meloney v. Edward T. Hallett, 29 Apr 1859. Whitlock, trained as a lawyer, was tide waiter, searcher, and registrar of vessels at St Andrews: PANB RS13/A/10, Tilley to Whitlock, 21 Dec 1857. He was active in the militia and civic affairs and was famed locally for his garden, where he grew an 'immense' cucumber, 'the largest yet' (*Standard*, 10 Oct 1855). In 1863 he succeeded Jack as deputy treasurer and comptroller of customs at St Andrews (*Standard*, 11 Nov 1863) and became county treasurer in 1864 (CCGS Apr 1864).

121. CCGS 14 Apr 1798. Two more pilots lost their licenses at Common Pleas in 1820: *Herald*, 1 Aug 1820.

122. The pilots maintained that this refusal accounted for the grounding of the vessel *Nehemiah* while the *Standard*, 1 Oct 1835, defended the ship's captain and its owner, pointing out that 'The law does not oblige outward bound Vessels to take a Pilot, and even inwards they may refuse one by taking half fees. How far the insurance is affected depends on local and political circumstances.' The 1840 and later versions of the regulations entitled pilots to half-pilotage when their offers of service

the number of ships using the port declined along with the commercial importance of St Andrews, competition among pilots increased, as did friction with shipowners who resented their monopoly and fees.[123] Eight pilots complained to sessions in 1851 that they could not comply with the 1842 regulations then in force because of 'the very great expense' in fitting out suitable boats, 'the very few vessels that come to this Port,' and the fact that some of those who held licenses were nonresidents or made their livings running packets to and from the U.S. without buying shares in pilot boats, 'yet nevertheless avail themselves of their Branches in taking charge of all vessels coming in their way without any expense or outlay.'[124] Sessions issued a new set of regulations requiring pilot boats to be used exclusively for that service and pilots to live in the county and have an interest or standing in all or part of a pilot boat.[125] The 1850s saw increased contention among the pilots some of which resulted in litigation in Hatheway's court.[126] The regulations were revised more and more frequently through the decade although not always in the interest of the pilots[127] and in 1861 the justices refused their petition for more changes 'as the regulations were drawn up by some of the leading merchants and shipowners in connection with a committee after careful deliberation.'[128]

Enforcement of the pilot regulations was by civil process. Pilots could sue shipowners who refused their services or fees in defiance of the regulations. For example, in 1852 John Boyd of West Isles took out a capias against the captain of an American ship for half-pilotage, ap-

were refused on outward as well as inward bound vessels: PANB RS148/J/5, Pilot's Regulations, April 1840.

123. On the other hand when surplus pilots were permitted to go to Boston and New York to find ships one merchant complained of them 'leaving our own coast neglected' so that ships were 'beating about in the Bay, firing guns for twelve days in the fog, without being able to obtain a pilot': *Standard*, 17 Aug 1859.

124. PANB RS148/J/5/g, petition of William Cline et al., 7 Apr 1851, with an annotated list of 21 licensed pilots.

125. PANB RS148/J/5/g, 'Pilots Regulations,' passed CCGS Sep 1851.

126. In 1857 three pilots issued a 'caution to the public,' disclaiming liability for notes they had given to other pilots 'as we have not received value for the same.' *Standard*, 1 Jul 1857.

127. Revised regulations were promulgated in 1851, 1854, 1856, 1858, and 1860.

128. *Standard*, 17 Apr 1861.

pointing veteran pilot William Meloney as his agent and attorney.[129] Pilots who overcharged or undercut the regulated rate risked a £5 fine 'with costs, to be recovered before a Justice of the Peace; one moiety of the fine to be paid to the County Treasurer for the use of the County, and the other moiety to the prosecutor.'[130] This provision became a key weapon in the internecine struggle to stay in business as demand for pilots declined.[131] Thus in 1856 Hatheway ordered pilot Jarvis Clarke to pay prosecutor John F. Hanson £5 for 'demanding and claiming [from the captain of an American ship] a lesser sum for pilotage than the rates established by law in violation of 4th rule of Pilot Regulations.'[132] Obadiah Clarke sued fellow pilot James Clarke for a similar breach of the regulations but was nonsuited; a few months later when James sued Obadiah in return, plaintiff and defendant were represented by agent Sargent Meloney (a pilot) and lawyer R.M. Andrews respectively. Andrews objected that the complaint (a breach of rule 4 of the regulations) was indefinite, not stating clearly whether Obadiah was accused of taking too much or too little pilotage. Hatheway ruled that it made no difference as the regulation prohibited both offences, 'the fine being the same ... and the result to D must be the same in either case.'[133]

When Hugh Meloney sued Edward Hallett for forty shillings half-pilotage of his vessel (Hallett having refused to take him on board) both parties were represented by counsel. A.T. Paul, for the defence, contested the validity of Meloney's license, claiming it had been nullified by the statute 2 Geo.IV (1821) c.6, which repealed and replaced the former legislation for regulating pilots. B.R. Stevenson contended for the plaintiff that it was valid by virtue of the Revised Statutes 1854, c.162 s.11, which provided that all appointments continued in force

---

129. PANB RS148/B/1/a, 13 Oct 1852.

130. Sept 1851 regulation, s.4.

131. It was not the only weapon; groups of pilots continued to petition sessions not only for improved rates and privileges but also to have other pilots' licenses revoked. For example, PANB RS148/J/5/g, petition of William Cline et al., 4 Mar 1854.

132. PANB RS148/D/4/a, 24 Nov 1856.

133. O. Clarke v. J. Clarke, 8 Mar 1858; J. Clarke v. O. Clarke, 23 Jun 1858. Obadiah was part owner of the *John Conley* and James of the *Watchman*. In 1864 Obadiah, a Mason and 'one of the oldest and most active pilots belonging to this Port,' was lost at sea in a gale off Campobello: *Standard*, 9 Nov 1864.

after the repeal of the statute under which they were made.[134] A probably somewhat bemused Meloney produced a true copy of his license sealed by the clerk of the peace and Hatheway ruled that he was indeed a pilot. Next counsel turned their attention to Meloney's qualifications under the investment provision of the regulations. He had only recently returned to the piloting business and had not yet taken ownership of a share in a boat but he had given his note for £5 to Clarke for standing in the *Watchman.* The next issue was whether Meloney's gig boat was ready and suitable for service. He acknowledged that he had it caulked after Hallett refused his services but claimed, 'I could have gone down the Bay in my boat without caulking.' Whitlock agreed that 'it is not customary to take anything but gig boats to pilot vessel out.' Then Meloney proffered a notice signed by Hatheway in his capacity as chair of sessions issuing the new regulations, over Paul's objection. Finally Paul objected that Meloney had not proved his standing as pilot because he had not established that his boat was of the required tonnage. Meloney produced a bill of sale to show the tonnage of his gig boat but Hatheway drew a line through his note of this part of the evidence when Paul objected that the plaintiff had already closed his case. The protracted hearing was not about Hallett's refusal to take on a pilot or pay the fee—he had said he 'did not believe in pilotage' and entered his vessel at Eastport to avoid the St Andrews rules—but focused on whether Meloney was a pilot within the meaning of the regulations. The jury returned a verdict in Meloney's favour for thirty-three shillings and ninepence 'short pilotage or inner limit' plus twenty shillings threepence costs.[135]

It would be hard to argue that civil litigation materially assisted the resolution of the pilots' struggle to maintain their customary entitlements in the face of changing patterns of trade and transport technology.[136] Nevertheless Hatheway's court was as much a part of the

134. It is difficult to see what point Paul was attempting to make by citing the repeal provisions in the 1821 statute as Meloney completed his apprenticeship and received his branch license in 1835: PANB RS148/b/14/a, 4 Apr 1835.

135. Meloney v. Hallett, 29 Apr 1859.

136. Pilotage was calculated in part on the ship's draught and the newer American ships that entered the port of St Andrews had shallower draughts than the British vessels that had formerly been the mainstay of the pilots' incomes.

arena in which that struggle was waged as the fog-bound island inlets where the pilots waited on their boats for inbound ships or the sessions room of the courthouse where they directed their petitions and complaints. James Boyd's 1863 act to shift the regulatory authority from the county bench to a provincially-appointed commission may have promised, as the *Standard* enthused at the time, to 'relieve the Justices of no small amount of trouble, save much time and expense, as well as relieve the Pilots from constant changes of regulations, arising from a difference of opinion among themselves,' but it also marked another moment in the decline of the sessions system and local lay justicing.[137]

Taxes

The collection of county and parish rates and the enforcement of the (often monetized) statute labour obligation for the maintenance of highways and by-roads was by private civil process in the name of the responsible parish or county officer. William Craig, commissioner of roads, was plaintiff in eleven suits in the eighty-month period while highways commissioner Stephen McCurdy sued at least nine times.[138] Twelve of these twenty suits resulted in trials—a much higher proportion than the average in Hatheway's court—and all of them resulted in judgment for the plaintiff. Statute labour and its monetization was a recurring theme in Charlotte political discourse. Justice Abbot told a sessions grand jury that the substition of a money tax, while burdensome on the poor, had proved beneficial at St Stephen, producing 'at a much cheaper rate a greater improvement in the roads, streets and bridges than ever before.' The statute labour system might be inequitable, but this was not the fault of the magistrates: 'We have not the making of the Laws, neither do we or the Grand Jury come here to find fault with the Laws—but each in our own proper sphere to administer, fulfil, and obey them.'[139] The Highways Act was amended in 1850, increasing the scale of statute

137. *Standard*, 15 Apr 1863. For the legislation, see note 119 above.

138. The 1851 census listed two Stephen McCurdys at St Andrews, a farmer and a carpenter. Four suits were initiated by 'Stephen McCurdy, commissioner of highways' and of ten others by 'Stephen McCurdy' at least five were for statute labour.

139. *Standard*, 16 Apr 1845.

labour and cutting the commutation rate in half. 'One great benefit which will result ... is to relieve the poorer classes of society—persons having large incomes and owning much property, will now contribute more ...'[140] This did not stop 'Veritas' from decrying its inequity or 'Poor Man' from denouncing a system 'whereby a rich man can pay 1s 3d (25c) but the poor man has to work a full day.'[141] Hatheway's trial notes from later years include two statute labour cases. In one McCurdy had won a default judgment against a defendant who subsequently proved he had performed his statute labour in another parish. Discharged from the twenty shilling judgment he was nevertheless liable for nineteen shillings and ninepence costs.[142] The other was a complaint of assault against a roads surveyor in a dispute about whether the complainant's pickaxe and shovel were good enough to complete his statute labour. It illustrates the overlap between criminal and civil disputes, a topic to be considered in the next chapter.

Dog tax collector Hugh Morrison filed nine suits before Hatheway in the eighty-month period, all of them resolved in his favour. In 1856 he brought suit against wheelwright Edward Stentiford. Here is Hatheway's trial minute in full:[143]

> Hugh Morrison, collector of dog tax, to recover tax of 5/ from Edward Stentiford for a dog kept by him. Parties present. P: called on D for tax, he said he did not own a dog. The dog was lying in D's shop. D said the dog had been about the shop since last fall and belonged to the captain of the steam boat. P told D he was liable to tax as he harboured the dog. Came again and saw D's wife sitting and dog lying beside her. D took same position as before. Defence: [P] never saw D feed the dog, which might have picked up something that was thrown out the door. D agrees dog is very fat but says he does not know where he gets his food; denies liability for tax. Am of opinion that the D has harboured encouraged and kept the Dog in and about his premises and therefore liable to the tax and therefore adjudge him to pay 5/ tax and costs.

140. *Standard*, 1 May 1850.
141. *Patriot*, 2 Sep 1853, 15 Oct 1853.
142. McCurdy v. Miller, 23 Jul 1859.
143. Morrison v. Stentiford, 22 Apr 1856.

Chapter 8

Hatheway's crown docket, 1847-67

> By a statute passed in the reign of Philip and Mary, which has always been deemed in force and acted upon in this Province, Justices of the Peace are required, before they commit any prisoner for felony, to take the examination of the prisoner, and the evidence of the witnesses who can speak to the matter, and to put the same in writing, and to certify the same to the next Court of Gaol Delivery. They are also required to bind by recognizance all material witnesses to appear at such Court to give evidence, and in like manner to certify to the Court the recognizances of such witnesses, which are also to be in writing.
>
> This is one of the most important branches of the duty of a Justice of the Peace. Upon a skilful and faithful execution of it, the satisfactory administration of criminal justice essentially depends.

With these words to an 1831 grand jury, chief justice Chipman summed up the common law's understanding of the JP's role in felony prosecutions.[1] But to state the magistrate's role in the administration of criminal justice in this way was at the same time to obscure the extensive discretion it implied and to ignore the various means

1. *Courier*, 15 Jan 1831. The thrust of Chipman's address was to celebrate the province's adherence to the English program of criminal law reform described below.

by which justices of the peace acted to determine the great majority of criminal offences outside the system Chipman described. In Charlotte county criminal trials at the circuit court (presided over by a judge of the supreme court) were relatively few, especially after the criminal law reforms of the early 1830s (Table 8.1).[2] That there were not more is due to the justices who received the original complaints and managed them so as not to require supreme court trials or often any trial at all. Minor crimes like common assault[3] and petty theft could be tried by the justices with a jury at general sessions or summarily in their private offices. And of course a host of regulatory and morals offences under provincial statutes and local by-laws attracted criminal penalties (whipping, incarceration, fines) but were entirely within the justices' purview.

From the late 1820s when New Brunswick began to copy the English Peel Acts to reform the classification of crimes and the severity of punishments, summary proceedings before justices out of sessions increasingly overtook jury trials not only at the circuit court but at general sessions as well. Table 8.2 tracks the decline in arraignments at sessions, a proxy for trials by jury there. The 1828 statute reforming the law of offences against the person provided for summary trials before two justices in all cases of common assault.[4] The 1831

2. Supreme court judges on circuit tried both civil and criminal cases, the latter as the court of general gaol delivery. Circuit court minutes are missing for most of the period. The data in Table 8.1 are compiled from newspaper reports, official correspondence, and court minutes where available. In 1836 the justices and legal profession successfully petitioned for a second annual circuit court for Charlotte emphasizing the volume of civil business. 8 Wm.IV (1837) c.4 fixed the county's circuit court dates as the fourth Tuesday in April and the Tuesday following the fourth Tuesday in October, confirmed by 9 Vict. (1846) c.57. The second court was abolished after 1856 when civil business declined due to the commercial collapse: by 20 Vict. (1857) c.5 the county's single circuit court was to commence on the first Tuesday in August.

3. When the question whether the clerk of the crown had a monopoly of criminal prosecutions arose in 1841 Chipman and his fellow judges recommended the appointment of crown prosecutors except in trials before justices of the peace in which 'the ordinary Assaults and Batteries and other misdemeanors, *where the injury is rather of a private than a public nature*' should continue to be left to private prosecution: JLC 1842, App. 1, 402.

4. 9&10 Geo.IV (1829) c.21, s.15. The New Brunswick statute was based on [UK] 9 Geo.IV (1828) c.31.

Table 8.1 – Criminal trials at Supreme Court, Charlotte circuit (Includes special courts of gaol delivery, available dates: see note 2)

Year	Tried	Year	Tried	Year	Tried
1811	1	1847	4	1860	2
1821	1	1850	2	1861	2
1822	5	1852	2	1862	0
1825	3	1853	0	1863	4
1826	4	1854	0	1864	1
1827	8	1855	7	1865	2
1829	3	1856	0	1866	5
1834	0	1857	2	1867	3
1845	1	1858	0	1868	3
1846	1	1859	3	1869	0

Table 8.2 – Arraignments at General Sessions, five-year intervals

Year	Arraigned	Year	Arraigned	Year	Arraigned
1785	16	1820	16	1845	0
1800	3	1825	6	1850	1
1805	12	1830	3	1855	0
1810	10	1835	5	1860	0
1815	0	1840	3	1865	0

statute reforming the law about property crime gave three justices out of sessions the power to hold summary trials for larceny up to forty shillings; by 1858 the limit had been raised to five pounds.[5] The

5. 1 Wm.IV (1831) c.15, s.28; 21 Vict. (1858) c.22, s.5. Summary trials before three justices for minor offences including petty larceny had been available under certain circumstances as early as 1786 (26 Geo.III c.59) but the only penalties that could be imposed were corporal punishment and banishment from the county. Thus in 1786 five justices in special sessions sentenced Joshua Lock, who had confessed to stealing a pair of silver buckles from Phoebe Webb, to twenty lashes at the public whipping post and to remain out of the county for twelve months: CCSS 14 Aug 1786. In 1820 the justices ordered five petty thieves to receive thirty-nine lashes each and the four nonresidents among them to leave the county: *Herald*, 1 Aug 1820. Under

duties of justices out of sessions in criminal proceedings were 'clearly defined by positive enactment'[6] for the first time in 1849 when New Brunswick adopted its version of the Jervis acts along with a codification of indictable offences modelled on Brougham's failed English bill of the previous year.[7] The substance of the 1849 codification was borrowed by Nova Scotia's 1851 statute revision while the latter's form and structure, copied from New York and Massachusetts codes, became the basis for New Brunswick's revised statutes of 1854.[8] These included revised provisions governing the justices' summary jurisdiction along with a revision and restatement of their role in preliminary examinations, which Chipman had considered to be among the 'most important branches' of their duty.[9]

Against the scattering of jury trials before supreme court judges on the Charlotte circuit or the bench of magistrates at general sessions must be set the hundreds of criminal proceedings dealt with summarily by the county's justices out of sessions. C.R. Hatheway listed three hundred and sixteen such cases on the 'Crown side' of his docket between 1849 and 1866 and eighty-three more appear elsewhere in his papers.[10] Hatheway was an unusually active magistrate

---

the reformed law justices had the power to fine and incarcerate. By 1 Wm.IV (1831) c.18 the county bench could establish rules for imprisonment at hard labour. The provincial penitentiary was opened in 1841.

6. 12 Vict. (1849) c.31 (preamble).

7. 12 Vict. (1849) c.29 (codification), 12 Vict. (1849) c.30 (combining the preliminary examination reforms of [UK] 11&12 Vict. (1848) c.42 with eighty additional sections dealing with criminal procedure generally), and 12 Vict. (1849) c.31 (substantially reproducing the summary jurisdiction provisions in [UK] 11&12 Vict. (1848) c.43 and the protections for justices in [UK] 11&12 Vict. (1848) c.44). All this legislation was introduced in Council. Brougham's bill is discussed and paraphrased in *Justice of the Peace*, London, 10 and 24 Jun 1848.

8. Brown, *Genesis*, chapter 4.

9. The 1854 revision also included a new version of the law regulating the justices' civil jurisdiction. The preliminary examination and summary jurisdiction enactments are considered more closely below.

10. Hatheway turned Ledger 2 upside-down and around for his crown docket. The additional 83 cases (as well as additional documentation for some of those in the docket) appear in the record of 'complaints and trials of suits long ago settled' (1854-61) which follows the end of his civil docket in the same ledger and in loose papers in PANB RS148/D/3/a-g, D/4/a-c and D/5. For the exclusion of these cases from the docket, see further below. Unless otherwise indicated the cases discussed

but as we have seen there were other justices who declined to take on civil business but nevertheless participated actively in criminal justice.[11] In 1863 St Andrews justice B.R. Fitzgerald collected fines in 19 cases, most of them for drunkenness, assault, or abusive language, and charged fees to the county in 27 cases. Cases in which no fines were assessed and the county was not liable for costs went unrecorded in this accounting. St Stephen police magistrate W.J. Rose listed 30 'county' cases (including licensing offences, thefts, and several preliminary examinations in which the accused was committed for trial), 33 'alms house' cases (assaults, in which fines went to the overseers of the poor), and 58 'police' (mostly drunk and disorderly) cases for a total of 121 items in his return for the year ending March 1868.[12] Justices sitting alone or with one or two others handled the vast bulk of the criminal business in Charlotte county. Supreme court judges saw very little of it and grand or petit jurors not much more.

This chapter examines the administration of criminal justice by the Charlotte magistrates, emphasizing the middle years of the nineteenth century and based in large part on Hatheway's records. It aims to show that there was significant overlap in the ways that the justices dealt with crime, civil disputes, and local governance so that if keeping the peace was not entirely seamless it was nonetheless a single fabric. To vary the metaphor, just as Hatheway moved between civil and criminal matters by turning his record book over and opening it at the other end, so was there unity and continuity in the varieties of local justicing.

Discretion and the preliminary examination

It was long a matter of debate among lawyers and then among legal historians whether the Marian statutes which established the law of preliminary examinations left the justice of the peace any discretion

below are found in the 1849-67 docket ('Ledger 2') while cases found in the 1841-49 docket are identified as 'Ledger 1', and those in the short 1867-8 docket as 'Ledger 3.'

11. Chapter 7. The Charlotte county papers in PANB RS148/D include criminal proceedings before justices Hugh Mackay, Ker, Abbot, Craig, Fitzgerald, Hiltz, Crilley, W.F.W. Owen, Rose, and Curran among others.

12. The Fitzgerald and Rose accounts are in PANB RS148/D/4/c. See also Fitzgerald's account for 1862-3 in PANB RS148/D18/c.

about whether to commit the accused for trial.[13] Richard Burn's influential manual cited Dalton's *Countrey Justice* (1618) for the proposition that the examining magistrate should not dismiss the case even if he thought the prisoner to be innocent of the charge, 'for it is not fit that a man once arrested and charged with felony, or suspicion thereof, should be delivered upon any man's discretion, without farther trial.'[14] Notwithstanding Chipman's paraphrase of the Marian statutes in his 1831 charge, provincial legislation of that year seems to have contemplated the dismissal of felony charges at the examination stage. Mirroring British reforms, it instructed examining magistrates to commit the accused for trial where 'the evidence shall be such as not to warrant a dismissal of the charge.'[15] In Charlotte county, at any rate, committal for trial was not the inevitable outcome of arrest for an indictable offence.[16]

St Stephen police magistrate W.J. Rose's 'county account' return for 1867-8 included fourteen indictable offences, proceedings in which it was his role to conduct the preliminary examination (Table 8.3). In two of them the complainants did not appear—an exercise of

13. [Engl.] 1&2 P&M (1554) c.13; [Engl.] 2&3 (1555) P&M c.10. For a brief account of the intent and consequences of these statutes, Langbein et al., *Common Law*, 583ff.

14. Burn, *Justice*, I:536. This was the current edition when New Brunswick was established. Langbein et al., *Common Law*, 648, summarizes the disadvantages to defendants of the Marian pretrial. Beattie, *Crime and the Courts*, 268ff, discusses the eighteenth-century amelioration of English pretrial procedure, arguing that by mid-century, 'Magistrates began to feel more obligation to make some assessment of the evidence being presented and to assume more right to dismiss charges when they thought the case too weak to justify a trial' (274). Beattie points out that the implications were not 'fully registered in law until Jervis's Acts of 1848' (277) but see page 294 below.

15. 1 Wm.IV (1834) c.14, s.3, following [UK] 7 Geo.IV (1826) c.64 and [UK] 7&8 Geo.IV (1827) c.27. The reforms of the 1830s reduced the number of capital felonies, expanded the summary jurisdiction of justices in lesser offences, and broadened the middle range of indictable misdemeanors. References to indictable misdemeanors in the New Brunswick statutes include 1 Wm.IV c.15 (1831) s.20, and 19 Vict. (1856) c.52, s.11. Police court legislation for Saint John, Portland, and St Stephen provided for summary trials of what had formerly been indictable offences: for example, 11 Vict. (1848) c.12, s.18. The 1854 statute revision distinguished between indictable and summary offences: see further below.

16. For the corresponding practice in Upper Canada see Lewthwaite, 'Pre-Trial Examination.'

Table 8.3 – Indictable offences in W.J. Rose's 'county' account, St Stephen, 1867-8

Offence	Disposition
Suspected conceal birth	Dismissed
Intent to kill	Committed for trial
Intent to do bodily harm	Dismissed
Abusing horse	Committed for trial
Horse stealing	Sent to Fredericton on Mayor's warrant
Intent to cause bodily harm	Complainant did not appear
Attempt to do bodily harm	Committed to gaol
Detaining [?] a child	Complainant did not appear
Burglary	In lock-up, conveyed to Calais secretly
Suspected theft	Dismissed
Attempt to do bodily harm	Bound over to take his trial
Assisting [attempt bodily harm]	Dismissed
Theft	Bound over to take trial
Bigamy	Dismissed

discretion on their parts—and in two more the accused was removed from Rose's jurisdiction, one by warrant and the other by 'secret' conveyance across the international border. Of the remaining ten, five were committed for trial and five had their charges dismissed. Rose was operating under the 1854 rules which recognized a discretion in the magistrate to discharge an accused who in his opinion should not be put on trial.[17] But none of the outcomes he reported would have seemed amiss to Charlotte justices of earlier generations.

In 1786 five St Andrews justices met in special sessions to examine a prisoner arrested on suspicion of petty larceny. Finding there to

17. The 1849 administration of justice act had provided that 'when all the evidence offered upon the part of the prosecution shall have been heard, if the Justice ... shall be of opinion that it is not sufficient to put such accused party upon his trial for any indictable offence' the accused was to be discharged, but if there was sufficient evidence, 'or if the evidence given raise a strong or probable presumption of the guilt of such accused,' then the examining magistrate was to commit him for trial: 12 Vict. (1849) c.30, s.14. The 1854 version was shorter and plainer: 'Should the Justice after a full hearing be of the opinion that the accused should not be put on his trial, he shall discharge him as to that enquiry; but should he be of the contrary opinion, he shall then commit him by Warrant, or admit him to bail as hereinafter provided.' (RSNB 1854, c.156, s.12.) See below, at note 47.

be 'no foundation for the charge against him,' they ordered him discharged.[18] In 1823 the St Andrews magistrates held a special meeting to consider what to do about two men in their gaol whose clothing matched descriptions of stolen garments sent by an American correspondent. They agreed to inform the vice-consul at Portland, 'and further in case the Magistrates of Robbinston or Eastport will make the necessary arrangements to receive [them], that the Magistrates here will deliver them up at either of those places free of expence.'[19] The third member of this trio of 'abandoned scoundrels' was found aboard a fog-bound vessel near Lubec, Maine, by St Andrews jeweller William Paterson who brought him to St Andrews on suspicion of having burglarized his store. There he received three judicial whippings of 39 lashes each before being sent back to Lubec for trial at Portland.[20] The secret conveyance of Rose's burglar may have been a similar incident of informal extradition or extraordinary rendition.

The Charlotte magistrates had no hesitation in discharging accused whom they believed not to be guilty. In 1836 two Americans were arrested and examined by justices Ker, Wyer, Douglas, and Rait for passing counterfeit banknotes in St Andrews. One was committed to gaol to await his trial; the other 'proved his innocence and was liberated.' The *Standard* published correspondence between Rait and James Frink of the St Stephen bank describing the examination and attesting to the second suspect's good character: 'that the notes were passed by him is confessed, but he satisfactorily accounts for the manner in which they came into his possession, and left not the slightest grounds of blame or guilt attachable to him.'[21] Hatheway's records of trials in 1840 include two examinations pursuant to mittimus warrants in which the accused were discharged.[22]

Occasionally disagreements among the examining magistrates came to light. In 1839 Rait complained to the provincial executive

18. CCSS 14 Aug 1786.

19. CCSS 14 Oct 1823.

20. *Sentinel*, 27 Jul, 16 Nov 1822; *Courier*, 10 Aug 1822.

21. *Standard*, 5, 19 May 1836.

22. Chapter 6. Ledger 1, crown side, 25 Apr 1840 (two accused examined for 'felony' by three justices and discharged); ibid., 26 Oct 1840 (one accused examined by Hatheway alone for drunkenness and riotous conduct, discharged).

that the clerk of the peace had insulted him during the preliminary examination of William Eills by saying he had 'advocated the cause of a prisoner' and had 'acted more as a Council [*sic*] than as a Judge.' The complaint was referred to Harris Hatch for comment. He passed it on to the committing magistrate, William Ker, who reported having called in Hatch as his legal advisor when the prisoner was brought before him to be examined. Eills's 'particular friend,' apparently lawyer R.M. Andrews, sent for Rait to attend. In Ker's opinion Rait acted 'in favor of the prisoner during the whole of the examination.' Ker committed Eills for trial but when Judge Parker sent for the record Rait insisted on writing an explanatory letter and enclosing it in the packet. It was at this point that Wellington Hatch (who was to succeed his father as clerk of the peace in 1840) told Rait that 'it was all nonsence sending a Letter to the Judge and also said that if he had a cause to advocate he would employ him as he pleaded better for the Prisoner than the counsel.' At the end of the day the clerk made up the packet and sent it to the judge without a covering letter.[23]

Rait's was not the most egregious example of magisterial interference in a felony investigation. In 1848 relatives of a homicide victim accused Grand Manan patriarch Wilford Fisher JP of intentionally delaying proceedings and otherwise interfering in the course of justice so that the accused could escape to the United States. He was said to have at first refused to order the arrest of Gilmore, the man held responsible by a coroner's jury, and then to have put off his examination for several days; to have ordered the constable to keep him in his personal custody rather than commit him to the local lock-up; to have conversed privately with Gilmore for more than half an hour at the conclusion of the examination; and to have permitted him to return to his home. The erstwhile prisoner made off for Eastport and thence to Boston where the trail turned cold. The provincial executive commissioned Fredericton lawyer William Watts Jr to conduct a

23. PANB RS8 (Magistrates), Rait petition, 26 Feb 1839, endorsed 'communicated to H Hatch 5th March 1839'; PANB MC207, Ker to Hatch, 9 Mar 1839. There is another copy of the petition without endorsement in NBM NB Government Collection, S181, F105. Ten years later, Eills's name headed a petition against justices Ker and Boyd for failing to pay over fines to the county treasurer: PANB RS13/27/c.

formal enquiry, the third in Fisher's career as a magistrate.[24] Fisher boycotted the investigation, declining to return to the island from Eastport while it was under way. Watts concluded that Grand Manan magistrate Cochran Craig was guilty merely of 'amiable imbecility' in failing to stand up to Fisher during the inquest and subsequent preliminary examination but found Fisher to be so ignorant or negligent of his duty that he 'should not be left in a condition to repeat.' Fisher sent the executive two letters and a petition decrying the expense to which his enemies' complaints had subjected him and attacking the motives and credibility of adverse witnesses. His only comment on the substance of the allegations was to blame the constable in whose charge he had left the accused. Ignoring Watts's recommendation for his removal, the government kept Fisher in the commission of the peace until his death in 1868.[25] He was well-connected with the St Andrews junto, having served with Hatch and Wyer as a packet commissioner and militia officer.

Harris Hatch's involvement in the Eills case (1839) suggests that the 1849 provision directing county clerks of the peace to advise and assist justices in felony proceedings merely restated a long-standing practice.[26] On at least one occasion Hatch intervened to persuade a justice to proceed on a lesser charge in order to avoid a jury trial at the circuit court. In 1837 a Campobello constable complained to W.F.W. Owen JP about a crew from Lubec stealing cordwood, 'the property of the proprietor of the land'—Owen himself—and resisting arrest. Owen committed the ringleader to trial for 'riot and rout,' but relented at Hatch's suggestion:[27]

> The ends of justice will I conceive be perfectly answered by

24. Fisher had been investigated by W.B. Kinnear for the 1839 burning of the Anglican church and by Lachlan Donaldson for misconduct as militia captain and road commissioner two years later. For a possibly overly-sympathetic assessment of Fisher's career (which does not mention the 1848 investigation) see Ingersoll, 'Fisher, Wilford.'

25. PANB RS7, Fisher to Partelow, 4 Sep 1848, enclosing petition and a second letter of the same date; ibid., Watts report, 21 Sep 1848.

26. 12 Vict. (1849) c.30, s.19. The provision does not occur in the corresponding English act, [UK] 11&12 Vict. (1848) c.42.

27. PANB RS148/D/3/c, Farmer complaint, 3 Feb 1837; PANB RS148/J/1, Owen to Hatch, 27 Feb 1837.

> the most summary proceeding, which if it can be settled ... at once by two Magistrates will sufficiently satisfy my view of the Case. If I understand your explanation, it is to relinquish that part of the charge which relates to 'Riot & Rout' and confine to the other which relates to the assault on the Constables only, which can be adjudicated by two Magistrates.

In assault and larceny cases the justices had a built-in discretion to characterize the offence as falling within or without their summary jurisdiction—common assault versus assault with intent or in commission of a felony; larceny below the statutory limit or above it—and there is reason to believe that they sometimes adjusted their views of the evidence accordingly. For example the 'sundry articles of clothing' stolen from 'sundry persons' for which three justices sentenced John Thomson to four months' hard labour in the penitentiary in 1860 were valued at £4/15, just below the statutory limit of five pounds.[28] As will be seen below several complaints that amounted on their face to indictable aggravated assaults became simple summary offences in Hatheway's court; more than a few of these were subsequently settled, withdrawn, or resolved by having the accused enter into a peace bond.

There is no single reason why the Charlotte justices were so reluctant to commit accused for trial before a judge and jury. The cost of incarceration was a factor—'These persons are a very great charge to our County,' wrote Hatch to the attorney general in 1822, asking that a court be convened 'to relieve us from the burden as early as possible'[29]—and the remarkable porosity of the county gaol, not to mention the parish lock-ups, was likely another. Corrupt motives were sometimes alleged: Fisher was said to be 'under obligations' to Gilmore, and Eills may have been associated in one of Rait's many business enterprises. A major factor was the protective and proprietorial attitude of the more patriarchal justices towards the local community. Outside interference was unwelcome. This attitude was reflected in the insularity of local justice which responded to misconduct by strangers with extraordinary rendition and banishment from

28. PANB RS148/D/3/b, 16 Aug 1860.

29. PANB RS76/c/2, Hatch to Wetmore, 8 Apr 1822; similarly, CCGS 21 Sep 1825, CCGS 19 Apr 1836 (and see corresponding petition in PANB RS7).

the county. Outsiders received special treatment even from county juries in the circuit court. Only two convicts are known to have been executed in Charlotte before Confederation:[30] Richard and Maria Stewart, 'a negro man and woman,' went to the gallows for infanticide in August 1826. In pronouncing sentence Chipman made it clear that incest, 'although the fact was not distinctly proved,' deeply aggravated the offence.[31] Much was made in the press about the gravity of their crime and the 'awful example' the Stewarts' fate must serve to others who, while not guilty of the sin of incest, 'are strongly suspected of having taken away the lives of their own children, the fruits of their illicit amours.' What was not mentioned either in Chipman's remarks or the press reports was that at the very same circuit court a jury had refused to find another woman guilty of killing her illegitimate newborn, substituting instead a conviction for concealing the birth of a child.[32] When it came to crime within the community Charlotte tended to put the King's peace before the King's justice.

Summary justice

Among the almost four hundred complaints in Hatheway's records only seventeen were referred to the circuit court and ten (including seven bastardy cases) to general sessions (Table 8.4). Eighty per cent (ninety per cent if the undocketed complaints are not counted) were disposed of summarily whether by conviction (or other order) or by

30. Two men sentenced to death 'for committing a rape upon Mary Ann an Indian Woman' escaped from the St Andrews jail in 1829: CCSS 19 Nov 1832. Two men convicted of grand larceny at the August 1827 circuit took benefit of clergy and were each sentenced to two whippings of 39 lashes: PANB RS32/A/2.

31. It is not known whether the Stewarts were brother and sister or parent and child. That they were indicted and convicted for murder (rather than concealing birth) and hanged (rather than have had their sentences commuted) is a reminder of the casual racism of the time and place; here, however, the emphasis is on the harsher treatment of marginalized outsiders more generally.

32. *Sentinel*, 19, 27 Aug 1826; *Royal Gazette*, 29 Aug 1826 quoting *Herald*; PANB RS32/A/2, R v. Jane Cummins, tried 12 Aug 1826, sentenced the same day to three months' imprisonment. The Stewarts' trial followed immediately upon Cummins' sentencing. Newborn infanticide was more commonly prosecuted as concealing birth than as homicide in the nineteenth century. See, for example, Backhouse, 'Desperate Women' and M.E. Wright, 'Unnatural Mothers.'

Table 8.4 – Hatheway's crown-side dispositions, 1849-67
(399 crown-side cases)

Type	Count
Complaint only	36
Peace bond	128
Summary conviction or other order	200
To be tried at sessions	10
To be tried at circuit	17
Withdrawn/settled	4
Other	4

Table 8.5 – Justices sitting with Hatheway in summary trials, 1849-67
(56 summary trials)

Name	Count	Name	Count
Patrick Clinch	1	James Boyd	4
George Mckay	1	Charles Bradley	6
T.T. Odell	1	Harris Hatch	12
J.W. Street	2	W.C. McStay	13
William Whitlock	2	William Ker	18

Table 8.6 – Summary of offences tried by Hatheway, 1849-67
(Substance of charge in 200 crown-side summary judgments)

Type	Count
Assault	58
Contempt	8
Disturb peace	10
Drunk	75
Liquor sale	35
Profanity/abusive language	6
Theft	9
Other	11

binding the accused to keep the peace. These three hundred and twenty-eight cases included seven larcenies heard by three justices and forty-six assaults and three other offences heard by two justices (Table 8.5). In the rest Hatheway acted alone. Table 8.6 summarizes the subject matter of two hundred summary judgments. They include twelve assaults in which no other justice is named. In two of these cases Hatheway's record uses the word 'us' or 'we' suggesting the presence of an unnamed second magistrate. The remaining ten assault trials do seem to have been decided by Hatheway alone despite the statutory requirement for two justices. In several of them the accused was charged with an offence triable by a single justice—breach of the peace, abusive language—along with the assault. Hatheway may have convicted on the alternate charge alone. The remainder include some in which the accused were minors and three in which the accused were discharged: one for want of prosecution,[33] a second in which Hatheway found the complainant to have been the aggressor, and the last in which the accused had been arrested because a clergyman thought that he might be about to beat his wife. There are thirty-six cases in which the complaints (or such other pretrial documents as warrants) survive in the county papers but are not recorded in Hatheway's docket. Some of these may have been heard by another justice (with or without Hatheway's participation) but others likely went untried because the accused could not be found or the complaint was withdrawn or abandoned.

A group of cases involving cattle[34] suggests something of the range of Hatheway's activities in crown cases. He took bail to appear at the next circuit court for an accused charged with killing a horse.[35] He took bail for an accused charged with beating a cow but cancelled the recognizances when the complainant abandoned the prosecution on the eve of the circuit court. The accused and his witnesses had given exculpatory evidence at the preliminary examination.[36] He is-

33. RSNB 1854 c.138, s.10.

34. Defined by RSNB 1854, c.155, s.10 and s.11 as including 'every horse, mule, ass, sheep, pig, or goat ... and also every bull, cow, calf, or ox' as well as heifers.

35. R v. William Johnston, 23 Aug 1854.

36. R v. James Coakley on complaint of Andrew Elliot, 4 Jun 1861; Hatheway's notes of the preliminary examination are in PANB RS148/D/3/b.

sued a warrant for the arrest of an accused who had drawn a pistol and threatened to shoot the complainant's horse in a quarrel between neighbours over cutting timber on disputed land. When the constable brought him to court the accused denied the charge and asked for an adjournment to procure an important witness. He was bailed to appear a few days later but when the trial date arrived Hatheway noted, 'all settled.'[37] When two widows, both 'very poor and have small children,' complained of being terrorized by a dangerous red mare that their mutual neighbour permitted to run at large Hatheway wrote him a letter but 'nothing could be obtained.'[38] He fined another accused ten shillings for allowing a hog to run at large in the town.[39] When Francis O'Neal's cattle tried to break into James Gallaghar's enclosed field, Gallaghar started to drive them away. 'Francis O'Neal came suddenly out of the woods with a club in one hand and a large stone in the other,' struck at Gallaghar and swore that he would knock his brains out. Gallaghar complained to Hatheway, who issued a warrant to arrest O'Neal 'and carry him before some Justice of the Peace to shew cause (If any he has) why he should not find sureties for his keeping the peace and being of the good behaviour towards James Gallagar as prayed for in the annexed complaint.' Subsequently he ordered O'Neal to find bail for good behaviour, 'and he promised to do so the next day.' O'Neal must have defaulted on his promise for Hatheway issued a warrant of imprisonment two weeks later.[40]

All but the first of these six complaints were disposed of summarily although just one of them involved a summary trial. Two were abandoned by the complainants following the preliminary examina-

37. PANB RS148/D/4/a, R v. James Murphy on complaint of James Arvin, 16 Feb 1858. In an 1845 complaint about maltreating and injuring a cow, the parties 'compromised and settled' after Hatheway adjourned the trial to permit the accused to procure a material witness: Ledger 1, R v. Bridget Flinn on complaint of John Kent, 8 May 1845.

38. PANB RS148/D/3/a, complaints of Mary Ann Bartlett and Mary Greenlaw against Francis Dinsmore, 5 Sep 1866. In this case Hatheway charged the county seventy five cents for 'drawing compts and 2 Oaths & long complnts.'

39. Charles McQuaid, 8 Nov 1850. Half the fine was paid to the poor house commissioners, which suggests that the balance went to an unnamed informer.

40. PANB RS148/D/3/a, Francis O'Neal on the complaint of Charles Gallaghar, 20 Jul 1857.

tions and another by Hatheway himself when 'nothing could be obtained' of the accused; in one he levied a fine, probably on the accused's confession[41] but possibly after a trial; and in the last he imposed a peace bond, a remedy to be discussed in detail later in this chapter. Something of Hatheway's attitude to prosecution can be gleaned from his note to James Boyd who had sent him a written complaint against four men for (among other things) 'abusive language to myself while in the execution of my duty as a magistrate in endeavouring to quell a riot at the late fire on Saturday last and at other places.' Hatheway replied,[42]

> In the case against Meagher, the charge appears to me too vague to safely proceed thereon, some specific act should be named that the Justice can take action thereon such as Assault, Threats whereby the complainant is put in fear for safety of his person, family, or property, or if a Justice, obstruction in the execution of his office, or for drunkenness, as the case may be. I make these suggestions to prevent a failure in any case, which would give the Defendants an opportunity of *exulting*, which has a tendency to bring the authority into contempt.

The statute book imagined that there were two distinct processes, one by which the justice was responsible for proceedings before indictment and another by which he could convict an offender summarily. John Archbold thought that with the passage of the Jervis acts, on which New Brunswick's 1849 statutes were based, 'it is scarcely possible for a Justice of the peace now to err in the execution of his duties, either in respect to indictable offences, or in cases of convictions or orders.'[43] The 1854 revised statutes separated them so that summary conviction came under Part III, 'Courts and proceedings in connection therewith,' along with the justices' civil jurisdiction but the preliminary examination came under Part IV, 'The criminal law

41. RSNB 1854 c.138, s.11: 'When the defendant shall be present at the hearing, the substance of the information shall be stated to him, and if he admit the truth thereof, and show no sufficient defence, the Justice shall convict ...'

42. PANB RS148/D/4/b, Boyd to Hatheway with endorsement, 12 Sep 1859. On the reverse Hatheway wrote, 'Nov 4th nothing done.'

43. Archbold, *Jervis's Acts*, 14.

& the administration of criminal justice.'[44] In practice, however, the distinction could be hard to maintain. In each chapter the statute presented a linear procedure, but there were no signposts to indicate where or how they intersected. There were at least two sorts of problems. First, despite the efforts of the revisors to set out straightforward guidance in ordinary language with a compendium of useful forms, each statute was inherently ambiguous. Second, while to the law commissioners the justices' role in preliminary examinations was entirely distinct from their role in summary proceedings, from the standpoint of the working justice nothing could be further from the truth. After all, both sorts of proceedings typically began when someone in a private or public capacity came before the justice with an allegation. Assuming that it more resembled a criminal offence than a civil dispute (there will be more to say about this below) the justice had to decide whether to treat the applicant's narrative as a complaint prefatory to a preliminary examination or an information initiating the summary process. This was not a simple question of deciding whether the subject matter belonged to the class of indictable offences or offences punishable by summary conviction. These were not mutually exclusive categories but much turned on the distinction. Different procedural steps were called for depending on whether the applicant's problem was classified as an indictable or a summary offence.

Both chapters contained ambiguities and inconsistencies. In c.156, the indictable offences procedure, the most important of these was the role of defence evidence in the preliminary investigation.[45] The English and New Brunswick statutes both provided for the pros-

44. RSNB 1854, Part III, Title XXXVII, c.138 (civil jurisdiction in c.137); Part IV, Title XL, c.156.

45. The Marian statutes required justices to record the evidence taken in the preliminary examination, 'or as much thereof as shall be material to prove the felony.' Burn, *Justice*, I:537 quoted Dalton's suggestion, 'Yet it seemeth also just and right, that the justices who take information against a felon, or person suspected of felony, should take and certify as well such information, proof, and evidence, as goeth to the acquittal or clearing of the prisoner, as such as maketh against the prisoner: for such information, evidence, or proof so taken, is only to inform the king and his justices of the truth of the matter.' The Peel acts extended the pretrial to all indictable offences. In his commentary on the Jervis act pretrial procedure ([UK] 11&12 Vict. (1848) c.42, s.25), Archbold, *Jervis's Acts* says that the justice 'is not to try the prisoner, he is not to

ecution witnesses to be examined in the presence of the accused, who had the right to cross-examine them and then, under caution, to make a statement in his own defence. The New Brunswick revision departed from the Jervis act by an interpolation in s.12: 'Should the Justice *after a full hearing*[46] be of the opinion that the accused should not be put on his trial, he shall discharge him ... but should he be of a contrary opinion, he shall then commit him ...' This is followed by a sentence whose policy does not appear in any English act before 1867:[47]

> The Justice may take evidence on behalf of the accused, and transmit it with the other documents to the Clerk of the Crown on the Circuits, and the witnesses giving such evidence shall be bound by recognizance, if desired by the accused.

This provision might be read as meaning that defence evidence was to be taken only after the justice had decided to put the accused to trial (the only circumstance in which any documents were to be sent to the circuit clerk) yet he was to have a 'full hearing' before the justice decided whether to discharge or commit. On the other hand, to hear the defence case before making that decision would be to turn what was intended to be a preliminary enquiry into whether the prosecution had established a *prima facie* case into something more like a trial of

judge whether the evidence given is sufficient to convict him,' but simply whether it raises a presumption against him.

46. The phrase 'full hearing' does not occur in any nineteenth-century UK statute dealing with criminal procedure. It appears in the Nova Scotia revised statutes of 1851 in connection with lunatics (RSNS 1851 c.152) and of 1859 in connection with lunatics and apprentices (RSNS 1859 c.152; ibid., c.125) but not the criminal pretrial.

47. [NB] 12 Vict. (1849) c.30 reproduces [UK] 11&12 Vict. (1848) c.42, s.25, and then appends this proviso: 'that nothing herein contained shall be construed to require such Justice or Justices to hear evidence on behalf of any party so accused, unless it appear to him or them to be meet and conducive to the ends of justice to hear the same, in which case the evidence in behalf of the accused shall be transmitted [to the clerk of the crown]' but recognizances need not be taken from defence witnesses. The proviso is permissive, not restrictive. Stephen, *History of the Criminal Law*, I:220, gives a slightly misleading account of the Jervis act by implying that the provision for defence evidence at pretrial formed part of the 1848 legislation when in fact it was first enacted by [UK] 30&31 Vict. (1867) c.35, s.3, which he cites in a footnote. The other footnotes at that page all refer to the 1848 act.

the merits. Nor did the statute have anything to say about whether the prosecution was entitled to cross-examine the defence witnesses or whether the accused was entitled to counsel. This poorly-integrated interpolation in the New Brunswick statute was probably meant to legitimize what was already the well-established practice in the colony.

There were inconsistencies in c.138, the summary conviction statute, as well, although perhaps not as head-scratchingly bewildering as the c.156 treatment of defence evidence. For example, the text of the relevant sections referred to an information being 'laid' but the corresponding forms indicated that it was to be 'taken and sworn.' The only reference to an oath in these sections related to the service of an unanswered summons. The forms referred to information and complaint indifferently. The statute provided that 'the Justice shall hear the parties, and any evidence that may be produced,' (s.11) but gave no guidance about the procedure to be followed except that 'the parties in person, or by counsel, may conduct and defend their causes' (s.9). Although both sorts of proceeding had similar apparatus for requiring the attendance of the parties and their witnesses, they were not identical. The two hearings differed in several other formal respects apart from their ostensible purposes. Summary trials had to be public (c.138 s.9); preliminary examinations could be held in private (c.156 s.9). While both statutes indicated by capitalized letters the various forms to be used, they referred to different schedules and the one does not correspond to the other.[48] The revised statutes supplied separate schedules of justices' fees in civil suits and summary convictions but made no specific provision for their fees in preliminary examinations.[49] Overall, however, the effect of the New Brunswick versions of the Jervis acts was to blur the boundaries between the preliminary examination and the summary trial and to recognize thereby the broad discretion exercised by justices in handling crown matters.

Against this background, a detailed account of one of Hatheway's proceedings will illustrate some of the choices a justice had to make

48. For example, letter 'B' indicates a summons in c.138 but a warrant in c.156. The schedule of forms for summary proceedings is appended to c.138, while the schedule for c.156 appears at the end of Part IV, appended to c.160.

49. RSNB 1854 c.163, heads sixth and seventh.

in applying these provisions. On March 24, 1857, Barbara Davidson attended at Hatheway's office and made a statement on oath:[50]

> I have been hired by Josiah Craig as a housekeeper for a long time, that latterly he has made several attempts to have his will of me and used violent means to accomplish his purpose. I have always resisted him and declared to him that I would never submit to his wishes and requested him to pay me my balance of wages due to enable me to go away as I had no relations to go to nearer than Grand Manan. That yesterday he made another like attempt upon me, when I told him I would die before I would submit and upon failing to accomplish his purpose called me infamous names and used language to me too bad to be repeated, he took me by the throat, choked me and then knocked me down over a log and the bruises upon my head and face you can now see. I therefore request that the said Craig may be prosecuted for the said offence as the law requires.

Davidson complained that Craig had used violent means in his attempts to have sexual relations with her, including a 'like attempt' the day before. Among the indictable offences set out in c.149 of the revised statutes were carnal knowledge and abuse of a woman against her will and by force, a capital felony (s.7), and assault with intent to commit a felony, a misdemeanor punishable by up to two years' imprisonment or a fine at the discretion of the court (s.19). If Hatheway had understood Davidson's story as a complaint that Craig had committed the latter offence he was required by c.156 to conduct a preliminary examination. However, if he had understood Davidson's complaint to be that Craig abused her only after she had successfully resisted his sexual advances it would have been possible to construe the offence as a common assault punishable by summary conviction. Hatheway issued a warrant for Craig's arrest and summonses

50. PANB RS148/D/3/a, R v. Josiah Craig, 24 Mar 1857. Hatheway endorsed the original complaint, 'Queen vs Josiah Craig / Barbara Davidson / Complainant / Deft acquitted 4th Apl 1857.' At the bottom of the complaint he added his statement of costs: 'O[ath] C[omplaint] & W[arrant] 3/6 - 2 Summons 2/ - Trial 2 O[aths] 1/ - 400 words 2/6. {2 Summonses for Deft under Seal 2/ }.' There is no docket entry for this case.

to Davidson and another witness. On April 4 the parties appeared at Hatheway's office. He made these notes of the proceeding:[51]

> The Queen vs Josiah Craig for an assault & battery alleged to have been committed by him upon Barbara Davidson on or about the 23d March last.
>
> Barbara Davidson sworn says: I was hired by Deft as housekeep upwards of a year ago, left him for about 4 weeks and returned again last summer. The reason I stopped with D so long was to get my wages due if possible. About 23d Mch I went to the barn to milk the Cow when Deft came in, called me base names, vile language, made me so angry that I caught hold of the barn shovel and threw it at him, did not hit him. He abused me so with vile language that I threw an axe at him, did not hit him, upon which he ran up to me and I took a stick. I intended that if he took hold of me to hit him with the stick. He then caught me by the throat and choked me, struck me upon the right temple which raised a bruise, knocked me down across the end of a log and my side is still sore. [Cross-examined:] I know that I should be punished hereafter if I should swear to a falsehood and suppose I should be punished here.
>
> Defence. James Gow sworn. I know the complt & deft. I was at Deft Barn at the time spoken of. Complt was inside milking. Deft went into the barn to find his horses (as I supposed). In about a minute he came running out & the compt followed him with a shovel, chased Deft into the field & then threw the shovel at him. Compt then went to the barn, got her milk and went into the house. I followed her in. She swore she would leave her mark on him and take her pay that way. She then went out, brought in an axe and swore she would put it into his guts. In a minute or two Deft came in for his breakfast. Upon coming to the door compt threw the axe at him but did not hit him then caught a stick about 4 feet long, struck at Deft. He caught the stick and took it from her. He caught her by the hand and she pulled it away and struck D in the face two or three times. She scratched his face & made it bleed then caught him by his neck handchf & tried to choke him.
>
> Defendant discharged.

51. Ledger 2, 'complaints and trials of suits long ago settled' (see note 10). I have supplied sentence breaks and commas where needed to improve the sense.

What sort of a proceeding was this? Hatheway's endorsement on the complaint and bill of costs make it out to have been a trial leading to an acquittal, but the note of the hearing shows the outcome to have been a discharge. There was no preliminary examination in summary offences, but trials for common assault required two justices and Hatheway conducted this hearing by himself. It lacked some elements of the preliminary examination—Craig was not cautioned and no statement was taken from him—but Hatheway read over Davidson's and Gow's testimony to them and had them affix their marks, which he would not have done at trial. It lacked other elements of the summary trial, as for example the opportunity to acknowledge the offence before any evidence was taken.

We might be inclined to view the proceeding as a bumbling miscarriage by an 'amiable imbecile,' an illustration of how incompetent lay magistrates unwittingly undermined the rule of law. Alternatively, we might understand it as a moment in the construction of substantial justice by an experienced practitioner familiar with his community and alert to the real issues underlying the complaint. There is some evidence favouring this alternative view. Hatheway would have known that Craig was vulnerable to accusations of sexual predation because he had taken sureties from him in a bastardy prosecution a few years earlier.[52] He would also have noticed that one of the few consistencies between Davidson's original complaint and the evidence at the hearing was her claim for unpaid wages. On April 4 Hatheway heard not only Davidson's assault charge but also her civil suit in which Craig acknowledged owing her £2/13/6 balance of wages and Davidson received judgment for that sum plus costs.[53] It is easy to imagine that the criminal proceeding provided the leverage necessary to make Craig acknowledge the wages debt and pay it. Barbara Davidson received substantial justice because she and Hatheway understood how to use the justice system creatively. This reconstruction may also explain why the civil suit appeared in his docket but the criminal complaint did not.

52. 19 Apr 1853; CCGS 24 Sep 1853.

53. Ledger 2, civil side. Hatheway issued a summons to Craig on March 25, the day after Davidson swore her complaint. He issued an execution on April 6 and Craig made payment in full on May 3.

This case also shows that as much as the justices' role in preliminary examinations intersected with their summary jurisdiction, so did both of these with their authority to determine minor civil suits. Justicing was not so much a business of parsing the statute book as it was of preserving peace and order in the community. Quite a number of criminal proceedings before Hatheway might just as easily have come on as civil suits. Many of these appear in the record of 'complaints and trials of suits long ago settled' or in the loose papers but not in the docket, suggesting that they too might better be seen as gestures towards informal dispute resolution than as criminal proceedings in their own right. A few examples from the first six months of 1854: A farmer pays his hired man in bank notes, realizing too late that he has mistakenly given notes with a face value of five pounds instead of five shillings.[54] A man's brother gives him money to pay his debt to a third party, but the brother refuses to pay it over.[55] A farmer accuses the man from whom he had purchased two oxen of stealing them from his barn.[56] Someone accuses four others of theft for disassembling and carrying away pieces of his oxcart which he had left at the roadside overnight.[57] Similarly, several of the civil suits described in chapter 7 could as easily have originated in criminal informations.

Strong drink as offence and defence

More than half of Hatheway's summary judgments involved liquor sales or consumption. The liquor selling cases were straightforward breaches of the licensing regulations, several of them based on grand jury presentments referred to him for disposition by the general sessions. None of them seems to have arisen under either of the prohibition acts (discussed in chapter 11). Most resulted in convictions and fines, many of them on confession. A few reluctant witnesses were committed for contempt; in one case the prosecutor failed to appear and the accused liquor seller was discharged; in another, the prosecutor was 'nonsuited' [*sic*] and ordered to pay costs after three consta-

54. R v. Patrick Bury, 5 Jan 1854.
55. R v. Peter Halloran, 31 Jan 1854.
56. R v. Thomas McGuire, 8 Mar 1854.
57. R v. Walter McFarlan et al., 13 Jul 1854.

bles testified that they had not bought liquor from Mrs Sharkey, the accused, in that license year.[58] The accused's husband was among three tavern owners who had pleaded guilty to the same charge a few days earlier.[59] Another case was dismissed on the evidence of a boarder that he had not seen anyone purchase liquor from the accused in the past year.[60] On the same day, however, Lauchlan Doon was fined two pounds on a grand jury presentment when he acknowledged that the informer 'came to his house one night very dry, the little girl gave him some spirits and he gave her some money for it.'[61]

Judging from a file of papers supporting justice B.R. Fitzgerald's claim for fees the manner of proceeding against lists of alleged liquor sellers in grand jury presentments or town clerks' returns closely resembled Hatheway's civil debt collection practice.[62] In 1863 sessions ordered the clerk of the peace to 'call upon the Town Clerks of each Parish to furnish him the names of all persons who are or have been selling Liquor without Licence.'[63] Parish clerk John H. Rose sent in twenty-seven St Stephen names and three from Milltown, 'supposed

58. A fourth witness arrived too late to give evidence at trial but declared that he had not bought any either: R v. Mrs B Sharkey, 10 Jun 1858.

59. R v. Charles McGee, 21 May 1858; R v. John Langmaid [Langmuir], 22 May 1858; R v. William Sharkey, 8 Jun 1858. McGee and Langmuir were repeat offenders, suggesting that the old practice of collecting license fees in arrears by prosecution was still in operation (chapter 11). In one such case, Hatheway agreed to defer the execution to allow the defendant to appeal to general sessions, which remitted his fine: ibid., R v. William Tatton, 17 Nov 1849; CCGS Apr 1850.

60. R v. Joseph Smith, 4 Nov 1854.

61. Ibid., R v. Lauclan Doon, 4 Nov 1854. Doon, who said he did not want a trial, also admitted that his wife had been selling spirits and he had not interfered. Hatheway noted in the margin, 'This conviction not carried to [the docket] as usual D promising to pay in a few days.' However he issued an execution in December and a warrant of imprisonment on 26 March 1855; Doon paid the fine on April 4.

62. Chapter 7. Like Fitzgerald, Hatheway seems to have begun proceedings on liquor-selling complaints by corresponding with the accused: PANB RS148/D/1, Frink to Hatheway, 29 Apr 1847, on behalf of a St Stephen druggist who had received such a letter. Frink wrote that of the three informants, two had not entered the accused's shop in the last four years, 'not being on terms of intimacy,' while the third 'is not in the habbit of purchasing *White Eye*.'

63. CCGS Sep 1863. This probably reflected the increasing unwillingness of sessions grand juries to present offenders preferring instead to critique the county accounts: chapter 9. For earlier examples of grand jury presentments in liquor cases see PANB RS148/D/3/a.

to be selling without license.' Rose observed that some of them 'tell me they have licenses but they do not appear upon the list.'[64] The clerk of the peace handed Rose's list to St Andrews justice B.R. Fitzgerald presumably because no St Stephen justice was prepared to act.[65] He reported that some of those named indeed held licenses; as to the others, 'I took the trouble to write each of them on the subject.' Some confessed and paid their fines but ten did not. Fitzgerald asked Rose to send a list of witnesses, promising to keep his name out of it. The file contains replies to Fitzgerald's letters from the alleged delinquents, most of them claiming not to have sold any liquor in the past year or two although only one tendered evidence in his defence. Several complained of the hardship of having to attend court at St Andrews. 'If the steam boat was runing I would strive to you but for us gowing in a sleigh or stage it would I fear put an end to my days,' wrote Mrs Margarette Donoghue, 'but I want to spare my life as long as you is willing to spare me.' John Murphy wrote that the charge against him was unjust, and 'I am aware that you can put me to troubel and expence to defend any invstigason in St Andrews.'[66] Others pleaded the general issue: 'All in Milltown knowes my situation,' wrote Edward Fitzgerald, 'that I am blind these two years and cant go out of doares even to Church,' while Mrs D. Sullivan explained that she had not seen or heard from her husband for eighteen months, so 'you see what a hard chance is before me with eight little children to support with the assistance of god and my own little industry.' Fitzgerald collected $184 in fines from those he convicted, paid $160 to the county treasurer, and kept $24 for his services in managing the whole list. He had made himself quite unpopular. On the night of December 26 Fitzgerald's office was entered and 'all my provincial Statute Books together with my Record Book, account book feloniously and by malice aforethought taken from my office, conveyed to the Lower end

64. PANB RS148/D/4/a, Rose to Hatch, 4 Nov 1863. 'Kill them easy' appears at the bottom of the page.

65. Ibid., Fitzgerald to Rose, 'Confidential,' 17 Feb 1864. For the reluctance of justices in St Stephen to act in civil and criminal matters because they were 'so busily engaged with their own private affairs,' see *Standard*, 9 and 23 Aug 1865.

66. Rose wrote to Fitzgerald on Murphy's behalf, asking him to allow the complaint to be laid in St Stephen, 'to save the extra expense of hiring a team &c to go to St Andrews.'

of the Market Wharf by some persons unknown, then torn and hove into the tide.'[67] The grand jury at April sessions found his account against the county for fees in the liquor cases to be 'very strange' and the bench appointed a committee of three justices, one of them Fitzgerald's old rival James Boyd, to investigate.[68] It concluded that he should be allowed twelve dollars 'for his trouble' and pay over the rest and recommended 'that in future all complaints for breach of licence laws be prosecuted in the Parish where such breach takes place.' After September sessions, however, the *Standard* reported that some whose licenses had expired 'have not renewed them, preferring to "run the risk" of being fined.'[69]

Excessive drinking was not taken seriously as an offence until the rise of the temperance movement. Before then its only significance was sabbatarian. Being drunk on a Sunday was prohibited in 1786 when the legislature made it an offence, ambiguously, to 'be convicted of drunkenness, or the disturbance of the Public Worship of God, either on that or any other day ...'[70] A 1798 grand jury called for better 'Regulations ... to prevent Drunkenness on the Sabbath' along with others to prevent fowling and fishing on the Lord's day.[71] But by the late 1840s public drunkenness, not sabbath-breaking, was the gist of the offence. The criminal law consolidation of 1849 distinguished between 'drinking, or frequenting tippling houses' as an offence against religion (ch. II, s.2) and 'drunkenness' as an offence against 'public morals and decency' (ch. III, art.1).[72] The 1854 revised statutes provided for summary convictions for drunkenness 'either

67. PANB RS479/b/2.

68. PANB RS148/A/5/e/1, Grand Jury report, 11 Apr 1865; CCGS Apr 1865. Fitzgerald had presented a petition that led to Boyd's removal from the magistracy in 1850, and then kept him out of the assembly for almost three years before Boyd won the scrutiny in 1853: chapter 10. Fitzgerald was Charlotte county's first openly Catholic magistrate and assemblyman. He died suddenly in 1866: *Standard*, 4 Apr 1866.

69. *Standard*, 4 Oct 1865. The report continued: 'In justice then to those persons who have complied with the law, the Town Clerks should, after the license list is published, send a list of delinquents, to be dealt with according to law.'

70. 26 Geo.III (1786) c.5.

71. CCGS Apr 1798.

72. 12 Vict. (1849) c.29.

upon view, or on evidence before a Justice.'[73] Of the seventy drunkenness convictions in Hatheway's ledger, more than half (thirty-eight) were 'upon view.' Sometimes this meant that after encountering an apparent drunkard on the street, Hatheway would return to his office and write up a conviction to be served on the offender by a constable some time later. Thus on October 22, 1851, Hatheway convicted John Burns of drunkenness and sentenced him to pay ten shillings or be imprisoned for four days. Constable Haddock notified Burns of his conviction on November 3 and on November 5 he was committed to gaol for want of effects. Later that month Hatheway convicted butcher Thomas Healey of drunkenness on view, sentencing him to twenty shillings or four days in gaol. Constable Henan served notice on Healey two days later but the fine remained unpaid despite an execution issued in February 1852.[74] On other occasions Hatheway convicted drunks 'on view' when they were brought into his office by a constable or other informant. In August 1852 Healey, a repeat offender, was brought before Hatheway by Dr Gove 'and 2 or 3 Constables.' He was 'raving drunk' and 'was with difficulty prevented beating Doctor Gove in my office.' Hatheway committed him to gaol 'for present safety and security' and he was not released until he paid his fine from the previous November along with ten shillings for the latest offence.[75]

Slightly fewer than half of Hatheway's drunkenness convictions began with a complaint or information. Mary Caffrey complained that her husband Michael ill-treated and abused her and her children. The previous day he had come home 'crazy drunk,' broke their only table to pieces, and attempted to beat his grown daughter Eliza, who fled the house. Mary hid with her infant in her arms until Michael threatened to take her life when she too fled, spending the night out of doors. Michael, arrested on Hatheway's warrant, pleaded guilty to drunkenness. Hatheway fined him twenty shillings and ordered him

73. RSNB 1854 c.145.

74. 22 Sep; 3, 22 Nov 1851. Healey was evidently going through a bad patch. Hatheway sentenced him to three days in jail and a ten shilling fine for 'interrupting me in a judicial proceeding.' He served the jail time but constable Henan reported that the 'fine cannot be recovered': 20 Sep 1851.

75. 22 Nov 1851, 25 Aug 1852.

to find securities for good behaviour.[76] A few days later Mary returned to Hatheway's office and complained that Michael, who had left home after his previous conviction, had returned 'raving drunk.' He broke and destroyed their kettle, bakepan, and teapot and then beat her dreadfully until two men responded to her cries for help. Hatheway issued an arrest warrant and left Michael in gaol several days before bringing him up and offering to release him on bail on condition that he take the temperance pledge.[77]

Temperance logic held that strong drink was the efficient cause of bad acts by good (albeit weak) men. Michael Caffrey's brutal assaults on his wife and children were not his fault: the drink was responsible. Like others in his situation Caffrey was convicted of drunkenness but not charged with a crime of violence. Drink made men 'crazy' or 'raving' so that they were not fully responsible for their actions. Elizabeth Summers complained that her husband got drunk, 'acted like a crazy man, took an axe, swore he would put the axe into [her].' Her two children escaped out the window when they heard their father calling for the axe.[78] John Brien complained that his lodger John Graham 'has been repeatedly crazy drunk; last night so outrageous that it took five men to take him to gaol ... he is so violent that neither I nor my family dare silence him.'[79] James Chandler, convicted of an unprovoked assault on a fourteen-year-old boy he met in the street, was 'crazy drunk' at the time.[80] Peter Crawley, arrested for assaulting a special constable, had been drinking 'and was perfectly crazy.' Crawley ('a very quiet man when sober') claimed to have had 'no recollection of the transaction.'[81] Thus strong drink erased both responsibil-

76. Ledger 2, 'complaints and trials,' complaint of Mary Caffrey, 9 Oct 1854; Docket, 9 Oct 1854, indicating that the conviction was under the 1849 criminal law consolidation. Caffrey had an earlier conviction before Hatheway for drunkenness: 24 Aug 1852. According to the 1851 census the family had arrived from Ireland in 1848; Michael was a 'railroad labourer.' They may therefore have been among the *Star* immigrants discussed in chapter 10.

77. Ledger 2, 'complaints and trials,' complaint of Mary Caffrey, 29 Oct 1854; Docket, 30 Oct, 14 Nov 1854. One of Caffrey's sureties was tavern keeper Charles McGee.

78. 28 Aug 1854.

79. 20 Dec 1856.

80. PANB RS148/D/4/a, 10 Oct 1857.

81. 2 Mar 1859.

ity and memory. Daniel O'Haleran, committed for 'assaulting sundry persons and other acts of violence,' said he had 'no recollection of the affair.'[82] John McCarty, accused of breaking into the cellar where Eliza Cole, 'a woman of colour,' lived with her three children and attempting to 'take hold' of her, did not deny the truth of her complaint, 'but was drunk last evening and don't know anything about the matter.'[83] It is difficult to assess whether these defences mitigated the penalty—the outcomes ranged from committal for trial to discharge on a peace bond—but they were powerful ideological statements distinguishing good men from bad acts.[84]

John Burns, Thomas Healey, John Graham, and Michael Caffrey were all repeat offenders. Hatheway's papers include eighty-two convictions and complaints of drunkenness, involving fifty-two distinct offenders. Caffrey and Graham appeared before him three times, Healey five, but St Andrews' leading drunkard by this measure was lawyer Richard M. Andrews whom Hatheway convicted on view seven times between 1856 and 1859. Andrews had at one time been Hatheway's supporter—he signed the county lawyers' petition to have him reinstated in the magistracy—but the two had a falling out over Andrews's bill for legal work on Hatheway's behalf: 'I told him I considered it a sham and that I would not pay him for it.'[85] The quarrel came to a head in 1855, shortly after Andrews's office, library, and papers were consumed by fire.[86] He was uninsured. Thereafter An drews undertook to harass Hatheway at every opportunity. In March

82. 29 Sep 1855.

83. PANB RS148/D/3/b, 29 Sep 1865.

84. In two cases before three justices, the accuseds' claims to have been intoxicated at the time did not save them from penitentiary sentences for larceny; in one of them the prosecutor disputed the thief's claim to have been drunk: PANB RS148/D/4/a, R v. James Fergusson, 14 Jun 1866; ibid., R v. James Parks, 14 Dec 1866.

85. PANB RS148/D/3/b, 'A statement of transactions with and relating to Mr R M Andrews.' This was one of a number of similar statements and entries made by Hatheway documenting his quarrel with Andrews. The legal work involved the judicial review in Seelye v. Hatheway, discussed above in chapter 7 and in particular Andrews's failure to collect money Hatheway believed was due him. Similarly James Boyd complained that Andrews, a former friend, had attempted a 'gross imposition by an inflated bill of costs': PANB RS/13/54/c, Boyd to Partelow, 1 Jan 1850. Boyd reported that Andrews spent most of his time at Pheasant's Public House.

86. *Standard*, 25 Apr 1855.

1856 Hatheway was making an official inspection of the county gaol. He met Newton Seelye, confined there for refusing to testify before his nephew Henry Seelye JP in a liquor case. Andrews approached them, put one hand on Seelye's shoulder, pointed a finger in Hatheway's face, and said, 'Don't speak to him, he is a Magistrate, he is a liar, he tells lies.' Turning to Hatheway, he 'raised his voice, distorted his lips and said, "Yes, you are a liar, you tell lies, and I will attack you wherever I meet you in the Street and tell you that you are a liar and tell lies."'[87] Hatheway called on the gaoler for assistance, returned to his office, and entered a conviction against Andrews for drunkenness on view. Several incidents followed in which Andrews, intoxicated, met or stalked Hatheway in the streets of St Andrews and denounced him in the presence of various bystanders. Each time Hatheway entered drunkenness convictions against him. Constables Henan and Haddock warned Hatheway that Andrews might injure him in some way, even 'take a pistol and blow your brains out,' and urged that he put him under bonds. Hatheway asked mutual acquaintances to intervene with Andrews but without effect. For reasons unknown, the pattern ended after May 1859. Andrews appeared as a defendant in Hatheway's court on one later occasion, when Edwin Hatch complained that he had called him 'a damn liar and a rascally mean fellow.' Hatch withdrew the complaint when Andrews apologized.[88]

Perhaps the oddest intersection of temperance and crime in Hatheway's justice shop took place in February 1865 when Alexander Law, son of the county gaoler, laid a complaint of assault against Edward Elliot, son of the St Andrews town clerk. The two youths, both enrolled in the Temperance Society, met by chance in Saint John whereupon Elliot invited Law to join him in a glass of whiskey, saying 'all the Sons of Temperance here drink.' The two returned to St Andrews together and attended a meeting of the society where Law reported Elliot's lapse. When Law disregarded his warning to stay away from the investigating committee Elliot punched him in the back of

---

87. 8, 11 Mar 1856. An abbreviated version of the same account appears in PANB RS375/B/2, Hatheway's jail visitation notebook, entry for 11 Mar 1856. For the Seelyes, chapter 11.

88. PANB RS148/D/3/a, 10 Aug 1864. Edwin Hatch was a son of the late Harris Hatch and worked as a clerk for the St Andrews railroad company.

the head, knocking him down and saying 'he did not care if it cost him four or five dollars as he would be willing to pay it.' Hatheway issued a summons but Elliot barred his door against the constable who tried to serve it. Hatheway then issued a warrant for his arrest, at the same time asking the father to intervene. Andrew Elliot fetched his son; Hatheway sent for Charles Bradley as the second justice required in assault cases; and while they were waiting, Edward ran off, 'the Office being crowded, upwards of 30 persons being present.' He was arrested on a second warrant and brought before Hatheway and Boyd the next day. They fined him four dollars and costs and ordered him to find sureties for good behaviour but a week later Hatheway struck out his signature on the judgment noting, 'I hereby abandon all proceeding in this suit against Edward Elliot ... It appearing doubtful whether the Summons issued has been served on Deft.'[89]

St Andrews' bad boys

The same 1798 grand jury that deplored drunkenness on Sundays also called for regulations, 'to prevent Boys and Servants playing in the Streets in different parts of this Town which has long been complained of as a nuisance.' By the middle of the nineteenth century complaints that wayward youth were terrorizing the respectable inhabitants of St Andrews, jeering at band practices, interrupting town meetings, breaking windows with stones and snowballs, and mowing down pedestrians with their sleds had become the standard fare of newspaper correspondence columns, grand jury presentments, and proceedings before justices of the peace.[90] Parents could sometimes intervene on behalf of their children: one woman withdrew her complaint against a youth who had punched her in the mouth and taken her by the throat, 'in consequence of the explanations and solicitations' of his parents.[91]

Edward Elliot's assault on Alexander Law was atypical, both of them being sons of community stalwarts. Many youthful offenders

89. PANB RS148/D/3/b; PANB RS148/D/4/a, 17 Feb 1865.

90. For examples *Standard*, 5 Nov 1841, 1 Jul 1842, 8 Oct 1851; PANB RS148/A/5/e/1, Grand Jury, 16 Apr 1842.

91. PANB RS148/D/3/a, complaint of Sarah Smith, 13 Jan 1857.

were poor, illiterate, and Irish. They were not objects of pity nor was justice towards them much tempered with mercy. When a dozen or more boys gathered on a wharf one Sunday and threw stones at a barn Hatheway convicted four of them for disturbing the peace 'in desecration of the Lord's Day,' requiring them to find bail in ten pounds each or go to gaol.[92] Henry O'Neal had to put up five pounds bail for his son James, one of a crowd of boys found throwing stones at Thomas Healey's butcher shop.[93] James Fitzsimmons, arraigned for throwing rocks at Samuel Getty's shop, did not know his own age but thought he was thirteen. He could not read or write; his father was dead; he was homeless; his mother lived at St George with her married sister and went out washing for a living to support his three sisters and two brothers. Hatheway sent him to gaol until he could find bail for good behaviour.[94] John Leary, the larger of two boys found robbing apples from the poor house orchard, had no bail to offer and was committed to gaol.[95] A nineteen-year-old who acknowledged coming into town to beat two schoolboys who had struck his brother in the street was sent to gaol until he could find bail and then for ten days for nonpayment of costs.[96]

Patrick Behan, possibly the most incorrigible of St Andrews' bad boys, was convicted repeatedly for breaking sign poles and shutter hinges and other breaches of the peace. Constable Henan, who had several warrants for his arrest, finally caught him because 'he was so intoxicated that he could not run away.' It took Henan, two special constables and the high sheriff to overcome his resistance and convey him to the gaol with a 'great crowd of persons' following. Convicted of disorderly conduct under the town by-laws Behan was fined and bound to keep the peace. Barely a year later, convicted of an unprovoked assault in the street, he refused to pay his fine or find bail and spent nearly two months in gaol. Justice Ker deposed that Behan was 'a dangerous man to go at large' and that he was 'in great bodily fear

92. PANB RS148/D/3/a, complaint of John Bradford, 12 May 1857.
93. PANB RS148/D/3/g, 15 Oct 1857.
94. PANB RS148/D/3/a, complaint of Catharine McDennis, 3 Nov 1857.
95. 12 Sep 1854.
96. R v. Edward Morrison, 12 Feb 1856.

of him upon going out on the street at night.'[97] Behan was eighteen or nineteen years old at the time.

Untried complaints and the peace bond

A 'very feeble' widow complained to Hatheway that while she was asleep in her room one night a young man entered without knocking, stripped off her bedclothes, and took them outdoors where a crowd of people stood about laughing.[98] A woman who lived alone in a rented room complained that her grown-up son came in drunk and abused her, beating her about the head and loosening a tooth.[99] A woman who shared a house with two other families complained that they threatened and beat her children, used bad language, and assaulted her.[100] In all these cases, and many others, the complainants did not ask Hatheway to bring charges against the accused or punish them. They asked only for sureties to keep the peace. Male complainants might ask to have the accused bound to keep the peace but they usually pressed to have them prosecuted or punished as well. Women often sought peace bonds alone. In cases of domestic violence, where the imposition of a fine or jail time would lessen household resources, this is not surprising.[101] But the same was true of complaints against housemates and nonresident family members. When Mary Jane Hanson, who lived in St Patrick parish, complained that Margaret Hanson, her three children, and John Poppin with his wife and children were all squatting without permission at her property in St Andrews, 'and have cut down the barn and part of other buildings for fuel,' she insisted that she did not want to prosecute them for the offence, 'but merely to give security for their good conduct in future.'[102] Elizabeth

97. 19 Jun 1855, 31 May 1856, 2 Jun 1856.

98. Complaint of Elizabeth Conner, 24 Apr 1855.

99. Complaint of Mary Crowley, 23 Aug 1855.

100. Complaint of Ann Mooney, 9 Feb 1854.

101. Thus Elizabeth Summers, threatened with an axe by her drunken husband, asked only for sureties: above at note 78. Similarly PANB RS148/D/3/a, complaint of Mary McLaughlin that her husband gets drunk and beats her, 23 Nov 1857; ibid., complaint of Mary Sherman that her husband beats her drunk and sober, 9 Apr 1859.

102. PANB RS148/D/3/a, 19 Feb 1857. Poppin testified that he was paying rent to Margaret Hanson and made firewood of the furniture and barn at her request.

Seegee sought a peace bond from her stepmother who had broken down her door and threatened to 'put an axe into [her] skull.' She admitted having gone to Elizabeth's house with a club and threatened to burn the house down if she did not give her the iron pot she wanted.[103] Women were less reluctant to prosecute unrelated offenders. Jane Jones sought to prosecute the Reverend John Ross when he threw a stone to separate their dogs and it hit her in the shoulder.[104] Catherine Keley prosecuted John Highland for assault when the two of them struggled over a piece of driftwood: she was upset because he had complained to the priest about her.[105] Sarah Kerr wanted her neighbour Mary Leggen to be 'dealt with at law' for striking her with a pitchfork handle in an altercation over her hogs.[106] The real difference between men and women complainants may simply have been that more women's complaints than men's were against family members. Men were more likely to complain of assaults or abuse at work, in the tavern, or on the street; women at home.

About a third of the complaints before Hatheway ended with the accused entering into sureties to keep the peace to the complainant with no conviction recorded or penalty imposed.[107] (Peace bonds were also imposed along with fines in most assault, abusive language, and disorderly conduct convictions.) Even proceedings in indictable offences could terminate this way. Justice William Ker commenced a preliminary examination for assault to commit a felony and received the evidence of the complainant, Prudence McDonal, that while walking with her the accused put his arm around her waist, attempted to push her down, and asked her to 'give him a bit.' Ker neither discharged him nor sent him for trial; instead, he bound him over to keep the peace.[108] Where the accused were young children or married women, their parents or husbands might be ordered to find sureties for them.[109] All but a few accused were able to find guaran-

---

103. 5 Sep 1854, 15 Sep 1854.

104. PANB RS148/D/3/a, 18 May 1857.

105. 16 June 1854.

106. PANB RS148/D/3/c, 3 Oct 1845.

107. Taking into account undocketed complaints in which the outcome is unknown, the proportion may well have been higher.

108. PANB RS148/D/3/c, R v. Alexander Hartford, 13 Oct 1858.

109. For example when Elizabeth Greenlaw was convicted of striking a young girl

tors. Hatheway recorded the names of 264 sureties in the crown cases considered here. They included 180 distinct individuals: most gave bail just once or twice. Excluding the bastardy cases, nine individuals acted as sureties four or more times, none on more than eight occasions. Two were justices (Boyd and Fitzgerald) but they were also politicians and may have been standing bail for loyal constituents. The rest included two butchers, a grocer, a tavernkeeper, two farmers, and constable Henan.

Most of Hatheway's peace bonds bound the principal in £10 or £20 and one or two sureties in half that amount each.[110] These were promises to pay in the event that the condition was not met, a familiar instrument in a society built on credit and debt. The accused might have to pay the justice's costs but neither he nor his sureties had to come up with ready money in the amount of the bond.[111] It is not clear whether Hatheway investigated the sureties' credit-worthiness; in most cases he would have known them personally or by reputation. While the occasional accused was jailed for failing to find sureties there is no record of a proposed surety being rejected. The peace bond represented the community's endorsement of the accused's capacity for reintegration. Sureties were guarantors of future conduct who incurred a financial interest in the accused's compliance with the conditions of the bond. Although they could always liquidate their indebtedness by surrendering him to the sheriff during its term there is nothing to suggest that this was a common occurrence.

Most of the justice's powers derived from statute but his authority to impose peace bonds flowed directly from the commission of the

---

who was picking strawberries on the Greenlaw's grass field, Hatheway (sitting alone) ordered her husband to 'find sureties for his Wife's keeping the peace towards Alex'r Ridout's Wife and Children for one year and pay the costs of suit.' In the same case Hatheway declined to hear the testimony of Elizabeth's mother-in-law: 'says she is 79 years old, appears so violent and under such an excitement that I deem it improper to note or take her evidence.' PANB RS148/D/4/a, R v. Elizabeth Greenlaw, 13 Jul 1857.

110. Of 126 docketed cases 67 bound the accused and two sureties, 40 the accused and one surety, and 19 the accused alone. For an example of the latter, John Wentworth was 'recognized in £5 conditioned that he keep the peace and be of the good behaviour towards John Kelly . . . for one year and also towards the said Kelley's wife Sarah for one year,' 23 Jul 1850.

111. Compare Lermack, 'Recognizances,' 475.

peace. It directed the justices 'to cause to come before you, or any of you, all those who to any one or more of our people concerning their bodies, or the firing of their houses, have used threats, to find sufficient Surety for the Peace, or their good behaviour, towards us and our people; and if they shall refuse to find such security, then them in our prisons until they shall find such security to cause to be safely kept.'[112] While the older authorities distinguished between sureties for the peace, granted only to applicants who had reason to fear bodily harm or arson, and sureties for good behaviour,[113] which had a broader application,[114] nearly all of Hatheway's recognizances required the person bound to 'keep the peace and be of the good behaviour towards' the applicant and (often) his or her family, usually for six or twelve months.[115]

Constructing substantial justice

In theory the peace bond was a prospective remedy against reasonably apprehended violence. Yet, as we have seen, it was often used as a substitute for prosecution where violence, especially domestic violence, had already taken place. Along with the other means already considered for avoiding indictments and trials, the peace bond can be

112. PANB RS148/P/2/b, Commission of the peace for Charlotte, 25 Apr 1845, reproduced in Appendix B.

113. Security for good behaviour, unlike security to keep the peace, was thought to have had a statutory foundation in late medieval legislation. See Bacon, *Use of the Law*, 9. Burn, *Justice*, I:257-69, after a lengthy review of the authorities, deprecated the reliance on (Engl.) 34 Edw.III (1361) c.1, preferring the authority of the commission of the peace. Bonds for good behaviour, although not to keep the peace, were provided for by New Brunswick statutes proscribing public gaming (26 Geo.III (1786) c.26), keeping disorderly houses (9&10 Geo.IV (1829) c.8) or both (RSNB 1854 c.157 s.20, which also added bawdy houses).

114. Burn regretted that a remedy that had once been narrowly confined had expanded greatly as offences 'flowed in and multiplied' due to the judges' deferential attitude to lay justices. He urged that bonds for good behaviour should be imposed only with great caution as they interfered with the liberty of the subject. For a somewhat analogous U.S. 14th-amendment critique of the widespread use of the peace bond in colonial Pennsylvania, see Lermack, 'Peace Bonds,' 178.

115. There were variants, for example the recognizance of David Hopkins Jr, David Hopkins, and Jonathan Currie that Hopkins *fils* would 'keep the peace towards John Collins . . . and not to injure his property for one year . . .': Ledger 1, 6 Aug 1842.

viewed as a technique for constructing substantial justice. As much as laying informations and seeking security underscores the agency of complainants, often poor and at the margins of the local community, so too does it raise questions about the agency of the magistrate, the extent to which Hatheway and other justices shaped complaints to conform to their understanding of peace-keeping.[116] These are not easy questions to answer on the basis of the written informations that have survived. There are occasional hints, like Hatheway's caution to Boyd about giving accused cause to 'exult.'[117] Many would-be prosecutors were illiterate (or at least did not sign their names). Hatheway's notes routinely record that before administering the oath he 'first read and explained' the statement to the complainant, 'who appeared perfectly to understand same.'[118] He would not have had to 'explain' the statement if he had merely written it down at the complainant's dictation.

The informations taken by Hatheway were much less formulaic than those in the high courts but they contain enough boilerplate to leave little doubt that complainants negotiated their substance with the magistrate. Take for example James Arvin's information against James Murphy.[119] It begins with a factual account of Murphy's threatening behaviour so much more focused and succinct than the rambling narrative Arvin later gave *viva voce* at trial that it must owe a great deal to Hatheway's editorial shaping and polishing.[120] After this comes Hatheway's standard boilerplate for a peace bond request: 'Wherefore I am put in fear for the safety of my person and property from the violence of the said James Murphy and pray that he may be required to find sureties for his keeping the peace and being of the good behaviour towards me, and also, that he will not injure or destroy my property.' Compare, for example, the final part of Joseph

116. Compare King, *Crime, Justice*, part 1 (pretrial processes).

117. Above, at note 42.

118. For example Ann Mooney's information against Mary McIntee et al., 9 Feb 1854.

119. PANB RS148/D/a, 16 Feb 1858 and see above at note 37.

120. Arvin v. Murphy, Mar 1858. Hatheway's notes of testimony do not pretend to be an exact transcript. The magistrate undoubtedly contributed to the representation of the trial evidence as well, although to a lesser extent than in the information.

Kilpatrick's information against John Britt:[121]

> Wherefore I am put in fear of the said John Britt that he will do me some bodily harm and pray that he may be required to find sureties for his good behaviour and keeping the peace towards me.

By contrast, though, Thomas J. Sandford's information against Angus Kennedy concludes:[122]

> Wherefore I am put in fear for the safety of my person from the said Kennedy and pray that he may be prosecuted for the said offence and also required to find sureties for his keeping the peace and being of the good behaviour towards me.

If Hatheway used the peace bond to avoid formal convictions why was he unable or unwilling to negotiate such an outcome here? Sandford's testimony at Kennedy's trial before justices Hatheway and Street answers the question: 'I complained to Justice Hatheway against Defendant for the first offence and he said he would write to Defendant and afterwards said that he had not answered the letter.' In the result Kennedy was ordered to pay a twelve dollar fine to the commissioners of the poor and $2.95 costs to Sandford and to 'find sureties himself in $80 and two sureties in forty dollars each, for his good behaviour and keeping the peace for one year, and that he be *committed* to the common Gaol there to remain, until he shall comply with the terms of this conviction.'[123] This upheld Hatheway's authority and deprived Kennedy, who had ignored his letter, of any reason to exult.

If Hatheway's records of complaints and trials draw out the agency and interaction of both prosecutors and magistrates in shaping the narrative and outcome of disputes, they also demonstrate that lawyers played a very small part. Professional counsel are identified in only six of Hatheway's crown-side cases.[124] B.R. Stevenson ap-

121. PANB RS148/D/3/b, 18 Apr 1860.

122. Ibid., 21 Oct 1861.

123. Ibid., R v. Angus Kennedy, 22 Oct 1861, emphasis in original.

124. In the Sons of Temperance case discussed above at page 306, town clerk Andrew Elliot is identified as attorney for his son Edward. Elliot was a gardener by occupation.

peared for defendants twice, as did A.T. Paul, while R.M. Andrews and Wellington Hatch appeared once each. Paul and G.D. Street each appeared twice for the prosecution. These were all assault cases heard (with one exception) by two justices. In four of them the accused was convicted and fined. Judging by the trial records the lawyers had little to contribute. They were never present when the information was lodged. In one case the defendant's lawyer (Hatch) conducted an effective cross-examination of the prosecutor, managing to get his client off with just a peace bond; in another B.R. Stevenson attempted unsuccessfully to introduce evidence about title to land, which would have removed the case from the justices' jurisdiction.[125] The exceptional case was Arvin's complaint against Murphy, heard by Hatheway alone (presumably because the information sought a peace bond, not a criminal conviction) yet the only assault complaint in which both parties were represented by counsel (Street for the prosecution, Paul for the defence). The outcome suggests that counsel collaborated with the magistrate in mounting a masquerade to secure peace between two warring neighbours: 'Complainant & Defendant agree to withdraw and abandon all further proceedings upon this complaint and each pay their own costs.'

If the practising lawyers' contribution to shaping Hatheway's crown side cases was minimal, was the literature of the law any more significant? David Owen had acquired and used a copy of Richard Burn's English justicing manual, Pagan cited Burn once at sessions, and there are a few notes from 'Burns Justice by Chitty' in one of Hatheway's ledgers.[126] There was no comprehensive New Brunswick manual nor did Charlotte magistrates express a need for one.[127] In 1841 Saint John lawyer Peter Stubs, son of the former Charlotte JP, published *The New-Brunswick Manual; A compilation of forms and*

125. R. v. James Stephenson, 11 Sep 1854; R. v. Elliot Hume, 7 Jun 1860. For Hume's trial, PANB RS148/D/3/b. Compare the discussion of lawyers' participation in civil trials before justices in chapter 7.

126. At the front of Ledger 1 (1840-49) Hatheway made notes from this source about gaol fees, appointing special constables and the form of committment.

127. In 1822 a handful of justices, most from Saint John, petitioned the legislature for aid 'to allow them to compose a treatise on the Laws relating to their office and duties.' The only Charlotte signatory, the Rev. Jerome Alley, was never an active justice. PANB RS24 S30 P22; JLA 1822, p.19.

information designed for the use of Justices of the Peace, Merchants, Mechanics, &c.[128] It included a two-page précis of the justices' authority and a number of forms but it is not referred to in any of the Charlotte legal materials I have seen. Hatheway wrote out short extracts from various treatises in the endpapers of his ledgers.[129] By mid-century, Hatheway had copies of the provincial statutes and occasionally referred to them by page number in his notes of cases.[130]

Only twice in the record of Hatheway's crown-side practice did a significant point of law arise. On both occasions the issue was the legality of a local by-law. In March 1858, Hatheway fined R.M. Andrews £7/10 under the 1854 morality regulations for insulting him in the street, 'believing that his intention on this occasion was to irritate me and cause me to quarrel with him.'[131] When he learned that 'doubts were entertained' about the legality of the rule he repaid the fine with interest but in a memorandum about his feud with Andrews, Hatheway attempted to justify his reliance on the Sessions legislation:

> Previous to the Rules and Regulations aforesaid being passed in the Sessions, they were examined by the late Hon H Hatch,

128. The manual contained a good deal of material (lumber contracts, mortgages, wills, landlord and tenant, custom house forms, crown lands, immigration, American consulate) of more use to merchants and mechanics than to justices of the peace.

129. Along with the notes from Chitty's edition of Burn mentioned above, the front pages of Ledger 1 include an excerpt from 'Holt on Shipping' about the form of the contract between master and mariner and another from the 'Shipmasters Guide up to 1844' about seamen's wages and forfeitures. In the front of Ledger 2 (1849-67) Hatheway wrote out 'extracts from the Law on Contracts by Doctor Parsons Professor at Cambridge 1st vol 1853' dealing with competence to contract. There are no law extracts in Ledger 3 (1867).

130. Some of the annual volumes of New Brunswick statutes in the CIHM/Early Canadiana Online database have Hatheway's autograph on the title page. His colleague B.R. Fitzgerald also had copies of the statutes before his office was vandalized: see note 67 above. In some years the legislature made appropriations 'for extra copies of the Province Laws for the use of the Magistrates,' for example 3 Vict. (1840) c.59 (£10).

131. The regulations are discussed in chapter 11. Hatheway relied on Rule 4, which made it an offence punishable by a fine of up to £10 to 'use any obscene or profane language, violent cursing, or swearing, or ... by insulting language or behavior, taunting epithets, or threatening gestures, attempt to commit a breach of the peace, or incite others to do so ...'

> were also read over by G D Street, W Hatch and A T Paul Esqrs from whom, I understood, that they did not see anything objectionable in them. G J Thomson Esq examined them twice with much attention (apparently), said he highly approved of them and upon his application the Rules were extended to St Stephens and upon a similar application of some Justices residing at St George they were extended to a certain part of that Parish and subsequently, the Clerk of the Peace was ordered to get 100 copies of the Rules printed in which Justice Chandler concurred, those circumstances confirmed me in the belief of the legality of the Rules.

Six years later Hatheway convicted James Dougherty of abusive language in telling George Jackson, whom he claimed owed him fifty cents, that he was a 'damned robber' who 'ought to be with Henan,' that is, in the penitentiary.[132] A few days afterwards B.R. Stevenson wrote challenging his authority to assess Dougherty for five dollars costs in addition to the eight dollar fine. Stevenson drew Hatheway's attention to the 1862 local government amendment act whereby Sessions could make regulations 'to impose a penalty not exceeding eight dollars' for the offence, arguing that 'the penalty' meant both fine and costs.[133] Hatheway agreed to defer judgment for several days 'to comply with Mr S wishes' and then reduced the fine to two dollars, bringing the total to seven dollars and seventy cents including the costs of conviction.[134] Neither his appeal to the authority of the local bar in 1858 nor his meek acceptance of Stevenson's opinion in 1862 suggests that Hatheway was prepared to tackle a technical interpretation of the law when challenged. He was well aware of the current statutes—in sentencing Dougherty to one day in gaol for every forty cents of the fine if it remained unpaid he was following the latest legislative direction[135]—but deferred to professional interpretations of their mean-

132. Henan's downfall is explained in chapter 11.

133. 25 Vict. (1862) c.17 s.9. PANB RS148/D/1, Stevenson to Hatheway, 20 Apr 1864. Stevenson, who was later to become the province's attorney general, argued that notwithstanding 26 Vict. (1863) c.13, which provided for the payment of the 'fine or penalty' to the justice 'together with the costs,' the total of fine and costs could not exceed the eight dollar maximum penalty in the 1862 statute.

134. Ibid. (endorsement); PANB RS148/D/4/a, judgment dated 27 Apr 1864. The additional seventy cents costs presumably paid for Hatheway's reconsideration.

135. 26 Vict. (1863) c.13.

ing. On the very few occasions that they participated in Hatheway's court lawyers had little influence over the characterization of facts or issues but rather a lot over the ascribed formal meaning of the law.

It remains, then, to consider what 'substantial justice' amounted to. The 1810 small debts act protected proceedings before justices from being reversed or set aside on technical grounds 'where substantial justice has been done.'[136] This was a form of protection to lay justices acting reasonably and in good faith within the limits of their jurisdiction. Thus had Hatheway defended himself in 1826 against the complaint that he had acted as both complainant and judge in the statute labour cases: 'I thought I had done substantial justice.'[137] More generally, the term distinguished efforts to grapple expeditiously with the real substance of disputes from 'procedural justice' in the high courts, where outcomes were seen to depend on technical and formulaic niceties that might deliver absurd consequences at enormous expense.[138] Judging by Hatheway's practice in both civil and crown-side disputes, low law was cheap, expeditious, and accessible. It neither required nor encouraged the participation of legal professionals. Its outcomes were generally not de-

136. 50 Geo.III (1810) c.17 s.13. The same proviso appears in 42 Geo.III (1802) c.7, an act amending ICCP jurisdiction. 4 Wm.IV (1834) c.45 s.80 inverted the provision by making supreme court review of a justice's civil proceedings available for error 'by means whereof substantial justice has not been done.' RSNB 1854 c.137 s.44 provided for judicial review of justices' civil proceedings on the party's affidavit that 'he thinks substantial justice has not been done him.' The supreme court judge was then to 'decide the cause according to the very right of the matter, without regard to forms.' All these provisions protected civil proceedings before lay justices. Substantial justice was invoked as a privative protection of summary proceedings for breach of by-laws and local regulations before (typically lay) civic courts in incorporated Moncton (18 Vict. (1855) c.66, s.63), Woodstock (19 Vict. (1856) c.32, s.63), and Fredericton (22 Vict. (1859) c.8, s.86), all of which acts directed the court to make its determinations 'as the very right of the matter may appear, without regard to technical objections, imperfections, or defects which do not affect the substantial justice of the case.'

137. CO 188/35, Hatheway to Wetmore, 25 Jan 1826: see chapter 3.

138. 'In short I mean substantial Justice to be done, for their benefits; and the real interests of all parties concerned ...' CCA MC349, David Owen to Harris Hatch, 28 Mar 1820. Owen considered himself a lifelong victim of procedural justice, although he does not seem to have been a bona fide practitioner of the other kind. See also Bell, 'Legal Pluralism' and Marquis, 'Anti-Lawyer Sentiment.'

termined by formalities although it occasionally relied on technical considerations to deliver what seemed to be the right result in the circumstances. Low law was fact-driven although the facts that drove it might be derived not just from evidence led in court but from the justice's (and in many civil cases the jurors') knowledge of economic and social relations in the local community as well. While its remedial authority was limited it nevertheless attempted to structure outcomes to suit circumstances. Examples include Hatheway's clearinghouse practice for commercial debts, the widespread reliance on the peace bond, and idionsycratic remedies like requiring an abusive husband to take the temperance pledge.

Low law was cheap, expeditious, and accessible, but did it deliver substantial justice? From the strict rule-of-law perspective that was gaining ground not only within the expansive self-aggrandizing profession but also among the emerging patrician elements in provincial politics, it did not deliver 'justice' at all. It relied on local prejudice, the whims of puffed-up amateurs, the bumbling inanities of amiable imbeciles. It is difficult to find serious fault with Hatheway on these counts. His practice and judgments were for the most part orderly and predictable, although they may not have been the practices and judgments one would expect from a professional common law court. Hatheway's court, and the sessions system generally, provided a kind of 'community justice' derived from an organic, ultimately Tory, conception of a peaceful, orderly local society managed by its more respectable and responsible members.[139] In Charlotte county, at least until the mid-nineteenth century, a Loyalist ancestry and success in

139. Compare Sharpe, *Lazier Murder*. In this study of a murder prosecution in rural Ontario, Sharpe contrasts 'community justice,' based in local opinion and local interests and entrusted to amateur volunteer justices, coroners, and constables, with the emerging professional justice of full-time police detectives, crown attorneys, and the criminal bar. There are unresolved tensions in Sharpe's account of 'community justice'—for example, the wide gap between the bloodthirsty vengefulness of the local population generally (at least as reported in the press) and the local elite's efforts to have the death sentences commuted raises questions about the relationship between 'community opinion' and 'community justice,' while the readiness of the local authorities to offload their responsibilities to the professionals suggests that elite interest in controlling local affairs was more attenuated in municipally-incorporated Prince Edward in the 1880s than in sessions-system Charlotte in the 1850s and 1860s.

business or politics were the main proxies for respectability and responsibility. Hatheway himself was only marginally a member of this local elite, earning his place by his willingness to assume public duties that higher-ranking and more entrepreneurial figures eschewed. As a full-time lay justice, Hatheway was neither a casual amateur nor a professional police magistrate. But in contrast to a patrician like W.F.W. Owen (or a would-be patrician like James Boyd) he was undoubtedly a local paternalist.[140] The principal objects of low law in Charlotte county were to preserve peaceful social relations, maintain social and economic order, and retain local elite control of local affairs. All three were contested in mid-nineteenth-century New Brunswick. A grounded judgment as to whether 'substantial justice' was done must go beyond questions of accessibility and informality and take on the social, economic, and political context in which the sessions system flourished and decayed.

140. Despite his family connections with Saint John and Fredericton notables (including a future premier), Hatheway preserved a determinedly local outlook on provincial and national issues. See for example his address to the grand jury at April sessions, 1867, (*Standard*, 17 Apr 1867) from which the quotation on the facing page is taken.

Part III

The sessions system and its enemies

'And now comes upon us the Confederation of our Colonies, which of course will greatly increase our taxes.'

C.R. Hatheway JP, 1867

Part III: Introduction

Part III examines the magistrates' roles in county administration, in particular public works, social welfare, and the regulation of strong drink. One common denominator of these topics is public finance. Another is moral regulation, whether in determining conditions for prisoners in the county gaol, the proper scope of pauper relief, the appropriate number of tavern licenses, or the enforcement of prohibitory liquor legislation.

The justices' powers of taxation were limited both by statute and by economic circumstance. Assessments for public works and paying down the county debt required the consent of the legislature. Before about 1830 most assemblymen were prominent justices. From a public finance point of view the assembly functioned as an extension of the sessions system. Chapter 9 examines the breakdown of this institutional partnership.

The Irish famine emigration of the late 1840s and early 1850s brought hundreds of sick and incapable paupers to the county. Chapter 10 examines how the provincial executive's insistence on downloading responsibility for them to the parishes precipitated a violent division on the Charlotte bench and began the gradual demise of the sessions system through the transfer of authority from local to provincial officials.

Chapter 11 focuses on liquor regulation, a significant source of county revenue since its inception. The temperance movement reinforced divisions within the county as parochial demands for fewer licenses limited sessions' ability to pay for contingencies. In the mid-1850s prohibition reshaped provincial politics into parties of wet 'Rummies' and dry 'Smashers.' Along with partyism came patronage, diluting the active Charlotte bench with numerous partisan appointees and undermining its perceived dignity and authority.

Chapter 12 examines the consequences of these political changes. Although two attempts led by the upper parishes to replace the sessions system with elective municipal government failed, its scope and effectiveness were steadily undermined by other institutional changes. At Confederation the sessions system was still in place but in severely attenuated form. Ten years later it was finally abolished.

Chapter 9

Called to account: Justices, assemblymen, and ratepayers

As county governors, the bench of magistrates had significant responsibilities but limited access to resources. Under the province's poor law the court of sessions assessed the parishes for the relief of paupers. Under the liquor law it sold tavern and retail licenses and fined bootleggers. Under a variety of provincial acts the justices collected penalties for minor offences and used them to subsidize poor relief or county contingencies. For other purposes, including the major public works that every county was expected to supply, sessions had to seek the co-operation of the legislature both for direct appropriations from provincial funds and for permission to raise money by sale or lease of commons land or by special assessments on the county ratepayers. In the province's first forty years, when the House of Assembly most resembled a convention of county justices to divvy up the provincial treasury for local purposes, there was little effective opposition to the magistrates' financial management. By the mid-1830s this had changed. Tensions increased between the magistrates and the assembly as critics and reformers became more prominent in provincial politics. Even before pauper immigration and the temperance movement rocked the fiscal foundations of the sessions system,[1] uncontrolled expenditures on county building projects undermined the harmony and perceived legitimacy of the magistrates' rule. This chapter examines how the county gaol and courthouse were financed, and the emergent role of the grand jury as the tax-resistant ratepayers' check on the justices' money management.

The first gaol

The June 1785 charter that erected Charlotte county, 'for the due, orderly, convenient and speedy administration of justice,' contemplated the erection of a gaol and courthouse at St Andrews but said nothing about how they were to be paid for. James Campbell JP and others among the wealthier inhabitants lent money to build a gaol and more than three hundred and fifty pounds was expended for the purpose. The county members got a bill through the first session of the assembly to raise funds by lottery, only to see it rejected by council.[2] A small amount was secured by the sale of water lots and mill privileges licensed by the governor of Nova Scotia before the creation of the province but in 1788 the magistrates memorialized the legislature for a grant of £271/14/6, the balance outstanding, claiming that the county's inhabitants were wholly unable to bear an assessment.[3] The assembly voted one hundred pounds which sessions agreed, under some duress, to distribute proportionately among the gaol creditors.[4] The county had already acquired a set of stocks by Septem-

1. Chapters 10 and 11 respectively.

2. PANB RS24 S1-B21. The bill, introduced by Robert Pagan, proposed to raise £300 by a twenty per cent charge on ticket sales, so it anticipated gross proceeds of £1500. It is not clear who was expected to buy tickets; presumably not the inhabitants of Charlotte county, who were deemed incapable of bearing an assessment. (The preamble recited that it was 'inexpedient at present to raise money by a tax on the county.') The bill named William Paine, Jeremiah Pote JP, James Campbell JP, Robert Pagan JP, Peter Clinch JP, and Gillam Butler as 'managers' of the lottery. Paine, Campbell, Pagan, and Clinch were the county's MHAs. Butler was already under investigation for smuggling: chapter 2.

3. PANB RS24 S3-P3, 21 Jul 1788. By 26 Geo.III (1786) c.42 counties without gaols or courthouses were empowered to raise funds for them by assessment, but 29 Geo.III (1789) c.3 limited assessments for this purpose to £300.

4. 28 Geo.III (1788) c.10. James Campbell, who had advanced £172 towards building the gaol, signed the memorial 'on behalf of the petitioners,' and pressed

ber 1785 and a 'public whipping post' by the following August; the first mentioned committal to the county gaol was in March 1787.[5] Less than a month later came the first in a long series of grand jury presentments complaining of 'the ruinous state of the Common Gaol ... not being fit for the reception of prisoners.' The jurors' concern at this point was not the comfort and safety of inmates but rather that 'many persons apprehended and committed for capital offences have escaped.'[6] 'Many' may have been an exaggeration. Later that spring, though, two men broke out;[7] in August a special sessions committed their suspected liberator to the gaol and at about the same time a regular gaoler was appointed.[8]

Water lot proceeds continued to trickle in. Despite the remaining gaol debt, the magistrates decided to spend part of them on developing St Andrews streets and commons—this over the protests of two out-of-parish justices, David Owen and Hugh Mackay[9]—and on

sessions for repayment, was relying on the proceeds to settle his own debts, promising his Saint John lawyer to 'send you an order on my Agent for as much as I can' immediately following sessions, '& hope that will sise procedure agt me for a little time ... ': NBM Hazen, Campbell to Chipman, 9 Sep 1789.

5. The magistrates ordered two men set in the stocks at September sessions 1785, one for insulting the grand jury and the other for 'profane swearing in open court.' A special sessions in August 1786 sentenced Joshua Lock to twenty lashes and a year's banishment from the county for stealing a pair of silver shoe buckles, and another the following March committed Cornelius Ryan to the common gaol 'on suspicion of going down the Chimney of [a] Dwelling House ... and stealing from thence sundry articles at different times ... '

6. CCGS Apr 1787.

7. One of the escapees, John Dunbar, was according to legend 'the first person to suffer capital punishment in the county.' Convicted of having murdered his wife and stuffed her body into a herring barrel, he is said to have twice escaped the county gaol before finally being recaptured in Boston and returned to St Andrews for execution. The story puts his crime about 1798 and names a different accomplice than the man committed in 1787: Vroom, *Glimpses* LXXXVI, 12 Oct 1893.

8. The following year gaoler Adam Smith complained that he had been in office nine months without any allowance. Sessions awarded him £20 per annum from August 1787, 'to be paid as contingent funds of the County will admit,' although only in proportion along with other county officers, and allowed him to supplement his income by selling liquor to the prisoners and others about the gaol: CCGS Apr 1788.

9. Neither Owen's Campobello nor Mackay's St George would pay a penny of their county assessments for years to come.

constructing 'a Block House to make the Goal [*sic*] secure.'[10] The sorry state of the county's finances did not become fully apparent until after the death of William Garnett, who had acted as both clerk and treasurer. At a week-long special sessions called to sort out the mess, the first item of business was the gaol debt.[11] Fortunately the assembly had come through a second time, appropriating a hundred pounds 'towards defraying the expence of building and finishing the Court-House and Gaol.'[12] The magistrates decided to apply this windfall to the outstanding debt of £177/3/11, once again in proportion.[13] The water lot purchasers of 1785 still appeared to owe the county £188/9/6, more than enough to clear the gaol debt, but the new county treasurer reported that there was no likelihood of recovering these or other outstanding accounts, and that while some of the county's debtors had been sued and judgments obtained, 'he cannot discover how far they have been satisfied.'[14] The county was almost six hundred pounds in debt.[15]

Table 9.1 – Charlotte county assessment by parish, 1804

Parish	Amount*	Proportion	Population†	Proportion
St Stephen	98	21%	683	27%
St Andrews	84	18%	487	19%
St George	72	15%	400	16%
St David	60	13%	286	11%
St Patrick	51	11%	229	9%
West Isles	51	11%	117	5%
Campobello	27	6%	245	10%
Pennfield	26	5%	54	2%

* CCGS. Rounded to nearest pound (currency).

† 1803 estimate by Acheson, 'Denominationalism,' app. A.

10. CCGS Apr 1789.

11. CCSS 14-18 Jul 1801 and see chapter 2.

12. 41 Geo.III (1801) c.12. Similar appropriations were made for York, Queen's, Sunbury, Westmorland, and King's counties.

13. At September sessions, however, they voted to pay various small debts and accounts out of the appropriation before distributing most of the remainder to the gaol creditors.

14. PANB RS148/A/1, Henry Barlow Brown report on the state of county accounts, 17 Sep 1801.

15. CCGS Sep 1801.

In 1804 sessions finally decided to assess the county for debt relief. While the parishes had been taxed regularly for the poor rate,[16] typically in accordance with their own estimates of the amounts needed, this was the first assessment for general county purposes since Charlotte's foundation twenty years previously. The justices aimed to raise £468/4/0, well in excess of the three hundred pounds statutory limit on assessments for gaols and courthouses.[17] The minutes do not make it clear either why this sum was chosen—possibly it was the most recent estimate of the county's indebtedness[18]—or on what basis it was distributed among the various parishes, but in most cases it was roughly proportional to their estimated population (Table 9.1). The province's assessment law empowered justices in sessions 'by equal proportion to distribute and charge' the sums needed among the various parishes; the assessors (parish officers) were then to apportion the sum among the inhabitants 'as they in their discretion shall think just and reasonable,' and to issue precepts to the constables to levy and collect individual assessments.[19] Assessors and collectors were allowed a commission to reimburse them for their time and trouble. Sessions attempted to limit the assessors' discretion by recommending that they apportion the rate at two shillings for every hundred acres of land under grant, two shillings poll tax, and the remainder on other ratable property.[20] The assessment was not an unqualified success: by 1812, barely £185 had been collected, and some parishes had paid nothing at all (Table 9.2).

---

16. Chapter 10.

17. 29 Geo.III (1789) c.3. 26 Geo.III (1786) c.42 did not expressly authorize assessments for debt liquidation or county contingencies: on its face it was limited to contracts for building gaols and courthouses (s.1), repairing public works (s.2), and the county treasurer's salary (s.7). By 26 Geo.III (1786) c.43 the same machinery was also used to collect the parish poor rate.

18. David Owen complained to the secretary of state for the colonies that 'the County is in Debt nearly to the amount of five hundred pounds for a Gaol and Court House; for which [Nova Scotia] Governor Parr had made ample provision by the Sale of Mill privileges and Water Lots—and that the present Inhabitants are, contrary to the Grant, saddled with the Burthen.' CO188/12, Owen to Hobart, 29 Dec 1803.

19. 26 Geo.III (1786) c.42. The preamble to 3 Geo.IV (1822) c.24 suggests that the assessors' discretion under the 1786 act had been entirely unfettered, 'without regulation or appeal,' and produced wide discrepancies.

20. CCGS Apr 1804.

Table 9.2 – Charlotte county assessment by parish, 1812*

Parish	1804 Assessed	- Paid	- Interest	= Owing	+ 1812 Assessed	= Total
St Stephen	98	63	30	5	98	103
St Andrews	84	36	17	31	84	115
St George	72	0	0	72	72	144
St David	60	25	12	23	60	83
St Patrick	51	15	8	19	51	70
West Isles	51	29	14	8	51	59
Campobello	27	0	0	27	27	54
Pennfield	26	17	8	1	26	27
	468	185			468	655

* CCGS. All amounts rounded to nearest pound (currency).

In the mean time, the gaol's shortcomings remained clearly apparent. The justices ordered window sashes and a floor to be installed, 'in case any person should be confined therein during the approaching winter,' subject as always to the availability of funds. Three years later the work still had not been done. The gaoler's account was allowed (along with that of the coroner, clerk and sheriff) and ordered to be paid by the treasurer, 'as soon as he has sufficient funds in his hands.' The sheriff filed a formal protest 'against the insufficiency of the county gaol.'[21] There were two more gaol breaks[22] and yet another grand jury presentment about the gaol's 'insufficiency.'[23] September sessions 1809 adopted its grand jury's recommendation for a new gaol and courthouse to be funded by the sale of ungranted St Andrews town lots.[24] That winter a confined debtor was 'in such an uncomfortable situation, owing to the bad state of repair of the gaol' that the sheriff wanted to move him to a private house.[25] Armed with the provincial executive's approval and declarations by both the sher-

21. CCGS Sep 1800; Apr 1803; Apr 1804; Sep 1804.

22. CCGS Apr 1805; CCGS Sep 1807.

23. CCGS Apr 1807.

24. This required a grant of land from the province to the justices for this purpose: 26 Geo.III (1786) c.38.

25. Chipman's legal opinion was that this could not be done safely without the creditor's consent: NBM Hazen, Hitchings (St Stephen) to Chipman, 6 Dec 1809; Chipman to Armstrong, 12 Jan 1810.

iff and the grand jury that the existing gaol was 'unhealthy and dangerous to the lives of such as may be confined therein,' the justices put the lots up for public auction, solicited plans for a suitable building and appointed a committee to purchase boards and put them 'in a state of seasoning for use.'[26] A year later they adopted a report calling for an assessment on the county to pay for a new gaol and courthouse.[27] The final impetus came in August 1811 with yet another gaol break, this one apparently fuelled in part by the gaoler's rum ration.[28]

At April sessions 1812 the justices finally ordered the long-awaited assessment to pay for a new gaol and courthouse and reduce the county debt. The amount and distribution were to be the same as in 1804. Parishes were to be credited with eight years' interest on their 1804 payments, thereby reducing the amount owing on the former assessment (Table 9.2). Every aspect was controversial: the amount, the distribution, the 'interest' novelty.[29] But the justices had provided themselves with legislative insurance, a grant of £200 from the assembly and 'An act to authorise the justices of the peace for the county of Charlotte, to levy an assessment for paying off the county debt, and for finishing and compleating the county Gaol and Court House, lately erected in said county.'[30]

The second gaol

The act, sponsored by Charlotte members Robert Pagan JP, John Dunn (the former sheriff), and Donald McDonald (the county treasurer), recited in its preamble that the building 'now occupied' as a courthouse and gaol 'has so far gone to decay' that a new one

26. CCGS Apr 1810.

27. CCGS Apr 1811. The proceedings of a special sessions for this purpose are not in the minutebook.

28. NBM, Hazen, Chipman Benchbook, The King v. Jonathan Watson, Charlotte circuit, 23 Aug 1811. Watson, charged with participating in a riot that liberated three prisoners by breaking up the floor of the gaol, was acquitted but the prisoners (a debtor and two sailors) escaped.

29. CCGS Apr 1812. The names of dissenting justices were recorded for each of these items.

30. 52 Geo.III (1812) c.22 (appropriations) and c.10 (assessment).

was necessary.[31] It continued by acknowledging that although four hundred pounds had already been levied, more was needed 'which cannot be assessed agreeably to the Laws now in force ...' This amounted to an admission that the 1804 assessment had been unlawful, but no matter: section 6 of the act 'ratified and confirmed, and rendered firm and valid in the Law' that former assessment. The act permitted an additional assessment of up to eight hundred pounds to pay off the county debt and complete the new county gaol and courthouse.

Clearly the justices had anticipated a challenge to the new assessment and delayed it until they had secured the protection of the act. The challenge came in the form of a protest by St George magistrate Peter Clinch, who petitioned to have the act suspended pending a full accounting 'by disinterested persons ... or by the Grand Jury of the County.'[32] He raised a number of objections, some new but others long familiar. Pointing out the act's implicit acknowledgment that the 1804 assessment had been unlawful, he argued that it could not be rescued after the fact. The total assessment permitted was now three times the unlawful amount (and four times what the 1789 legislation allowed). But the legislature had already appropriated four or five hundred pounds for the Charlotte gaol, and sessions had other sources of income including liquor licenses ('screwed up as high as the law will admit') and the sale of land ('for the Bench of Justices deal largely in Lands'). In fact, Clinch argued, the assessment was not for one gaol and courthouse, but for two, the old and the new. The old one should have been paid for long ago by the legislative appropriations and the sale of water lots and mill privileges.[33] Clinch next objected to the act's 'lumping together' gaol building and the county debt, 'thereby tending to involve both in obscurity.' He traced the origin of the debt to the expenses of the Penobscot Association which had settled St Andrews, 'incurred before New Brunswick was a

31. JHA 1812. McDonald brought in a bill to assess Charlotte for a new gaol and courthouse on Feb 18; the next day Pagan brought in a bill that included paying off the county debt, and it was this that passed the House without amendment. Pagan and Dunn were appointed to carry it to council for concurrence on Feb 22.

32. PANB RS24 S23-P10 (1814).

33. Compare David Owen's 1803 complaint at footnote 18.

Province or Charlotte a County,' and argued that current inhabitants who had nothing to do with the Association could not be held liable for its debts, the more so as the sale of water lots and mill privileges had been intended to defray them. Members of the Association had been rewarded with valuable grants and situations and so had been reimbursed for their expenses.

Clinch argued that the Charlotte justices had exceeded their powers in other respects as well: 'They have directed notes of hand to be given, they have conducted themselves as a Body Corporate, they have dabbled in Interest as well as Lands' (instancing the credit allowed for former payments in the 1812 assessment, which he argued amounted to an additional burden on the other parishes). He claimed that his own parish, St George, had been overrated with no effective recourse, and that because owners of property in more than one parish were rated in just one, the wealthier inhabitants could escape being fully taxed: 'if a man had ten times more property in other parishes than in the one wherein he resided, he had nothing to pay for it.' The act was an attempt to evade the statute of limitations. The twenty-year delay in assessing the county imposed the burden on recent arrivals of paying for benefits they had never enjoyed and subsidizing former inhabitants who had since departed 'life or the county.'

Clinch was himself a long-serving magistrate: why had he not acted to prevent these evils? Like other justices from the country parishes, he had found himself 'a mere pageant upon the Bench:'

> He never knew a question of any importance carried against the St Andrews Gentlemen—thus in every thing relating to the assessment, they were virtually the Acts of the Magistrates of St Andrews. [He] would not presume to say that they in these instances have made any corrupt use of their power—but they were at least so situated, that their Interest was in opposition to their duty ...

Clinch's petition was referred to a blue-ribbon committee, pillars of the establishment all: attorney general Thomas Wetmore, solicitor general John Murray Bliss, and William Botsford, former judge of vice-admiralty (and future solicitor general, speaker of the assembly, and supreme court justice). In an unusually lengthy and detailed report they found Clinch's complaints to be without merit, a foregone conclusion in light of the 1812 act which had amply legitimized all that had gone before and authorized what followed. They found that the Penobscot Association expenses had been fully defrayed by the sale of water lots and mill privileges before Charlotte county came into existence, so that not only had no debt been carried over but 'a considerable balance carried to the public stock of the County, which has been applied towards discharging the debts incurred in building the first Gaol and Court House.' This finding could not have been accurate: it flies in the face of the justices' own claims in the first few years of the province and of the accounting made on Garnett's death. The committee dismissed Clinch's argument about the hegemony of the St Andrews justices, observing correctly that the details of the assessment were approved by 'the Magistrates of the County at large, at a very general meeting of them.'

As for Clinch's claim that the assessment was to pay for two gaols, not one, and that the cost had amounted to the 'preternatural sum' of £1200 or more, the committee concluded that, 'no other sum of money, except the said sum of *four hundred pounds* has ever been levied or assessed upon the County for the building of either of the two Gaols and Court Houses, or for any other County purposes ...' This was true as far as it went in reference to the 1804 assessment but ignored the new assessment provided for by the 1812 act, the real object of Clinch's protest, as well as the other sums expended at least notionally for the purpose. The 1804 assessment had realized £185; the 1812 assessment including discounts and delinquencies amounted to £655; the legislature had appropriated £400 by 1812 and would appropriate £500 more by 1818; the sale of water lots had netted at least £180; other town lots had been put to auction, although the proceeds are unknown—so the presumptive cost of the two buildings was close to two thousand pounds, surely a 'preternatural sum.'

Although Clinch's protest was dismissed in no uncertain terms—'Upon a review of all the circumstances your committee cannot refrain from noticing the asperity and peculiarity of the language of the petitioner so unwarranted as it regards the Magistracy of the County, and so incompatible with the respect due to this House.'[34]—it is im-

34. JHA 1814, 30f.

portant both for its substantive critique of the assessment law and as another illustration of the tension between the St Andrews junto and the magistracy in the other parishes. In 1822, when the assembly revised the province's assessment legislation, several amendments reflected points in Clinch's 1814 critique. Nonresident real estate was made subject to assessment. Assessors' proceedings were regulated and their discretion reduced. These changes were reiterated and strengthened by further enactments in 1825 and 1831.[35] The Charlotte magistrates also drew a lesson from Clinch's protest and its demand for a disinterested audit of county accounts. For the next fifteen years they scrupulously avoided public disclosure of county revenue and expenditure other than the parish poor rate. Sessions minutes record receiving county treasurers' reports but have little or nothing to say about what they contained or what was done about them.

The new courthouse and gaol was not finished until 1818 or later (if ever, as will appear below) and required the infusion of an additional five hundred pounds from the assembly.[36] The gaol was occupied in 1814 but work remained to be done: the grand jury's call for improvements was referred to Peter Clinch (!) and Peter Cristy whose recommendations resulted in an additional two hundred pounds assessment. Two years later sessions ordered the gaol yard to be fenced in and a drain to be made for the gaol's 'necessary'. More (unspecified) expenditures were ordered in 1819 after another grand jury presentment but a month later a special sessions was called to review a list of improvements and repairs for which the county had no funds. The justices resolved to meet again before the legislature convened to prepare a petition for yet another appropriation.[37] In 1821 the St Andrews magistrates ordered the criminals' room in the gaol to be made as secure as funds permitted.[38] Then in 1822 an inquest on an imprisoned debtor found that his death was 'hastened, in consequence

35. 3 Geo.IV (1822) c.24; 6 Geo.IV (1825) c.15; 1 Wm.IV (1831) c.26 (and see further below).

36. 56 Geo.III (1816) c.30 granting £300 to the justices 'towards finishing the gaol and courthouse'; 58 Geo.III (1818) c.22, granting £200 to secure the criminals' and debtors' rooms.

37. CCGS Sep 1814; Sep 1816; Sep 1819; CCSS 6 Oct 1819, but there is no record of such a meeting or petition.

38. CCSS 1 May 1821.

of his confinement in the lower room of the gaol, where he was exposed for three months to a *pestilential effluvia* arising from the vault in said room, ... which occasioned insanity and disease, by which he came to his death.'[39] A few months later sessions resolved to build a new gaol—and in the mean time, to dig a drain for the old one.[40]

The stone gaol

In January 1826 the justices sought permission from the legislature to sell the existing gaol lot, it being 'very low and unhealthy,' and to use the proceeds to build a new gaol on 'a more elevated and healthy site.'[41] They were successful, although the preamble to the bill had nothing to say about the unsanitary condition of the old gaol but only that it had 'but two apartments wherein Debtors and Criminals of every denomination can be imprisoned.'[42] In the event, and more than ten years later, the old gaol was refitted as the town's market house and public meeting hall.[43] In 1830 the legislature authorized a thousand pound assessment to build the new gaol.[44]

No sooner had the first half of the new gaol assessment been levied than five St Andrews magistrates called a special sessions to build a new courthouse on the same block as the gaol and to seek authorization for an additional assessment of three thousand pounds as well as a legislative grant in aid.[45] When Wyer introduced the petition for a new assessment in the assembly it was immediately met by

39. *Sentinel*, 10 Aug 1822, copying *Herald* (emphasis in original).

40. CCGS Apr 1823.

41. PANB RS24 S34-P24, 6 Jan 1826.

42. PANB RS24 S34-B20; 7 Geo.IV (1826) c.7.

43. Wellington Hatch bought the property for £260 at public auction in October 1839 'to hold for the benefit of the Town' pending reimbursement: CCSS 21 Oct 1839; CCGS Apr 1841. An article on the renovation reported that 'the partitions and floors of the old gaol were lined with iron bars about six inches apart and double planked over timber, notwithstanding which several places can be seen where we are informed persons have cut their way through and made their escape out of holes barely a foot square.' *Standard*, 17 Jun 1842.

44. 10&11 Geo.IV (1830) c.13, limiting it to no more than £500 in any year.

45. This 'special sessions or meeting of the magistrates' on 28 Jan 1831 attended by Colin Campbell, Thomas Wyer, John Wilson, C.R. Hatheway, and David Mowatt, essentially an executive session of the junto, resolved to call a special sessions to take the matter into consideration. This took place on 10 Feb 1831 while the legislature

two opposing petitions, one from St George and Pennfield, signed by justices Mackay, Vernon, and Jones and introduced in the House by Patrick Clinch, and the other from St Stephen, St David, and St James, introduced by James Brown and signed by justices Moore, Upton, and Armstrong, of whom the latter two had attended the February special sessions. When Wyer rose the following day to move an assessment bill it was to finish the gaol only and for no more than a thousand pounds. Merged at the committee stage with a bill to erect lock-up houses in St George and St Stephen, it shuttled back and forth between assembly and council twice before receiving assent along with a seven hundred and fifty pound appropriation.[46] The proposed new courthouse would have to wait another decade.

This was not the end of the stone gaol story. In 1834, 1836, and 1838 the justices received approval for three more thousand-pound assessments just to complete the gaol and pay down the debt.[47] In all, the county was assessed five thousand pounds for the new gaol and to service the associated debt (Table 9.3): the legislature also appropriated more than a thousand pounds for the project between 1831 and 1835. There were the usual difficulties in collecting the rate, and some delinquent collectors found themselves committed to gaol until payment was made.[48] The St George assessors—Patrick Clinch among them[49]—defended their failure to act by claiming that the sessions warrant was defective and the assessment excessive and so ille

was in session. Two St Stephen justices attended along with St Andrews JPs Wilson, Ker, and Hatheway. Two petitions were sent to Fredericton, the first (for the assessment) in the name of the justices of the peace for the county, the second (for an appropriation) in the name of the sheriff and magistrates, members of the bar, and officers of the court and other public departments.

46. 1 Wm.IV (1831) c.36 allowed assessments of £1000 for the gaol and £200 to build the parish lock-ups. Over protests the £200 was assessed on the parishes concerned rather than the county as a whole.

47. 4 Wm.IV (1834) c.25; 6 Wm.IV (1836) c.17; 1 Vict. (1838) c.25.

48. CCGS Apr 1834.

49. Patrick was Peter's eldest son and succeeded him as one of the St George magistrates and as MHA (1828-9, 1830-7). In 1836 he defended his alleged delinquency as an assessor of rates: 'My method of proceeding for some years past with the different Collectors & which I have good reasons for adopting has been to take no kind of responsibility on myself in recovering from the different Defaulters but merely to issue Summonses against such persons as they require & after Judgment is obtained, to issue Executions with directions to the Constable to pay over the money

Table 9.3 – Gaol and debt assessments by parish, 1831-8*

Parish	1831	1832	1834	1835	1836	1838†	Total
St Stephen	141	141	210	110	230	215	1048
St Andrews	194	194	210	105	190	175	1068
St George	100	100	130	75	180	198	783
St David	75	75	100	50	115	158	573
St Patrick	60	60	75	40	90	85	410
West Isles	45	45	60	23	30	30	233
Campobello	30	30	50	15	25	15	165
Grand Manan	30	30	50	25	50	43	228
Pennfield	30	30	55	28	40	41	224
St James	45	45	60	30	50	42	272
	750	750	1000	500	1000	1000	5000

* CCGS. All amounts rounded to nearest pound (currency).

† As revised: see text.

gal. They were convicted at a special sessions and fined ten pounds each but execution was stayed until the next court when the fines were remitted on payment of costs and they were ordered to refund overcharges to the collectors. The same sessions ordered the new St George assessors to assess themselves, which they had 'omitted to do.' All these orders were rescinded at the next court, but to what effect is not known.[50]

Assessment rolls survive for half the parishes taxed for the new gaol in 1831.[51] There was new legislation setting out procedures in great detail and supplying a form for the assessors' use.[52] The act re-

when levied to the Collectors—receiving no part myself except my own fees. So that if there is any deficiency I don't consider myself at all accountable for it.' PANB RS148/a/1, Clinch to W. Hatch, 1 Sep 1836.

50. CCSS 29 May 1834; CCGS Sep 1834, Apr 1835.

51. There are rolls for St Andrews, St David, St Patrick, Grand Manan, Pennfield, and West Isles. The Pennfield rolls indicate only the amount to be taxed without showing the basis or rate of taxation. (For Pennfield's assessment method in 1820, which rated cleared acreage, livestock, and sawmills, see Holmes, *Loyalists to Canada*, 244.) Including Pennfield, these rolls account for 58% of the assessment; without it, 54%. A partial roll for St George has survived as an incomplete collector's return for about one-fifth of the parish's assessment (RS148/C/3/n/1), but too much is missing for it to be included in the analysis here.

52. The Grand Manan assessors blamed their delay in filing on 'our not being

quired one-eighth of the total assessment to be raised by a poll tax on all male residents over the age of twenty-one (except paupers), and the balance on 'visible' real and personal property within the parish and income 'from any office, profession, trade, or occupation' or 'any salary or income payable out of funds in this province' received by an inhabitant of the parish.[53] There were detailed rules about the valuation of real and personal property, which were to be rated at twenty per cent of their value. Income was to be assessed on the basis of 'clear profit' from professions, trades, and occupations, although 'farming and merchandizing' were exempted. Inhabitants were to be taxed on the sum of their rated property and income; nonresidents were to be taxed solely on the value of their real estate in the parish.[54] Despite the detailed statute, there was still a good deal of variation in the ways that different parishes approached the task. The poll tax ranged from eightpence in St Patrick to two shillings in Pennfield.[55] All the parishes charged (and presumably collected) more in poll tax than the one-eighth permitted by the statute. Pennfield and St Patrick charged a third more than they should have, St David about half as much again, St Andrews three-quarters, and West Isles well over twice the authorized amount.[56] The effect, of course, was to reduce the tax on wealth. Here too the nominal rates varied widely, from a half-penny in the pound in St Patrick to three times that rate or more in St David and Grand Manan. The parishes also differed in how they assessed property and incomes. The West Isles assessors identified just one resident with income (C.H. Jouett, the local customs officer),

---

in possession of the late Assessment Law and that had it not reached us through the Public Prints we should still have had much difficulty in proceeding'; PANB RS148/C/3/f/1, Fisher to Hatch, 2 Sep 1831.

53. 1 Wm.IV (1831) c.26, s.1. This would seem to exempt the amounts due half-pay officers like C.R. Hatheway, Thomas Jones, and others whose payments were issued in England.

54. Ibid., s.2.

55. The St George poll tax was 2/7 on an assessment to raise £100 for a parish lock-up and £75 for the poor in addition to the £100 for the county gaol, so the gaol portion of the poll tax was slightly more than 11d.

56. West Isles collected the county tax together with the poor tax in a ratio of 3:1, so I have calculated the county poll tax at three-quarters of the 2s charged, or 18d. At this rate the excess poll tax on the 170 eligible taxpayers amounted to 127 per cent of the permitted proportion of the assessment.

Table 9.4 – Gaol assessment, 1831: Wealth distribution by quintile

Parish	Payers	Rated	Q1	Q2	Q3	Q4	Q5	PT Only*
St Andrews								
(town†)	386	£49,360	64.2	15.6	9.6	6.3	4.6	23.3%
(country)	301	£16,440	47.8	18.7	13.1	11.0	9.5	46.0%
St David	301	£11,482	44.1	22.4	14.4	12.1	6.5	1.7%
St Patrick	382	£26,353	61.6	21.3	12.7	4.7	0.0	29.6%
West Isles	183	£2,875	63.1	17.3	5.7	1.4	0.0	27.3%
Gr. Manan	185	£3,616	70.9	18.3	8.1	2.8	1.2	3.3%

* As a proportion of polltax-eligible taxpayers. For St Andrews this includes propertyless taxpayers notionally assessed at £30 income.
† Individuals: excludes Charlotte County Bank.

presumably equating the fishery which employed most residents with 'farming and merchandizing,' and they dispensed with the twenty per cent rule on property. The St Andrews assessors seem to have taken it as a rule of thumb that almost everyone with no real or personal property (but not a pauper) must have thirty pounds in annual income and assessed them accordingly. St Andrews was the only parish to assess a corporation: the 'president and directors of the Charlotte County Bank' was rated at £2800 on £14,000 of the bank's personal property.[57] There was no assessment of the bank's income or profit. Some parishes seem to have been more alert than others to the assessment of nonresident property. There were no nonresidents assessed in St Andrews but fifty-six in St Patrick where nonresident magistrate John McMaster tied with resident magistrate James Allanshaw as the largest property owners in the parish at £2280, representing more than eleven thousand pounds each. There was wide variance in the commissions allowed assessors and collectors.

To the extent that the rated property and income can be relied upon, these assessments also illustrate some of the county's fiscal inequalities. Among the five parishes St Andrews, with sixty per cent of the wealth, carried only forty-eight per cent of the tax burden. St Patrick had twenty-four per cent of the wealth but only fifteen per cent of the tax burden. The other three parishes were heavily over-

57. They were also assessed separately as individual ratepayers.

Table 9.5 – Gaol assessment, 1831:
Difference between top and tenth ratepayer by parish

Parish	Top-Rated	Tenth-Rated	Difference (%)
St Andrews			
(town*)	2500	630	397
(country)	600	200	300
St David	180	101	178
St Patrick	2280	272	838
West Isles	270	66	409
Grand Manan	270	80	338

* Individuals: excludes Charlotte County Bank.

taxed.[58] Clearly the method of distributing the county assessment according to parish population gave a significant advantage to ratepayers in the wealthier parishes. These assessments also demonstrate the wide disparities not only among parishes but within them (Table 9.4). Everywhere but St David, the top twenty per cent of ratepayers enjoyed more than half of the parish wealth. Except in St David and Grand Manan, a quarter or more of non-pauper adult male residents had no ratable property or income. There was a huge discrepancy in St Andrews parish between the town and the countryside; in the latter nearly half the taxable residents were propertyless.

The unequal distribution of wealth within each parish as shown in Table 9.4 is muted by the analysis of quintiles. There were substantial, indeed substantive, differences within the top twenty per cent. Table 9.5 shows the assessed value of the top-rated and the tenth-rated taxpayer in each parish. A small elite controlled a large proportion of the county's wealth. The top-rated taxpayer in the five parishes was Harris Hatch, the clerk of the peace and bank president in St Andrews. Hatch was also assessed as a nonresident property owner in St David (where his holdings made him the nineteenth-highest rated taxpayer) and St Patrick. Hatch was only four times as wealthy as

58. The ratios of tax burden to wealth for St David, West Isles, and Grand Manan are 19:10, 11:3, and 7:3 respectively. These and the ratios reported in the body of the paragraph might be different if we had comparable data for the missing parishes.

the tenth-rated taxpayer in St Andrews, sheriff Elisha Andrews, but he was nine or ten times richer than the wealthiest ratepayer in most other parishes. The second-rated taxpayer in St Andrews, Thomas Wyer JP, local agent for Lloyds of London, was assessed as a nonresident in St Patrick and St David. William Frankland JP was the sixth-rated taxpayer in Grand Manan, where the second-rated Wilford Fisher was to be appointed to the commission of the peace the following year. There were three justices, one of them a nonresident, and the nonresident sheriff Andrews among the top eleven ratepayers in St Patrick. John Wilson JP, number twenty in St Patrick as a nonresident, was number three at home in St Andrews.

This analysis suggests not only that the magistrates as a body had a vested interest in preserving the lop-sided assessment system, but also that there was merit in some at least of the complaints by country justices about the unfair advantages to St Andrews. All this, of course, takes the assessments at face value; it is not possible to evaluate them systematically on the surviving evidence. The 1831 act provided for self-assessment by ratepayers, who were to hand in statements of property and income subject to the assessors' review for cause.[59] There is nothing to show whether the assessors had such statements before them, nor is it possible to know whether their proceedings overcame the complaint of the preamble to the act, that the broad discretion formerly allowed 'has been productive of great dissimilarity in the mode of apportioning and assessing the rates . . . and has also created dissatisfaction in many instances, on account of the irregularity in the apportionment of such rates among the inhabitants of the several towns or parishes.' It is worth noticing, however, that in every parish the assessors were drawn almost exclusively from the first quintile and included some of the wealthiest ratepayers.[60] One of

59. 1 Wm.IV (1831) c.26 s.5.

60. The sole exception among the five parishes was St Patrick where one of the three assessors was from the second quintile; his family, however, was well-represented in the first quintile. The top-rated assessors in each parish were John Cotterell (rated 3rd in St David), Samuel McFarlan (4th in St Patrick), James Chaffey JP (13th in West Isles), Wilford Fisher (2nd in Grand Manan), and Dr Samuel Frye (15th in St Andrews in 1832). The St Andrews assessment for 1831 is unsigned and there is no surviving parish list for that year. Frye was an assessor in 1832 as well as a physician, bank director, and president of the county agricultural society.

the 1831 assessors was already a magistrate; others, including Samuel McFarlan, Wilford Fisher, James Brown, and Josephus Moore, were later to become justices of the peace.[61]

The stone gaol project took more than ten years to realize from the decision to sell the former property until the new building was completed in 1836.[62] The original plan was to build on a hill lot purchased from the estate of Jeremiah Pote (father-in-law of both Robert Pagan and Thomas Wyer Sr) but when a largely-attended meeting of magistrates decided that the gaol should go on a property big enough to accommodate a separate courthouse as well, the Pote lot was put up for sale and the magistrates purchased a site on Frederick street owned by judge Neville Parker, one of Wyer Jr's brothers-in-law.[63] Sessions had appointed a committee of magistrates and other local notables to approve specifications, supervise construction, and borrow money at interest to pay the contractor.[64] Even before the site was chosen they agreed with Donald D. Morrison to erect a stone building with cells on the ground floor, debtors' rooms upstairs, and quarters for the gaoler with a cellar beneath, at a contract price of three thousand pounds.[65] Morrison entered into a bond secured by Wyer and St Andrews entrepreneur John Aymar.[66] The specifications reflected a strong interest in security—granite walls thirty inches thick on rubble foundations, eighteen-inch-wide iron cell doors, small windows with bars four inches apart—and some concern for sanitation, although

61. For the relationship between high parish office, appointment to the magistracy, and election to the assembly see also Klein, 'Paths to the Assembly.'

62. The magistrates held special sessions at the gaol in December 1835 to petition the legislature for an assessment. The building remained in use as a gaol until 1979; it currently houses the Charlotte County Archives.

63. Parker, a former resident of St Andrews, was master of the rolls. For his not very distinguished career, P. Buckner, 'Parker, Neville.'

64. PANB RS148/F/2/c/1, 'Order respecting New Gaol and assessment,' CCGS Apr 1832.

65. PANB RS148/F/2/c/1, 'Articles of Agreement . . . ,' 29 Jun 1831.

66. Aymar, a blockmaker by trade, had the St Andrews waterworks privilege by 10&11 Geo.IV (1830) c.18. He was rated 22nd in the 1831 St Andrews town assessment, below the leading merchants, lawyers, and customs officials, but ahead of the county treasurer and several of the lesser magistrates. Morrison was rated 2nd in the St Andrews country assessment at £460: this placed him in the top twenty for the parish as a whole.

the detailed notes about drains and sewers in the draft had by the final specification become, ominously, 'the Drains of the Cells to be considered hereafter.'[67]

The gaol project more than exhausted the county's funds. In April 1835 the treasurer reported six hundred pounds in bank debt, seven hundred and fifty pounds owing the members of the gaol committee, and a hundred and twenty-five pounds in unpaid accounts, for a total debt of nearly fifteen hundred pounds. On the credit side he had less than twenty pounds in hand. More than four hundred and fifty pounds of the previous year's assessment remained uncollected, but even should that come in the county was still a thousand pounds in the red and quite unable to pay operating expenses and salaries.[68] The justices had borrowed from the Charlotte County Bank and the St Andrews Savings Bank, which is to say largely from themselves.[69] Three bank directors, Messrs. Hatch, Stubs, and Frye, made up the gaol committee. The bank's proprietors charged the county six per cent annual interest to service its debt and awarded themselves a four per cent half-yearly dividend on the capital stock.[70] Despite sessions' 1835 resolution to divide the proceeds of that year's assessment evenly between the gaol debt and county contingencies there was not enough in hand to pay for gaol operations. In April 1836 sessions resolved to put every penny it could collect towards contingencies and leave the bank debt to accrue interest for the time being. The magistrates met in special sessions to authorize the borrowing of forty pounds to advance the gaoler for food and supplies in December 1835; two hundred pounds from the funds of the Commissioner of Buoys and Beacons (i.e., Thomas Wyer, twice brother-in-law of county treasurer David W. Jack[71]) to pay the gaoler and constables in September 1836; more from the county bank to buy fuel in October 1837 and provisions in November; and a note of hand at six months sight from James Rait JP for bread for the prisoners.[72]

67. PANB RS148/F/2/c/1, 'Copy of original specification ...' as tendered; 'A specification for the New Stone Gaol ...' as contracted for.

68. *Standard*, 21 Apr 1835.

69. Chapter 6.

70. *Standard*, 5 Apr 1835.

71. Jack's first and second wives were Wyer's sisters.

72. CCSS 10 Dec 1835; CCGS Sep 1836; CCSS 29 Oct 1837; CCSS 15 Nov 1837;

It is hardly surprising that the competence and integrity of the justices' financial management was again put in question. James Brown, the liberal MHA from St David, denounced the excessive and 'unjust exactions' of the gaol and debt assessments and introduced a bill to require the justices and treasurer to have the county accounts audited by the grand jury with the power to compel witnesses and the obligation to present delinquent assessors and collectors along with anyone else who misused public funds. It 'would fully expose, and therefore prevent the irregularities and frauds which have heretofore prevailed.'[73] This had been one of the remedies urged by Peter Clinch in 1814 and repeatedly recommended without success by Charlotte grand jurors since.[74] Bills calling for the vetting of public accounts by grand juries or for their publication had been introduced from time to time since then, but always failed.[75] This time the measure passed.[76] The first grand jury report on the Charlotte accounts was delivered at April sessions 1835 but despite a great deal of interest and 'contrary to general expectation,' it was not published until a year later.[77] While it

---

CCSS 19 Nov 1837.

73. 'Speech of Anthony Hobnail Esquire, in the House of Assembly ...,' *Standard*, 29 Nov 1834. Brown and Patrick Clinch were close allies in the fight over the civil list bill: *Standard*, 6 Apr 1837.

74. *Herald*, 2 Apr 1822, letter of 'an inhabitant of St Stephen'; PANB RS24 S31-P1.

75. See letter of 'P. P.', *Standard*, 15 Nov 1834.

76. 5 Wm.IV (1835) c.28, providing for the accounts to be presented to the grand jury at the sessions where parish officers were appointed. This was amended by 7 Wm.IV (1837) c.17 to make it the next succeeding sessions. Addressing the grand jury in April 1837, Wyer praised the change as relieving the busy spring jury from this 'tedious task' and referring the accounts instead to the fall court 'when perfect leisure prevails to inspect them minutely.' The *Standard* (13 Apr 1837) took a different view, arguing that the change made the grand jury's inspection of accounts 'a mere nullity' because it would happen after the money already had been paid out. The next year Wyer introduced a bill in the assembly to restore the original 1835 provision in Charlotte only; a similar bill originating in the legislative council was enacted (1 Vict. c.28) and this difference between Charlotte and the other counties was preserved by 3 Vict. (1840) c.23 and continued by 8 Vict. (1845) c.36. Following 13 Vict. (1850) c.30, RSNB 1854 c.55 reverted to the original provision province-wide (s.4) and provided as well for grand jury approval of any assessment for county contingencies (s.1). Similarly, RSNB 1854 c.54 required a grand jury presentment before sessions could order an assessment for gaols or courthouses (s.1) but not for record offices (s.2, limit £300).

77. *Standard*, 23 Apr 1835, 21 Apr 1836.

was critical of the tax collection process and the 'very large balances unpaid by the respective parishes on the County assessments,' and raised an eyebrow at Harris Hatch's practice of charging 'commission and salary for the performance of the same duty' (collecting commons and market wharf rents),[78] it was scathing in its treatment of the gaol which, it said after taking a view, 'appears sufficiently strong for any thing where strength alone is required, but on the principle that imprisonment should not be torture and death (which must ensue if Prisoners are put into the cells during winter) ... it appears totally unfit for the purpose it was intended to serve.' Not only was the place unclean, but it was 'absolutely necessary that something be done in the way of a *drain or Sewer* to carry off the filth accumulating about such an establishment.' The present method of carting it away was a 'monstrous expense,' as too was the charge for carrying bread from the baker to the gaol, 'which actually amounts to more than the cost of the bread.'

The report was no less scathing about the cost of building the gaol. The justices had allowed Morrison an extra two hundred and fifty pounds 'although no satisfactory statement was ever rendered by the contractor to the building committee ... thereby saddling the County unnecessarily with that sum in addition to the £3000 as per contract for [a] building which has from first to last been considered a most exorbitant tax, having actually cost double what a building in every way more suitable could have been erected for ...'[79] The jury noted that it had purchased a book in which to record its review of the public accounts, which it recommended to be exhibited at each sessions for the information of successive grand juries. The unexplained disappearance of this record was to become a minor scandal some

78. On publishing the report a year later, the *Standard* (21 Apr 1836) noted 'that Mr. Hatch gave a most satisfactory explanation to the Magistrates, and also to individuals of the Grand Jury after the Report was read; but unfortunately that body had terminated its legal existence so that no correction could be made.' A related issue unremarked by the grand jury was addressed by awarding Hatch a salary increase in lieu of some fees: CCGS 21 Sep 1835.

79. Several years later a committee of magistrates 'appointed to examine and report on the accounts for building the stone gaol' concluded that 'no greater allowance was made to the contractor than what the contract authorised': PANB RS148/A/5/d, 7 Apr 1841.

years later.

The second grand jury report on county accounts, delivered in April 1836 and published shortly thereafter in accordance with its own recommendation, was milder in tone than the first, but again the gaol and the gaoler came in for special censure. Supplying bread was still much too expensive, and the need for drains and sewer no less pressing: the report pointed out that the gaoler's charge 'for emptying the common tubs' (£26/4/6) 'is nearly equal to the interest on £450!' While several improvements had been made, 'the character of the building appears incapable of being made suitable to the comfort, cleanliness and health of the inmates.' If, as seems unlikely, the grand jury at September sessions 1837 even saw the county accounts, its report was not published.[80] In April 1838, though, the grand jury delivered its most scathing report to date. It began, 'The imperfect returns and Public Accounts laid before the Grand Jury ... and the total want of system or arrangement in those they have received, render it impracticable for them to take a general view of the County affairs,' and ended, 'the Grand Jury cannot avoid concluding that their time has been trifled with, and that they would be acting in a manner unbecoming the duty they owe to the County should they fail to express their reprehension of this state of things, and their surprise that effectual measures have not yet been taken to fulfil the intentions of the statute.'[81] But the report dealt almost entirely with the imperfections of the process by which the accounts were prepared and put before the jury, and had little or nothing to say about the financial circumstances of the county.

It seemed at that April sessions that the St Andrews junto might be losing its grip. When the court opened as usual on the second Tuesday of the month there were only four justices present, all residents of St Andrews. As the senior justice in attendance Wyer presided and addressed the grand jury. The court adjourned until the next day when only Wyer and James Douglas attended. It adjourned to Thursday, and then again to Friday when the grand jury presented

80. See note 76. The *Standard* barely mentioned September sessions; its columns were fully taken up with the general election then in progress. There is nothing in the CCGS minutes to suggest that such a report was received.

81. *Standard*, 12 May 1838.

Table 9.6 – Division on electing chair; committee membership, CCGS April 1838

Justice	Parish	Q 1	Q 2	Audit	Assess
Owen	Campobello	○	○	✓	✓
Moore	St David	○	○	✓	✓
Mackay	St George	•	•		
Vernon	St George	○	○		
Clinch	St George	○	○	✓	
Knight	Pennfield	○	○	✓	✓
Albee	St Stephen	○	○	✓	✓
Ker	St Andrews	○	○		
Mowatt	St Andrews	•	•		
Rait	St Andrews	•	○	✓	
Wilson	St Andrews	○	○		✓
Wyer	St Andrews	•	•		
		8:4	9:3		

○ 'Yea' • 'Nay'

Q1: 'whether a chairman shall be elected by the Magistrates to conduct the business of the Session.' (Clinch/Owen)

Q2: 'whether they have a right to appoint a chairman to conduct the business of the Session.' (Owen/Clinch)

two bills. On Saturday Wyer, apparently the only justice present, discharged the grand jury, the minutes having made no mention of its report on the county accounts. Finally on the Monday of the second week a sizeable group of justices attended, the majority from other parishes. The first item of business was an unprecedented motion by W.F.W. Owen and Patrick Clinch that the bench elect a chairman to conduct the session. The recorded votes (Table 9.6) demonstrated the division within the St Andrews group and between St Andrews and the parishes. Justices Ker and Wilson voted against Wyer while outside of St Andrews, only Hugh Mackay voted with him—and as the senior justice in the county he would preside if the motion was lost. Although James Rait had deserted Wyer on the second question, he reclaimed the day by quickly putting a third motion: that Mackay be appointed chair of the session. It passed unanimously.

Figure 9.1 – St Andrews courthouse and stone gaol (Paul Craven, 2009)

This symbolic rebuke was quickly followed by a more substantial one with the election of committees to audit the county accounts and to distribute the thousand-pound assessment amongst the parishes. No-one who had voted against an elected chair was appointed to either committee. The assessment committee's report was received and adopted the same day. Later that evening sessions resumed after a brief adjournment. It is not clear who among the magistrates remained. St Andrews justices Wyer, Rait, Ker, and Wilson were present, as was James Frink (St Stephen).[82] They resolved to reconsider the assessment, 'to levy on those Parishes which are delinquent from the last assessment those sums in addition to the sums apportioned to them' in the committee report, and to 'reduce the assessment apportioned to the non delinquent Parishes proportionately.' The main effect was to reduce the St Stephen assessment by forty pounds and to increase those on St George and St David by twenty-five and fifty-one pounds respectively.[83] With this accomplished, sessions adjourned until the next day and proceeded with routine business. On the final day of the court Mackay, Wyer, Rait, Owen, Clinch, and Moore attended. They revisited two former decisions. The St George poor assessment was increased by a hundred pounds. On a reconsideration of the Magaguadavic timber boom rates adopted earlier in the session, Wyer alone opposed the change.

The new courthouse

On circuit in 1834 judge Chipman, deprecating the courtroom in the old gaol building as 'confined, low, and quite unfit for the advanced state of the population,' had urged that 'something might be suggested by the grand Jury which would lead to the erection of a new

82. The clerk did not record attendance when court resumed that evening. The names listed are those who moved or seconded resolutions; there were no recorded votes. Mackay might have been present as chair; the first item in the minutes when court resumed was a motion of thanks (Ker/Rait) 'for his impartial conduct as the senior justice occupy[ing] the Chair for many years past,' but an obscure annotation by the clerk suggests that this vote may have been taken just before the adjournment.

83. There were slight reductions for all the other parishes but West Isles, which was unaffected by the change.

Court House.'[84] The grand jury had obliged by delivering the desired recommendation, on the fanciful theory that the cost of erecting another building on the commodious new gaol lot would be met by the proceeds of selling the old property.[85] When the assembly next met Wyer introduced a bill to assess the county for the purpose.[86] While several acts passed in the interim for assessments to pay down the county debt, it was not until 1839 that the legislature addressed the need for a new Charlotte courthouse. The act permitted the justices to enter into contracts for up to twelve hundred pounds, half of which could be raised by assessment. The legislature appropriated six hundred pounds to support the project.[87]

At September sessions 1838 there was no talk of electing a chair. W.F.W. Owen moved that 'a Committee be appointed to take to their assistance professional men to examine and report to the Bench on tomorrow the present state [of the courthouse]; if the present building is defective its deficiencies in arrangement. Whether there be any objections to the present site and what they are and to point out for the consideration of the bench any more appropriate site.' Five members were elected, only one of them from St Andrews. Their report was unanimously accepted and a committee consisting of justices Owen (Campobello) and Marks (St Stephen), St Andrews lawyer A.L. Street, sheriff Campbell, and clerk of the peace Hatch was appointed to carry it into operation. Later in the session, Owen was appointed to a similar committee (without Marks) for 'procuring plans and estimates for sufficient drains and sewers to carry filth from the Gaol ...' Despite his recent arrival in the county Owen was emerging as its new leader in public works and public finance.

In the mid-1830s Owen, one of Britain's most celebrated naval surveyors, reinvented himself as a New Brunswick landlord and developer.[88] Captain (later Vice-Admiral) William Fitz William Owen,

84. *Standard*, 7 Aug 1834.

85. PANB RS148/A/5/c. The same idea had been advanced to finance the stone gaol: above at page 334. When it was finally sold at auction in 1839 the old gaol site fetched £260: note 43 above.

86. JHA 1835, 362. The bill was ordered to be published in the *Standard* and consideration postponed to the next session.

87. 2 Vict. (1839) c.22; JHA 1839, 354.

88. Among several accounts of Owen's naval career the most extensive is Bur-

the younger son of Campobello's original grantee William Owen and cousin of its late resident proprietor David Owen, having settled with his brother and other relations, became sole proprietor of the island estate. Arriving in the province in September 1835, he lived on the island until 1852 when he remarried and moved to Saint John with his second wife, the widowed daughter of former Charlotte justice Moses Vernon. In the folklore of Campobello's late-nineteenth-century tourist trade, W.F.W. Owen is cast as noble joviality in contrast to David's cranky peevishness.[89] In his own mind W.F.W. became 'the Quoddy hermit,' a high church recluse struggling no less with his self-confessed propensity for 'the licentious practice of indiscriminate sexual intercourse' than against evangelical incursions among his tenants.[90]

He made his first entry onto New Brunswick's public stage wearing his late cousin's shoes. David Owen's first act on Campobello soil had been to serve eviction notices on the residents. W.F.W.'s was to demand payment for arrears of rent.[91] In his portrayal, the 'outrage' that followed foreshadowed the end of Empire and amply vindicated cousin David's dim view of the government and law officers at Fredericton. The nub of Owen's complaint was that a gang of armed Americans—approximately ten of them in the first round of correspondence, twenty in the sequel—had crossed under cover of dark-

---

rows, *Owen.* See also Cornell, 'Owen, William Fitz William.' Owen Sound, Ontario, is named for him.

89. Wells, 'Quoddy Hermit' and *Campobello* and others cited elsewhere.

90. Owen admitted that his 'vicious tendencies were inordinately indulged for some time ... I was never cured of it perfectly until late in life.' W.F.W. Owen, *Quoddy Hermit,* 29, 30. His barely-veiled autobiographical disclosures so embarrassed Owen's family that they tried (unsuccessfully) to buy up and destroy the entire press run.

91. MSA, Owen Register, 24 Jun 1835. When Owen's agent, J.B. Mather, arrived on the island he found it 'in a poor state, owing to neglect, and to the death of the leading people ... who when alive furnished employment for a number of artisans and laborers. These people have now left Welshpool for other places where work can be procured, leaving a miserable remnant of poor fishermen about 400 in number, very few of whom are I fear able to pay rent otherwise than in produce, i.e. dried fish or potatoes.' Similarly the mill rent could only be taken in boards. At this point Owen seems to have contemplated bringing as many as a hundred families with him to resettle the island: ibid., Mather to Owen, 29 Jun 1835. Mather instructed A.L. Street to proceed against some of the tenants: ibid., Mather to Street, 10 Aug 1835.

ness from Lubec[92] to Snug Cove, Campobello, where they had broken into a house, confined its occupants for several hours, and made off with a quantity of salt. As it turned out, they were merely recovering their own salt which they had stored in the cellar where it had been distrained by Owen for his tenant's unpaid rent and which he had refused to sell back to them. In the end, Owen had to content himself with a civil suit in the Maine courts and abandon his efforts to have the men convicted of 'piratical and lawless aggression.'[93]

Nevertheless as Charlotte magistrate, assemblyman, and legislative councillor, Owen stood for fiscal rationality and administrative accountability. He was first appointed to the Charlotte magistracy on November 25, 1835: his was the only new name in the commission of the peace, which removed several former magistrates who had died, been appointed to incompatible offices (Colin Campbell's shrievalty), or were otherwise unsuitable (Peter Stubs's embezzlement). He was appointed JCP in 1838, the same year that he took his seat in the assembly on a successful challenge, and became a legislative councillor following his defeat in the 1842 election. In contrast to his uncle, W.F.W. went out of his way to charm the provincial elite, cheerfully advising the lieutenant governor about harbours and fortifications. He was appointed Commissioner of Light Houses in the Bay of Fundy in 1838 and 1842. He participated actively in county business, particularly between 1836 and 1843 when he attended all but one April sessions (where most of the financial business of the county was done) and several September and special sessions. He sat on the audit or assessment committees or both in most of these years. Beginning in the mid-1840s, however, Owen reduced his role in county affairs in favour of his son-in-law, John J. Robinson RN, who was first appointed to the commission of the peace in 1840 and took over the Campobello estate

92. Lubec, the eastern-most community in the U.S., is separated from Campobello by 'the Narrows,' spanned since 1962 by the Roosevelt Campobello International Bridge.

93. PANB RS8, Owen to Odell, 22 Apr 1836. Owen received a judgment in his favour from the Maine Supreme Judicial Court for Washington County in June 1836. I am grateful to Arthur Dostie of the Maine State Archives for identifying the docket in Owen v. Boyle (replevin, docket #167) and confirming that no other record of the case survives. For another example of Owen's punitive instincts moderated see chapter 8.

when Owen retired to Saint John.[94]

Owen advocated a new professionalism in county management, exemplified by his 1838 motion that 'professional men'—lawyers—be brought in to assist the magistrates in planning for the new courthouse. When his committee reported the following April it laid out the basic requirements,[95] limited expenditure, and established a method for apportioning the cost among the various parishes. It recommended that a committee consisting of the county treasurer, the clerk of the peace, and A.L. Street (none of them magistrates)[96] be appointed to oversee the project with broad authority to contract and decide the details within the broad mandate of the report. They were also authorized to arrange for the sale of the old courthouse land and building and the purchase of the remaining lots on the new gaol and courthouse block. What had previously been considered the direct responsibility of the magistrates (often but not aways assisted by the clerk of the peace) was now delegated to county staff and outside professionals.[97]

At the same time that the justices' financial autocracy was coming under some pressure both externally, as the ratepayers on the grand jury attempted to oversee expenditures, and internally, from managerial reformers like Owen, a more dramatic change was under way in the relationship between sessions and the assembly. From 1803 until 1831 all or at least a majority of the county's four MHAs were in the commission of the peace, and most of them were active

---

94. Robinson was less active than Owen in county affairs, in part because he was absent on naval duty in the early 1840s. He succeeded Owen as lighthouse commissioner in 1846 and was elected to the assembly for a single term in 1851.

95. These were a judgment hall, sessions room, grand jury room, two petit jury rooms, a room for the judges, and another for the barristers, all in a building not to exceed seventy by fifty-five feet on the lot adjacent to the new stone gaol.

96. In March 1840 Harris Hatch was to retire as clerk of the peace and of the inferior court of common pleas in favour of his son Wellington, who had been performing 'the principal duties of both offices' for the last three years: *Standard*, 17 Apr 1840. Hatch senior became a legislative councillor in 1841 but was not appointed to the commission of the peace until 1844/5.

97. CCGS Apr 1839. Although the report was adopted, direct magisterial involvement was reintroduced the following year when James Allanshaw JP replaced A.L. Street, who had left the county: CCSS n.d. (probably 24 Apr 1839); Owen was not present.

participants in sessions business.[98] In financial matters, the assembly functioned largely as an extension of the sessions system, sharing the public purse among the various counties and parishes by annual appropriations and specific local enactments, both driven by petitions. Once sessions had resolved to request legislative aid for county (sometimes parish) purposes the clerk of the peace would draw up the petition and if necessary draft a bill which might be referred to the grand jury for review. When the legislature convened (usually a month or two before April sessions) one of the county members tabled the petition, introduced the bill, and with the aid of his county colleagues shepherded the request through the assembly. Beginning with the 1831 election, however, this relationship began to change. While the underlying causes were complex and far-reaching, the immediate reasons were simple enough. The county's senior magistrate, Hugh Mackay, who had served in the assembly for more than thirty years, retired from politics, although not from sessions, at age eighty. Colin Campbell, who had sat in the House almost as long as Mackay, had to resign from both the commission of the peace and the legislature upon becoming county sheriff.[99] James Brown, the rising star of reform from St David, won a seat, as did St Stephen lawyer George Stillman Hill. Neither was a justice of the peace. Thomas Wyer, a county member since 1828, retained his seat and was joined by novice MHA Patrick Clinch JP. Throughout the 1830s Wyer managed to keep the special relationship between sessions and the assembly alive. Legislative control of crown lands created a surplus of one hundred and fifty thousand pounds in 1837.[100] Total appropriations for Charlotte were larger than they had ever been during that decade, and they were never to be as large again thereafter.[101] Then

98. Appendix, A.3.

99. Sheriffs were disqualified from the commission of the peace because they were county officers directed and paid by sessions although appointed by the executive: chapter 1, note 77. Colin Campbell's efforts to regain his commission once he lost the shrievalty are discussed in chapter 5. I have not found express contemporary statutory authority disabling sheriffs from sitting in the assembly, but as the sheriff had the management of elections the two offices were clearly incompatible: 31 Geo.III (1791) c.17.

100. Whalen, *Local Government*, 20.

101. Before 1857 the legislature passed omnibus appropriation bills itemizing ev-

in late 1839 Wyer accepted appointment to the legislative council.[102] In the by-election that followed, James Boyd resoundingly defeated Wyer's former colleague Patrick Clinch in a populist campaign attacking the 'imaginary rights' and 'assumed prerogative' of sessions and its financial mismanagement.[103] Clinch, whose platform seems to have consisted of complaints about his treatment during the previous election, acknowledged that Wyer's elevation had broken up 'the

---

ery by-road grant and school subsidy along with individual salaries, pensions, grants in aid of various public and private works, and so on. It is impossible to allocate all these grants on a county basis with precision because many of them crossed county boundaries, for example the great road between St Andrews and Fredericton, the stagecoach between St Andrews and Saint John, or the annual subvention for lighthouses in the Bay of Fundy. I estimate that annual appropriations for individuals and works in Charlotte (excluding grants for roads, bridges, and schoolteachers but including the grammar school grant) averaged about £400 before 1831, £2500 between 1831 and 1842, and £1400 thereafter until 1857 when the 'Smasher'-dominated assembly adopted the British system of appropriation whereby the government initiated money bills. 'The hoary and highly individualistic system by which hard-bargaining assemblymen came to Fredericton to answer in the most direct manner possible the extremely practical demands of their constituents fell into disuse in 1857': MacNutt, *New Brunswick*, 365. For the 'Smashers' see chapter 11 below.

102. There was some dissatisfaction in the county as it was felt that Charlotte was already well represented there by Allanshaw and Hatch and overdue for a seat on the executive council. Petitions came from various parts of the county (but not, apparently, St Andrews) asking that Wyer be appointed to the executive council instead: PANB RS344, petition of Rev. Skeffington Thomson and 60 others including Samuel Abbot JP, Robert Lindsay JP, John Porter JP, Josephus Moore JP, and G.S. Hill 'M.P.P.,' 28 Aug 1839; ibid., petition of inhabitants of St David, 30 Aug 1839; ibid., petition of Wilford Fisher JP, Cochran Craig JP, and others, 6 Sep 1839. These were unavailing. The provincial secretary replied to Thomson, saying his petition could not be entertained because it had 'so direct a tendency to interfere with the exercise of H.M.'s Royal Prerogative': PANB MC1001/MS2/II/A3, G.S. Hill papers, Political Correspondence, Odell to Thomson, 13 Sep 1839. Wyer took his council seat on September 20, 1839: *Courier*, 29 Sep 1839.

103. Boyd's election address, *Standard*, 28 Sep 1839. His critique of the fish bounties was a direct swipe at Wyer, who had championed them. Boyd campaigned on strengthening grand jury oversight of county affairs (*Standard*, 23 Nov 1839): 'As regards the law respecting the auditing and passing the County accounts, as it now stands it amounts to a perfect farce. We must insist on greater powers to be given to the Grand Juries, in order that when the accounts have passed their hands, their doings on them may be final; and I feel satisfied that in such hands and with proper management, that in a very short space of time the affairs of the County will assume a totally different aspect.'

old copartnership.'[104]

The evidence for this was not long in coming. Sessions petitioned for a two thousand pound assessment to pay down the county debt and a bill to this effect was introduced in the House. The three county members who were not in the commission of the peace 'were so frightened at the amount that they stopped the bill and said they would send to St Andrews for the accounts to see how it was possible that such an immense debt could arise.'[105] They united to reduce the amount to seven hundred and fifty pounds by assessment and a six hundred pound appropriation. At April sessions the grand jury expressed alarm at increasing county expenditures, 'extravant' salaries of some public officials, 'highly reprehensible' expense claims by constables, and the compound interest charged by the bank on the county debt. It complained again about the magistrates' reluctance to comply with its predecessors' recommendations. When the legislature met in 1841 there were petitions to make a new county of St Stephen, St David, and St James parishes, and another to do the same for Campobello, West Isles, and Grand Manan. As one supporter put it, the outer parishes wished 'to separate ourselves from the usurped thraldom under which [St Andrews] have held us in subjection.'[106]

Sessions had asked for a grant to pay off the courthouse and a thousand pound assessment for the county debt. The four Charlotte MHAs once again demanded to see the accounts and then refused to support an assessment for any amount. They secured a £250 grant to pay the courthouse contractor's overdue account. Brown, Boyd, and Owen all spoke out in the assembly to denounce the county's financial mismanagement. Brown pointed out that a third of the last assessment remained to be collected and wondered why half the county's expenditure consisted in payments to magistrates and constables.[107] Boyd called for a commission to investigate the accounts for the last ten years since the building of the stone gaol. Owen told

104. *Standard*, 23 Nov 1839.

105. *Standard*, 29 Feb 1840, legislative correspondence of 'Jack Robinson.'

106. *Standard*, 5 Feb 1841, along with an editorial rejoinder to this correspondent and further letters in the edition of 12 Feb 1841. Separation had long been a favoured remedy for domination by St Andrews: chapter 3.

107. Several speeches by members from other counties emphasized the iniquity of magistrates taking fees for county business. It had been, and continued to be,

the House,

> Since he had been appointed a magistrate, he had endeavored to induce his coadjutors to have the accounts investigated, but notwithstanding the exertions he had made to obtain a clear insight into them, he had not succeeded ... If the extent of mismanagement were known, he was satisfied a commission would be appointed to examine the subject; but which should not be done by persons selected from among the magistrates, as the duty would be extremely onerous and painful.

Brown summed up: not every magistrate was to blame, many came to sessions from different parts of the county, but a few at St Andrews 'managed matters after they were gone, and the people were not satisfied.'[108] The same day, Boyd introduced a bill to audit the county; later in the session it was given the three-months' hoist on a close division, the Speaker casting the deciding vote.[109]

Notwithstanding the £250 granted in 1841 to pay off the contractor, the county petitioned again in 1842 for £320 still owing for the courthouse and for eighty pounds more to put a fence around it, complaining that the assembly's refusal to grant an assessment the previous year had caused 'great embarassment to your Petitioners, under the circumstances.'[110] The legislature allowed a thousand pound assessment but appropriated only one hundred fifty pounds: a warrant issued for one hundred forty and it took another year before the re-

common practice in Charlotte for justices to charge the county for statutory fees in criminal and regulatory cases where costs could not be recovered otherwise. In April 1839 sessions resolved that 'Whereas many accounts come before the bench from Magistrates and Constables for expences and fees in criminal cases which add very materially to the charges on the County (which can ill afford it) and as it has appeared that these expences may in very many cases be recoverable from the parties themselves. It is recommended to all the Magistrates to use all legal means of diminishing all such charges and we suggest that all fines adjudged in cases of assault and battery are available for fees and costs.' (Appropriating fines in assault cases to pay the justices would reduce the amount available for poor relief.) The means suggested included seizing property found on the person of anyone arrested on a criminal information and taking bonds from private prosecutors to guarantee that they would proceed and pay expenses.

108. *Standard*, 12 Mar 1841, 'from Mr. Ward's Reports' for 23 Feb 1841.

109. JHA 1841, 147. The Charlotte members all voted to proceed with the bill.

110. PANB RS345/b/1, 23 Feb 1842.

maining ten pounds was made available.[111] This marked the end of legislative grants for Charlotte's building projects. In the same year the assembly refused the justices' petition for aid towards paying off the county debt.[112] There were further assessments for debt and contingencies in later years: a thousand pounds in each of 1844 and 1846; four hundred in 1847 and 1848; three hundred in 1849; and one hundred seventy-five in 1850.[113] But the old system of substantial provincial appropriations for local projects was foundering as the economy moved towards crisis. As early as 1842 the provincial secretary warned Boyd against asking for money for a St Andrews sewer.[114] The government issued a circular 'to impress upon Magistrates that from the state of the public finances there is at present no prospect of obtaining sums of money, from the public revenue, for the prosecution of local public works.'[115] By 1850 the provincial deficit exceeded one hundred thousand pounds.[116]

There was just one election after 1831 in which justices made up a majority of Charlotte's MHAs, that of 1847 following Brown's and Boyd's appointments to the commission of the peace. Brown was never an active justice and rarely attended sessions. Boyd was active enough but usually found himself on the outs with his fellow magistrates, apparently taking pride in his ability (as he put it in his 1839 election address) 'to give serious offence' to his colleagues. There was to be a major rift in 1850 leading to Boyd's forced resignation from the bench and temporary ouster from the assembly.[117] The 'old copartnership' was well and truly over. At least in the short term, it was replaced by parsimony. Addressing the grand jury at April sessions 1843 Owen urged 'retrenchment and economy in all the County busi-

---

111. 5 Vict. (1842) c.14; JHA 1843, 231.

112. JHA 1843, 144.

113. 7 Vict. (1844) c.4; 9 Vict. (1846) c.13; 10 Vict. (1847) c.35; 11 Vict. (1848) c.37; 12 Vict. (1849) c.15; 13 Vict. (1850) c.L-14. 24 Vict. (1861) c.34 authorized a £300 assessment on St Andrews for the town debt.

114. PANB RS13/A/4, Odell to Boyd, 26 Aug 1842: 'in the present state of the province there can be little prospect that this can be derived from Public Grants unless as an advance on Security of a Local Rate for its reimbursement.'

115. *Standard*, 28 Dec 1842.

116. Whalen, *Local Government*, 20.

117. Chapter 10.

ness.'[118] The cuts were expected to be deep: sessions resolved not only to reduce salaries and 'introduce the strictest economy' in all county services but also, 'that both water closets in the courthouse be removed and be sold for the benefit of the county.'[119]

There were renewed complaints about a few magistrates monopolizing money matters and failing to publish the public accounts. The St Andrews *Standard*, which had never taken a controversial position on anything, published a shocking editorial: 'The public affairs of Charlotte County have been so long directed by a certain Clique, who have preyed without mercy upon their unresisting victims, that we now see the people borne down with Taxes ... ' The next week's issue sheepishly acknowledged that it had been copied without attribution from the *St Stephen Courant*, but the damage had been done and an unprecedentedly lengthy debate ensued among the paper's correspondents. 'There has been from time to time a goodly amount raised to pay off the County debt,' wrote 'A Freeholder,' 'but it appears to me to be larger now than ever, and I wish to know when it will be less.' Boyd responded in the next issue, blaming the justices for suppressing the accounts and pointing out that his bill to enhance the power of the grand jury had passed the assembly only to be refused by council. The ratepayer revolt continued. 'We are heavily taxed every year, and we wish to understand why it is so, and also to know if we can be compelled to submit to these exorbitant taxes.'[120] At September sessions Wyer promised to have the accounts published 'in full immediately,' but then criticism turned to the make-up of the grand jury. It was 'highly improper,' wrote 'A Taxpayer,' 'to have persons who are known to have the expenditure of public money, or have accounts against the county or parish as the case may be, placed year after year on the April grand jury, when there are plenty of intelligent and disinterested men, who have not been on, perhaps more than once, in five years, if ever.'[121] The sheriff was to blame, he said; the justices

118. *Standard*, 3 Apr 1843.

119. CCGS 20 Apr 1843.

120. *Standard*, 8 Jun 1843; 7, 14, 21 Aug 1844; 2 Sep 1844.

121. *Standard*, 18 Sep 1844. By my count, of the 124 grand jurors at April sessions 1840-1845, one served four times, two three times, and twenty twice, so while about eighteen per cent of the jurors served more than once in six years, only

were not corrupt but overgenerous; those from the upper parishes as much so as in St Andrews. What was really needed was a Charlotte seat on the executive council, someone to whom the honest magistrates could complain about their misconducting brethren. 'A Countryman' responded, 'I have no disposition to screen the Magistrates in any act of extravagance but am averse to condemning anyone unheard.' Nonsense, replied 'A Taxpayer': 'The cause of the County debt is as well known to be the extravant expenditure of the County money by the Justices.' The grand jury law was useless: 'It is an insult to intelligent men, to hand them a parcel of accounts after being passed and ordered to be paid by the Justices six months previously; it is a mockery! to tell them to look at accounts over which they can have no control, no matter how outrageous or extravagant they may appear.'[122]

By now the legislature was back at work. Sessions had forwarded a petition for another assessment. Boyd introduced two grand jury bills, one to continue the existing act which was due to expire; the other to permit the jury to 'examine, audit and allow' the accounts. Both bills passed the House, the second having been amended to apply only to Charlotte county. Boyd and Hill declared that if council rejected it they would oppose the assessment.[123] Council rejected the second bill,[124] and when the Charlotte assessment bill reached the committee stage, Boyd moved the three months' hoist.[125] Once again the Charlotte members had defeated the Charlotte justices.

Nevertheless at September sessions 1850 Charlotte county was finally pronounced debt-free. This success probably had less to do with retrenchment, economy, or more efficient tax collection than with the fact that the county had not embraced any substantial public works projects in the past decade. There was enough money on hand or awaiting collection to pay expenses until the new *County and Parish*

Thomas Berry, who was a grand juror in 1841, 1842, 1843, and 1844, could be said to have served 'year after year.' Berry, the contractor for the courthouse, was a St Andrews poor house commissioner in some of these years: see chapter 10.

122. *Standard*, 16, 30 Oct 1844; 13 Nov 1844 (and note 102 above); 5, 12 Feb 1845.

123. *Standard*, 2 Apr 1845, legislative correspondence of 'Jack Robinson.'

124. Wyer, Hatch, and Owen were present but the division was not recorded: JLC 1845, 305f.

125. JHA 1845, 257 (27 Mar).

Act came into operation.[126] The new act did away with the need for legislative sanction of assessments for county buildings, provided for the election of parish officers, and made assessments for county contingencies subject to prior approval by the grand jury.[127] A comprehensive reworking of town and county governance, the act was a step on the way to municipal incorporation.[128] But *plus ça change*, as 'An Old Tax Payer' returned to the correspondence columns in 1868 to point out:[129]

> It appears to me we are getting from bad to worse, and that we have forgotten the lessons of the past, which were recorded in the old Grand Jury Book, which has been missing for several years, abstracted I have long believed, by an interested party, whose malfeasance was recorded therein …

126. *Standard*, 25 Sep 1850.
127. 13 Vict. (1850) c.30.
128. 14 Vict. (1851) c.38; *Standard*, 29 Oct. 1851, and chapter 12.
129. *Standard*, 15 Dec 1868.

Chapter 10

Three ships: Poverty, paternalism, and politics at mid-century

In May 1847 the St Andrews justices sent an urgent appeal to the lieutenant governor. Five vessels loaded with destitute emigrants from Ireland were expected within days; the poor house commissioners[1] disclaimed all responsibility for their support; the town's inhabitants were much alarmed; no-one had authority to act. The magistrates called on the provincial executive to ensure that 'some efficient means may be taken to meet the emergency.' They enclosed a report from the commissioners, who said they were advancing money out of their own pockets for support of the local poor and that there would be nothing left over to relieve newcomers. 'We have expected for the last several weeks,' they wrote, 'to see the appointment of an Emigrant Agent for this Port officially announced, having understood it to be the intention of the Government to make such an appointment, and being aware that a large sum of money was appropriated by the Legislature at the last Session ... for the relief & assistance of destitute Emigrants as they arrived at the several ports in the Province.'[2]

1. The poor house commissioners were the overseers of the poor for St Andrews parish: see further below.

2. PANB RS555, Hatch et al. to Prov. Secty., 21 May 1847 and encl.

The government's reply was not encouraging. It was impossible to appoint or pay for an emigrant agent. The legislative grant was intended only to reimburse local overseers of the poor for necessary advances to sick and destitute emigrants. The overseers were the legal guardians of the poor and must do whatever was needful.[3]

On June 3, the *Elizabeth Grimmer*, a St Stephen-built timber ship temporarily converted to carry 229 passengers from Londonderry, arrived off St Andrews.[4] Doctor Frye inspected the vessel and reported to the magistrates that eight of the emigrants had died on the passage, eight more were sick with fever, and many of the rest were feeble. The ship was ordered to quarantine at Hospital Island, where the passengers were landed on June 5.[5] There were now nine or ten sick with fever and another had died.[6] The quarantine station was grossly inadequate: Dr Frye complained about the lack of beds, the 'promiscuous disorder,' the shortage of fresh water, the lack of accommodation for the medical attendant.[7] The commissioners of the poor declared themselves incapable of providing for the sick and destitute: 'We consider it no part of our duty ... to take charge of Paupers who may arrive at this place from distant countries.'[8] Three days later Dr Frye released the vessel from quarantine along with most of the emigrants, keeping seventeen sick and convalescent on the island. The magistrates met to deal with the inhabitants' alarm about the sudden influx of enfeebled paupers, naming Hatheway, Boyd, and James Street to a committee to find and supervise their accommodation.[9]

When the *Elizabeth Grimmer* arrived at St Stephen a week later it produced another local panic, coroner David Rose writing to St Andrews to complain that the ship had not been properly disinfected when in quarantine there. Several emigrants were sick and one more had died. The St Stephen magistrates lacked a copy of the county

3. PANB RS148/a/6, Prov. Secty. to Hatch et al., 24 May 1847.

4. For an account of these events that emphasizes the plight of the Irish emigrant, Rees, *Some Other Place.*

5. PANB RS148/a/6, Frye to magistrates, 3 Jun 1847; PANB RS555, Jack to Prov. Secty., 5 Jun 1847.

6. PANB RS555, Wyer to Prov. Secty., 8 Jun 1847.

7. PANB RS148/a/6, Frye to magistrates, 9 Jun 1847.

8. PANB RS148/a/6, Commrs of Poor to Magistrates, 8 Jun 1847.

9. Ibid., special meetings of magistrates, 9 and 15 Jun, 1847.

health regulations and doubted their authority to convene a special sessions. The ship's owner, ignoring their orders to moor away from the wharves, was presently discharging cargo: 'I am told that the smell from her is so disagreeable that it is impossible to remain any length of time in her hold.' Rose's son, along with the ship's captain and most of the crew, had come down with fever.[10] That Rose's olfactory evidence came at second-hand was telling. At St Andrews James Boyd complained that the whole burden of dealing with the sick, 'an arduous and dangerous duty,' fell on himself alone, 'my colleagues of the Committee declining to go near the infected.' Boyd's own agenda was transparent: 'There should have been and there still ought to be some one person appointed to attend to the whole duty, who could make his own arrangements much more satisfactorily than to be constantly interfered with by persons who give themselves very little trouble in such matters.'[11]

The parish poor

Responsibility for the poor in colonial New Brunswick fell on the parish authorities in accordance with the province's unreformed version of Elizabethan poor law.[12] Fines and forfeitures levied for a variety of regulatory and petty criminal offences were assigned in part or whole to the use of the poor.[13] Any shortfall had to be made up by local taxation. Tension between charity and frugality was inevitable. Reverend Samuel Andrews memorialized the county bench in 1793, lamenting the lack of permanent provision for the indigent: 'there are Overseers of the poor appointed by the community, but they are left

10. PANB RS148/a/6, Rose to W. Hatch, 23 Jun 1847. Dr Frye rebutted Rose's complaints about the St Andrews quarantine, although he acknowledged that the ship's lower hold had not been cleaned as it was full of cargo for St Stephen: ibid., Frye to Magistrates, 25 Jun 1847.

11. PANB RS555, Boyd to Prov. Secty., 22 Jul 1847.

12. Greenhous, 'Paupers and Poorhouses.'

13. Thus in April 1832 the poor house commissioners reported receiving £26/7/9 from justices Hatheway and Stubs in fines for assaults and liquor offences and decried the failure of the town's hog reeves to charge the owners of swine running at large in the streets, thereby depriving the parish of an additional source of revenue: PANB RS148e/4/a.

without strength; as the Community who appointed them put nothing into their hands to distribute.'[14]

The fundamentals of the system were enacted in 1786. In each county, at the first general sessions of every year, the justices were to appoint three overseers of the poor for each parish.[15] Each year the outgoing overseers were to report on 'the state and condition of the Poor in their several districts.' The justices would audit these accounts and issue warrants of assessment for each of the parishes accordingly.[16] For example, at April sessions 1831, the justices ordered poor assessments ranging from fifteen to one hundred pounds for all the parishes but Grand Manan, where 'none [was] applied for.'[17]

---

14. CCGS Sep 1793.

15. 26 Geo.III (1786) c.28 provided for their appointment and 26 Geo.III (1786) c.43 for their powers and duties. In practice, the parish officers including the overseers of the poor were nominated by the resident magistrates, sometimes following a public meeting, and the parish clerk submitted the list for approval at general sessions. This approval was not entirely *pro forma*, as on several occasions the assembled justices struck out some names and substituted others, either of their own motion or in response to parishioners' petitions. (For an example of a successful petition, CCGS Apr 1845 (St George); for an unsuccessful one, CCGS Apr 1844 (St Stephen).) After 1850, most parish officers, including three overseers of the poor, were to be elected by the ratepayers at a public meeting and then confirmed by the bench: 13 Vict. (1850) c.30; 13 Vict. (1850) c.47.

16. An amending act, 33 Geo.III (1793) c.6, enabled the justices to audit the poor accounts and assess the parishes at any general sessions. This subsequently became the model for school assessments, substituting trustees for overseers: 56 Geo.III (1816) c.23, s.5. 41 Geo.III (1801) c.8, made perpetual by 50 Geo.III (1810) c.19, permitting Saint John to levy a dog tax for the 'further and better support of the poor' of that city, was extended to Fredericton and St Andrews by 9 Geo.IV (1828) c.23. 58 Geo.III (1818) c.18 authorized the justices of St Andrews to lease a portion of the town commons to support the parish poor. In 1841, the justices authorized the St Andrews poor house commissioners to act as their bailiffs in collecting arrears of rent from the commons lessees: CCGS Sep 1841. When part of the common was sold in the early 1860s, interest on the proceeds was ordered to be paid to the overseers of the poor semiannually: CCGS Apr 1863. A dispute later emerged over whether this income belonged to the whole parish of St Andrews or just the town: CCGS Apr 1867.

17. CCGS Apr 1831. The parishes were to be assessed as follows:

St Stephen	£75	St Andrews	£100	St George	£75	St David	£20
St James	£15	Gr Manan	—	West Isles	£25	Campobello	£30
Pennfield	£50	St Patrick	£20				

See also an administrative order for the preparation of poor accounts in duplicate so that the magistrates resident in each parish could determine the assessment

The overseers were to act preemptively by obliging 'any idle, or disorderly person or persons ... who have no visible means of support, and who are likely to become chargeable to the parish,' to work for anyone willing to employ them, and by binding out poor children as apprentices.[18] They could establish workhouses for paupers who could not earn their own living, or farm them out to whomever would take them for a yearly allowance (hence the 'pauper auctions' at which care for the parish indigent was assigned to the lowest bidder).[19] In practice, the overseers often made small supplemental grants (for example, for medical attendance) to support the working poor.[20] Paupers denied support by the overseers, and people whose accounts for taking care of the poor had been refused by them, could appeal to the justices in general sessions.[21] On one such occasion, the justices ordered the overseers to admit a man to the St Andrews poor house, 'on account of his helpless state, during the time it may be found necessary to keep his wife in gaol.'[22]

The justices in sessions approved each parish's list of officers, received their accounts, supervised the parish assessors and tax collectors, and heard assessment appeals.[23] Many examples might be given of sessions policing the parish poor tax apparatus, but a few

required each year before coming to general sessions: CCGS Apr 1840.

18. In one case (CCGS Sep 1801) the Charlotte justices released an apprentice from his indentures because of mistreatment by his master, putting the boy 'under the directions of the overseers of the poor to be provided for.'

19. 26 Geo.III (1786) c.43 directed the overseers 'to put the said poor in the hands of the person who shall offer to keep them for the least expense, having at the same time a regard to the character of the person who offers, so that the poor may not be inhumanly treated nor the public abused.' See also Aiton, 'Selling Paupers.'

20. Thus in 1819 the St Andrews overseers noted that James Goswelling 'works for his victuals, the Parish supply him with clothes': PANB RS148/m/20/a.

21. For example, CCGS Apr 1844 ordered the overseers of Pennfield to pay Thomas Sparks £6 'for keeping Edward Black a Pauper.' A counterpetition failed because the parish overseers had already complied with the order: CCGS Apr 1845.

22. CCGS Apr 1837.

23. Appeals took the form of a petition by the ratepayer, a show-cause order to the assessor, and a final determination in sessions: for example, James Boyd's petition filed at CCGS Sep 1844 was put over to the next general sessions to allow time for the reply. After taking into account assessor G.D. Street's submission the bench decided at CCGS Apr 1845 that 'there ought to be no deduction made in the amount he was assessed last year.'

will suffice. A long-running series of disputes among successive St Stephen overseers of the poor, assessors, and rate collectors came to general sessions on several occasions in the late 1820s and early 1830s, culminating in an order for arbitration.[24] In 1834 sessions investigated the delinquent tax collectors of St George parish 'for the last ten years,' audited the overseers of the poor's accounts for two years past, and issued processes 'to punish' five parish officials. Three assessors, prominent members of the community of whom two were later to be promoted to the magistracy, were censured for neglect of duty and ordered to be prosecuted before a single JP 'not belonging to the Parish of St George.'[25] Although the overseers of the poor escaped prosecution, they were criticized for crediting the parish with a 'note of hand in lieu of Rates' and ordered to collect the outstanding amount 'forthwith.'

Although the 1786 poor act did not define who was 'likely to become chargeable to the Town or Parish where they reside,' it was understood that the local community was to care for its own. Destitute incomers could be returned to their home parishes for support, as the St Andrews justices had reminded David Owen in 1788 when his servant left a Campobello pauper on Robert Pagan's doorstep.[26] Similarly in 1797, when the St Andrews overseers complained that a pauper had been landed overnight from a Saint John vessel, the justices met in special sessions to order him sent back whence he came.[27] The magistrates at general sessions decided disputes between the overseers of different parishes about which was responsible for maintaining particular paupers. In 1832 sessions ordered the St Stephen over-

24. CCGS Apr 1832. During the recession of the early 1840s a delinquent St Stephen collector of rates was committed to jail until he rendered a satisfactory account and paid over the amounts collected in full: CCSS 3 May, 3, 6, 8 Jun 1843.

25. CCGS Apr 1834. Isaac Knight and Robert Thompson were to become magistrates; the third, Peter Clinch, was also prosecuted (with two others) for breach of duty as commissioners of highways. A St George constable was prosecuted for neglecting to levy an execution for an unpaid parish rate. Warrants issued against three additional former officers of the parish at the close of the session. Despite holding the warrants to be defective and the assessment illegal, St Andrews magistrate Peter Stubs gave judgment against the three for ten pounds each. Several orders made against them at CCGS Sep 1834 were all rescinded at CCGS Apr 1835.

26. Chapter 2.

27. CCGS 13 Jan 1797.

seers to provide for a woman petitioner 'as other paupers are' and a year later ordered them to pay a St Andrews constable for returning her to St Stephen.[28]

The overseers of the poor were responsible for the support of children born to unwed mothers who were unable to provide for them. If a mother was able but unwilling, sessions would order her to 'maintain her bastard child.'[29] The putative father was to be apprehended on a justice's warrant and committed to gaol for up to six weeks following the birth unless he either indemnified the parish against having to support the child or gave security to appear at the next general sessions.[30] The adolescent Thomas Wyer Jr, the county's future senior magistrate, assemblyman, and legislative councillor, made his first formal appearance at Charlotte general sessions in April 1800 to enter into a £300 bond for child support.[31] The case began as an application for a filiation order by the mother's father but continued as a complaint by the overseers of the poor. Justice Thomas Wyer Sr did not attend court that day: Thomas Jr appeared by his 'guardians' Robert Pagan and Maurice Salt, overseers of the poor, who formally resigned that office for the occasion. Three hundred pounds was a great deal of money, befitting Wyer Sr's standing: in 1817 a putative

28. CCGS 29 Sep 1832, 24 Sep 1833. Other pauper settlement cases at general sessions included 'the appeal of the Church Wardens and Overseers of the Poor of the Parish of St Stephen against the removal of Catharine Sykes from the Parish of St Andrews' (Apr 1816) and an order to maintain 'the pauper Jane Ferguson' from the St Stephen poor rates, 'during the time that she may be obliged to reside in the parish of St James' (CCGS Sep 1825).

29. For example, CCGS Sep 1823.

30. 32 Geo.III (1792) c.3, which was 'copied from the British Statute': CO 188/4, Carleton to Dundas, 2 Jun 1792. Mothers were to be examined on oath by one or more justices to identify the putative father, but they could not be required to undergo such an examination until at least one month after delivery of the child, nor was it lawful 'to compel any woman before she shall be delivered, to answer to any questions relating to her pregnancy.' The province's bastardy legislation was amended by 2 Vict. (1839) c.48, 4 Vict. (1841) c.28, 8 Vict. (1845) c.75, and consolidated in 13 Vict. (1850) c.30 and RSNB 1854, c.57.

31. This was to indemnify the overseers and their successors against 'all manner of Costs, Taxes, Rates, Assessment and charges whatsoever, for or by reason of the Birth, Education, or Maintenance of the said Child and of and from all actions, Suits, troubles and other charges whatsoever touching or concerning the same.' CCGS 10 and 11 Apr 1800.

father had to give only one hundred pounds security to indemnify the parish.[32] Later in the century it became common to specify the amount of child support. For example in two 1835 cases each man was ordered to pay the overseers four pounds and a few shillings for charges incidental to the birth, five shillings weekly while his child was 'at the breast,' and half that amount each week thereafter so long as the child remained chargeable to the parish.[33] Breach of a support order usually resulted in the father's committal to jail.[34]

The St Andrews overseers applied to April sessions 1803 for a 'remedy' for their expenditures on behalf of three sailors who had been landed at the port suffering from frostbite. The justices resolved that the parish was 'not by law bound to relieve the said persons as Paupers thereof.'[35] New legislation in 1820 made the overseers responsible for the care of sick and disabled seamen although they were not paupers of the parish. Ships arriving in the province were liable for a tax of one penny per registered ton annually for the sick and disabled seamen's fund, payable at the port of entry before breaking bulk or discharging ballast. Crews of vessels owned in the province had sixpence per month deducted from their wages towards the tonnage duty. The overseers were to relieve the seamen in need, rendering their accounts to the justices in general sessions who then sent them on to the provincial treasurer.[36] In 1826 the legislature transferred responsibility for sick and disabled seamen at St Andrews to three commissioners to be appointed, not by the local justices, but

32. CCGS Apr 1817.

33. CCGS 18 Apr 1835, 21 Apr 1835. In 1851 Hatheway took a bond from a putative father to indemnify the parish until the child reached the age of seven years: Ledger 2, crown side, 13, Alfred McCurdy bond.

34. CCGS Sep 1841; CCGS Sep 1849; CCGS Sep 1852; CCGS Sep 1861. Putative fathers were also jailed when they failed to post bond to appear at an adjourned hearing: CCGS Apr 1862, CCGS Sep 1862.

35. CCGS Apr 1803.

36. 60 Geo.III (1820) c.15; 2 Geo.IV (1821) c.10; 3 Geo.IV (1822) c.27. The latter made 'more permanent provision' for such seamen at the port of Saint John by establishing a marine hospital for 'the care, cure, attendance, and support' of its seafaring patients and a pest house for the quarantine of those with infectious diseases. Overseers at other ports could send their sick and disabled seamen to Saint John if the duties paid at their ports exceeded local requirements and were transferred to the marine hospital's funds.

by the provincial executive.[37] In 1830 the justices were authorized to lease part of the St Andrews common for a local marine hospital.[38]

Among the other responsibilities of the overseers of the poor was the management of lunatics' estates to cover 'the reasonable charges of removing, and of keeping, maintaining and curing' them while sequestered (and if necessary restrained in chains) by the order of two justices of the peace, 'during such time only as such Lunacy or madness shall continue.'[39] In 1842 the sheriff charged the county for bedding and glass destroyed by two prisoners 'confined on account of Lunacy,' but recommended that the overseers of their parishes be made to refund the money: 'The Parishes, you are aware, can be assessed by your Worships, the County not without an Act of the Legislature.'[40] Once the provincial lunatic asylum was established at Portland (Saint John) the overseers were responsible to pay for the maintenance of inmates sent there from their parish and for the cost of transporting them to (and perhaps occasionally from) the asylum.[41] On at least one occasion sessions agreed to dip into county funds to pay a constable for taking a lunatic to the asylum, the man in question 'not belonging to any parish in the county.'[42] In 1845 the bench ordered all accounts for taking lunatics to the asylum to be paid out of county funds when the legislature refused to reimburse the parishes for this service.[43]

These various duties of the parish overseers were increasingly institutionalized over the first half of the nineteenth century. The char-

37. The justices protested the 'inconvenience' of this initiative and urged the government to appoint three of the poor house commissioners to the new commission: CCGS Sep 1826.

38. 10&11 Geo.IV (1830) c.11; see also PANB RS13/a/2, Odell to commissioners Hatch, Ker, and Jack, 28 Oct 1831.

39. 5 Geo.IV (1824) c.9.

40. PANB RS148/b/2/e, sheriff's report, CCGS Apr 1842.

41. A temporary provincial lunatic asylum was established at Saint John in 1837 (1 Vict. (1838) c.4 reimbursed the magistrates for their outlays) and provision was made for a permanent institution ten years later: 10 Vict. (1847) c.55.

42. CCGS Sep 1841.

43. CCGS Apr 1845. The St Andrews overseers had petitioned the province unsuccessfully for reimbursement of £38/9/3 expended in the past three years for conveying insane persons to the asylum: PANB RS345/b/4, 22 Feb 1844; JHA 1844, 100, 224.

acteristic institution was the work house, known by that name or as the poor house or alms house—whatever it was called, the function was the same.[44] An 1818 bill to provide for 'the erection of a poor House and Work House' at St Andrews to serve the whole county was not adopted. A second bill would have allowed the Charlotte justices to sell off part of the town common to pay for a poor house. After extensive amendments, it became an act to permit the justices to lease part of the common and put the proceeds to the use of the St Andrews parish poor.[45] In 1820 the justices in sessions ordered the St Andrews overseers to 'endeavour to hire a house suitable to keep the poor in.'[46] The following year a poor house was completed at the private expense of John Dunn and Christopher Scott, who vested its management in the rector, churchwardens, vestry, and overseers of the poor of the parish.[47] At the next session of the legislature a bill was introduced to incorporate the St Andrews poor house trustees but consideration was postponed until it could be read to the grand jury at sessions.[48] An act passed the following year providing for between five and seven commissioners (of whom no more than two could be justices of the

---

44. Saint John had such an institution before 1819, for in that year the legislature authorized the justices to assess the city £750 to replace one destroyed by fire; this proved insufficient and two further assessments had to be allowed: 59 Geo.III (1819) c.3; 60 Geo.III (1820) c.14; 2 Geo.IV (1821) c.1. The York county alms house was established at Fredericton in 1822: its commissioners, appointed by the justices in sessions, could compel the idle poor to live there 'and do all such work as they shall think them able and fit for.' The York commissioners could contract with the overseers of any parish in that or any adjoining county for the maintenance of their poor: 3 Geo.IV (1822) c.25. In 1838 the legislature declared the York model to have been 'found by experience to be less expensive than the general system ... and to be productive of industrious, sober and moral habits among that class of people' and therefore applicable to Saint John: 1 Vict. (1838) c.17. It does not appear that any Charlotte parish sent its poor to the York work house.

45. JHA 1818, 9, 11, 22, 29, 67, 77; PANB RS24 S26-B10; 58 Geo.III (1818) c.18. This initiative coincided with the first significant arrivals of impoverished Irish immigrants at St Andrews which heavily strained local resources: see further below.

46. CCGS Sep 1820.

47. *Royal Gazette*, Fredericton, 7 May 1822. Scott, a St Andrews merchant, later paid for the erection of a Presbyterian church and manse there: *Royal Gazette*, Fredericton, 9 Nov 1822.

48. JHA 1823, 32. The bill was introduced by Peter Stubs. There is no mention of it in the sessions minutes that year.

peace) to superintend and manage the institution, receive applicants for relief, compel the entry of idlers and beggars, and set the inmates to work, along with the other responsibilities of parish overseers. The commissioners had the discretion to 'inflict such correction and punishment' as they considered necessary on inmates who refused to work or otherwise misbehaved. The proceeds of the inmates' work were to be applied towards their support and maintenance.[49] The St Andrews poor house was supported by fines, local assessment, commons rents and, after 1828, a tax on dogs.[50] Sessions agreed to assess St Stephen for a parish poor house in 1845.[51] In 1858 the legislature authorized an expenditure of up to £1500 for the purpose and provided for commissioners, who were appointed the following year.[52] In 1866 St George parish was assessed $200 towards the erection or purchase of an alms house there.[53]

It is not clear how the St Andrews poor house was managed in its earliest years. By April 1831 sessions evidently thought there was something amiss for it appointed justices Hatheway, Ker, and Wyer 'to act in concert with the commissioners of the poor house to devise the most expedient method of providing for the poor of the parish ... and the government of the poor house and lot belonging thereto.' For the rest of the decade the membership of the poor house commission remained remarkably consistent (Appendix A.4).

49. 5 Geo.IV (1824) c.10. By 10&11 Geo.IV (1830) c.20, the justices and commissioners were authorized to establish a house of correction at the St Andrews poor house, 'wherein persons convicted of certain offences, and rogues and vagabonds, might be confined and kept at hard labour, instead of being imprisoned in the county gaol,' but they do not appear to have done so.

50. Note 16 above. Dog taxes for support of the parish poor were made available to county benches throughout the province by 9 Vict. (1846) c.14; the predecessor local acts were repealed by 10 Vict. (1847) c.10.

51. CCGS Apr 1845.

52. 21 Vict. (1858) c.56; PANB RS148/c/1/a, Grimmer to Hatch, 14 May 1859, addressing a dispute between the St Stephen magistrates and general sessions over the appointment of the commissioners once the alms house was completed.

53. CCGS Apr 1866. St George had had disproportionately high poor assessments for a number of years—in 1863 more than St Andrews and St Stephen combined—although its population was smaller than either. The reasons are unclear but probably had more to do with cumulative indebtedness arising from decades of tax arrears and collector delinquency than with unusually high pauperism in the parish or exceptionally generous outlays for relief.

Henry O'Neil, Thomas Sime,[54] and William Babcock—respectively a butcher, a baker, and a ship's chandler—served together continuously for nine years;[55] commission agent James Boyd joined them for the first four and general merchant Thomas Turner for the last six. They employed a manager to run the poor house and farm at £50 per annum.[56] In 1832, the commissioners reported a considerable reduction in the poor house debt, claiming that their efforts demonstrated 'that under proper management, the Farm and the Income of the Commons is sufficient to maintain the Poor of this Parish, unless attended with some extraordinary visitation.' Although some thought them hard, they had refused to relieve paupers outside the poor house as outdoor relief would 'create idleness and be highly injurious to the Parish.'[57] Among the additional efficiency measures they recommended was setting aside part of the poor house lot for burials, 'as the bringing to town, and other charges, is an expense that can be saved to the Parish.' They found the weekly cost of keeping a pauper to be two shillings and elevenpence three farthings. In concluding their report, they asked the justices to assess the parish £100 to pay off the remaining debt, 'which we trust will be the last assessment required for the supporting the Poor of this Parish.' It was not (Figure 10.1).

Like other offices the poor house commission offered its incumbents opportunities for both public service and commercial advantage. For example in 1836-7 William Babcock submitted his account for £15/4/6½ for a variety of goods including tea, trousers, pots,

---

54. Sime had been keeper of the county gaol through the 1820s and in that capacity billed £39 for boarding poor debtors between 1820 and 1828 (twelve debtors for a total of ninety eight weeks at 7/6 per week; the justices allowed him just £10/10/0): PANB RS148/e/5/h, account dated 20 Sep 1828.

55. Sime and Babcock owned adjoining properties on the bay side of Water Street; O'Neil's butcher shop was directly across the street.

56. He was allowed a live-in servant, the keeper being responsible for her wages and the commissioners for her board and lodging. PANB RS148/e/5/h, Morrison to Trenholm, 18 Apr 1836; ibid., Trenholm petition to sessions, 18 Apr 1836, with W.F.W. Owen's endorsement on reverse. Trenholm's predecessor as poor house manager had been dismissed by the commissioners in 1831: PANB RS148e/4/a.

57. In 1845 sessions refused to allow more than ten pounds for the support of any poor except those in the poor house, 'as they cannot see any necessity of supporting any outdoor paupers at all': CCGS Apr 1845.

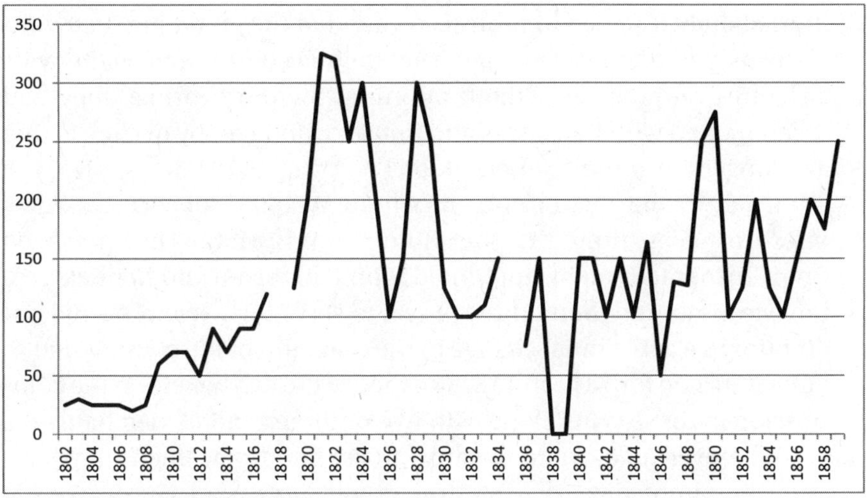

Figure 10.1 – St Andrews parish poor assessments, 1802-59

brooms, rope, cotton for a shroud, candles, brandy, fish oil, blankets, socks, meal, and window glass, taking in part payment a pig from the poor house farm valued at six shillings and threepence. The previous year he had billed £29/18/5 for a similar range of supplies.[58] In 1835 and 1836 the grand jury adjudged the poor accounts to be 'very correct and satisfactory,' which is not surprising as their foreman was William Babcock. In 1838 it approved the poor commissioners' 'correct and satisfactory accounts' showing a balance of £800 in favour of the parish, and recommended that the former assessment be refunded to the ratepayers.[59] No new assessment was ordered in that or the following year. The tax holiday was short-lived, however, and in April 1841 the grand jury declined even to review the poor accounts, recommending 'that an alteration be made in the appointment of the Overseers of the Poor—that no grocer be appointed to act as such Overseer, and that a change be made of at least two every year.'[60] Three of the commissioners—Sime, Turner, and O'Neil—

58. PANB RS148/e/5/h.
59. *Standard*, 12 May 1838.
60. PANB RS148/a/5/e/1/g, grand jury report, 19 Apr 1841. The principle of re-

immediately resigned in protest, saying that the grand jury had doubly censured them (first by ignoring their accounts, and again by its strictures on grocers) without affording them a hearing: they had 'been treated with harshness and injustice and hereby decline acting any longer as Commissioners of the Poor.'[61]

It fell to the magistrates, of whom William Babcock was now one,[62] to reconstitute the poor house commission. They prevailed upon Turner to remain, appointed John Parkinson, another baker, to replace Sime, and found three others to serve for a year. This did not amount to a substantial change in the make-up of the commission.[63] Sime returned for 1842 and 1843 so there were two bakers on the commission in those years along with two or three general merchants.

Whatever its attitude towards grocers and placemen may have been, the immediate cause of the grand jury's 1841 censure is not hard to discover. The eight hundred pounds surplus of 1838 had disappeared. In 1839 the commissioners petitioned the legislature for reimbursement of more than six hundred and fifty pounds expended on support of 'the transient poor'; by 1843 they were more than five hundred pounds in debt for the same reason.[64] As the local economy went into decline later in the decade, increasing the need for parish relief and reducing the ratepayers' ability to meet assessments, an influx of destitute emigrants—an 'extraordinary visitation' like that foreseen by the commissioners in their 1832 report—threatened to exhaust parish and county resources.

---

placing two commissioners each year had been ordered by the magistrates in 1837, 'with the view of interesting this Community more generally in the welfare of Public concerns' (CCGS Apr 1837) but it had not been followed.

61. PANB RS148/a/5/e/1/g, Sime et al. to Hatch, 24 Apr 1841.

62. Babcock was appointed fireward in 1839 and JP in 1840. He served in that capacity until moving to the United States in 1844 or 1845.

63. Turner and Lochary were merchants, as Babcock had been. Miles S. Hannah and Peter Smith had joined with Sime to petition the legislature for compensation following the collapse of the Charlotte County Savings Bank after Peter Stubs's defalcation: JHA 1837-8, p.17.

64. PANB RS344, petition of Sime et al., 31 Jan 1839; PANB RS345/b/3, petition of Chandler et al., 11 Jan 1843.

The transient poor

Local responsibility for the local poor was firmly established. But who was responsible for the transient poor who had no established claims on any community in the province?[65] The issue was first addressed by the legislature in the aftermath of the 1812-14 war when it appropriated nearly four hundred pounds to reimburse the Saint John overseers for their outlays on behalf of 'transient Poor and Black Refugees lately brought into the Province, and who remained in the City,' and another sixty pounds to the overseers of neighbouring Portland for their expenses in supporting disbanded soldiers. The following year the legislature granted £173/1/2 to reimburse the St Andrews overseers 'for money advanced by them, for medical aid and maintenance of distressed Emigrants from Ireland, thrown upon the Parish last fall, and for medical aid to seven families in St Andrews, reduced to sickness and distress, by receiving those diseased Emigrants into their houses, at the request of the Overseers of the Poor, and for the support of disabled Seamen in that Parish, as stated in their Petition, with vouchers accompanying the same.'[66]

This established a pattern of legislative grants to parish authorities for the relief of poor transients and immigrants, paid retroactively to cover previous outlays accounted for by the petitioning overseers. Table 10.1 lists such provincial appropriations to the St Andrews poor house commissioners by the year of the grant which in every case was to reimburse expenses incurred a year or more beforehand. Table 10.2 lists similar appropriations to other Charlotte county parishes, and Table 10.3 to individuals for similar purposes.

In the ten years 1836-45, the St Andrews overseers received more than four thousand pounds from provincial funds to cover relief costs for nonresidents. In 1838, the year of the eight hundred pound 'surplus,' almost a thousand pounds of provincial money had come from this source. The 'surplus,' and the two-year tax holiday that followed,

65. Impoverished transients might be jailed as vagrants under the colony's pass law. 26 Geo.III (1786) c.27 provided punishment for 'all idle and wandering persons, who shall not have a pass or testimonial from some Justice of the Peace, setting forth from whence such ... persons shall have come, and the place to which they are to pass...'

66. 57 Geo.III (1817) c.11, 58 Geo.III (1818) c.22.

Table 10.1 – Appropriations for emigrant relief, St Andrews

Year	Amount	Fund*	Act
1818	£173		58 Geo.III c.22
1820	89		60 Geo.III c.17
1821	113		2 Geo.IV c.24
1822	50		3 Geo.IV c.35
1823	66		4 Geo.IV c.32
1833	59		3 Wm.IV c.3
1834	124	•	4 Wm.IV c.3
1835	155	•	5 Wm.IV c.2
1836	443	•	7 Wm.IV c.3
1837	300	•	8 Wm.IV c.18
1838	991	•	1 Vict. c.4
1839	350	•	2 Vict. c.4
1840	376		3 Vict. c.59
1841	504	•	4 Vict. c.36
1842	383	•	5 Vict. c.37
1843	441	•	6 Vict. c.41
1844	150	•	7 Vict. c.45
1845†	150		8 Vict. c.83
1846	26	•	9 Vict. c.56
1847	41		10 Vict. c.49

* Emigrant Fund (see text).

† Grant to former commissioners of the poor.

Table 10.2 – Appropriations for emigrant relief, other parishes

Year	Parish	Amount	Fund*	Act
1823	Pennfield	£6		4 Geo.IV c.32
1836	St George	64	•	7 Wm.IV c.3
1838	St George	40	•	1 Vict. c.4
1838	St Stephen	75	•	1 Vict. c.4
1839	St George	20	•	2 Vict. c.4
1839	St Stephen	50	•	2 Vict. c.4
1840	St Patrick	17		3 Vict. c.59
1840	St Stephen	88		3 Vict. c.59
1841	St George	29		4 Vict. c.36
1841	St Stephen	110	•	4 Vict. c.36
1842	St George	46	•	5 Vict. c.37
1843	St Stephen	82	•	6 Vict. c.41
1844	St Stephen	45	•	7 Vict. c.45
1845	St Stephen	25	•	8 Vict. c.83
1848	St Patrick	10		11 Vict. c.5
1848	St George	109		11 Vict. c.7
1848	St Stephen	28		11 Vict. c.7
1849	St Stephen	35	•	12 Vict. c.33
1850	Pennfield	7		13 Vict. c.21

* Emigrant Fund (see text).

Table 10.3 – Appropriations for emigrant relief, individuals

Year	Recipient	Parish	Amount	Purpose	Act
1840	S Frye	St Andrews	£100	vaccination, medical attendance	3 Vict. c.59
1847	T Turner*	St Andrews	120	support sick & destitute emigrants	10 Vict. c.49
1847	J Orr	St Patrick	9	support a sick & destitute emigrant	10 Vict. c.49
1848	M Baldwin	St Andrews	20	widow of Hospital Island attendant	11 Vict. c.5
1848	M Tufts	St Andrews	20	widow of Hospital Island attendant	11 Vict. c.5
1848	J Boyd	St Andrews	50	charge of sick & distressed emigrants	11 Vict. c.7
1848	S T Gove	St Andrews	45	medical attendance	11 Vict. c.7
1848	S Frye (late)	St Andrews	130	medical attendance	11 Vict. c.7
1849	W McStay†	St Andrews	73	medical attendance	12 Vict. c.33
1849	S T Gove†	St Andrews	25	medical attendance	12 Vict. c.33
1849	E Bayard†	St Andrews	40	medical attendance	12 Vict. c.33
1849	J Boyd	St Andrews	150	Acting Emigration Agent	12 Vict. c.33
1850	J Boyd	St Andrews	75	Acting Emigration Agent	13 Vict. c.21
1850	S T Gove†	St Andrews	3	medical attendance	13 Vict. c.21

* St Andrews was to be assessed £110 to repay Turner's advances: 10 Vict. (1847) c.69.

† From emigrant fund.

represented a subsidy to local ratepayers who were relieved of the burden of paying for the local poor by a provincial subvention for destitute emigrants.

Various provincial schemes to attract and settle desirable British immigrants had been mooted from time to time. For example in 1816 the assembly voted a thousand pounds for assisted passages from Britain and Ireland. Legislation of 1820 empowered county-level committees to recommend immigrants of good character for location tickets.[67] There was substantial Irish immigration in the 1820s and 1830s: the *Standard* complained about fraudulent advertising by emigrant agents, quoting one Limerick pamphlet which claimed that from St Andrews, 'it is only a day's walk to Saint John's, Miramichi, Pictou or the United States.'[68] In 1840 the legislature awarded the North American Colonial Association of Ireland one hundred thousand acres of land for settlement.[69] But the mounting concern about Irish emigration had its origin, not in settlement schemes, but in worries over public health and public finance. In 1818 the St Andrews overseers told the legislature that owing to the 'extraordinary influx of Emigrants from Ireland' last season the parish had 'been incumbered with the maintenance of a Number of aged, feeble and diseased persons, and in some Instances whole Families, in a most wretched and distressed situation.' They sought reimbursement for their advances and recommended the passage of an act requiring emigrants to indemnify the parish at which they arrived, 'having found from Experience that a large proportion of those who possess the Means of removing, have gone to the United States, leaving behind only such as your petitioners have been obliged to provide for.'[70]

In 1827 the secretary of the Charlotte County Agricultural and Emigrant Society complained that the brig *William Henry*, 'owned

67. 56 Geo.III (1816) c.30; 60 Geo.III (1820) c.22, cont'd 3 Geo.IV (1822) c.10. The Charlotte justices advertised accordingly: *Herald*, 5 May 1820.

68. *Standard*, 19 Jun 1834.

69. 3 Vict. (1840) c.2. The lieutenant governor promoted the establishment of county emigration societies: PANB RS13/a/3, Odell circular to Sheriffs, 27 Jul 1841; ibid., Odell circular to Emigrant Societies, 24 Aug 1841.

70. PANB RS24 S26-P2. The overseers petitioned again the following year, 'that the continued influx of Emigrants principally from Ireland has thrown a great many distressed and sick persons on the Parish': PANB RS24 S27-P24.

by N Marks of St Stephen, but chartered by a Dublin House, arrived here last month with 250 Passengers (from Dublin), had no Surgeon, an insufficient supply of Provisions and bad water. Their sufferings were dreadful—of the number 39 are chargeable to the Parish, two have died and others are not considered out of danger.' A large proportion were 'of the most useless description, mere beggars, squalid, loathsome, dejected.'[71] In the 1830s several incidents of smallpox, cholera, typhoid fever, and other contagious ship-borne diseases at Saint John, St Andrews, and other port towns led to the establishment of local boards of health, quarantine regulations, and facilities for disinfecting ships and passengers.[72] By an act of 1832 passenger vessels from Great Britain and Ireland were to pay head money into an emigrant fund, 'to be expended by grants of the legislature towards relieving destitute and diseased passengers and emigrants and in assisting them to reach their several places of destination within the province.'[73]

At St Andrews the magistrates ordered infected vessels to anchorage away from the town.[74] When the provincial executive recommended that all ships arriving from Europe be placed under 24-hour

71. CO188-35, Stubs to Simonds, 1 Aug 1827.

72. At CCGS Apr 1793 the Charlotte magistrates upheld a grand jury presentment opposing smallpox innoculation. Later innoculation became the standard response to outbreaks: *Sentinel*, 10 Jun 1823; *Royal Gazette*, 24 Jun 1823, and see further below. The *Mars* was quarantined in 1821 after some smallpox-infected passengers had already disembarked: *Sentinel*, 25 Aug, 1 Sep 1821. The St Andrews magistrates fined the captain of the *Hibernia* £50 for landing passengers with smallpox in 1832: *Courier*, 16 Jun 1832. For the magistrates' management of a smallpox incident at St Stephen in 1859, see PANB MC243, file 'Political Correspondence and Papers, 1859.' Cholera was thought to have reached St Andrews on the *Susan*: *Courier*, 12 May 1832, copying *Courant*, 11 May 1832.

73. 2 Wm.IV (1832) c.36, providing for double head money on vessels that arrived without a certificate of fitness. Such certificates proved to be unobtainable in Britain and the provision was repealed when new Imperial regulations were enacted: 7 Vict. (1844) c.9. Four years later, in the face of the 'extremely burthensome' arrival of 'large numbers of destitute and diseased emigrants' the former act was suspended and replaced by more detailed and costly head money provisions: 11 Vict. (1848) c.10. Legislation in 1850 required vessels arriving from Europe to post bonds indemnifying the province against their passengers becoming a public charge: 13 Vict. (1850) c.3, s.5 and s.6.

74. CCGS Sep 1831.

quarantine to stop the spread of cholera, sessions struck a committee to complete the 'pest house' on Little Hardwood Island, a small island without fresh water a few miles from the town which was to become, as 'Hospital Island,' St Andrews' quarantine station.[75] Two years later the Charlotte board of health was convened to deal with a smallpox outbreak amid news of another cholera scare at Saint John.[76] The magistrates established committees in each parish and appointed visiting physicians to examine all vessels arriving at ports in the county. Dr McStay, visiting physician for St Andrews, advertised 'cholera medicine in small packages fit for families.' October 8 was declared a day of public fast and humiliation. In the newspaper that week, under the banner 'Health Secured,' James Boyd advertised his sole agency for Morrison's Vegetable Universal Medicine.[77] The provincial executive agreed to the local board of health's request for £150 to cover the emergency, emphasizing that the grant was without precedent and not contemplated by law. The board members were held personally accountable for the money.[78]

In the later 1830s and early 1840s when arriving emigrant ships brought health scares and demands for emergency relief the Charlotte magistrates held special sessions to revise the quarantine regulations and to order ships to Hospital Island on the advice of the visiting physician.[79] The commissioners of the poor at St Andrews and the overseers in other parishes regularly petitioned for and received reimbursements from the emigrant fund.[80] Provincial assistance was routine. In 1846, for example, when Wyer reported the arrival at St Andrews of a ship carrying smallpox, the provincial secretary directed deputy treasurer David W. Jack, as acting emigrant agent,[81] to seek an

75. PANB RS13/a/2, Odell to Hatch, 6 Apr 1832; CCGS Sep 1832. Hatheway was a member of the committee. The magistrates borrowed £200 to defray the cost of dealing with the cholera ship *Susan* and then met in special sessions to draw up quarantine regulations for the county: CCSS 2 Nov 1832.

76. *Standard,* 7 Aug, 25 Sep, 2, 9 Oct 1834.

77. *Standard,* 25 Sep, 9 Oct 1834.

78. PANB RS13/a/2, Odell to Wyer, 4 Sep 1834.

79. CCSS 21 Jan 1841; CCSS 21 May 1842; CCSS 12 Apr 1846.

80. Tables 10.1 and 10.2.

81. Jack had been serving in this unpaid capacity since 1841, making quarterly returns of passenger ship arrivals. When he asked to be paid for this task on top of

order from the magistrates to remove all infected persons to the quarantine station and to 'call on the Commissioners of the Poor to make the necessary provision for the medical care and comfortable accommodation of the sick,' promising to reimburse them upon receipt of their account. He also enquired about the availability of vaccine at St Andrews, sending a packet of lymph 'fresh from the pustule this day' to the visiting physicians.[82]

But by the time the *Elizabeth Grimmer* arrived barely a year later this system had broken down. The trouble began as early as 1842 when the St Andrews commissioners complained that although the legislature had appropriated almost four hundred pounds to reimburse them for supporting emigrants they had been unable to realize one shilling from the warrant in the hands of the provincial treasurer. More than sixty emigrants were in the poor house; the commissioners had no funds to pay for their keep; their provisions contractor was refusing advances until the previous year's bill was paid. The problem arose out of St Andrews' situation on the international boundary, making it 'an understood place of deposit for the wives and children of Emigrants, who, either from choice or necessity leave them here, while the Husbands and Fathers proceed elsewhere for employment.' The province's poor law never contemplated that the parish commissioners should take charge of distressed paupers who arrived upon their shores, although they had done so from charitable motives. If funds were not provided, they would 'be compelled, however reluctantly, to open the doors of the Alms House and expel from thence the present Emigrant inmates of the Establishment.'[83]

A year later, the commissioners petitioned again. The alms house was originally intended for the benefit of the parish poor but it had started to admit destitute emigrants about fifteen years previously

---

his ten per cent commission as deputy he was told that the emigrant agency was to be separated from the revenue department and someone else appointed: PANB RS345/b/3, Jack petition, 2 Feb 1843, and endorsement.

82. PANB RS13/a/5, Saunders to Jack, 18 Jun 1846; Saunders to Wyer, 18 Jun 1846; Saunders to Gove, 25 Jun 1846; Saunders to Frye, 27 Jun 1846.

83. The petition was endorsed by justices Wyer, Boyd, Garnett, and Hatheway: PANB RS7, vol. 115, 6 Jul 1842. A few days later the provincial treasurer was instructed to pay the commissioners £383/4/6 'out of the first monies in the Treasury': PANB RS13/a/3, Odell to Prov. Treas., 11 Jul 1842.

on the understanding that the province would repay their expenses. The poor house would be self-supporting with commons rents and a small local assessment were it not for the numbers of emigrant poor and the long delays in receiving provincial grants. 'The effect has been to enhance the prices of supplies, occasion frequent assessments, and produce general dissatisfaction among the parishioners.' The commissioners were now five hundred pounds in debt. They received no compensation for duties which had become so onerous that they could no longer perform them without neglecting their private businesses. It was time to separate the emigrant from the parish poor. Emigrant paupers should be placed in a separate establishment 'under the exclusive control of suitable persons to be appointed for that purpose.' Alternatively funds should be placed at the hands of the commissioners to repay advances as they accrued. The present system was unendurable, and unless it was changed no more emigrants would be admitted to the poor house.[84]

The matter came to a head at general sessions the following year. The magistrates refused to pass the poor commissioners' requisitions unless they accounted for the parish poor separately from the emigrant poor. Then they divided on a resolution, 'That the Magistrates do not feel authorized to assess the Parish of St Andrews for the support of the Emigrant Poor.' Five justices voted in favour; Wyer alone voted against and William Babcock abstained. Next came a vote to reconsider the St Andrews parish list. On a similar division the old poor house commissioners were ousted and the justices appointed replacements. After passing a £100 poor assessment, sessions resolved to put the poor house up for tender to 'the highest and most suitable persons capable of taking charge of the same for the term of three years *for the support of the Poor of said Parish.*'[85] The policy of

84. PANB RS345/b/1, 11 Jan 1843.

85. CCGS Apr 1844, emphasis supplied. CCGS Sep 1847 ordered the renewal of the lease. The lessee received five shillings a week for each pauper inmate along with the proceeds of the farm. He was responsible for clothing and bedding, but not for maintaining the buildings. In January 1849 there were ten inmates. Despite the justices' order of April 1845 that no more than £10 per year be expended on outdoor relief the commissioners were supporting 39 individuals in 11 families outside the poor house: CCGS Apr 1845; CCGS Sep 1847; PANB RS346/i, Report of Asa Coy, Jan 1849 [Coy Report].

the sessions resolutions was essentially the same as that of the commissioners' 1843 petition: there should be a strict separation of parish and emigrant poor, physically, fiscally, and administratively.

One immediate consequence of these decisions was that they left the ousted commissioners without any means of reimbursement for their personal outlays. The provincial treasurer refused to pay them the appropriation because they were out of office.[86] They sued the county, obtaining a rule nisi to assess the parish, but the justices retained counsel to show cause against them 'on the grounds that accounts furnished are unsatisfactory extravagant and illegal.'[87] A partial resolution came at next April sessions, which allowed a balance of about one hundred and sixty pounds to the former commissioners and assessed the parish accordingly.[88] When sessions refused their petition for more they turned to the legislature, saying that the magistrates had rejected their appeal 'on the ground that they were not by law bound to provide for expenses and outlays incurred in the maintenance of Emigrant Poor, but for Parish Poor only.'[89] They asked for more than one hundred and ninety pounds but were voted only fifty pounds 'in full of all claims.'[90] They persisted, petitioning the legislature again in 1847 for almost two hundred and fifty pounds to reimburse Thomas Turner for money expended in 1842, 1843, and 1844.[91] This produced a further grant of one hundred and twenty pounds along with an order for a special assessment on the parish of St Andrews to repay the balance of Turner's advances.[92]

The larger issues of who was to be responsible for emigrant paupers and how to pay for them were still not resolved. Then as news of the impending arrival of the *Elizabeth Grimmer* and other emigrant ships reached St Andrews the magistrates asked the commissioners of the poor whether they intended to take charge of sick and destitute arrivals. When they replied that it was entirely out of their power

86. PANB RS13/27/c.

87. CCGS Sep 1844; Wyer, Wilson, and Hatheway were appointed to oversee this litigation.

88. CCGS Apr 1845.

89. PANB RS345/b/6, 27 Jan 1846.

90. 8 Vict. (1845) c.83.

91. PANB RS345/b/7, 26 Jan 1847.

92. 10 Vict. (1847) c.49; 10 Vict. (1847) c.69.

to do so the magistrates applied to the province for emergency assistance.[93] The government's response merely reiterated the unsatisfactory status quo:[94]

> The Overseers of the Poor being the legal guardians of the Poor, it will devolve on these Officers in their respective Parishes where Emigrants may arrive to make the necessary disbursements and on the transmission of their Accounts of all charges legitimately incurred they will be duly paid.

But when the commissioners of the poor nevertheless refused to have anything to do with the emigrants, the magistrates struck a committee to look after them. Hatheway summarized the year's statistics: 270 sick emigrants had arrived at St Andrews, of whom forty had died. Three of the town's inhabitants, including Dr Frye, had died of fever while attending the sick.[95] By October, the emigration season well over, the magistrates were providing hospital care in town for the few sick immigrants who remained. If there was now little sickness, there was still much destitution. Many of the men went looking for work in the United States leaving their families behind. David Jack reported that 'much distress at present therefore prevails among the Emigrants and besides the daily calls upon families for relief, street begging prevails to a greater extent than I have witnessed for many a year.'[96]

The railroad navvies

By the late 1840s, when the potato famine and estate clearances were depopulating Ireland and high American head taxes were diverting U.S.-bound emigrants to British North American ports, the New Brunswick economy was seriously stressed. Crop failures were immiserating farmers and inflating food prices; the forest industry was

93. PANB RS555/b/2/e, Commissioners of Poor to Justices Hatch, Wyer, Wilson, and Ker, 21 May 1847; ibid., Wyer et al. to Prov. Secty., 21 May 1847.

94. PANB RS13/a/5, Prov. Secty. to Hatch et al., 25 May 1847.

95. PANB RS555/b/2/c, Hatheway to Prov. Secty., 27 Jan 1848. At the time of his death, Frye was chairman of the agricultural society and president of the Charlotte County Bank.

96. PANB RS555/b/2/1, Jack to Prov. Secty., 21 Oct 1847.

in cyclical decline; money was scarce and bankruptcies high.[97] As early as 1842 the Charlotte magistrates met in special sessions to consider the distressed state of the rural economy.[98] In 1845 the county agricultural society advised the government that the potato crop had failed and grain crops were attacked by rust and rot.[99] The magistrates estimated that there would be barely a bushel of potatoes per inhabitant, 'and in consequence of the very high price of bread stuffs great distress will ensue in the County.' Anticipating hardship they reduced the commons rents for the duration. The destruction by fire of a rope walk and a ship under construction at St Andrews further increased unemployment in the town.[100]

There was one bright star on Charlotte county's economic horizon however. The St Andrews & Quebec Railroad, enthusiastically promoted for many years by John Wilson, seemed at last to be becoming a reality. G.N. Smith and C.R. Hatheway had completed a preliminary survey from St Andrews to the Canadian border in 1834. Detailed surveys followed, legislation was procured in both provinces, a London board was established, stock was optioned, and by the spring of 1847 construction was about to begin. The president of the London board, Earl FitzWilliam, decided to combine the interests of his Irish landholdings and his New Brunswick company by clearing out his tenants and shipping them to St Andrews to build the railroad. He told Wilson to expect one hundred navvies to arrive by the ship *Star* in the spring of 1848. FitzWilliam promised to purchase enough stock in the company to cover their wages for twelve weeks' work at two shillings and sixpence local currency per day.[101]

---

97. For a brief survey of historians' views about the impact of recession on Charlotte County in the late 1840s, see Campbell, 'Smashers,' 95.

98. PANB RS148/a/2/b/8; CCSS 27 Jul 1842. The meeting was called in response to a government circular (PANB RS13/a/3, Odell to Clerks of Peace, 18 Jul 1842) aimed at 'ascertaining the real condition of the people' and asking whether the magistrates were able to guarantee funds to be raised at the county level. The Charlotte justices replied that they had no funds at their disposal and suggested the immediate issue of by-road and other warrants, 'the expenditure of which amounts, would greatly alleviate the suffering that now exists.'

99. PANB RS13/2/24, Frye to Prov. Secty., 21 Jan 1845. A provincial grant to make repayable loans and distribute seed potatoes followed: CCGS Sep 1845.

100. CCSS, 8 Dec 1845; Coy Report.

101. Ibid.

In the mean time the provincial government was casting about for a solution to the emigrant supervision problem. It turned to James Boyd, who had (or claimed to have had) taken on the whole burden of the emigrant ships arriving at St Andrews the previous year. Boyd had offended imperial sensibilities with his criticism of British port officials for clearing the *Elizabeth Grimmer* to sail, occasioning an investigation and a stiff reprimand from the colonial secretary. But he had dealt with the situation on the ground quite efficiently, 'getting rid,' as he put it, of many of the destitute by advancing them small sums for passage to Eastport and Boston.[102] In May 1848 the provincial secretary asked Boyd, 'In case there be necessity for the services of some person to take charge of Emigrants at St Andrews this season, ... whether you could have any objections to discharge such duties as may devolve on you in that capacity.'[103] When Boyd agreed he was advised that should the *Star* arrive at St Andrews before council approved his appointment he should act 'as far as may be necessary under the circumstances.'[104]

We first encountered James Boyd as captain of the St Andrews Rifles, sent to put down apprehended riots at Campobello in the last days of David Owen, and then as one of C.R. Hatheway's accusers in the wake of the Spearman affair. He took credit for breaking Hatheway as a magistrate in 1832 and tried to keep him from a surveyor general's deputation in 1843.[105] An auctioneer and commission merchant, he had been one of the poor commissioners for several years in the early 1830s and town clerk in 1833. He won the by-election

102. For Boyd's criticism, the investigation and the reprimand, PANB RS555/b/2/2, despatches from Earl Grey, 3 Nov 1847, 10 Nov 1847, Boyd to Jack, 7 Dec 1847, Jack to Prov. Secty., 7 Dec 1847; PANB RS 13/a/6, Ramsay to Wolcott, 22 Feb 1848, Prov. Secty. to Boyd, 15 Apr 1848, Boyd to Prov. Secty., 20 Apr 1848. Unrepentant, Boyd promised in the last that, 'should it be my lot again to have anything to do in the care and management of Emigrants, I will take care to have sufficient proof to substantiate any charges I may have to make.' For Boyd's activity on the ground, PANB RS555/b/2/2, Boyd to Prov. Secty., 22 Jul 1847.

103. PANB RS13/a/6, Prov. Secty. to Boyd, 12 May 1848.

104. Ibid., 23 May 1848. Boyd's appointment as 'acting emigration officer' was confirmed a few days later, 'with the understanding that the remuneration to be received will depend on the amount of services which you shall have performed in the opinion of the Legislature': ibid., 31 May 1848.

105. Chapters 4 and 5 respectively.

for Wyer's vacated seat in 1843 and was re-elected to the assembly in 1847.[106] In 1845 he became a justice of the peace. Boyd's emergence as St Andrews emigration officer in 1848 was to have profound repercussions for the local magistracy and county politics. He was a leading opponent of the Wyer-centred junto that had dominated St Andrews affairs since its founding. It was entirely predictable that he should fall out with the majority of the local bench whose role in managing the *Star* crisis was deeply compromised by its connections with the railroad company and its support for the poor commissioners' refusal to relieve the emigrants. As the split between Boyd and his fellow magistrates deepened, the stage was set for the failing junto's last grasp at power.

The *Star* arrived off St Andrews on Sunday afternoon, May 28. When Edwin Bayard, the visiting physician appointed by sessions, went to the ship the following morning he found three hundred and seventy-five passengers on board, twenty-two of them sick with typhus; nine others had died on the voyage. He reported to the magistrates, who issued a quarantine order and instructed him to visit the ship at Hospital Island and take charge of landing the passengers and cleaning the vessel. The following day, however, as Bayard set off for the island he met James Boyd who told him that he had taken charge as Emigration Officer, that he had appointed doctors Gove and McStay to look after the emigrants, and that the magistrates had nothing further to do in the matter.[107] The magistrates immediately objected to Fredericton that Boyd was defying their authority under the infectious diseases act and the county quarantine regulations. Boyd's actions were causing 'great confusion and embarrassment.'[108] Anticipating this protest Boyd argued that he had to take immediate action, 'more particularly as Magisterial bodies move slowly,' and claimed that the magistrates' 'jealousy arises particularly from the circumstance that Dr Bayard is connected by marriage in the family of John Wilson Esq, ... and his friends express a strong anxiety

106. Chapter 9.

107. PANB RS148/a/6, Bayard to magistrates, 29 May 1848.

108. PANB RS148/a/6, St Andrews magistrates to Saunders, 2 Jun 1848. The letter was signed by justices Hatch, Wyer, Wilson, Street, Ker, and Hatheway.

to find employment for him on that account.'[109] The government denied the magistrates' request to constitute a board of health and told Boyd that 'the whole of the duties connected with Emigration and the care of the sick will devolve upon you.'[110]

The *Star* passengers were all landed on Hospital Island by June 3. There were six new cases of fever and four more deaths. Further embarrassment and confusion arose when Boyd and the magistrates sent conflicting orders to the ship's captain. By June 5, fifty-nine emigrants had been hospitalized with fever and dysentery and one more had died. Many others were being sent to a landing prepared by the railway company for their reception. Boyd complained that 'they are a most desparate band to manage ... They are very foul in their persons ... There are quite a number of old people, who I am afraid will be chargeable for a long time.' To add to his troubles a group of widows and orphaned children arrived from Saint John: 'I am beset with them night and morning; and to get rid of them have paid the passages of several of them across the River to the American side ... I had either to do so or maintain them, as the Commissioners of the Poor would do nothing for them.'[111]

As soon as Boyd had reported the refusal of the poor house commissioners to provide for the emigrants the government had referred the question to the crown law officers.[112] They reported that it was beyond doubt that the parish officials 'are bound to look after and take charge of all poor—being indigent paupers—whether natives or emigrants ... and to afford them such relief as their necessities may require.'[113] On the face of it, this would seem to conflict with the government's direction that Boyd was to have exclusive control of the *Star* emigrants. In transmitting the opinion to the St Andrews poor commissioners, Saunders stressed that the lieutenant governor did not 'wish or expect that you should take special charge of the Emigrants as such, but he desires that you should be informed of what the Law

109. PANB RS555/b/2/2, Boyd to Saunders, 31 May 1848.

110. PANB RS13/a/6, Saunders to Boyd, 2 Jun 1848; ibid., Saunders to Wyer, 3 Jun 1848.

111. PANB RS555/b/3/b/3, Boyd to Saunders, 5 Jun 1848.

112. PANB RS13/a/6, Saunders to law officers, 2 Jun 1848.

113. PANB RS555/b2/2, Report of the law officers, 6 Jun 1848.

requires of you in cases of urgent necessity and complete destitution, whether of Emigrants or others.'[114]

The government had also asked for a report on the dispute between Boyd and the magistrates over the appointment of a visiting physician. The attorney general having given his opinion that the magistrates had the statutory authority they claimed, the government asked Boyd to 'co-operate cordially' with them.[115] A memorandum prepared by or for the lieutenant governor reveals the executive's view of the matter:[116]

> McStay is a Catholic and has practised in St Andrews for very many years. Bayard has only recently come there. For these reasons (& the Emigrants being all Catholic) perhaps Mr Boyd deemed it best to employ him—this however is mere conjecture. Dr Bayard may be the most skilful of the two, and the Magistrates have the right to appoint—provided they take charge of the Emigrants, or rather that the Overseers of the Poor take charge of them—if the Magistrates insist on their legal rights and are willing to take the responsibility.

In the mean time, several of the sick had been transferred to a makeshift infirmary at O'Neil's farm near the railway works. Boyd's idea of cordial co-operation is apparent in a note he sent to Wellington Hatch on June 12: 'Understanding that the Magistrates or some part of them have authorized Dr Bayard to attend to the sick at O'Neils, I wish you as Clerk of the Peace to inform those gentlemen that I conceive their interference with my duties a very improper one, and an interference that I will not submit to.'[117] Bayard complained to the magistrates that 'Dr McStay has for three days successively visited the sick at ONeils and administered medicines to them after I had been there and ordered medicine for the patients—if an immediate stop is not put to this interference I must resign all further charge of the patients . . . It is really trifling with the lives of individuals and plac-

114. PANB RS13/a/6, Saunders to Overseers, 10 Jun 1848.

115. PANB RS148/a/6, attorney general's opinion, 9 Jun 1848; ibid., Saunders to Boyd, 9 Jun 1848. Saunders also sent the opinion to the magistrates and asked them to co-operate cordially with Boyd: PANB RS13/a/6, 10 Jun 1848.

116. PANB RS342/a/4 (n.d.).

117. PANB RS148/a/6, Boyd to Hatch, 12 Jun 1848.

ing my professional reputation at stake.'[118] Boyd assured the government that he would endeavour in future to get along with the magistrates, 'although I am aware I shall find it a difficult task.' He continued:[119]

> If these Gentlemen had been actuated in the first instance by a desire to perform their public duties (and I speak advisedly) and not allowed themselves, some from personal pique, some from disappointment at my being invested with the authority that I have been, no difficulty would have happened.

For their part, the magistrates advised that they 'should be most happy to act cordially with Mr Boyd as Emigrant Agent, but we are impressed with the idea that this cannot be done, as Mr Boyd and Dr McStay lately appointed are Magistrates, and upon any discussion with reference to the quarantine law we are apprehensive of collision which would be embarrassing and which would render meetings of the Magistrates doubtful.' Moreover, 'the expenses have been greatly increased by two parties acting in opposition to each other.'[120]

The magistrates' letter also complained that the railway company had to supply provisions to emigrants who 'from debility' were unable to work. In the letter as transmitted they wrote, 'It is quite inconvenient for the Company to continue this charity, and, therefore, we ask, where are we to look for means to defray the daily expences that must necessarily arise ... ' A surviving draft, signed by all six justices, has 'they' instead of 'we' in both places, pointing up the close identification between the magistrates (especially Hatch and Wilson, who were officers of the company) and the railway.[121] Nevertheless, the magistrates did seem to have the law on their side. They regretted that the attorney general had considered only section 6 of the infectious distempers act,[122] which provided for the appointment of vis-

118. PANB RS555/b/2/c, Bayard to magistrates, 12 Jun 1848.

119. PANB RS555/b/2/b/3, Boyd to Saunders, 13 Jun 1848.

120. PANB RS148/a/6, Magistrates to government, 13 Jun 1848, signed by justices Hatch, Wyer, Wilson, Hatheway, Ker, and Street. Nevertheless, by June 15 Boyd and the justices had come to an accommodation whereby Dr McStay was to remain at Hospital Island while Dr Bayard was to have charge of thirty-six sick emigrants at the railway station: PANB RS555/b/2/c, Boyd to Sauders, 15 Jun 1848.

121. The draft and final versions are both in PANB RS148/a/6.

122. 1 Wm.IV (1831) c.40.

iting physicians. The magistrates relied as well on section 7, which authorized three or more justices to order the landing, management, and release of passengers on quarantined vessels. In their view, which was certainly not inconsistent with that provision, 'under the law, the Magistrates are bound to provide for them, until released from quarantine.' The government at Fredericton never responded to this assertion which, if upheld, would have undermined its delegation of responsibility for the emigrants to Boyd.

By mid-July both Dr Bayard and Dr Gove had caught the fever. Dr McStay was in permanent attendance at Hospital Island so neither the residents of St Andrews nor the emigrants landed there and at O'Neil's farm had access to a physician. James Boyd had also come down with the fever,[123] leaving his son Kempt in charge of the emigrants.[124] The magistrates arranged with the surgeon of a visiting naval vessel to help in the emergency. Dr McStay decided to leave the quarantine station: Boyd *fils* surmised he was afraid of the fever.[125] By the end of the month Boyd was convalescent although still dyspeptic and feeling 'as one just risen from the dead.' Although 'suffering the most excruciating torment from piles,' he was preparing to bring his accounts to Fredericton. Forty sick emigrants remained: 'I am heartily tired of them.' Kempt had managed them remarkably well and was 'as capable in detecting impostures as I could have been.'[126]

By the end of the month Boyd could report that he was 'getting rid of the Emigrants very fast.' There were fourteen left on Hospital Island, three or four of whom were not expected to live, and fourteen at O'Neil's farm 'or Rail Road Hospital,' nine with typhus, one con-

123. Harris Hatch blamed 'this fellow' Boyd for the spread of fever by preventing the magistrates from enforcing quarantine and by his 'constant communication' with the sick at Hospital Island and O'Neil's farm: PANB RS555/b/2/c, Hatch to Saunders, 1 Jul 1848.

124. James Kempt Boyd, the eldest of at least six sons, died at Los Angeles in 1861 aged 39.

125. PANB RS555/b/2/c, J.K. Boyd to Saunders, 21 Jul 1848.

126. 'Thirteen days deprived of my reason and brought to the lowest stage of existence, for four days my life was despaired of . . . I was down thirty days; since I was allowed to sit up and go out a little I have mended very fast, but such is the disordered state of my Bowels that they require much watching': PANB RS13/15/b/7, Boyd to Fulton, 25 Jul 1848. Robert Fulton was a clerk in the provincial secretary's office.

valescing, 'and four complaining.' In all there had been twenty-two deaths, two of them hired attendants on the island.[127] Boyd brought his accounts in at the beginning of August, hoping for early payment to cover his advances. As soon as he returned to St Andrews he removed the remaining emigrants from Hospital Island and had the buildings scrubbed and boarded up. Eleven sick and five convalescing remained at O'Neil's: 'I think I shall finally get rid of the sick in a month.'[128]

By mid-September the 'Rail Road Hospital' was empty but Boyd still had charge of thirty-three widows and orphans for whom he budgeted two shillings and sixpence per week each.[129] He announced that he intended to send them all to the poor house despite the commissioners' objections:[130]

> They complain that they have not the means of supporting them, even though an assessment should be ordered at the September Sessions. The difficulty of collecting it at a period of such great depression is so apparent that I do not think myself it could be collected. Our Tradesmen and Labourers have little or nothing to do at present, therefore money could not be got from them. In the event of their going to the Poor House, the expense would be double what I am now allowing them.

Sessions approved Dr Bayard's account against the province but made no provision for an assessment.[131]

The St Andrews railway company had expected to receive one hundred Irish labourers fit to work on the road for twelve weeks. 'But to our surprise,' as John Wilson wrote, 'with the one hundred men

127. PANB RS555/b/2/c, Boyd to Partelow, 27 Jul 1848. The legislature voted £20 each to Margaret Baldwin and Margaret Tufts whose husbands had died of typhus fever while attending emigrants at Hospital Island, St Andrews: 11 Vict. (1848) c.5.

128. PANB RS555/b/2/c/2, Boyd to Partelow, 7 Aug 1848.

129. According to receipts in PANB RS555/b/2/b/3, the railroad company paid £6 rent for O'Neil's farm to Aug 1 and also paid for carpentry, building supplies, 'sundries for sick emigrants,' water transport, meat, bread, and a coffin.

130. PANB RS555/b/2/b/3, Boyd to Partelow, 12 Sep 1848.

131. Bayard requested prompt payment, 'as being a young man just commencing the world, and having been ill for several weeks with Fever contracted during my attendance upon the Emigrants, I require all the means I can collect': PANB RS555/b/2/c, Bayard to Partelow, 20 Sep 1848.

sent out were two hundred and seventy seven old men, women, and children, and the whole afflicted with sickness, death, and poverty.'[132] The St Andrews directors were not blameless. They had done little to prepare for the *Star*'s arrival. Too few shanties had been built to accommodate the labourers, let alone their families. Some were crowded into sheds, others into rented rooms around St Andrews. 'Nearly all are very miserably provided for and the destitution of some beyond description. Widows with small children, husbands with sick wives, &c. ... With these unfortunate Emigrants the R R Company have a hard bargain.'[133] Some of the men petitioned for land and DLS Mahood was assigned to locate them pending council approval.[134] Margaret Jones petitioned from St Andrews for relief. She had been sent to the province by Earl FitzWilliam with her husband and six children. Her husband had died of ship fever, her oldest child had scarlet fever, and she was destitute. When she applied for admission to the poor house she was turned away although the commissioners offered to send her and her children to Eastport.[135]

In early January 1849 the railway company informed Boyd that it had supplied employment for Earl FitzWilliam's emigrants for twice as long as originally agreed and that 'owing to the inclemency of the weather and unproductiveness of their work at this season, the Company cannot think of maintaining them any longer.' The company wished to know when the Emigrant Officer would be pleased to take charge of them.[136] Advised of this application, the government maintained that Boyd's appointment had ended at the close of the emigrant season. 'The persons referred to, in His Excellency's opinion, differ in no respect from other poor, and if destitute the responsibility of relieving them will fall on the Overseers of the Poor, and on the local funds.'[137] The provincial secretary informed the railway company that while the lieutenant governor regretted the condition of

132. PANB RS555/b/2/b/3, Wilson to Coy, 21 Jan 1849.

133. PANB RS555/b/2/b/3, Coy to Partelow, 11 Jan 1849.

134. PANB RS13/2, Hatch to Prov. Secty., 4 Aug 1848; PANB RS13/a/6, Partelow to Hatch, 9 Aug 1848.

135. PANB RS346/b, Petitions, 1849.

136. PANB RS555/b/2/b/3, J.H. Whitlock to Boyd, 2 Jan 1849.

137. PANB RS13/a/6, Partelow to Boyd, 10 Jan 1849. The letter was copied to the poor commissioners.

these unfortunate people, 'it does not appear to His Excellency that they can properly be considered as "Emigrants" at the present time in such a sense as to throw them on the Provincial funds.'[138]

It was in these circumstances that the government appointed Asa Coy, a Fredericton attorney, to investigate conditions at St Andrews including the state of the parish finances. He found that the poor commission's annual income, independent of assessments, amounted to about £140 in commons rents 'not very punctually paid,' £4 in dog tax, and £10 in fines. The parish had been assessed £100 in 1848, all of which was collected, but almost all the proceeds went to pay off the previous year's outstanding balance. The working commissioner was paid £10 for his services and small amounts were expended on law charges and in 'assisting indigent persons to remove from the County.' The commissioners had recently had to borrow £80 from the Charlotte County Bank to pay the keeper of the alms house and to provide for outdoor paupers, whose number was rapidly increasing. There were privations in the countryside and beggars in the streets of St Andrews. 'These circumstances, added to the general depression in Mercantile business in which St Andrews deeply participates, warrant the opinion, which was pressed upon me, that a Parish Assessment could not be levied if ordered.' Turning next to the circumstances of the seventy-nine *Star* emigrants who were about to be discharged by the railway company, Coy concluded 'with regret' that there could be little doubt that many of them would have to be supported by public funds. Though this was unfortunate, neither the railway company nor the local officials could be blamed.[139]

Boyd, as was his way, took a different view. The railroad company had 'misstated facts' about the terms of the engagement with Earl FitzWilliam. Despite its claims the company was never out of pocket when the men were unwell because Boyd took charge of all the sick. The company had drawn on FitzWilliam for £1165/13/0 but paid out only £925 in wages. It claimed to have urged the men to leave for the United States when their three months was up but in fact had encouraged them to stay, assuring them of employment through the winter. Some difficulty arose and the men stopped work, but they

138. Ibid., Partelow to Whitlock, 10 Jan 1849.
139. Coy Report.

were employed again and had behaved themselves ever since:[140]

> While writing, I am this moment surrounded by the whole tribe of the Rail Road men, who complain that this morning they were put on half time and this coupled with the inclemency of the weather will not allow them to work much more than three half days in the week. These people are really in a most deplorable situation scarcely half clad and many of them with families of from six to ten Children and all they could earn even if employed full time deducting losses for bad weather is scarcely sufficient to provide them with the coarsest description of food to say nothing of Shoes and other clothing, there are but four Shanties built for them to live in consequently a great number are living in hired Rooms the rent of which they will be unable to pay.

It was true that the local commissioners of the poor had neither money nor credit, and there was no work to be had in St Andrews. Were he to be placed in charge and given £150 to spend over the winter, Boyd suggested, it would be more economical and a greater saving to the province than to hand them over to the poor commissioners under the terms of their contract with the alms house keeper. 'If I am to do anything for them I can make all the necessary arrangements before I leave for Head Quarters and my son can manage the men under my directions from time to time.'

Boyd left for Fredericton to attend the legislature. In February he sent forty overcoats and a hundred pairs of shoes to be distributed by Kempt among the *Star* emigrants.[141] A month later the railroad company discharged the last of them. The magistrates endorsed a petition for location tickets and a year's advances or transportation to Canada West: the government allowed £50 from the emigrant fund 'for immediate relief without any pledge for the future.'[142] Justices Ker, Street, and McStay pleaded with the lieutenant governor for aid: 'There are now about two hundred and fifty persons, including women and children, who are completely destitute, and rambling about the streets, almost in a state of starvation, and are now threatening, if they are

140. PANB RS555/b/2/b/3, Boyd to Partelow, 'Private,' 15 Jan 1849.
141. PANB RS555/b/2/b/3, J.K. Boyd to J. Boyd, 21 Feb 1849.
142. PANB RS346/j, 31 Mar 1849.

not relieved, to plunder the Inhabitants.'[143] Upon Boyd's return to St Andrews to attend April sessions he was 'surrounded by the half famished Emigrants . . . Some of them grow quite turbulent, I however soon put a stop to that. Something more must be done for them or they really will starve. They are sitting about in groups in the most extreme distress . . .'[144]

The provincial government paid out dribs and drabs to Boyd, £25 here and £30 there, all the while imposing conditions—that relief be given as much as possible in exchange for work, that by-road grants be used to create employment for the emigrants—which were impossible to meet in the circumstances. Boyd found some work for them in making a road through the commons and in deepening a sewer, but it was far from enough: 'These people I shall change every third day in order to afford all a share of employment.'[145] Fearful that giving cash to the emigrants, no matter how small the amounts, was leading the town's 'hucksters and petty shop keepers' to encourage them to remain, Boyd struck upon a new plan. He used the government's latest grant to buy a ton and a half of Indian meal at Eastport and distributed seven pounds of it to each individual along with a small quantity of molasses as a week's allowance. 'This course has raised some considerable outcry against me, but I saw no other way of getting rid of them.'[146] When this did not suffice he promoted a new scheme: that the government advance £150 to pay for passages to Boston or other American ports. Any emigrant who refused to go would forfeit further relief. The amount might be repaid eventu-

143. PANB RS555/b/2/b/3, Ker et al. to Head, 4 Apr 1849.

144. PANB RS555/b/2/2, Boyd to Partelow, 'Private,' 14 Apr 1849. His official letter (ibid., 16 Apr 1849) was to similar effect: sessions had voted to raise £400 to relieve the poor, 'and from all appearances shall have to make another assessment in September.' The sessions minutes give the St Andrews assessment as £250. Boyd attended only the last two days, after the assessments had been decided. There was no second assessment. In September the collector of rates was ordered to pay Boyd £4/8/9 'for his expenses in going to Fredericton to request the Govt to advance a sum of money to send out of the County the Emigrants by the Star': CCGS Sep 1849.

145. PANB RS555/b/2/2, Boyd to Partelow, 16 Apr 1849; PANB RS13/a/6, Partelow to Boyd, 23 Apr 1849; PANB RS 555/b/2/2, Boyd to Partelow, 27 Apr 1849.

146. Ibid., and PANB RS555/b/2/b/3, Schedule of relief given to Star Immigrants, 29 Apr 1849, listing quantities of meal and molasses for each family. For cornmeal as a deterrent form of poor relief elsewhere, Fingard, 'Winter's Tale.'

ally by an assessment on St Andrews, although not at present 'owing to the poverty of the inhabitants and the almost total stagnation of business.' In the mean time Boyd reduced the weekly allowance of meal.[147] It did not take the government long to respond: Boyd's proposal to pay passages to the U.S. could not be entertained and there would be no further provision for the *Star* emigrants' relief after May 29, the anniversary of their arrival.[148] Then, on May 12, the barque *Susan* arrived off St Andrews.

The idle, worthless, and dissipated

The *Susan* made two trips to St Andrews in the service of emptying Irish poor houses, one in May 1849 and the other in September 1850.[149] One hundred and nine passengers arrived in 1849 (one born on the voyage) of whom all but seven were so miserably poor as to meet Boyd's stringent standard for relief. They received meal and molasses. Although they were in good health Boyd decided to keep them at Hospital Island, 'as the owners of houses in the town will not let them in when they have no money.' Most were women and children; few spoke English.

The remaining *Star* emigrants were still in town. In his letter reporting the arrival of the *Susan* Boyd asked again that 'something be done to get them away,' as he was having 'a hard time with them but have managed to keep them in pretty good subjection.' The government notice that there was to be no further support arrived before he sealed the letter so he added a postscript acknowledging its receipt and undertaking to show it to the 'local authorities' the next day.[150] The St Andrews magistrates held a special meeting and again resolved to petition the government for aid. It was to no avail: 'The Emigrant fund has already borne a charge at least equal to the justice of the case, and His Excellency and the Council are of opinion that the liability of the Commissioners of the Poor of St Andrews must be held

147. PANB RS555/b/2/b/3, Boyd to Partelow, 7 May 1849.

148. PANB RS13/a/6, Partelow to Boyd, 9 May 1849.

149. Likely a different vessel than the 1832 cholera ship of the same name.

150. PANB RS555/b/2/b/3, Boyd to Partelow, 12 May 1849.

such as to enforce on them the consequences of any neglect to give legal relief.'[151]

The government paid off Boyd for his services as emigrant agent[152] and the following spring, just before the season opened, appointed Charlotte sheriff Thomas Jones as assistant emigration officer for St Andrews.[153] Several ships were expected. Jones inspected the decaying facilities on Hospital Island and pressed for repairs and improvements.[154] He called on the overseers of the poor, warning them that he had no funds to support destitute emigrants should any arrive: 'I have reason to believe that it is the intention of the Government to enforce the performance of that duty from you.'[155] They immediately repudiated his advice: 'We do not intend to assume what we conceive to be the duty of the Emigration Officer.' The legislature had established the emigrant fund; the parochial authorities had no control over it; the responsibility lay with the government. The poor assessment was insufficient to provide even for the local poor, so the commissioners 'most positively decline being burdened with the destitute of two or three cargoes of Emigrants' unless funds were provided.[156]

On September 23 the *Susan* arrived with eighty paupers from the Cork Union workhouse and a draft worth seventy pounds currency for their support. Twenty seven were seriously ill, many nearly blind from eye infections caught during the voyage. Jones hired a house in town for a temporary hospital, engaged a nurse, and procured medical attendance, supplies, and provisions. Fifteen had come out under contract to the railway but only one of them was actually em-

151. PANB RS13/a/6, Partelow to Hatch, 12 Jun 1849.

152. PANB RS13/a/6, Partelow to Boyd, 24 Jul 1849

153. PANB RS555/b/2/3, Perley to Jones, 18 Apr 1850. Unlike Boyd, who had communicated directly with the provincial secretary, Jones reported to provincial emigration agent Moses Perley at Saint John.

154. Boyd had been waiting for instructions about improvements at Hospital Island. The legislature had appropriated £150 from the Emigrant Fund for badly needed repairs and new construction there, but as late as May 1850 the warrant had not been issued: 12 Vict. (1849) c.33; PANB RS555/b/2/c/2, Kelly to Partelow, 15 May 1850, enclosing Thomas Jones's detailed account of the state of the facility.

155. PANB RS555/b/2/3, Jones to Overseers, 23 Aug 1850.

156. Ibid., Ker, O'Neil, Stevenson, Lochary, and Dimock to Jones, 23 Aug 1850.

ployed and he was soon in the hospital, his ankle crushed by a railroad wagon.[157] Jones had to pay for the funeral of another. Two more were expected to die. By mid-November the seventy pounds had been long spent. Endorsing his request for additional funds, Saint John emigrant agent Moses Perley noted that Jones 'has also had to advance for sick and destitute emigrants of last year, transferred to him by Mr Boyd.'[158] Perley suggested that any money expended might be charged back to the Cork workhouse guardians; the government, however, in authorizing a warrant for £100 to attend to the emigrants' 'urgent wants,' warned that, 'If they are in the opinion of the Law Officers persons the burthen of whose maintenance should by law be defrayed by the Parish and not from the Emigrant fund the Attorney General will be instructed to enforce any future claim against the Parish Officers.'[159]

According to Jones's annual report, three emigrant ships had arrived at St Andrews. The first carried a few 'young women of respectable appearance' who had been sent for by relatives and found homes immediately after landing. The second carried poor Irish destined for the United States: they had been duped by a dishonest shipping agent who told them that St Andrews was 'within a stone's throw' of New York. Jones arranged for those who had funds to be transferred directly from the ship to a vessel he hired at their expense to carry them to an American port. The rest disembarked at St Andrews where they remained until remittances arrived or they had earned enough to cross the border. The exceptions were two women with several children for whom he paid passage 'to prevent them becoming chargeable for the whole winter' and six others who had hired themselves out as servants and remained in the county.

Those who arrived by the *Susan* were a different matter. About half were active young men and women who soon found employment, but the rest mostly 'Do-No-Goods of a large city, idle, worthless and dissipated, ... the worst description of immigrants that ever came to this port.'[160] Jones was personally out of pocket more than

157. PANB RS555/b/2/c/2, Jones to Perley, 29 Mar 1851.
158. PANB RS555/b/2/b/3, Perley to Partelow, 16 Nov 1850.
159. PANB RS555/b/2/3, Prov. Secty. to Perley, 21 Nov 1850.
160. Ibid., Jones to Perley, 31 Dec 1850.

two hundred and thirty pounds on their account and he hoped that the government would make some allowance over and above these expenses, 'for the loss of time, trouble, expense, and responsibility' incurred in supervising the repairs to Hospital Island and managing so many sick and destitute emigrants.[161]

By mid-September 1851 there were still six Cork Union emigrants in hospital at St Andrews, who would 'probably be a public charge as long as they live.' The government told Jones to do nothing for them after September 23, the anniversary of their landing, and the magistrates that it was against the law 'to treat as Emigrants persons who have been in the province twelve months.'[162] Conflict over who was to pay for offshore paupers continued intermittently for the rest of the decade. In 1852, when the owners of a passenger ship refused to pay the visiting physician's bill on the ground that there was no law making them liable for the cost of inspection, the St Andrews magistrates could find no authority for charging it to the county and wrote to the provincial secretary and the Saint John emigrant agent for instructions. They received no reply. The following year, faced with a boycott of ship inspections by the St Andrews medical fraternity, the lieutenant governor decided that the doctors could be paid out of the emigrant fund.[163] Friction with the railway company also continued:[164]

> Two children, Stephen and Lawrence Gaynor, have been [chargeable to the Province] from December to the end of April, when I found persons willing to take them off my hands. They were frostbitten and otherwise sick most of the winter.

---

161. PANB RS555/b/2/c/2, Jones to Perley, 29 Mar 1851. By 1858 he was entitled to an annual salary as assistant emigration officer at St Andrews, but it was payable only in the event of emigrant arrivals: PANB RS 13/a/10, Tilley to Jones, 29 May 1858.

162. PANB RS555/b/2/b/3, Perley to Partelow, 12 Sep 1851; PANB RS13/a/7, Partelow to Jones, 15 Sep 1851; ibid., Partelow to W Hatch, 15 Sep 1851.

163. PANB RS555/b/2/c, Kelly to Partelow, 20 Jun 1853, and endorsement; PANB RS13/a/7, Partelow to Perley, 24 Jun 1853, indicating that 'visits of medical men for quarantine purposes of an ordinary kind connected with emigrants' were to be paid for by the county but where no provision was made the charge could be paid from the emigrant fund; ibid., Partelow to Hatch, 24 Jun 1853, demanding to know why the county has not provided for payment of visiting physicians per 13 Vict. (1850) c.30.

164. PANB RS555/b/2/3, Jones to Perley, 26 May 1854.

> Their father, an old man, could obtain no kind of employment from the 19th Feb'y to 28th March, after that period he occasionally was employed, when I reduced his rate of boarding from 11/3 to 6/ per week. Goggin with the two Doyles and Sullivan were similarly situated, with this difference, that Doyle was injured on the Rail Road and Sullivan was badly frozen. All these people would have proceeded to Quebec had they not been induced to remain [at St Andrews] with the expectation of finding permanent work on the Rail Road.

By the late 1850s wrangling among the parish overseers, the county, and the province over responsibility for destitute emigrants had spilled over to St Stephen. In November 1857, the overseers there submitted their detailed account of £39/10/0 expended on behalf of David Caughie. It began with tea, sugar, soap, and barley furnished in June 1856, continued through oatmeal, molasses, and matches in the summer and fall, proceeded to castor oil, tincture of opium, and Holloway's ointment in the winter, and ended in February with medical attendance, coffin, grave-digger's fee, hearse rental, and shroud.[165] Provincial secretary Tilley returned the account to the local deputy treasurer: 'there is no proof whatever before the Government that David Caughie was really an Emigrant ...'[166] The overseers supplied a certificate showing him to have really been an emigrant, which Tilley found satisfactory—'but there are at present no funds at the disposal of the Government.'[167] At last, in January 1859, the government agreed to reimburse the parish on account of Caughie 'so far as may be deemed reasonable and just.'[168]

As for the local poor, the 1850s were business as usual. There were now just three overseers or poor house commissioners, elected by the ratepayers at a town meeting subject to sessions approval. Their names were different, but their backgrounds, policies, and practices seem to have been much the same. In 1851 alms house keeper James McCarty reported twelve inmates, seven of them Irish-born.[169]

165. PANB RS555/b/2/f/1, Account sworn by Lawrence Ryder, 18 Feb 1857.

166. PANB RS13/a/10, Tilley to Watson, 12 Dec 1857.

167. Ibid., Tilley to Overseers, 28 May 1858.

168. Ibid., Tilley to Grimmer, 27 Jan 1859.

169. R.F. Fellows, *Census, 1851*. Only three of the Irish-born inmates had arrived in the province after 1840.

By 1857 the commissioners were lamenting the 'very decayed condition' of the poor house and farm—'the piggeries and sheds are all rotten and blown down . . . The fire ladders are also unsafe'[170]—but in 1859 the magistrates again prohibited outdoor relief in St Andrews except on medical grounds. The following year they resolved that groceries for the poor house, along with doctors' visits and medicine, must be put to tender and the lowest bid accepted. The same order the following year provided expressly that none of the overseers was to enter a bid. Three years later, after having to tell the outgoing overseers to hand over 'all the books papers and monies appertaining to the poor house' to their successors, sessions issued a still more detailed order that 'flour and meal, meat whether fresh or salted, dry and pickled fish, groceries, dry goods, boots and shoes, and all other articles of whatsoever nature or kind for the use of the indoor and outdoor paupers in the parish of St Andrews, be procured by the commissioners . . . by public competition and further that no person being a commissioner as aforesaid shall be a competitor for any of the articles required for the use of the said paupers.'[171] In April 1867, on the eve of Confederation, the justices in general sessions assessed St Andrews seven hundred dollars for the use of the poor, issued a support order in a bastardy case, petitioned for an amendment to the commons lease legislation, and rated the dog tax on Grand Manan at one dollar per year.[172]

The junto's last stand

When the first of our three ships, the *Elizabeth Grimmer*, arrived at St Andrews in May 1847, the magistrates had appointed James Boyd, C.R. Hatheway, and James W. Street to supervise its cargo of sick and destitute Irish emigrants. Hatheway's petition to be paid for his services was passed over in silence by the 1848 legislative committee on emigrant appropriations but it voted fifty pounds to Boyd, who

170. PANB RS148/e/4/a, Poor Commissioners' report, 16 Apr 1857.

171. CCGS Apr 1859, Apr 1860, Apr 1861, Apr 1862, Apr 1864. The St Stephen poor house commissioners were also ordered to tender for supplies: CCGS Apr 1862.

172. CCGS Apr 1867.

claimed to have taken the whole burden on his own shoulders.[173] The following year Hatheway petitioned again, claiming to have been much occupied with emigrant affairs in the summer of 1847 'when the duty was extremely onerous and attended with great personal danger.' He pointed out the grant to Boyd and requested compensation for his own efforts.[174] J.W. Street also petitioned, complaining that although his account for twenty-five pounds had been approved by the magistrates in 1848 and submitted along with Boyd's, he had not been paid.[175] The legislative committee to which the Hatheway and Street claims were referred reported against them on the ground that their services were of the sort 'usually performed gratuitously.'[176] The only Charlotte member of the 1848 and 1849 select committees on emigrant appropriations was James Boyd.

Intermittent sniping between Boyd and the St Andrews junto occurred throughout the famine immigration crisis and continued after Wyer's death in 1849. Wyer's complaint that Boyd was causing embarrassment and confusion and Harris Hatch's, that 'this fellow' was preventing the magistrates from enforcing the law, have already been cited. Alongside their strictures about Boyd's role as emigrant agent they mounted an attack on his membership in the commission of the peace. As the junto sought to recapture its weakening grip on county affairs, personal enmities reflected structural realignments in community power. Behind the competition for resources and the conflict-

---

173. JHA 1848, 9 (committee constituted); 92 (petition referred); 292 (bill #111 reported). The emigrant appopriations bill, which included Boyd's £50, was enacted as 11 Vict. (1848) c.7.

174. PANB RS346/b, Hatheway petition, 25 Jan 1849. Along with membership of the committee to find housing for the *Elizabeth Grimmer* emigrants, attendance at several meetings of the magistrates, and sponsorship of two petitions to constitute a board of health, Hatheway had hosted a special sessions at his office in July 1847 to order the brig *James* into quarantine and attended another a few days later to release the vessel, so there was at least some foundation for his claim: PANB RS148/a/6, 7 and 12 Jul 1847. He cited the statistical summary of emigrant arrivals he had sent the government in January 1848 as additional evidence of his activity.

175. PANB RS346/i, Street petition, 1 Feb 1849. Boyd's and Street's accounts had been certified at a special meeting of the magistrates held 31 Jul 1847: PANB RS148/a/1. A month later the provincial secretary advised Boyd that a warrant had issued in favour of both of them: PANB RS13/a/6, Saunders to Boyd, 26 Aug 1847.

176. JHA 1849, 260-1.

ing personal agendas lay an accelerating shift in the locus of control from the county (dominated as it still was by the St Andrews magistrates) to the provincial government. Emigrant arrivals in the 1830s and early 1840s had been managed by parish officers under the supervision of the county bench although the provincial government, and the emigrant fund in particular, paid the tab. The executive's attempt to download the cost of emigrant support to the parish in the face of unprecedentedly needy arrivals foundered on the shoals of fiscal incapacity, but in its grudging acceptance of responsibility for short-term emergency relief the government at Fredericton took away from the local officials their authority for managing the emigrant poor, delegating it at first on an ad hoc (and likely illegal) basis to Boyd and then assigning it in more regular bureaucratic fashion to the provincial emigrant agent and his local assistants. The selection of Thomas Jones, who as high sheriff represented the executive authority of the lieutenant governor in the county, was symbolically appropriate.[177] That he and his predecessor as emigrant officer had long been identified with opposition to the St Andrews junto was no less symbolic and their appointment surely no accident. The junto was not about to take this lying down.

In November 1849, in the midst of the emigrant crisis, fifty-three Charlotte freeholders complained to the lieutenant governor that justices Boyd and Ker were withholding public funds and 'that there are many other degrading charges made against the above named Justice Boyd in a paper called the *Charlotte Gazette* ... which your Petitioners have no reason to disbelieve, and if true would tend to bring the Magistracy into contempt.' The complaint about Ker did not amount to anything, but those against Boyd led the government to call on the county bench for a full investigation.[178] The justices held eleven days of hearings in December 1849 and January 1850.[179]

---

177. At one point Jones applied for the vacant post of immigration officer at Saint John but withdrew his name upon learning that there was to be no imperial grant for the post: PANB RS346/j, Jones to Prov. Secty., 25 Jun 1855.

178. PANB RS13/27/c/1849, Petitions, 7 Nov 1849; PANB RS13/A/6, Partelow to W Hatch, 4 Dec 1849. On December 10, Hatch published a notice in the *Standard* calling a special sessions for December 29: 'All the Justices are requested to attend and all the parties concerned.'

179. CCGS Apr 1850; CCGS Sep 1850. I have been unable to find minutes or other

Along with the complaint about withheld fines there was a panoply of charges against Boyd: discouraging a constituent from establishing a hay scale in competition with his own; profiteering in his former position as emigrant officer; misconduct in office as Grand Manan packet commissioner; combining the offices of prosecutor and judge in a liquor case. There were almost certainly other charges as well but the issues of the *Charlotte Gazette* in which they appeared have not survived and all that remains as evidence is Boyd's attempted rebuttals in private correspondence and, more significantly, in several issues of the St Andrews *Standard*. What caught the attention and concern of the provincial executive, though, was not so much the charges themselves—for the most part they were petty and politically motivated—but the extraordinarily vituperative and vindictive tenor of Boyd's (and his son's) responses to them in the public press. Just as in the Gilbert Ruggles–Warren Hatheway affair of the 1820s, Boyd's flamboyant public utterances were incompatible with his gravitas as a magistrate.

The *Charlotte Gazette* was a St Andrews weekly published since 1846 by John McLachlan. McLachlan had arrived in the province from Scotland in 1825, about twenty-five years of age.[180] Seven years later he was elected a director of the Charlotte County Bank[181] and appointed to the magistracy. He was omitted from the commission of the peace in 1845, when Boyd and J.W. Street were appointed. It is not clear why the government decided to remove McLachlan. There was a petition against him for issuing an execution on a judgment despite a stay of proceedings pending appeal,[182] but when McLachlan asked the executive why he had lost his commission the only answer he received was that it had nothing to do with that complaint.[183] There were no other particulars in the petition, but it did refer darkly to

---

notes of these hearings, which were almost certainly held *in camera*.

180. NB Census, 1851.

181. *Courier*, 12 May 1832.

182. PANB RS7, vol. 106, Daniel J. Morrison petition, 10 Mar 1845.

183. PANB RG8 (Magistrates), McLachlan to Reade, 7 May 1845; Reade to McLachlan, 10 May 1845; McLachan to Colebrooke, 20 May 1845 (in this letter, protesting his removal from the commission without a hearing, McLachlan told the lieutenant governor that his father had been thirty years in the Navy and served at Trafalgar and Copenhagen); RS13/a/4, Reade to McLachlan, 22 May 1845.

McLachlan's 'notoriously intemperate habits,' saying that 'his whole character and conduct are such as to bring into disgrace and contempt the office of magistrate.'

As the Boyds' jibes make plain, McLachlan's public image was sullied not just because he was a drinking man but also by his real or imagined relations with his black housekeeper, referred to by Boyd *fils* as 'Phebe.'[184] J.K. Boyd openly portrayed McLachlan as a violent drunkard and Phebe as his 'sable Dulcinea' or 'sooty satellite' or 'poor negro wench.'[185] The overt racism of Kempt's published attacks on McLachlan was broadly hinted at in his father's repeated epithets. In James Boyd's letters to the *Standard* the editor of the *Charlotte Gazette* was 'sooty Jack,' 'Black Jack,' 'filthy,' and 'dirty.'[186] McLachlan's relationship with Phebe had put him beyond the pale. 'It is well known that no person in the community who has any regard for his own standing, will admit the Editor into his domestic circle. From such society he has long been a banished man. Indeed he has arrived at that pitch when man ceases to be a man, and is now become a mere butt for the boys ...' Perhaps this is why McLachlan's name was left out of the 1845 commission of the peace.

Boyd's *ad hominem* defence against the *Charlotte Gazette*'s charges extended to all his accusers. Andrew Elliot, the town clerk who had criticized Boyd's conduct of liquor cases, was motivated by 'his own ugly, vindictive spirit ... I ought not to notice such vermin.'[187] Former alms house commmissioner John Bradford, who complained that Boyd had used his authority as magistrate to pre-

184. J.K. Boyd correspondence, *Standard*, 10 Oct 1849. In this sketch, Boyd imagines an argument between McLachlan and Phebe in the back garden of McLachlan's house. There was a later legend recounted in 1910 by R.E. Armstrong that this house was haunted by the ghost of the housekeeper who had burned to death within its walls. 'After the tragedy McLachlan deserted the house and for years it stood alone and abandoned upon the mountain side.' ('History of Journalism in St Andrews,' *St Croix Courier*, 27 Jan 1910. I am grateful to David Sullivan of St Andrews for a copy of this source.) When the census of 1851 was taken McLachlan was living as a lodger in the home of wheelwright Robert Alexander. The only woman enumerated in the house was Alexander's wife Margaret.

185. *Standard*, 3 and 10 Oct 1849.

186. *Standard*, 3, 10 Oct 1849. These were Boyd's second and third replies to the *Charlotte Gazette*; his first, in the *Standard* for 26 Sep 1849, has not survived.

187. Ibid.

vent him from erecting a set of hay scales in competition with Boyd's, 'has many good points, but when he mixes himself up with such a miserable, worthless drunken wretch as John McLachlan, he must be prepared to take what those get who lie down with dogs.'[188] Hatheway came in for two helpings of obloquy. Boyd junior, recounting McLachlan's attempt to have him bound to keep the peace after he had threatened 'to so handle him that a certain dingy intimate of his should find it difficult to recognize him,' had this to say:[189]

> On the next day, Justice Hatheway sent a constable to me, politely inviting me to come to his office and find sureties of the peace toward the Editor of the Gazette.
>
> This was mighty like Mrs. Bond in the old song, crying to the ducks, 'Dilly, dilly, dilly, come and be killed.' So thought I, and I waited upon Mr Hatheway to tell him that I demanded an examination before two Justices, thanking him at the same time for what I ignorantly supposed was his courtesy. He refused this, unless I would take upon me to assure him beforehand that I could controvert the statements made by Mr McLachlan in his affadavit. He read to me the complaint, in which the Editor insinuates that I had concealed weapons, and that, being afraid to meet his prowess fairly, I would take undue advantage to injure him. I again refused to find sureties on those terms, and on Saturday morning Mr Hatheway came to me and asked me to go to his office. There I found the Ethiopian Editor; and Mr Hatheway very modestly proposed to go into an examination among ourselves three. But I had heard that it was unsafe to go to a certain warm country to hold lawsuits with its ruler, and conceiving that such would be my predicament if I consented, I again refused, except I might have an examination before two Justices. Mr Hatheway, strong in the law, issued a warrant for my apprehension. This warrant I at once obeyed, and entered into the requisite sureties before Mr Justice Ker, not choosing to have my liberty restrained for so long a period as Messrs Hatheway and McLachlan would have inflicted upon me.

188. Ibid., 3 Oct 1849.
189. J.K. Boyd correspondence, *Standard*, 3 Oct 1849.

In comparison Boyd senior's observation, published in the same issue of the *Standard*, that Hatheway 'made himself somewhat conspicuous in the matter' of the hay scales, seems almost benign. In private, James Boyd was more forthcoming:[190]

> I lay the whole blame on C.R. Hatheway Esq. This gentleman has been hostile to me since the commencing his career in this place as a Magistrate, [I] having been one amongst others of the most respectable people then in this town [who were] compelled to make a complaint of his conduct to Sir Archibald Campbell during his administration of the Government and for which Mr H was deprived of his commission, but some years afterwards restored on the petition of Messrs Hatch, Wyer, Ker and others of the then Magistrates and none have had more cause to regret his reappointment than Messrs Hatch and Ker and which they now openly acknowledge.[191]

Hatheway, he reported, had engineered the revelation about Boyd's withheld fines, having been 'pimping round the constables to get information as to what monies had been collected,' and arranged for an intoxicated McLachlan to be present in the sessions room when the matter came up. 'The Justices present at the time exonerated Mr K and myself from all censure and there I supposed the matter would have rested, but on the appearance of the Gazette paper the next week out came a falsified [account] of the affair and amongst other things charging us with having corruptly withheld County and Parish monies, and to which I was foolish enough to reply.'

The November 1849 petition referred to charges appearing in four October issues of the *Charlotte Gazette*. Boyd's admission that he had made a mistake in answering them came in private correspondence with the provincial secretary. Characteristically, Boyd defended himself by attacking the petitioners:[192]

---

190. PANB RS7, vol. 107, Boyd to Partelow, 'Private,' 15 Dec 1849.

191. Although there was some tension at the time between Hatch and Hatheway over who was to succeed to the colonelcy of the Charlotte militia when Hatch retired, the trouble was short-lived and in 1855 Hatch recommended Hatheway for promotion to the Common Pleas because he wanted another St Andrews JCP to join him on the ICCP bench: PANB RS7, Hatch to Tilley, 30 Mar 1855.

192. Ibid.

> The notorious William Eills who signs at the head of the petition is a would be candidate for the next Election, and who a few years since was tried for an attempt to commit a Highway Robbery and Murder and who only escaped by the ingenuity of Counsel, he it is who went round with the petition and after two days trial he succeeded in getting his friend Fitzgerald and another miserable being by the name of Fauls (who has been frequently through my court) to sign it, his next step was to go to St Stephen and there not one person would sign it, from there to two other parishes, where he succeeded in getting three more, and at last was compelled to send to his own neighbourhood, where by bullying lying and other false pretences he [got] some parties to sign.

In his official response to the petition, Boyd claimed that he had made several applications to Harris Hatch as senior magistrate for an investigation of the complaints against him but he and justice Wilson were afraid to comply because to do so would encourage McLachlan to 'commence heaping abuse' on them. Boyd understood that the justices had written to the attorney general asking to be 'excused from such a delicate duty' and to have an independent commissioner appointed. 'They need have no delicacy so far as I am concerned. I court the most rigid scrutiny, and trust that the Magistrates of the County will be directed to attend to their duty, so that I may be relieved from such foul and scandalous charges.'[193]

The executive had already directed the clerk of the peace to call a special sessions to investigate the petitioners' charges, having first confirmed the authorship of the newspaper correspondence.[194] Before the investigation could commence, more charges came to light. Edward Snell, the contractor for the weekly mail boat running between St Andrews, Campobello, and Grand Manan, came to Hatheway to swear out a deposition against Boyd.[195] The legislature had appropriated one hundred pounds for the Grand Manan packet and

193. Ibid., Boyd to Partelow, 15 Dec 1849. (Another letter of the same date as the one marked 'Private.')

194. PANB RS13/a/6, Partelow to W Hatch, 4 Dec 1849. This letter and the text of the petition were published together in the *Standard,* 9 Dec 1849; the signatories were identified in the 26 Dec 1849 issue.

195. PANB RS7, vol. 107, Snell deposition, 18 Dec 1849.

appointed Boyd and John Farmer as commissioners. By his contract Snell was entitled to quarterly payments. He applied to Boyd for the money twice but was given various reasons why he had not yet received it. In the interim, Boyd offered to advance funds at ten per cent interest per month. 'I told him I could not take much at that rate, but I wanted ten dollars to pay one of my men; this amount he gave me on my promise to pay him eleven dollars when I received my quarterly payment.' Three weeks later, when the provincial money arrived, Boyd took eleven of the twenty-five pounds to satisfy Snell's debt, charging him two and a half per cent commission on the balance. When the next due date arrived, Snell went to Boyd for his money and was again told that he had nothing in hand. Snell believed, although he could not prove, that Boyd had been using the packet money for private speculations in flour and other imported goods. He asked the government for redress because he needed the money and a lawsuit would mean delay and uncertainty.

The government sent a copy of Snell's complaint to Boyd and directed him to produce receipts for his payments.[196] Boyd's response was first to deny Snell's version of the facts and then to explain them away. Snell was the 'dupe of designing men.' His attorney, R.M. Andrews, used to be Boyd's friend until he 'attempted a gross imposition by an inflated bill of costs.' As for Hatheway, 'every man in the County of Charlotte knows that I never had a greater enemy. He has never been known to let slip an opportunity for annoying me. I have charged him with acting corruptly as a magistrate, and no wonder that he is anxious to drag me into the same pit with himself.'[197] Assuring Snell that Boyd had not yet received the first quarterly payment when Snell requested it and that he had applied a few days early for the second payment, the government decided that there was insufficient cause for it to interfere.[198]

By now, the magistrates' investigation was well under way. As it

196. PANB RS13/a/6, Partelow to Boyd, 27 Dec 1849.

197. PANB RS13/54/c, Boyd to Partelow, 1 Dec 1850. Boyd surmised that he had given offence by refusing to permit Snell to use the packet to smuggle rum from Eastport to Grand Manan where Hatheway intended to treat the island militia and so to influence them against Hatch.

198. PANB RS13/a/6, Partelow to Snell, 9 Jan 1850.

proceeded more charges emerged, most particularly that Boyd had bought a round of drinks in an unlicensed tavern, informed against its proprietor, and prosecuted him before himself. After eleven days of hearings the justices reached their conclusion and communicated it to the lieutenant governor.[199] A numerously-signed petition, headed by R.M. Andrews and transmitted by B.R. Fitzgerald, called for Boyd's removal from the magistracy, asserting that he had been shown to have been 'in the habit of peculating the County and Parish monies,' that he had made unlawful charges for his services, that he had falsified his records, and that his arbitrary, violent, and vindictive conduct 'tended to bring the Magistracy into contempt, and lessen that body in public confidence.'[200] Boyd was beside himself. '[T]he whole was a deep laid scheme to destroy my character and thereby my popularity in the County.'[201] By now April general sessions was approaching and the government still had not acted. Boyd was in Fredericton for the sitting of the legislature but he wrote to the grand jury in St Andrews undertaking to prosecute eight of the witnesses against him for perjury.. The justices pressed the lieutenant governor for a decision as Boyd's appearance at general sessions would place them in a 'false and inconvenient position.'[202] The letter in the provincial secretary's files is endorsed, 'Mr Boyd has resigned his seat. New commission.'

In fact Boyd had resigned before the letter was even written. His scribbled note on a torn half-sheet of paper, stating only 'I hereby tender my resignation of my seat on the Bench in the County of Charlotte,' was dated April 1, 1850.[203] The following day, lieutenant governor Head reported to the executive council that he had met with Boyd to communicate council's conclusion: not all the charges had been maintained, the motives of some of the parties may have been questionable, but 'upon the whole they think enough was established to show that Mr Boyd cannot, with advantage to the public service or satisfaction to himself retain his position on the Bench as a Mag-

199. Boyd and the petitioners were represented by counsel: *Standard*, 30 Jan 1850.

200. PANB RS346, Petitions, n.d.; PANB RS13, Fitzgerald to Partelow, 24 Jan 1850.

201. PANB RS13/54/c/1850, Boyd to Partelow, 28 Mar 1850.

202. CCGS Apr 1850; PANB RS13/54/c/1850, Wilson to Lt. Gov., 11 Apr 1850.

203. PANB RS7, vol. 96, Boyd resignation.

istrate.' It would be preferable that he should resign but otherwise, 'however painful to his own feelings,' the lieutenant governor should have to act. Boyd thereupon tendered his resignation and Head accepted it.[204]

But this was not the end of the matter. In September, sessions complained to the government that Boyd had still not paid over the fines he had been found to have retained.[205] Boyd also memorialized the government saying he had resigned from the magistracy out of frustration and now regretted it. He had tried to prosecute the witnesses against him for perjury but at the September circuit court judge Parker was doubtful that the magistrates' investigation had the power to take sworn testimony. In October Boyd consulted the attorney general and on his advice brought one of the witnesses before justice Ker, 'where the complaint was fully sustained.' The attorney general came to St Andrews and after examining the depositions taken by Ker told Boyd it was no use proceeding further because there could be no conviction for false swearing before such a tribunal as the magistrates' investigation. Boyd entreated the government to restore him to the county bench, 'not that I have any wish or desire to exercise any functions as such, but that my enemies may know that they have not accomplished all their object.'[206]

In the mean time, Boyd found himself in trouble on the electoral front. When he told the House that 'penny papers were doing more harm than good by propagating unsound principles,' he was met by this response:[207]

> The honest members of the Assembly have nothing to fear from the press; only such men as Mr Boyd, who was recently tried by a special commission at St Andrews for embezzling the public funds, need fear and tremble. If one half of the allegations contained in the Charlotte Gazette against this member

---

204. PANB RS6, minutes, 2 Jan 1850.

205. CCGS Sep 1850; PANB RS13/54/c, copy of resolution transmitted by W Hatch. Boyd does not appear to have paid over the money before December 1851: PANB RS13/a/7, Partelow to Boyd, 31 Dec 1851.

206. PANB RS13/54/c, Boyd to Lt. Gov., n.d.

207. *Standard*, 27 Mar 1850, copying *New Brunswicker* report of 'Legislative Doings' for March 21, quoting William End (debate on newspaper postage rates).

> be true, he should at once be stripped of his Magisterial honours and sentenced to condign punishment.

At the general election in June 1850 he was narrowly defeated for the fourth Charlotte seat by B.R. Fitzgerald. Boyd pressed for a scrutiny (there were only seven votes between them) but for the time being he was out of office. He was finally seated in place of Fitzgerald in March 1853—and promptly petitioned for and was awarded the travel and incidental expenses he would have received had he been in the House all along. A few days later he asked again to be reinstated in the magistracy but was told that a resignation, once accepted, could not be withdrawn.[208] Boyd kept his seat in the upset election of June 1854 and topped the Charlotte polls in July 1856, and then again applied for reinstatement as a justice so that he could join in the good fight against 'the temperance magistrates' at the upcoming general sessions.[209] A new commission of the peace issued a few days before September sessions opened, reinstating Boyd but leaving the October 1855 commission otherwise unchanged except for Harris Hatch and John Snell, both of whom had died in the interim.

Defeated in the 1857 election, Boyd was returned in 1861 and 1865. He occupied various public offices. One in particular— government director of the St Andrews & Quebec Railroad—clearly signified the transfer of local power to the provincial executive.[210] Although Boyd remained in the commission of the peace and participated regularly in general sessions, he never lost his disdain for the local bench. Opposing an 1865 bill to increase their civil jurisdiction to £10, he told the House, 'This is putting a dangerous weapon in the hands of the Magistrates, and will double the number of their offices. I would just as soon lose a debt as to go into some of those offices to collect it.'[211]

---

208. PANB RS13/a/7, Partelow to Boyd, 8 Apr 1853.

209. Chapter 11.

210. PANB RS13/a/9, Wilmot to Boyd, 28 Nov 1856; Fulton to Boyd, 14 Jan 1857; Wilmot to Lt. Gov., 5 Mar 1857; Tilley to Thompson, 25 Sep 1857. His subsequent claim for compensation for past services was denied, 'on the ground that it has already been received by you': RS13/a/10, Tilley to Boyd, 4 Dec 1857.

211. PANB RS4, Debates 1865, p.98. I am grateful to David Bell for this reference.

Chapter 11

The temperance magistrates: License and prohibition

Alcohol was an important ingredient of Charlotte county society, economy, and politics and an ongoing concern for its magistrates and other low law officials.[1] The sale of liquor licenses was one of the relatively few sources of county, as distinct from parish, revenue which the bench could control without seeking special dispensation from the provincial assembly. Spirits figured among the common articles of contraband smuggled across the Passamaquoddy narrows and so attracted the attention of the local customs establishment.[2] Alcohol was important as an item of trade and a component of wages, both of which meant that the businessmen-justices had a commercial as well as a public regulatory interest in licensing and enforcement. In the middle of the nineteenth century a powerful temperance movement swept across the international border at St Stephen and carried the abolitionist banner throughout the province.[3] Alcohol's political and moral repercussions overtook its fiscal and commercial significances. With temperance, the kinds of liquor cases commonly

1. For a wide-ranging social history of alcohol in Canada, Heron, *Booze.*

2. Benedict Arnold's application to manufacture rum at Saint John had been denied due to West Indies planters' fears that it would serve as a conduit for American rum smuggled into the province: chapter 2.

3. For the temperance movement in the maritime colonies generally Noel, *Canada Dry*, chapters 2 and 3.

heard by the magistrates in their judicial capacity shifted away from breaches of the license laws to drunk-and-disorderly and other public order/morals offences. At the same time drunkenness (although not yet alcoholism) emerged as a mitigating factor in criminal cases and a central feature of discourse about domestic violence.[4] The temperance movement carried two prohibitionist measures through the provincial legislature and in the process transformed the character of New Brunswick politics.[5] In helping to give birth to a true party system in the Assembly, temperance undermined the traditional role of the county members (many of them magistrates) and thereby contributed to the shift from patriarchal to patrician styles of magisterial paternalism, to changes in the ways justices were recruited, and more generally to the decline and eventual demise of the sessions system.

A licensed magistracy

The province's earliest liquor legislation, 'An Act for regulating Innholders, Tavern-keepers, and Retailers of Spirituous Liquors,'[6] enacted by the first session of the legislature, was concerned exclusively with restricting sales to soldiers, sailors, servants, and apprentices, who were not to be allowed credit or to give goods in pawn for liquor. It was followed a year later by legislation empowering the justices of each county, in general or special sessions, to license 'such persons as they in their discretion shall think fit,' to keep taverns, or to sell 'wine, brandy, rum, beer, ale, or any strong liquors whatsoever' at retail in quantities less than five gallons.[7] The justices were given an equally broad discretion to set a license fee between ten shillings and four pounds. The proceeds, after allowing the county clerk two shillings and sixpence 'for his trouble' in issuing each license, were to be used by general sessions to defray the county's contingent expenses. Licensees were required to enter into bonds with two sureties to keep an orderly house and obey whatever rules and regulations sessions

4. Chapter 8.

5. Campbell, 'Smashers'; Marquis, 'Contesting Prohibition.'

6. 26 Geo.III (1786) c.36. The restrictions on retailers, although not on tavern-keepers, were relaxed by 34 Geo.III (1794) c.5.

7. 27 Geo.III (1787) c.6. The act did not apply to the city of Saint John where licensing was governed by the city charter and common council enactments.

adopted for them. The act imposed a five pound fine for every unlicensed sale and provided two avenues of enforcement. Offenders could be prosecuted on complaint before a single justice, in which case the fine was to be split between the informer and the overseers of the poor for the parish in which the offence occurred. Alternatively, proceedings against offenders could be taken by the justices in general sessions upon the presentment of the grand jury, in which case the fines were to be paid into county funds and disbursed in the same way as license fees. To this end the license act was to be given a public reading at the opening of every court of general sessions, following which the grand jury received a list of licensees and instructions to 'make diligent enquiry and presentment' of offenders. While a few other statutes and proclamations received occasional public readings at sessions, only the license act had to be read aloud there twice in each and every year.

These regulations were tightened up in 1814 by requiring tavern licenses to be issued only by general sessions, and then for a full year, and by forbidding retailers to sell in quantities less than a pint on penalty of a twenty shilling fine for each offence. Tavern keepers and retailers became liable to a forty shilling fine for selling liquor on Sundays (except to travellers).[8] The maximum fee for a license became ten pounds in 1825 and the penalty for retailing less than a pint was raised to five pounds. In 1831 all the existing license legislation was repealed and reenacted in consolidated form along with the provisions restricting sales to soldiers, sailors, and servants, with only minor amendments: the minimum license fee was raised to twenty shillings; tavernkeepers could no longer go surety for one another; and it became an offence for retailers to allow customers to consume liquor on their premises. Another repeal and reenactment in 1835 preserved the existing system while raising the minimum license fee to forty shillings except for taverns in remote locations, which could be licensed for as little as twenty shillings if they were deemed nec-

---

8. 54 Geo.III (1814) c.6. The act also gave the justices power to transfer a license on the death or removal of the licensee and imposed the usual bonding requirements on the new holder. Originally in force for two years, it was continued by 56 Geo.III (1816) c.19, 60 Geo.III (1820) c.4, 4 Geo.IV (1823) c.2 (confirmed by 5 Geo.IV (1824) c.6), and (with the 1825 amendments) by 9 Geo.IV (1828) c.10.

essary for the accommodation of travellers.[9] The new act removed the 1831 limitation on sureties. Fines for some offences, which had previously been fixed, could now range from forty shillings to ten pounds at the convicting justice's discretion. It became an offence, punishable by a five pound fine and revocation of the license, knowingly to sell illegally imported liquor. Licensees convicted of crimping offences ('enticing, seducing, harbouring or concealing' articled seamen or apprentices) could be disqualified from holding a license for one year. The statute abolished *qui tam* prosecutions (charges brought by an informer for a share of the fine) and provided that all penalties recovered under the act were to be paid into the county treasury. This diverted funds formerly destined for the parish poor to the county's general revenues. Other amendments followed: in 1838 the justices were empowered to enforce their local tavern regulations by fines of ten shillings to five pounds; a year later they were empowered to compel the attendance of witnesses in such proceedings;[10] a further repeal and reenactment in 1840 made minor changes to license fees and penalties, gave an enforcement role to town (parish) clerks for the first time, strengthened the powers of sessions grand juries to compel the attendance of witnesses (although not to require them to criminate themselves), and regularized the forms and fees for proceedings before justices in liquor cases.[11] Despite these various accretions and refinements, by 1850, on the eve of the first prohibition act, the province's liquor legislation had the same policy and broadly similar administrative details as the original acts of 1786 and 1787.

The Charlotte magistrates hastened to take advantage of the first license act, convening a special sessions for the purpose in July 1786. They set license fees at thirty shillings for tavernkeepers and large retailers and fifteen shillings for smaller retailers, delegated authority to issue licenses to the county clerk, and required applicants for retail licenses to be recommended by two neighbouring justices. At April general sessions two years later, the grand jury presented two Grand Manan widows for keeping disorderly houses and several other peo-

9. 6 Geo.IV (1825) c.13, 1 Wm.IV (1831) c.24, 5 Wm.IV (1835) c.3.

10. 1 Vict. (1838) c.33; 2 Vict. (1839) c.50.

11. 3 Vict. (1840) c.47, amended by 5 Vict. (1842) c.13, empowering justices to issue subpoenas, and continued by 8 Vict. (1845) c.24 and 13 Vict. (1850) c.14.

ple for retailing without licenses.[12] The bench directed the clerk to summon those among the people presented 'as have not been considered by him as licensed' to September sessions, and ordered that any payments for license fees made by the offenders in the interim would be offset against their fines. This sort of retroactive licensing of defaulters was to be a common response to grand jury presentments for many years. In April 1791 three informers complained about two unlicensed retailers on Moose Island (Eastport), possibly in an effort to reinforce the county's claim to jurisdiction over that disputed territory. In 1798 the sessions grand jury considered a letter from the Anglican rector of St Andrews calling for the suppression of vice and immorality. The jury presented a 'lament that the Regulations heretofore made to prevent Drunkeness [*sic*] on the Sabbath has not had the desired effect,' and recommended that church wardens visit public houses during divine service, presumably to denounce or inveigle Lord's Day tipplers. Sabbatarianism aside, alcohol was not seen as a serious moral issue or social problem. Until 1807, when he was paid fifty shillings in lieu, the county gaoler had a retail license for the convenience of inmates.[13] Grand juries in the first years of the nineteeth century complained of retailers using illegal measures or selling in quantities under five gallons without a license, and that the statutory distinction between tavernkeepers and retailers was not being observed.[14] The latter was probably a reference to retailers who permitted customers to drink on the premises: in response, the bench passed a 'standing rule' clarifying the licensing requirements but decided, on account of 'the want of a Right conception of the Regular mode of taking out Licenses heretofore,' to remit fines that session for offenders who paid their license fees and court costs.

One of the reasons for the bench's solicitude for license offenders became apparent at the April 1801 general sessions. Daniel McMaster JP was on the bench when the grand jury came into court and presented him for retailing without a license. His brother justices released him from the presentment without a fine but issued an order

12. CCSS 18 Jul 1786; CCGS Apr 1788. The minutes do not identify the retailers but they are alluded to in the paragraph headed 'Licenses.'

13. CCGS Apr 1791, Apr 1798, Sep 1807.

14. CCGS Apr 1802, Apr 1801, Apr 1803.

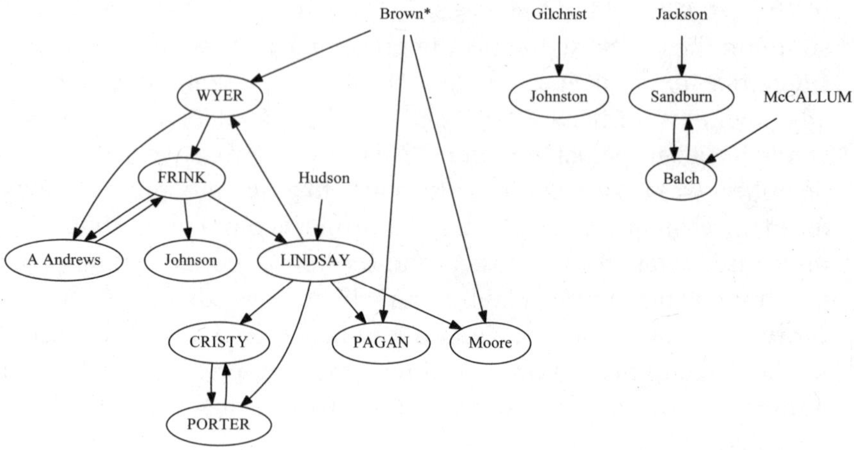

Figure 11.1 – Tavern and retail licensing, April 1803. Capitalized names are current justices. Enclosed names are licensees. Arrows run from surety to licensee. * H.B. Brown was acting county clerk until March 1803, when he became county treasurer. (Source: PANB RS148/j/3/a.)

clarifying the five gallon rule. Several justices were licensees, and a significant proportion of licenses were held by justices. The twenty-one names in the 1802 license list included eight justices.[15] The following year another justice, Warren Hatheway, was presented by the grand jury for retailing without a license and ordered to pay twenty shillings and the clerk's fee, which amounted to taking out a license after the fact,[16] and in 1807 sessions quashed the grand jury's presentment of David Owen for retailing without a license.[17] The licensed justices often served as sureties for one another: Figures 11.1 and 11.2

15. PANB RS148/J/2/j. Peter Cristy JP held separate licenses for his mill and his landing.

16. CCGS Apr 1803. Warren Hatheway's justicing career is described in chapter 3. Similarly, when a Mr Foster, presented for retailing without a license, entered a guilty plea, the justices accepted his proposal that he pay eight pounds, five for the fine and three to be licensed for the balance of the year: CCGS Sep 1804. Thomas Armstrong, presented along with Foster, was discharged upon paying the license rate and fee.

17. CCGS Sep 1807.

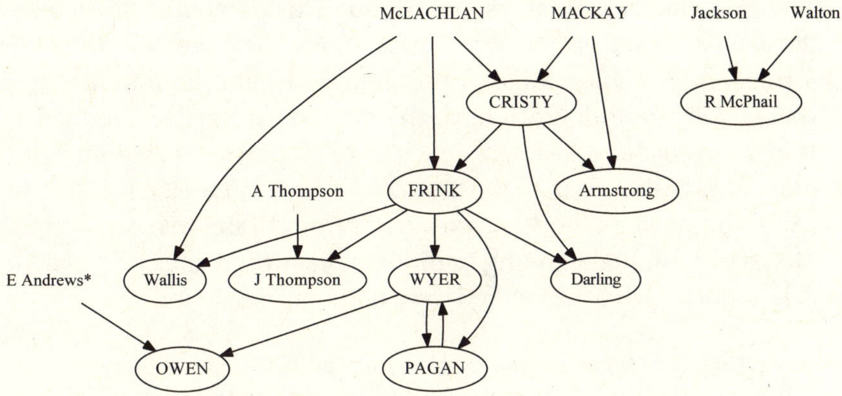

Figure 11.2 – Tavern and retail licensing, April 1804. Capitalized names are current justices. Enclosed names are licensees. Arrows run from surety to licensee. * Elisha Andrews was a justice until March 1803, when he became county sheriff. (Source: PANB RS148/j/3/a.)

show the web of licensee-surety relations in 1803 and 1804. There was a dense web of licensees linked together by common sureties and often serving as sureties for one another. Six of twelve licensees in 1803 and five of ten in 1804 were justices. Three 1803 licensees and just one in 1804 were not part of this web. Only one justice acted as surety for a licensee outside the web and he did so for just one. The sole outlier in 1804 is an interesting case. In April 1802 the sessions grand jury presented St Andrews tavernkeeper John McPhail for retailing liquor with illegal measures and the clerk of the market was ordered to investigate. In September of the following year the grand jury presented McPhail again, this time for retailing without a license and keeping a disorderly house. The justices ordered that he be forbidden to keep a tavern in future. In April 1804 John McPhail appeared at sessions to confess to the retailing charge and was fined five pounds and costs. At the same sessions Rebecca McPhail was granted a tavern license.[18]

This pattern of licensed magistrates and regular presentments for

18. CCGS Apr 1802, Sep 1803, Apr 1804.

licensing offences, often resolved by applying part of the fine towards the license fee retroactively, continued for many years. As late as 1835 former justice Gilbert Ruggles, presented for selling liquor unlawfully, successfully petitioned to have the amount of his fine credited towards the cost of a license.[19] Sessions practice respected the spirit, if not always the letter, of the license law. Soon after Harris Hatch became county clerk, he received a letter from Grand Manan patriarch Moses Gerrish JP defending traditional practices against the 'rigid legal moralists' whom he feared were dominating sessions:[20]

> Dear Sir, I turned to the Law long ago, and well knew what it required of those who wished to keep Taverns or to retail spirituous Liquors; but during the Clerkship of the late Mr McDonald, it was the custom here for a person desirous of retailing spirituous Liquors to wait on him with £3/2/6; sometimes this person was recommended by me only, not always, and I believe the same inattention to the adherence of Law was frequently practised with regard to Sureties; and we heard no more about retailers until the year expired. I acknowledge this to be a lax mode of doing business, but a small deviation from the letter of the Law, where no injury is done, if not justifiable, cannot be deemed very criminal; as in the present case, if the money received for licenses was safely deposited, accounted for, and converted to the use of the County, no real injury could arise from this irregularity.

Gerrish had little to fear, at least in the short run. At the next April sessions the bench responded to the grand jury's presentment of 'sundry persons that have not strictly complied' with the licensing regulations by ordering that the offenders were to be warned when next they took out licenses that if they offended again their bonds would be estreated, 'and in case of future applications for licenses the fitness of the person . . . should be taken into consideration.'[21]

Nevertheless by the 1820s more restrictive regulation was beginning to appear. Sessions decided that St Stephen shopkeepers

19. CCGS April 1835. For Ruggles, see chapter 3.

20. PANB MC207, Gerrish to Hatch, 17 Jul 1816. Gerrish studied law at Harvard before the revolution.

21. CCGS Apr 1817.

were ineligible for tavern licenses in the parish; a similar order for St Andrews came a few years later.[22] New regulations called for the posting of handbills identifying license-holders and signs identifying taverns.[23] License fees were raised although widows were given a break.[24] Fearing that there were too many licensed taverns in St Andrews the magistrates tightened up the application procedures. After an 1829 grand jury called for a reduction in the number of licenses the bench adopted yet more stringent rules, requiring all applicants for tavern licenses to get recommendations from a majority of the magistrates in their parish and striking a committee to look over St Andrews applications.[25] Similar restrictions were adopted for retail licenses in 1831, when the grand jury presented that 'the number of Shops authorised to sell spirituous liquors, have a manifest tendency to corrupt the morals of the People and to bring want, ruin, and every concomitant evil, upon many decent and respectable families.'[26]

This was the language of the temperance movement. A Temperance Society formed at Saint John in the fall of 1830. Temperance meetings were held in St Andrews and St Stephen in May 1834 and became regular weekly, then monthly, gatherings.[27] In that year sessions received a petition from Grand Manan requesting that no licenses be granted to anyone on the island. The magistrates complied in 1835 and also ordered 'on motion of Mr Justice Porter, that no Retailing or Tavern License shall be granted for the Parish of St Stephen this session.'[28] The following year Grand Manan petitioned successfully again. After reading a similar petition from Pennfield the magistrates appointed constables for each parish 'for informing against

22. CCGS Apr 1821, Apr 1824.

23. CCGS Apr 1821, Apr 1826.

24. CCGS Sep 1826, setting the fee at £5 in St Andrews and Milltown; widows paid £1/12/6.

25. CCGS Sep 1828, Apr 1829, Sep 1829. Additional measures, including quarterly inspections of all taverns, were adopted in April 1830. However, the rule requiring recommendations from magistrates was rescinded in 1832 and many new licenses were issued the following year: CCGS Apr 1832, Apr 1833.

26. CCGS Apr 1831; PANB RS148/a/1, Grand Jury report, 21 Sep 1831.

27. *Courier*, 4 Sep 1830; *Standard*, 8 May, 29 May, 11 Sep 1834 & seq.

28. This was Porter's sole reported appearance at general sessions in his thirty-six years on the commission of the peace.

persons selling Liquor' illegally and agreed to reward them with 40s for each offender convicted. They raised tavern license fees at several locations to £6/12/6 (reserving discretion over widows' fees). At April sessions 1838 the rate was raised to £10, £5 for widows, but this was so high that several former licensees could not afford to renew. They petitioned September sessions, acknowledging that they had been selling without licenses in the interim, and were permitted to pay a reduced fine, 'provided they come forward and pay the same before being sued.'[29]

By the early 1840s temperance had become the shibboleth of officialdom. The lieutenant governor circularized county benches for regulations requiring tavernkeepers to keep such nonintoxicating beverages as tea, coffee, spruce beer, and ginger ale in stock at all times.[30] The names of William Babcock, newly appointed to the bench, and Hatheway, recently reappointed, headed the list of petitioners for legislation to restrict the number of licenses.[31] James Boyd served on the executive committee of the St Andrews Total Abstinence Society and chaired its annual meeting.[32] The conservative St Andrews newspaper lent its voice to the cause. Reporting a fire at the house of an 'inebriated' local resident, the *Standard* recommended relief for his wife, 'a very deserving, industrious woman,' and membership in the total abstinence society for her husband. It gave free publicity to temperance meetings throughout the county and published temperance verses and an original short story entitled 'The Cup of Woe' as well as such object lessons as the tale of a farmer from St Patrick who came to St Andrews in good health, got drunk, fell off the wharf and drowned—'a solemn warning to those who persist in

29. CCGS Apr 1834, Apr 1835, Apr 1836, Apr 1837, Apr 1838, Sep 1838.

30. PANB RS13/a/3, Odell to clerks of peace, 17 Jun 1841 and 7 Jul 1841; the Charlotte copy (endorsed with W. Hatch's undertaking to lay it before the sessions) is in PANB RS148/B/1/a.

31. PANB RS24/1842/Pe no. 185. The petitioners included doctors Gove and Frye, John Wilson, and some of the leading storekeepers and artisans of St Andrews. It was read in the assembly and tabled: JHA 1842, 91.

32. *Standard*, 3 Sep 1845. During the debate on an 1849 bill to abolish tavern licenses, Boyd told the assembly 'of the individual benefit he had received from joining the Total Abstinence Association,' and that 'he had never been himself, and able to stand up in that House like a man, until the present Session.' *Standard*, 4 Apr 1849.

the ruinous and degrading vice of intemperance.'[33]

Nor was this empty thunder. The first annual meeting of the St Andrews Total Abstinence Society learned that in the space of a year its membership in town had grown from a mere hundred to two hundred and fifty-four, exclusive of those expelled for repeated violations 'after having been expostulated with from time to time, upon the subject.' A St Andrews parish society had another two hundred members and measures were being taken to form a Temperance Union with Saint John. A Catholic total abstinence society formed at St Andrews. The Oak Bay Young Men's Temperance Society had two hundred and fifteen members in good standing while only three had been expelled for repeated violations of the pledge. The St Croix Total Abstinence Society held its annual meeting at the Baptist church in St Andrews: it had a hundred and twenty-two members in good standing and one who was not. A St Stephen temperance speaker told a meeting at St Andrews that there were only seventeen people in all of Milltown who had not signed the pledge.[34]

While interest in the local temperance organizations began to decline by the middle of the decade—the Total Abstinence Society had to charge admission to defray the expenses of an 1847 lecture because of the insufficiency of 'the usual collection at the meetings heretofore'[35]—it revived again when the American fraternal organization, the Sons of Temperance, marched into Charlotte county 'to unite total abstinence and benevolence.'[36] A St Andrews chapter formed in 1847 and A.T. Paul, the local lawyer who was secretary of the Total Abstinence Society, promptly became its leader. It quickly formed links with branches at St Stephen, Calais, Eastport, Fredericton, and Saint John. There were branches in St David and St George. The St Stephen 'Sons' applied to the legislature for incorporation and the Grand Division for the whole province met at Milltown in 1849. Paul also headed the committee of adults supervising the St Andrews branch of the Cold Water Army, the temperance youth organization. Hatheway's eighteen-year-old son Clements was president and his fourteen-year-

33. *Standard*, 1 Dec 1843, 24 Jul 1844, 13 Nov 1844.
34. *Standard*, 26 Aug 1845, 6 Jan 1843, 10 Dec 1845, 25 Mar 1846, 6 May 1846.
35. *Standard*, 6 May 1846, 17 Mar 1847.
36. Chapman, 'Temperance Movement.'

old brother Bradshaw was a member.[37]

As temperance agitation increased so did the pressure on sessions to limit the number of liquor sellers. Some St George petitioners argued 'that the evils of intemperance and consequent increase of pauperism in this part of the county is mainly to be attributed to the facility with which Licenses are obtained,' and urged that a single tavern was all that their small community required. A petition from Milltown recited that 'much good has resulted' from a temporary halt to liquor sales there and asked that no licenses be granted for the village. A group of St David petitioners, 'convinced that the use of intoxicating liquors are unfavorable to the moral and religious principles of the Community and detrimental to the best interests of Society,' asked that no licenses be issued for the parish. Another petition from St George, maintaining that 'immediate and powerful measures are required for the removal' of the evils of intemperance, urged that no licenses be issued. Even admitting that 'Ardent spirits are beneficial to travellers,' they considered that for every glass sold to bona fide travellers twenty were sold at the same place to parish residents, 'thereby the benefit which might be afforded to travellers is materially overbalanced by the evils before mentioned.' A petition from Pennfield, headed by the signature of Joshua Knight JP, called for no licenses to be granted in the parish because, 'the facility of procuring intoxicating drink, too often tempts the sober man from the path of duty ...' Abolishing licenses would be a panacea for all social ills:

> [T]he laws would be less often violated, crime cease to be an every day occurrence, their Parish in a great measure relieved from the burden of its poor, and themselves and their families, be enabled to live in greater harmony and good will with each other, were the traffic in ardent spirits not sanctioned by law.

A large petition from St Patrick, endorsed but not signed by Peter McCallum JP, gave another set of grounds for withholding licenses: 'the bad examples set ... before the youth of our land, the loss frequently experienced ... in consequence of their hired men, being incapaci-

37. *Standard*, 28 Apr, 5, 26 May, 16, 24 June, 1 Sep, 25 Aug 1847; 17 Feb, 10 Jan, 1 Aug 1849; 22 Mar 1848. Like the Sons of Temperance, the Cold Water Army originated in the northeastern U.S.

tated for their employment ..., the profanation of the Sabbath.' A petition from Mascarene (in St George) complained 'that there is established almost in the heart of the settlement a house licensed to retail spirituous liquors, and which answers no other purpose than to lead the inexperienced youth of this community to profane the sabbath, destroy all regard for moral and religious rectitude and to train them probably for the drunkard's grave.' The solution was to deny licenses. Moses Vernon JP and sheriff Jones joined with the Baptist and Presbyterian ministers and several leading citizens of St George in asserting that 'upwards of five thousand gallons of spirituous liquors' were retailed in the parish each year, a quantity 'vastly greater than is necessary for the accommodation of travellers, if such necessity at all exists,' and urging that no licenses be issued. While most of the petitions were cast in generalities some held up specific innkeepers for obloquy. Thus the Oak Bay Young Men's Temperance Society petition, endorsed by Josephus Moore JP, urged that no license be awarded to Robert Deacon who was 'totally incompetent.' Other petitions against licenses came in from St Patrick, St Stephen, Milltown, and St David.[38] In 1847 numerous copies of a standard form of petition decrying the forty-two licensed taverns still operating in the county came in from various parishes, many of them signed by local magistrates.[39]

A few of these petitions were not read at sessions for want of a sponsor but most were presented to the justices or the grand jury. Some, although by no means all, were granted. This led to a new round of petitions from the favoured localities seeking to preserve their tavern-free status. They ranged from the obsequious—'we duly appreciate the favor ... and would again approach your worships with humble confidence to solicit a continuance of the same consideration' (Oak Bay, St David)—to the combative (Milltown, Middle Landing, and Upper Mills, St Stephen):

> That the public sentiment of this portion of the Parish is strongly in favor of temperance principles. That there is not a *licensed* grogshop or other place for the sale of spirituous

38. CCGS Apr 1846, Sep 1846, Apr 1847.
39. The petitions are in PANB RS148/J/6.

> liquors in it—and has not been for years—and further, that not one is needed or wanted as we still go in for improvement, for advancing on the ascending line, and have no disposition to take the *first retrograde step* towards *rum and ruin*—A *licensed* tavern therefore or other place for the sale of spirituous liquors in this portion of the Parish, would be a *gross outrage* upon the feelings of this community—and would be a marked reprobation of all their laudable efforts in the cause of temperance.

An 1854 petition from the same part of St Stephen and to the same end, albeit in gentler language, was signed entirely by women.[40]

In 1848 James Boyd introduced a bill to abolish tavern licensing. 'He might, no doubt, be told that the Justices of the Peace exercised a sound discretion in granting these licenses; but he was sorry to say he could not agree with those who held this doctrine.' Acknowledging that licenses were a large source of county revenue, he said it was a revenue 'too dearly bought.' Editorials commented that it was a bit paradoxical for such a bill to be brought in by a member who was rarely seen after dinner (and Boyd acknowledged his own propensity to join in 'a friendly glass' or two) but it was generally recognized that he was serving his Charlotte constituents what they wanted.[41]

The magistrates were well aware that refusing licenses came at a cost. Already by 1844 Thomas Wyer noted that license revenue, which had typically added two hundred and thirty pounds to the county coffers, now amounted to only sixty pounds. The following spring Samuel Abbot told the sessions grand jury that at one time the liquor revenue had covered the county expenses, but as the expenses had grown so had the revenue shrunk, 'which is indicative of that great moral reform which under the influence of our "Temperance Societies" is now so happily pervading this community.' A year later Wyer reported that license revenue was down to fifty pounds, owing, he supposed, 'to the effects of the Temperance Societies.'[42]

---

40. See also the petition of the 'Ladies of Milltown,' Sep 1856.

41. *Standard,* 1 Mar 1848 reporting assembly debate of 22 Feb; JHA 1848, 183. The bill was stopped in committee, three of the Charlotte members voting against the resolution to postpone and one (Thomson) in favour.

42. *Standard,* 18 Sep 1844, 16 Apr 1845, 15 Apr 1846.

Table 11.1 – Votes on no-license motions, April sessions, 1849 and 1852 (justices who attended one or both sessions, by parish)

Justice	Parish	1849	1852	1852R*
J Brown	Campobello	-	◎	■
J Snell	Campobello	☐	☐	■
J Knight	Pennfield	■	■	☐
J Boyd	St Andrews	◎	-	-
J Chandler	St Andrews	◎	-	-
CR Hatheway	St Andrews	◎	☐	■
W Ker	St Andrews	◎	☐	■
H Hatch	St Andrews	-	◎	◎
WC McStay	St Andrews	☐	☐	■
D Mowatt	St Andrews	-	■	☐
JW Street	St Andrews	☐	☐	■
J Wilson	St Andrews	◎	■	☐
J Moore	St David	◎	■	☐
J Young	St David	-	■	☐
P Clinch	St George	☐	-	-
D Gilmore	St George	☐	-	-
G Mackay	St George	☐	☐	■
R Thompson	St George	-	◎	■
AJ Wetmore	St George	-	◎	■
A McCallum	St Patrick	■	■	☐
S McFarlane	St Patrick	-	☐	◎
J Frink	St Stephen	☐	■	◎
J Grimmer	St Stephen	■	■	◎
N Marks	St Stephen	◎	☐	■
J Porter	St Stephen	■	-	-
DA Rose	St Stephen	◎	■	◎
RM Todd	St Stephen	■	■	☐

* Vote to reconsider: see text.

☐ Nay. - Absent from Sessions.

■ Yea. ◎ Attended but did not vote.

Among the leaders of the bench at St Andrews, John Wilson's was the only sanguine voice. In 1849 he attributed the county gaol's empty cells and vacant debtors' room 'mainly to the spread and dissemination of temperance principles,' and only regretted that the efforts of former grand juries had failed to persuade his colleagues to abolish licenses altogether. The magistrates divided on the grand jury's recommendation to grant no licenses that session. The resolution was moved by two newly-appointed St Stephen justices and when it was narrowly lost by a vote of seven to five the bench made an unprecedented order to publish the names of those on either side in the local press.[43] The most remarkable thing about this vote was the preponderance of magistrates from outside St Andrews who participated. Many of the shiretown justices attending sessions (including Hatheway, Ker, Boyd, and even John Wilson, whose address had spurred the grand jury recommendation) avoided the vote (Table 11.1). The following year Wilson told the grand jury that he opposed granting licenses—'the sale of liquor was a great evil'—and pointed to the 'peaceable and happy' example of dry Milltown.[44]

At April sessions 1852, shortly after a nine-thousand-name petition against the liquor traffic reached the provincial legislature, Wilson moved that no licenses be granted. Seconded by the active St Stephen magistrate David Rose, the motion carried by a vote of ten to eight, with St Andrews justices Hatheway, Ker, McStay, and Street among the opposition. The next day McStay and Ker moved for reconsideration which carried ten to seven in the absence of several supporters (Table 11.1) but no licenses were approved that session.[45] The following spring, in the shadow of the province's first prohibition bill, the *Standard* worried about the cost:[46]

> We learn that for the last four years the County revenue derived from licenses amounted to £150 per annum. What is to supply the deficiency in the revenue? The internal expenses of the County have, with strict economy, amounted to £400 per annum. The assessment for the present year is £300. Where is

43. *Standard,* 11 Apr 1849; CCGS Apr 1849.
44. *Standard* 10 Apr 1850.
45. CCGS Apr 1852.
46. *Standard,* 20 Apr 1853.

Figure 11.3 – License fees as proportion of county revenue, 1840-67

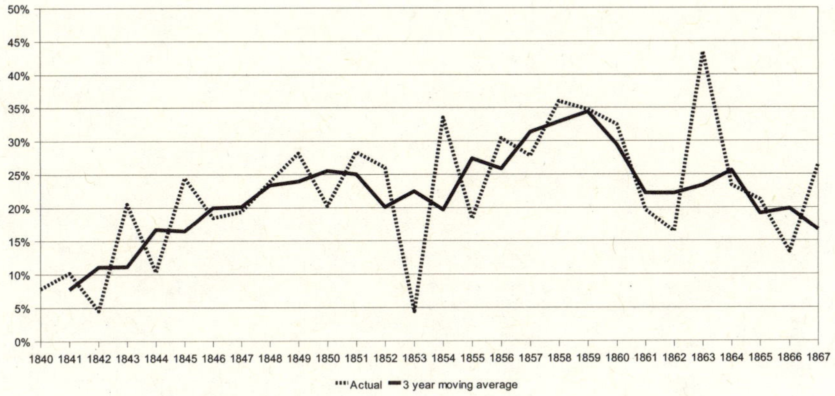

> the other £100 to come from? . . . Let us not be misunderstood; we advocate a strict compliance with the law—as it is probable that the "liquor law" will go into effect in June; but how is the falling off in the County funds to be made up?

In fact, however, the trend was for license fees to increase as a proportion of county revenue from 1840 to 1860 (Figure 11.3) notwithstanding the prohibition statutes of 1852 and 1855. License fees accounted for the smallest proportion of revenue in the early 1840s, amounting to about five per cent in 1842 as compared with a high of nearly eighty per cent in 1829. These wide apparent swings were exaggerated by a number of factors, including delays in paying for licenses (so licenses taken out one year showed in revenue the following year) or one-time special grants that inflated revenues (so that license fees made a smaller proportional contribution that year.) Despite the *Standard*'s worries about 'the other £100,' after 1844 license revenue fell below one hundred pounds just once—in the prohibition year 1853—and that was made up for by a surge in licensing the following year. Actual license revenue peaked in 1856 with the repeal of prohibition but the declining trend in license fees as a proportion of general revenue after 1860 is best explained by an increase in other forms of revenue as actual license income remained relatively stable although still

Figure 11.4 – Attendance at Sessions by parish of residence, 1836-55

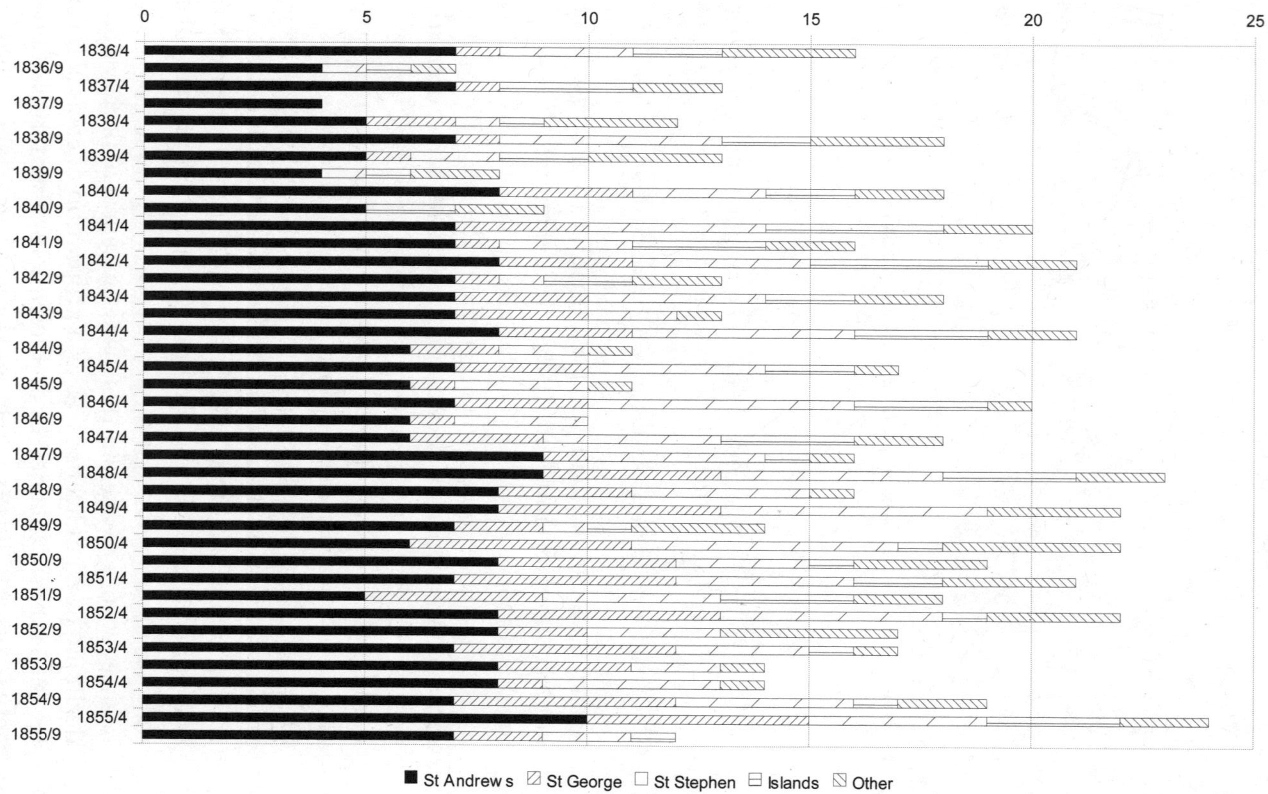

below the highs of the mid-1830s. Actual revenues from licenses in the early 1840s were only about half what they had been in the mid-1830s, and a substantial proportion of the difference must have been due to the sanctioning of parish temperance petitions, a kind of informal local option without plebiscites, enabled by the increased participation of justices from St Stephen and the outlying parishes at sessions in those years (Figure 11.4).

Enforcement

'Would to God, Mr Editor, such were the *true* cause,' a correspondent replied to Samuel Abbot's claim that declining liquor revenues reflected pervasive moral reform. 'There are as many persons selling liquor throughout this County as in "years gone by"—and that the falling off of the revenue from the decrease of the issue of Tavern Licenses is now more attributable to the neglect of the Magistrates in bringing the open violators of the License Law to justice—than from the progress of the Temperance cause.'[47] Temperance advocates put pressure on the bench to enforce the licensing regulations, not only because liquor sellers were public enemies but also to enhance the diminishing revenue.

Policing was a problem. When Hatheway and Babcock petitioned the legislature for more stringent licensing rules they included a plea for stipendiary magistrates and a paid professional police, 'the constabulary force throughout the Province being generally composed of that class who rather sympathise with than suppress the disorderly.'[48]

---

47. *Standard*, 30 Apr 1845.

48. PANB RS24/1842/pe, no. 185. The idea of stipendiaries was in the air. In 1843 the legislature received the report of Capt. John Ross RN (made to the lieutenant governor in 1840) on 'the state of the fisheries, the condition of the light houses, the contraband trade, and various other matters in the Bay of Fundy,' recommending the appointment of 'an intelligent, active, honest man, unbiased by party feeling, unprejudiced by conflicting petty interests' to be stipendiary magistrate and superintendent of fisheries. The same session received two petitions from Saint John, one headed by Edward Jarvis advocating the appointment of a stipendiary magistrate and the other from the mayor and aldermen opposing it: JHA 1843, cxxxiv, 86, 90. 16 Vict. (1852) c.2 provided for police magistrates along the line of the E&NA railway to be paid by the government, exercise the juridiction of two JPs out of sessions, and supervise a force of stipendiary constables. See further chapter 12, note 64 below.

Ten years later Harris Hatch told the grand jury that the license law 'at present was nugatory, as no-one would inform against delinquents, and pointed out the necessity of having a paid police, whose duty it would be to inform against persons violating that law.'[49] Charlotte county had relied entirely on parish constables for its policing until 1829 when the volunteer rifle corps (commanded by James Boyd) was called out as a *posse comitatus* to assist the sheriff in making arrests at Campobello.[50]

Later that year when Boyd was assaulted in the street at St Andrews the *Herald* called for a night watch.[51] Nothing was done about it until September sessions 1831 when the grand jury repeated the call 'in consequence of recent and nightly attempts to commit depredations.' The magistrates sanctioned the recommendation but had no authority to pay the two shillings and sixpence allowed nightly to each of two men on patrol. A public subscription was taken up in December: Hatheway and Ker each donated five shillings; Wilson and Wyer fifteen shillings; Boyd and Hatch twenty.[52] Once the proceeds were spent the watch seems to have been suspended until new fears were aroused by an attempted arson at Garnett's store in 1834, when a public meeting appointed Boyd and two others to organize a 'nightly watch for the protection of the lives and properties of the inhabitants.' Within a few days Wyer was able to tell the grand jury at sessions 'that an extensive volunteer guard has been organized, which furnishes a nightly patrol of six persons for the maintenance of peace and the security to property.' After a few weeks of active vigilantism—'It has had the salutary effect of breaking up several dens of great iniquity and crime, and has the tendency of rendering the streets quiet and deserted even at very early hours'[53]—enthusiasm for the watch seems to have waned. A special sessions called to deal with unruly boys 'insulting females and committing depredations' at St Andrews ap-

49. *Standard*, 22 Sep 1852. He had made a similar comment at April sessions.

50. *Courier*, 31 Jan 1829, copying *Herald*; see chapter 3.

51. *Sentinel*, 5 Aug 1829, copying St Andrews *Herald*.

52. PANB RS148/D/18/a, nightly watch account and receipt, Nov 1832.

53. *Standard*, 11, 18, 25 Sep 1834. Constable Pike's account against the county for 1834 included five shillings for 'attending at the trial of 7 persons taken up by the nightly watch': PANB RS148/D/18/b.

pointed a constable to patrol the streets at two shillings and sixpence per day.[54] This must not have lasted long because a correspondent who complained to the *Standard* in 1842 about the 'mob' of youths who gathered to disrupt amateur band rehearsals urged, 'It is but a short time since their worships were under the necessity of appointing a nightly watch to preserve order in our streets, and it is now a matter of surprise that with so much more cause they tacitly permit the continuance of misconduct, which could at once be put down by the presence of a single constable.'[55]

A growing concern for public order—including efficient supervision of drinking establishments—conflicted with the ratepayers' interest in strict economy. As early as 1835 the grand jury, auditing the county accounts, criticized the 'enormous sums' paid to constables.[56] When the attorney general introduced his bill for the election of parish officers in 1850 he proposed to make an exception for constables who should continue to be appointed by the magistrates in sessions. James Boyd expressed his opposition in his usual style, saying 'he himself knew of Constables who were appointed from year to year, who, when a riot or disturbance occurred, would not lift their finger to put it down.' This elicited an editorial defending the peaceable character of the county—'During a residence of twenty years ...we have never heard of a riot having taken place ... unless an exhibition of feeling between parties at an election may be called such, and this Mr Boyd knows well.'—and a riposte by 'J.K.B.,' Boyd's son Kempt, no stranger to the public prints, explaining that by 'riot' Boyd had meant 'the noisy and tumultuous assemblage of those popularly known among us as *rowdies*' and of whom, he insisted, there were many. Later that year the justices named William Henan and Robert Shaw as special constables for the town of St Andrews, 'to act in the capacity of police.'[57] When the next town meeting elected just four constables under the new legislation the sheriff, county coroner, clerk of the peace, and other leading citizens petitioned sessions to complain that 'the number is insufficient, and that by the said

54. CCSS 1 Jun 1840.
55. *Standard*, 29 Jun 1842.
56. CCGS Apr 1835, published in *Standard*, 21 Apr 1836.
57. *Standard*, 6, 20 Mar; 2 Oct 1850.

Election the Constabulary of this Town will not be in as efficient a state as it was last year.' The magistrates agreed and reappointed William Henan, who had been left off the town meeting's list.[58] A contest over who was to pay for special constables resulted in a decision to charge the town rather than the parish.[59] Continued tension between the ratepayers and the magistrates over the merits of 'Chief Constable' Henan, as he was called by the *Standard* in an article praising his 'prompt and efficient' capture of two men accused of stealing from the firm of Odell & Turner in 1861, came to a head two years later when the same paper, true to its apparent editorial policy of 'mind your own business,' hinted that 'a case is undergoing examination of a most disgraceful nature, which we trust, for the credit of the county, may not come before the public as there are grave doubts as to the correctness of the complaint.'[60] The examination before James Boyd resulted in William and James Henan being committed for trial at the circuit court, where the 'Chief Constable' was sentenced to three months in penitentiary for obstructing constable Richardson Haddock and a further six months for receiving stolen goods.[61]

An 1852 grand jury had endorsed Hatch's proposal for a professional force, 'as the Railroad, now in construction, causes a greater influx of strangers'[62] but the company pressed for legislation to appoint its own Railway Police. 'The principle reason for its introduction, I gather, is that liquor is sold in some places near the Line, and that the men very often "go on a spree," particularly after "pay day" and consequently become insubordinate.'[63] In 1856, anticipating the repeal of

58. PANB RS148/P/3/h, letter, 14 Apr 1851; ibid., constable list 1851 with Henan's name added in a different hand.

59. CCGS Apr 1851.

60. *Standard,* 20 Feb 1861, 29 Jul 1863.

61. Two of his sons also received penitentiary sentences for larceny and for assaulting constable Haddock: *Standard,* 12 Aug 1863, giving no further details. There are no surviving issues of other Charlotte newspapers for the relevant months. The circuit minutes for 1863 have not survived and the case does not appear to have been reported in the Saint John, Fredericton, or Eastport press. For Boyd's involvement see constable Morrison's account for services in PANB RS148/D/4/c, 11 Apr 1864: 'Aug 3, 1863 - Committing Wm Heanan and James Heanan by order of Justice Boyd.'

62. *Standard,* 29 Sep 1852.

63. *Standard,* 10 Mar 1858. The bill, which originated in the executive council,

prohibition, the grand jury recommended 'that a suitable person be appointed ... to guard against any infringement of the Liquor Law,' but opposed 'the embodiment of a Police Force, under the present peaceable aspect of the County, as we consider it would entail an unnecessary expense.'[64] With its declining population St Andrews had to continue to make do with special constables and intermittent volunteer vigilance despite continuing complaints about the 'disgraceful conduct' of the town's boys and young men.[65] 'The duty of Magistrates does not compel them to parade the streets at night and act the part of policemen,' the *Standard* pointed out to one correspondent. 'His suggestions with reference to a Police force are well enough, but the legal course must be taken before any such body can be organized.'[66] During the Fenian scare of 1865-6 troops were posted to St Andrews and the citizens organized a 'Home Guard' which maintained a nightly patrol. The volunteer rifle company was called out for active paid service, James Boyd having been temporarily relieved of command.[67] The crisis over, St Andrews returned to the old system. An 1868 special sessions to discuss establishing a town police force adjourned without any decision being taken.[68]

At St Stephen, on the other hand, where agitation for better policing is first heard of in connection with sabbath-breaking in the mid-1850s,[69] a professional police force was established in 1864.[70] Sessions adopted police regulations for St Stephen in 1866 and the following year a special sessions reappointed the town's two officers by

was enacted as 21 Vict. (1858) c.28, and a special sessions appointed four constables to be paid by the company: CCSS 17 Nov 1860.

64. *Standard*, 30 Apr 1856.

65. For example, *Standard*, 30 Aug 1865, 14 Mar 1866, 13 Feb 1867.

66. 24 Oct 1866.

67. 'Capt. James' company of Home Guards will now be filled up without any delay, and we understand, they have an assurance that they will not be compelled to serve under Col. Boyd, who is represented as so unpopular in the Battalion that the Commander-in-Chief has deemed it necessary to appoint Col. Willis to its temporary command.' *Standard*, 21 Mar 1866.

68. CCGS 29 Jan 1868.

69. *Standard*, 23 Aug 1854.

70. 27 Vict. (1864) c.55. A bill to erect gas lamps in the town's streets was introduced in the same legislative session. PANB RS148/B/2/e contains accounts for the payment of the St Stephen night watch in 1865.

the slimmest of majorities after 'quite an animated discussion.'[71] In 1868, following another spate of store robberies at St Andrews, the *Standard* editorialized that 'a Police force is required, the same as at St Stephen, where they attend day and night, though it is not the Shire-town.'[72]

As the references to larcenies, rowdies, sabbath-breaking, and abusive language make plain, the pressure for more effective policing was not restricted to liquor law enforcement. Nevertheless, a generalized disquiet about social order formed part and parcel of the moral rearmament of the temperance campaigns. There was far more anxiety than real crime in the streets of St Andrews, where the *Standard*'s encomiums to the night watch were typically accompanied by assurances that the cells remained empty. While there had been occasional references to the moral order earlier in the century—the royal proclamation for the suppression of profanity and immorality read at the opening of sessions in 1811; a sessions committee in 1842 that recommended 'making some Constabulary arrangements, which might at all times secure for the Town tranquility, Peace & good order with a strict attention to the morals of the rising generation'[73]—it was not until the height of the temperance agitation that questions of public morality were pushed to the fore. In part this was due to the rhetoric of the abolitionist cause, which made abstinence a necessity for the weak and an exemplary duty for the strong, and in part an expression of the increasingly confident middle-class feminism institutionally invested in the temperance movement and exemplified by 'Aurora''s and 'Fanny''s letters to the *Standard* denouncing a male correspondent's purported scriptural and historical authority for keeping women out of the public sphere.[74] Concerns about gender rela-

71. CCGS Sep 1866; *Standard*, 15 May 1867.

72. *Standard*, 4 Nov 1868.

73. CCGS Apr 1811; PANB RS148/A/5/g, 16 Apr 1842.

74. This extended correspondence in the fall of 1855 was brought to a close by the editor's advice to Lydia Eastman that she 'give herself no further trouble, as her remarks are sufficiently plain and do not require explanation or defence.' 'JSM' was allowed the right of one further reply, however, following which the *Standard* opined that had he made it sooner, 'this "vexed question," as it is termed by a contemporary, would not have assumed that importance which it has done in the opinions of our correspondents, whose time and talents might have been occupied with subjects

tions, sexual propriety, and public decency were expressed in a variety of contexts including the 'unseemly sights and inconveniences' of the covered tollbridge between St Stephen and Calais; the appointment of an officer to 'examine into the sanitary condition of the yards, cellars &c in this Town'; the youths 'improperly exposing their persons' when bathing at the Market Wharf near the steamboat landing; boys 'coasting' on toboggans and using 'obscene and profane language which offends the ladies'; regular congregations of young men annoying 'night schools and religious meetings' (the amateur musicians having long since disbanded) and 'perambulating the streets at night in a state of intoxication, singing songs, making hideous noises, and latterly breaking windows.'[75] Queen Victoria's royal proclamation for the encouragement of piety and virtue (1860), published at St Andrews on the eve of the Prince of Wales' visit to the province, called on 'all persons of honor, or in place of authority' to serve as good examples to others, and on justices of the peace in particular 'to be very vigilant and strict in the discovery and the effectual prosecution and punishment of all persons who shall be guilty of dissolute, immoral, or disorderly practices ...'[76]

This upwelling of outrage and concern was met by new regulations. In 1854 sessions adopted a code of 'rules and regulations for preventing vice, immorality, disorderly conduct and indecency in the thoroughfares, Alleys, and other public places,' first for St Andrews but soon extended to St Stephen, part of St George, and by 1860 the whole county.[77] The regulations imposed a fine of up to ten pounds for a wide variety of offences including breaking windows or lamps, throwing stones or snowballs, 'inscribing' or 'delineating' obscene graffiti, cutting shrubbery, discharging firearms, setting off fireworks, lighting bonfires, sliding or coasting on ice or snow, playing ball or other games, fighting, using profane language, violent cursing, in-

vastly more edifying and interesting to our readers.' *Standard,* 1, 22, 29 Aug; 5, 12, 26 Sep; 3 Oct 1855.

75. *Patriot,* 29 Jul 1853; *Standard,* 9 Aug 1854, 16 Aug 1854, 18 Mar 1857, 24 Oct 1866. The sanitary inspection was inspired by a cholera outbreak.

76. *Standard,* 25 Jul 1860, copying *London Gazette,* 18 Jun 1860.

77. CCGS Sep 1854; *Standard,* 18 Oct 1854; CCGS Apr 1860. PANB RS148/A/7/d is the proof copy prepared for publication.

decently exposing one's person (or any part thereof), using insulting language or taunting epithets or threatening gestures, inciting breaches of the peace, being drunk, pretending to be drunk, bawling, yelling, screaming, singing or shouting, turning a horse loose, setting a dog to bark, riding or driving furiously, wantonly ringing doorbells, knocking at doors without lawful excuse, extinguishing lamps, and throwing or heaping offensive matter or allowing it to run from any manufactory, brewery, bakery, slaughterhouse, dunghill, hogsty, or privy.[78] The regulations empowered one or more justice to impose a fine of up to ten pounds upon complaint, confession, or view, the proceeds going 'to defray the County contingencies.' Nor did these local regulations stand alone. The 1854 revised statutes provided for convictions for drunkenness 'either upon view, or on evidence before a Justice.'[79] The following year's prohibition act provided that intoxicated persons could be arrested on view and kept in gaol until sufficiently sober to be brought before a magistrate and required to disclose who had sold them the liquor, failing which they could be fined forty shillings or committed to gaol for ten days.[80] Other rules and orders followed. Persons convicted of 'drunkenness and riotous conduct' henceforth were to be 'confined in a cell and fed upon bread and water.' Penalties for using insulting or abusive language were amended to conform to new provincial legislation.[81] Town and parish clerks were ordered to provide the names of persons selling liquor without licenses. A streamlined version of the regulations adopted in 1866 reinstated the justice's power to convict upon view, 'as the law admits,' but dropped drunkenness from the list of offences.[82] In 1868 sessions banned billiard tables from licensed premises as they had 'a

78. There is considerable overlap between this list of offences and those set out in the Portland (Saint John) police act, 11 Vict. (1848) c.12, ss. 11 and 13.

79. RSNB (1854) c.145, 'Of offences against public morals and decency.' The other morals offences were incest, adultery, disorderly houses, and lotteries.

80. 18 Vict. (1855) c.36, s.18. Following the repeal of prohibition, however, the local regulations were amended to eliminate convictions by a justice on view: CCGS Apr 1859.

81. CCGS Apr 1862, Sep 1863 (implementing 25 Vict. (1862) c.17, s.9 and 26 Vict. (1863) c.13) and see chapter 8 for B.R. Stevenson's objection to Hatheway's application of the penalty provisions.

82. CCGS Sep 1866; *Standard*, 7 Nov 1866.

very injurious effect in leading young men and others who frequent such places, into habits of gambling and other evil practices.' It is not clear whether the same considerations informed the similar regulation for barbershops.[83]

It is one thing to have regulations and another to police them. The *Standard* told a correspondent that the rule against coasting had rarely been enforced because few complaints were made; indeed, the paper's usual response to morals complaints was that the offended party should go to a magistrate and file an information. Nonsense, replied 'Another Native,' citing the case of a woman who had been 'run down' by a sled: 'What young lady of any sensibility would not suffer even a personal inconvenience of this kind rather than appear in a Magistrate's court with a rabble of lawless boys.—So much for another stupid enactment.' As he saw it, 'the Magistrates are afraid of provoking the ire of the boys!—probably bearing in mind the treatment the late Editor of the Charlotte Gazette received at their hands, because he dared to oppose them and reprove their misconduct.'[84]

Some idea of the extent of enforcement of the liquor and other morals regulations can be gathered from the county accounts because constables filed expenses and magistrates made returns of fines (as well as claiming fees in some cases). It is hard to assess how meticulously these statements were made; the 1850 investigation of James Boyd for peculation was unusual and had more to do with his lack of collegiality than his finances.[85] Nevertheless, these accounts and returns furnish some of the best evidence now available for the scope of policing.

In the mid-1830s enforcing the liquor laws represented a variable but not insignificant proportion of the fees and expenses charged the county by constables and justices. Thus in September 1835 constable Peacock charged the county £5/1/7$\frac{1}{2}$ of which £3/8/0 was for seventeen days' court attendance. The remainder was accounted for by services in specific crown cases, including eight shillings for serv-

83. CCGS Apr 1868; *Standard*, 6 May 1868.

84. *Standard*, 18 Feb, 18 Mar 1857. For the *Charlotte Gazette* and its editor John McLachlan see chapter 10.

85. Chapter 10. Following an audit of his returns in 1840 William Ker made a series of payments to reimburse the county for previously unreported fines.

ing a summons on Samuel Nixon 'for selling rum without license' and seven shillings and sixpence for serving a subpoena on a witness in that case. Constable McNall submitted a half-yearly account for one pound court attendance and £4/3/6 in crown cases, none of them involving liquor. His account for £6/2/0 in the following half year included £3/8/0 for court attendance and several items relating to liquor law enforcement: 8/6 for fifteen miles' travel to serve a subpoena on a witness in the Nixon case, 3/6 for apprehending an accused for 'druckness and bad behaviour,' and the same amount for summoning an accused and two witnesses in a disorderly house complaint. Constable Pike's account for the former period, amounting to £5/11/0 exclusive of court attendance, included two shillings and sixpence for assisting in one committal for 'duckness,' presumably drunkenness.[86] Constable Peacock's account for the six months ending April 1836 included service of thirteen summonses and the same number of subpoenas in liquor cases, the bulk of his duties in that period. Magistrate William Ker's charges for the first half of 1835 amounted to £8/7/6 including eleven shillings justice fees in Nixon's case (annotated 'witness run away to States'), the only liquor prosecution he listed. In the next half-year, however, Ker issued nine summonses for selling liquor without a license and several subpoenas in those cases, accounting for £1/2/0 of his £11/15/0 charge against the county in crown cases.[87] Costs in another nine liquor cases comprised the whole of Wilford Fisher's account for 1835, the first year that no licenses were issued for his parish, Grand Manan. There were no liquor cases in Joshua Knight's charges for 1835-6. Fines for selling liquor without a license contributed £32 to the county coffers in 1836, as compared to £235 in license fees.[88]

From 1840 on there is a consistent run of county accounts showing receipts of fines for liquor and other offences. Unfortunately, and especially in the earlier years, the offence for which the fine was levied is not always given. Figure 11.5 shows the amount of fines paid over to

86. PANB RS148/D/18/b, 18 Sep, 16 Apr, 17 Sep, 18 Apr 1835. The grand jury passed all these constables' accounts but noted that it considered them 'exhorbitant, generally speaking': ibid., John Pike account, 15 Apr 1835.

87. Ibid., Apr 1836, 14 Sep 1835, 7 Apr 1836.

88. PANB RS148/B/2/a, Apr 1836; PANB RS148/D/18/b; PANB RS148/B/2/a.

Figure 11.5 – Fines received by county treasurer by offence type, 1840-67 (pounds): see text.
(Source: PANB RS148/B/2/c (1840-56), RS148/B/2/d (1850-67)

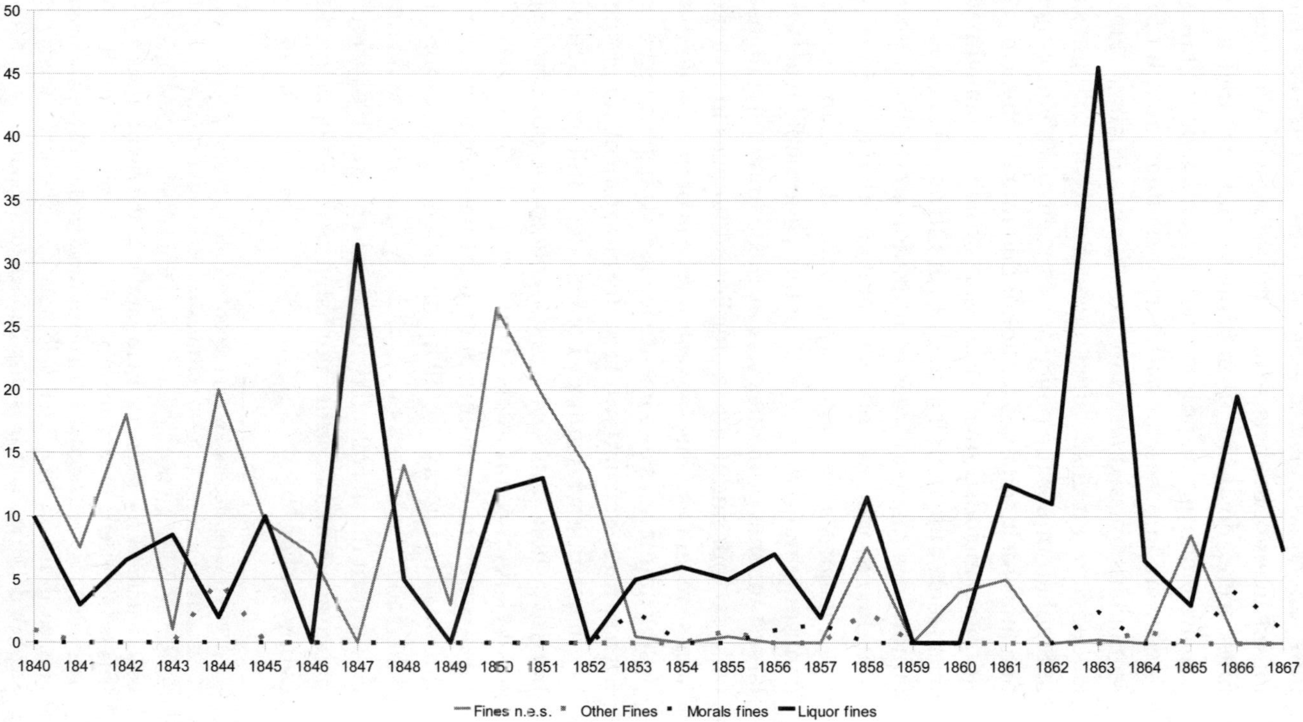

the county treasurer each year until 1867. 'Liquor fines' included fines for breaches of the license law and selling without a license; 'morals fines' were mostly for 'drunkenness' but included a few fines for abusive language, disorderly conduct, and Sabbath-breaking. 'Other fines' were imposed for harbouring seamen, breach of the pilotage regulations, missed jury duty, and 'furious driving.' 'Fines n.e.s.' included fines for unspecified offences and (in 1865) fines collected at St Stephen under the police act. It seems likely that these unspecified fines included fines for liquor and morals offences. (They would not have included fines for assault, which remained payable to the overseers of the poor in each parish.) In any event it is apparent that liquor fines made a larger contribution to the county treasury than fines for other known offences, and also that fines (of all kinds) were not a major source of county revenue. In many years they did not contribute more than twenty pounds and rarely reached thirty. The largest income from fines was in 1863, amounting to just over forty-eight pounds and nearly all for liquor offences in a year of declining license revenues. This suggests a revival of the former practice of imposing liquor fines as a license fee for not having taken out a license. Even so these accounts understate the extent of liquor fines even if every magistrate who imposed one made a full return to the treasurer. In cases where a moiety was payable to the prosecutor (usually the town clerk) the county received only part of the fine.[89] While fines for breaches of the license law went (in whole or part) to the county, this was not the case for all morals offences. Fines for 'drunkenness' collected at St Andrews went directly into the general revenue of the county but those collected at St Stephen after 1864 went to a special police account and so are not listed as fines on the credit side of the county ledger.[90]

89. A few entries indicate receipt of a 'moiety' or 'proportion' of a liquor fine.

90. The great majority of the fines returned by St Stephen magistrate W.J. Rose 'on police account' in 1867-8 were for 'drunkenness': PANB RS148/D/4/c. Fines collected under the police act were payable to the county treasurer but were to be held 'as a separate fund ... to be paid over by him from time to time' as sessions ordered: 27 Vict. (1864) c.55 s.7. This meant that they did not necessarily appear as fines payments on the receipts side of the county ledger. Several entries for the St Stephen police account are struck through in the county accounts, suggesting the treasurer's belated compliance with the statutory requirement for a 'separate fund.'

Party and bench

New Brunswick political historian Gail Campbell has argued that the temperance movement transformed New Brunswick politics by replacing sectional (parish, religious, ethnic, or occupational) with partisan interests essential to the electoral functioning of a party system. In the 1850s New Brunswickers began to vote according to their support for 'Rummies' or 'Smashers,' the emerging conservative and liberal parties in provincial politics. While nearly everyone could agree with 'temperance' as a general social good there was a deep divide between those who felt the necessity for state enforcement of total abstinence and those who believed in a more limited role for public policy. Campbell acknowledges that the turn to party politics required as well a party organization and a party in office ('caucuses, floor leaders and whips') but sees in the temperance agitation the formation of 'the party in the electorate,' the voters who regularly supported it at the polls. Her study of votes cast in Charlotte county's open ballot elections from 1846 to 1857 demonstrates the evolution of voter attachment to partisan positions, and concomitant detachment from sectionalism.[91]

Along with the turn to partisan politics, these years saw a related shift from county to province as the main locus of political activity. In the past, local interests had been paramount. Magistrates on the county bench governed in and out of sessions with considerable autonomy from the provincial executive and judiciary. The assembly, limited in its fiscal capacity and subject to executive supervision, was little more than a brief annual gathering of local patriarchs to divvy up road and bridge money and authorize county assessments. Many assembly members were county justices and their legislative meetings were in many respects extensions of sessions. In the 1840s this began to change. Imperial free trade, the emergence of responsible government provincially and ratepayer democracy locally, along with the inability of local authorities to cope with the commercial crisis and the pressure of famine immigration, combined to shift the locus of politics to the provincial assembly. We have already seen this exemplified in the conflict between old-style local patriarchs like Wyer

91. Campbell, 'Smashers.'

and Hatch and new-style patricians like Boyd during the immigration crisis of the early 1850s.[92]

During the 1850s there was an increasing divergence between the old local sessions system and the new institutions of partyism and responsible government. One of the preconditions for province-wide initiatives like prohibition (and, as we shall see, municipal incorporation and the dismantling of the sessions system) was a reorganization of the structures of local power. In Charlotte county, where sessions had previously been dominated by the St Andrews junto, the greatly increased participation of justices from other parishes reflected not only the impact of temperance principles on local elites but also the determination of both temperance activists and businessmen in competing localities (often the same people) to dilute the shiretown's influence by appointing their supporters to the county bench. In no small degree this was an artefact of the patronage that accompanied partyism and made it possible but it also reflected a policy of undermining the sessions system in the interest of a broad reorganization of provincial politics. In this sense, the new politics was truly a politics of 'smashers.'

Until mid-century, the Charlotte magistracy sought to reproduce itself by lobbying the provincial executive for appointments of like-minded loyal and respectable men of substance to the commission of the peace. Justices and others wrote to the provincial secretary from time to time recommending names to be added to the commission. Their letters were usually either politely ignored or referred to one of the judges for comment.[93] Before the mid-1830s most of the justices seem to have been more agitated about their precedence in the commission than about new recruits. Contestation over the class standing and moral character of candidates for the magistracy arrived with the early stirrings of agitation for responsible government.

92. Chapter 10.

93. For example, when David Owen recommended Cadwallader Curry and John Paterson to sit with him as justices for Campobello, provincial secretary Odell acknowledged his letter, informed him that no new appointments could be made except by issuing a new commission for the county, and mentioned that he had spoken to the chief justice about Owen's candidates: Owen to Odell, 9 Nov 1824, and Odell's undated note of his reply, both in CO 188/35.

When Moses Vernon and W.F.W. Owen recommended a tanner and a blacksmith as justices for St George, parish patriarch Hugh Mackay objected 'that neither of these persons are in nowise qualified to discharge the duties of the Office . . . that they have neither the education, influence, nor such Standing in Society as to entitle them to such distinction being conferred about them . . . '[94] When forty-seven Deer Islanders complained of the inconvenience of having no resident magistrate and submitted the endorsements of all four Charlotte assemblymen for their recommendation that Charles William Garrison be appointed, lieutenant governor Harvey sent the papers to the chief justice for inquiry by the judge of the next Charlotte circuit. Judge Parker reported that Garrison was an honest, respectable man and of good character, but making him a magistrate would conflict with his occupation as parish schoolmaster, in which he was 'to a certain extent under the control of the Trustees of Schools' and his pupils' parents: '[I]t is much to be feared that a person holding the situation of a Schoolmaster appointed to the Magistracy would soon seek to make up by Justice fees the falling off in his School emoluments which would be the natural consequence of the interference of the two offices.' Moreover, the man had a 'bodily defect, . . . which ought not to be passed over, when we consider the necessity of maintaining proper respect.' W.F.W. Owen had similar reservations about Garrison, referring to him forthrightly as 'a Schoolmaster and by nature a Cripple,' but admitted he was a respectable man and better qualified than anyone else in the parish who was willing to be named to the commission.[95] Garrison was not appointed.

By the mid-1840s, the Temperance stamp frequently appeared on correspondence about candidates for the magistracy. James Brown proposed two names from St David, both of them Methodists and 'active promoters of Temperance and Morality.'[96] W.B. Chandler opposed a nominee because he was 'a man given to that worst of all vices

94. PANB RG8/2/a, Mackay to Odell, 15 May 1838.

95. PANB RG8/2/a, petition of James Chaffey et al., Dec 1837; endorsement letter, Fredericton, 2 Jan 1838; Odell to Chief Justice, undated; Parker to Chief Justice, 10 May 1838; W.F.W. Owen to Odell, 8 June 1838.

96. PANB MC1001/MS2/ii/E/b/5, Brown to Rankin, 12 Apr 1847. All the correspondence quoted in this paragraph was found in the private papers of George Stillman Hill, a St Stephen barrister who served as MHA (1830-46), executive councillor

Drinking and his circumstances are very limited and there are other things about him equally objectionable.'[97] Joshua Knight opposed George Mackay's nomination because 'he can scarcely write a common order or receipt, frequently comes home in Liquor, and from being engaged in fights, with his face cut and clothes torn.' He rejected a second candidate because 'a JP should be a man of veracity, have some property in his own name, and should pay his just debts without compulsion, and not have the tongues and frowns of his neighbours continually upon him,' proposing instead the names of two 'honorable sober (Temperance members) religious men of property and universally respected,' although one of them was American-born and unnaturalized.[98] When this proved to be the latter candidate's downfall, Knight proposed a third name as the only one in the parish who 'would do': 'We have many who appear well in the Street or among strangers as long as they keep *sober*; but how would a drunkard or a knave do for a peace maker?' Threatening to resign from the magistracy were his nominee not to be appointed, Knight acknowledged

---

(1847-54), and legislative councillor (1849 until his death in 1858). Lawyer Hill was a master of the leading question. In 1841, as chairman of the legislature's committee of inquiry 'into the extent, causes and effects of intemperance,' he prepared thirty questions to be circulated in the community, including:

> 10. Is not the difficulty of procuring and managing Seamen in the merchant service chiefly to be attributed to their habits of intemperance?—and would it not be a great pecuniary benefit to this service, if Seamen were universally sober men?
>
> 11. Are not the wages of labour, and consequently the cost of the necessaries and comforts of life, greatly enhanced by the generally prevailing use of intoxicating drinks?
>
> 21. What have been the most remarkable benefits, within your own knowledge, to individuals and families, who have become members of a Total Abstinence Society?

When Hill became an executive councillor in 1847, legislative councillor Wyer advised him that 'everything depends on having Respectable Sober and Independent Magistrates and you should insist on your Recommendations for your own County being Complyed with.' Ibid., Wyer to Hill, 8 Jun 1847, 'confidential.'

97. Ibid., A1, Chandler to Wyer, 2 Jun 1847.

98. Ibid., E/b/5, Knight to Hill, 25 Aug 1847. For Hill's defence of James Albee JP against critics of his American birth, see his undated draft for publication in the Saint John *Courier* (not the *St Croix Courier* as stated in the finding aid): ibid., G/1/a.

that he was his brother-in-law, 'but only by my first wife.'[99]

As Temperance began to shape partyism and electoral outcomes in the mid-fifties, appointments to the magistracy became the coveted currency of political patronage. James Brown, newly elected in the Liberal-Temperance cause in 1854 after a spell in the legislative council, lamented the tide of requests for places in the commission, 'as the appointment of *one* is the disappointment of *many* ... There is such a large number proposed and indeed demanded that I think we must revise the whole Commission.'[100] His attempts to do so were frustrated in part by the competing demands of his political allies.[101] Even so, thirteen new justices were appointed in 1855, by far the largest accretion to the bench that the county had ever seen, although Brown had to leave out St David, St Andrews, and St Patrick claimants for the time being.[102] After the 1857 election, when the 'Smashers' made a clean sweep of Charlotte's four seats, another thirteen new justices joined the commission.[103] At this rate, the *Standard* editorialized, the courthouse must be enlarged. The appointees were competent, but 'this wholesale system of creating Magistrates savours strongly of political partisanship.'[104] J.G. Lorimer's new pa-

99. Ibid., Knight to Wyer, 29 Feb 1848.

100. PANB MC243, Brown to A.H. Gillmor, 15 May 1855. Brown, a farmer from St David, served in the assembly from 1830 until 1850, when he accepted the legislative council seat vacated by Wyer's death. He resigned in 1854 to run for the assembly. Arthur Hill Gillmor was a son of Daniel Gillmor JP, a lumberman later implicated in the crown lands scandal of the 1860s during Brown's surveyor generalship (chapter 5). Arthur was first elected to the assembly in 1854.

101. PANB MC243, Brown to Gillmor, 3 Oct 1855: 'I trust I shall be able to get your nominees appointed at our next meeting, which will be about ten days hence. I cannot get the whole number appointed who were on the list sent to you in a former letter, and must therefore leave some places unsupplied. I have just received a letter from our fellow Candidate, Chandler, saying that he had been informed that the Catholics in our County were much dissatisfied, because we had neglected them. It was my intention to appoint four of them for Magistrates, but against this McAdam and a large number of our most influential friends decidedly protest. So that Sullivan, my own nominee, whom I formerly recommended, I am thus compelled to omit, and Bradley also, as I cannot be allowed any one at present from St Andrews.'

102. Ibid., Brown to Gillmor, 29 Oct 1855.

103. The net increase was twelve as Henry Seelye had resigned in the mean time; see below.

104. *Standard*, 31 Mar 1858.

per, *The Investigator*, was less restrained, its indignation overtaking its syntax:[105]

> Look at the new Batches of Magistrates that come forth with every Gazette! That alone, that ridiculous farce, is in itself enough to blast the reputation of any Government! Such an exemplification of silly childish pandering to the wishes of partisans who love to have Esq. and J.P., to names which many of them can hardly scrawl (write is out of the question), and such a manifest desire to strengthen themselves by such absurd and ludicrous means, renders superbly contemptible!

This politicization of the commission was not just a figment of the journalists' imagination. Henry Seelye (of whom more below) urged 'a thorough change' in county officials, beginning with the removal of all magistrates appointed by the defeated government: 'I hold the Executive of the Province should exercise a special supervision over the Bench of each County, as in no other way can a respectable Magistracy be maintained.'[106] According to Brown it was the new government's policy 'to confine the dismissals to such persons as had been notoriously and avowedly opposed to our party in the late struggle.' Against critics who said this did not go far enough he argued that 'in Charlotte, we had made 38 new appointments, and dismissed 10 from office; and that whatever might be said to the contrary, we were really about the greatest *smashers* in the Province!'[107] Quizzed by the lieutenant governor about his proposed addition of nine more justices for the county in 1859, however, Brown privately admitted that 'the multiplication of Magistrates in the way we have done of late is farcical and ridiculous.'[108] Nevertheless when council met after prorogation in 1861 he recorded that there was to be 'a number of Magistrates appointed after the Election.'[109] In an 1866 editorial decrying the politicization of the bench, the *Standard* quoted an 'old, respectable and

105. Reprinted in *Standard*, 30 Jun 1858.

106. PANB MC243, Seelye to Gillmor, 24 Feb 1858.

107. Ibid., Brown to Gillmor, 2 Apr 1858, reporting the substance of his correspondence with David Upton. Brown's count included coroners, surveyors, and other officials as well as justices.

108. PANB MC295, diary, 27 May 1859.

109. Ibid., 27 Apr 1861. PANB MC243 includes several letters from partisans demanding the commissions they had been promised before the election: for exam-

well qualified' justice's observation that 'there was a time when it was considered an honor to have a seat on the bench; that now neither ability nor respectability were looked to, but, that an active polical hack or whipper in at elections, was all that was required to entitle a person to be appointed a JP.'[110]

A model temperance magistrate

New Brunswick enacted two major pieces of temperance legislation in the 1850s. The first, a government bill to end the liquor traffic, passed in 1852 and came into effect on June 1, 1853. In Charlotte it produced a surge in imports of 'London porter, stout and pale ale' and the establishment of the county's first steam-powered brewery at St Andrews since beer was exempted from this first attempt at a prohibitory liquor law.[111] It was a half measure that satisfied neither the temperance organizations nor their critics, and the government quickly repealed and replaced it with a new licensing statute before calling the 1854 election.[112] The Smashers made a strong showing in 1854. In Charlotte they captured three of the county's four seats, leaving only James Boyd to represent the 'High Church & Tory party and rum interest.'[113] Soon afterwards, and despite the *Standard*'s claim that the 1852 fiasco had taught temperance leaders, 'by attempting to get too much, we lose all,'[114] Samuel Leonard Tilley, Most Worthy Patriarch of the Sons of Temperance and provincial secretary in the new government, introduced a more draconian and comprehensive prohibitory bill. Despite widespread opposition and criticism it passed both assembly and legislative council with a majority of three in each

ples, Timothy Riordan to Gillmor, 18 Feb 1863 (and, refusing to take 'no' for an answer, 30 Mar 1863); James Bogue to Gillmor, 6 Mar 1863; Henry Leeman to Gillmor, 18 Mar 1863.

110. *Standard*, 28 Aug 1866.

111. *Standard*, 18 May 1853 (J.W. Street advertisement); ibid., 21 Sep 1853 (Patent Steam Brewery advertisement).

112. 15 Vict. (1852) c.51; 17 Vict. (1854) c.15. 18 Vict. (1855) c.23 addressed the difficulty of enforcing the 1854 licensing act by providing for penalties to be levied under the province's summary convictions legislation, RSNB 1854 c.138.

113. PANB MC243, Upton to Gillmor, 19 Jul 1854.

114. Ibid., 28 Apr 1854.

chamber.[115] At St Andrews the *Standard* called on everyone to petition the lieutenant governor to exercise the veto: '[W]e are still deserving of the name of Britons, and are not to be dictated to, as to what we shall eat, drink, or avoid, by any small minority belonging to Temperance Societies.'[116] This having proved unavailing the paper promoted an address to the Queen praying that she refuse her assent: it 'can be seen at the Steam Brewery, where signatures may be attached to it.' When it became clear that the act was to be left to its operation the new brewery prepared to shut its doors, offering to store customers' final orders in its cellars free of charge.[117] On Christmas Day a town meeting chaired by James Boyd resolved to bind county members to vote for repeal.[118] The *Standard* advised obedience to the law, 'unjust, obnoxious and impolitic' though it was, counselling that a two-month trial should be enough to demonstrate its futility.[119] It took five.

Prohibition came into effect on January 1, 1856. At St Andrews it was business as usual. Liquor shops remained open; no-one complained to the justices; revenue officers left smugglers alone.[120] In mid-January the *Standard* reprinted a lengthy report of the first prosecution under the act at Saint John as well as a brief account of a seizure from a shop at St Stephen.[121] Next came 'a most disgrace-

115. 18 Vict. (1855) c.36. For the history of the act and the constitutional crisis it provoked, Marquis, 'Contesting Prohibition.'

116. *Standard*, 4 Apr 1855. The paper qualified its criticism of temperance societies, 'whose works, as long as they do not extend to Legislative enactments, shall receive, as they have always done, our best and sincerest wishes.'

117. Ibid., 16 May, 26 Dec 1855. Charles Thompson petitioned for compensation, saying that he had sold his commission to emigrate and build the brewery, that he had invested £4000 in machinery and equipment he imported from England, and that he stood to lose £800 a year on account of the legislation: PANB RS347/c, 8 Feb 1856, endorsed 'no funds at H[is] E[xcellency]'s disposal for the purpose.'

118. Ibid., 2 Jan 1856. Boyd presented a repeal petition signed by 984 Charlotte electors when the assembly opened in February. Despite a requisition signed by 918 electors the other county members voted against the repeal bill introduced on the first day of the session. 'We admit their consistency as Sons of Temperance, but have they not acted contrary to the expressed wishes of a large majority of their constituents?' (ibid., 20 Feb 1856).

119. Ibid., 26 Dec 1855.

120. Ibid., 9 Jan 1856.

121. Ibid., 16 Jan 1856 copying *Courier*, 7 Jan 1856 and *Patriot*, 11 Jan 1856.

ful as well as illegal proceeding' at St Stephen, where Mrs Quinn's dwelling house was forcibly entered and searched 'from cellar to garret' for liquor without result. When she was nevertheless arrested and brought before a magistrate the case was dismissed because the witnesses did not answer their subpoenas.[122] Against the background of massive agitation for repeal,[123] attempts to enforce the prohibitory law had begun, drawing a sharp line between the shiretown and the upper parishes. When newly-minted St George magistrate Henry E. Seelye visited St Andrews, he was 'surprised to find the Town universally opposed to the Government, but what better could be expected of St Andrews?'[124]

Henry Edward Seelye was a son of Henry Seelye, an Irish-born British soldier who had married a daughter of St George founder Peter Clinch in 1815. Henry *père*, an unsuccessful businessman with interests in land and lumbering, served as a militia officer and parish by-roads commissioner before leaving for California in 1850. His eldest daughter, Lucretia, was married to deputy surveyor William Mahood. Henry Edward was about thirty-five years old when he was made a magistrate in Brown's 1855 batch. A temperance activist and Gillmor partisan, he was apparently without a regular occupation although he had briefly set up shop as a daguerreotypist at St Andrews in 1847.[125]

---

122. Ibid., 2 Feb 1856. By s.15 of the act, a justice was to issue a search warrant on the complaint of one 'reputable person, resident in the County' that he believed liquor was being kept for illegal sale on the premises, except in the case of a stand-alone dwelling occupied by a family, which could only be searched on the written testimony of three reputable witnesses under oath and liable to two years' imprisonment for knowingly making false statements. For the subpoena power see below.

123. The *Standard* reported mass meetings at Saint John and Fredericton (where Tilley was burned in effigy): 16 Jan, 23 Jan, 6 Feb 1856. Even in such a temperance stronghold as Grand Manan there were 'petitions afloat in all quarters': PANB MC243, Fisher to Gillmor, 18 Feb 1856.

124. Ibid., Seelye to Gillmor, 29 Feb 1856.

125. Seelye was among the signatories of an 1849 address against free trade ('depriving us of the advantages of the British connection in the way of commerce') on the occasion of the lieutenant governor's visit to St George. When the 1851 census was taken he and his wife (also named Lucretia) were lodging with a grocer there. R. Fellows, *First Families*; *Standard*, 9 Jun 1847; 9 Sep, 3 Oct 1849, 2 Nov 1850, 28 Apr 1852; PANB RS13/A/6, Saunders to Seelye, 5 Aug 1847; PANB RS346/b, 3 Sep 1849; PANB MC243, Upton to Gillmor, 19 Jul 1854, Brown to Gillmor, 15 May 1855 and 29 Oct 1855; PANB RS7, vol. 95, 17 Oct 1855.

Seelye's personal mission as a magistrate was to become the scourge of St George liquor-sellers. In a series of almost daily letters to Gillmor he described his preparations—'I have had my large Store cleared up and it makes a first rate Court room'—his demeanor—'I was perfectly calm and unmoved and when all was tumult and noise as you may well conceive it was I with a single command restored perfect order and even the boys were still'—his inspiration—'the Lord I firmly believe has given me a double amt of wisdom & strength'—and his attitude—'I was determined my Court should be respected and feared if not loved'—culminating in two shaky convictions for selling liquor contrary to the act.[126]

Within a few days of Mrs Quinn's escape from justice at St Stephen Seelye had pressed Gillmor to ask the attorney general whether the subpoena powers in the *Summary Convictions Act* applied to liquor cases: 'if it cannot the law *must* be amended for without the right to compel witness to attend it is void.'[127] A few days later he heard his first case, involving a man who got drunk on cherry bitters: 'I tasted the Bitters and concluded it is about one half rum, no doubt mixed up on purpose to evade the "Maine Law."'[128] The parties concerned were dismissed with a warning but, 'We expect to have a trial of the law here in a day or two and I think some of the *drink* will be poured out.' Then came 'rather an exciting day for St George generally and myself particularly,' the trial and impending conviction of two rum sellers. Despite his want of 'good advice' on the spot and no opinion

126. PANB MC243, Seelye to Gillmor, 19, 21, 29 Feb; 1, 4, 5, 8 Mar 1856.

127. PANB MC243, Seelye to Gillmor, 19 Feb 1856. RSNB 1854 c.138, provided in s.6 for compelling the attendance of material witnesses who failed to answer a summons and for committal of witnesses who refused to testify on oath. The act applied to proceedings before a justice in respect of 'any offence punishable by summary conviction' (s.1). There was no express power to compel witnesses set out in the 1855 prohibition act nor did it refer to 'summary conviction' per se, although s.25 provided that all 'penalties, foreitures, and convictions' under the act were to be tried before a justice of the peace. Seelye continued to press Gillmor for attorney general Fisher's opinion but decided when nothing was forthcoming to proceed in any event: PANB MC243, Seelye to Gillmor, 29 Feb, 4 Mar 1856.

128. Ibid., Seelye to Gillmor, 21 Feb 1856. In the same letter Seelye warns Gillmor about Boyd's repeal petition, suggesting that many of the names were forged and that it was being represented as the product of a county meeting when in fact the resolution was adopted at a St Andrews town meeting.

from the attorney general, Seelye decided to summon witnesses under the *Summary Convictions Act* and threatened to commit any who refused to testify.[129] The next day he convicted Richard McGee Jr and Henry Murphy for selling liquor and sentenced them to pay a fine of ten pounds and twenty shillings costs each or spend three months in jail.[130] Both immediately gave notice of appeal. Two other cases were adjourned so that Seelye could compel the testimony of witnesses who had either 'skulked' to avoid answering their summonses or, in one case, appeared but refused to testify. The following day he had them 'carried into the court by main force and commanded to swear or go to Gaol.' Another of Gillmor's correspondents, Michael Walsh, described the outcome:[131]

> Their cases were adjourned, I think four times, and had to be dismissed for want of Witnesses. There were warrants issued for several, all of whom kept out of the way except N Seelye[132] who was forced into Court as was also Ned Knight. They refused to swear and were sentenced to jail. Newton Seely was confined 4 days but Toad shouldered Knight cralled out of the way ... [H.E. Seelye] certainly performed his part in a very handsome manner. Enough to say he acted mildly but with dignified firmness quite impartially and strictly just. He received notice on Monday last from Judge Parker in arrest of judgment.

129. Ibid., Seelye to Gillmor, 21 Feb (with postscript re petition dated 27 Feb), 29 Feb, 4 Mar 1856.

130. The complainant in McGee's case was Louis Messenett, whose brother Claudius was another of the baker's dozen of 1855 JP appointments: PANB RS148/D/4/a, Charlotte County judgments, 5 Mar 1856. I have not found the judgment or identified the complainant in Murphy's case.

131. Ibid., Walsh to Gillmor, 2 Apr 1856.

132. Newton Seelye was the magistrate's uncle: 'Poor old Col Hatch ... I don't know he is sorry he voted for the "prohibitory law" particularly when that law authorizes a Magistrate "to send his *own* Uncle to gaol" – Couldn't there be some Magistrates made who have got no uncles?': ibid., Seelye to Gillmor, 6 Apr 1856, emphasis in original. In his letter to Gillmor (ibid., 2 Apr 1856) Walsh reported that 'N Seelye I believe has cut stick I consider him a bad man and I think his absence will be no loss to the community.' Hatheway encountered Newton Seelye in the debtors apartments of the St Andrews jail where he had been confined for 'refusing to give Evidence before Justice Henry Seelye': PANB RS463/A/2, 11 Mar 1856; PANB RS375/B/2, 11 Mar 1856 and see chapter 8.

The Rummies' response was not long in coming. Walsh surmised that a perjury charge against a liquor complainant brought before three tory 'Just Asses' had been 'got up through feelings of malice and revenge.' He told Gillmor that Murphy, whom Seelye had convicted, and Newton Seelye, whom he had committed for refusing to swear, had given informations against Francis Hibbard (another temperance magistrate in the 1855 batch), Louis Messenett, and Seelye himself for smuggling: 'a large amount of goods were seized on Hibbard but the others got clear.' Justice Seelye told Gillmor that 'the *Parson*'—presumably Skeffington Thomson, the Anglican rector of St Stephen and father of tory magistrate and politician Dr Robert Thomson—'is so enraged at our proceedings that his recovery is considered doubtful, he has volunteered to back both Ned Nite & Newt Seelye in carrying on a prosecution against me, and to oppose it the [Sons of Temperance] Division have pledged their whole fund to carry on the war—exciting times I assure you.'[133]

With his liquor cases pending before the judges, Seelye set out to St Andrews for April sessions where he hoped to forestall the Rummies' anticipated attempt to appoint one of the accused as agent for the sale of 'liquors for medicinal, mechanical, chemical or sacramental purposes' under the prohibitory act.[134] The temperance trio—Seelye, Claudius Messenett, Hibbard—were the only St George magistrates to attend sessions: 'the *Old* Justices would not condescend to sit with the *new*.' Seelye was elected to the three-member committee for appointing liquor agents. He drafted regulations for the agents' conduct and secured the appointment of his own nominee for the parish.[135] Nevertheless there was a cloud on the horizon. There had been an attempt to adjourn Sessions for a week 'to meet the emer-

133. PANB MC243, Seelye to Gillmor, 8 Mar 1856. In 1858 Seelye urged Gillmor to remove Dr Thomson from the coronership on partisan grounds: ibid., 24 Feb 1858. Seelye enlisted Gillmor's help in getting St Stephen barrister George Grimmer to represent him in the liquor appeals: ibid., 6 Apr 1856.

134. It is not clear whether the 'Dick McGee' named by Seelye as the candidate for appointment was the father, whose case was abandoned for lack of evidence, or the son, whom he had convicted. Ibid., Seelye to Gillmor, 9 Apr 1856.

135. This was 'old Nick Mealing' whom Seelye had earlier told Gillmor 'would make the best Agent here and wants it and it would do him a great benefit in a pecuniary way.' Ibid., Seelye to Gillmor, 9 and 13 Apr 1856; CCGS Apr 1856.

gency that might arise in case the liquor law should be repealed.' If some measure could not be taken to make the *Summary Convictions Act* apply to liquor cases, Seelye worried, 'I fear we are in a worse fit than if the law had been repealed.' Barely a month later, when the government resisted his insistence that it either enforce the liquor law or repeal it, the lieutenant governor dissolved the legislature and sent the province to the polls.

In July, with a slim Rummy majority in the new assembly—the Charlotte representation was evenly split on party lines—prohibition was formally repealed. Seelye promptly resigned from the bench on the principle, he later explained, that magistrates appointed by defeated governments should be removed.[136] He took as his reward the secretaryship of the provincial railway appraisers along with appointments for his brother as a surveyor and an uncle—not Newt—as coroner. In 1862 he left Charlotte county for British Columbia where he worked as a pro-Confederation journalist, accompanied the BC delegates to Ottawa to negotiate the terms of entry, and in 1872 accepted an appointment in the Dominion Customs. He died at Kootenay in 1876.[137]

When sessions opened in September 1856 Seelye was gone but 'political viper' Boyd was back on the bench.[138] He arrived at St Andrews in time to debate the regulations under the new licensing act. There were two petitions from Milltown, one for and the other against issuing tavern licenses for the village. The justices agreed to charge five pounds for an annual license and to publish the names of all licensees in the local press. Somewhat tardily, fifty-seven names appeared.[139] Peace had been restored.

---

136. PANB RS13/A/9, Tilley to Seelye accepting his resignation dated 25 July, 6 Aug 1857; PANB MC243, Seelye to Gillmor, 24 Feb 1858.

137. Ibid., Gillmor to Seelye (copy), 22 Mar 1859; PANB RS 13/A/10, Tilley to Jardine, 26 Oct 1858; *Saint Croix Courier*, 18 Jul 1872; *Standard*, 24 May 1876.

138. Boyd had been restored to the commission of the peace in September 1856 to oppose the temperance magistrates: chapter 10. Walsh called him a 'political viper' in correspondence with Gillmor: PANB MC243, 2 Apr 1856.

139. CCGS Sep 1856; *Standard*, 1 July 1857.

COMMENCEMENT OF THE ST. ANDREW'S AND QUEBEC RAILWAY.

Figure 12.1 – St Andrews & Quebec Railroad groundbreaking, 1847 [PANB P110-64, RS22-44]

Chapter 12

The sessions system in decline

From a St Andrews viewpoint the health of the sessions system was closely associated with the prosperity of the town, and that in turn with the fortunes of the St Andrews & Quebec Railroad scheme. From its founding in October 1835 the railroad was promoted by the most prominent businessmen-magistrates, most of them also directors of the Charlotte County Bank.[1] This first railway promotion in British North America proposed to link the ice-free port of St Andrews with Quebec City, replacing twelve hundred miles of seasonal navigation with some two hundred miles of track operable year-round.[2] Following an exploratory survey by *Standard* editor G.N. Smith DLS and C.R. Hatheway, resolutions were passed in the New Brunswick and Lower Canada legislatures, a blue ribbon 'standing committee' organized, the lieutenant governor's approval obtained, and envoys sent to London to lay the scheme at the foot of the throne.[3] Just as arrangements for a detailed survey were in train, Washington objected that the proposed route passed through disputed territory. The im-

1. The railroad committee consisted of Allanshaw, Wyer, Hatch, Wilson, Rait, Frye, and J. McMaster, with Adam Jack as secretary-treasurer.

2. [Anon.], *Account of the St A&Q.*

3. For the survey see chapter 5. The standing committee included the chief justice, provincial secretary Odell, crown lands commissioner Baillie, judge Botsford, W.F.W. Owen, and G.F. Street, among others.

perial government ordered all activity suspended until the boundary question was finally settled. The Ashburton treaty of 1842 gave the territory to the United States.

In 1845 the railroad company reorganized at St Andrews, elected a board dominated by Charlotte notables, and established a company to raise capital in England.[4] Its stock was widely subscribed in Charlotte although few local investors were able to meet the calls when they came. A new route was selected and construction began on the St Andrews to Woodstock section. By 1851 four miles had been completed from Harris Hatch's wharf at St Andrews to John Wilson's mills and quays at Chamcook. Two years later twenty-five miles had been laid, the company was close to broke, and its prospects were shadowed by the opening of the St Lawrence & Atlantic from Montreal to Portland, Maine. New financing allowed construction to continue until 1855 when the contractors threatened to take over the road for nonpayment. The British shareholders intervened, proposing that the St Andrews directorate transfer control to London. While many Charlotte investors thought this would be the salvation of the company, John Wilson resisted. In president Hatch's absence he managed to get resolutions through the local board to give him interim control of the road and its equipment (allegedly so that he could get timber he had cut on speculation out to market) and a gratuity of £1600 for past services.

When the St Andrews *Standard* published letters and editorials criticizing his motives Wilson sued for libel. The majority of local investors voted to transfer control. A few weeks later, ousted from the venture he had championed for twenty years and alienated from his colleagues and community, Wilson died. The railway's reorganization as the New Brunswick & Canada under a London board seemed to hold out new hope for St Andrews—the St Stephen *Patriot* called it 'the resuscitation of a dying town'[5]—but competing schemes with powerful backing in Saint John and St Stephen undermined it: 'An impenetrable darkness overshadows the vision of our public men, and

4. The board elected in 1846 consisted of Harris and Wellington Hatch, Wilson, Frye, St Andrews postmaster G.F. Campbell, W.F.W. Owen, D.S. Morrison, R. Walton, J. Rodgers, W. Porter (St Stephen), and four Woodstock directors.

5. 30 Sep 1853.

the reason is that an overwelming selfishness and localism pervades every nook and corner of the country.'[6] The railway reached Woodstock in 1862 but the company collapsed the following year, dragging down with it the Charlotte County Bank and St Andrews' remaining aspirations for commercial significance. The road's fate was sealed in 1868 when the imperial government approved an Intercolonial Railway route that bypassed it entirely; it was finally absorbed by the CPR in 1890.

The businessmen of St Andrews had seen a long series of entrepreneurial hopes raised and dashed since the leaders of the Penobscot Association planted the town in the 1780s only to find it blocked from its hinterland by the surveyor of the King's woods. A commercial strategy based on the triangle trade came to grief with the repeal of the navigation acts and the admission of American ships into West Indies ports. The repeal of the colonial preference undermined their expectations for the timber trade. The separation of the port of St Andrews from that of Saint John raised hopes briefly but within a few years liberalized customs rules allowing vessels to clear at the outports left St Andrews in the doldrums. The town's harbour proved too shallow for the new deep-draught technology of ocean-going steamships but, without the projected railway, freight volumes were too small to justify the cost of dredging a deep-water port. Since the 1790s the businessmen of St Andrews had relied on their role as county governors based in the shire town to offset these and other disadvantages. But by the mid-1850s even that advantage was slipping away. The slow demise of the sessions system was neither cause nor consequence of St Andrews' decline but it contributed to the town's malaise and played its part in the intraregional competition that increasingly favoured St Stephen. Ten years after John Wilson died his estate at Chamcook became the residence of Charlotte county's new clerk of the peace, George S. Grimmer, a lawyer from St Stephen.[7]

We have already encountered many of the institutional shifts that undermined the sessions system. As the assembly gained control of the public purse its function changed and so did the opportunities it offered to men of ambition. At one time the House had been little

6. Letter of 'Monitor,' *Standard*, 14 Nov 1855.
7. *Standard*, 5 Apr 1865.

more than a committee of county governors to divide appropriations for local purposes; now it essentially governed a province and did so by taking control of executive and administrative functions that had traditionally been the province of sessions. The modernization of the criminal law had increased the volume of cases heard summarily by individual justices at the expense of the criminal jurisdiction of general sessions and its grand and petit juries. The development of the party system had made commissions of the peace tools of patronage, greatly expanding the roster of JPs while undermining their prestige. Popular democratic reforms like the secret ballot and elective parish office not only limited the authority of the county bench but made appointed county governorship seem anachronistic at best, corrupt and perverse at worst.

While in some respects the decline of the sessions system was a side-effect of other institutional changes, in others it was programmatic. For the Smashers the old regime was anathema and had to be replaced. This was to be accomplished not only by shifting authority from the local bench to provincially-appointed boards and commissions and by dismantling local institutions like the inferior courts of common pleas, but also by reconstituting local government. Nevertheless the old ways persisted alongside the new for a long time. The sessions system did not give up easily. From the late 1840s until the decade after Confederation the two systems coexisted, not peacefully but in a state of tension and conflict. This helps to explain how it was possible, for example, for the provincial government to prohibit the manufacture and sale of 'intoxicating liquors' while the county continued to derive revenues from tavern and retail licenses. It helps to explain the ineffectiveness of such provincial initiatives as prohibition and municipal incorporation in the years leading up to Confederation. It also helps to explain the deterioration of confidence in the workings of the sessions system as shown, for example, by the decline in the role of the grand jury. Efforts at reforming local governance were met by efforts to resist change.

The great fight for clean government

'The utter want of municipal institutions giving the people any control over their local affairs, may indeed be considered as one of the main causes of the failure of representative government, and of the bad administration of the country.'[8] Thus wrote Lord Durham, whose vision, filtered first through Sydenham's utilitarianism[9] and again through Baldwin's pragmatism, ultimately became the *Municipal Corporations Act* of Canada West in 1849. This did away with the Canadian version of the sessions system, substituting electoral ratepayer democracy for appointed officialdom at the county, town, township, and even village levels.[10] While the initiative spoke to local concerns about the quality and availability of JPs[11] and the opportunities for elite patronage, municipal incorporation in Canada West was at least at first a top-down project driven by imperial reformers and their colonial vice-regents.[12] 'It seems to have been left to English reforming Whigs to recognize the functional connections between colonial and municipal government, and indeed to foist it upon their Canadian counterparts.'[13]

Similar pressures were felt in New Brunswick, where in 1842 the lieutenant governor told the legislature at the opening of the session that he had become convinced 'of the paramount importance of providing for the introduction of those principles of Municipal Government... which I am persuaded will be found peculiarly adapted to the situation of the people of this Province.'[14] Nothing came of this first sally. At St Andrews a correspondent cautioned readers of the *Standard* that popular election of local governors 'affords no guarantee that one set of men will act with more prudence and ability than the

8. Craig, *Durham Report,* 67. Whebell, 'Baldwin and Decentralization' points out that for Edward Gibbon Wakefield and Durham's secretary Charles Buller, the colonies themselves were mere municipalities.

9. Radforth, 'Sydenham.'

10. I am indebted to Mary Stokes for her insights into municipal incorporation in Ontario. See in general Aitchison, 'The Municipal Corporations Act of 1849.'

11. 'The shortage of justices is the most important fact about the local government of Upper Canada'—ibid., 111.

12. Whebell, 'District Councils Act,' 185; Radforth, 'Sydenham.'

13. Whebell, 'District Councils Act,' 188.

14. JHA 1842, 6.

other' and warned that corporation government must mean higher taxes.[15] Writing in 1846, Calvin Luther Hatheway claimed that New Brunswickers were generally happy with the existing system, 'and when it was, a few years since, proposed in our Legislature to alter the system and establish Municipal Corporations, it was opposed by the majority of that Body. When we look at the workings of Municipal Corporations in the United States, see their constant or continued elections, and witness the ruinous effects of their numerous taxes, we see nothing desirable in their system, and feel much better content with our own.'[16]

Again in 1848, commenting on the incorporation of the city of Fredericton, the lieutenant governor reminded the legislature of his conviction that by adopting 'the English principle of voluntary Incorporation' the province would gain 'great advantages.'[17] This top-down pressure mounted in 1850 with the tabling of despatches from Downing Street saying that 'the establishment of a system of Municipal organization' was 'most urgently wanted.'[18] Earl Grey's conception of how this might work in New Brunswick was somewhat undermined by his proposal to give local municipalities control of land and timber revenues to be expended on local improvements. This, lieutenant governor Head had to point out, 'would be hardly practicable, since the receipts from these sources in different Counties of the Province are so extremely unequal as far to exceed what would be necessary in one County, whilst another would be left almost without funds.'[19]

At the next session of the legislature reform of municipal institutions was back on the agenda as a corollary to parliamentary government at the provincial level. The assembly resolved to give the exec-

---

15. *Standard*, 16 Dec 1842.

16. Hatheway, *History of New Brunswick*, 67-8. One of Charles Reid's elder brothers, he was a DLS, a JP in Saint John and then Sunbury counties, and a major in the Saint John militia. His son George Luther Hatheway was to become premier of New Brunswick in 1871.

17. JHA 1848, 346. Despite frequent references to English constitutional principles by promoters of New Brunswick reform, no English county was incorporated before the 1889 *County Councils Act*.

18. JHA 1850, 112, Grey to Head, No. 148, 23 Jul 1849.

19. JHA 1850, 113, Head to Grey, 17 Sep 1849.

utive the right to initiate money bills on imperial 'principles of Responsible and Departmental Government,' and while an amendment to postpone implementation until 'Municipal Corporations shall be in efficient working throughout the Province' was lost nevertheless the House considered 'the establishment of Municipal Bodies to control and distribute the funds for local objects and other purposes of self government' to be 'intimately connected' with the change in the machinery of supply.[20]

While in Canada it was a fundamental premise of the Baldwin act that there should be no unincorporated municipal bodies larger than the police village, the New Brunswick assembly proposed to make incorporation optional by providing for 'such bodies in all localities where they may be demanded by the People.'[21] There was a petition before the legislature from the Carleton grand jury, endorsed by several magistrates and the county sheriff, to give 'to the inhabitants of the said County the sole control of their local affairs, by means of Municipal organization.'[22] A bill for county-level incorporation by local option was introduced and extensively amended in committee. It provided for a requisition to the county sheriff signed by at least fifty resident ratepayers calling for a public meeting to consider incorporation. After giving due notice and publication the sheriff was to preside at a meeting of at least one hundred ratepayers; if at least two-thirds of those voting were in favour he was to certify the result to the lieutenant governor in council who was thereupon to issue a charter. An attempt to provide for opting out of incorporation instead of opting in garnered only two votes. Most of the debate on this section was over the franchise and the proportion of votes required. The bill defined the municipal franchise as 'resident Freeholders and Householders of the County, paying rates upon property.' An attempt to restrict it to freeholders only was lost, the Charlotte members evenly split on either side of the question. An attempt to replace the two-thirds requirement with a simple majority also lost with three Char-

20. JHA 1851, 355; ibid., 14.

21. Ibid., 14. Canadian police villages were regulated by the incorporated townships that contained them along with boards of trustees for local purposes.

22. Ibid., 68. Several additional petitions from Carleton followed: ibid., 138.

lotte members against and one in favour.[23] The bill passed the assembly on April 1, 1851, and received council approval. At the close of the session the lieutenant governor told both Houses that he 'rejoice[d] sincerely to find that the first step has been made towards the general introduction of Municipal Institutions throughout the Province.'[24]

The *Standard* welcomed the legislation, editorializing that 'the people are anxious to have the power of electing those who are to manage the County affairs, as the present rulers are considered irresponsible, and there appears to be a growing desire among the people for self-government.'[25] Nevertheless the grand jury at April sessions declined to give an opinion on incorporation but wondered, since 'the affairs of this County are now well conducted, whether it would not be inexpedient to give up a certainty for an uncertainty.'[26] The editor of the *Standard* served on the grand jury at September sessions, and it recommended putting the question to the test.[27] A requisition duly appeared with one hundred and forty-one names including those of three justices—Wilson, Hatheway, and Todd—assemblyman Fitzgerald, and assemblyman-in-waiting James Boyd.[28] As the date of the public meeting approached the *Standard* gave room to opposing opinions. 'Freeholder' urged caution in setting 'local demagogues' against the magistrates, while 'A Tenant and Taxpayer in the West End,' railing against the fire engine tax, prophesied that 'the day of retributive justice is at hand, when these poor ratepayers will teach their rulers a lesson of wisdom through the ballot box, under the Municipal Act.'[29] A satirical piece lampooned 'Squire Dodge' who was 'opposed to anything that would enlighten the mass of the people who are not far enough advanced in civilization to govern them-

---

23. Fitzgerald supported the wider franchise and the simple majority; Robinson was for the wider franchise but the two-thirds majority; Porter and Thomson voted for the narrower franchise and the two-thirds majority.

24. JHA 1851, 395.

25. *Standard*, 19 Mar 1851.

26. Ibid., 23 Apr 1851.

27. Ibid., 1 Oct 1851.

28. Ibid., 24 Dec 1851. Earlier accounts in the *Standard* had said there were two hundred signatories; on 14 Apr 1852, a week before the vote, it said there were 'upwards of one hundred and fifty.'

29. *Standard*, 15 Oct 1851; 27 Aug 1851.

selves.'[30] While continuing to oppose 'old-fashioned systems of mismanagement,' the editor wanted people to weigh the measure carefully and not adopt it blindly.[31] A few days before the public meeting the grand jury at April sessions pronounced in favour of municipal incorporation as 'a boon offered to all persons interested therein, which, if properly appreciated, will have a tendency to afford them the full enjoyment of their rights and privileges as British subjects.'[32]

The Charlotte meeting was called for noon on April 22, 1852, at the county courthouse in St Andrews. After a public reading of sections of the municipal act the sheriff announced that only householders paying rates were entitled to vote. He handed over the chair to magistrate Ker who introduced a series of speakers. Dr Thomson MLA and justices Patrick Clinch, George Thomson, and G.D. Street all spoke against incorporation; somewhat surprisingly, B.R. Fitzgerald MLA also opposed it 'at the present time.' The speakers in favour included John Wilson, Lachlan Donaldson, F.A. Babcock, James Boyd, William Smith, and H.E. Seelye. 'Had the weather not been so stormy and the freshets so high on our rivers,' the *Standard* explained, 'many intelligent persons from the upper Parishes would have been present, who are decidedly in favor of incorporating the County, and carried the measure by an overwhelming majority, even beyond the two-thirds vote.' As it was, however, there were one hundred and sixty-nine votes in favour and one hundred sixteen opposed, so the measure was defeated by a margin of twenty-one. The *Standard* contented itself by reprinting an editorial from the Carleton *Sentinel* deploring 'that the same deception and misrepresentations are practiced [in Charlotte] to defeat the Municipal Act that were employed' at Carleton, the province's first incorporated county.[33]

Support for municipal incorporation was indeed much higher in the 'upper parishes,' St Stephen especially, than in St Andrews or the islands. Table 12.1 shows the proportion of signatories by parish for the 1851 requisition as well as a subsequent requisition in 1854 and

30. Ibid., 31 Mar 1852. See also ibid., 7 and 14 Apr 1852.
31. Ibid., 29 Oct 1851; 19 Nov 1851.
32. Ibid., 21 Apr 1852.
33. Ibid., 28 Apr 1852.

Table 12.1 – Municipal incorporation support by parish, 1851-4

	1851	%	1853	%	1854	%
Campobello	1	1	0	0	0	0
Pennfield	2	1	23	23	1	1
St Andrews	38	27	0	0	27	26
St David	19	13	1	1	2	2
St George	2	1	16	16	1	1
St James	2	1	1	1	1	1
St Patrick	12	9	0	0	11	11
St Stephen	62	44	59	58	58	56
West Isles	3	2	2	2	2	2
Parish known	141		102		103	
Total	141		141		136	
% known	100		72		76	

two petitions in 1853.[34] Although the petitioners styled themselves the ratepayers of Charlotte the petitions appear to have circulated only in St Stephen, St George, and Pennfield. Directed to the assembly, they complained that the municipal act was inoperative because it compelled ratepayers to cast their votes at the shiretown: 'this evil was seriously felt at the meeting held in this County in April last for the adoption or rejection of said Act, in consequence of which but a partial vote was secured.'[35] They sought to have the incorporation vote held like a general election at polling places in the various parishes. The petitions were tabled in the assembly but no amending bill was proposed.

The *Standard* kept up the pressure for incorporation but the St Stephen *Provincial Patriot* was a more constant champion. It ran a series of letters signed 'Public Good' systematically setting out the case for incorporation and rebutting the arguments against it.[36] Since 'the people' would control offices and salaries there would be no tax increases unless the people decided they wanted them. The legisla-

34. Names were compared to the 1851 and 1861 censuses and, where available, assessment rolls. Adults with the same name in more than one parish were excluded from the 'known' total on which the percentages were calculated.

35. PANB RS24/1853/pe, nos. 139 and 266.

36. *Patriot* 2, 9, 16, 23 and 30 Sep 1853.

ture's time would no longer be wasted on local matters. There would be a great advance in public education as schools were the most important duty of county councils. By-road money would be spent efficiently as the commissioners would no longer be the MLAs' placemen 'maintained year after year against the unanimous wish of the immediate neighbourhood.' It was wrong for the legislature to approve municipal corporations without imposing them universally 'on a constituency governed by a Magistracy as irresponsible (it would perhaps, be harsh and uncharitable to say *despotic*) as so many autocratic plenipotentiaries.' It was time for Charlotte to follow the example of Canada, Australia, and Carleton county:

> too long [Carleton] played concubine to the unhallowed desires of her lordly Magistrates, and having gained the embrace of a chaste and frugal partner *by a Corporation*, she advises her sister, coy and reluctant Charlotte, to come out from the Magisterial harem and 'do likewise.'

Another series, signed 'Veritas,' challenged the view that incorporation would raise taxes by arguing that county and parish funds were mismanaged under the present system.[37] The existing county tax went to pay officers 'known only to the office-holders in St Andrews, and the Magistrates with their satellites who batten on the County funds.' No-one knew the size of the county debt or how long it would take to pay it off. 'The tax-payers know they have to pay this tax, but they know no more about its distribution than a Patagonian.' As for tavern and retail licenses, 'into what vortex this money has been cast, few can tell, except the Magistrates and the official compact in St Andrews.' Similarly the poor tax and the road tax. Was it unfair that tenants in St Andrews had to contribute towards a fire engine? Was it imbecilic for St Stephen's magistrates to have built the lock-up house on the public market slip? Was the commutation system for statute labour a 'legal swindle' on the 'great mass of the people'? Municipal incorporation was the cure for every complaint.

Like the *Standard*, the *Patriot* gave some space to the opposition. An insightful conservative commentary observed that New

37. Ibid., 7, 14 Oct, 4 Nov, 1 Dec 1853.

Brunswick faced the 'singular and anomalous spectacle of having Republican institutions forced upon it by the monarchical government of England.' The assembly had become all-powerful at the expense of the Crown prerogative and the government had to exercise patronage to stay in power, so it was driven to such measures as prohibition, municipal incorporation, vote by ballot, 'elective everything,' which if adopted would bring the province 'to the lowest depths of Democracy from which there would be no return.'[38] 'Thersites' argued that the combination of growing population, universal suffrage, and municipal incorporation must lead to increased taxation on the 'middle class'—'if you raise an evil spirit you must find something for it to do.' The new system must necessarily reproduce all the failings of the old, magnified by greater opportunities for corruption. Expanding the local franchise from freeholders to all ratepayers would not improve the system: 'Is all virtue concentrated in the Rabble?' And it was an anachronism to blame the St Andrews magistrates for while at one time they had an 'unfair preponderance' they no longer controlled county management.[39]

Unsuccessful attempts were made in the legislature in 1852 and 1854 to amend the voting procedure so that a simple majority would suffice for incorporation. There were only two votes in favour in 1852 but twelve two years later. All the Charlotte members voting were opposed in both years. There was a second opportunity to revisit the act later in the 1854 session when chapter 42 of the Revised Statutes reached committee of the whole. Once again an amendment was moved to incorporate by a simple majority of ratepayers voting at the public meeting. It attacted seven 'yeas' including that of James Boyd, newly installed in place of Fitzgerald. Thomson and Porter voted against the amendment, which was lost. Then another amendment was moved to require the sheriff to call public meetings simultaneously in each parish. The committee split evenly with Boyd voting in favour and Thomson against; the amendment was defeated on the chair's vote.

But at the same session a new bill was passed for public meetings in each parish with a recorded vote to be tallied at the shire town and

38. Ibid., 1 Dec 1853.
39. Ibid., 30 Dec 1853.

incorporation to follow if two-thirds of the total vote was in favour. This meant that there were two incompatible municipal incorporation acts on the province's statute books at the end of the spring 1854 session. The *Revised Statutes* included Title VI, Chapter 42, 'Of the establishment of municipal authorities,' providing for a requisition by fifty resident freeholders and householders, a public meeting of one hundred ratepaying householders at the county courthouse, and a two-thirds vote. The *Public Statutes* included 'An Act to alter and amend the Act providing for the establishment of Municipal Authorities in this Province,' which repealed section 1 of the 1851 statute and provided for a requisition by one hundred resident freeholders and householders, public meetings at the parish polling places used for general elections, voters' lists compiled from parish assessment rolls, recorded votes, and a two-thirds majority of those voting in the county as a whole.[40]

A new requisition for a Charlotte incorporation meeting announced in March 1854 was delayed when the sheriff, uncertain whether 'freeholders and householders' meant all freeholders and all householders or just freehold householders, referred the question to the law officers. The *Standard* hoped that the legislature would amend the act for a simple majority before the Charlotte vote: 'Under the present system, when a two thirds vote was necessary, the old fogies that infest every County could, by the exercise of their influence, and by misrepresentations, obstruct the vote.'[41] Charlotte's second municipal incorporation meeting, an exceptionally 'disorderly and noisy' one, took place at St Andrews on June 30, 1854, after the general election polls closed but before the results were announced. It began with efforts by J.W. Chandler and James Boyd to show that the requisition and meeting were illegal because they were initiated under section 1 of the 1851 municipal act which had since been repealed: 'the Meeting should be dismissed, a new Requisition might be prepared, when all the people in the different Parishes might vote at their own doors.' Nevertheless the people insisted on voting, four hundred and forty-three in favour, three hundred and forty against,

40. 17 Vict. (1854) c.8.
41. 15 Mar 1854.

and incorporation was defeated by seventy-nine votes.[42]

The newly-elected Smasher government revisited the municipal corporations act, repealing the inconsistent sections of both 1854 statutes and replacing them by a provision for meetings at all parish polling places and incorporation by a simple majority.[43] But the heart had gone out of the county incorporation movement in Charlotte and no further requisitions were made. In 1856 the attorney general introduced a bill to make county incorporation mandatory throughout the province but in its final form the act preserved the system of incorporation by requisition and public meeting.[44] Charlotte was not alone in its diminished enthusiasm for municipal reform. Carleton, York, and Sunbury counties incorporated; in Victoria the initiative led to rioting and a legislative inquiry;[45] but on the whole the measure was met with indifference.[46] As one correspondent put it, 'Were there any Demonstrations made by the people demanding such changes? Were there any reform Clubs? Any monster Meetings?'[47] An 1857 assembly committee regretted the expense of 'useless' private and local bills cluttering the legislative agenda but concluded 'that until Municipal Institutions are more generally adopted in the Province' nothing could be done about it.[48]

And in Charlotte nothing further was done until after Confederation.[49] In 1871 the Town of Saint Stephen was incorporated and given a stipendiary police magistrate, its elected mayor and councillors to

42. *Standard*, 5 Jul 1854.

43. 18 Vict. 1854, c.3.

44. *Standard*, 9 Apr 1856; 19 Vict. (1856) c.37.

45. JHA 1854 (1st), 251ff.

46. JHA 1853, Appendix, cxviii, Report of W.P. Dole, Inspector of Schools, Saint John, reporting 'the indifference which has been manifested throughout the greater part of the Province, in regard to the establishment of Municipal Corporations.' School reformers alert to the Canada West experience considered municipal incorporation a *sine qua non* of educational improvement: see for example, JHA 1854 (2d), Appendix, cxlii, Report of John Davidson, York County: 'When the Municipal Act is generally adopted throughout the Counties in this Province, or better still, by the Parishes, and the people learn the great advantages to be derived from managing their own affairs, then an improved system of education might be carried out ...'

47. *Patriot*, 1 Dec 1853.

48. JHA 1857, 177.

49. Bell, 'Confederation Issue' concludes that 'standard explanations of New Brunswick's strangely fluctuating response to confederation have little relevance to

be justices of the peace during their terms of office but not required to act judicially 'unless at pleasure.'[50] Milltown followed suit two years later and Upper Mills in 1874.[51] Finally in 1877 *An Act relating to Municipalities* provided that 'The Ratepayers of every County not heretofore incorporated shall be a body politic and corporate under this Act,' which also abolished courts of Quarter [*sic*] Sessions throughout the province.[52] The sessions system was no more.[53]

The death of a thousand cuts

The decline and eventual demise of the sessions system proceeded on two fronts simultaneously. The first was its wholesale substitution by municipal corporations which took a generation and profound constitutional change to achieve. The other was the piecemeal ongoing revision of practically every component of the old system. While a few of these reforms, like the introduction of county courts, were substantial changes, most were minor in themselves but cumulatively significant. For example, the removal of pilotage from the sessions jurisdiction to that of a provincially-appointed commission, championed by James Boyd and discussed in chapter 7, was one among many small subtractions from local authority which amounted altogether to a much larger shift. Another aspect of reform was the trend away from local legislation (Appendix A.5) to general enactments for the whole province which tended to transfer regulatory and administrative authority from sessions to provincial bodies. This, together with a mid-century penchant for consolidation and systematization, replaced specific and particularistic rules with abstract and universal ones that were less accommodating to local circumstances and preferences and more resistant to variation by the exercise of local discretion.

Charlotte County,' where electors had 'a positive regard for the status quo.'

50. 34 Vict. (1871) c.20. The town's gaol was to remain the county gaol at St Andrews (s.69).

51. 36 Vict. (1873) c.103; 37 Vict. (1874) c.60.

52. 40 Vict. (1877) c.3.

53. For the operation of county government under the 1877 act see Whalen, *Local Government*, chapter 4.

The *County and Parish Act* of 1850 consolidated and amended a hundred and fifteen local government statutes. It provided for the direct election of many parish officers by the ratepayers at town meetings.[54] From one point of view this merely recognized a long-standing although informal practice in some parishes; from another it undermined the authority of sessions to oversee parish offices. It also provided that justices, clerks of the peace, and coroners could not serve as county treasurer or auditor or hold any office fiscally accountable to sessions. It regularized compensation by salary, commission, fee, allowance, and reward for various local government services, itemized sessions' regulatory jurisdiction and powers of enforcement, and eliminated the need for legislative sanction of certain county public works. It enhanced the power of the grand jury to approve assessments for county contingencies and audit county accounts and of the ratepayers to review parish finances before electing officers. By limiting discretion, increasing oversight, and regularizing methods and practices the act bureaucratized the administrative role of the justices in sessions and undermined the personal authority of the county or parish patriarch. Subsequent amendments expanded the list of parish officers to be elected (thereby further diminishing the appointive power of sessions), empowered the sessions grand jury to elect its own foreman, required performance bonds from some county and parish officers, and subjected certain regulatory measures within sessions jurisdiction to provincial approval.[55] Other amendments tightened up the rules and procedures for policing rates collection, setting out sanctions for misconduct or neglect by JPs and other officials.[56] More legislation in the decade following Confederation continued these trends.[57]

The *County and Parish Act* dealt with the administrative functions of sessions; it was accompanied by an act to consolidate numer-

54. 13 Vict. (1850) c.30.

55. 14 Vict. (1851) c.25; 15 Vict. (1852) c.47; 16 Vict. (1853) c.45; R.S.N.B. 1854, vol.2, c.12; 19 Vict. (1856) c.38; 23 Vict. (1860) c.38; 25 Vict. (1862) c.17; 30 Vict. (1866) c.11.

56. 25 Vict. (1862) c.30; 26 Vict. (1863) c.12; 29 Vict. (1866) c.3 (JPs to act in a parish or county notwithstanding that they are personally ratable there).

57. For example, 38 Vict. (1875) c.10 included timber driver on the list of elective parish offices and provided that only ratepayers in the parish were qualified to serve.

ous local statutes about local justice, particularly the inferior court of common pleas.[58] In 1854 the assembly received a report recommending the abolition of the common pleas and of jury trials at sessions:[59]

> This plan will require all criminal and civil suits to be tried at the Circuit Courts over which a Judge of the Supreme Court would preside. The Sessions could either at the same time in a different apartment transact their ordinary local, fiscal and municipal business, or adjourn to a more convenient day. They would, as well as the Grand Jury, receive the advice and the instruction of the presiding Judge; and the ordinary Criminal business of a Circuit, with the supervision of the County Accounts, might be disposed of in the time generally occupied by a Grand Jury under the present system, who are often delayed by the local officers.

This proposal to bring the central institution of the sessions system under the immediate supervision of the supreme court bench was not immediately acted upon.[60] However in 1867 the *County Courts Act* abolished both common pleas and the sessions petit jury and erected a county court with jurisdiction over personal actions up to two hundred dollars, tort up to one hundred dollars, and all actions against justices of the peace for anything done by them in the execution of their office. It was also empowered to review civil proceedings before justices. The presiding judge was to be a barrister of at least seven years' standing. Charlotte shared a county court judge with Carleton and Victoria: the court was to sit four terms in each county annu-

58. 13 Vict. (1850) c.47.

59. JHA 1854, 'Third report of the law commissioners,' 31. Former attorney general Fisher had reported in 1851 that municipal government reform also entailed the elimination of local courts: 'Instead of electing between a multitude of smaller Courts, which exist in older and more populous Counties and the trial of causes by ignorant and inexperienced men, the Supreme Court, under such a system, could be so remodelled as to try causes of any amount exceeding five pounds, at an expense proportioned to the amount in dispute.' JHA 1851, 311.

60. In 1861 the Charlotte grand jury recommended abolishing juries at September sessions, recognizing that the job of reviewing county accounts took place at April sessions and that there were so few criminal trials at sessions that the petit jury could be dispensed with in September.

ally.[61] This stripped sessions of its criminal jurisdiction (indictments found by the sessions grand jury were to be tried in the county court), dispensed with the office of JCP, and imposed a closer supervision of the JPs both in and out of sessions than formerly. An 1868 act gave the county courts concurrent criminal jurisdiction with the circuit courts in all non-capital 'crimes, offences and misdemeanors' and allowed them to hear appeals from summary convictions by JPs.[62]

The *County Courts Act* was not the only or even the first attempt to professionalize what had long been lay justice. As early as 1848 a failed bill 'to provide for the more effectual administration of the office of a justice of the peace' proposed to appoint salaried police magistrates to sit six days a week at the shire towns.[63] The City of Saint John acquired a salaried police magistrate appointed by the provincial government in 1849.[64] Similar appointments for other towns and cities accompanied or followed municipal incorporation.[65] While these enactments did not require police magistrates to be lawyers the experience of other jurisdictions suggests that this would be the next step. Other post-confederation legislation was aimed at JP appointments and responsibilities. An act of 1869 permitted the lieutenant governor in council to include several names in a commission of the peace or issue commissions to each person individually and to remove any justice of the peace by notice in the *Royal Gazette*.[66] Justices could be summoned to serve on county court juries. Penalties

---

61. 30 Vict. (1867) c.10. After 1874 the same judge also sat for Madawaska: 37 Vict. (1874) c.11.

62. 31 Vict. (1868) c.13. The county court clerk's role and remuneration in criminal matters was regulated by 32 Vict. (1869) c.5. See also 33 Vict. (1870) c.20, s.17 which barred the clerk from acting as a magistrate in preliminary examinations.

63. Assy 1848, bill #73. Introduced by York MHA James Taylor the bill disappeared after second reading.

64. 12 Vict. (1849) c.68. This act required imperial confirmation as it amended the city charter. The Saint John parish of Portland had petitioned successfully for a stipendiary police magistrate in 1848 (JHA, 135; 11 Vict. (1848) c.12). In 1849 James Boyd and others reported in favour of appointing one for Grand Manan: JHA 1849, 336. C.R. Hatheway petitioned the government to be appointed stipendiary magistrate for Charlotte in 1852: PANB RS9/1852-12-15/7.

65. For example, 34 Vict. (1871) c.20 s.45, appointing a police magistrate for the incorporated Town of St Stephen.

66. 32 Vict. (1869) c.92 (printed in 1870 volume).

were introduced for justices who failed to make returns of summary convictions and the county court was empowered to compel justices to provide copies of their proceedings to appellants.[67]

The *County Courts Act* ended the justices' monopoly on small claims but it did not eliminate their civil jurisdiction.[68] As we have seen the scope of civil proceedings before a justice sitting alone or with a three-man jury had been contested since at least 1802 when lieutenant governor Carleton urged disallowance because the five pound limit was excessive and the justices' monopoly infringed on the authority of the supreme court.[69] There was more resistance to interfering with this aspect of the justices' role than any other except the wholesale replacement of the sessions system by municipal incorporation. In 1865 the assembly passed a bill prohibiting attorneys or barristers of the supreme court from acting as justices of the peace in civil suits but it was given the three-months' hoist in council.[70] In the same year assembly and council agreed to make bail more readily available in civil proceedings on capias but council rejected the assembly's effort to extend the justices' civil jurisdiction to ten pounds.[71] In 1867 the assembly passed a bill requiring civil suits to be heard by justices resident in the same parish as one of the parties and limiting witness fees but it too was lost in council.[72]

Legislation in the decade following Confederation included a prohibition on constables acting as agent or attorney for either party,[73] an enactment positively affirming that no JP was exempted from the civil jurisdiction because he was an attorney,[74] and another regulating set-offs in suits before justices.[75] Then in 1876 the *Parish Courts Act* established small claims courts (debt to $40, tort to $15 damages) in every parish that lacked a resident stipendiary or police magistrate with civil jurisdiction. The new court was presided over by a Commis-

67. 33 Vict. (1870) c.2; 35 Vict. (1872) c.6; 36 Vict. 1873 c.13.
68. For justices after Confederation, Prime, 'Forgotten Magistrates.'
69. Chapter 1.
70. PANB RS24/1865/b/#89; JLC 25 May 1865.
71. 28 Vict. (1865) c.15; PANB RS24/1865/b/#70; JLC 3 Jun 1865.
72. PANB RS24/1867/b/#10.
73. 31 Vict. (1868) c.4.
74. 33 Vict. (1870) c.1.
75. 38 Vict. (1875) c.18.

sioner with the powers and procedures of a justice's civil court and the additional power to tax attorney fees where the amount sued for exceeded $20. All these changes left the justices' civil jurisdiction more or less as it had been in 1802 but now in competition with the county and parish courts and subject to appellate review. It was becoming increasingly difficult to discern a boundary between lay low law and professional high law in minor civil litigation although the practices of lay justices may still have differed from those of county and parish court professionals.[76] Unlike other aspects of the sessions system the demise of the justices' civil jurisdiction depended upon it remaining essentially unreformed. As Prime points out, the unaltered debt jurisdiction of JPs (it was still $20 as late as 1952) meant that their courts became increasingly irrelevant as prices, wages, and indebtedness increased over time.[77]

Four themes

These institutional trends inevitably bring to mind Max Weber's foundational account of centralization, bureaucratization, professionalization, and the shift from charismatic to rational authority.[78] Weber famously equated the 'patriarchal, summary and highly irrational'[79] English justice of the peace with the Muslim 'khadi' as epitomizing traditional substantive justice guided by values-based reaction to individual circumstances without regard to universal legal principles. This was in contrast to the formalism of the common law courts and marked the legal system as class-divided: 'a dual judicial policy of formal adjudication of disputes within the upper class, combined with arbitrariness or de facto denegation of justice for the economically

76. Couturier, 'Courts and Business Activity' relies on Gloucester circuit and county court records. He mentions the parish courts in passing but does not notice the civil jurisdiction of justices of the peace. More work in this period would be required to estimate the relative volume of cases going to lay justices or parish courts and any differences in their practices or procedures from those of county and circuit courts. See also Prime, 'Forgotten Magistrates,' 11-12. In chapter 3, Prime examines the civil and criminal practice of Quaco (Saint John county) justice W.H. Moran in the late nineteenth and early twentieth centuries.

77. Ibid., 86.

78. Gerth et al., *From Max Weber.*

79. Rheinstein, *Weber on Law,* 317.

weak.' There was an 'insoluble conflict' between formal and substantive justice roughly paralleling the tension between the propertied and the underprivileged. The emerging bourgeois interest was in 'a rational procedural system and therefore in a systematized and unambiguously formal and purposefully constructed substantive law which eliminates both obsolete traditions and arbitrariness and in which rights can have their source exclusively in general objective norms.'[80]

In the introductory chapter I identified four related themes running through this history of low law and petty justice in Charlotte county: private interest and public office; the discretion and autonomy of low law officials; the problem of supervising and controlling them; and tensions between local and external forces in shaping low law institutions. In this concluding section I want to draw these threads together in the service of my earlier contention that the sessions system was a functioning institutional whole that transcended the mere sum of its parts, a few of which survived the disassembly of the system in attenuated form.

Weber's 'dual judicial policy' and his distinction between formal and substantive justice reflect the separation of high law from low law. His strictures on 'arbitrariness or de facto denegation of justice' in the low law realm reveal a top-down view which neglects to weigh the relative merits of the distinct logics of high and low law. They are based in different values: 'universality of application, singularity of meaning, rightness'[81] in the former case; local particularism ('community justice'), circumstantial interpretation, perceived fairness in the latter. High law pursues impersonal justice; low law preserves community peace. Both are inherently conservative—social peace and social harmony reinforce existing power relations—but at the same time each is potentially disruptive of the other. The thickness or permeability of the boundary between them is constituted by degrees of judicial and executive deference, legislative protectiveness, the capacity of low law providers to insulate their proceedings from scrutiny (for example by trial-avoidance), and the willingness of low law consumers to accept its outcomes. Either of these institutions may ap-

80. Ibid., 230, 319, 231.
81. Tomlins, 'Introduction,' 2.

pear arbitrary and justice-denying from the perspective of the other. Neither is immune from arbitrariness and denial of justice in its own terms: compare David Owen's experience as a supreme court litigant on the one hand and his practice as a JP on the other.

The traditional English ideal of the gentleman rural justice activated by paternal *noblesse oblige* and spurning fees as beneath his station (or leaving them for his clerk) began to fall afoul of politicized appointments and the increasing press of business as early as the mid-seventeenth century.[82] In more populous areas or where the gentry was increasingly reluctant to participate actively in popular justice it became necessary to staff the magistracy from less elevated ranks with men willing to undertake a significant volume of petty business for the fees it produced. Borough justices—serving mayors and aldermen—were likely to be well-off artisans and shopkeepers. In eighteenth-century greater London the 'trading justice' was a well-understood phenomenon. There petty criminal justice was a competitive entrepreneurial business prone to barratry and corruption at the margins, its leaders exploring techniques of self-regulation to avoid external supervision and control which nevertheless eventually came with the appointment of stipendiaries and the abolition of fees.[83]

In the colonial setting of early New Brunswick there was no real equivalent to the English landed gentry despite the presence of a scattering of pretenders and remittance-men of whom David Owen was Charlotte's most prominent example. A thin upper layer of 'professional' Loyalists carried vestiges of aristocratic culture, as did official appointees from 'Home' including some lieutenant governors, supreme court judges, army and customs officers, and a few others.[84] A handful of them served as justices or sheriffs but the great majority of those and other local offices were filled from the outset by other ranks, so that the gentility of the magistracy was at a low concentration to begin with and was further diluted over time. The business-

82. Landau, *Justices*, chapter 6.

83. Landau, 'Trading.'

84. For a stimulating discussion of the role of aristocratic culture in pre-modern administration and of its replacement by a measurement-based management culture see Allen, *Institutional Revolution.*

men, traders, and professionals who staffed the Charlotte sessions system and other low law positions typically viewed public office as an adjunct to private entrepreneurship. As justices they took fees; as commissioners they took commissions; and those for whom involvement in public business detracted from private profit restricted their activity accordingly. At St Andrews where the political economy of debt generated a good deal of minor civil litigation this created the opportunity that Charles Reid Hatheway seized. His status as the son of a Loyalist family, his prior service as a British junior officer, and his half-pay income all meant that he could turn justicing into a remunerative business without sacrificing respectability.

Despite his forced sabbatical from the magistracy as a side-effect of the conflict between aristocratic and bourgeois values exemplified by Spearman's supposed challenge to Wyer, itself a sideshow of the assembly's efforts to gain control of Crown revenues, Hatheway's conduct as a fee-for-service purveyor of petty justice bore little resemblance to his portrayal as a villainous trading justice in lieutenant governor Campbell's despatches. Nor was his practice characterized by 'arbitrariness or de facto denegation of justice' although it met the Weberian standards of summary and substantive decision-making. Hatheway's practice, like that of the Jamaica stipendiaries studied by Diana Paton, cannot easily be classified between 'premodern' and 'modern' law but belonged to 'a more hybrid juridical formation in which the magistrates both attempted to enforce a precisely rule-bound "rule of law" and, at the same time, aimed to bring the parties involved in the disputes to an agreement on how to proceed.'[85] In both criminal and civil matters Hatheway encouraged disputants to settle their differences without trial, making extensive use of peace bonds in the former and duns in the latter. When trials were necessary their outcomes were generally predictable. Creditors received judgments against their debtors; tax evaders were ordered to pay up; assailants were fined; thieves were punished. Hatheway had no patience for technical niceties, devised straight-forward procedural short-cuts (for example the clearinghouse approach to mul-

85. Paton, *No Bond but the Law*, 75. The stipendiaries were appointed by the imperial authorities and recruited in Britain to substitute for the planter magistracy during the 'apprenticeship' period that followed the abolition of slavery.

tiple actions involving the same party as both debtor and creditor), and in more complex cases tried to focus on the real issue in dispute. This was certainly a substantive approach which might have been construed as procedurally arbitrary or justice-denying from the perspective of the legal professional but the local clamour for his reinstatement and his continuing success in the business point to general approval at least by plaintiffs and prosecutors in the community notwithstanding occasional attacks by James Boyd and other would-be patricians.

If the Charlotte experience was at all typical, the social ordering or 'peace' of early colonial New Brunswick was largely defined by the sessions system and its personnel rather than by either the assembly or the executive. Partly in consequence of group settlement with its predefined leadership, partly due to the importance of local entrepreneurship and competition in the early accumulative stages of the province's development, and partly because of the uncertainties created by shifting imperial policy, the local setting became a site of real economic power and political authority poised both to exploit opportunities emanating from, and to mitigate adverse consequences of, executive and imperial decisions. In these early years the assembly was more an extension and consortium of local sessions systems than a central legislative body in its own right. This was the period in which the St Andrews junto flourished. It was able to silence protests, contain its critics, and overrule contestation from other parts of the county, imposing and keeping its 'peace' through sessions, the assembly, and summary civil and criminal justice while pursuing its developmental and competitive agenda. The junto and its allies effectively screened access to the county bench (although it was less successful in controlling the shrievalty) and proved more capable than either the high courts or the executive in disciplining defiant members of the magistracy.

Beginning in the 1840s a number of external and indigenous factors converged to shift the locus of political and economic authority first to the assembly and then to the emergingly responsible provincial government. Changes in imperial policy gave American shippers access to West Indies and other colonial ports and ended New Brunswick products' protection in British markets, thereby undermining the junto's developmental strategy and threatening its prosperity. The executive insisted on downloading at least part of the cost of depopulating the Irish countryside to New Brunswick parishes and dealt with local resistance by substituting provincial for local officials. The assembly's new access to former crown revenue sources produced a decade of rapid spending succeeded by a crippling public indebtedness and growing demands for greater accountability and oversight. Economic and social disruption contributed to the rapid rise of the temperance movement which helped to transform the make-up of the assembly, the magistracy, and ultimately the provincial government. The emergence of party politics and the increasing trend towards provincial management of what had previously been local institutions and perquisites fostered opportunities for patrician critics to compete effectively with local patriarchs.

These changes undermined the sessions system and eventually replaced it by subordinating elected municipal councils to a parliamentary provincial government. What faded vestiges of the old system remained were increasingly irrelevant in comparison to their new institutional competitors. As elsewhere in the new Confederation, as also in Britain and other colonies and dominions, the old low law regime of local government and popular justice by appointed officials was dismantled only to be replaced by a new low law of appointed agencies, boards, and commissions answerable to the party in power.

But how representative was the Charlotte experience? In his study of the transformation of English local governance, David Eastwood takes issue with the traditional view that the sessions system fell victim to its own inefficiency, irrationality, and corruption so that centralization and reform were historical necessities: 'In practice the system was more coherent and efficient than its critics (whether they be Whig, Utilitarian, or Fabian) have alleged.' Its institutions and practices were adapted to a particular social formation and its hierarchy of power relations. 'The transformation of the institutions and political culture of rural England should thus be seen not as a necessary consequence of the modernization of the English state but rather as a particular consequence of [a] specific history of state modernization.'[86] So too in Charlotte, where the sessions system in the period of its full articulation was coherent (although contested), efficient (in getting its way), and adapted to local circumstances (although decreasingly capable of adapting itself dynamically to changed circumstances). Sectional jealousies and interpersonal rivalries aside—and apart from such outliers as David Owen or Richard Waycott, indicted for sedition in 1832 for shouting in public that the magistrates at St Andrews 'ought to be damned for appointing such constables, God damn them, God bugger them'[87]—county residents by and large seem to have accepted the legitimacy of the system (if not of all its personnel) or at least preferred it to the available alternatives. Other New Brunswick counties seem to have had broadly similar experiences but not so nearly identical that their specific histories can be ignored. (For example, what explains the early adoption of municipal incorporation in Carleton county?) The same can be said in varying degrees of cognate arrangements in other parts of British North America, elsewhere in the empire, and in Britain itself. An emphasis on the local and particular can provide a richly textured account of the reciprocal influences of character and circumstance on events and institutions in the broader context. Particularism need not be exceptionalism.

Nevertheless the sessions system and its components were not unique to Charlotte county or New Brunswick so it is reasonable to ask how closely its local expression there resembled others elsewhere. Certain defining aspects are close to universal: the appointed volunteer magistracy with blended judicial, administrative, and legislative jurisdiction in periodic courts of session; its responsibility for keeping the peace; the statutory foundation of its multifarious responsibilities in and out of sessions; its role in the preliminary stages of criminal procedure. Other elements, for example the exclusive jurisdiction over small debts, are much less widely distributed. Then there are aspects of the system—for example the proportion of appointed justices who were active in or out of sessions; the extent to which petty sessions was institutionalized; the nature and extent of judicial and executive supervision—that vary not only across colonial

86. Eastwood, *Governing Rural England*, 3.
87. PANB RS148/D/3/g; CCGS Apr 1832.

or provincial settings but along the history of each of them. Our capacity to make these comparisons depends, of course, on how well we know the various local systems, how many of them have been studied, and in what aspects. So we have a number of detailed studies of how justices of the peace and other magistrates exercised their criminal jurisdiction in several British counties and British North American colonies[88] as well as some other places in the empire. There has been one attempt at a comprehensive overview of their role in employment relations supported by a number of detailed studies of particular settings.[89] So it is possible to say that the sessions system in Charlotte was fairly typical in its handling of criminal cases, relying heavily on the peace bond to avoid trials and convictions and using the preliminary inquiry to deflect cases from the high court, and also that in the employment sphere the limited scope of New Brunswick's master and servant legislation was likely offset by the justices' broad civil jurisdiction in managing workplace disputes.

About other aspects of the Charlotte system it is much more difficult to make systematic comparisons, mostly because they have not been much investigated elsewhere. Charlotte's were not the only justices and other low law officials to have used their positions in the service of their private business and family interests, but it is impossible to say whether they were more or less venal than their counterparts in other New Brunswick counties, let alone elsewhere in North America, Britain or the empire. We do not know whether the close integration of sessions and assembly that characterized the height of the Charlotte system obtained in every New Brunswick county or had parallels elsewhere.[90] Nor are we able yet to make systematic comparisons between the operation of the sessions system and other forms

88. For Britain see among other sources the cited works by Beattie, Eastwood, Hay, King, Landau, and the Webbs. For North America see among others the sources cited in chapter 1, note 33. Studies of mid-nineteenth-century and later urban justice demonstrate a shift towards the rapid summary disposition of petty criminal and regulatory cases in permanent professional courts. Several of these are reviewed in Marquis, 'Contours'; see also Craven, 'Law and Ideology' and among more recent writing Glasbeek, *Feminized Justice*; for the United States, Willrich, *City of Courts*.

89. Hay and Craven, *Masters, Servants* and the works cited therein.

90. Eastwood, *Governing Rural England*, chapter 5, discusses relations between parliament and the magistracy during poor law reform.

and institutions of local law and governance: it would be instructive to examine Charlotte's post-Confederation experience as a municipal corporation. More broadly, few of the institutions of contemporary low law—the quasi-judicial, regulatory, and administrative agencies, boards, and commissions that proliferate in modern societies—have been closely investigated by historians. One suspects that despite their widespread capture by legal professionals and closer supervision by the courts they may have more in common with the local justice of the ancien regime than is generally recognized.

Appendices

Appendix A

Reference tables

A.1 Selected powers of New Brunswick JPs, 1786–1832

Act	Power	Juris'n
26 Geo.III c.5	Sabbath observance - To enforce	Single
26 Geo.III c.13	Weights & measures - To enforce	Single
26 Geo.III c.27	Rogues & vagabonds - To issue pass	Single
26 Geo.III c.27	Rogues & vagabonds - To examine/commit	Single
26 Geo.III c.27	Rogues & vagabonds - To remove from parish	Double
26 Geo.III c.28	Town & parish officers - To appoint	Sessions
26 Geo.III c.28	Town & parish officers - To enforce service	Double
26 Geo.III c.30	Open fire regulations - To enforce	Single
26 Geo.III c.34	Timber booms - To order removal	Double
26 Geo.III c.35	Taverns - To enforce regulations about servants	Single
26 Geo.III c.36	Master & servant	Single
26 Geo.III c.38	Public lands - To receive in trust	Sessions
26 Geo.III c.38	Commons - To regulate	Sessions
26 Geo.III c.42	Rates for county purposes - To assess	Sessions
26 Geo.III c.42	Rates - To enforce collection	Single
26 Geo.III c.43	Poor Law - To assess rates	Sessions
26 Geo.III c.43	Poor Law - To supervise overseers (consent req'd)	Double
26 Geo.III c.49	Markets - To enforce forestalling & regrating	Triple
26 Geo.III c.53	Seamen - To enforce articles (employment contracts)	Single
26 Geo.III c.54	Criminal - To try offences under grand larceny	Triple
27 Geo.III c.6	Taverns - To grant licenses	Sessions
27 Geo.III c.6	Taverns - To enforce licenses	Single
28 Geo.III c.8	Markets, Ferries - To make regulations	Sessions

31 Geo.III c.5	Marriages - To solemnize where no Anglican vicar	Single
32 Geo.III c.3	Bastard children - To order maintenance	Single
32 Geo.III c.6	Dogs - To hear complaints of sheep-killing	Single
33 Geo.III c.2	Dumping of ballast - To enforce restrictions	Double
33 Geo.III c.3	Deserters from military - To imprison	Single
33 Geo.III c.3	Deserters from military - To punish persons aiding	Single
33 Geo.III c.6	Hogsheads of lime - To enforce standards	Single
33 Geo.III c.9	Fisheries regulations - To enforce	Double
34 Geo.III c.2	Warrants - To endorse those issued in another county	Single
34 Geo.III c.9	Cattle at large - To enforce restrictions	Single
34 Geo.III c.9	Cattle gates - To erect	Sessions
39 Geo.III c.7	Hay - To make regulations for weighing	Sessions
39 Geo.III c.7	Hay - To enforce regulations for weighing	Double
39 Geo.III c.8	Quarantine - To make regulations	Sessions
39 Geo.III c.8	Quarantine - To enforce regulations	Single
41 Geo.III c.4	Beacons - To punish destruction or defacing	Double
43 Geo.III c.7	Butter - To appoint inspectors	Sessions
45 Geo.III c.4	Alien importers of merchandise - To try	Single
45 Geo.III c.12	Schoolmasters - To arrange payment	Sessions
45 Geo.III c.15	Timber Booms - To regulate	Sessions
47 Geo.III c.7	Minor offences by disorderly persons - To punish	Single
47 Geo.III c.8	Cattle - To punish failure to post notice of strays	Single
47 Geo.III c.13	Fishery - To regulate	Sessions
50 Geo.III c.6	Highways - To appoint commissioners and surveyors	Sessions
50 Geo.III c.6	Highways - To supervise commissioners and surveyors	Double
50 Geo.III c.6	Highways - To swear in commissioners and surveyors	Single
50 Geo.III c.6	Highways - To enforce statute labour obligation	Single
50 Geo.III c.18	Traffic - To regulate pedestrian and vehicle	Sessions
50 Geo.III c.24	Ferries - To establish	Sessions
52 Geo.III c.7	Assize of bread - To regulate	Sessions
52 Geo.III c.7	Assize of bread - To enforce	Sessions
54 Geo.III c.5	Partridges - To preserve	Single
56 Geo.III c.23	School Trustees - To appoint	Sessions
57 Geo.III c.5	Bread corn bounty - To administer oath	Single
57 Geo.III c.9	Firewards - To enforce their orders	Single
58 Geo.III c.2	Fish offal - To punish throwing into water	Single
59 Geo.III c.12	Timber Regulations - To enforce fines to £5	Single
59 Geo.III c.12	Timber regulations - To enforce fines to £10	Double
59 Geo.III c.14	Fish trade regulations - To enforce fines up to £10	Double
59 Geo.III c.15	Herring fishery - To make regulations	Sessions
59 Geo.III c.15	Herring fishery - To enforce to £10	Double
2 Geo.IV c.10	Disabled Seamen - To enforce duty for support	Single
3 Geo.IV c.25	Alms and Work houses - To erect and assess for	Sessions
3 Geo.IV c.28	Harbour Masters - To appoint	Sessions
3 Geo.IV c.28	Harbour Regulations - To make	Sessions

3 Geo.IV c.28	Harbour Regulations - To enforce	Double
3 Geo.IV c.29	Town and Parish offices - To fill vacancies	Double
5 Geo.IV c.8	Market Wharf at Saint Andrews - To regulate	Sessions
5 Geo.IV c.8	Market Wharf regulations - To enforce	Single
5 Geo.IV c.9	Lunatics - To restrain	Double
5 Geo.IV c.10	Poor House commissioners - To appoint	Sessions
6 Geo.IV c.18	Militia Oath - To administer	Single
6 Geo.IV c.18	Militia Exercises - To punish wilful interruptions	Single
6 Geo.IV c.18	Militia Assessments - To enforce against aliens	Single
6 Geo.IV c.19	Militia Act - To enforce fines	Single
8 Geo.IV c.11	Smoked Herrings - To appoint inspectors	Sessions
8 Geo.IV c.11	Smoked Herring regulations - To enforce	Single
8 Geo.IV c.15	Timber Drives - To regulate and appoint commissioners	Sessions
9 Geo.IV c.19	Bear Bounty - To administer oath and destroy the noses	Single
9 Geo.IV c.19	Bear Bounty - To certify claims	Sessions
9 Geo.IV c.23	Dog Tax - To appoint collector and pass his accounts	Sessions
9 Geo.IV c.23	Dog Licenses - To enforce at suit of collector	Single
9 Geo.IV c.28	Fire Regulations - To enforce	Single
9&10 Geo.IV c.8	Bawdy-house - To bind keepers to appear at Sessions	Single
9&10 Geo.IV c.21	Common Assault - To try summarily	Double
9&10 Geo.IV c.25	County Accounts - To publish annual statements	Sessions
9&10 Geo.IV c.27	Pedlars and Chapmen - To enforce licensing	Single
10&11 Geo.IV c.10	Salt and Coals - To regulate measures	Sessions
10&11 Geo.IV c.10	Cartage Rates - To regulate	Sessions
10&11 Geo.IV c.10	Cartage - To enforce rates and regulations	Single
10&11 Geo.IV c.12	Sawmill Waste - To enforce prohibition of discharge	Single
10&11 Geo.IV c.19	Conveyance of Criminals - To arrange between Counties	Double
10&11 Geo.IV c.20	Houses of Correction - To establish	Sessions
10&11 Geo.IV c.22	Maiming Cattle - To try summarily	Double
1 Wm.IV c.9	Fences and Pounds - To regulate and establish	Sessions
1 Wm.IV c.9	Fences and Pounds - To enforce regulations	Single
1 Wm.IV c.14	Accused Persons - To examine and commit or take bail	Single
1 Wm.IV c.15	Search Warrants - To issue in criminal cases	Single
1 Wm.IV c.15	Larceny, Receiving Stolen Goods - To try	Sessions
1 Wm.IV c.18	Hard Labour - To regulate punishment	Sessions
1 Wm.IV c.31	Gaol Limits - To set and extend	Sessions
1 Wm.IV c.42	Auctioneers - To set license fee	Sessions
2 Wm.IV c.36	Landing Fees - To enforce	Double

A.2 Charlotte JPs by area of residence, 1784–1857

Commission	Islands	Pennfield†	St Andrews	St David	St George	St Patrick†	St Stephen†	Total
1784:Aug	-	-	5	-	-	-	-	5
1785:Jun	2	2	6	-	2	-	3	15
1799:Oct	-	-	5	-	-	1	5	11
1818:Oct	5	-	8	-	1	2	3	19
1821:Nov	7	1	12	1	2	2	3	28
1822:Aug	7	1	10	1	2	2	2	25
1826:May	6	1	9	1	2	3	3	25
1830:Mar	4	1	11	1	3	3	5	28
1832:May	2	-	7	1	3	3	3	19
1832:Dec	6	1	11	1	3	3	5	30
1835:Nov	5	1	9	1	2	3	5	26
1836:May	6	1	11	1	2	3	5	29
1837:Nov	6	1	11	1	3	3	5	30
1838:Mar	7	1	11	2	2	3	8	34
1838:Nov*	10	1	11	2	3	2	8	37
1839:Dec*	10	1	11	2	3	3	8	38
1840:Mar*	6	1	10	2	3	3	9	34
1840:Nov	8	1	6	2	4	2	7	30
1845:May	9	1	9	2	3	2	9	35
1846:Jan	8	1	9	3	4	2	9	36
1848:May	8	1	11	4	7	1	9	41
1850:Apr	7	1	10	4	7	1	9	39
1855:Mar	7	-	11	4	7	1	9	39
1855:Oct	7	3	12	3	9	-	12	46
1856:Sep	7	3	10	3	9	-	12	44
1857:Apr	9	4	12	3	11	-	17	56

* One non-resident magistrate (William Boyd Kinnear) was named in these commissions.
† Includes areas subsequently set off from original parish.

A.3 Charlotte MHAs, 1786–1862

• – In the commission of the peace ⊙ – Not in the commission of the peace

Name	1786	1793	1796	1803	1810	1817	1820	1821	1828	1831	1835	1837	1843	1847	1851	1854	1856	1857	1862
Boyd J												(⊙)	⊙	•		•	•		•
Brown J										⊙	⊙	⊙	⊙	•		•		•	
Campbell C					•	•	•		•										
Campbell Jas	•		•																
Campbell Jon							•	•											
Chandler J W																		⊙	
Clarke J N								•	•										
Clinch Peter	•	•																	
Clinch Patrick										•	•								
Dunn J					⊙														
Fitzgerald B R															⊙				
Gillmor A H																⊙	⊙	⊙	⊙
Grimmer G S																			⊙
Hill G S										⊙	⊙	⊙	⊙						
Lindsay N			(•)	•															
Mackay H		⊙		•		•	•	•	•										
McAdam J																⊙	⊙	⊙	
McDonald D					•														
McMaster D		⊙																	
Mowatt D			⊙																
Owen D			(⊙)[1]																
Owen W F W												(•)							
Pagan R	•	•	•	•	•	•													
Paine W	⊙																		
Porter J				•		•	•												
Porter W														⊙	⊙				
Robinson J J															•				
Stevens J G																			⊙
Street G D																	⊙		
Stubs P								⊙											
Thomson R												(⊙)[2]	•	•	•				
Wyer T									•	•	•	(•)[3]							

[1] Removed by petition for nonattendance; replaced by N Lindsay in by-election.
[2] Expelled 1838 for tampering with evidence in scrutiny; replaced by challenger W F W Owen.
[3] Seat vacated on appointment to Legislative Council; replaced by Boyd, by-election Nov 1839.

A.4 St Andrews poor commissioners, 1832–50

Name	1832	1833	1834	1835	1836	1837	1838	1839	1840	1841	1842	1843	1844	1845	1846	1847	1848	1849	1850	N
R M Andrews													•	•	•	•	•			5
C A Babcock													•	•						2
W Babcock	•	•	•	•	•	•	•	•	•											9
J Bailey													•	•	•	•	•			5
H Beamish					•															1
T Berry											•	•				•	•			4
J Boyd	•	•	•	•																4
D Bradley																		•	•	2
J W Chandler								•	•		•	•								4
C W Dimock															•				•	2
M S Hannah										•					•					2
J Irwin																		•		1
H H Hatch																		•		1
R Ker																•	•		•	3
J Lochary										•									•	2
D Morrison			•	•																2
H O'Neil	•	•	•	•	•	•	•	•	•										•	10
J Parkinson										•	•	•								3
A T Paul																		•		1
J Paul																•	•			2
G Ruggles	•	•																		2
T Sampson																		•		1
T Sime	•	•	•	•	•	•	•	•	•		•	•								11
P Smith										•	•	•								3
T Turner					•	•	•	•	•	•			•	•						8
R Walton													•	•	•					3
S Watts						•	•													2

A.5 Local and private acts for Charlotte

See 5 Wm.IV (1835) c.17, which makes all Acts of Assembly public acts, and also 13 Vict. (1850) c.19 regulating printing and distribution of Acts, repealed 15 Vict. (1852) c.2. Distinctions among public, local, and private/personal acts first made by 13 Vict. (1850) c.19 are reflected in the organization of that year's statute volume.

Local acts for a particular county or part of a county were often later extended to other parts of the same county, to other counties, or to the province as a whole with or without repeal of predecessor local statutes. For example, 9 Vict. c.14, 'An act relating to dog tax in the several counties of this province,' was followed by 10 Vict. c.10, 'An act to repeal several acts now in force relating to laying a tax on dogs in certain counties in this province,' repealing the various local acts (which it recites) and making the 9 Vict. c.14 the sole and general statute.

26 Geo.III	1786	c.34	An act for securing the navigation of the river Maggagauguaudavick.
34 Geo.III	1794	c.4	An act for altering the times of holding the Inferior Court of Common Pleas and General Sessions of the Peace in the county of Charlotte.
41 Geo.III	1801	c.4	An act for the better securing the Navigation of Passamaquoddy Bay within Deer Island.
45 Geo.III	1805	c.5	An act to continue [41 Geo.III c.4].
		c.7	An Act to alter and amend [26 Geo.III c.34].
		c.14	An Act for the regulation of booms for securing masts, logs, and lumber, in the County of Charlotte.
47 Geo.III	1807	c.13	An act to empower the Justices of the Peace for the County of Charlotte, in their General Sessions, to regulate the fisheries in the said county.
50 Geo.III	1810	c.3	An act to revive, continue and amend [41 Geo.III c.4].
		c.22	An act to prevent the destruction of moose on the island of Grandmanan.
52 Geo.III	1812	c.7	An act to authorise the Justices of the Peace for the Counties of York and Charlotte, respectively to regulate the assize of bread in the towns of Fredericton and St Andrews.
		c.10	An act to authorise the Justices of the Peace for the County of Charlotte, to levy an assessment for paying off the county debt, and for finishing and compleating the County Gaol and Court House, lately erected in said county.
53 Geo.III	1813	c.7	An act to enlarge the limits of the parish of St Stephen, in the County of Charlotte.

54 Geo.III	1814	c.11	An act to authorise the rector, church wardens and vestry of St Andrews' Church, in the parish of St Andrews, to convey to the King's Majesty, a certain piece of glebe land of the parish, for the purpose of erecting military fortifications thereon.
		c.15	An act to enlarge the limits of the parishes of St Patrick and St George, in the County of Charlotte.
56 Geo.III	1816	c.10	An act to constitute the island of Grand-Manan and its appurtenances in the County of Charlotte into a distinct Town or Parish.
57 Geo.III	1817	c.9	An act for appointing firewards in the towns of Fredericton and St Andrews, and ascertaining their power and duty, and more effectually to prevent fires in the said towns.
58 Geo.III	1818	c.18	An act to empower and authorise the Justices of the Peace for the County of Charlotte, to lease a certain piece of common land in the parish of St Andrews, and to invest the proceeds towards the support of the poor of the said parish.
59 Geo.III	1819	c.16	An act to regulate the herring fisheries in the parishes of West-Isles, Campo-Bello, Pennfield, and St George, in the County of Charlotte.
60 Geo.III	1820	c.2	An act for granting further aid in support of the grammar school in the town of St Andrews.
2 Geo.IV	1821	c.2	An act for the better extinguishing fires which may happen in the towns of Fredericton and St Andrews.
		c.4	An act to authorize the Justices of the General Sessions of the Peace of the County of Charlotte, to levy an assessment to enable them to pay off the county debt.
		c.8	An act to extend the provisions of [59 Geo.III c.16] to the parish of Grand-Manan.
		c.16	An act to authorize the rector, church wardens, and vestry of St Andrews Church in the parish of St Andrews, to convey a certain piece of glebe land of the said parish, and to dispose of the money arising from the sale thereof, in the purchase of other lands.
3 Geo.IV	1822	c.3	An act to continue [59 Geo.III c.16] and [2 Geo.IV c.8].
		c.5	An act to continue [50 Geo.III c.22].

		c.14	An act for the better securing of the inner bay of Passamaquoddy, and to indemnify the Deputy Province Treasurer at St Andrews, against any demands for monies collected for tonnage duties since the former acts for this purpose expired.
		c.17	An act in addition to [2 Geo.IV c.2].
		c.19	An act to regulate the cutting of saw logs on the river Magaguadavic and its various branches.
4 Geo.IV	1823	c.7	An act in addition to [45 Geo.III c.14].
		c.11	An act for erecting a part of the parish of St Stephen and the country adjacent, in the County of Charlotte, into a separate and distinct town or parish.
		c.15	An act to continue [60 Geo.III c.2].
		c.20	An act to amend [2 Geo.IV c.2].
5 Geo.IV	1824	c.2	An act to continue [3 Geo.IV c.3].
		c.3	An act for erecting and maintaining a lighthouse upon one of the islands or rocks near the south-east coast of the island of Grand-Manan.
		c.8	An act to authorize the Justices of the Peace for the County of Charlotte, to make regulations for the market wharf at St Andrews.
		c.10	An Act to provide for making rules and regulations for the management of the poor-house in the parish of St Andrews.
		c.13	An act to provide for the erection of fences with gates, across the highway leading through Deer Island, in the parish of West-Isles and County of Charlotte.
6 Geo.IV	1825	c.11	An act to authorize the Justices of the General Sessions of the Peace for the County of Charlotte, to levy an assessment to enable them to pay off the county debt.
		c.12	An act to incorporate sundry persons by the name of the president, directors and company of the Charlotte County Bank.
7 Geo.IV	1826	c.2	An act to continue [3 Geo.IV c.19].
		c.7	An act to authorize and empower the magistrates of the County of Charlotte, to sell the County Gaol and gaol lot, in the town of St Andrews, and to erect a more suitable building in the said town, in lieu thereof.
		c.17	An act to incorporate the minister and elders of the Kirk of Scotland in the town of St Andrews.

		c.20	An act to authorize the rector, church wardens and vestry of Christ Church in the parish of St Stephens, to dispose of a part of a tract of glebe land in that parish, and to vest the proceeds in other lands more productive to the rector.
8 Geo.IV	1827	c.3	An act further to continue [60 Geo.III c.2].
		c.11	An act to regulate the herring fishery in the parishes of Grand Manan, West Isles, Campo-Bello, Pennfield, and St George, in the County of Charlotte, and to provide for the inspection of smoked herrings in the said parishes.
		c.15	An act to empower the Justices of the County of Charlotte to make regulations for driving timber and logs down the rivers St Croix, Magaguadavic, and Digdeguash, and their branches.
		c.22	An act to continue until the first day of May, in the year 1829, [2 Geo.IV c.2], so far as relates to the said town of St Andrews.
9 Geo.IV	1828	c.3	An act to continue and amend the acts for the better securing the navigation of the inner bay of Passamaquoddy.
		c.9	An act to continue [5 Geo.IV c.13].
		c.23	An act to lay a tax on dogs in certain parts of the parishes of Fredericton and St Andrews.
		c.28	An act to repeal the laws now in force for appointing firewards, and for the better extinguishing of fires in the town of St Andrews, and to make regulations more suitable to the said town; and for other purposes therein mentioned.
9&10 Geo.IV	1829	c.16	An act to continue [8 Geo.IV c.15].
		c.24	An act to repeal [5 Geo.IV c.3].
10&11 Geo.IV	1830	c.11	An act to authorize the Justices of the Peace for the County of Charlotte, to lease a certain piece of common land in the parish of St Andrews, for the purpose of erecting thereon a suitable building for an hospital for sick and disabled seamen.
		c.12	An act for the better and more effectual securing the navigation of the river St Croix, in the County of Charlotte.
		c.13	An act to authorize the Justices of the Peace for the County of Charlotte, to assess the inhabitants, for erecting a Gaol in the said county.
		c.18	An act to grant John Aymar the privilege of supplying the town of St Andrews with water by pipes.

		c.20	An act to establish Houses of Correction within the counties of York and Charlotte.
		c.23	An act to provide for the maintenance of the light house established upon the island of Campo-Bello, near Head Harbour, in the County of Charlotte.
		c.26	An act to confirm a division made of certain lands, situated at Chamcook, in the parish of St Andrews, granted to the Justices of the County of Charlotte, in trust for the use and benefit of the rector or minister, and parish school of the same parish.
1 Wm.IV	1831	c.2	An act to regulate the cutting of saw logs on the river Magaguadavic and its branches.
		c.5	An act to make perpetual [9 Geo.IV c.23].
		c.8	An act to amend [8 Geo.IV c.11].
		c.22	An act relative to trespasses by horses and swine in the parish of Fredericton and the town of St Andrews.
		c.31	An act to authorize the extension of the gaol limits in the County of Charlotte.
		c.36	An act to authorize the Justices of the Peace for the County of Charlotte further to assess the inhabitants of said county for the completion and finishing a Gaol, and for the erection of lock-up-houses in said county.
		c.40	An act to make more effectual provision for preventing the importation and spreading of infectious distempers within the towns and settlements in the counties of Charlotte and Northumberland.
2 Wm.IV	1832	c.3	An act to continue the acts relative to the herring fishery in the County of Charlotte.
		c.5	An act to empower the owners of the saw mill at the rolling dam on the river Digdeguash, in the County of Charlotte, to erect a boom for the securing of saw logs on the said river.
		c.16	An act to amend [1 Wm.IV c.23] so far as the same relates to the parish church of St Andrews.
		c.17	An act to amend [1 Wm.IV c.40].
3 Wm.IV	1833	c.5	An act to continue [10&11 Geo.IV c.12].
		c.6	An act to continue [8 Geo.IV c.15].
		c.7	An act to alter and amend [3 Geo.IV c.14].
		c.34	An act to authorize the Justices of the Peace for the County of Charlotte to assess the Inhabitants of St Stephen in the said county for the purpose therein mentioned.

4 Wm.IV	1834	c.10	An act to continue [2 Wm.IV c.5].
		c.11	An act to continue [9 Geo.IV c.28].
		c.16	An act to contine and amend the acts relative to the herring fishery in the County of Charlotte.
		c.25	An act to authorize the Justices of the Peace for the County of Charlotte to levy an assessment towards paying off the county debt, and for other purposes therein mentioned.
5 Wm.IV	1835	c.20	An act to authorise the Justices of the Peace for the County of Charlotte to assess the inhabitants of the parish of Grand Manan for the erection of a Lock-up House in the said parish.
		c.22	An act to authorise and empower the Justices of the Peace for the County of Charlotte to lease a part of the public landing at salt water in the parish of St Stephen.
		c.31	An act to regulate the driving of timber and saw logs down the river Magaguadavic and its branches.
		c.36	An act for the appointment of firewards and the better extinguishing of fires which may happen in that part of the parish of St Stephen commonly called Mill Town and its immediate vicinity.
		c.41	An act relating to the navigation of the inner bay of Passamaquoddy.
		c.44	An act to authorise an assessment on the inhabitants of the County of Charlotte towards paying off the debts due from the said county.
5 Wm.IV	(2d.)	c.4	An act to authorise the rector, church wardens and vestry of All Sts' Church in the parish of St Andrews in the County of Charlotte, to sell and dispose of certain land in the said parish.
6 Wm.IV	1836	c.12	An act to amend and explain [5 Wm.IV c.22].
		c.17	An act to authorise the magistrates of the County of Charlotte to levy an assessment to pay off the county debt.
		c.31	An act to incorporate The St Andrews and Quebec Rail Road Company.
		c.32	An act to incorporate sundry persons by the name of The President, Directors and Company of the St Stephen's Bank, in the County of Charlotte.
		c.42	An act to establish the road leading from Connick's, at Waweig in the County of Charlotte, to the lower bridge over the river St Croix, as one of the great roads of communication.

		c.46	An act in addition to [5 Wm.IV c.36].
		c.69	An act to incorporate The St Stephen's Whale Fishing Company.
		c.70	An act to incorporate The Chamcook Mill and Factory Company.
7 Wm.IV	1837	c.16	An act to repeal [3 Wm.IV c.7].
		c.20	An act further to continue [9&10 Geo.IV c.12] and also further to continue [8 Geo.IV c.15].
		c.36	An act relating to the herring fisheries in the County of Charlotte.
		c.38	An act to amend [6 Wm.IV c.31].
		c.47	An act to incorporate certain persons by the name of The President, Trustees and Proprietors of the St Stephen's Academy.
		c.48	An act to incorporate The Campo Bello Mill and Manufacturing Company.
8 Wm.IV	1837	c.9	An act in addition to [6 Wm.IV c.32].
		c.10	An act in addition to an in amendment of [6 Wm.IV c.69].
		c.18	An act to provide for the relief of poor emigrants in the town of St Andrews in the County of Charlotte.
1 Vict.	1838	c.19	An act to provide for the erection of fences with gates across the highways on Deer Island in the parish of West Isles in the county of Charlotte.
		c.25	An act to authorize the magistrates of the county of Charlotte to levy an assessment to pay off the county debt.
		c.28	An act to amend the law relating to the inspection of public accounts by grand juries, so far as relates to the county of Charlotte.
		c.29	An act in addition to an act, intituled 'An act to make more effectual regulations relating to pilots within this province,' so far as regards the county of Charlotte.
		c.40	An act for the incorporation of *The St Andrew's and Saint John Stage Coach Company*.
2 Vict.	1839	c.22	An act to authorize the justices of the peace for the county of Charlotte to levy an assessment for the building a new Court House in the said county.
		c.40	An act to empower the commissioners of the Marine Hospital at St Andrews, in the county of Charlotte, to purchase a lot of land for the benefit of the said hospital.
		c.46	An act to revive and continue [5 Wm.IV c.31].
3 Vict.	1840	c.2	An act to continue [7 Wm.IV c.36].

		c.25	An act to continue the act relating to church wardens and vestrymen, and to persons having voices in their election, so far as relates to the parish church of St Andrews.
		c.26	An act to continue [5 Wm.IV c.41].
		c.28	An act to regulate the assize of bread in the towns of St Andrews and St Stephen, in the county of Charlotte, and to repeal the acts now in force relating to the town of St Andrews.
		c.29	An act to continue [9 Geo.IV c.28].
		c.33	An act to amend and continue [5 Wm.IV c.36].
		c.36	An act to authorize an assessment on the inhabitants of a part of the parish of St Stephen, in the county of Charlotte, for the purpose therein mentioned.
		c.66	An act to incorporate the Chamcook Mill and Factory Company.
		c.67	An act to authorize the justices of the peace for the county of Charlotte to levy an assessment to pay off the county debt.
4 Vict.	1841	c.10	An act to provide for more effectually repairing the streets and bridges in a part of the parish of St Stephens.
		c.11	An act to authorize the justices of the peace for the county of Charlotte to assess the parish of St Stephen, in the said county, for the erection of a wharf on the public landing at salt water in the said parish.
5 Vict.	1842	c.2	An act to authorize the justices of the peace for the county of Charlotte to make regulations for the market wharf in the parish of St Stephen.
		c.6	An act to continue [1 Vict. c.19].
		c.7	An act to establish the line of road from Oak Bay, in the county of Charlotte, to the mouth of Eel River in the county of York, as one of the great roads of communication in this province.
		c.14	An act to authorize Her Majesty's justices of the peace for the county of Charlotte, to levy an assessment to pay off the county debt.
		c.16	An act relating to the appointment of firewards and the better extinguishment of fires in a part of the parish of St Stephen, in the county of Charlotte, therein mentioned.
		c.29	An act to incorporate the St Stephen Log and Timber Sluice Company.
		c.30	An act to incorporate the St Andrews Marine Assurance Company.

		c.40	An act to incorporate the St Stephen's Marine Assurance Company.
6 Vict.	1843	c.7	An act to repeal so much of [9 Geo.IV c.23] as relates to the owners of dogs residing on the commons and glebe in the parish of St Andrews.
7 Vict.	1844	c.3	An act to authorize the justices of the peace for the county of Charlotte to make further provision for the payment of the treasurer of that county.
		c.4	An act to authorize the justices of the peace for the county of Charlotte to levy an assessment to pay off the county debt.
		c.14	An act to continue and amend [6 Geo.IV c.12].
		c.25	An act to revive certain acts relating to the prevention of the importation and spreading of infectious distempers within the counties of Charlotte and Northumberland, and to extend the provision of the same to the counties of Gloucester and Restigouche.
8 Vict.	1845	c.22	An act to continue [10&11 Geo.IV c.18].
		c.23	An act to continue [10&11 Geo.IV c.12] and also further to continue [8 Geo.IV c.15].
		c.27	An act to continue [3 Vict. c.25].
		c.28	An act to continue several acts relating to the appointment of firewards and the better extinguishment of fires in a part of the parish of St Stephen, in the county of Charlotte.
		c.35	An act to continue [3 Vict. c.28].
		c.37	An act to continue [9 Geo.IV c.28].
		c.38	An act to continue [5 Wm.IV c.41].
		c.45	An act to continue [3 Vict. c.2].
		c.51	An act to amend [6 Geo.IV c.12].
		c.52	An act to incorporate the St Croix Bridge Company.
		c.53	An act to incorporate the St Andrews Whale Fishing Company.
		c.54	An act to incorporate the St Andrews Steam Mills and Manufacturing Company.
		c.58	An act to repeal [10&11 Geo.IV c.12] and to make other and more effectual provision relating to the same.
9 Vict.	1846	c.13	An act to authorize Her Majesty's justices of the peace for the county of Charlotte to levy an assessment to pay off the county debt.
		c.35	An act to alter the great road from Fredericton to St Andrews.

		c.37	An act to continue [7 Vict. c.25].
		c.49	An act for the incorporation of the St Croix River Canal Company.
10 Vict.	1847	c.23	An act to incorporate the Charlotte County Agricultural Society.
		c.27	An act further to amend and extend the provisions of [6 Wm.IV c.31].
		c.28	An act to incorporate the St Andrews Benefit Society.
		c.35	An act to authorize Her Majesty's justices of the peace for the county of Charlotte to levy an assessment to pay off the county debt.
		c.45	An act to amend [9 Geo.IV c.28].
		c.63	An act further to continue [7 Wm.IV c.36].
		c.69	An act to authorize the justices of the peace for the county of Charlotte to assess the inhabitants of St Andrews, to pay expenses incurred in the support of emigrant poor in said parish.
		c.84	An act to facilitate the making of a rail road from St Andrews, in the county of Charlotte, to Woodstock, in the county of Carleton, and branches thereof.
11 Vict.	1848	c.37	An act to authorize her majesty's justices of the peace for the county of Charlotte to assess the inhabitants of said county to pay off the county debt, and to provide for the contingent expenses thereof.
		c.42	An act to provide for the more effectually repairing the streets and bridges in the town plat of St Andrews.
		c.43	An act to empower and authorize the justices of the peace for the county of Charlotte to lease a certain piece of common land in the parish of St Andrews, and to invest the proceeds towards the support of the poor of the said parish.
		c.48	An act in addition to and amendment of [10 Vict. c.27].
		c.63	An act to extend the provisions of [11 Vict. c.84].
12 Vict.	1849	c.8	An act to establish the road leading from Roix' farm, on the great road between St George and St Andrews, to the great road between Fredericton and St Stephen, as one of the great roads of communication.
		c.12	An act to legalize the conveyance of water to Turner's grist mill, in the parish of St Patrick, in the county of Charlotte.

		c.15	An act to authorize her majesty's justices of the peace for the county of Charlotte to assess the inhabitants of said county to pay off the county debt, and to provide for the contingent expenses thereof.
		c.28	An act to provide for the more effectually repairing the roads and bridges in the Parish of Campo Bello and Grand Manan.
		c.60	An act in further amendment of the acts relating to the incorporation of the St Andrews and Quebec Rail Road Company.
		c.68	An act to incorporate the St Stephen Upper Mills Boom Company.
		c.74	An act further to facilitate the making of a rail road from St Andrews to Woodstock, with a branch to St Stephen.
13 Vict.	1850	c.L-14	An act to authorize the justices of the peace of the county of Charlotte to levy an assessment to pay the county debt and contingent expenses of said county.
		c.L-16	An act to continue [11 Vict. c.42].
		c.P-1	An act relating to the St Andrews and Quebec Rail Road.
		c.P-15	An act to continue [2 Wm.IV c.16].
		c.P-18	An act to authorize the trustees of the Church of Scotland, in the town of St Andrews, to sell certain lands, and vest the proceeds in other lands.
14 Vict.	1851	c.L-8	An act to amend [4 Vict. c.10].
		c.P-11	An act to incorporate the St Stephen Rail Road Company.
		c.P-13	An act to incorporate the Orthodox Congregational Church at Mill Town, in the Parish of St Stephen.
		c.36	An act to facilitate the construction of a railway from St Andrews to Quebec.
15 Vict.	1852	c.20	An act to incorporate the St Patrick Central Agricultural Society.
		c.60	An act to amend [13 Vict. c.36].
		c.70	An act to continue [6 Wm.IV c.32].
		c.74	An act to continue [12 Vict. c.68].
		c.75	An act to incoporate the St Andrews Steam Ferry Boat Company.
		c.77	An act to incorporate the St Stephen Middle Boom Company.
16 Vict.	1853	c.3	An act to amend [13 Vict. c.36].

		c.15	An act to unite a portion of a school district in the parish of St David to the parish of St James, in the county of Charlotte.
		c.16	An act to authorise the justices of the peace for the county of Charlotte to assess the inhabitants of the parish of St Stephen for the erection of a lock-up house in the said parish.
		c.17	An act to assess a certain district in the parish of St Stephen, in the county of Charlotte, to defray the expense of a fire engine, engine house, and other articles connected therewith.
		c.18	An act for the better and more effectual securing the navigation of the River St Croix, in the county of Charlotte.
		c.39	An act to revive and amend [59 Geo.III c.16].
		c.47	An act to authorise the rector, church wardens and vestry of St Mark's church, in the parish of St George, in the county of Charlotte, to sell and dispose of certain glebe lands in said parish, and invest the proceeds in other lands.
		c.50	An act relating to the St Andrews and Quebec Rail Road Company.
		c.52	An act to increase the capital stock of the St Stephen's Bank, in the county of Charlotte.
17 Vict.	1854	c.38	An act to provide for the more effectually repairing the highways, streets, and side walks in the Milltown highway district, in the parish of St Stephen.
		c.56	An act to incorporate the Milltown Acqueduct Company, in the parish of St Stephen.
		c.57	An act to incorporate the Middle Landing Mills Company in St Stephen.
		c.60	An act to incorporate the St Andrews Gas Company.
18 Vict.	1855	c.42	An act to continue [11 Vict. c.42].
		c.43	An act to continue [12 Vict. c.28].
		c.58	An act to authorize the rector, church wardens, and vestry of St David's Church, in the parish of St David, in the county of Charlotte, to sell and dispose of certain lands in the said parish, and invest the proceeds in other lands.
		c.62	An act relating to the St Stephen Railroad Company.
		c.71	An act to incorporate the St Stephen Lower Bridge Company.

19 Vict.	1856	c.7	An act to authorize the rector, church wardens, and vestry of St Paul's Church, in the parish of Grand Manan, in the county of Charlotte, to sell and dispose of certain lands in the said parish, and invest the proceeds in other lands.
		c.19	An act relating to the St Andrews and Quebec Railroad Company.
		c.24	An act relating to the fire department of St Stephen, in the county of Charlotte.
		c.25	An act to erect the upper part of the parish of St Patrick, in the county of Charlotte, into a separate town or parish.
		c.27	An act relating to the public burial grounds in the town of St Andrews.
		c.28	An act to incorporate the St Stephen Rural Cemetery.
		c.30	An act to incorporate the St Stephen's Gas Light Company.
		c.69	An act for further facilitating the making of part of the St Andrews and Quebec Rail Road.
		c.70	An act in addition to and in amendment of [19 Vict. c.19].
20 Vict.	1857	c.5	An act to alter the time of holding the circuit court in the county of Charlotte.
		c.8	An act to repeal [12 Vict. c.28] so far as it relates to the parish of Grand Manan.
		c.9	An act to erect the eastern part of the parish of Pennfield, in the county of Charlotte, into a separate town or parish.
		c.18	An act to authorize the rector, church wardens and vestry of All Sts Church, in the parish of St Andrews, in the county of Charlotte, to sell and convey the glebe and church lands in the said parish, and reinvest the proceeds in other lands or securities.
		c.21	An act relating to the public burial grounds in the parish of St Stephen.
		c.26	An act to incorporate the St Andrews Rural Cemetery Company.
		c.27	An act to incorporate the St Stephens Academy.
		c.30	An act to incorporate the First Universalist Society at Milltown in the parish of St Stephen.
21 Vict.	1858	c.55	An act to provide for the more effectually repairing the roads and briges in the parishes of West Isles and Campo Bello, in the county of Charlotte.

		c.56	An act to authorize the justices of the peace for the county of Charlotte to assess the parish of St Stephen, in the said county, for the erection of an Alms House therein, and to provide a site for the same, and for making rules and regulations for the management thereof.
		c.64	An act to incorporate the St Andrews Mechanics' Institute.
		c.65	An act to incorporate the Middle Bridge Company at St Stephen.
		c.66	An act to incorporate the Milltown Lower Dam Company in the parish of St Stephen.
		c.67	An act to incorporate the St Stephen Water Company of Milltown.
22 Vict.	1859	c.52	An act to establish Mark's Street, in the parish of St Stephen, in the county of Charlotte, as a public highway.
		c.56	An act to authorize the rector, church wardens, and vestry of St Paul's Church, in the parish of Grand Manan, to sell a certain part of the glebe land in said parish, and invest the proceeds in other lands.
23 Vict.	1860	c.13	An act to continue [16 Vict. c.18].
		c.51	An act to extend the time for the completion of the Rail Road from St Andrews in the county of Charlotte, to Woodstock in the county of Carleton.
		c.56	An act to authorize the justices of the peace for the county of Charlotte to sell and dispose of a part of the commons land in the parish of St Andrews to the St Andrews Rural Cemetery Company.
		c.67	An act to continue [17 Vict. c.38].
		c.68	An act to empower the president and directors of the public grammar school in the town of St Andrews, to sell certain lots of land in the said town, and invest the proceeds in landed securities.
		c.88	An act to incorporate the Campo Bello Mining Company.
24 Vict.	1861	c.20	An act further to extend the time for the completion of the railroad from St Andrews in the county of Charlotte, to Woodstock in the county of Carleton, and for other purposes.
		c.34	An act to authorize the justices of the peace for the county of Charlotte to levy an assessment to pay off the debt due by the town of St Andrews.

		c.35	An act to authorize the justices of the peace for the county of Charlotte to sell certain lands in the parish of St Andrews, and invest the proceeds in government securities.
		c.36	An act to enable the firewards of the parish of St Stephen, in the county of Charlotte, to increase the number of firemen attached to the St Stephen Volunteer Fire Engine Company Number Two.
		c.37	An act to authorize the justices of the peace for the county of Charlotte to assess the inhabitants of the parish of St Stephen for the erection of a lock-up house in the Milltown, in the said parish.
		c.38	An act in addition to [20 Vict. c.21].
		c.49	An act to incorporate sundry persons by the name of the St Andrews Water Company.
25 Vict.	1862	c.44	An act to enable the justices of the peace for the county of Charlotte to sell certain lands and invest the proceeds in other securities.
26 Vict.	1863	c.36	An act relating to rules and regulations for the government of pilots in the county of Charlotte.
		c.37	An act to repeal [11 Vict. c.42].
		c.47	An act relating to certain exemptions from duty at the port of St Stephen.
27 Vict.	1864	c.22	An act to provide for more effectually repairing the streets, bridges and sidewalks in the lower highway district in the parish of St Stephen.
		c.23	An act to provide for the erection and maintenance of a poor house and alms house in the parish of St George, in the county of Charlotte.
		c.55	An act for establishing and maintaining a police force in the the parish of St Stephen, in the county of Charlotte.
		c.56	An act to incorporate the St Stephens Branch Railroad Company.
28 Vict.	1865	c.20	An act to provide for the preservation of deer on the island of Grand Manan.
		c.40	An act to incoporate certain persons holders of property in the lower district of St Stephen, for the purposes therein mentioned. [railroad bonus]
		c.42	An act to repeal [5 Geo.IV c.2].
		c.43	An act to revive and continue [8 Vict. c.52].
		c.44	An act relating to the Charlotte County Bank.
		c.45	An act in addition to [27 Vict. c.56].

		c.46	An act to amend [27 Vict. c.55].
29 Vict.	1866	c.11	An act to incorporate the St Andrews Friendly Society.
		c.21	An act to facilitate the construction of a deep sea wharf at or near the southeastern end of Water Street in the town of St Andrews, in the county of Charlotte.
30 Vict.	1866	c.29	An act to revive and continue [8 Vict. c.52].
		c.15	An act to repeal [26 Vict. c.47].
		c.22	An act to amend [27 Vict. c.56].
		c.33	An act in addition to [28 Vict. c.45].
		c.52	An act to provide for the more effectually repairing and improving the streets, bridges and sidewalks in the lower highway district in the parish of St Stephen.
		c.60	An act to revive [5 Geo.IV c.10].
		c.67	An act to incorporate the St Andrews Deep Sea Wharf and Railway Company.
		c.69	An act for the further increase of the capital stock of the St Stephens Bank in the county of Charlotte.
		c.79	An act to provide for the erecting of a town hall in the parish of St David, in the county of Charlotte.
		c.80	An act relating to the firemen of Milltown, in the parish of St Stephen, in the county of Charlotte.
		c.87	An act to repeal section 4 of [19 Vict. c.27].

Appendix B

Commission of the Peace, 1845

Know Ye, that We have assigned you, jointly and severally and every one of you our Justices to keep our Peace, in our County of Charlotte, in the Province of New-Brunswick, and to keep, and cause to be kept all Ordinances, Laws and Statutes, for the good of the Peace, and for the preservation of the same, and for the quiet rule and government of our People made, in all and singular their articles in our said County (as well within liberties as without) according to the force, form, and effect of the same; and to chastise and punish all persons that offend against the form of those Ordinances, Laws or Statutes, or any one of them, in the aforesaid County, as it ought to be done according to the form of those Ordinances, Laws and Statutes; and to cause to come before you, or any of you, all those who to any one or more of our people concerning their bodies, or the firing of their houses, have used threats, to find sufficient Surety for the Peace, or their good behaviour, towards us and our people; and if they shall refuse to find such security, then them in our our prisons until they shall find such security to cause to be safely kept.

We have also assigned you and every two or more of you (of whom any one of you the aforesaid [names of those in quorum] we will shall be one) our Justices to inquire the truth more fully, by the oath of good and lawful men of the aforesaid County, by whom the truth of the matter shall be the better known, of all and all manner of felonies, trespasses, forestallings, regratings, ingrossings, and extortions whatsoever; and of all and singular other crimes and offences, of which the Justices of our Peace, may or ought lawfully to inquire, by whomsoever, and after what manner soever, in the said County, done or perpetrated, or which shall happen to be there done, or attempted, and also of all those who in the aforesaid County, in companies against our peace, in disturbance of our people, with armed force, have gone or rode, or hereafter shall presume to go or ride; and also of all those who have there lain in wait, or hereafter shall presume to lie in wait, to maim, or cut, or kill our people; and also of all victuallers, and all and singular other persons, who in the abuse of weights or measures or in selling victuals, against the form of the Ordinances, Laws and Statutes, or any one of them therefore made, for the common benefit of our said Province of New-Brunswick, and our people thereof, have offended or attempted, or hereafter shall presume in the said County to offend or attempt; and also of all Sheriffs, Bailiffs, Stewards, Constables, keepers of Gaols, and other Officers, who in the execution of their offices about the premises, or any of them, have unduly behaved themselves, or hereafter shall presume to behave themselves unduly, or have been, or shall happen hereafter to be careless, remiss or negligent in our aforesaid County; and of all and singular articles and circumstances, and all other things whatsoever that concern the premises, or any of them, by whomsoever, and after what manner soever, in our aforesaid County, done or perpetrated, or which hereafter shall there happen to be done or attempted in what manner soever; and to inspect all indictments whatsoever, so before you or any of you, taken or to be taken, or before others late our Justices of the Peace in the said County made or taken, and not yet determined; and to make and continue processes thereupon, against all and singular the persons so indicted, or who before you hereafter shall happen to be indicted, until they can be taken or surrender themselves, and to hear and determine all and singular the felonies, trespasses, forestallings, regratings, ingrossings, extortions, unlawful assemblies, indictements aforesaid, and all and singular other other the premises, according to the Laws and Statutes of that part of our United Kingdom of Great Britain and Ireland called England, and of our said Province of New-Brunswick, as in the like case it has been accustomed, or ought to be done; and the same offenders, and every of them, for their offences, by fines, ransoms, amerciaments, forfeitures, and other means, as according to the Law and custom of that part of our United Kingdom of Great Britain and Ireland called England, and of our said Province of New-Brunswick, or form of the Ordinances, Laws and Statutes aforesaid, it has been accustomed, or ought to be done, to chastise and punish.

And therefore we command you and every of you, that to keeping the Peace, Ordinances, Laws, Statutes, and all and singular other the premises, you diligently apply yourselves; and that at certain days and places, which you, or any such two or more of you, as is aforesaid, shall appoint for these purposes, into the premises ye make enquiries; and all and singular the premises hear and determine, and perform and fulfil them in the aforesaid form, doing therein what to justice appertains, according to the Law and custom of that part of our United Kingdom of Great Britain and Ireland called England, and of our said Province of New-Brunswick. Saving to us the amerciaments, and other things to us therefrom [belong]ing.

And we command by the tenor of these presents our Sheriff of our said County of Charlotte that at certain days and places, which you, or any two or more of you, as is aforesaid, [shall make] known to him, he cause to come before you, or such two or more of you as aforesaid, so many and such good and lawful men of his Bailiwick (as well within liberties as without) by whom the truth of the matter in [the premises] shall be the better known and inquired into.

Appendix C

Sources cited

C.1 Archives

CO188 Colonial Office Original Correspondence—New Brunswick. (PANB MC416)

CCA - Charlotte County Archives, St Andrews

MC349	Harris Hatch fonds.
MC378	C.E.O. Hatheway, Book No. 3, 1879-82.
Uncat.	Survey of lots on Deer Island by C.R. Hatheway, 3 Dec 1825.

MHS – Massachusetts Historical Society, Boston

Ann Appleton Storrow Papers, 1790-1796.
Ann Appleton Storrow Papers addition, 1782-1804.

MSA - Maine State Archives, Augusta

Register Book Deeds Leases, Etc for the Estate of Campo Bello, Prop. of Capt. W.F.W. Owen.

NBM - New Brunswick Museum, Saint John

Charles Reid Hatheway Papers.
Hugh T. Hazen Collection, Chipman Papers.
Nathaniel Hubbard Papers.
Jarvis Family Papers.
William Mahood Journals.
New Brunswick Government Collection.

NLW - National Library of Wales, Aberystwyth

Glansevern estate papers

NYPL - New York Public Library

George Chalmers papers, 1606-1812

PANB – Provincial Archives of New Brunswick, Fredericton

MC207	Hatch family fonds
MC243	Arthur Hill Gillmor family fonds
MC295	James Brown fonds
MC416	Colonial Office collection : [1784-1920]
MC642	The humble address of the Learned Goose, Hannah, and Company
MC873	Charlotte County Bank fonds
MC996	H. M. Customs and Excise (Plantation) records : [1766-1855]
MC1001	Hill, Upton family fonds
MC1081	Nehemiah Marks family fonds
RS1	Published Journals of the Proceedings of the Legislative Assembly of New Brunswick
RS6	Executive Council: Minutes and Orders-in-Council
RS7	Executive Council: Ottawa Microfilm Series
RS8	Executive Council: New Brunswick Microfilm Series
RS9	Executive Council: Cabinet Meetings Records
RS13	Provincial Secretary: Correspondence
RS23	Provincial Secretary: Customs House Administration Records

RS24	Legislative Assembly: Sessional Records
RS32	Supreme Court Minutes
RS36	Supreme Court Circuit Courts Records
RS42	Supreme Court Original Jurisdiction Case Files
RS76	Records of the Minister of Justice and Attorney General
RS148	Charlotte County Council Records
RS157	Sunbury County Council Records
RS330	Records of Thomas Carleton, Lieutenant Governor
RS339	Records of Ward Chipman, Colonial Administrator
RS342	Records of William Black, Colonial Administrator
RS343	Records of Archibald Campbell, Lieutenant Governor
RS344	Records of John Harvey, Lieutenant Governor
RS345	Records of William M. G. Colebrooke, Lieutenant Governor
RS346	Records of Edmund W. Head, Lieutenant Governor
RS347	Records of John H. T. Manners-Sutton, Lieutenant Governor
RS375	Charlotte County Jail Records
RS431	Charlotte County Court Records
RS463	Charlotte County Magistrates Records
RS479	Charlotte County Justices of the Peace Records
RS538	Provincial Secretary: Warrants, Appointments and Commissions
RS539	Provincial Secretary: Judicial Administration Records
RS555	Provincial Secretary: Immigration Administration Records
RS559	New Brunswick Militia Records
RS623	Provincial Secretary: Banks Administration Records
RS637	Records of the Surveyor General
RS686	New Brunswick Land Grant Records
RS687	Crown Lands Survey Records

UNB - University of New Brunswick Archives & Special Collections, Fredericton

MG/H46a	Office of the Surveyor General 1807-1813

C.2 Newspapers

Since several of the Charlotte newspapers survive in broken runs (if at all) I have also cited items from missing issues of the local press that were copied in other papers, giving both the original and reprint sources. Newspaper titles changed frequently: generic titles are listed here. For additional details see the entries by reference number in Council of Head Librarians of New Brunswick, *New Brunswick Newspaper Directory, 1783-1996*, 2d edition (Fredericton, 1996).

Citation	Generic Title	Ref.#
St Andrews		
Bay Pilot	Bay Pilot	621
Charlotte Gazette	Charlotte Gazette	623
Courant	St Andrews Courant	632
Herald	St Andrews Herald	625, 628, 629
Provincialist	Provincialist/Charlotte County Advertiser	627
Standard	St Andrews Standard	634–640
St Stephen		
Patriot	Provincial Patriot	653
St Croix Courier	St Croix Courier	654, 655
Saint John		
Chronicle	Weekly Chronicle	544, 592
Courier	New Brunswick Courier	475
Daily Sun	The Daily Sun	393, 546
Gazette	The Saint John Gazette	423, 515–517
Globe	Saint John Globe	385, 518
New Brunswicker	The New Brunswicker	481, 482
Royal Gazette	The Royal Gazette [to 1815]	505, 506
Morning Telegraph	Morning Telegraph	470
Fredericton		
Head Quarters	The Head Quarters	132, 133
Royal Gazette	The Royal Gazette [from 1815]	148, 155
Eastport, ME		**ISSN**
Sentinel	Eastport Sentinel	2325-5749, -5757

Bibliography

Acheson, T.W. 'A Study in the Historical Demography of a Loyalist County.' In: *Histoire Sociale/Social History* 1 (Apr. 1968), pp. 53–65.

— 'Denominationalism in a Loyalist County: A Social History of Charlotte, 1783-1940.' M.A. thesis. University of New Brunswick, 1964.

— 'New Boston to New Brunswick: Anonymous Loyalists in New Hampshire.' In: *Acadiensis* 27.1 (1997), pp. 3–26.

— *Saint John: The Making of a Colonial Urban Community.* Toronto: University of Toronto Press, 1985.

— 'The 1840s: Decade of Tribulation.' In: *The Atlantic Region to Confederation: A History.* Ed. by Phillip A. Buckner and John G. Reid. Toronto: University of Toronto Press, 1994, pp. 307–332.

Aitchison, J.H. 'The Municipal Corporations Act of 1849.' In: *Canadian Historical Review* 30.2 (1949), pp. 107–122.

Aiton, Grace. 'The Selling of Paupers by Public Auction in Sussex Parish.' In: *Collections of the New Brunswick Historical Society* 16 (1961), pp. 93–110.

Allen, Douglas W. *The Institutional Revolution: Measurement and the Economic Emergence of the Modern World.* Chicago: University of Chicago Press, 2012, p. 267.

[Anon.] *A Statement of Facts relative to The Standfasts and The Runaways …* pamphlet. 1802.

— *An Account of the Saint Andrews and Quebec Railway, being the Original Intercolonial Railway, From its First Inception in 1835 to the Present Time.* Saint John, 1869.

Anon., ed. *Elections in New Brunswick 1784-1984.* Fredericton, 1984.

[Anon.] *The Elector's Mirror; or, Truth Unveiled.* pamphlet. 1802.

— *The Question respecting the right of the United States of America, to the Islands in Passamaquoddy-Bay, By virtue of the Treaty of 1783, considered in the Case of the Sloop Falmouth …* pamphlet. [1806].

Archbold, J.F. *Jervis's Acts, 11 & 12 Victoria, cc. 42, 43, & 44 Relating to the Duties of Justices of the Peace Out of Sessions as to Indictable Offences, Convictions, and Orders : and to the Protection of Justices in the Execution of their Duties…* 3rd. London: Shaw & Sons, 1851.

Arthurs, H.W. 'Labour Law without the State?' In: *University of Toronto Law Journal* 46.1 (1996), pp. 1–45.

— *'Without the Law': Administrative Justice and Legal Pluralism in Nineteenth-Century England.* Toronto: University of Toronto Press, 1985, p. 312.

Backhouse, Constance B. 'Desperate Women and Compassionate Courts: Infanticide in Nineteenth-Century Canada.' In: *University of Toronto Law Journal* 34.4 (Fall 1984), pp. 447–478.

Bacon, Francis. *The Use of the Law. Provided for Preservation of our Persons, Goods and Good Names. According to the Practice of the Lawes, and Customes of this Land.* London, 1635.

Baker, Howard. 'Small Claims, Communal Justice, and the Rule of Law in Kingston, Upper Canada, c.1785-1819.' LL.M. thesis. Osgoode Hall Law School, 1993.

Barto, Martha Ford. *Passamaquoddy: Genealogies of West Isles Families.* Saint John, NB: privately printed, 1975.

Beattie, John M. *Crime and the Courts in England, 1660-1800.* Princeton, NJ: Princeton University Press, 1986.

— *Policing and Punishment in London, 1660-1750: Urban Crime and the Limits of Terror.* Oxford: Oxford University Press, 2001.

Bell, David Graham. 'A Perspective on Legal Pluralism in 19th-Century New Brunswick.' In: *University of New Brunswick Law Journal* 37 (1988), pp. 86–93.

— 'The Confederation Issue in Charlotte County, New Brunswick.' M.A. thesis. Kingston: Queen's, 1976.

Berton, G.F.S., comp. *The Acts of the General Assembly … From the Twenty Sixth Year of the Reign of King George the Third to the Sixth Year of the Reign of King William the Fourth.* Fredericton, 1838.

Brown, Desmond H. *The Genesis of the Canadian Criminal Code of 1892.* Toronto: University of Toronto Press. Published for the Osgoode Society, 1989, p. 253.

Buckner, Phillip. 'Parker, Neville.' In: *Dictionary of Canadian Biography.* Vol. 9. University of Toronto Press/Université Laval, 1976.

Buckner, Phillip A. and John G. Reid, eds. *The Atlantic Region to Confederation: A History.* Toronto: University of Toronto Press, 1994.

Burn, Richard. *The Justice of the Peace and Parish Officer.* 15th. London, 1785.

Burrows, E.H. *Captain Owen of the African Survey: The Hydrographic Surveys of Admiral W.F.W. Owen on the Coast of Africa and the Great Lakes of Canada, His Fight against the African Slave Trade, His Life in Campobello Island, New Brunswick, 1774-1857.* Rotterdam: A.A. Balkema, 1979.

Bushman, Richard Lyman. 'Farmers in Court: Orange County, North Carolina, 1750-1776.' In: Tomlins, Christopher L. and Bruce H. Mann. *The Many Legalities of Early America.* Chapel Hill: University of North Carolina Press. Published for the Omohundro Institute of Early American History and Culture, Williamsburg, VA, 2001, pp. 388–413.

Campbell, Gail. ''Smashers' and 'Rummies': Voters and the Rise of Parties in Charlotte County, New Brunswick, 1846-1857.' In: *Historical Papers / Communications Historiques* 21.1 (1986), pp. 86–116.

Carroll, Francis M. *A Good and Wise Measure: The Search for the Canadian-American Boundary, 1783-1842.* Toronto: University of Toronto Press, 2001.

Chapman, J.K. 'The Mid-Nineteenth-Century Temperance Movement in New Brunswick and Maine.' In: *Canadian Historical Review* 35.1 (1954), pp. 43–60.

Chitty, Joseph. *A Practical Treatise on the Criminal Law: Comprising the Practice, Pleadings, and Evidence Which Occur in the Course of Criminal Prosecutions* ... London, 1816.

Clarke, M. St. Clair and D.A. Hall, comp. *Legislative and Documentary History of the Bank of the United States, including the original Bank of North America.* Washington, 1832.

Condon, Ann Gorman. '1783-1800: Loyalist Arrival, Acadian Return, Imperial Reform.' In: *The Atlantic Region to Confederation: A History.* Ed. by Phillip A. Buckner and John G. Reid. Toronto: University of Toronto Press, 1994, pp. 184–209.

— 'Leonard, George.' In: *Dictionary of Canadian Biography.* Vol. 6. University of Toronto Press/Université Laval, 1987.

Conley, John A. 'Doing It by the Book: Justice of the Peace Manuals and English Law in Eighteenth Century America.' In: *Journal of Legal History* 6.3 (1985), pp. 257–298.

Cornell, Paul G. 'Owen, William Fitz William.' In: *Dictionary of Canadian Biography.* Vol. 8. University of Toronto Press/Université Laval, 1985.

Couturier, Jacques Paul. 'Courts and Business Activity in Late 19th Century New Brunswick: A View from the Case Files.' In: *Acadiensis* 26.2 (Spring 1997), pp. 77–95.

Craig, G.M., ed. *Lord Durham's Report: An Abridgement* ... Toronto: McClelland and Stewart, 1963.

Craven, Paul. 'Law and Ideology: The Toronto Police Court, 1850-80.' In: *Essays in the History of Canadian Law II.* Ed. by David H. Flaherty. Toronto: University of Toronto Press for the Osgoode Society, 1981, pp. 248–307.

Davies, Wayne K.D. 'A Welsh Landlord on a Canadian Frontier: David Owen of Berriw, Cambridge and Campobello, 1754-1829.' In: *National Library of Wales Journal* 31.3 (2005), pp. 217–241.

— 'Capt. William Owen and the Settlement of Campobello: Montgomeryshire's Connection with New Brunswick, Canada.' In: *National Library of Wales Journal* 31.3 (2000), pp. 217–241.

Dictionary of Canadian Biography. University of Toronto Press/Université Laval.

Donovan, Kenneth. 'The Origin and Establishment of the New Brunswick Courts.' In: *Journal of the New Brunswick Museum* (1980), pp. 57–64.

Eastwood, David. *Governing Rural England: Tradition and Transformation in Local Government, 1740-1840.* Oxford: Oxford University Press, 1994.

— *Government and Community in the English Provinces, 1700-1870.* New York: St. Martin's Press, 1994.

Edwards, Laura F. *The People and Their Peace: Legal Culture and the Transformation of Inequality in the Post-Revolutionary South.* Chapel Hill: University of North Carolina Press, 2009.

Facey-Crowther, David R. *The New Brunswick Militia 1787-1867.* Fredericton, NB: New Brunswick Historical Society and New Ireland Press, 1990.

— comp. *The New Brunswick Militia Commissioned Officers' List, 1787-1867.* Fredericton, NB: New Brunswick Genealogical Society, 1984.

Fellows, Robert. *Genealogies (First Families) at the Provincial Archives of New Brunswick, Canada.* 6th. Fredericton, NB: New Brunswick Genealogical Society and Provincial Archives of New Brunswick, 2006.

— 'The Loyalists and Land Settlement in New Brunswick, 1783-1790: A Study in Colonial Administration.' In: *Canadian Archivist / L'Archiviste Canadien* 2.2 (1971), pp. 5–15.

Fellows, Robert F, comp. *The New Brunswick Census of 1851, Charlotte County.* 2 vols. Fredericton: Provincial Archives of New Brunswick, 1974.

Fingard, Judith. 'The Winter's Tale: The Seasonal Contours of Pre-Industrial Poverty in British North America, 1815-1860.' In: *Historical Papers / Communications Historiques* 9.1 (1974), pp. 65–94.

Frank, Christopher. ''Let But One of Them Come before Me, and I'll Commit Him': Trade Unions, Magistrates and the Law in Mid-Nineteenth Century Staffordshire.' In: *Journal of British Studies* 44.1 (Jan. 2005), pp. 64–91.

Fyson, Donald. *Magistrates, Police and People: Everyday Criminal Justice in Quebec and Lower Canada, 1764-1837.* Toronto: University of Toronto Press for The Osgoode Society for Canadian Legal History, 2006, p. 464.

Gerth, H.H. and C. Wright Mills. *From Max Weber: Essays in Sociology.* New York: Oxford University Press, 1946, p. 490.

Girard, Philip. 'The Rise and Fall of Urban Justice in Halifax, 1815-1886.' In: *Nova Scotia Historical Review* (1988).

Glasbeek, Amanda. *Feminized Justice: The Toronto Women's Court, 1913-34.* Vancouver: UBC Press, 2009.

Godfrey, W.G. 'Glenie, James.' In: *Dictionary of Canadian Biography.* Vol. 5. University of Toronto Press / Université Laval, 1983.

Goebel, Julius and T. Raymond Naughton. *Law Enforcement in Colonial New York: A Study in Criminal Procedure, (1664-1776).* Montclair, NJ: Patterson Smith, [1944] 1972.

Greenhous, Brereton. 'Paupers and Poorhouses: The Development of Poor Relief in Early New Brunswick.' In: *Histoire Sociale / Social History* 1 (Apr. 1968), pp. 103–128.

Grose, Francis, comp. *A Classical Dictionary of the Vulgar Tongue.* London: S. Hooper, 1785.

Hatheway, Calvin Luther. *The History of New Brunswick from Its First Settlement.* Fredericton, 1846.

Hay, Douglas. *Criminal Cases on the Crown Side of King's Bench: Staffordshire, 1740-1800.* Stafford, UK: Staffordshire Record Society, 2010.

— 'Dread of the Crown Office: The English Magistracy and King's Bench, 1740-1800.' In: *Law, Crime and English Society, 1660-1830.* Ed. by Norma Landau. Cambridge: Cambridge University Press, 2002, pp. 19–45.

— 'Legislation, Magistrates, and Judges: High and Low Law in England and the Empire.' In: *The British and Their Laws in the Eighteenth Century.* Ed. by David Lemmings. Woodbridge, UK: Boydell Press, 2005, pp. 59–79.

— 'Patronage, Paternalism and Welfare: Masters, Workers and Magistrates in Eighteenth-Century England.' In: *International Labor and Working-Class History* 53 (Spring 1998), pp. 27–48.

— 'Time, Inequality, and Law's Violence.' In: *Law's Violence.* Ed. by Austin Sarat and Thomas R. Kearns. Ann Arbor: University of Michigan Press, 1992, p. 171.

Hay, Douglas and Paul Craven, eds. *Masters, Servants, and Magistrates in Britain and the Empire, 1562-1955.* Chapel Hill: University of North Carolina Press, 2004.

Heron, Craig. *Booze: A Distilled History.* Toronto: Between the Lines, 2003.

Higginson, Thomas Wentworth. *Cheerful Yesterdays: A Cambridge Boyhood.* Boston: Houghton, Mifflin, 1898.

Hill, Isabel Louise. *Some Loyalists and Others.* 1977.

Holbrook, James, comp. *A Census of the Population of New Brunswick, in the Year 1840, Compiled and Arranged from the Official Returns made by the respective Clerks of the Peace of the several Counties.* [Fredericton]: John Simpson, Queen's Printer, [1841?].

Holmes, Theodore C. *Loyalists to Canada: The 1783 Settlement of Quakers and Others at Passamaquoddy.* Camden, ME: Picton Press, 1992.

Ingersoll, L.K. 'Fisher, Wilford.' In: *Dictionary of Canadian Biography.* Vol. 9. University of Toronto Press/Université Laval, 1976.

— 'Owen, David.' In: *Dictionary of Canadian Biography.* Vol. 6. University of Toronto Press/Université Laval, 1987.

Johnson, J.K. *Becoming Prominent: Regional Leadership in Upper Canada, 1791-1841.* Toronto: University of Toronto Press, 1989.

Karsten, Peter. *Between Law and Custom: High and Low Legal Cultures in the Lands of the British Diaspora – the United States, Canada, Australia, and New Zealand, 1600-1900.* Cambridge: Cambridge University Press, 2002.

Kilby, William Henry, comp. *Eastport and Passamaquoddy: A Collection of Historical and Biographical Sketches.* Eastport ME, 1888.

King, Peter. *Crime, Justice, and Discretion in England, 1740-1820.* Oxford: Oxford University Press, 2000.

Klein, Kim. 'Paths to the Assembly in British North America: New Brunswick, 1786-1837.' In: *Acadiensis* 39.1 (2010), pp. 133–157.

Landau, Norma, ed. *Law, Crime and English Society, 1660-1830.* Cambridge: Cambridge University Press, 2002.

— *The Justices of the Peace, 1679-1760.* Berkeley: University of California Press, 1984.

— 'The Trading Justice's Trade.' In: *Law, Crime and English Society, 1660-1830.* Ed. by Norma Landau. Cambridge: Cambridge University Press, 2002, pp. 46–70.

Langbein, John H., Renée Lettow Lerner, and Bruce P. Smith. *History of the Common Law: The Development of Anglo-American Legal Institutions.* New York: Aspen/Wolters Kluwer Law & Business, 2009.

LaVorgna, Koral. 'The Irish in St. Patrick's Parish, Charlotte County, New Brunswick, 1831-1881.' M.A. thesis. U.N.B., 1995.

Lemmings, David, ed. *The British and Their Laws in the Eighteenth Century.* Woodbridge, UK: Boydell Press, 2005.

Lermack, Paul. 'Peace Bonds and Criminal Justice in Colonial Philadelphia.' In: *Pennsylvania Magazine of History and Biography* 100.2 (Apr. 1976), pp. 173–190.

— 'The Law of Recognizances in Colonial Pennsylvania.' In: *Temple Law Quarterly* 50.3 (Spring 1977), pp. 475–512.

Lewthwaite, Susan. 'Law and Authority in Upper Canada: The Justices of the Peace in the Newcastle District, 1803-1840.' Ph.D. dissertation. University of Toronto, 2001.

Lewthwaite, Susan. 'The Pre-Trial Examination in Upper Canada.' In: *Criminal Justice in the Old World and the New: Essays in Honour of J.M. Beattie.* Ed. by Greg T. Smith, Allyson N. May, and Simon Devereaux. Toronto: Centre of Criminology, University of Toronto, 1998, pp. 85–103.

Macmillan, David S. and Roger Nason. 'Pagan, Robert.' In: *Dictionary of Canadian Biography.* Vol. 6. University of Toronto Press/Université Laval, 1987.

MacNutt, W.S. 'Baillie, Thomas.' In: *Dictionary of Canadian Biography.* Vol. 9. University of Toronto Press/Université Laval, 1976.

— *New Brunswick: A History, 1784-1867.* Toronto: Macmillan of Canada, 1963.

Mann, Bruce H. *Republic of Debtors: Bankruptcy in the Age of American Independence.* Cambridge MA: Harvard University Press, 2002.

Marquis, Greg. 'Anti-Lawyer Sentiment in Mid-Victorian New Brunswick.' In: *University of New Brunswick Law Journal* 36 (1987), pp. 163–174.

— 'Contesting Prohibition and the Constitution in 1850s New Brunswick.' In: *The Grand Experiment: Law and Legal Culture in British Settler Societies.* Ed. by Hamar Foster, Benjamin L. Berger, and A.R. Buck. Vancouver: UBC Press for the Osgoode Society for Canadian Legal History, 2008.

— 'The Contours of Canadian Urban Justice, 1830-1875.' In: *Urban History Review* 15.3 (Feb. 1987).

Marsh, Herbert. *Memoir of the Late Revd. Thomas Jones.* Cambridge, 1808.

Mowat, Grace Helen. *The Diverting History of a Loyalist Town: A Portrait of St. Andrews, New Brunswick.* Brunswick Press, 1953.

Murray, David. *Colonial Justice: Justice, Morality and Crime in the Niagara District, 1791-1849.* Toronto: University of Toronto Press for The Osgoode Society for Canadian Legal History, 2002.

Nason, Roger. 'Meritorious but Distressed Individuals: The Penobscot Loyalist Association and the Settlement of the Township of St. Andrews, New Brunswick, 1783-1821.' M.A. thesis. University of New Brunswick, 1982.

Noel, Jan. *Canada Dry: Temperance Crusades before Confederation.* Toronto: University of Toronto Press, 1995.

Nowlan, Alden. *Campobello: The Outer Island.* Toronto: Clarke, Irwin, 1975.

Owen, David. *A Statement of the Transactions Respecting the Possession of Robert and Mary Wilson, On the Island of Campo-Bello, Now Owned by the Surviving Grantee.* Privately printed pamphlet. May 1822.

Owen, William. *Narrative of American Voyages and Travels of Captain William Owen, R.N. and Settlement of the Island of Campobello in The Bay of Fundy 1766-1771.* Ed. by Victor Paltsits [and W.F. Ganong]. New York, 1942.

— *The Journal of Captain William Owen R.N., During his Residence on Campobello in 1770-1771, together with other documents and notes on the History of the Island.* Ed. by W.F. Ganong. Saint John, 1897.

Owen, William Fitz William. *The Quoddy Hermit; or, Conversations at Fairfield on Religion and Superstition.* Boston, 1841.

Palmer, Robert C. *English Law in the Age of the Black Death, 1348-1381: A Transformation of Governance and Law.* Chapel Hill: University of North Carolina Press, 1993.

Paton, Diana. *No Bond but the Law: Punishment, Race, and Gender in Jamaican State Formation, 1780-1870.* Durham, NC: Duke University Press, 2004.

Phillips, Jim, R. Roy McMurtry, and John T. Saywell, eds. *Essays in the History of Canadian Law X: A Tribute to Peter N. Oliver.* Toronto: University of Toronto Press for The Osgoode Society for Canadian Legal History, 2008.

Prime, Russell J. 'Forgotten Magistrates: Historical Glimpses of New Brunswick's Community Justices, 1870-1980.' M.A. thesis. Carleton University, 1996.

Radforth, Ian. 'Sydenham and Utilitarian Reform.' In: *Colonial Leviathan: State Formation in Mid-Nineteenth Century Canada.* Ed. by Allan Greer and Ian Radforth. Toronto: University of Toronto Press, 1992, pp. 64–102.

Ramsay, Iain. 'Consumer Law, Regulatory Capitalism and the 'New Learning' in Regulation.' In: *Sydney Law Review* 28.1 (2006), pp. 9–35.

Raymond, W.O., comp. *Winslow Papers, A.D. 1777-1826.* Saint John, 1901.

Rees, Ronald. *Some Other Place ... than Here: St. Andrews and the Irish Emigrant.* Fredericton, NB: New Ireland Press, 2000.

Rheinstein, Max, ed. *Max Weber on Law in Economy and Society.* Trans. by Max Rheinstein and Edward Shils. Cambridge, MA: Harvard University Press, 1954.

Sabine, Lorenzo. *Biographical Sketches of Loyalists of the American Revolution, with an Historical Essay.* Originally published in 1864. Port Washington, N.Y.: Kennikat Press, 1966.

Scott, Leonard. *Early Reminiscenses. A Poem Recounting Incidents Occurring in the Youth of the Author and Describing Country Life in the Province of New Brunswick, Forty Years Ago.* New York, 1864.

Searby, Peter. *History of Cambridge.* Vol. 3, 1750-1870. Cambridge: Cambridge University Press, 1997.

See, Scott W. *Riots in New Brunswick: Orange Nativism and Social Violence in the 1840s.* Toronto: University of Toronto Press, 1993.

Sharpe, Robert J. *The Lazier Murder: Prince Edward County, 1884.* Toronto: University of Toronto Press for the Osgoode Society for Canadian Legal History, 2011.

Skryme, Sir Thomas. *History of the Justices of the Peace.* 3 vols. Chichester: Barry Rose, 1991.

Sloan, Robert Wesley. 'New Ireland: Loyalists in Eastern Maine during the American Revolution.' Ph.D. dissertation. Michigan State University, 1971.

Smith, Douglas W. 'Berriew and Trinity : Thomas Jones (1756-1807) and his contemporaries.' In: *Montgomeryshire Collections (Transactions of the Powys-land Club)* 79 (1991), pp. 121–34.

Smith, Joshua M. *Borderland Smuggling: Patriots, Loyalists, and Illicit Trade in the Northeast, 1783-1820.* Gainesville: University Press of Florida, 2006.

— 'The Rogues of 'Quoddy: Smuggling in the Maine-New Brunswick Borderlands, 1783-1820.' Ph.D. dissertation. University of Maine, 2003.

Snell, Ronald Kingman. 'The County Magistracy in 18th-Century Massachusetts: 1692-1750.' Ph.D. dissertation. Princeton University, 1970.

Stephen, James Fitzjames. *A History of the Criminal Law of England.* London: Macmillan & Co., 1883.

Stone, Arthur J. 'The Admiralty Court in Colonial Nova Scotia.' In: *Dalhousie Law Journal* 17.2 (Fall 1994), pp. 363–429.

Stubs, Peter. *The New Brunswick Manual: A Compilation of Forms and Information, Designed for the Use of Justices of the Peace, Merchants, Mechanics, &c.* Saint John, NB, 1841.

Thomson, Don W. *Men and Meridians: The History of Surveying and Mapping in Canada.* Ottawa: R. Duhamel, Queen's Printer, 1966.

Todd, Alpheus. *The Practice and Privileges of the Two Houses of Parliament with an Appendix of Forms.* Toronto: By order of the House of Assembly, 1840.

Tomlins, Christopher L. 'Introduction: The Many Legalities of Colonization: A Manifesto of Destiny for Early American Legal History.' In: Tomlins, Christopher L. and Bruce H. Mann. *The Many Legalities of Early America.* Chapel Hill: University of North Carolina Press. Published for the Omohundro Institute of Early American History and Culture, Williamsburg, VA, 2001, pp. 1–20.

Tomlins, Christopher L. and Bruce H. Mann. *The Many Legalities of Early America.* Chapel Hill: University of North Carolina Press. Published for the Omohundro Institute of Early American History and Culture, Williamsburg, VA, 2001.

Trevelyan, George Macaulay. *Trinity College: An Historical Sketch.* Cambridge: Trinity College, 1943.

Vaughan, Norma. 'At Campobello, 'Just over the Line'.' In: *Boston Home Journal* (1903).

Venn, J.A., comp. *Alumni Cantabrigienses: A Biographical List of All Known Students, Graduates and Holders of Office at the University of Cambridge, from the Earliest Times to 1900.* Vol. 2:4. Cambridge: Cambridge University Press, 1922.

Vroom, James, comp. *Glimpses of the Past.* 1892–5. URL: http://members.shaw.ca/caren.secord/index.html.

Weaver, John C. *Crimes, Constables, and Courts: Order and Transgression in a Canadian City, 1816-1970.* Montreal and Kingston: McGill-Queen's University Press, 1995.

Webb, Sidney and Beatrice Webb. *English Local Government from the Revolution to the Municipal Corporations Act.* London: Longmans, Green, 1906–1929.

Weiler, Paul C. 'The 'Slippery Slope' of Judicial Intervention: The Supreme Court and Canadian Labour Relations, 1950-1970.' In: *Osgoode Hall Law Journal* 9.1 (Aug. 1971), pp. 1–79.

Wells, Kate Gannett. *Campobello: An Historical Sketch.* pamphlet. Boston, 1892.

— 'David Owen, of Campobello, New Brunswick.' In: *Acadiensis* 1.1 (Jan. 1901).

— 'The Quoddy Hermit.' In: *Atlantic Monthly* 55.332 (June 1885), pp. 821–826.

Whalen, H.J. *The Development of Local Government in New Brunswick.* Fredericton: Department of Municipal Affairs, 1964.

Whebell, C.F.J. 'Robert Baldwin and Decentralization, 1841-9.' In: *Aspects of Nineteenth-Century Ontario: Essays Presented to James J. Talman.* Ed. by F.H. Armstrong, H.A. Stevenson, and J.D. Wilson. Toronto: University of Toronto Press in association with the University of Western Ontario, 1974, pp. 48–64.

— 'The Upper Canada District Councils Act of 1841 and British Colonial Policy.' In: *Journal of Imperial and Commonwealth History* 17.2 (1989), pp. 185–209.

Willrich, Michael. *City of Courts: Socializing Justice in Progressive Era Chicago.* Cambridge: Cambridge University Press, 2003.

Wilson, Barry K. *Benedict Arnold: A Traitor in Our Midst.* Montreal and Kingston, ON: McGill-Queen's University Press, 2001.

Wilson, James K. 'The Court of General Quarter Sessions of the Peace: Local Administration in Pre-Municipal Upper Canada.' M.A. thesis. McMaster University, 1991.

Winslow Papers Online. URL: http://www.lib.unb.ca/winslow/index.html.

Woodfall, William. *An Epitome of the Law of Landlord and Tenant.* London, 1803.

Wright, Esther Clark. *The Loyalists of New Brunswick.* Fredericton, NB, 1955.

Wright, Mary Ellen. 'Unnatural Mothers: Infanticide in Halifax, 1850-1875.' In: *Nova Scotia Historical Review* 7.2 (1987), pp. 13–29.

Wynn, Graeme. 'Population Patterns in Pre-Confederation New Brunswick.' In: *Acadiensis* 10.2 (1981), pp. 124–138.

— *Timber Colony: An Historical Geography of Early Nineteenth Century New Brunswick*. Toronto: University of Toronto Press, 1981.

Index of Names

Topical Index

PUBLICATIONS OF THE OSGOODE SOCIETY FOR CANADIAN LEGAL HISTORY

2014 Christopher Moore, *The Court of Appeal for Ontario: Defining the Right of Appeal, 1792–2013*
Paul Craven, *Petty Justice: Low Law and the Sessions System in Charlotte County, New Brunswick, 1785–1867*
Thomas GW Telfer, *Ruin and Redemption: The Struggle for a Canadian Bankruptcy Law, 1867–1919*
Dominique Clément, *Equality Deferred: Sex Discrimination and British Columbia's Human Rights State, 1953–1984*

2013 Roy McMurtry, *Memoirs and Reflections*
Charlotte Gray, *The Massey Murder: A Maid, Her Master, and the Trial that Shocked a Nation*
C. Ian Kyer, *Lawyers, Families, and Businesses: The Shaping of a Bay Street Law Firm, Faskens 1863–1963*
G. Blaine Baker and Donald Fyson, eds., *Essays in the History of Canadian Law, Volume XI: Quebec and the Canadas*

2012 R. Blake Brown, *Arming and Disarming: A History of Gun Control in Canada*
Eric Tucker, James Muir, and Bruce Ziff, eds., *Property on Trial: Canadian Cases in Context*
Shelley Gavigan, *Hunger, Horses, and Government Men: Criminal Law on the Aboriginal Plains, 1870–1905*
Barrington Walker, ed., *The African Canadian Legal Odyssey: Historical Essays*

2011 Robert J. Sharpe, *The Lazier Murder: Prince Edward County, 1884*
Philip Girard, *Lawyers and Legal Culture in British North America: Beamish Murdoch of Halifax*
John McLaren, *Dewigged, Bothered, and Bewildered: British Colonial Judges on Trial, 1800–1900*
Lesley Erickson, *Westward Bound: Sex, Violence, the Law, and the Making of a Settler Society*

2010 Judy Fudge and Eric Tucker, eds., *Work on Trial: Canadian Labour Law Struggles*
Christopher Moore, *The British Columbia Court of Appeal: The First Hundred Years*
Frederick Vaughan, *Viscount Haldane: 'The Wicked Step-father of the Canadian Constitution'*
Barrington Walker, *Race on Trial: Black Defendants in Ontario's Criminal Courts, 1858–1958*

2009 William Kaplan, *Canadian Maverick: The Life and Times of Ivan C. Rand*
R. Blake Brown, *A Trying Question: The Jury in Nineteenth-Century Canada*
Barry Wright and Susan Binnie, eds., *Canadian State Trials, Volume III: Political Trials and Security Measures, 1840–1914*
Robert J. Sharpe, *The Last Day, the Last Hour: The Currie Libel Trial* (paperback edition with a new preface)

2008 Constance Backhouse, *Carnal Crimes: Sexual Assault Law in Canada, 1900–1975*
Jim Phillips, R. Roy McMurtry, and John T. Saywell, eds., *Essays in the History of Canadian Law, Volume X: A Tribute to Peter N. Oliver*
Greg Taylor, *The Law of the Land: The Advent of the Torrens System in Canada*
Hamar Foster, Benjamin Berger, and A.R. Buck, eds., *The Grand Experiment: Law and Legal Culture in British Settler Societies*

2007 Robert Sharpe and Patricia McMahon, *The Persons Case: The Origins and Legacy of the Fight for Legal Personhood*
Lori Chambers, *Misconceptions: Unmarried Motherhood and the Ontario Children of Unmarried Parents Act, 1921–1969*
Jonathan Swainger, ed., *A History of the Supreme Court of Alberta*
Martin Friedland, *My Life in Crime and Other Academic Adventures*

2006 Donald Fyson, *Magistrates, Police, and People: Everyday Criminal Justice in Quebec and Lower Canada, 1764–1837*
Dale Brawn, *The Court of Queen's Bench of Manitoba, 1870–1950: A Biographical History*
R.C.B. Risk, *A History of Canadian Legal Thought: Collected Essays*, edited and introduced by G. Blaine Baker and Jim Phillips

2005 Philip Girard, *Bora Laskin: Bringing Law to Life*
Christopher English, ed., *Essays in the History of Canadian Law: Volume IX – Two Islands: Newfoundland and Prince Edward Island*
Fred Kaufman, *Searching for Justice: An Autobiography*

2004 Philip Girard, Jim Phillips, and Barry Cahill, eds., *The Supreme Court of Nova Scotia, 1754–2004: From Imperial Bastion to Provincial Oracle*
Frederick Vaughan, *Aggressive in Pursuit: The Life of Justice Emmett Hall*
John D. Honsberger, *Osgoode Hall: An Illustrated History*
Constance Backhouse and Nancy Backhouse, *The Heiress versus the Establishment: Mrs Campbell's Campaign for Legal Justice*

2003 Robert Sharpe and Kent Roach, *Brian Dickson: A Judge's Journey*
Jerry Bannister, *The Rule of the Admirals: Law, Custom, and Naval Government in Newfoundland, 1699–1832*

George Finlayson, *John J. Robinette, Peerless Mentor: An Appreciation*
Peter Oliver, *The Conventional Man: The Diaries of Ontario Chief Justice Robert A. Harrison, 1856–1878*

2002 John T. Saywell, *The Lawmakers: Judicial Power and the Shaping of Canadian Federalism*
Patrick Brode, *Courted and Abandoned: Seduction in Canadian Law*
David Murray, *Colonial Justice: Justice, Morality, and Crime in the Niagara District, 1791–1849*
F. Murray Greenwood and Barry Wright, eds., *Canadian State Trials, Volume II: Rebellion and Invasion in the Canadas, 1837–1839*

2001 Ellen Anderson, *Judging Bertha Wilson: Law as Large as Life*
Judy Fudge and Eric Tucker, *Labour before the Law: The Regulation of Workers' Collective Action in Canada, 1900–1948*
Laurel Sefton MacDowell, *Renegade Lawyer: The Life of J.L. Cohen*

2000 Barry Cahill, *'The Thousandth Man': A Biography of James McGregor Stewart*
A.B. McKillop, *The Spinster and the Prophet: Florence Deeks, H.G. Wells, and the Mystery of the Purloined Past*
Beverley Boissery and F. Murray Greenwood, *Uncertain Justice: Canadian Women and Capital Punishment*
Bruce Ziff, *Unforeseen Legacies: Reuben Wells Leonard and the Leonard Foundation Trust*

1999 Constance Backhouse, *Colour-Coded: A Legal History of Racism in Canada, 1900–1950*
G. Blaine Baker and Jim Phillips, eds., *Essays in the History of Canadian Law: Volume VIII – In Honour of R.C.B. Risk*
Richard W. Pound, *Chief Justice W.R. Jackett: By the Law of the Land*
David Vanek, *Fulfilment: Memoirs of a Criminal Court Judge*

1998 Sidney Harring, *White Man's Law: Native People in Nineteenth-Century Canadian Jurisprudence*
Peter Oliver, *'Terror to Evil-Doers': Prisons and Punishments in Nineteenth-Century Ontario*

1997 James W.St.G. Walker, *'Race,' Rights and the Law in the Supreme Court of Canada: Historical Case Studies*
Lori Chambers, *Married Women and Property Law in Victorian Ontario*
Patrick Brode, *Casual Slaughters and Accidental Judgments: Canadian War Crimes and Prosecutions, 1944–1948*
Ian Bushnell, *The Federal Court of Canada: A History, 1875–1992*

1996 Carol Wilton, ed., *Essays in the History of Canadian Law: Volume VII – Inside the Law: Canadian Law Firms in Historical Perspective*
William Kaplan, *Bad Judgment: The Case of Mr Justice Leo A. Landreville*

Murray Greenwood and Barry Wright, eds., *Canadian State Trials: Volume I – Law, Politics, and Security Measures, 1608–1837*

1995 David Williams, *Just Lawyers: Seven Portraits*

Hamar Foster and John McLaren, eds., *Essays in the History of Canadian Law: Volume VI – British Columbia and the Yukon*

W.H. Morrow, ed., *Northern Justice: The Memoirs of Mr Justice William G. Morrow*

Beverley Boissery, *A Deep Sense of Wrong: The Treason, Trials, and Transportation to New South Wales of Lower Canadian Rebels after the 1838 Rebellion*

1994 Patrick Boyer, *A Passion for Justice: The Legacy of James Chalmers McRuer*

Charles Pullen, *The Life and Times of Arthur Maloney: The Last of the Tribunes*

Jim Phillips, Tina Loo, and Susan Lewthwaite, eds., *Essays in the History of Canadian Law: Volume V – Crime and Criminal Justice*

Brian Young, *The Politics of Codification: The Lower Canadian Civil Code of 1866*

1993 Greg Marquis, *Policing Canada's Century: A History of the Canadian Association of Chiefs of Police*

Murray Greenwood, *Legacies of Fear: Law and Politics in Quebec in the Era of the French Revolution*

1992 Brendan O'Brien, *Speedy Justice: The Tragic Last Voyage of His Majesty's Vessel Speedy*

Robert Fraser, ed., *Provincial Justice: Upper Canadian Legal Portraits from the Dictionary of Canadian Biography*

1991 Constance Backhouse, *Petticoats and Prejudice: Women and Law in Nineteenth-Century Canada*

1990 Philip Girard and Jim Phillips, eds., *Essays in the History of Canadian Law: Volume III – Nova Scotia*

Carol Wilton, ed., *Essays in the History of Canadian Law: Volume IV – Beyond the Law: Lawyers and Business in Canada, 1830–1930*

1989 Desmond Brown, *The Genesis of the Canadian Criminal Code of 1892*

Patrick Brode, *The Odyssey of John Anderson*

1988 Robert Sharpe, *The Last Day, the Last Hour: The Currie Libel Trial*

John D. Arnup, *Middleton: The Beloved Judge*

1987 C. Ian Kyer and Jerome Bickenbach, *The Fiercest Debate: Cecil A. Wright, the Benchers, and Legal Education in Ontario, 1923–1957*

1986 Paul Romney, *Mr Attorney: The Attorney General for Ontario in Court, Cabinet, and Legislature, 1791–1899*

Martin Friedland, *The Case of Valentine Shortis: A True Story of Crime and Politics in Canada*

1985 James Snell and Frederick Vaughan, *The Supreme Court of Canada: History of the Institution*

1984 Patrick Brode, *Sir John Beverley Robinson: Bone and Sinew of the Compact*

David Williams, *Duff: A Life in the Law*

1983 David H. Flaherty, ed., *Essays in the History of Canadian Law: Volume II*

1982 Marion MacRae and Anthony Adamson, *Cornerstones of Order: Courthouses and Town Halls of Ontario, 1784–1914*

1981 David H. Flaherty, ed., *Essays in the History of Canadian Law: Volume I*